The Complete
Financial History
of Berkshire Hathaway

Every owner of a physical copy of this edition of

The Complete
Financial History
of Berkshire Hathaway

can download the eBook for free direct from us at
Harriman House, in a DRM-free format that can be read
on any eReader, tablet or smartphone.

Simply head to:

ebooks.harriman-house.com/
financialhistoryBerkshireHathaway

to get your copy now.

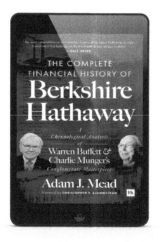

The Complete Financial History of Berkshire Hathaway

A Chronological Analysis of
Warren Buffett and Charlie Munger's
Conglomerate Masterpiece

Adam J. Mead

HARRIMAN HOUSE LTD
3 Viceroy Court
Bedford Road
Petersfield
Hampshire
GU32 3LJ
GREAT BRITAIN
Tel: +44 (0)1730 233870

Email: enquiries@harriman-house.com
Website: harriman.house

First published in 2021.
Copyright © Adam J. Mead

Hardback ISBN: 978-0-85719-912-6
eBook ISBN: 978-0-85719-913-3

British Library Cataloguing in Publication Data
A CIP catalogue record for this book can be obtained from the British Library.

For Shelly, Abigail, and Julia

Dedicated to teachers and lifelong learners

Contents

About the author

Adam J. Mead is a lifelong student of business and capital allocation.

He is the CEO and Chief Investment Officer of Mead Capital Management, LLC, a New Hampshire-based Registered Investment Advisor he founded in 2014.

Adam spent over a decade in banking in commercial credit, including observing first-hand the after-effects of the Great Recession and the long credit expansion afterward.

Adam has been investing in public securities markets since 2004. He owned two small businesses (non-financial) during college, and grew up in a family of small business owners. In addition to managing assets for his clients at Mead Capital, he is involved with numerous local non-profit organizations.

Adam holds a Master of Business Administration from Southern New Hampshire University, from which he graduated Summa Cum Laude in 2013. Previously he graduated Summa Cum Laude from Southern New Hampshire University in 2008 with an undergraduate degree in Business Studies and a Minor in Economics.

A native of Derry, NH for his entire adult lifetime, Adam lives in Derry with his wife Shelly, their two daughters, and their two dogs.

Acknowledgments

This book could not have happened without much help, support, encouragement, and luck. First and foremost, I thank Warren Buffett and Charlie Munger, whose business creation is topped only by their genuine skill and passion for teaching. I'm grateful for the many founders, managers, and employees who carefully built each part of Berkshire into what it is today, and for those who will continue its legacy.

I'm lucky to follow in the footsteps of some incredible Berkshire scholars. Not least among them is Lawrence Cunningham, who went above and beyond to find me financial filings at the Library of Congress, in addition to reading an early draft of the manuscript. The staff at the Boston Public Library were incredibly helpful in researching Berkshire's early history. A special thank you to Todd Wheeler for lending me his signed copy of Phil Beuth's *Limping on Water* and recounting the story of his career at Capital Cities/ABC—these provided invaluable insights into the management philosophy of Tom Murphy and Dan Burke. Thank you to Carol Loomis for her early help with this project.

My good friends Andrew Wagner and Carter Johnson provided ideas, support, and guidance throughout the process of crafting Berkshire's history. I'm thankful for Guy Spier's friendship and support—and his reminder of just how special Berkshire's culture is. Chris Bloomstran provided invaluable suggestions and helped me find the right voice to convey Berkshire's long history. Jonathan Brandt suggested improvements to key parts of the manuscript. Marcy, Margaret, and Sarah Hawley, along with John Baskin, provided great ideas and helped me better understand the world of publishing. Jessie Rancourt enthusiastically read a draft of the manuscript and provided excellent feedback. Jeff Annello's detailed critique not only made the book better but helped me clarify its intended audience. Gautam Baid shared his experience writing and publishing *The Joys of Compounding* and encouraged me to paint my own canvas. I'm also thankful for Ron Lazaro's encouragement and keen eye on a later draft of the manuscript.

I wouldn't have found my new friends at Harriman House without Dan Pecaut and Austin Pierce. Craig Pearce at Harriman was a joy to work with and shared my enthusiasm for bringing the full story of Berkshire Hathaway to life in a first-class way. Chris Parker created a beautiful cover that conveys the feeling of Berkshire in one concise snapshot. The care and devotion of the typesetting work done by Chris Wild shows on every page.

Eric Wing and Leakana Ly at MetroCreate crafted a beautiful companion website at theoraclesclassroom.com. They found ways to bring my particular and exacting ideas to life, which I know wasn't easy.

My editor, Erika Alison Cohen, became a trusted partner and friend along this long journey. Her work can only be fully appreciated next to the raw material I provided her. She proved not only an excellent editor but a patient teacher as well.

Two individuals not directly related to this project deserve attention for their contributions. The first is my high school welding instructor at Pinkerton Academy, Mr. Copp. He taught his students that a weld could be the best and strongest in the world, but if it looked sloppy no one would fully appreciate it. I've used that lesson as a metaphor in every walk of life since leaving his class. I must also thank Gary Vaynerchuk. He doesn't know it yet, but his message of pursuing one's passions with empathy and energy, no matter how small the audience, kept me going to the finish line.

Finally, and most important of all, I thank my wife Shelly. I'm incredibly lucky to have a loving partner who supports my endeavors, even ones that turn out bigger and much longer than originally envisioned. No project of this magnitude could be completed without a trusted companion by one's side to keep the rest of the world in order while pouring heart and soul onto the page.

For all this help, many mistakes and omissions undoubtedly remain. To someone now accustomed to the world of electronic media, a printed book preserving these faults in time is a terrifying prospect. They are mine alone.

Foreword by
Christopher Bloomstran

The Library of Congress contains more than 200 volumes devoted to Berkshire Hathaway and the two gentlemen adorning the cover of this book. Add in newspaper and magazine articles, research reports, investment letters, social media messages, and Berkshire's own financial reporting and archives of its annual meetings, and it is safe to conclude that more has been written on the company and the two men running it than on any other business over the past three decades, perhaps over all time. The question must therefore be asked, "Why another book?"

I know I speak for countless others when I say Warren Buffett and Charlie Munger are my mentors—not in the classic sense, but for having had such a profoundly positive impact on my life as an investor and as a citizen.

It's hard to believe for the quarter-century following 1965, when Mr. Buffett bought control of Berkshire Hathaway, that he and the company were genuinely flying under the radar. Despite having compounded Berkshire's book value per share at 24% and its shares by 28% annually, against only a 10% return for the Standard & Poor's 500 index, Berkshire, Buffett, and Munger were not household names in the late 1980s and early 1990s. Today, of course, Messrs. Buffett and Munger are world-wide rock stars and Berkshire Hathaway is no longer just a company but a cult. Back then, I never heard those names uttered when I studied finance. Outside of the MBA program at Columbia University and a handful of schools with oddball professors, early Berkshire cultists to be sure, these three didn't exist on campuses. Following school, I worked at a large midwestern bank in trust investments. We didn't own or even follow Berkshire. To the old guard it was regarded as, "just an insurance company that's really no more than a leveraged mutual fund." When I studied for the CFA designation in the early 1990s, I only first learned of Berkshire when reading about the efficient market hypothesis and a highly regarded finance academician pointing to the company and to Mr. Buffett as aberrant, lucky anomalies.

In 1996 those aberrant anomalies issued their class "B" shares to the public and I set out to learn about the unusual company that would, on the first page of the offering document, admonish prospective shareholders that:

- The shares being offered are not undervalued.
- The company will not grow as fast prospectively as in the past.
- The shares in recent years advanced faster than intrinsic value so to expect underperformance.
- The offering size is tailored to meet expected demand so to not expect a quick profit.

Who does this? I found and purchased a copy of the reprinting of the fourth edition of Benjamin Graham's *The Intelligent Investor*, on the cover of which Mr. Buffett claimed, "By far the best book on investing ever written." It is. The copy also contained bonus material, a new introduction and also an appendix, both written by Mr. Buffett. The appendix was an edited transcript of a talk given at Columbia University in 1984 commemorating the fiftieth anniversary of Ben Graham and David Dodd's *Security Analysis*. The speech was titled, "The Superinvestors of Graham-and-Doddsville." In a modern context it would be an "instant classic." As has been the case for so many investors, that was it. I read the entire book that night and read it again the following night. The light had gone on, a common occurrence for those first encountering this Grahamian, Buffett approach for the first time.

From Graham it was immediately on to Berkshire Hathaway. Despite having a research library nearly as large as a basketball court, the bank didn't have any annual reports on the Buffett-led conglomerate. Those were the days when you had to call a company to get reports. The 1993 to 1995 annuals, the three I'd requested, contained the most unusual Chairman's letters, which not only informed but taught. Ben Graham taught. It was obvious that Mr. Buffett modeled his own approach from his mentor and took it upon himself to educate as well, a giving back so contrary to what most would do. In a field as competitive as investments, why give away the secret sauce, the formula for Coca-Cola, when it would be so easy to copy? Back then, one could write to Berkshire's offices in Omaha and the company would mail you a three-volume bound set of Chairman's letters dating back to 1977. I can't recall how many times I've read these letters. Those pages contained pure gold for the young, aspiring investor. Value investing took on an entirely new meaning. Nowhere else could you learn so logically about accounting (good and bad), valuation, stock-based compensation, corporate governance, the vagaries of inflation and taxes, derivatives as weapons of mass destruction, and the list goes on and on.

I bought shares of Berkshire Hathaway for the first time in February 2000. The stock had fallen by half from 1998 and offered seeming value. How much value I would only appreciate as the years passed (and the position size and my affection for all things Berkshire abounded…). The annual shareholders meeting by then had become a "thing," so off to Omaha as a first-time shareholder that April 29th I went. I've only missed one meeting since, the following year when my firstborn arrived just days prior to the meeting. Every year my understanding accumulated, taking in the wisdom offered so selflessly by the sages on the dais. Some would diligently scribe every word and provide transcripts of the discussion. I owe tremendous thanks to those that did, and so many of you are now great friends. Now the video recordings of these meetings have been graciously provided to CNBC and a wonderful online archive of every meeting back to 1994 is available free of charge and beautifully done. Even at critical moments, often at times of uncertainly or panic, Mr. Buffett would take to *Fortune* magazine and pen articles that put fears to rest or reset expectations. Mr. Munger would host his own annual meetings in Pasadena and Los Angeles for Wesco Financial and more recently the Daily Journal. Transcripts and recordings of the long Berkshire archive abound.

So again, "Why another book?" When you read this monumental effort by Adam Mead, the answer will be obvious. Despite all of the annual reports, all of the letters, all of the books, all of the interviews and annual meetings, none have done what history required. We the investors, the students of capital allocation, history really, needed the complete chronology of Berkshire Hathaway, dating to its days pre-Buffett when the original textile businesses that became today's Berkshire thrived, and then did not. With Mr. Buffett's encouragement, Adam has written the complete *business* and *investment* history of the company, leaving no acquisition, no investment, no cycle uncovered. He assimilated all of the annual reports, meeting transcripts and myriad other information and compacted it into this terrific, readable work. Biographies can be interesting and entertaining, but this detailed history of the greatest company and "Greatest of All Time" investors the world has ever seen was necessary.

The reader should pay special attention to the evolution of Mr. Buffett and of Berkshire. Over time, the business has undergone dramatic change. From the early pivot away from its New England textile origins to insurance, to subsequent well-timed transitions to and away from common stocks, to the outright ownership of businesses, the allocation of capital was brilliant. The book captures an evolving genius and ability to be presciently and invariably ahead of the crowd. It's as though Berkshire became the embodiment of the epigraph introducing *Security Analysis*, from Horace's *Ars Poetica*, "Many shall be restored that now are fallen, and many shall fall that are now in honor."

You will find the book arranged in a manner where information and details can be easily located and referenced. But read cover to cover, both the uninitiated to Berkshire and its most ardent followers will derive enormous utility and satisfaction from it. Privileged to get an early preview of the manuscript, despite my 25 years as a now self-described Berkshire cultist, I learned so many new and important things about Berkshire and its history. It is my pleasure to encourage you to enjoy this gem. I owe so much of my investment career and investing framework to the lessons of Warren Buffett and Charlie Munger. We all owe a heartfelt thanks to Adam Mead for writing the book on Berkshire that needed to be written.

Well done, Adam!

Christopher P. Bloomstran
President and Chief Investment Officer
Semper Augustus Investments Group

Introduction

Saturday, May 5, 2012. Omaha, Nebraska. 5:30 a.m. I am waiting in line to get into the arena for the Berkshire Hathaway Annual Meeting. I am a first-timer. A group of guys from Cincinnati, Ohio, welcomes me into their ritual of charging in to get seats on the floor close to Warren Buffett and Charlie Munger. We charge with the politeness of men in suits and the excitement of teenage girls seeing The Beatles in concert for the first time. I'd just found 40,000 friends who share a love for Berkshire.

On that day, I never could have imagined I'd have the chutzpah (to use a Charlie Munger term) to someday write a book on Berkshire Hathaway. Yet that first meeting was the beginning of a journey that led to what you now hold in your hands. I listened intently to the Oracle of Omaha and the witty Munger for hours and experienced first-hand the 200,000 square-foot exhibition hall which was truly a one-of-a-kind blend of celebration, reunion, trade show, and shopping spree. Dinner at Gorat's that evening with my new companions from Cincinnati solidified friendships which remain to this day. I've attended every Annual Meeting since, including the virtual one in 2020 due to Covid-19, and my friendships with wonderful people from all over the world are now too numerous to count.

Over the years, I've had the great fortune to meet fellow Berkshire shareholders, operating managers, and some directors during the Annual Meeting weekend. Two highlights were shaking Warren's hand during one of his stints working as salesman "Crazy Warren" at Borsheims and shaking the hand of investing great Jack Bogle. The bigger names like Buffett and Bogle garner press beyond the business world. Others like Ron Olson, Irv Blumkin, Tony Nicely, Todd Combs, and Ted Weschler occupy fame within the Berkshire and investing community. Countless others, like Kathy Sorensen at Johns Manville, Gregg Renner at MiTek, and the many managers, employees, and members of the Berkshire home office team, are lesser known but equally critical in creating the fabric that make up Berkshire's culture.

My insatiable curiosity and thirst for everything Berkshire grew as I collected Annual Meeting passes, books about Berkshire, and new friends. Yet even with the volumes of books written about Berkshire, I found myself pining for something more. I wanted to go deeper than Warren's Chairman's letters and see the numbers that made him so excited about the businesses and Berkshire's future. I wanted to understand the accounting and the reasons why certain acquisitions were made. I wanted to see how the company evolved from a struggling textile company to a respected Fortune 500 company. I wanted to follow its evolution chronologically in one place. Not finding such a volume anywhere, I set out to create it using my knowledge of Berkshire and my skills as a former commercial loan officer and current investment manager. I've long harbored the idea of a project that would take years to complete and perhaps test the limits of my penchant for deferred gratification. Half a decade wasn't my original plan, but here we are …

I formalized my quest in 2016, which took me on a journey digesting over 10,000 pages of written material, including Moody's Manuals on the early Berkshire predecessor companies dating to the 1920s, each Berkshire Hathaway Annual Report from 1955 to 2019 (totaling some 4,000+ pages, including 900+ pages of Chairman's letters), most of Berkshire's 10Ks, and many of the 10Qs. I listened to and read the transcripts of each Annual Meeting from 1994 to 2020 (140+ hours of video and 3,000+ pages), analyzed financial filings and annual reports from subsidiary companies where they were available, read newspaper and magazine accounts, books on subsidiary companies, and of course, the multitude of other works on Berkshire completed over the decades.

The structure of this book follows my deep-seated inclination toward logic and order. The foundation rests on the Annual Reports and, especially during the Buffett years, on the Chairman's letters. The goal was to add to Buffett's analysis of each year and not outdo him, but go deeper and ask why and how. Each decade leads with a financial snapshot including key acquisitions and noteworthy events. Each decade ends with a review of the major events, key lessons, and appendices with detailed financials. In this way, the book is a guide through fifty-five years of history, both in long form and in review. This book is the synthesis of many materials filtered through the mind of one individual. It's not perfect and it is biased. With so many facts, figures, and calculations covering many years it is certain that errors exist. (I'd be grateful to know where I erred; please email me at brkbook@gmail.com.)

The longtime Berkshire shareholder or well-versed student will recognize additional possible shortfalls. When a business conglomerate covers more than five decades, even an exhaustive history requires cutting. What deserves to remain or be eliminated is not an easy task. The calculations in charts could lead to questions, as could information left out. I hope the book provides a single place to satisfy those looking to drink from the firehose that is all the wonderful details of Berkshire Hathaway. Perhaps future editions will include additional information deemed critical, and the true fanatic can (and should) go through as much original source material as possible.

I envision two broad audiences for this book. One is the new student of Berkshire or investing who wants to live through the company's history as it happened, year by year. That individual will gain an incredible appreciation for the process and decisions that transformed a struggling textile company into what it is today. They will better understand how to think about businesses, which will undoubtedly make them better at investing. (To use another Munger-ism, how could it be otherwise?)

The second broad audience is the longtime student or shareholder of Berkshire. For this audience, the book may serve more as a reference guide, a refresher on a particular year or years quickly digestible compared to the full financials. With a chronological layout, the book is compartmentalized to allow easy study of a particular year or decade.

The layout of the chapters may seem an odd choice at first, but there's a logic to it. Using Buffett's arrival in 1965 as the point of origin, I first went back a decade to see what the company looked like between 1955 and 1964. When I sent the first chapter to Warren, he suggested going back even further to examine the brief respite of profitability the predecessor companies experienced during WWII before resuming their economic slide. Having made the jump back in time, I couldn't stop. My curiosity wanted to know where *all* the predecessor companies came from. Thus, the book starts in the eighteenth century and follows the development of the textile industry.

The first chapters examine the rise of the textile industry in New England, from its origins combining proprietary textile manufacturing technology taken from England with seed capital harvested from a declining whaling industry. We see the shift of textile dominance to the South as technology changed the economics of the industry. We follow the Berkshire predecessor companies through the 1930s and 1940s and see the challenges of the 1930s wipe out a host of textile companies before WWII showers profits on those that remained. Then we see the struggles return as foreign competition slowly begins decimating another once-powerful industry.

The year 1955 conveniently begins the decade Berkshire Fine Spinning Associates and Hathaway Manufacturing merged to create Berkshire Hathaway. Most surprising of all are the capital allocation decisions made by Buffett's predecessors. While Berkshire Hathaway was a business in decline and its managers stubborn, they acted rationally by shrinking the business and returning capital to shareholders. Those actions weren't enough to keep the stock price from falling below a level that attracted a young investment manager who saw a price/value discrepancy to exploit.

We begin in earnest in 1965, the year Buffett gained control of Berkshire and learned how hard it was to make money in textiles. Working capital and physical plant must do the job, not just the market's reevaluation of those assets in relation to the stock price. The textile business would drag down Berkshire's operating results and cause headaches for another twenty years. Yet those challenges provided crucial business lessons. One lesson was that even the most talented management team can't save a business with bad economics. Another was how swiftly capital allocation could shift the fortunes of a company for the better, which in this decade were the two large acquisitions of National Indemnity (1967) and the Illinois National Bank and Trust of Rockford (1969). These bold moves represented 28% and 44% of Berkshire's average equity capital at the time of purchase, respectively. By 1974, Berkshire was well on its way to changing course.

Between 1975 and 1984, Berkshire grew exponentially through acquisitions and investments, most notably the increased investment in and eventual merger with Blue Chip Stamps. With Buffett and Munger in control of Blue Chip, it purchased See's Candies in 1972, began purchasing Wesco in 1973, and acquired *The Buffalo News* in 1977. Berkshire also merged with Diversified Retailing in 1978. This decade is highlighted by Berkshire's entrepreneurial push into insurance and its entry into reinsurance.

Berkshire hits its stride in the 1985–1994 decade. Ajit Jain joins Berkshire and begins building an insurance powerhouse focused squarely on profitability. This is the decade where float swells and investment income far surpasses any underwriting losses. The leveraged buyout fad of this time allows Berkshire to acquire Scott Fetzer (itself a mini-conglomerate) and Fechheimer. It also provides an opportunity for Berkshire to back Capital Cities in its bid for ABC. Berkshire invests $1.3 billion in Coca-Cola during this decade, a cost basis that remains unchanged today. The decade was also marked by challenges, most notably the Salomon Treasury bid-rigging episode which required nine months of Buffett's time while he worked to rescue Berkshire's $700 million investment and his reputation. Berkshire's investment in USAir nearly collapses, and its investment in footwear quickly deteriorates.

The 1995–2004 decade sees Berkshire build out the framework of its future. The acquisition of the remaining half of GEICO that it didn't already own solidifies its presence in primary insurance, and its acquisition of General Reinsurance brings initial headaches but creates a reinsurance powerhouse. Both moves add to the huge amounts of capital Buffett and Munger can allocate. One outlet for capital is the utilities sector, which provides predictable returns and the ability to invest large sums but with limited upside potential. The boom and subsequent bust of the dot-com wave also creates opportunities for Berkshire to welcome discarded but cash-generating businesses into its protective umbrella.

The 2005–2014 decade—the fifth under Buffett's control—sees additional large non-insurance acquisitions, including a major international one. The Great Recession mid-decade provides Berkshire an opportunity to put large amounts of capital to work in a short period of time. It also tees up the acquisition of Burlington Northern Santa Fe, which expands upon the utility platform acquired the prior decade by adding another large company with regulated investment returns and a place to make big investments. The largest reinsurance deals in history highlight Berkshire's willingness to use its capital strength when opportunities present themselves.

Finally, a half decade period covering 2015–2019 proves Buffett's assertion that Berkshire's incredible past record would weigh on future returns. Over 40% of the change in shareholders' equity between 1965 and 2019 occurred in these five years and proved the power of compounding. Berkshire's rate of return, however, falls to its lowest level in its modern history—a poor result only in comparison to its own record and impressive considering the size of the conglomerate and its conservative balance sheet, including huge holdings of Treasuries. Berkshire makes several large investments during this period, including a partnership that takes control of Heinz and Kraft Foods. Its $35 billion investment in Apple demonstrates Berkshire's consistent pattern of making concentrated investments. Yet cash continues to build in an economy where private transactions and public equity markets are expensive by historical standards. Berkshire thus increasingly returns capital to shareholders in a series of share repurchases that may be the pattern for the remainder of the decade. The world is given a glimpse into succession with the promotions of Greg Abel and Ajit Jain to Vice Chairmen. Yet Warren Buffett and Charlie Munger, aged 89 and 95 respectively at the end of 2019, show no sign of slowing down.

Taking a step back we see Berkshire Hathaway among the greatest of human achievements. Berkshire's financial outcomes were a result of business mastery, the perfection of a system that cultivated human potential. The capitalist system put in place by America's Founding Fathers and the incredible tailwinds of the mid-twentieth century provided the rich soil to allow the genius of Warren Buffett and Charlie Munger to flourish. The full story of Berkshire Hathaway is worth understanding for what it can teach us about continuing timeless methods of excellence in business and in life.

As long as this book is, I hope to continue to add more to the understanding of Berkshire Hathaway over time. To that end, I have created a website called The Oracles Classroom (www.theoraclesclassroom.com) which contains an Excel file with the financial statements presented in the chapter appendices, an interactive Berkshire timeline, an archive of Berkshire and subsidiary financials, book recommendations, a blog, and more. I look forward to hearing from readers, shareholders, students, and others, as we all continue our journey as students of this remarkable conglomerate and its creators.

Adam Mead
Derry, New Hampshire
November 2020

Chapter 1
Textile Conglomerate

A proper history of Berkshire Hathaway prior to Warren Buffett taking control in 1965 could occupy an entire book unto itself. When we think of the conglomerate that is Berkshire Hathaway today, we think of a widely diverse enterprise spanning a multitude of different industries. The 1965 version was a large textile company comprised of many companies with stories of their own.

The Rise and Fall of an Industry

What gave rise to those textile companies and the industry itself is fascinating and instructive. We must therefore start at the beginning.* Samuel Slater brought the first water-powered textile mill to the United States in 1789. Slater snuck out of England** with the know-how to build a viable water-powered mill and did so with financial backers in Pawtucket, Rhode Island.[1] By 1809 there were twenty-seven Slater-type mills in New England.[2]

The next major innovation was financial and operational. Francis Cabot Lowell, a wealthy Boston merchant used a joint-stock corporation to create the Boston Manufacturing Company in 1813. He was the first to integrate his mills, the first of which was in Waltham, Massachusetts. It housed all operations needed to turn raw cotton into finished cloth.[3] They were profitable almost immediately. Lowell had thus discovered the optimal combination of size and integration to generate economies of scale out of the cotton mill. Not surprisingly, this innovation spread rapidly.

---

* The very beginning was handmade textiles. Workers would spin fibers of wool or cotton into yarn, and then would hand weave the fabric into clothes. This book is chiefly concerned about the large-scale, industrial textile manufacturing industry in the United States.

** England had attempted to ban the export of its trade secrets by banning emigration of skilled workers until 1825, and the export of machinery until 1843. (Behemoth)

Having wrested all the power they could out of the Charles River in Waltham, the investors in the Boston Manufacturing Company (sometimes referred to as the Boston Associates) turned their sights on a new location. They chose a site on the Merrimack River in what was East Chelmsford, Massachusetts, and formed the Merrimack Manufacturing Company.* In Lowell, the company was more than just mills; it was a company town that by the 1840s had over 8,000 employed.[4] They used the surrounding farmland to build a boardinghouse, churches, company stores, and other infrastructure for the many workers required to operate the mills. Many of the workers were women.

The next major improvement in textile mill operations came from the Amoskeag Manufacturing Company, formed in the late 1830s in Manchester, New Hampshire, along the Merrimack River. Whereas the Lowell-type mills were individually owned, the Amoskeag mills operated under one corporate umbrella. This allowed for bulk purchasing, sales, and other economies of scale.[5]

Why the North?

The early mills in the United States were thousands of miles from cotton fields, which raises a key question: Why develop the textile industry in the North? In short, the South did not find it immediately economical to do so, and the North had some distinct advantages, at least initially. Two initial Northern advantages were access to capital and a cheap power source.

Availability of capital was possibly the deciding factor as to why the textile industry first took hold in the Northeast. When Francis Cabot Lowell formed the Boston Manufacturing Company, he was already a successful businessman. He and his Boston Associates had access to capital from the whaling business.[6] By the mid-1800s, a large store of capital accumulated during the boom times of whaling was unleashed as whaling declined and the textile business grew.[7]

Other early advantages of the North were geographic. New England has many strong-flowing rivers that unleashed vast amounts of power as they descended to the ocean.[8] These rivers also provided a convenient means of transporting goods to and from the mills.[9] Secondly, the North's proximity to New York City, known as the fashion capital, may also have played a part since the Northeast knew sooner which products were most popular. (After all, information travelled much more slowly then.)[10]

According to *The Decline of a Textile City: A Study of New Bedford*, "the New England region obtained a virtual monopoly" in textiles with 70% of the active spindles in the United States housed there. By 1880, New England boasted more

---

* Later, after Francis Cabot Lowell died in 1817, the town was renamed in his honor.

than 80 percent of active spindles.[11] This would prove to be the height of success for New England textile manufacturing—it would only go down from there. This time also saw increased competition due to the formation of many new textile companies looking to get into the then-prosperous industry. Quick additions to capacity would be the hallmark of the textile industry during good times. It would ultimately lead to depressed prices.

Between the 1880s and the late 1920s, the North slowly lost its supremacy in textile manufacturing. As the economic landscape shifted, early advantages turned into shackles that accelerated the industry decline in the North. A major factor was a slow, grinding technical obsolescence. While the South first found it advantageous to grow the raw material to supply the Northern mills,[12] the South's late entrance allowed it to incorporate newer, more efficient machines such as automatic looms and ring spindles. Owners of northern plants found it hard to justify the new expenditures given their plants' marginal profitability. Over time, the gap between the North and the South widened, hastening the shift South.[13]

The shift away from water-powered plants also hurt the North. The North's strong rivers gave it an advantage over the South in the early days, but the rivers could only provide so much power. The South, by contrast, soon incorporated steam power into its mills, aided by a proximity to coal. When electricity became a viable source of energy to power the mills, the South too had a slight advantage as large electrical power plants were less prevalent in the North.

Other deciding factors favoring the South over the North were lower labor costs (including the effects of unionization) and lower taxes.[14] Later, the addition of air conditioning neutralized the North's advantage over the unbearable heat of the South.[15] The gap was also due to increasing demand for long-fiber cotton from west of the Mississippi, which saw no shipping advantages in the North over the South.*

Perhaps because the decline of the North's advantages was slow, it didn't see the long-term trends happening in plain sight. Periods of prosperity occasionally happened, such as during shortages of cotton caused by natural events or war. And when new uses for textiles were found, such as incorporation into billiard balls, tires, conveyor belts, and typewriter ribbons,[16] Northern mills quickly grabbed the business. But as had been the case before, the good times quickly led to bitter competition. By the time some of the Berkshire Hathaway predecessor companies were merging in 1929, the industry was facing mostly headwinds. The North would try, but fail, to reclaim its dominance in the industry that defined the region for decades. The first step entailed a series of mergers and acquisitions that diminished the sheer number of competitors.

---

* Finer-quality finished textiles required long-fiber cotton, initially produced only in the North, which was grown west of the Mississippi. The difference in shipping costs to the South versus the Northeast were negligible according to Wolfbein (p. 64).

Berkshire Fine Spinning Associates, Inc.

The oldest predecessor company with identifiable direct connections to the Berkshire Hathaway of today is the Valley Falls Company. According to the Woonsocket, Rhode Island, history,[17] the Valley Falls Company was formed by Oliver Chace in 1839. The Chace family built a textile empire that brought prosperity to the villages of Cumberland and Central Falls, Rhode Island, as the family built and expanded its mills along the river.

From there, the history unfolds through a series of companies throughout New England as outlined below.

- 1929: Five companies, including Valley Falls Company, merged to form Berkshire Fine Spinning Associates, Inc. The other four were:
  - Coventry Co., formed in 1864 in Coventry, Rhode Island
  - Greylock Mills, formed in 1880 in Pittsfield, Massachusetts
  - Fort Dummer Mills, formed in 1910 in Brattleboro, Vermont[18]
  - Berkshire Cotton Manufacturing Company, formed in 1889 in Adams, Massachusetts

Berkshire Cotton Manufacturing was the largest of the five, so the new entity was named Berkshire Fine Spinning Associates, Inc.*

- 1930: King Philip Mills, formed in 1871 in Fall River, Massachusetts; and Parker Mills, formed in 1895 in Fall River, Massachusetts, merged into Berkshire Fine Spinning. (Parker Mills had merged with Hargraves Mills in 1921 after both Parker and Hargraves fell into financial difficulties.[19])
- 1955: This myriad group of textile mills and companies merged with the Hathaway Manufacturing Company to create Berkshire Hathaway.

Hathaway Manufacturing Company

The history of the Hathaway side of Berkshire Hathaway is more straightforward. It was formed in 1888 at the height of textile manufacturing in New England; incorporated in 1889 in New Bedford, Massachusetts; and operated independently until the 1955 merger with Berkshire Fine Spinning. Hathaway was formed with

---

* According to the 1930 Moody's Manual entry on Berkshire Fine Spinning Associates, the balance sheet for the company as of September 30, 1928 (which must have been a pro forma accounting since the mergers did not happen until 1929) had $13 million of total capital (preferred, common, and surplus). According to the separate Moody's account for Berkshire Cotton Manufacturing as of the same date, it had $6.9 million of total capital.

$400,000 of initial capital from Horatio Hathaway* and several partners looking for their next business venture after the decline of New Bedford's sperm whaling industry, according to filings with the Massachusetts Secretary of State. One of those partners was Hetty Green, the rich heiress to a New Bedford shipping fortune.[20]

1930s

The two Berkshire Hathaway predecessor companies, Berkshire Fine Spinning and Hathaway Manufacturing, operated on parallel tracks throughout the 1930s. They largely faced the same struggles as New England-based textile manufacturers, including the relentless march south and the growing influence of overseas competition.

The Great Depression in the 1930s acutely affected New England textile manufacturers. The mills that had survived that far had largely done so by shifting production away from coarser goods and toward the finer textiles that the South had not yet mastered. The Great Depression softened demand for these higher-priced discretionary fine goods. Many mills saw production of such fine goods fall by over 50%, while volumes of coarser-grade staples fell less than 1%.[21]

New England mills, including the Berkshire Hathaway predecessor companies, also shifted some production to silk and rayon during the 1930s. These two cotton substitutes were naturally suited for manufacturing in the North, at least initially, due to their similarities to fine-grade cotton. Hathaway Manufacturing shifted to these substitutes earlier, making it and another New Bedford mill that did the same, the Gosnold Mill, the most profitable in the region.[22]

Since material costs for cotton and its substitutes was largely market-driven, mill owners looked to the next largest cost, wages. Workers responded with strikes and walkouts, including the Uprising of '34 in which a general textile strike impacted the entire industry. While both North and South were affected, the strike was more concentrated in the South.[23]

During the Uprising of '34, 500,000 mill laborers walked off the job. The North self-interestedly lobbied against working conditions in the South. The South had lower wages and did not have the same restrictions against child labor, working hours, or working conditions that the North had imposed. With the implementation of the Fair Labor Standards Act of 1938, a standard uniform wage nationwide mitigated the labor differential between the North and the South. The North rejoiced, but it was bittersweet since the legislation came too late. As described in *The Decline of a Textile City: A Study of New Bedford*, the new law could not "bring back mills which were already liquidated, whose machinery was sold at auction, and whose buildings had been torn down."[24] It also did nothing to stop the growing impact of overseas competition.

---

* Horatio Hathaway earlier formed the Acushnet Mill in New Bedford, Massachusetts. (*The Snowball*, p. 267.)

Some efforts to stem the shift of production to the South succeeded, but the forces against the North were strong. Data on spindles in place, a measure of industry capacity, illustrates the shift. Figure 1.1 shows the overall decline of the industry between 1914 and 1938, and the large gains by Southern cotton-growing states over that period.

Figure 1.1: Millions of spindles in place by year and location

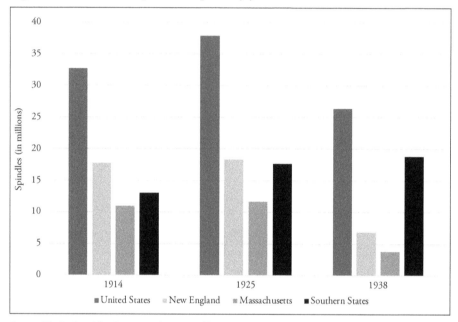

Source: *The Decline Of A Cotton Textile City* (Wolfbein p. 161).

The US share of spindles in place in New England fell from 54% in 1914 to 26% in 1938—less than half its 1914 share. Meanwhile, the Southern cotton-growing states experienced the opposite trend, growing from 34% of spindles in place in 1914 to 71% of the total—a gain 1 percentage point greater than New England's loss. It is interesting to note that in 1925, the peak of textile production, production was almost evenly split, with 46% in the South and 48% in the North.

Data for Berkshire Fine Spinning Associates and Hathaway Manufacturing during the 1930s conform to the industry trends. Though early 1930s data is scarce, one can assume that the Berkshire Hathaway predecessor companies fared similar to industry and regional counterparts. Beginning with 1934, data on both constituent companies can be examined, and that is when differences start to appear.

Table 1.1: Comparative operational data for Berkshire Fine Spinning Associates and Hathaway Manufacturing

	Berkshire Fine Spinning	Hathaway Manufacturing
1934		
Net revenues *($ millions)*	$16.3	$3.9
Equity capital *($ millions)*	$13.8	$2.1
# spindles	900,000	79,000
# looms	20,000	3,200
1939		
Net revenues *($ millions)*	$18.4	$7.3
Equity capital *($ millions)*	$13.1	$2.2
# spindles	748,000	62,000
# looms	15,000	2,800
1935–1939 (average)		
Return on equity	0%	6.10%
Profit margin	(0.40%)	2.10%
Revenues/average equity[1]	$1.31	$3.15

Footnote: Revenues/average equity calculation is from 1936–39 because no data is available for 1935 for Hathaway Manufacturing.

Note: No data on 1939 for BFS, but spindles/looms same in 1938 and 1940.
Sources: Moody's Industrial Manuals 1934-40 and author's calculations.

The most obvious difference is operational size. Berkshire had ten times more spindles than Hathaway and over six times more looms. This production capacity, though, did not translate into profitability. The last five years of the 1930s, a short but illuminating period, shows how Hathaway had a positive return on equity—and Berkshire had none. The natural question is, why? Both mills produced largely the same products of finer-grade cotton, and both had picked up silk and rayon production.

While five years is probably the shortest time for an examination of this sort (since many factors can come into play in the short run), the answer is likely due to two elements. Hathaway's mills were all located in New Bedford, Massachusetts, and all had the relative advantage of proximity to sea transport. Some Berkshire mills were close to the sea, but the company also had plants as far as Western Massachusetts and Vermont. The transport disadvantages of those geographically diverse plants, coupled with Berkshire managing an interstate network of plants, likely weighed on profitability.*

---

* The locational advantage Hathaway enjoyed is highlighted by its higher capital efficiency. Between 1936 and 1939, its revenues per dollar of average equity average was $3.15. Berkshire by contrast produced just $1.34. This magnified the average Hathaway margin on revenues (profit margin) of 2.1% that much more.

1940s

The difficult operating conditions of the northern textile mills in the 1930s likely would have continued unabated throughout the 1940s if it weren't for one major event. World War II created a temporary boom for the entire textile industry and offered the remaining mills in the North a brief flash of extreme profitability. Profits continued for northern mills, albeit briefly, through the 1940s, as the US economy brought itself out of the Great Depression aided largely by consumers' ability and willingness to spend. Very short flickers of profitability would periodically happen after this, but the 1940s would prove to be the last hurrah for the northern mills.

The 1940s wartime boom might have dissipated profitability for individual firms if it weren't for the many failures during the preceding decade that led to mill closures and decreased competition. Just in New Bedford, Massachusetts, twenty mills went out of business between 1930 and 1939.[25]

The firms that remained found themselves positioned to benefit enormously. The war effort required an immense production of textiles for military use including powder bags, camouflage cloths, ponchos and mosquito netting. The large-scale use of parachutes in the war required production of nylon, a relatively new material that was both lightweight and strong. The textile mills were initially hesitant to commit to large-scale production. It was only after Berkshire Fine Spinning made a large commitment that other mills followed suit. Berkshire Fine Spinning alone produced 5 million yards of nylon fabric for the war effort, and it and others found a new outlet for their many languishing spindles and looms.[26]

The effect on the northern mills' profitability was apparent, as seen in Figure 1.3. Berkshire's profit margins, which had been slightly negative in the five years ended 1939, increased to 4.9% for the five years ended 1944.

Figure 1.2: Revenues at Berkshire Fine Spinning and Hathaway Manufacturing from 1940–1949

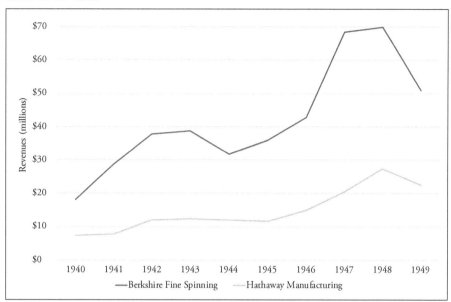

Sources: Moody's Industrial Reports and Berkshire Hathaway Annual Reports.

Figure 1.3: Profit margins at Berkshire Fine Spinning and Hathaway Manufacturing from 1940–1949

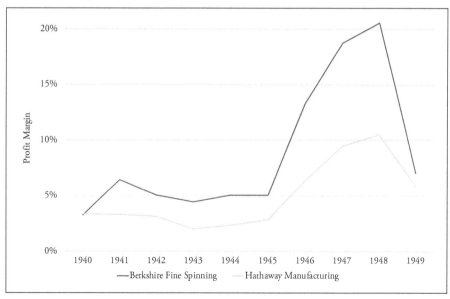

Source: Moody's Industrial Reports and Berkshire Hathaway Annual Reports.

Figure 1.4: Return on equity at Berkshire Fine Spinning and Hathaway Manufacturing from 1940–1949

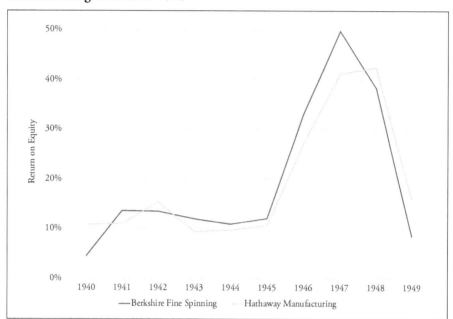

Sources: Moody's Industrial Reports and Berkshire Hathaway Annual Reports.

Hathaway Manufacturing experienced even greater gains in profitability. Its net profit margin averaged just 2.8% between 1940 and 1944, which was just 0.7 percentage points higher than the average of the preceding four years. But because of Hathaway's greater capital efficiency (it generated an average of $4.04 in revenues per dollar of equity between 1940 and 1944, compared to Berkshire's $2.20 during the same period), its return on average equity during those years averaged 11.2% compared to Berkshire's rate of 10.9%. (Remember, Berkshire's return on equity from 1935 to 1939 was zero.)

The latter half of the 1940s saw textile profitability reach greater heights than during the war years. The US economy boomed during the peace time that followed WWII. Real disposable personal income per capita (a measure of dollars available to consumers to spend) fell from $7,361 in 1929 to $6,468 in 1935. It then grew to $10,754 in 1944 before declining slightly to $9,927 in 1949 as the US entered another recession.[*]

The US consumer, with almost a third more income at their disposal in the 1940s than in the previous decade, began spending liberally. Goods formerly eschewed as being unnecessary, such as the fine-woven products made by the Northern textile mills, were once again in demand.

---

[*] Data from the Federal Reserve Bank of St. Louis using chained 2012 dollars.

This was the real boom for the Berkshire Hathaway predecessor companies. High sales in the late 1940s led to greater margins. Net margins at the two companies exploded, with Berkshire averaging 12.9% between 1945 and 1949 and Hathaway reaching 7.0%. The combination of higher revenues and higher margins resulted in a dramatic increase in returns on shareholders' equity. At Berkshire its return on average equity was 28% per year during the 1945–49 period. Hathaway averaged a slightly lower—though by no means disappointing—27% per year during that same period.

1950–1954

The data on Berkshire Fine Spinning is sparse for this period. So the analysis of the next five-year period uses the pro forma consolidated financial information provided in the first combined Berkshire Hathaway Annual Report in 1955. The boom experienced during the 1940s did not exactly go bust in the 1950s; rather, it fizzled. The temporary profitability, caused by strong demand from World War II and a reinvigorated consumer after the war, faded to the background as the fundamental disadvantages of northern textile production became apparent.

Beginning in 1950, the Berkshire Hathaway predecessor companies experienced rapid declines in revenues and profitability, as shown in Figure 1.5. Having come from what was the peak of $97 million of combined revenues in 1948, revenues rebounded slightly in 1951 to $92 million but never recovered. The companies quickly lost their healthy profit margins too.

Figure 1.5: Pro forma profit margin and return on equity for Berkshire Hathaway 1950–1955

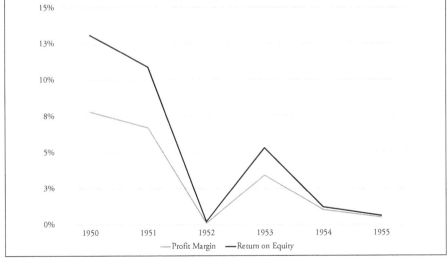

Sources: Moody's Industrial Reports and Berkshire Hathaway Annual Reports.

The decline in northern textile production can also be seen in the statistics of active spindles* shown in Figure 1.6. The graph highlights the decline of the industry overall but shows the South held its ground, while the North continued to see losses.

Figure 1.6: Millions of active spindles by location 1940–1955

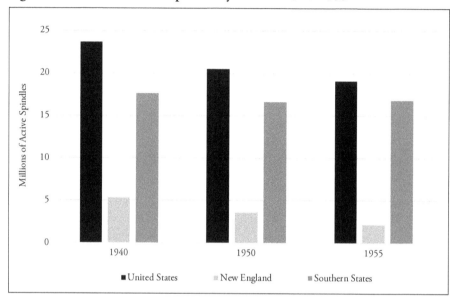

Note: Active spindles are different than spindles in place. The former is a measure of usage; the latter is a measure of capacity.

Source: *Changes in American Textile Industry*, Technical bulletin No. 1210. US Dept. Agriculture, Issued November 1959, p. 72, accessed via Google Books.

While New England states fell from 22% of total active spindles in 1940 to 12% in 1955, the South's share increased from 75% in 1940 to 88% in 1955. It is interesting to note that between 1950 and 1955, the inroads of the South were such that despite the US shrinking overall, it grew the number of active spindles—at the expense, of course, of the North.

---

* Note that the term active spindles is a slightly different metric than spindles in place. The latter is a measure of capacity, whereas the former is a measure of usage. A more finely tuned measure of usages, active spindle hours, is also sometimes seen referenced.

Berkshire Hathaway, Inc.

The final merger that would impart the name on today's modern conglomerate occurred in 1955 when Berkshire Fine Spinning merged with Hathaway Manufacturing. The merger resulted primarily from continued relentless industry pressures. But it was set in motion by a flooding of the Hathaway Mill on Cove Street in New Bedford, Massachusetts, which was significantly damaged by Hurricane Carol in September 1954. Eager to remain in business, Seabury Stanton, Hathaway's leader, pursued a merger with Berkshire Fine Spinning. The merger was finalized on March 14, 1955.

Leading the new enterprise were John H. McMahon as chairman of the board, Seabury Stanton as vice chair, and Malcolm G. Chace, Jr., as president. The managers were upbeat, writing in the first annual report in 1955:

> "The purpose of the combination of the two companies was to effect operating economies and greater diversification of products for each. The new Company can now supply the market not only with plain fine combed cotton goods, but also with fancy colored box loom fabrics and with rayon, nylon, dacron and other synthetic fabrics."

Unfortunately, that report also contained a portentous warning. Shortly after the merger, in July of that year, a strike caused a thirteen-week shutdown. The next month, Hurricane Diane severely damaged several plants in Rhode Island. These early episodes would set the stage for the many troubles and tough decisions that would be faced during the ensuing decade.

Conclusion

The many corporate mergers that occurred prior to the formation of the combined Berkshire Hathaway, Inc. (as we know it today) created a textile conglomerate. The business had locations throughout New England and was quite large with combined revenues of over $65 million in 1955. In 1956, the year after its combination, Berkshire Hathaway was 431st on the Fortune 500 list of the largest US companies, though it was far from being the largest textile company of its day.[*27]

The constituent companies that labored separately before joining largely faced the same headwinds leading up to the 1955 merger. Early advantages of the North during the nineteenth century turned into disadvantages in the twentieth century as

---

* There were others ahead of Berkshire Hathaway on the Fortune 500 in 1956. For example: Burlington Industries ranked 70th with revenues of $515 million, Cannon Mills ranked 184th ($194 million), Textron ranked 187th ($189 million), Cone Mills ranked 208th ($164 million), Riegel Textile ranked 344th ($86 million), and Pepperell Manufacturing ranked 352nd ($85 million).

the South built newer, more efficient plants. The North fell further behind as lower labor and energy costs accrued to the South. A major (though temporary) return to profitability after the Great Depression occurred during World War II in the 1940s. The fire the war lit under the economy quickly turned to cinders once it ended. The lower input cost advantages of the South reappeared in full force in the 1950s, leading to renewed industry decline and consolidation in the North.

Active spindle data for the country reflects the industry decline as it relates to world events and industry changes, as seen in Figure 1.7.

Figure 1.7: Active spindles (usage) versus spindles in place (capacity), 1925–1955

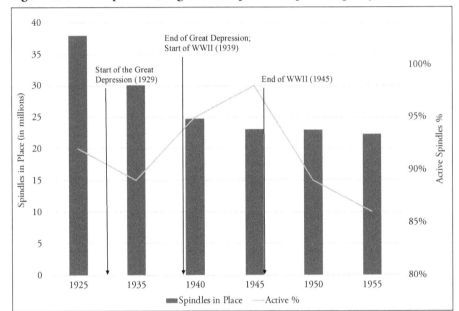

Figure 1.7 shows that in times of tight industry capacity firms did well. But when supply exceeded demand, excess capacity lowered profits and oftentimes caused the weakest firms to falter and reduce production or close entirely.

Geographical differences are also telling. By running multiple shifts, sometimes around the clock, the South rang up a 122.6% utilization rate of its spindles. The North, by contrast, utilized just 78.6%, with Massachusetts the worst at 70.4%.[28] These types of statistics show the advantages the South had over the North, and how the South used them to grow profits. The small degrees of advantages in labor costs and better technology, coupled with high degrees of plant utilization, resulted in a distinct competitive advantage over the North.

As an interesting aside, the accounting practices of the textile mills could also have played a factor in their extended demise. Many mills (in both locations) improperly accounted for depreciation of plant and equipment. This would have made it seem the mills were operating at an economic loss under conditions of apparent profit. It also would have had the effect of distribution of capital that should have been reinvested in plant upkeep and modernization.[29] Proper accounting, of course, would not have prevented the economic reality from taking place. But it might have led to more rationality on the part of mill owners, however, who might have stopped money-losing operations sooner.

Despite the clear advantages of the South, textile operations in the North, and New England in particular, did not entirely disappear. Berkshire Hathaway did not cease all operations until 1985. One company, Burlington Industries, even weathered the storm up through the New Millennium, struggling mightily along the way with intense foreign competition.[*][30]

The Berkshire Hathaway that existed a decade before Warren Buffett taking control was a melting snowball trying to maintain its size by furiously appending other wet, melting snow. Instead of recognizing the heat and seeking shelter or changing course, the managers of the 1955 Berkshire Hathaway conglomerate stayed on the same path, hoping for a different result. Some managers surely recognized the structural industry changes taking place, but most only knew one business, textiles. It would take one man, and a quirk of history, to turn a faltering business into one of the world's most admired companies.

Lessons: Textile Beginnings to 1954

1. Knowledge can only confer a temporary advantage to a business. Eventually all industry participants have access to best practices. Even governmental protections cannot stop the spread of valuable information.
2. Sometimes the second mover has an advantage over the first mover. The South gained an advantage over the North by using the latest know-how when building from scratch.
3. Business mergers cannot alter a fundamentally disadvantaged economic position or trend. The many textile mergers that culminated in the creation of Berkshire Hathaway were the result of a shrinking industry and could delay, not stop, the inevitable.

---

* Burlington Industries would ultimately find itself filing for bankruptcy in late 2001. Berkshire actually bid for it at auction, but the deal fell through and its business was split apart and sold. It remains today, at least in name, as part of the International Textile Group, which purchased its assets out of bankruptcy in 2003.

Figure 1.8: The Beginnings of Today's Berkshire Hathaway, Inc.

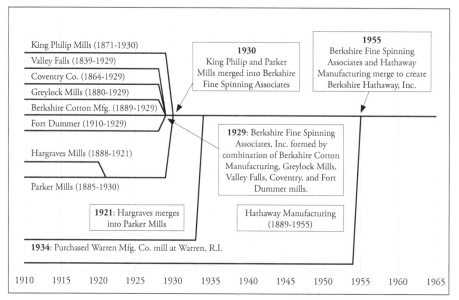

Sources: Moody's Manual reports and Massachusetts Corporate Card Files accessed via the Boston Public Library.

Appendix Note: Source data for 1934–1945 are from Moody's Industrial Manuals accessed via Mergent Online. Source data for 1946–1955 come from the first Berkshire Hathaway Annual Report for the combined entity. The reader should be aware that data for net income and equity don't exactly match the sum of the constituent parts in years where there are both combined and individual data available.

Table 1.2: Berkshire Fine Spinning Associates and Hathaway Manufacturing Company, select data, 1945–1955

Berkshire Fine Spinning Associates	1955	1954	1953	1952	1951	1950	1949	1948	1947	1946	1945
Revenues (*$ thousands*)					$60,987	$63,466	$50,912	$69,890	$68,445	$42,861	$36,043
Net income					3,141	4,099	3,570	14,358	12,842	5,690	1,814
Equity					45,193	44,262	41,691	42,530	32,444	19,187	15,294
Key Ratios											
Revenue growth					(3.9%)	24.7%	(27.2%)	2.1%	59.7%	18.9%	13.7%
Revenues / avg. equity capital					$1.40	$1.48	$1.31	$2.23	$3.07	$2.49	$2.40
Return on revenues (net margin)					5.2%	6.5%	7.0%	20.5%	18.8%	13.3%	5.0%
Return on average equity					7.0%	9.5%	8.5%	38.3%	49.7%	33.0%	12.1%

Hathaway Manufacturing Company	1955	1954	1953	1952	1951	1950	1949	1948	1947	1946	1945
Revenues (*$ thousands*)		$21,227	$27,463	$19,749	$30,862	$26,158	$22,446	$27,288	$20,538	$14,997	$11,622
Net income		(373)	482	(80)	1,836	1,702	1,312	2,858	1,949	952	328
Equity		11,012	11,490	11,608	10,968	9,732	8,629	7,892	5,597	3,867	3,166
Key Ratios											
Revenue growth		(22.7%)	39.1%	(36.0%)	18.0%	16.5%	(17.7%)	32.9%	36.9%	29.0%	(3.5%)
Revenues / equity capital		$1.89	$2.38	$1.75	$2.98	$2.85	$2.72	$4.05	$4.34	$4.27	$3.67
Return on revenues (net margin)		(1.8%)	1.8%	(0.4%)	6.0%	6.5%	5.8%	10.5%	9.5%	6.3%	2.8%
Return on average equity		(3.3%)	4.2%	(0.7%)	17.7%	18.5%	15.9%	42.4%	41.2%	27.1%	10.7%

Table 1.3: Berkshire Fine Spinning Associates and Hathaway Manufacturing Company, select data, 1934–1944

Berkshire Fine Spinning Associates	1944	1943	1942	1941	1940	1939	1938	1937	1936	1935	1934
Revenues (*$ thousands*)	$31,696	$38,679	$37,772	$28,747	$18,163	$18,442	$14,351	$19,389	$18,951	$16,031	$16,335
Net income	1,602	1,724	1,907	1,852	592	284	(517)	1,418	73	(1,228)	209
Equity	14,766	14,638	14,311	14,035	13,173	13,098	13,094	13,611	13,629	12,635	13,825
Key Ratios											
Revenue growth	(18.1%)	2.4%	31.4%	58.3%	(1.5%)	28.5%	(26.0%)	2.3%	18.2%	(1.9%)	
Revenues / avg. equity capital	$2.16	$2.67	$2.67	$2.11	$1.38	$1.41	$1.07	$1.42	$1.44	$1.21	
Return on revenues (net margin)	5.1%	4.5%	5.0%	6.4%	3.3%	1.5%	(3.6%)	7.3%	0.4%	(7.7%)	
Return on average equity	10.9%	11.9%	13.5%	13.6%	4.5%	2.2%	(3.9%)	10.4%	0.6%	(9.3%)	

Hathaway Manufacturing Company	1944	1943	1942	1941	1940	1939	1938	1937	1936	1935	1934
Revenues (*$ thousands*)	$12,045	$12,409	$11,949	$7,796	$7,329	$7,307	$3,889	$8,470	$6,985	Unknown	$3,937
Net income	278	250	378	259	246	230	(19)	177	253	(0)	54
Equity	2,988	2,766	2,572	2,356	2,350	2,219	2,059	2,193	2,118	1,953	2,072
Key Ratios											
Revenue growth	(2.9%)	3.8%	53.3%	6.4%	0.3%	87.9%	(54.1%)	21.3%			
Revenues / equity capital	$4.19	$4.65	$4.85	$3.31	$3.21	$3.42	$1.83	$3.93	$3.43		
Return on revenues (net margin)	2.3%	2.0%	3.2%	3.3%	3.4%	3.1%	(0.5%)	2.1%	3.6%		
Return on average equity	9.7%	9.4%	15.4%	11.0%	10.8%	10.8%	(0.9%)	8.2%	12.4%	0.0%	

Table 1.4: Berkshire Fine Spinning Associates and Hathaway Manufacturing Company, pro forma combined, select data, 1945–1955

	1955	1954	1953	1952	1951	1950	1949	1948	1947	1946	1945
Revenues ($ thousands)	$65,498	$66,929	$86,414	$68,293	$91,849	$89,625	$73,358	$97,177	$88,982	$57,858	$47,665
Net income	301	660	2,921	99	6,175	7,008	5,031	17,722	16,193	6,868	2,142
Equity	51,400	53,354	55,153	54,990	57,524	55,359	51,670	51,756	38,868	24,878	18,459
Key Ratios											
Revenue growth	(2.1%)	(22.5%)	26.5%	(25.6%)	2.5%	22.2%	(24.5%)	9.2%	53.8%	21.4%	9.0%
Revenues / equity capital	$1.27	$1.25	$1.57	$1.24	$1.60	$1.62	$1.42	$1.88	$2.29	$2.33	$2.58
Return on revenues (net margin)	0.5%	1.0%	3.4%	0.1%	6.7%	7.8%	6.9%	18.2%	18.2%	11.9%	4.5%
Return on average equity	0.6%	1.2%	5.3%	0.2%	10.9%	13.1%	9.7%	39.1%	50.8%	31.7%	11.8%

Table 1.5: Berkshire Fine Spinning Associates and Hathaway Manufacturing Company, pro forma combined, select data, 1934–1944

	1944	1943	1942	1941	1940	1939	1938	1937	1936	1935	1934
Revenues ($ thousands)	$43,740	$51,088	$49,721	$36,543	$25,492	$25,749	$18,240	$27,859	$25,936		$20,272
Net income	1,880	1,974	2,286	2,111	838	514	(536)	1,595	326	(1,229)	263
Equity	17,754	17,404	16,883	16,390	15,523	15,317	15,153	15,804	15,747	14,588	15,897
Key Ratios											
Revenue growth	(14.4%)	2.7%	36.1%	43.4%	(1.0%)	41.2%	(34.5%)	7.4%			
Revenues / equity capital	$2.46	$2.94	$2.94	$2.23	$1.64	$1.68	$1.20	$1.76			
Return on revenues (net margin)	4.3%	3.9%	4.6%	5.8%	3.3%	2.0%	(2.9%)	5.7%			
Return on average equity	10.7%	11.5%	13.7%	13.2%	5.4%	3.4%	(3.5%)	10.1%	2.2%	(8.1%)	

Chapter 2
1955–1964

Table 2.1: Decade snapshot: Pre-Buffett years

	1954*	1964
Business:	Textile manufacturing	Textile manufacturing
Key managers:	Chairman: John H. McMahon; Vice Chairman: Seabury Stanton; President: Malcolm G. Chace, Jr.	Chairman: Malcolm G. Chace, Jr.; President: Seabury Stanton
Annual revenues:	$66.9 million	$50 million
Stockholder equity:	$53.4 million	$22.1 million
Book value per share:	$23.25	$19.46

*Pro forma for the combined Berkshire Fine Spinning Associates, Inc. and Hathaway Manufacturing Company, which merged on March 14, 1955 to form Berkshire Hathaway, Inc.

Key capital allocation decisions:
1. Purchased the stock of Bourne Mills for $3.4 million (1956).
2. Closed unprofitable divisions and plants in response to ongoing losses.
3. Reduced investment in working capital by $19.8 million (-58%).
4. Reduced net investment in property, plant, and equipment by $9.7 million (-57%).
5. Returned $22.3 million to shareholders in the form of dividends and buybacks.

Noteworthy events:
1. Warren Buffett begins buying shares for Buffett Partnership Limited in 1962.

Introduction

An analyst or shareholder comparing Berkshire Hathaway's 1955 and 1964 Annual Reports would have come away with two conclusions. First, profitability was down. The company that existed in 1964 earned about half of what was earned in 1955. Second, the company's financial condition, although not necessarily in bad shape, had materially changed. What was formerly a company flush in cash and excess liquid resources at the end of 1954 became a company with substantially lower levels of cash and marketable securities, about half the investment in physical assets, and some debt. What transpired to cause Berkshire Hathaway to become half of its former self?

Note on year-ends: Berkshire Hathaway reported on a fiscal year basis until it adopted a calendar year in 1967.[*]

Table 2.2: Select information 1955–1964

	1955	1956	1957	1958	1959	1960	1961	1962	1963	1964
BRK book value per share - % change	(3.6%)	0.1%	(4.9%)	(11.1%)	6.0%	16.3%	(3.7%)	(10.3%)	(6.7%)	3.3%
US GDP Growth (real %)	7.1%	2.1%	2.1%	(0.7%)	6.9%	2.6%	2.6%	6.1%	4.4%	5.8%
10-year Treasury Note (year-end %)	3.0%	3.6%	3.2%		3.9%	4.7%	3.8%	4.1%	3.9%	4.1%	4.2%
US inflation (%)	(0.3%)	1.5%	3.4%	2.7%	0.9%	1.5%	1.1%	1.2%	1.3%	1.3%
US unemployment (%)	4.4%	4.1%	4.3%	6.8%	5.5%	5.5%	6.7%	5.6%	5.6%	5.2%

Sources: Berkshire Hathaway Annual Reports 1955–1964 and Federal Reserve Bank of St. Louis.

1954

Let's turn first to the balance sheet and assess the financial condition of the company that existed at year-end 1954. Because the merger between Berkshire Fine Spinning Associates, Inc. and Hathaway Manufacturing Company was not consummated until March 1955, this is actually an accounting look at what the companies would have looked like had they operated as one a year earlier (pro forma to use the modern jargon). The 1955 combined Berkshire Hathaway, Inc. report contained a lookback for comparison purposes, as shown in Table 2.3.

---

[*] It appears the method was inclusive of the last full week in September. This produced the oddities such as September 27, 1958 (a Saturday) and October 3, 1959 (also a Saturday).

Table 2.3: Berkshire Hathaway balance sheet, 1954

(*$ thousands*)	9/30/54	%
Current assets		
Cash	$4,977	9%
Marketable securities	2,963	5%
Accounts receivable, net	3,200	5%
Inventories	27,669	48%
Other current assets	394	1%
Total current assets	39,202	67%
Property, plant & equipment, net	17,249	30%
Other assets	1,778	3%
Total assets	$58,230	100%
Current liabilities		
Notes payable	878	2%
Accounts payable	2,296	4%
Accruals & other	1,702	3%
Total current liabilities	4,875	8%
Long-term liabilities	0	0%
Shares outstanding (000's)	2,295	
Total stockholders' equity	53,354	92%
Total liabilities and stockholders' equity	$58,230	100%

Note: Amounts are rounded from actual dollars which may cause totals to differ slightly.
Source: Berkshire Hathaway Annual Report 1955.

A company's assets can be overly simplified into two general components: short-term assets and long-term assets. Short-term assets fall into three main categories: inventories (in Berkshire's case raw materials such as cotton, silk, and rayon; product in the process of being converted into finished product; and finished goods such as fabric); accounts receivable (monies owed from customers for goods sold on credit); and cash. At the end of 1954, these current assets made up about two-thirds of Berkshire's total assets.

Long-term assets, usually grouped under property, plant, and equipment, are the land, buildings, and equipment necessary to run the company. The 1955 Berkshire Hathaway Annual Report listed the following locations, whose land, buildings, and equipment would have been classified under long-term assets:

- Executive offices in Providence, Rhode Island
- Two sales offices in New York City

- Nine operating plants: five plants in Adams, North Adams, Holyoke, Fall River, and New Bedford, Massachusetts; three in Albion, Anthony, and Warren, Rhode Island; and one plant in Brattleboro, Vermont
- Bleachery & Dye Works in Lonsdale, Rhode Island
- Curtain factories in Warren, Rhode Island and Fall River, Massachusetts
- A laboratory and machine shop in Warren, Rhode Island

That $17.2 million figure for long-term assets, as shown in Table 2.3, may not seem large today, but adjusting for inflation it would be equal to over $150 million in 2020 dollars. In short, Berkshire Hathaway halfway through the sixth decade of the twentieth century owned a lot of property.

Looking next to the other side of the balance sheet, we can see how those assets were financed. Again, to grossly simplify, a company's funding sources can be grouped into two broad categories: owners (otherwise known as equity) and non-owners. The non-owners category can be further delineated into borrowed monies (debt) and spontaneous liabilities (usually short-term funds provided by trade partners and others in the general course of business). In Berkshire's case, at year-end 1954, the company's owners recorded an investment of $53.4 million, which financed a substantial portion of its assets. The remaining balance of just 8% was made up of accounts payable (likely owed to suppliers of raw materials); accrued wages, salaries, and taxes; and a small number of short-term notes payable.*

At the end of 1954 Berkshire had no long-term debt. In short, its financial condition could be described as excellent.

The trouble begins when we start assessing the returns generated by Berkshire's asset base. We will take up this analysis with data from 1955.

1955

Using data from 1954 and 1955, we can assess the return on capital generated by Berkshire. Even though its balance sheet was in good shape early in the decade, its profitability was not, and this would lead in turn to a deterioration in its balance sheet.

---

* The amount of short-term funding required by a business is called working capital. Its definition varies depending on the analyst, but broadly speaking working capital is the difference between a company's current assets and its current liabilities. The working part becomes apparent when the sales cycle of a business is examined. While plant and equipment will remain stationary, working capital comes and goes. Cash might be used to buy inventory, which is turned into a credit sale, that ends up as a receivable, which is collected in cash. The more inventory required or unsold, and the more accounts uncollected, the larger the investment. Reducing the required investment is the spontaneous liabilities such as accruals or accounts payable, which have the effect of providing funds to the business.

Going into fiscal year 1955 (starting September 30, 1954), the management team at Berkshire Hathaway had $53 million of invested capital.* During the next year, Berkshire generated annual revenues of $65.5 million. That sounds like a lot of money, and it is, but remember, revenue is only one side of the picture. The capital it takes to produce that revenue, and the margins earned on each dollar of revenue, are equally important. In 1955, the ratio of capital to revenues was high,** meaning Berkshire was a capital intensive business. Basically, it took a lot of money to sell a lot of product.

Why was Berkshire so capital intensive? Textile manufacturing required a lot of land and equipment, and many production lines—with inventory tied up in each step. Additionally, a portion of its sales were on credit. This required an investment in accounts receivable as it waited to collect cash from customers. And since its material suppliers and employees would not go long without being paid, there were only modest offsetting liabilities to reduce working capital requirements.

Berkshire Hathaway reported net income of $301,000 on revenues of $65.5 million in 1955. The resulting net profit margin, or the ratio of net income to revenues, was 0.46%. Every dollar in revenues required an investment of about $0.81, so to bring in $100 in revenues required approximately $81. Earning $0.46 on an investment of $81 equals a return on capital of about 0.6%. Even in an era of long-term interest rates around 3%, as was the case in the mid-1950s, this was not an inspiring return.

A high capital-to-revenues ratio is not necessarily bad in and of itself. There are, of course, many good businesses, such as today's Berkshire Hathaway-owned Burlington Northern Santa Fe Railroad and Berkshire's utility businesses, that use such a model. But these modern subsidiaries have higher margins and enjoy some form of protection from competition. The textile business was a commodity business that suffered from high domestic and international competition, without any government-sanctioned price protection. As seen in Chapter 1, Berkshire Hathaway also had the added disadvantage of being in New England, with high labor and electric costs. Unsurprisingly, margins were thin. In short, it had no competitive advantages.

Warren Buffett was not yet associated with Berkshire Hathaway in 1955, but the situation Berkshire found itself in alludes to his future involvement. Berkshire's weak profitability would ultimately attract his attention as a "cigar butt"*** stock he could turnaround for a quick gain. After he instead went all in on Berkshire, the subpar

---

* Here I am using the average of 1954 and 1955's equity plus debt capital (the same figure presented in the appendix at the end of this section). Another approach would be to arrive at the same figure by averaging its short- and long-term assets, and then subtracting the average spontaneous liabilities. The case could be made to deduct surplus liquid assets from the calculation, which would improve the capital-to-revenues ratio. Either way, the fact remains the business was capital intensive.

** This equated to a revenues-to-capital ratio of $1.24. Said another way, it took $0.81 of capital to generate a dollar of revenues.

*** Buffett has frequently referred to his early approach of buying stocks selling for below their working capital as akin to finding a cigar butt on the ground. They aren't pretty but the last puff or two are free.

economics would provide painful but important lessons. He would learn the extreme difficulty in operating a commodity-type business and the benefits of looking for companies with a "moat"—a metaphor for a sustainable competitive advantage that protected a company's return on capital.

Any business can expect ups and downs. Unfortunately for the 1955 Berkshire Hathaway, its problems were both structural and cyclical. Like riding on a roller coaster, Berkshire experienced wild swings in profitability ultimately headed in one direction: down. It did experience brief respites of actual increases in profitability and returns when the stars aligned, but these too were only temporary. More typically, tough industry conditions were followed by attempts to resize, realign, or retool, followed by a brief period of improved profitability when inventories were low industry-wide, followed by industry overcapacity as firms raced to take advantage of what looked like a return to normal—all against a backdrop of increasing foreign competition.

The 1955 Annual Report contained clues as to the future profitability of the enterprise. In the jointly signed report by Chairman of the Board John H. McMahon, Vice Chairman Seabury Stanton, and President Malcolm G. Chace, Jr., the leaders noted several operational and competitive issues plaguing the company. Reading the report, it was clear Berkshire Hathaway was in a firefight, and they were losing.

A thirteen-week strike completely shut down operations mid-year. The strike was resolved with "slight concessions that have decreased the difference in labor costs between ourselves and many of our competitors." Additionally, a flood further caused a three-week shutdown.

Even the good news had a bad tinge. Management expected the new federal minimum wage of $1.00 per hour, up from $0.75, would help narrow the spread between Berkshire Hathaway's labor costs and those of its southern competitors. But the federal law would be of little help against foreign competitors. They noted the "flood of Japanese fabrics coming into the United States in ever increasing volume" and remarked upon the Japanese labor costs the equivalent of 15 cents per hour. They hoped governmental action (read: import tariffs) would help.

Not to end on a down note, the 1955 report concluded with expectations of improved future profitability due to "synergies" from the newly combined companies, though they didn't use that modern buzzword. McMahon, Stanton and Chace anticipated that a diversified product line, combined with cost reductions from the newly combined enterprise and relative labor cost parity with the rest of the United States, would result in a return to profitability. Unfortunately, that was not to be.

1956

In 1956, Berkshire Hathaway's management team acquired Bourne Mills of Tiverton, Rhode Island, for $3.4 million to diversify its product line. The Bourne plant was likewise in the textile manufacturing business and produced carded sateens, a different product from Berkshire's main lines. The Bourne acquisition also came with a subsidiary that had a wide distribution network reaching into Canada, and Berkshire management thought it might be useful for Berkshire's other products. Year-end results for 1956 provided management with some positive feedback for their capital allocation decisions: The company earned $923,000 that year—though the return on capital was just 1.7%. Industry developments also bolstered their confidence. "As a result of the recent increase in wages in the textile industry located in the South, our competitive position has been substantially improved, and we look to the future with confidence," management concluded in the Annual Report to shareholders.

But everything was not well. That same year cracks were widening in the core business. Labor shortages caused management to consolidate two plants in the Adams/North Adams, Massachusetts area. This would be the start of a long road of division and plant shutdowns followed by divestitures. It was the opposite of a growing, prosperous enterprise. The trouble was that the textile business in the United States was stuck in a long, slow decline into oblivion—it would just take a while to get there.

1957

During 1957, in response to depressed market conditions for textiles, Berkshire Hathaway took steps to maintain profitability. It curtailed some production rather than keep workers busy building excess inventories. The company also consolidated operations, eliminated higher cost plants, and invested in equipment to modernize operations in the remaining plants. In the 1957 letter to shareholders, Chairman Malcolm Chace, Jr. and President Seabury Stanton, stated, "With the operating economies resulting from our consolidation and modernization program, your company will be in a strong competitive position, and we expect that profitable operations will be resumed during 1958." It was not a great forecast.

1958

Profits were elusive in 1958. There was a severe depression in the industry, which necessitated numerous additional plant closures. The company closed the Greylock division in North Adams, Massachusetts; the Berkshire division in Adams,

Massachusetts; the Holyoke division in Holyoke, Massachusetts; the Fort Dummer division in Brattleboro, Vermont; and the curtain factory, repair division and warehouse buildings in Warren, Rhode Island. The 1958 Annual Report to shareholders made clear that the remaining divisions would be expected to be profitable going forward.

Table 2.4: Select period data

	Sept. 27, 1958	Jan. 1, 1957	% Change
Spindles	480,980	874,332	(45%)
Looms	12,610	19,214	(34%)
Plants	8	14	(43%)

Source: Berkshire Hathaway Annual Report 1958.

Management anticipated operating losses during this reorganization, but expected the cash freed by reducing working capital would help cover reorganization costs and operating losses. But no reorganization could help Berkshire Hathaway get rid of equipment it wasn't using—equipment no one wanted to buy. This is what happens when downsizing amid a systemic industry contraction. Many companies are all trying to sell equipment that no one could put to profitable use. The task was extremely difficult, maybe even impossible. "The market for second-hand textile machinery and buildings has been overloaded for the past several years, owing to the large number of mill liquidations which have taken place in all sections of the country," management concluded in the 1958 Annual Report, "and it has been extremely difficult to find customers for our machinery and properties."

The year ended in a sea of red ink: The company reported a net loss of $5 million in 1958.

1959

Buoyed by a general economic recovery, the following two years brought a brief respite of profitability. Operating costs were lower because of the rationalizing of plant assets in prior years, and textile prices were higher due to low industry-wide inventories. From the horrendous $5 million loss incurred in 1958, the bottom line rebounded to a $1.3 million profit in 1959. This likely gave management the confidence to maintain its policy of reinvesting in the business where they could "take full advantage of all technical improvements."

1960

The 1960 Annual Report informed owners of a change of business strategy. Management stated that, except for curtain fabrics and handkerchief fabrics, the company's entire production would now be sold in the gray (unfinished) state. This would be the operating plan going forward and would reduce risks associated with carrying finished goods.

The plan appeared to be initially successful. Though sales dropped almost 10%, profits swelled to $4.6 million, a net profit margin of 7.4% and a return on capital of 12%. Remember, this company had a net margin of 0.6% just five years earlier.

Spirits were high. Berkshire Hathaway was still debt free. However, as Buffett would later discover, such high points were a mirage. They merely served to keep everyone, owners and management alike, trudging forward.

The 1960 Annual Report noted an industry slowdown along with weakening prices. But with low inventories at the manufacturing level, satisfactory operating results were expected in the future. Again, management would be disappointed. It didn't take long for industry conditions to revert to a state of overproduction and low prices.

1961

Management stated in the 1961 Annual Report that sales volumes dropped materially and prices declined substantially, driven in part by continued imports of foreign textiles. Revenues declined almost 24% that year, to $48 million, and the company reported a $393,000 loss. This was not a terrible result given the significant contraction in revenues—but it was an indication of the pain to come.

1962

Choppy seas continued in 1962 with no signs of calm waters. Costs remained high and the company posted a $2.2 million loss, despite a 12% increase in revenues. That was not the worst of it. The company also recorded a $1.4 million charge for the "estimated loss on properties to be sold." In effect, it wrote down the value of its soon-to-be-divested plant assets but made the income statement look better (less bad, really) by recording the value as a charge to equity rather than flowing the loss through the income statement. Therefore, what would have been a $3.6 million loss was reduced by an accounting maneuver.* This ignored a dangerous undercurrent lurking below the surface.

---

* This may have been allowed by accounting conventions of the time, but management should have explained what was going on to owners in its communication to shareholders. Just a few years later Buffett would bring more candor to his communications to Berkshire Hathaway shareholders.

Management's response to the negative industry trends was to again change course, though within the textile industry. A new three-year modernization program began on October 1, 1962, the beginning of fiscal year 1963. Walking back on its concentration on unfinished products, it ceased unprofitable production* of these gray goods. Initial success in selling finished curtains and handkerchiefs led management to focus on selling more of those items. They were simple to produce and thus had lower labor costs. For these new products, which had a "semi-proprietary interest" with less competition, management established a Home Fabrics division which sold throughout the US and Canada.

With hindsight we can see the relative ease of entry into these finished goods provided no true protection from competition, only a delay of the inevitable. Buffett spoke of this years later in his 1985 Chairman's letter, the year Berkshire decided to permanently close the textile division. "Should you find yourself in a chronically-leaking boat, energy devoted to changing vessels is likely to be more productive than energy devoted to patching leaks."

A note of historical significance is appropriate here. Buffett began purchasing shares of Berkshire Hathaway for his investment partnership, Buffett Partnership, Ltd., in 1962. These first shares were purchased for $7.50, which translated into a market capitalization of about $12 million—about one-third of book value and less than working capital.

1963

Reflecting on the year 1963, management reported the company lost $685,000, but that there was a trend toward profitable operations. The company continued to invest in its new Home Fabrics division, which showed a "satisfactory profit". Digging deeper revealed clues that business was much worse than the reported net loss would indicate. The letter to shareholders explained that the company had permanently closed its Valley Falls division, and discontinued operations in the Berkshire King Phillip A division in Fall River, Massachusetts. What the letter failed to note was a $1.5 million charge to equity, like the one taken in 1962. Had it been recorded in the income statement, the net loss would have ballooned to $2.2 million.

1964

The final year in our decade under review, 1964, again saw mixed results. On the surface the company had returned to profitability. The company permanently closed its Berkshire King Philip A and E plants in Fall River, Massachusetts, leaving three

---

* Berkshire closed the Coventry and Bourne Mills divisions in Anthony and Tiverton, Rhode Island, respectively; Valley Falls, in Albion, Rhode Island closed shortly after year-end.

manufacturing plants in New Bedford, Massachusetts, and one in Warren, Rhode Island. A small profit of $176,000 was reported and management told shareholders that, "all divisions of the company were operating on a profitable basis at the end of the final quarter." Management also noted that the government subsidy program that existed since 1956, which subsidized foreign purchases of US cotton (to encourage exports and alleviate surplus production), was altered and allowed US manufacturers to obtain the same discount. If owners had not learned to dig deeper at this point, they should have. Another $3 million write-down to plant assets was recorded to equity. Likewise, if this was included as a true loss—as it most certainly should have been—it would have wiped out the small profit reported that year.

Decade in Review

With the decade concluded, let's take another assessment of Berkshire Hathaway in 1964. We find a business roughly half the size of its former self and one with a much weaker balance sheet.

Table 2.5: Select data from 1955 and 1964

(*$ thousands*)	1964	1955	$ Change	% Change
Revenues	$49,983	$65,498	(15,515)	(24%)
Cash	920	4,169	(3,249)	(78%)
Working capital	14,502	33,022	(18,520)	(56%)
Plant, property, and equipment	7,571	16,655	(9,084)	(55%)
Debt	2,500	0	2,500	n/a
Shareholders' equity	22,139	51,400	(29,261)	(57%)

Sources: Berkshire Hathaway Annual Reports 1955 and 1964.

The shriveled number of offices and plant locations at the end of 1964 illustrates the degree to which the business had contracted over the preceding decade. Save for one plant, operations had contracted to New Bedford, Massachusetts, including the executive offices and laboratory. The company still had two sales offices in New York City, and three Home Fabrics stores in Toronto, New York City, and Los Angeles. The report listed four plant locations, though three of those (the Hathaway Box Loom division, the Hathaway Synthetic division, and the Home Fabrics division) were in New Bedford, Massachusetts. The fourth was the King Philip D division, located in Warren, Rhode Island.

So, what happened over the decade? Between 1955 and 1964 Berkshire Hathaway generated aggregate revenues of $595 million yet its shareholders were punished for this with five separate years of losses that outstripped any profits made in better years. Worse yet, if the below-the-line write-downs to plant and equipment taken in 1962–1964 are included, the true economic result is even worse.

Table 2.6: Reconcilliation of shareholders' equity 1955–1964

($ thousands)	Change	% Change
Beginning equity 1955	$53,354	
Net income	(4,118)	13%
Asset write-downs	(5,900)	19%
Dividends	(9,174)	29%
Share repurchases	(13,090)	42%
Bourne Mill gain	887	(3%)
Tax adjustments	180	(1%)
Change in equity during period	(31,216)	100%
Ending equity 1964	$22,139	

Sources: Berkshire Hathaway Annual Reports 1955–1964.

Aside from the Bourne Mills acquisition in 1956, management acted rationally in shrinking the business, rather than continuing to acquire other mills in hopes of finding ever-elusive synergies. Over the course of the ten years ended in 1964, a net of $22.3 million, or about 42% of shareholders' equity from the beginning of the period, was sent to shareholders in the form of dividends and share repurchases. (Approximately $1.1 million of positive adjustments to equity were recorded over the decade relating to positive tax adjustments and an excess of assets acquired over the purchase price of the Bourne Mills acquisition.)

Table 2.7: Property, plant, and equipment: 1954–1964

($ thousands)	
Balance, end of 1954	$17,249
Depreciation	(17,809)
Plant write-downs	(5,900)
Capital expenditures	14,031
Balance, end of 1964	$7,571

Sources: Berkshire Hathaway Annual Reports 1955–1964.

Another key capital allocation decision (or rather a series of decisions) should be noted. Although management did shrink the company's investment in property, plant, and equipment over the decade, it had to spend money maintaining its fixed assets and investing in the latest technologies. Those decisions were expensive. Even though net property, plant, and equipment shrunk due to scaled-back operations, just maintaining existing equipment cost $14 million over that time.*

In short, management initially tried to make a go of it in the textile business by investing in new technology and merging with other mills. Instead, it found contraction—basically by half—was the only means of survival.

The Berkshire Hathaway that existed in 1964 was basically the same undiversified textile manufacturer that existed decades before. The business required large amounts of capital, had high labor requirements, and experienced low profits. In sum, it was a poor business in an industry whose glory days had passed.

Over the decades preceding Buffett's control, Berkshire Hathaway and its predecessors suffered a long, slow decline in operating performance. The cause of the deterioration is generally attributed to a commoditization of the industry coupled with intense competition. While attempts were made to remain competitive, such as cutting expenses and investing in more efficient machinery, the efforts were futile. In addition to strong competition from other American textile manufacturers, there was also overseas competitors. American textile manufacturers in the South were destined to suffer intensely from competition overseas, but the fact remained that both groups of domestic and foreign competitors had advantages over Berkshire Hathaway.

The main advantage to an overseas textile manufacturer in the 1950s and 1960s was a familiar culprit: lower labor costs. Advances in the logistics of global commerce coupled with know-how from experts worldwide created favorable economics for importing textiles to the United States. American textile manufacturers countered this trend with investments in more efficient machinery but to no avail.

Compounding this general malaise was the fact that Berkshire Hathaway was a New England-based company. Differences in the electricity costs between the Northeast and South meant Berkshire was at an added disadvantage. And since textiles were, as Charlie Munger noted later, just "congealed electricity," the only way to compete was with better technology. But because that better technology was available to all competitors, the playing field was leveled. Buffett would later comment in the 1985 Annual Report on the illusory benefits of such capital investments:

"Viewed individually, each company's capital investment decision appeared cost-effective and rational; viewed collectively, the decisions neutralized each other and were irrational (just as happens when each person watching a parade decides he can see a little better if he stands on tiptoes). After each round of investment, all the players had more money in the game and returns remained anemic."

---

* Berkshire's experience during its textile years illustrates quite clearly Buffett's assertion that depreciation is a meaningful expense.

In sum, all the gains from the investment flowed to the customer in the form of lower prices. Very little, if any at all, ended up, as Charlie Munger later said, "sticking to the ribs of owners."

If Berkshire Hathaway was to avoid a repeat of the decade ending in 1964, it would have to change course entirely, not just do something different within the textile industry. Fortunately for shareholders of Berkshire Hathaway going into 1965, Warren Buffett was about to enter the scene. Things would be very different going forward.

Lessons: 1955–1964

1. Qualitative indicators can lead to clues about a business's future.
2. The newest technology won't necessarily help a business, in terms of profitability, if that technology is available to all industry participants and that industry is commoditized.
3. Owners should always dig deeper into financial statements. Even if plant write-downs recorded in 1962, 1963, and 1964 were in accordance with accounting principles at the time, they were not trivial amounts. Management should have explained why $5.9 million was chopped off the value of their investment in property, plant, and equipment over three years.
4. Capital-intensive businesses can be difficult, if not protected by meaningful competitive advantages. With high amounts of capital required to generate each dollar of revenues, declining margins translate to declining returns on capital more forcefully.
5. Profit margins are important, but their absolute level is relatively unimportant. The more important metric is return on capital. A low margin business can produce a satisfactory return on capital provided capital requirements are low. Conversely, a business requiring a lot of capital can produce a satisfactory return if it achieves high margins. A business requiring a large capital investment with low margins (like the textile business during this decade), in an industry with surplus capacity and competitive disadvantages, was doomed.

Table 2.8: Berkshire Hathaway, Inc. consolidated balance sheets, year-end 1954–1964

($ thousands)	10/03/64	09/28/63	09/29/62	09/30/61	10/01/60	10/03/59	09/27/58	09/30/57	09/30/56	09/30/55	09/30/54
Current assets											
Cash	$920	$660	$1,445	$939	$1,535	$1,987	$2,473	$2,003	$2,554	$4,169	$4,977
Marketable securities	0	0	0	0	3,248	4,464	0	163	482	4,333	2,963
Accounts receivable, net	7,451	7,670	7,052	6,852	7,645	7,070	7,184	8,051	7,136	4,343	3,200
Inventories	11,689	18,011	19,281	20,880	14,920	15,655	22,411	24,066	30,842	22,977	27,669
Other current assets	191	237	321	275	495	433	0	875	0	1,000	394
Total current assets	20,250	26,579	28,099	28,947	27,843	29,608	32,068	35,157	41,015	36,822	39,202
Property, plant, and equipment, net	7,571	12,825	15,913	16,232	14,389	12,842	15,021	16,806	17,131	16,655	17,249
Other assets	65	43	77	100	162	211	939	1,696	1,812	1,722	1,778
Total assets	$27,887	$39,448	$44,089	$45,279	$42,394	$42,661	$48,028	$53,659	$59,958	$55,200	$58,230
Current liabilities											
Notes payable	$2,500	$5,400	$6,900	$4,150	$0	$0	$4,500	$3,350	$4,300	$0	$878
Accounts payable	2,097	2,415	3,316	3,371	2,583	2,424	2,267	3,836	2,185	2,334	2,296
Accruals & other	1,152	1,353	1,409	1,582	1,830	1,325	1,333	1,569	3,104	1,466	1,702
Total current liabilities	5,748	9,169	11,625	9,103	4,412	3,749	8,100	8,756	9,589	3,800	4,875
Long-term liabilities	0	0	0	0	0	0	0	0	0	0	0
Shares outstanding (000's)	*1,138*	*1,607*	*1,607*	*1,607*	*1,626*	*1,936*	*2,106*	*2,106*	*2,246*	*2,295*	*2,295*
Total stockholders' equity	22,139	30,279	32,464	36,176	37,982	38,912	39,928	44,903	50,370	51,400	53,354
Total liabilities and stockholders' equity	$27,887	$39,448	$44,089	$45,279	$42,394	$42,661	$48,028	$53,659	$59,958	$55,200	$58,230

Note: Amounts are rounded from actual dollars which may cause totals to differ slightly.

Sources: Berkshire Hathaway Annual Reports, 1954–1964.

Table 2.9: Berkshire Hathaway, Inc. consolidated income statements, 1954–1964

($ thousands)	10/03/64	09/28/63	09/29/62	09/30/61	10/01/60	10/03/59	09/27/58	09/30/57	09/30/56	09/30/55	09/30/54
Net revenues	$49,983	$50,591	$53,259	$47,722	$62,609	$69,512	$61,956	$66,098	$68,043	$65,498	$66,929
Expenses (excluding depreciation)	48,354	49,419	53,373	46,145	56,274	66,369	64,409	68,241	64,517	63,370	65,370
Depreciation	1,101	1,717	1,905	2,129	1,713	1,637	1,941	1,971	1,896	1,799	See note
Operating profit / (loss)	528	(545)	(2,019)	(551)	4,622	1,506	(4,394)	(4,114)	1,630	329	1,559
Other income / (expense)	(352)	(140)	(132)	86	2	(184)	(582)	(14)	160	384	(172)
Pre-tax income	176	(685)	(2,151)	(465)	4,624	1,322	(4,975)	(4,128)	1,790	713	1,386
Provision for taxes / (refund)	0	0	0	(72)	0	0	0	(870)	867	412	726
Net income / (loss)	$176	($685)	($2,151)	($393)	$4,624	$1,322	($4,975)	($3,258)	$923	$301	$660

Notes: Amounts are rounded from actual dollars which may cause totals to differ slightly. 1954: Depreciation included in expenses in line above.
Sources: Berkshire Hathaway Annual Reports, 1954–1964.

Table 2.10: Berkshire Hathaway, Inc. consolidated reconciliation of shareholders' equity, 1955–1964

($ thousands)	10/03/64	09/28/63	09/29/62	09/30/61	10/01/60	10/03/59	09/27/58	09/30/57	09/30/56	09/30/55
Prior year-end equity	$30,279	$32,464	$36,176	$37,982	$38,912	$39,928	$44,903	$50,370	$51,400	$53,354
Current year net income / (loss)	176	(685)	(2,151)	(393)	4,624	1,322	(4,975)	(3,258)	923	301
Current year dividends	0	0	(161)	(1,206)	(1,715)	(464)	0	(1,108)	(2,276)	(2,245)
Change in common	0	(3,436)	0	0	0	0	0	0	0	(3)
Change in paid in capital	0	(2,738)	0	0	0	0	0	2	887	(7)
Treasury stock	(5,316)	7,766	0	(208)	(3,838)	(1,874)	0	(1,267)	(579)	0
Revenue agent net asset adjustment	0	0	0	0	0	0	0	0	15	0
Reduction in provision for prior years' taxes	0	0	0	0	0	0	0	165	0	0
Estimated loss on properties to be sold	(3,000)	(1,500)	(1,400)	0	0	0	0	0	0	0
Retirement of treasury stock	0	(1,592)	0	0	0	0	0	0	0	0
Ending Equity	$22,139	$30,279	$32,464	$36,176	$37,982	$38,912	$39,928	$44,903	$50,370	$51,400

Note: Amounts are rounded from actual dollars which may cause totals to differ slightly.
Sources: Berkshire Hathaway Annual Reports, 1954–1964.

Table 2.11: Berkshire Hathaway, Inc. selected data and ratios, 1954–1964

	10/03/64	09/28/63	09/29/62	09/30/61	10/01/60	10/03/59	09/27/58	09/30/57	09/30/56	09/30/55	09/30/54
Working capital (*$ thousands*)	$14,502	$17,411	$16,474	$19,844	$23,430	$25,859	$23,968	$26,401	$31,427	$33,022	$34,327
Current ratio	3.52:1	2.90:1	2.42:1	3.18:1	6.31:1	7.90:1	3.96:1	4.02:1	4.28:1	9.69:1	8.04:1
Operating margin	1.06%	(1.08%)	(3.79%)	(1.15%)	7.38%	2.17%	(7.09%)	(6.22%)	2.39%	0.50%	
Net margin	0.35%	(1.35%)	(4.04%)	(0.82%)	7.39%	1.90%	(8.03%)	(4.93%)	1.36%	0.46%	
Average invested capital[1] (*$ thousands*)	$30,159	$37,521	$39,845	$39,154	$38,447	$41,670	$46,341	$51,462	$53,035	$52,816	
Revenues / avg. invested capital	$1.66	$1.35	$1.34	$1.22	$1.63	$1.67	$1.34	$1.28	$1.28	$1.24	
Avg. invested capital / rev. (inverse of above)	$0.60	$0.74	$0.75	$0.82	$0.61	$0.60	$0.75	$0.78	$0.78	$0.81	
Debt-to-equity ratio	11.29%	17.83%	21.25%	11.47%	0.00%	0.00%	11.27%	7.46%	8.54%	0.00%	
Return on avg. invested capital	0.58%	(1.83%)	(5.40%)	(1.00%)	12.03%	3.17%	(10.74%)	(6.33%)	1.74%	0.57%	
Return on average equity	0.67%	(2.18%)	(6.27%)	(1.06%)	12.03%	3.35%	(11.73%)	(6.84%)	1.81%	0.59%	
Book value per share	$19.46	$18.84	$20.20	$22.51	$23.37	$20.10	$18.96	$21.32	$22.43	$22.40	$23.25

Footnote:
1. Average invested capital calculated based on the average of the sum of the prior and current year's equity and debt capital.

Sources: Berkshire Hathaway Annual Reports, 1955–1964, and author calculations.

Chapter 3
1965–1974

Table 3.1: Decade snapshot: 1964–1974

	1964	1974
Business:	Textile manufacturing	Textiles, insurance, banking, candy, publishing
Key managers:	Chairman: Malcolm G. Chace, Jr.; President: Seabury Stanton	Chairman & CEO: Warren E. Buffett; President: Kenneth V. Chace
Annual revenues:	$50 million	$101.5 million
Stockholders' equity:	$22.1 million	$88.2 million
Book value per share:	$19.46	$90.02

Major Capital Allocation Decisions:

1. Purchased National Indemnity Company and National Fire and Marine Insurance Company (collectively National Indemnity) for $8.6 million (1967).

2. Purchased The Illinois National Bank & Trust Company of Rockford for $17.7 million (1969).

3. Contributed approximately $25 million of additional equity capital to the Insurance Group to support its growth.

4. Borrowed $20 million in long-term debt to repay existing debt, provide capital for the Insurance Group, and maintain liquidity for future opportunities.

5. Purchased a 26% interest in Blue Chip Stamps for approximately $15 million (various).

6. Reduced working capital and fixed assets in the Textile Group to maintain an appropriate level of capital investment in relation to sales.

7. Allocated Insurance Group float into undervalued securities.

8. Returned $2.6 million to shareholders in the form of dividends ($0.1 million) and share repurchases ($2.5 million).

Noteworthy Events:

1. May 10, 1965: Warren Buffett gains control of Berkshire and is elected Chairman.

2. Price controls instituted by the Nixon Administration (1970).

3. United States abandons the gold standard (1971).

Introduction

A mere 12.5 cents set off the long chain of events that led Warren Buffett to go all-in on Berkshire Hathaway and ensured its (and his) place in history. Buffett first acquired shares in Berkshire for his investing partnership, Buffett Partnership Limited, using a playbook executed countless times before: find a business selling for less than its liquidating value and wait for a temporary market correction to sell at a profit. Berkshire had a history of share repurchases that Buffett saw as a catalyst to monetize his current holdings. He anticipated future repurchases and even struck what he thought was a deal with Seabury Stanton to tender his partnership's shares for $11.50 per share. The official offer came at $11.375, or 12½ cents less. Feeling slighted, Buffett set out to seek control of Berkshire.[31]

Buffett made additional stock purchases on behalf of himself and his partnership, and gained the support of other existing shareholders, including Otis Stanton (Seabury's brother) and the Chace family. On May 10, 1965, Seabury and his son, Jack, resigned. The board immediately gave Warren Buffett control and placed Ken Chace in charge of operations. Berkshire thus became another investment vehicle through which Buffett could allocate capital.

Berkshire became Buffett's primary investment vehicle when he wound down Buffett Partnership Limited in 1969. Buffett took a deep value approach to investing, and the rise of the "nifty-fifty" and other high-priced growth stocks in the 1960s were completely at odds with that. He and some of the partners took Berkshire shares distributed during the liquidation of the partnership. Aside from some other outside investments (which as we will see eventually worked their way into Berkshire), Berkshire Hathaway remained as a permanent base of capital—the foundation on which Buffett's future business deals would be placed.[*]

This first decade of Berkshire Hathaway under Warren Buffett's control (1965–1974) is in some respects the most important. Like a caterpillar that morphs into a butterfly, Berkshire began a transition from a textile company to a conglomerate almost unrecognizable from its former self. Warren Buffett would learn many lessons during this decade, from the difficulty of commodity businesses to the benefit of starting with a good business. Buffett proved that over a relatively short period of time and with a careful, guiding hand, skillful capital allocation could help any business reach its highest potential. Also, he demonstrated that capital was a fungible commodity, not pre-destined to remain in the business or industry where it was originally invested.

---

[*] Buffett later wrote that using Berkshire as his investment vehicle was a mistake. He said he should have purchased better businesses using a private partnership rather than effectively share the upside with others outside of the partnership (Berkshire's other shareholders).

Table 3.2: Select information 1965–1974

	1965	1966	1967	1968	1969	1970	1971	1972	1973	1974
BRK book value per share - % change	23.8%	20.3%	11.0%	19.0%	16.2%	12.0%	16.4%	21.7%	4.7%	5.5%
BRK market value per share - % change	49.5%	(3.4%)	13.3%	77.8%	19.4%	(4.6%)	80.5%	8.1%	(2.5%)	(48.7%)
S&P 500 total return	10.0%	(11.7%)	30.9%	11.0%	(8.4%)	3.9%	14.6%	18.9%	(14.8%)	(26.4%)
US GDP Growth (real %)	6.5%	6.6%	2.7%	4.9%	3.1%	0.2%	3.3%	5.3%	5.6%	(0.5%)
10-year Treasury Note (year-end %)	4.6%	4.8%	5.7%	6.0%	7.7%	6.4%	5.9%	6.4%	6.7%	7.4%
US inflation (%)	1.6%	3.0%	2.8%	4.2%	5.4%	5.9%	4.2%	3.3%	6.3%	11.0%
US unemployment (%)	4.5%	3.8%	3.8%	3.6%	3.5%	5.0%	6.0%	5.6%	4.9%	5.6%

Sources: Berkshire Hathaway Annual Reports 2018, 2019 and Federal Reserve Bank of St. Louis.

1965

The 1965 Berkshire Hathaway letter to shareholders, although signed by Chairman Malcolm Chace and President Kenneth Chace (no relation), was written by Warren Buffett. Reading that letter, one can begin to see Buffett's subtle influence, starting with its communications to shareholders.

From the beginning Buffett was transparent about company finances—sharing financial details usually hidden within below-the-line charges to shield the income statements from taking a hit. He also explicitly explained an important accounting change that would provide a more realistic, but less rosy, view of the financial picture.

In the very first paragraph, the reader learns that the earnings as reported do not contain any non-recurring losses sustained from closing two plants. The second paragraph of the letter alerts shareholders to an important accounting change. Because of losses incurred in previous years, Berkshire did not have to pay federal income taxes on its pre-tax earnings of $4.3 million in 1965. Reporting Berkshire's profits without taxes, however, might mislead shareholders as to the true earning power of their company. An estimate of taxes that would have been payable without the loss carryovers was therefore deducted. The $2 million charge, "equivalent to federal income taxes," reduced reported net earnings to $2.3 million.

Though subtle, the fact that a manager would intentionally choose to report earnings almost 50% lower than they *could* have was a loud signal to those paying attention. It was also in marked contrast to accounting practices of the previous decade, whereby below the line charges were taken to equity. This had shielded the income statement from reporting losses on disposed plant and equipment, keeping shareholders out of the loop. Buffett chose the reverse. The charge taken for taxes was not actually payable due to the loss carryovers, and it was added back to equity in the reconciliation of accounts.

Operationally, Berkshire performed better in 1965. Revenues were flat compared to 1964 at $49.3 million, though profits grew to $2.3 million pre-tax.* In the letter to shareholders, Buffett noted a substantial reduction to overhead, and the company continued its program of investing in new technology to reduce costs and improve quality. Importantly, the economic results during the year represented a much-improved return on equity of 9.8%.**

Together the profits and capital freed as a result of reducing inventories allowed Berkshire to pay off $2.5 million in bank loans and repurchase 120,231 of its outstanding shares, or over 10% of the company.***

Buffett the capital allocator had arrived.

1966

On the surface, the year 1966 looked very similar to the prior year. Revenues totaled $49.4 million compared to $49.3 million in 1965; operating profit was up modestly to $4.8 million, from $4.7 million. But difficulties remained. Let's start with the product mix. Sales in the Synthetics division fell, though Home Fabrics increased. Box Loom gained, while sales within the King Phillip D division slackened. Then, the worst news: The latter half of 1966 was "one of generally depressed markets," not a good turn of events for an industry with generally depressed sales.

This story was unfortunately familiar. Overproduction in acetate fabrics and imports of nylon created oversupply. Anticipating future pain, the 1966 Annual Report noted that given the preceding weakness in synthetics, competitors were likely to increase cotton production. This would hurt the company's King Phillip D division. Rather than keep running at full steam, the company curtailed production for a week during October 1966 and noted that further shutdowns might be necessary to avoid inventory buildup.

Continued development in the new Home Fabrics products, a bright spot during the year, was meant to counter those slowdowns. But growth has a cost and would entail additional investment in inventories and receivables. It was the same old story, but one worth repeating: It takes money to make money. How much money? Buffett estimated up to $7 million.

---

* $4.3 million before the provision for taxes noted above. I've used the Buffett-adjusted figure.
** Using the lower $2.3 million figure.
*** Technically these repurchases can be attributed to the tender offer made by Stanton that irked Buffett and led him to seek control.

Buffett operated the company under a policy of self-sufficiency, both for philosophical reasons and because of the challenges of the textile industry. He said outside funding was virtually unobtainable, which was one reason Berkshire maintained reserves of cash and marketable securities to have resources on hand. "Present uncertainties such as war, tax rates and decreased level of business activity also all combine to emphasize the continuing need for a strong financial condition," he wrote. It's worth noting that this approach has never changed and neither have the uncertainties, though diversification has lessened the risk to the overall enterprise.

The 1966 Annual Report concludes with a section entitled Dividends. Due to the state of the company's balance sheet and the fact that it was profitable, Berkshire declared a dividend of $0.10 per share. This dividend, payable in 1967, was the last the company would pay—and likely will ever pay—under Buffett's control. Buffett would later codify his thinking into a principle.* The capital under his stewardship was best retained if Berkshire could deliver more than a dollar of market value for each dollar of retained earnings, he explained. Paying a dividend not only deprived shareholders of the ability to have that dollar remain and compound on their behalf but was also tax inefficient.**

1967

The trouble anticipated the prior year was realized in 1967. In response to steep declines in sales volumes and pricing, Berkshire cut production by 15% to avoid building up inventories. But cutting production created another problem: the loss of trained labor. Because it couldn't afford to maintain idle employees on the payroll while waiting for good times to return (if they returned at all), Berkshire was forced to lay off skilled labor. If Berkshire ramped up production in the future, it would face higher training costs to onboard new employees.

The ongoing weakness in the market for textiles necessitated the closing of another plant in 1967. The King Philip D plant in Warren, Rhode Island, which had a one-week shutdown in 1966 to avoid building excess inventories, closed permanently. The plant efficiently manufactured fine-combed lawns, but there was no longer demand for the product as cotton lawn products were being replaced by polyester blend fabrics. Further, there was little to no adaptability of the equipment for new uses.

There were some bright spots in textiles. The Home Fabrics division expanded to a wider variety of fabrics, and Berkshire began an Apparel Fabrics division which sold finished yarn products into the women's apparel market. Both were profitable,

---

* This is referring to the 1996 Owner's Manual, which has been kept up-to-date (though changing very little) since that time.

** Shareholders wishing to keep their share of earnings in the company would first have to pay tax and reinvest the balance, possibly at a premium. This imposed one policy for all shareholders.

but since the production orders were smaller and required more loom shifts, higher manufacturing costs reduced profits. By Buffett's own admission, company management and employees were hardworking and creative individuals.

Insurance

Buffett started allocating capital outside of the textile business—and in doing so, changed the face of Berkshire Hathaway forever.* The seminal event in 1967 was the acquisition of National Indemnity Company and its sister company, National Fire and Marine Insurance Company (considered together as National Indemnity**). The purchase of National Indemnity was perhaps the most important event in Berkshire's history, as it would provide a strong platform for future growth. More immediately it provided an outlet for the cash freed up by shrinking Berkshire's textile operations.

Jack Ringwalt and his brother Arthur founded National Indemnity in 1940. It was an unusual insurance company. The product didn't make it unusual. Insurance was and is a commoditized business with almost free entry. What made National Indemnity different was its philosophy of insuring risks other insurers rejected. The company began by insuring taxis. In addition to less-than-perfect drivers (the bulk of its business), the company insured risks others shunned entirely. The philosophy is best summed up by a quote from Jack Ringwalt: "There's no such thing as a bad risk, only bad rates." Ringwalt was willing to insure almost any risk, given an appropriate price. This included circus performers and lion tamers.[32] Even with more traditional risks, the insurance industry was like a pendulum, swinging between cycles of optimism and pessimism. National Indemnity's willingness to accept higher risks (at higher rates) led to doing business when others walked away. It was a strategy built on discipline and a relentless attention to minimizing costs. It is no wonder Buffett was impressed.

Buffett was no stranger to insurance. He famously took a trip to Washington, D.C., as a Columbia University student to learn more about GEICO, which would later play a starring role at Berkshire. After the visit Buffett penned "The Security I Like Best", featuring GEICO. National Indemnity operated in a different risk pool than GEICO (which focused on government employees with good driving records). But it had the basic characteristic of all insurance companies: a bucket of capital Buffett could allocate into undervalued businesses.

---

* This process had already started with Buffett allocating Berkshire's marketable securities portfolio into his favorite stocks including American Express, Disney Productions, Florida Light & Gas, Investors Diversified Services A, John Blair & Co., Mass. Indemnity & Life Insurance Co., and Sperry & Hutchinson.
** I use National Indemnity to refer to them collectively, although technically National Indemnity Company was the larger of the two and all but completely eclipsed its smaller affiliate.

National Indemnity was on Buffett's radar because of its headquarters in his hometown of Omaha. Buffett knew Ringwalt and had even tried unsuccessfully to persuade him to invest in the Buffett partnership years earlier. This time Buffett wanted to buy. He liked Ringwalt's reputation as a manager and understood the business well. When an opportunity arose to buy National Indemnity, Buffett pounced. He also persuaded Ringwalt to stay on to manage the business, an acquisition strategy he became known for, and developed a friendship with him.

Buffett agreed to pay $8.6 million for National Indemnity, a $1.9 million premium over the tangible net worth of the company. Why would Buffett, whose personal fortune through that time was made largely by buying companies for less than their net worth, pay almost a 30% premium? The answer lay in the nature of the business and in Ringwalt.

Insurance is unlike most other businesses in that its assets are almost entirely comprised of securities. In the most basic construction of an insurance company balance sheet its assets are funded by policyholders (unearned premiums and claims waiting to be paid) and the balance is shareholders' equity. Buying National Indemnity with Berkshire Hathaway meant Berkshire could allocate capital into securities it would buy anyway and, for a modest premium, also gain access to a well-run insurance operation. If Ringwalt (the expert insurance operator) could continue to earn an underwriting profit, those profits would pay for the upfront premium. Any additional gains Buffett could achieve by putting to work the $19.4 million of investable float (explained more fully in the section on 1968) would be gravy.[33]

With hindsight we know this was one of the most important and attractive business acquisitions in Berkshire's history. But even Buffett admits it took him a while to realize just how good a deal National Indemnity was.

The 1967 Annual Report had little discussion of insurance company financial operations.* Berkshire's 1967 consolidated statement of earnings reported only National Indemnity's after-tax income: a $791,938 equity in earnings of unconsolidated subsidiaries. The report also disclosed a $100,147 after-tax realized investment gain attributable to National Indemnity's investment portfolio. Still, one sentence in the insurance discussion stood out: "All earnings of the insurance subsidiaries are being retained to build additional capital strength." It was a reminder that the dividends of 1967 would not return because Buffett's strategy was to invest in growth to bring more value to shareholders.

One final note should be made about 1967. Effective December 30, 1967, Berkshire changed its accounting year to a calendar year. As a result, the Annual Report for 1967 covered fifteen months. It reported the results for the twelve months that ended

---

* The entire 1967 Annual Report was eight pages long and typical of the limited disclosures provided to investors in those years.

September 30, 1967, and the "stub" three-month period ending December 31, 1967. Efforts were made to provide shareholders with comparative figures to allow proper insight into business operations.*

1968

The 1968 letter to shareholders led off with a short, two-sentence paragraph starting this way: "Total operating earnings in relation to stockholders' investment still are not satisfactory... ." Buffett was alerting shareholders that in investing it's not the absolute level of profits that matter; it's whether the earnings are appropriate in relation to the amount invested. Berkshire's return on average shareholders' equity that year was 13.8%. This was not a poor result, and it was certainly better than Berkshire was accustomed to earning, but it was still below what Buffett considered satisfactory.

Textiles

Results for 1968 were separated into two paragraphs each for textiles and insurance, plus two additional paragraphs under a section titled, Marketable Securities and Acquisitions. Textiles that year were, not surprisingly, mixed. Revenues were up 14% to $46 million, led by Home Fabrics and Menswear Linings. The report pointed out that those areas were historically the most consistently profitable. Perhaps because of this, Berkshire had installed a new 150-inch loom for the coming year. Berkshire also held options on additional looms should volume materialize.

The Box Loom division was not part of that growth. Unlike Berkshire's more finished lines, the Box Loom division had historically suffered due to heavy imports and weak prices. Rather than continue operating in this area, Berkshire decided to phase out its operations of greige goods (raw textiles that are woven though not yet dyed or bleached). Additional losses from this division were forecast, though Berkshire anticipated improved overall results from textiles because of the change in strategy.

Insurance

The space devoted to commenting on the new insurance division (two paragraphs, like the textile division), clearly understated Buffett's enthusiasm for this new line of business. The division was performing so well that Berkshire would invest additional equity capital into operations and lay off less risk to reinsurers. (Reinsurers essentially

---

* To reconcile the new accounting with the old, the earnings from the three-month stub period are included as an adjustment to the December 31, 1967 reconciliation of shareholders' equity in the accompanying summary financials.

buy a portion of the volume of business written by the primary insurer so that the primary insurer can continue to write business at levels appropriate in relation to its capital.) Buffett even suggested the possibility of entering the reinsurance field in the future.

After praising Jack Ringwalt for delivering a "splendid operating performance", Buffett explained the operating philosophy and strategy for the group. The focus would be on operating profits, not volume or market share. It was possible to operate at an underwriting loss like the industry as a whole and make up the difference with investment income, but Berkshire's insurance operations would seek underwriting profits first and foremost. It's worth noting that Berkshire still employs this strategy.

The financial disclosures for the Insurance Group in the 1968 letter were decidedly wanting. Despite owning 99% of the insurance businesses, the results were not consolidated with the parent company financial statements. Instead, a line item on the balance sheet indicated an "investment in unconsolidated subsidiaries" of approximately $12.8 million. And the income statement only contained a line item for "equity in earnings of unconsolidated insurance companies" of $1.79 million (operating profits after tax) and $707,000 of after-tax investment gains.

It is unclear why more detailed results for the Insurance Group were not presented in 1968. However, complete statements for National Indemnity were included in 1969, with 1968 presented for comparison. Shareholders reading the 1968 Annual Report did not have the benefit of more detail, though fortunately we can examine each business more thoroughly during our review.

We will not venture into the fine detail of each insurance business but will instead look at the combined operations of the two subsidiaries as if they were one. Still, remember that National Fire and Marine was about one-tenth the size of National Indemnity, with premiums earned of $2.3 million compared to National Indemnity's $20.3 million.

In 1968, combined premiums earned were just over $22.6 million. Net premiums written as a percentage of average equity were 221%. The Insurance Group was writing a significant volume of business. More importantly, it was being written profitably.

The single most important measure of profitability for an insurance company is captured in what is called the combined ratio. The combined ratio is made up of the loss ratio (amounts paid out to cover losses to insureds), and the expense ratio (expenses incurred to conduct operations and write additional premium volume, such as salaries and rent).

Equation 3.1

Combined ratio = loss ratio + expense ratio

or

$$Combined\ ratio = \frac{loss\ expenses}{earned\ premiums} + \frac{underwriting\ expenses}{written\ premiums}$$

In 1968, these ratios were 65.4% (loss ratio) and 32.1% (expenses), producing a combined ratio of 97.5%. It may seem counterintuitive, but a ratio below 100% is generally good and means an insurer is operating at an underwriting profit. In this case, Berkshire got to keep 2.5% of the insurance premiums it took in from policyholders, in addition to money earned from investing those funds.

It was not uncommon for insurers, then and now, to operate at an underwriting loss so long as investment earnings produced a satisfactory overall result. These investment operations are conducted with the monies collected by policyholders, but not yet paid out in claims. This pool of funds is called float and can contribute an enormous amount of value to an insurance operation since any profits from investing the float accrues to the insurer.[*] It is often self-serving for the managers of an insurance business to think they can write unprofitable business, and therefore capture more market share and make it up in the investment operations.

While this strategy could work, most insurance executives are poor investment professionals since they lack training in that area.[**] These two tendencies combine to produce subpar results for many insurance industry shareholders. Fortunately for Berkshire Hathaway shareholders, they had a profitable underwriting operation *and* a world-class investor working for them.

Concluding the 1968 Annual Report was a note on two acquisitions completed just after the year ended. At the beginning of 1969, Berkshire acquired 100% of Sun Newspapers and its related printing business, Blacker Printing Company, both based in Buffett's hometown of Omaha, Nebraska. The newspaper business of today pales in comparison to the industry that existed several decades ago. Back then, the business was profitable with high returns on capital for dominant papers. Buffett would build on this initial foray into the industry to earn strong profits for Berkshire shareholders.[***]

---

[*] It is liable for any losses too, which is why insurance is so heavily regulated.

[**] Their focus is usually on sales of additional policies to drive premium volume.

[***] *The Sun* was smaller than the *Omaha World Herald* and economically not as attractive. Buffett loved newspapers and admittedly stretched for it, paying $1.25 million for an initial yield of about 8% (*The Snowball* p. 325).

1969

The Berkshire Hathaway of earlier years could not call itself a conglomerate, but the present company could. Buffett wanted shareholders to understand why this classification was so important and did so by opening the 1969 letter with a discussion of business strategy.

"Four years ago your management committed itself to the development of more substantial and more consistent earning power than appeared possible if capital continued to be invested exclusively in the textile industry." The paragraph goes on to explain that through two major acquisitions (the insurance subsidiaries, and a banking subsidiary acquired in early 1969), Berkshire averaged about a 10% return on shareholders' equity. This included the returns from the textile division, which were below 5%. For these reasons, the letter referred to the relatively new conglomerate as "reasonably successful"—when compared to other textile companies that remained or expanded solely in the textile industry. The underlying suggestion was clear: True success in textiles only would be hard or impossible to find.

Textiles

Despite this, textiles remained Berkshire's primary business operation, at least for now, and led off the first section of the letter. Not surprising for shareholders, textile sales in 1969 declined—12.1% to $40.4 million. The Box Loom division was shut down, causing substantial operating losses. The industry was in the throes of a recession worse than had been seen in many years because of an overall lack of demand.

In addition to closing the Box Loom division, Textile Group management instituted two-week shutdown periods to avoid building excess inventories. If a business believes demand will return in relatively short order, it may continue to produce product and store it for later sale. This keeps employees busy, but requires additional capital investment. Considering the severity of the 1969 slowdown, this would not have been wise. Even with the losses from Box Loom, the textile segment (after taxes) reported only a slight decrease in earnings, from $1.6 million in 1968 to $1.5 million a year later.

Insurance

Buffett led the insurance operations segment of his letter with praise for Jack Ringwalt and his team. (Buffett may have already been following his mantra of praise by name, criticize by category.) Under Ringwalt's leadership, Berkshire's insurance operations produced an underwriting profit, compared to substantial underwriting losses for the fire and casualty insurance industry. This was a direct result of Ringwalt's policy of underwriting for a profit and not just for volume (recall the strategy discussion from 1968).

One interesting note as it pertains to Buffett's statement on underwriting profits is that the letter states the figure was an adjusted amount. This contrasted to the financial statements, which showed a combined (National Indemnity Insurance Company and National Fire & Marine Insurance Company) pre-tax underwriting *loss* of about $153,000. This is when it pays to read the fine print. The notes to the financial statements for the insurance companies contain the likely answer to these conflicting statements. Note 1, the Basis of Presentation, states that the financials are presented using insurance accounting principles, rather than Generally Accepted Accounting Principles (GAAP). While there are many specifics as to how these differ, the main takeaway is that insurance industry reporting standards are stricter. In other words, more conservative.*

A specific item worth noting from Note 1 is: While premium income is recorded pro rata over the period of the policy, the costs associated with writing the business are expensed immediately. Buffett knew that despite reporting losses that year, the business the insurance segment was underwriting would likely generate a profit over the lives of the policies. Spending money to bring in more business caused expenses to balloon, and there was no accounting convention for separating monies spent on expansion versus those for maintaining existing levels of business. Buffett needed shareholders to understand that Berkshire was investing in its insurance businesses with the expectation of future profit, reported profits falling where they may. A look at the combined ratio, which was below 100%, indicates a profitable year. **

A new surety department was doing well. It entered workman's compensation insurance with an office in Los Angeles, California and its reinsurance division was off to a strong start. Commenting on the latter, Buffett wrote that due to the nature of the business, it would take years before an intelligent verdict could be rendered. Berkshire had plans for a new Home State insurance operation (an insurance company operating in one state for regulatory reasons), and concluded, "Expectations are for continued growth in our insurance operations."

Insurance results for 1969 illustrate Buffett's excitement about the segment. Premiums were growing at a double-digit rate, and the business was profitable, as judging by the sub-100% combined ratio.***

---

* This makes sense given insurance commissioners' primary goal is to protect policyholders, not the owners of the insurance company.

** This is an instance where the combined ratio of 96.2% indicates profit, yet the financial statements show a loss. This is due to the fact that the expense ratio is calculated on written premiums, while only earned premiums show up in the financial statements.

*** Note the discrepancy between the reported underwriting loss of $0.2 million and the 96.2% combined ratio. Such a ratio reflects an underwriting gain of approximately $1 million.

Table 3.3: Select Berkshire Hathaway insurance company data, 1968–69

($ millions)	1969	1968	Change
Premiums written	$28.8	$22.7	27%
Premiums earned	25.3	22.6	12%
Premiums written to average equity	215%	197%	18pts
Loss ratio	64.8%	65.4%	-0.7pts
Expense ratio	31.4%	32.1%	-0.6pts
Combined ratio	96.2%	97.5%	-1.3pts

Sources: Berkshire Hathaway Annual Report 1969 and author's calculations.

It's worth pausing to discuss the two premium figures contained in Table 3.3. Premiums written reflect the amount of business written during any given year. These are a direct consequence of the insurance company's sales force. Premiums earned are different. A policy written today that covers the next two years will be reflected in today's written results, but half will not be earned until the next year. Therefore it takes many years for underwriting skill to become apparent. Anyone can write a policy, but it takes an intelligent manager to write profitable business today while looking at tomorrow's risks.

Another major reason insurance premiums earned might differ from those written is due to reinsurance. Reinsurance is simply the practice of laying off or ceding some of the written policies to another insurer. This allows an insurance company to share some of the risk it undertakes and maximize its sales force. (In general, salespeople like writing business and don't like to stop because the insurer has too many policies on the books.) The amount of reinsurance can vary from substantial to negligible or nothing at all depending on the need or desire to diversify or maintain capital levels. Berkshire would not only look to retain the business it was writing, but grow naturally by taking on additional risk through its own reinsurance operations. In its inaugural year, Berkshire wrote $2.7 million of reinsurance business.[34]

Banking

The major acquisition of 1969 was the purchase of the Illinois National Bank & Trust Company. Banking, like insurance, involves prudently managing risks that take time to materialize. A bank's long-term record tells a compelling story. Buffett provided a short history of the bank for shareholders, which is worth repeating here:

"This bank had been built by Eugene Abegg, without addition of outside capital, from $250,000 of net worth and $400,000 of deposits in 1931, to $17 million of net worth and $100 million of deposits in 1969. Mr. Abegg has continued as Chairman and produced record operating earnings (before security losses) of approximately $2 million in 1969. Such earnings, as a percentage of either deposits or total assets, are close to the top among larger commercial banks in the country which are not primarily trust department operations."

To achieve such a growth rate over the preceding 38 years would have required an almost 12% return on equity, and an annual growth rate of 15.6% in the deposit base. Given the long history of sound and profitable operations, Buffett could rightfully conclude that, like Ringwalt, Abegg knew what he was doing.

The purchase price of the bank was not detailed, but we can back into it using the financial information contained in the Annual Report (see Table 3.4). This information shows that Berkshire paid approximately 1.05 times book value for the bank—a very attractive price given the quality of the bank.* This came to $17.7 million.

Table 3.4: The Illinois National Bank & Trust Co. of Rockford, acquisition analysis

($ millions)	
1969 ending carrying value	$18.9
Less: 1969 earnings	1.2
Berkshire purchase price	17.7
1968 Bank book value	16.8
Purchase multiple	1.05

Sources: Berkshire Hathaway Annual Report 1969 and author's calculations.

Buffett used Berkshire's now strengthened balance sheet to fund the purchase of the bank. Marketable securities were almost completely sold, raising approximately $11 million.** The shrinking textile operations provided almost $4.6 million through reductions in working capital and physical plant investment. Berkshire also augmented its funds by borrowing an additional $4.75 million.***

---

* The average return on assets (ROA) in 1969 was 1.68% (after tax, before securities gains/losses).
** Berkshire's marketable securities portfolio amounted to $5.4 million on the year-end 1968 balance sheet and was reduced to just under $300,000. The net proceeds were much higher. Due to the accounting rules at the time, which carried the value of the marketable securities at cost, funds raised were likely over $11 million. We know the value was $11.8 million at year-end 1968 but we cannot know for sure how the value changed between then and the liquidation.
*** A $6.25 million term loan replaced a $2 million bank loan. Quarterly principal payments of $375,000 were due until the $3.375 million balance matured on June 30, 1972. The interest rate was 0.50% over the prime rate for 90-day commercial loans of The First National Bank of Boston (which was the agent bank).

Berkshire, under the leadership of Warren Buffett, was becoming a very different company.

1970

Berkshire's mix of businesses produced equally mixed results in 1970. Its newly acquired bank did very well, insurance was mixed, and textiles were, unsurprisingly, mediocre.

Textiles

Still, the textile division's management team deserved compliments. Calling out Ken Chace by name, Buffett praised Chace and his group for their efforts to turn around the division while "swimming against a strong tide." That tide was the confluence of factors making the economics of textiles in New England unsustainable: high relative labor and electricity costs, coupled with stiff overseas competition.

In response to poor demand in both menswear linings and home fabrics, the division reduced production. This meant making sure inventories did not grow too far out of line from current sales levels. Over the preceding five years, inventories had averaged 25% of sales. With sales down 39% to $24.6 million in 1970, the ratio ballooned to 34%. Fluctuations in sales are not atypical in business, and if a manager expected a return to higher sales levels inventories might be maintained at the same dollar levels as before. With textiles though—a commodity whose finished products were subject to style trends, expensive to make, and where demand had dropped over time—waiting was not an option.

Despite the large drop in sales, the division eked out a tiny $107,000 profit. A good result relative to the large drop in sales, and certainly better than a loss, but far from satisfactory in relation to the capital employed in the business: $11.1 million in average non-cash working capital and $2.8 million in average property, plant, and equipment.

Insurance

The insurance segment turned in mixed, though generally satisfactory results, in 1970. Buffett said growth was outstanding, with premiums written and earned up over 55% to $45 million and $39 million, respectively. That included $7 million of written premiums in the reinsurance segment (over two and a half times the volume done the year before). But he was quick to point out that the growth in premiums was "accompanied by a somewhat poorer underwriting picture." This led to an underwriting loss of $330,000 for the Insurance Group, which meant that any earnings from the segment had to come from investing.

It is clear Buffett's enthusiasm for insurance remained strong despite the higher loss ratio. This is because he understood how the business worked. The operating philosophy of National Indemnity was to catch waves of business when it became profitable. That year a "surge of volume" resulted from more restricted markets (meaning other insurance companies pulling back after losing money).

Ringwalt's development of Home State insurance operations in 1970 signaled the future operational mantra of Buffett and Berkshire. The first operation was Cornhusker Casualty Company in Nebraska, a 100% owned subsidiary of National Indemnity. It wrote premiums of $249,000 that year. Buffett noted its "big-company capability and small-company accessibility," demonstrating the advantages of decentralized operations. Today, decentralization is the operating philosophy in all of Berkshire's operations. As the Berkshire Annual Reports would later remark, Berkshire's operations are managed via "delegation just shy of abdication." If readers were not yet convinced of Buffett's enthusiasm for this operation and for Ringwalt, Buffett let them know first that Ringwalt brought the concept to life and that there were plans to form more companies under the Home State banner.

Banking

Turning to Berkshire's new banking operation, Buffett was all praise for Illinois National Bank. He noted that the bank's operating return was the sign of "an exceptionally well-managed banking business." The bank earned a strong 1.9% return on average assets (ROA[*]) in 1970.[**]

It's worth pausing to note that while a 1.9% return may appear very low on an absolute basis—even lower than that of a basic savings account at the time—the economics of banking are such that it was truly an indication of a well-managed bank. Because banks have the advantage of using leverage (meaning they hold many more dollars in deposits than they do in equity capital), that 1.9% return on assets turned into a return on average equity (ROE) of 12.5%.

The concept is similar to the return on capital calculations used elsewhere in this book with leverage factored in. See the equations below:

---

[*] For the more technical reader here I am using return on average assets but keeping the ROA verbiage rather than ROAA.

[**] Buffett's comment in the Chairman's letter was on the bank's return on deposits. This is a somewhat archaic metric. Buffett later began using return on assets.

Equation 3.2

$$Bank: \frac{operating\ income}{assets} \times \frac{assets}{equity} = return\ on\ equity$$

Return on assets

$$Non\ bank: \frac{profit}{revenues} \times \frac{revenues}{total\ capital} \times \frac{total\ capital}{equity} = return\ on\ equity$$

Return on capital

Using the figures from the Illinois National Bank, we can see how its ROA is an indication of good economics and translates into a satisfactory ROE. Because the bank had nearly seven times the amount of assets as it did equity capital, the ROA is multiplied or leveraged by that same factor. While the use of leverage in the bank may seem (and is) high compared to other businesses, from a banking perspective it is on the conservative side. Today's banks routinely use ten- or twelve-times leverage. This creates higher returns on equity but brings additional risk and is one reason why banks are so tightly regulated.

Table 3.5: Illinois National Bank, return on assets and return on equity calculation, 1970

($ thousands)	
Operating income, after-tax	$2,221
Average assets	119,758
Return on assets	1.9%
Average equity	17,704
Avg. assets / avg. equity	6.8
Return on equity	12.5%

Sources: Berkshire Hathaway Annual Report 1970 and author's calculations.

The results from Illinois National Bank were achieved while maintaining high levels of liquidity. Its average loans to deposits ratio was just 49%. For perspective, today's banks routinely loan up to 80% of deposits. The remainder of Illinois National Bank's assets were in the investment portfolio or sitting in cash, with a small portion in premises and equipment, and other assets.

In short, Illinois National Bank was a conservatively run bank that managed its costs exceptionally well and as a result was highly profitable. This was a testament to Eugene Abegg and his management team.

Having just acquired Illinois National, Berkshire learned it would be required to sell it. At the end of 1970, Congress amended the Bank Holding Company Act of 1956 to include one-bank holding companies. The law prohibited these companies from owning non-bank companies. This meant Berkshire would not only need to sell the bank it had just purchased, but also be subject to oversight by the Federal Reserve Board and have restrictions on its acquisition activity. But Berkshire had some time. The law gave Berkshire ten years to sell, spin off, or otherwise dispose of Illinois National. In the meantime, as we'll see, Berkshire enjoyed the fruits of its ownership of Illinois National, and entered the banking business in other ways.

1971

In his opening paragraph to the 1971 Annual Report, Buffett included a reminder of his management objective. That objective was "to improve return on total capitalization … as well as the return on equity capital." Buffett noted that Berkshire's return on equity that year was 14%, which was above the average of corporate America. He highlighted his goal to improve return on total capitalization (the sum of long-term debt plus equity) as a reminder that Berkshire would not go about achieving high returns on equity by leveraging the balance sheet through excess borrowing. Although Berkshire would borrow funds at the parent level from time to time (and did so in 1971), these amounts would be very conservative. Notably, the satisfactory return on equity of 14% in 1971 included drag from inadequate earnings of the textile division. This highlights the success of the strategy to redeploy capital to greener pastures.

Textiles

Notwithstanding considerable efforts to reduce costs, the textile division struggled with low gross margins. A mild industry pickup was thought to be on the horizon, with more favorable volume and mix of business in the coming year.

The inadequacy of the Textile Group's returns is evident in its financial performance during the year. The meager operating profit represented a pre-tax return on capital of just 1.9% (see Table 3.6). No wonder Buffett was so quick to move on.

Table 3.6: Textile division, select data, 1971

(*$ millions*)	1971	1970
Revenues	$26.0	$24.6
Operating profit	0.233	0.107
Capital employed	12.1	14.5
Return on capital, pre-tax	1.9%	0.7%

Source: Berkshire Hathaway Annual Reports 1970, 1972.

Insurance

Quite contrary to the industry headwinds experienced in textiles, the insurance division (whose financials were now reported together under Insurance Group) had a considerable tailwind in 1971. As a result of some significant good fortune, the industry experienced reduced auto accident frequency, higher premium rates, and an absence of major disasters. For Berkshire this translated into 47% growth in premiums written, to $66 million, and a solid 95% combined ratio that brought in $1.4 million of underwriting profits.

This was all good news if you took it at face value, but when viewed as the calm before the storm, it carried a warning. Buffett knew this and was quick to point it out. "We shared in these benefits, although they are not without their negative connotations," he wrote. These strong results would bring more competitors into the marketplace. Those competitors would drive premiums to the point of unprofitability. It was only when competitors faced losses that they would either raise rates, pull back on writing business, or both. Until then, Berkshire's insurance managers would focus on underwriting profitability—volume be as it may.

Keeping the focus on the long term, Berkshire continued the expansion of its Home State operations. During 1971 it formed Lakeland Fire & Casualty Company in Minnesota and Texas United Insurance in Texas (which legally formed in 1972). The Home State business accounted for just $1.5 million in premium volume, but volume was expected to double in 1972 with these new additions.

Another area of insurance growth in 1971 was the acquisition of Home & Automobile Insurance Company in Chicago on September 30.* With volume of $7.5 million a year, Buffett highlighted the similarities between its founder, Victor Raab, and Berkshire's own star managers, Jack Ringwalt and Eugene Abegg. While National Indemnity accepted just about any risk from almost anyone (requiring pricing one-off policies), Raab focused on insuring those within Chicago's urban areas, a more

---

* The only information we can glean from the financial statements of the purchase is a $364,000 premium paid over the net assets of the business.

statistical-type operation. Buffett saw so much potential in this new acquisition that he added capital to the business because Raab was continually up against capital limits that hindered growth.

Although we do not know the precise amount added to Home and Auto because it was consolidated with Berkshire's other insurance operations, an additional $8.5 million in equity was added to the Insurance Group to support its burgeoning premium volumes.[*] This amount was partially funded by a new $9 million loan.[**] (A portion of the proceeds repaid the outstanding balance of a prior note.)

Commenting on this debt financing in the latter part of the 1971 Chairman's letter, Buffett stressed that Berkshire wouldn't overburden its balance sheet. Berkshire's insurance and banking subsidiaries possessed a special fiduciary relationship with the public, and this required Berkshire to always remain very strongly financed. This meant that, at both the parent and the subsidiary level, Berkshire would always "unquestionably fulfill our responsibilities." From the consolidated balance sheet at year-end 1971, Berkshire owed a total of $9.6 million compared to equity of $56.2 million—a debt-to-total capital ratio of just 15%.

Banking

Berkshire's banking division faced a tough year in 1971. Interest rates declined, which caused a corresponding decrease in interest income for the bank. Compounding the challenges on the income side was the nature of Illinois National Bank's deposit base. Its deposits were becoming more time-based as opposed to demand-based. Time-based funding (e.g. certificates of deposits) are much more expensive to a bank than demand deposits (checking accounts) which typically pay little or no interest. Nonetheless, Abegg and his team continued to hold the line on expenses and maintained the bank's conservative investment strategy of high-quality loans.

1972

Buffett described 1972 as a highly satisfactory year in large part due to the 19.8% return on beginning shareholders' equity. Each division contributed to the overall success, although the Insurance Group led the charge, partially due to the "unusual convergence of favorable factors"[***] described in 1971.

---

[*] Net premiums written to average equity in the Insurance Group fell from 272% in 1970 to 241% in 1971 in part due to the additional equity capital contributed.

[**] This loan called for quarterly principal payments of $500,000 beginning on June 30, 1973 with the balance of $3 million due on June 30, 1976. The interest rate was 0.50% over the prime rate for 90-day commercial loans of The First National Bank of Boston (which was the agent bank).

[***] Low auto accident frequency, moderate severity, and absence of major catastrophes.

Before moving into a more detailed review of each division, Buffett took the time to comment on the past eight years of his direct management of Berkshire. Since he took control in May 1965, operating earnings were substantially higher, and the diversification and redeployment of capital outside of the textile industry "established a significantly higher base of normal earning power" for shareholders. Shares outstanding had been reduced by 14% through repurchases, and book value, which was $19.46 per share at year-end 1964, had climbed 16.5% annually, ending 1972 at $69.72 per share. Lest Buffett be accused of claiming the credit for himself, he praised Jack Ringwalt, Eugene Abegg, and Victor Raab, the individuals operating National Indemnity Company and National Fire & Marine Company, Illinois National Bank, and the Home & Auto Insurance divisions, respectively.

Textiles

It's worth pausing to examine some figures relating to the textile division for 1972. Inventories increased at a double-digit rate, but the increase in revenues was much more modest. Furthermore, a reduction in accounts receivable coupled with increases in payables, freed up capital from the textile division. Capital requirements were controlled through careful inventory management and suggested a positive outlook for 1973.

Another item deserving attention is the increase in payables. Because payables are monies owed to suppliers, the textile division was effectively borrowing from suppliers to finance its operations. This released capital from the division that could be reallocated by Buffett elsewhere. The practice could not go on forever, as suppliers must eventually be paid, but it is common. For example, Walmart has taken this financial management strategy to an extreme, using its large purchasing power to extract long terms from suppliers. This means suppliers are financing Walmart's balance sheet as the price for doing business with the retail giant.

In sum, combining the capital tied up in net working assets, fixed assets, and an estimate of the cash needed to operate the division, total capital employed in the textile division decreased by $1.5 million. This decrease in required capital coupled with the improvement in operating performance translated into a 16% return on capital (see Table 3.7)—by far the best in many years and clearly a positive aberration.

Table 3.7: Textile division—select data

($ millions)	1972	1971
Revenues	$27.7	$26.0
Operating profit	1.697	0.233
Capital employed	10.5	12.1
Return on capital, pre-tax	16.1%	1.9%
Inventories	6.8	6.0
Inventories as % revenues	25%	23%
Accounts receivable (AR)	4.1	5.1
AR as % revenues	15%	20%

Sources: Berkshire Hathaway Annual Report 1972 and author's calculations.

Insurance

The textile industry had a very good year, but it dimmed in comparison to the insurance industry. Although overall premium volume declined, profits swelled due to very favorable loss experience. This included:

- National Indemnity's specialized business wrote premiums of $35 million (down 26%)
- Reinsurance wrote premiums of $11 million (down 24%)
- Home State operations had written premiums of $4.3 million (up more than 2.5 times)
- Home and Auto delivered written premiums of $6.9 million. Those were substantially higher than the $2 million written the prior year for Berkshire but down from $7.7 million written during the full year (remember Home and Auto was acquired on September 30, 1971).

Recall that a combined ratio of less than 100% is a good thing. The 1972 combined ratio was 93.7%. This meant that Berkshire's Insurance Group was being *paid* over 6% to do business with customers. This was on top of the money it made investing the float that came with holding its customers' money until loss claims came in. Float at the end of 1972 amounted to $70 million. High interest rates meant Berkshire enjoyed an enormous economic advantage holding onto these funds.* Additionally,

---

* It is worth noting that the footnotes to the Insurance Group in 1972 first disclosed Berkshire's initial investment in Blue Chip Stamps, and by extension that of See's Candies. Buffett would have much more to say on See's in the future. For now, all that shareholders could glean was that they, via Berkshire's insurance subsidiary, owned a 17% stake in Blue Chip Stamps, up from 6% the year prior. (No additional disclosure was then made, as Blue Chip Stamps was simply one of many marketable securities.)

Berkshire's bond portfolio had unusually good call protection, which would protect the high yields on those investments.

Table 3.8: Insurance Group—select data

(*$ millions*)	1972	1971
Premiums written	$58.0	$66.5
Premiums earned	59.6	60.9
Pre-tax underwriting gain	4.3	1.4
Pre-tax net investment income	6.6	5.0
Return on average equity	22.2%	21.6%
Loss ratio	62.0%	67.0%
Expense ratio	31.7%	28.1%
Combined ratio	93.7%	95.1%

Sources: Berkshire Hathaway Annual Report 1972 and author's calculations.

The extremely good profitability enjoyed during 1972 almost immediately attracted competition. Resulting volume declines starting in 1972 brought expectations of lower pricing for the near future. Although premiums earned fell only 2%, premiums written fell 13%. Berkshire would continue writing insurance at the right price, but would let volumes shrink if market rates were too low. Basing rates on long-term expectations, and accepting lower volume short term, was the best path to above-average long-term results.

If Berkshire was pulling back writing insurance business in the near term, it surely was not taking its foot off the gas in terms of building its *capacity* to write insurance. Berkshire planned to build on its acquisition of Home and Automobile Insurance of Chicago with new operations in Dade County, Florida and Los Angeles. Home State expanded with new ventures in Minnesota and Texas. All of these moves were made with an eye toward capturing more business when it materialized at appropriate prices.

Banking

Like Berkshire's Insurance Group, Eugene Abegg and his team at Illinois National Bank were excellent underwriters of risk and rightfully deserved Buffett's annual praise. Charge offs, or loans deemed uncollectible, were a mere 1/20th of those at other commercial banks. In 1972, the Bank wrote off $4,669 (no zeros omitted), or 0.0078% of its almost $60 million in loans, an exceptional banking record in any period.

1973

The Chairman's letter in 1973 contained a flurry of information for shareholders. First, however, Buffett led off with his customary quantitative disclosure of Berkshire's return on beginning shareholders' equity. That year's result, a gain of 17.4%, was down from the prior year's 19.8%. But Buffett was quick to point out that it was the *rate* of increase in book value, not the dollar amount, that mattered. Indeed, earnings per share had increased from $11.43 to $12.18. Buffett reiterated, "management's objective is to achieve a return on capital over the long term which averages somewhat higher than that of American industry generally—while utilizing sound accounting and debt policies." From the vantage point of history, we know this objective was achieved by a wide margin.

Textiles

The textile division reported strong results in 1973. High demand brought the trendline above average for Berkshire's textiles but still just average when judged from an absolute sense.[*]

Table 3.9: Textile division, select data

($ millions)	1973	1972	% Change
Revenues	$33.4	$27.7	21%
Operating profit	2.8	1.7	65%

Source: Berkshire Hathaway Annual Report, 1973 and author's calculations.

Partially holding back the Textile Group's performance were the Nixon Administration's Cost of Living Council's price controls.[**] Buffett said these "served to cut down some of the hills while still leaving us with the inevitable valleys." Textiles is a highly cyclical industry. Having a capped upside with unlimited downside was good for consumers, but terrible for a business owner.

In response to inflationary pressures on raw materials, the Textile Group changed its accounting from FIFO to LIFO.[***] LIFO, or last-in-first-out, is a method of

---

[*] A precise value for capital employed is not readily calculable due to the aggregation of many figures in Berkshire's consolidated financial statements. It's highly likely the 1973 result was better than the 16% pre-tax return on capital employed achieved in 1972. Buffett called the 1973 textile results "reasonably commensurate with our capital investment."

[**] Put in place in an effort to try and slow inflation. They didn't work.

[***] The accounting of inventory is important so that a business understands what its true costs, and therefore its true profits, are. In an inflationary environment the method of accounting causes a divergence in reported profits for the very same economic activity.

accounting for inventory that matches most recent costs against current revenue. This was a change from FIFO, or first-in-first-out, which matches old costs against current revenue. If Berkshire had remained under FIFO, the rising price environment would leave it assigning low values to costs as it sold products, and thus incurring higher taxes. While other managements might have enjoyed the reported profitability boost that FIFO produced (since low cost = higher profit and vice versa), Buffett preferred the more favorable economic result, even if it depressed reported profits.

Insurance

Insurance results were generally very good, although not without difficulties. National Indemnity and sister company National Fire and Marine had an exceptionally fine year, Buffett said, a fitting capstone for Jack Ringwalt, who retired as president after thirty-three years at the helm (he remained CEO). National Indemnity reported a $4.4 million underwriting profit on earned premiums of $30 million. That is impressive considering earned premiums fell 21% from the prior year. Buffett praised his successor, Phil Liesche, as having the same qualities as Ringwalt.

The Reinsurance Group experienced similarly satisfactory results during the year. Unfortunately, it experienced slightly lower volumes due to the influx of competition chasing yesterday's good results. Underwriting profit came in at $353,000 on earned premiums of $12 million.

Overall, the Insurance Group wrote 13% less in premium volume and earned 11% less than the prior year. Its profitability remained intact, with the combined ratio increasing slightly, but still very satisfactory, to 95.3%. This was good for $3.3 million of underwriting profits. (National Indemnity's profits subsidized underwriting losses at Home and Auto and Home State.)

Additional challenges in the Insurance Group came from managerial issues. The Home State companies had good results in Nebraska and Minnesota, along with an expansion into Iowa, which combined with other successes provided optimism. But Texas was a problem that required a restart almost from scratch.

Another area of weakness was in Home and Auto's Chicago operations. Even after borrowing funds to bolster its capacity to write business,* it experienced very poor results from underwriting. The cause: inadequate rates. Inflation caused medical and repair costs to escalate rapidly. Such costs were borne by the insurer, which had to live with the premiums its insureds had paid for the coverage, even if they became inadequate. Another threat to insurance profitability was higher jury awards paid by insurance companies to insureds. These juries tend to be very sympathetic to

---

* In March 1973, Berkshire borrowed $20 million at 8% from a consortium of twenty banks in order to provide the Insurance Group with additional financial resources to support its growth.

claimants. Insurance companies can and do include estimates for such costs in their policy rates, but if costs rise dramatically during the year, the difference can result in subpar profitability.

Offsetting those inflationary costs was an ongoing oil crisis, which created higher gasoline prices and led consumers to take fewer long car trips. This in turn lowered accident frequency. Buffett told shareholders he was not as optimistic as some competitors that lower accident frequency would offset the inflation seen in repair and jury costs.

A weakness in the accounting system at Home and Auto highlighted the impact data quality has on insurance profitability. Information was not brought to management's attention in a timely manner and policies were being written at rates that did not adequately reflect the cost of doing business. Buffett assured shareholders the situation was being addressed. Home and Auto expanded into Florida and California as planned, though an assessment of the results through 1973 was too preliminary to determine its effectiveness.

Investments

A large portion of Berkshire's investment portfolio resided on the books of the Insurance Group. The bear market that began in 1973 (coinciding with an economic recession) negatively impacted Berkshire's investments. Over $12 million in unrealized losses that occurred during 1973 represented a distressingly large portion of the $67 million average common stock portfolio within the Insurance Group. Despite such large reported losses, Buffett expressed confidence in the portfolio:

> "Nevertheless, we believe that our common stock portfolio at cost represents good value in terms of intrinsic business worth. In spite of the large unrealized loss at year-end, we would expect satisfactory results from the portfolio over the longer term."

Perhaps intentionally not stated in the letter to shareholders (for fear of arousing nervousness), Berkshire invested significant sums during 1973. The Insurance Group's financial reports show that over $15 million in bonds and preferred stocks were liquidated in order to invest over $32 million in common stocks and over $1.5 million in Blue Chip Stamps. One notable investment made in 1973 was $10.6 million for 467,150 shares in *The Washington Post* that declined to $7.9 million at year-end.* Berkshire could make such investments because it had both the resources and ample capacity to do so.**

---

* Two other notable investments were National Presto shares that cost $3 million and were worth $2.6 million, and Vornado, Inc., which cost $4.4 million and were worth $1.3 million at year-end 1973.

** Insurance volume in 1973 represented just 89% of average equity (computed on a GAAP basis for consistency with prior years). Using statutory capital the ratio is 121%.

Diversified Retailing

After two short paragraphs with the usual praise for Berkshire's banking subsidiary, Buffett turned his attention to a proposed merger with Diversified Retailing. If one had only been reading Buffett's reports to shareholders over the past nine years, you might have never heard of Diversified Retailing. The company ran a chain of women's apparel stores in addition to a reinsurance business.* The unusual reinsurance business line was the handiwork of Buffett, the controlling shareholder of Diversified. Buffett and Charlie Munger would weave such a complicated web of business lines and business ownership that the SEC would later investigate them for fraud. (Their dealings were above board, of course, though most financial fraud is accompanied by intricate accounting maneuvers meant to cover up misdeeds.) A merger would simplify much of the cross-ownership that got them into trouble in the first place.

The proposed merger, approved by Berkshire's directors, would be funded by issuing 195,000 Berkshire shares. Because Diversified owned 109,551 shares of Berkshire (you can see how a regulator might begin to suspect something was awry), dilution at Berkshire would be less than 86,000 shares. On 980,000 then outstanding Berkshire shares, dilution would come to less than 10%. Presumably, Berkshire would be receiving at least as much in business value as it was giving up.

Buffett told shareholders that "its [Diversified] most important asset is 16% of the stock of Blue Chip Stamps." Berkshire itself owned some Blue Chip Stamps shares directly. Post-merger, Berkshire's ownership in Blue Chip would increase from 22.5% to 38%.

With or without the Diversified Retailing merger, exceeding the 20% ownership mark required Berkshire to report its proportional share of Blue Chip's earnings on its financial statements. Blue Chip's year ended in February,** compared to Berkshire's calendar year. Berkshire had to decide which period to include. One option, blessed by Berkshire's auditors, was to use the earnings and ownership level as of Blue Chip's prior audit. This would mean including the twelve months ended February 1973*** in Berkshire's results for the twelve months ended December 31, 1973. Buffett said that "such an approach seemed at odds with reality" considering the ten-month lag. He chose to use the unaudited results of Blue Chip for the twelve months ended November 1973. Even though Berkshire auditors couldn't officially okay them, this choice resulted in just one month of Blue Chip's results falling outside of Berkshire's, instead of ten.

---

* The 1973 Diversified Retailing 10K reveals the reinsurance unit to be Columbia Insurance Company. Columbia's sole business was engaging in reinsurance transactions with National Indemnity, which would have allowed National Indemnity to write that much more business.
** Technically it was the Saturday closest to February 28, which sometimes caused the year-end to fall into the beginning of March.
*** Technically March 3, 1973.

Figure 3.1: Blue Chip's consolidation into Berkshire's financials

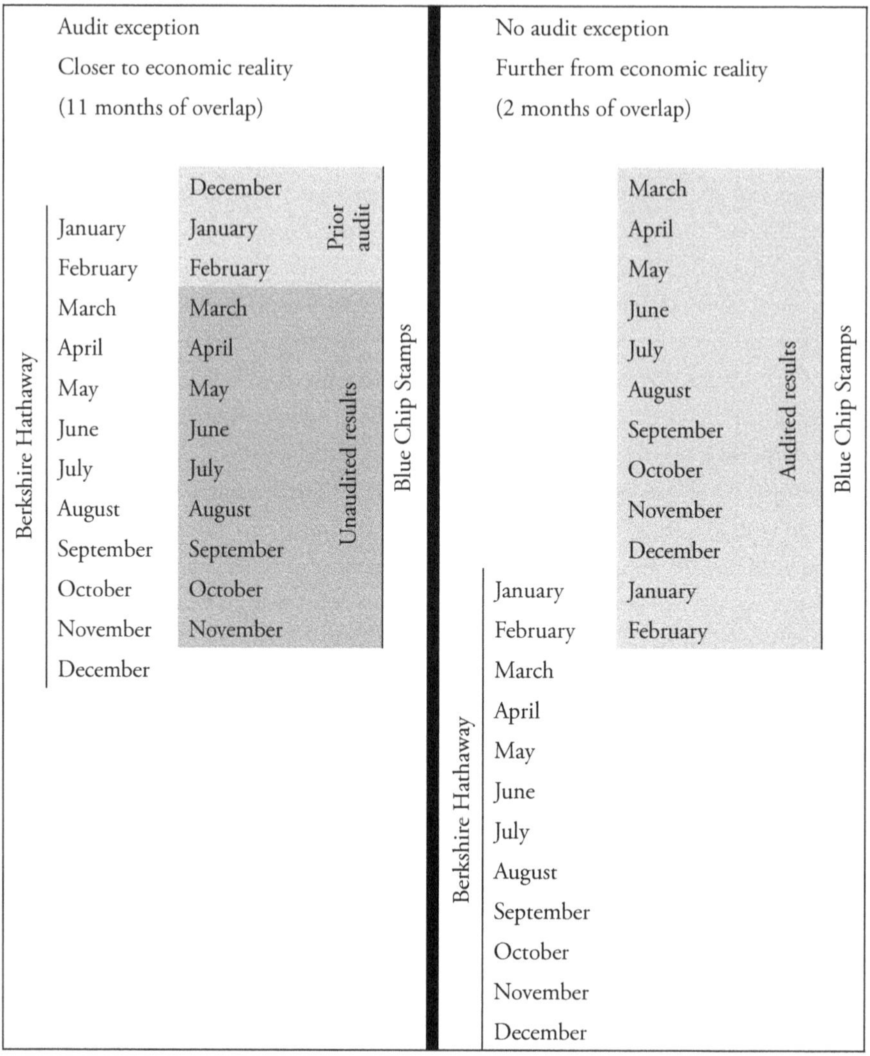

Audit exception	No audit exception
Closer to economic reality	Further from economic reality
(11 months of overlap)	(2 months of overlap)

Left block — Berkshire Hathaway / Blue Chip Stamps:

Berkshire Hathaway: January, February, March, April, May, June, July, August, September, October, November, December

Blue Chip Stamps: December (Prior audit), January, February, March, April, May, June, July, August, September, October, November (Unaudited results)

Right block — Blue Chip Stamps / Berkshire Hathaway:

Blue Chip Stamps (Audited results): March, April, May, June, July, August, September, October, November, December, January, February

Berkshire Hathaway: January, February, March, April, May, June, July, August, September, October, November, December

Buffett noted that Blue Chip had "important sources of earnings power in its See's Candy Shops subsidiary as well as Wesco Financial… ." Wesco was a 54%-owned subsidiary of Blue Chip that operated a savings and loan business. Charlie Munger would serve as Wesco's Chairman for many years until it was brought under Berkshire's umbrella in a 2011 transaction (Wesco and its subsidiaries will be discussed later in the book).

Concluding the 1973 letter was a note on the Pulitzer Prize-winning Sun Newspapers. That group was last mentioned by Buffett in the 1969 Annual Report, though because of its small size got little attention. Despite this, the paper earned a Pulitzer, the highest honor in newspapers, for exposing the incredible story of fraud at Boys Town, a local Omaha-based charity that was hoarding money but claimed poverty. Buffett praised the paper's management, journalists, and editorial staff for their achievement and signed off for the ninth time.

1974

Buffett wasted no time getting to the major driver of the relatively poor results achieved during 1974. Surprisingly, it was not the textile division. This time it was insurance. In his opening sentence to shareholders, Buffett shared that insurance underwriting had been dismal. Weakness was anticipated in his 1973 letter, but the extent of the 1974 reversal took him by surprise. Offsetting the weakness in insurance were quite satisfactory performance by both the Textile Group and the bank, the net result of which was a 10.3% return on beginning shareholders' equity for Berkshire as a whole. Results for 1974 underscored the value in having numerous sources of operating earnings, a benefit Berkshire lacked before Buffett transformed the company using his capital allocation skills.

Textiles

Textiles achieved fleeting profitability in 1974 before signs of weakness appeared. The division operated at one-third of capacity, which would result in future operating losses in the coming year if sales volumes remained depressed. Despite this, the division's $2.7 million in operating income, though down somewhat from the $2.8 million posted a year earlier, was something to celebrate.

As of 1974, the group primarily produced curtains, which were not necessities and thus sensitive to economic conditions. The ongoing recession caused consumers to defer purchases of such non-essential goods. Additionally, housing starts were down, which meant fewer windows needing curtains. If that wasn't enough, retailers were also trimming their inventories and making fewer purchases from Berkshire.[*]

Insurance

The confluence of competition, the trend of inflation running at approximately 1% per month,[**] and several mistakes that came to light in 1974, caused insurance underwriting results to deteriorate significantly. Battling competition that was very wary to increase premium rates to combat the rising costs of paying its insureds,

---

[*] The recession started in 1973 and lasted until the beginning of 1975. Unemployment was 7% at the end of 1974 and would peak at 9% in early 1975.

[**] This was not the general rate of inflation but the cost of insurance. Buffett cited auto repair, medical payments, and compensation benefits.

Berkshire pulled back writing what it saw as unprofitable business. Each line of business reported an underwriting loss. The combined ratio, which had been in profitable territory at or below 100% since entering that business, now jumped to 111%. The $6.9 million underwriting loss wiped out three-quarters of the cumulative underwriting profits made in Berkshire's short seven-year history.

Premiums written and earned were $61 million, up 21% and 14%, respectively. But Berkshire's Insurance Group was writing far less business that it could have been. Since 1970, when net premiums written to average equity peaked at 272%, this ratio had declined steadily to 88% by 1974.* Whether due to a desire to maintain premium volume or simply because they had to,** the industry continued to write unprofitable business. Berkshire intelligently remained on the sidelines. It had both the ability and the willingness to reduce its volumes short term to remain profitable long term.

Though general industry conditions and stiff competition hurt results during the year, nothing was more painful than self-inflicted losses. After telling shareholders of plans to expand into the Florida market, Buffett now informed his partners that the decision to expand Home and Auto to that state "proved disastrous". Buffett calculated the financial cost of the mistake at $2 million, most of which was realized in 1974.*** He summed up the mistake in one sentence: "In retrospect, it is apparent that our management simply did not have the underwriting information and the pricing knowledge necessary to be operating in the area."

Still, there was reason for optimism. The Home State group continued to grow premiums (up 9%) while getting a handle on costs, and the restart in Texas appeared to be working. Long-term success came with temporary setbacks. Berkshire had the patience, and perhaps more important, the capital strength, to ride out the storm.

Berkshire's advantage, largely by design, was its large capital base invested in high-quality assets. As noted earlier, Berkshire wrote just a fraction of its capital base each year in premium volume, far below its competitors percentage wise. Though profitability was down, the group still reported net operating income during the year thanks to net investment income more than offsetting the underwriting losses.****

Weak operating results during the year had one, if not positive, at least mitigating consequence. On a consolidated basis, Berkshire incurred no tax expense during the year, and in fact it booked a tax credit. Although textiles and banking were strong and generated taxable income, these earnings were reported along with all of Berkshire

---

* Using GAAP figures for consistency. The 1974 ratio based on statutory capital was 164%.
** Even an unprofitable contract brings cash in the door on day one.
*** Written premiums in Florida were $1.7 million in 1974 or about 25% of Home and Auto's total. Some of Buffett's $2 million figure would have included underwriting expenses, but it appears pricing was very inadequate.
**** The $136 million investment portfolio in the Insurance Group earned $7.9 million pre-tax, more than offsetting the $6.9 million pre-tax underwriting loss.

for tax purposes. The tax loss in the Insurance Group was available to shield income from other parts of the business.

The Insurance Group overall reported a profit, but the components of that profit were taxed differently. For example, it held certain tax-exempt issues, and its dividends were taxed at a lower rate. This meant it could use the underwriting loss to shield taxable income elsewhere within Berkshire. In later years, Berkshire would gain enormous similar tax benefits from owning utilities under the same corporate parent, maximizing every benefit of the conglomerate structure.

Banking

Separate financials for the bank* reflected the tax advantage it received as a subsidiary of Berkshire. On pre-tax, pre-securities gain income of $4.2 million the Bank accounted for just $220,000 of income tax, a rate of about 5% and far below the federal statutory rate of 48%. This was a direct result of tax credits from the Insurance Group. Clearly this low level of taxation was not normal, and the Bank would have paid much more had its parent at the time not been Berkshire Hathaway. The benefit to the Bank and Berkshire was real.

Accounting

Being owned by a conglomerate clearly created tax complications. Perhaps for this reason, or to remove the effect of changing tax rates over time, Buffett frequently commented on and used pre-tax profitability in his analysis of business results. At the end of the 1974 Annual Report was a new section entitled Management's Discussion and Analysis of the Summary of Operations. This new section was mandated by accounting standards[35] and contained additional details for readers of the financial statements. One sub-section contained a chart titled, Sources of Net Income, with data going back five years. The chart, reproduced in the appendix, separated each contributing source of income from corporate administrative and interest expense, realized investment gains/losses, and income taxes.

Elsewhere readers could see detail of the insurance premiums broken down by line. The section was largely a reproduction of the data Buffett had been giving readers all along. It would not be the first time Buffett was ahead of the accounting standards.

The new supplementary report also contained a section explaining the difference between statutory and GAAP accounting for the Insurance Group. Insurance authorities use a separate accounting system to analyze insurance companies

---

* Audited financials for the bank and the Insurance Group were reported at the end of the Berkshire Hathaway Annual Report.

that focuses on the insurance company's real ability to pay its claimants. Its aim is not economic reporting, but conservatism. That conservatism was important to understand because it placed restrictions on how much business the insurer could write and how its assets could be invested.

One of these adjustments was for deferred policy acquisition costs. These were the costs of acquiring new customers and included such expenses as brokers' commissions and marketing expenses. From an economic perspective, these expenses were assigned to the policies they sought to gain. As such, GAAP accounting placed some of the expense on the balance sheet as an asset, which was reduced over time as the insurer earned the policies. For statutory insurance accounting purposes, however, they were not included, since the monies had already been spent and would not be available in the event the resources were required to pay policyholders.

A reconciliation of Berkshire's statutory accounting surplus to that under GAAP for 1974 highlights many of the big differences between the two accounting standards. These included:

- Unrealized gains on equity securities
- Excess carrying value of subsidiaries
- Goodwill
- Deferred policy acquisition costs (mentioned above)
- Excess statutory liability loss reserves
- Certain insurance receivables
- Other non-admitted assets
- Certain other tax effects and adjustments (relating to depreciation and write-offs, for example)

Table 3.10: Reconciliation of statutory surplus to GAAP shareholders' equity, 1974

($ thousands)	
Policyholder statutory surplus	$37,202
Unrealized gains on equity securities (excluding Blue Chip Stamps)	16,450
Excess of carrying value in Blue Chip Stamps	9,176
Deferred policy acquisition costs	4,400
Excess statutory liability loss reserves	1,851
Net recoverable from unauthorized reinsurers	1,788
Sundry nonadmitted assets	1,043
Income tax effects and adjustments	(1,678)
Capital stock and surplus - GAAP	$70,231

Source: Berkshire Hathaway Annual Report 1974.

Diversified Retailing

Disappointingly, the proposed merger with Diversified Retailing, which was approved by the directors of each company the prior year and put to a shareholder vote, had been terminated because the Securities and Exchange Commission (SEC) hadn't given its okay.*[36] Shareholders would have to wait until 1977 for the deal to finally close. That didn't stop Berkshire from increasing its ownership in Blue Chip Stamps to 25% at year-end.

Listed at the end of the 1974 Annual Report were Berkshire's Directors and Executive Officers. It stood out for the small number of individuals listed: Buffett, as board chair and CEO of Berkshire; Ken Chace, as president of Berkshire and COO of the Textile Group; Malcolm Chace, Jr., retired former Berkshire chairman; and J. Verne McKenzie, as VP, secretary, and treasurer. For a company with over $200 million in assets and annual revenues north of $100 million, it was a lean team. Buffett preferred it that way.

Decade in Review

Perhaps at no other time in Berkshire Hathaway's history did the company experience more change. Berkshire had seen dramatic ups and downs before as its textile business went through violent business cycles. But the change experienced in the decade ending in 1974 was noteworthy for its shift in business strategy and capital allocation. Rather than continue solely in textiles, Berkshire under Buffett was redeploying capital into new industries. Buffett was shaping Berkshire into not the best *textile* company, but the best company—period.

The extent of the change Berkshire experienced during the preceding decade under Warren Buffett's leadership cannot be overstated. Once a dying textile business, Berkshire now had many sources of earnings power. Owners of Berkshire in turn owned an insurance operation, a bank, a newspaper, and, through Blue Chip Stamps, an interest in a trading stamps business, another bank, and a candy company.

Beginning the decade (year-end 1964) Berkshire was a textile company with $22 million of equity and diminished earning power. Such a sorry state of affairs weighed on the stock price, which traded between $8.50 and $13.50 per share during 1964 despite being backed by a book value of $19.46 per share.[37] Fast forward a decade and Buffett had nearly quadrupled Berkshire's consolidated equity. The stock followed suit with the price during the fourth quarter of 1974 ranging from a low of $40 to a

---

* This was only the start; Buffett and Munger would be investigated by the SEC because it appeared, through their complex web of ownership between the many companies they controlled, they were intentionally trying to cover up unlawful behavior.

high of $49 (down from a high of $93 during the first quarter of 1973 before the bear market did its damage).

Berkshire's stock price and valuation at the end of the decade reflected the general pessimism of the bear market of 1973/74. Despite the substantial progress made building value in the underlying business, the stock traded at a lower price to book value than it did at the beginning of Buffett's tenure (See Figures 3.2 and 3.3).

Figure 3.2: Berkshire Hathaway stock price, 1965–1974

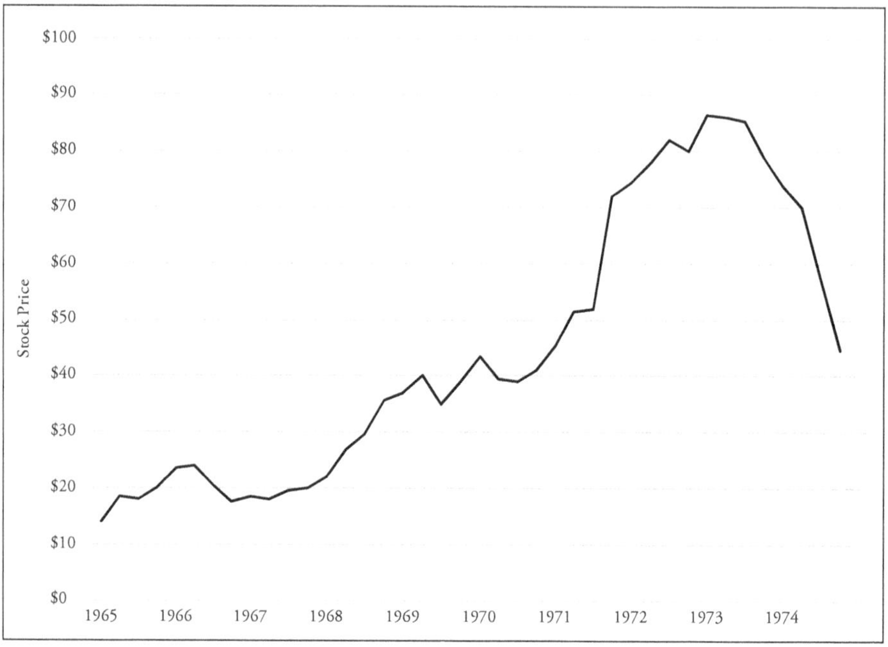

Sources: *Of Permanent Value* (Kilpatrick), Berkshire Hathaway Annual Reports 1965–1974, and author's calculations.

Figure 3.3: Berkshire Hathaway price to book ratio, 1965–1974

Sources: *Of Permanent Value* (Kilpatrick), Berkshire Hathaway Annual Reports 1965–1974, and author's calculations.

The capital allocation decisions made between 1965 and 1974 resulted in significant earnings, of which a portion was returned to shareholders in the form of dividends and share repurchases. The equity adjustments made in 1965 and 1966,* and other minor adjustments, made up the difference. To say that Berkshire had been transformed would be an understatement. Berkshire had a metamorphosis.

---

* Made because of Buffett's desire to report earnings closer to economic reality, even though they were lower. Because Berkshire owed no actual tax, the amounts were added back to equity in the equity reconciliation section.

Table 3.11: Reconciliation of shareholders' equity 1965–1974

($ millions)	Amount	% Change
Net income - operations	$57	86%
Net income - realized gains	7	11%
Unrealized appreciation of investments	0	0%
Mergers/divestitures	0	0%
Dividends/treasury stock	(3)	(4%)
Other/misc.	4	7%
Change in equity during period	66	100%
Beginning of period shareholders' equity	22	
End of period shareholders' equity	$88	

Sources: Berkshire Hathaway Annual Reports 1965–1974 and author's calculations.

Examining Berkshire's balance sheet in greater detail we can see some of the major changes that occurred. Comparing 1964 to 1974, the reader will notice that the Insurance Group's assets and liabilities were now listed on Berkshire's consolidated balance sheet (see Table 3.15). Because of its size, the group was now presented on a consolidated basis. Essentially everything was disaggregated and presented alongside the Textile Group, rather than just the equity component being presented separately like The Illinois National Bank & Trust of Rockford, and Blue Chip Stamps.

The marketable securities portfolio stands out first. Now totaling $136 million, this important asset made up almost two-thirds (63%) of Berkshire's total consolidated assets (see Table 3.15). Offsetting these assets were the sizable sums on the liability side of the balance sheet, including the $73 million of losses and loss adjustment expenses, and the $22 million of unearned premiums. These two items, major components of the all-important float, were (and are) liabilities. However, they are liabilities without a specific due date and cannot be called by policyholders.

That float was the result of work building and expanding the Insurance Group. Buffett saw the success of National Indemnity and wished to expand on it. Reinsurance was the first logical step. The Home State companies were another logical expansion, as was the desire to expand beyond Home and Auto's base in Chicago into other urban areas. Both expansions were fraught with challenges and losses. They highlighted Buffett's entrepreneurial zeal and willingness to take calculated risks. The lessons learned during those expansionary years were crucial learning points for the entire insurance organization, Buffett included. And he was not shy about sharing his and the organization's failures in his annual communications with shareholders.

Table 3.12: Insurance Group, select information 1969–1974

($ thousands)	1974	1973	1972	1971	1970	1969	1968
Premiums written							
Specialized auto and general liability	$36,738	$28,617	$35,354	$47,794	$37,820	$26,034	$22,620
Reinsurance	12,204	10,184	11,436	14,953	7,017	2,742	
Urban Auto[1]	6,613	6,571	6,874	2,040	249		
Home State companies	5,442	5,000	4,286	1,668			
Premiums written	60,997	50,372	57,950	66,455	45,086	28,776	22,620
Underwriting gain/(loss)							
Specialized auto and general liability	(1,939)	4,409	4,329				
Reinsurance	(2,068)	353	561				
Urban Auto	(2,183)	(878)	62				
Home State companies	(702)	(565)	(667)				
Underwriting gain(loss)	($6,892)	$3,319	$4,285	$1,409	($330)	($153)	$568
Combined ratio (statutory)	111.1%	95.3%	93.7%	95.1%	96.6%	96.2%	97.5%

Footnote:
1. Urban Auto from September 30, 1971, the date of acquisition. The full year results for the entity acquired were $7,669.

Source: Berkshire Hathaway Annual Reports 1973, 1974.

Other important assets on the 1974 consolidated balance sheet were the $22 million Investment in Bank subsidiary (Illinois National Bank), and $16.9 million common stock of Blue Chip Stamps.

What about the textile division? We can make an approximation of the capital employed in this group based on the known information on the balance sheet and detail provided in the Annual Report. Comparing data from 1964 and 1974 in Table 3.13, we can see that capital employed in the business shrunk by $14 million, or 57%. Perhaps more important, capital efficiency was increased by over 52% as the division eked out more volume with less capital investment.

Table 3.13: Textile division, select data

($ millions)	1974	1964
Cash[1]	$0.8	$0.9
Accounts receivable	4.4	7.5
Inventories	6.0	11.7
Plant, property & equipment	2.3	7.6
Less: current liabilities[2]	(3.1)	(3.2)
Capital employed in textile division	$10.4	$24.4
Textile revenues	$32.6	$50.0
Revenues / capital	$3.13	$2.05
Footnotes:		
1. 1974 cash estimated at 2.5% of revenues.		
2. 1974 current liabilities estimated by deducting Insurance Group from the consolidated financial statements.		

Sources: Berkshire Hathaway Annual Reports 1964, 1974 and author's calculations.

Readers already familiar with Berkshire's history may wonder why there was no lengthy discussion of See's Candies in this chapter given its importance. I have left this for later when Buffett discusses See's in his Chairman's letter. In this way, the reader following along chronologically will have the same information shareholders had. As far as shareholders might have known at the time, given the lack of disclosure other than minor details in the footnotes, See's was just one of many investments.

Lessons: 1965–1974

1. Capital allocation is a continuous, ongoing process. Not only must opportunities within an existing business be examined, options in entirely different industries must also be considered. If additional opportunities for investment are not available, management should consider returning capital to shareholders via buybacks and/or dividends.
2. Owners should focus on the rate of return they are earning from a business, not the dollar amount. Higher earnings, or higher earnings per share, can be achieved through a low rate of return, which does not serve investors well over the long run.
3. Satisfactory business results can be achieved without undue risk or leverage (Illinois National Bank).
4. Mistakes in capital allocation, such as the losses experienced in Florida and Texas in Berkshire's Insurance Group, do happen. The key is making sure bad investments don't put the larger enterprise at risk, learning lessons from those mistakes, and communicating candidly with shareholders about them.

Note: The reader should be aware that Berkshire's fiscal year-end beginning in 1967 was changed to the Saturday closest to December 31. As a result, 1970 has two periods; one for the year ended January 3 (1969 results), and another for December 31 (1970 results).

Table 3.14: Sources of Net Income table from the 1974 Berkshire Hathaway Annual Report

($ thousands)	1974	1973	1972	1971	1970
Insurance	$892	$10,249	$10,701	$6,372	$2,639
Textile	2,660	2,837	1,697	233	104
Unconsolidated bank subsidiary	4,093	2,782	2,700	2,192	2,973
Blue Chip Stamps	1,164	1,124	142	68	0
Interest and corporate administrative expenses	(2,324)	(1,966)	(770)	(648)	(581)
Pre-tax operating earnings	6,485	15,026	14,470	8,217	5,135
Realized investment gain (loss)	(1,908)	1,331	1,359	1,028	(301)
Extraordinary item	0	0	0	0	282
Total pre-tax income	4,577	16,357	15,829	9,245	5,116
Less: Total income taxes (credit)	(2,466)	3,497	3,703	1,559	551
Net Earnings	$7,043	$12,860	$12,126	$7,686	$4,565

Notes:

1. Years rearranged for consistency of presentation.

2. Operating earnings line added.

Source: Berkshire Hathaway Annual Report 1974.

Table 3.15: Berkshire Hathaway consolidated balance sheets, 1964–1974

($ thousands)	12/28/74	12/29/73	12/30/72	12/31/71	12/31/70	01/03/70	12/28/68	12/30/67	10/01/66	10/02/65	10/03/64
Current assets											
Cash	$4,231	$2,886	$4,998	$962	$1,352	$1,793	$1,606	$835	$629	$776	$920
Bonds	82,639	74,474	88,148								
Preferred stock	2,855	2,298	2,942								
Common stock	50,670	49,757	17,412								
Total marketable securities	136,164	126,530	108,503	0	0	294	5,421	3,825	5,446	2,900	0
Accounts receivable, net, textiles	4,378	5,148	4,055	5,100	3,916	6,397	7,563	7,572	8,114	7,423	7,451
Accounts receivable, net, other	13,513	8,908	8,799	0	0	0	0	0	0	0	0
Inventories, textiles	6,000	7,137	6,827	6,031	8,472	9,270	12,333	11,586	12,239	10,277	11,689
Property, plant & equipment, net textiles	2,333	2,063	1,966	2,209	2,494	3,014	3,863	5,640	6,307	6,617	7,571
Property, plant & equipment, net, non-textile	1,581	1,605	1,674								
Investment in bank subsidiary	22,417	21,003	20,473	20,117	19,878	18,868					
Investment in insurance subsidiaries				33,502	19,065	15,315	12,755	10,259			
Common stock of Blue Chip Stamps	16,924	13,717	11,287								
Investment in other subsidiaries	1,187	1,334	1,259	1,259	1,261	1,261	0	0	0	0	0
Deferred insurance premium acquisition costs	4,400	5,240	5,624				0				
Other assets	3,087	561	645	110	200	345	200	224	162	230	256
Total assets	$216,214	$196,132	$176,110	$69,290	$56,637	$56,557	$43,740	$39,941	$32,896	$28,222	$27,887

Continued…

… Continued from prior page.

Current liabilities

Losses and loss adjustment expenses	$72,761	$61,676	$60,275								
Unearned premiums	21,705	21,282	23,839								
Funds held under reinsurance treaties	2,857	1,318	958								
Amounts due for purchase of securities	294	460	674								
Accounts payable & accrued expenses	4,435	4,727	4,384	3,305	2,015	3,804	4,257	5,434	2,979	3,260	2,883
Income taxes, current	164	262	3,576	174	248	1,443	637	323	423	442	365
Income taxes, deferred	3,044	3,297	3,214								
Current portion of long-term debt	0	0	0	0	1,500	1,500	0	0	0	0	0
7.50% debentures due 1987	556	599	641	641	641	641	641	641	0	0	0
Notes payable to banks	0	0	9,000	9,000	3,750	5,250	2,000	2,000	0	0	2,500
8.00% senior notes due 1993	20,000	20,000	0	0	0	0	0	0	0	0	0
8.00% promissory note due 1988	1,274	0	0	0	0	0	0	0	0	0	0
Total financial debt	21,830	20,599	9,641	9,641	5,891	7,391	2,641	2,641	0	0	2,500
Other	924	1,356	1,253								
Total liabilities	128,015	114,976	107,815	13,121	8,154	12,638	7,535	8,398	3,401	3,702	5,748
Shares outstanding (000's)	980	980	980	980	980	980	985	985	1,018	1,018	1,138
Total stockholders' equity	88,199	81,155	68,295	56,169	48,483	43,918	36,205	31,543	29,495	24,520	22,139
Total liabilities and stockholders' equity	$216,214	$196,132	$176,110	$69,290	$56,637	$56,557	$43,740	$39,941	$32,896	$28,222	$27,887

Sources: Berkshire Hathaway Annual Reports 1964–1974.

Table 3.16: Berkshire Hathaway consolidated income statements, 1964–1974

($ thousands)	12/28/74	12/29/73	12/30/72	12/31/71	12/31/70	01/03/70	12/28/68	09/30/67	10/01/66	10/02/65	10/03/64
Insurance premiums earned	$60,574	$52,929	$59,627								
Insurance losses and loss adjustment expenses	47,120	32,836	36,987								
Insurance underwriting expenses	20,346	16,774	18,356								
Net underwriting gain/(loss), insurance	(6,892)	3,319	4,284								
Insurance investment income (excl. gain/loss)	7,880	7,283	6,644								
Textile revenues	32,592	33,411	27,742	26,011	24,569	40,427	46,002	39,056	49,372	49,301	49,983
Operating profit/(loss), textiles	2,660	2,837	1,697	233	107	1,455	1,567	56	4,849	4,687	528
Realized investment gains, net of tax	(1,340)	930	929	745	58	3,718	2,174	100	0	0	0
Equity in earnings of insurance subsidiaries				5,222	2,052	2,278	1,789	792			
Equity in earnings of Banking Subsidiary	4,093	2,782	2,700	2,167	2,614	1,537	0	0	0	0	0
Equity in earnings of Blue Chip Stamps	1,052	1,008	111								
Net interest, taxes, and other expense	(409)	(5,298)	(4,239)	(681)	(266)	(1,035)	(868)	160	(2,086)	(2,407)	(352)
Net income	$7,043	$12,860	$12,126	$7,686	$4,565	$7,953	$4,662	$1,107	$2,763	$2,279	$176

Sources: Berkshire Hathaway Annual Reports 1964–1974.

Table 3.17: Berkshire Hathaway consolidated reconciliation of shareholders' equity, 1964–1974

($ thousands)	12/28/74	12/29/73	12/30/72	12/31/71	12/31/70	01/03/70	12/28/68	12/30/67	10/01/66	10/02/65	10/03/64
Prior year equity	$81,155	$68,295	$56,169	$48,483	$43,918	$36,205	$31,543	$29,495	$24,520	$22,139	$30,279
Current year net income/(loss)	7,043	12,860	12,126	7,686	4,565	7,953	4,662	1,107	2,763	2,279	176
Current year dividends	0	0	0	0	0	0	0	(102)	0	0	0
Change in common	0	(190)	0	0	0	0	0	0	(601)	(2,348)	0
Change in paid in capital	0	0	0	0	0	0	0	0	0	0	0
Treasury stock	0	817	0	0	(0)	(240)	0	(577)	1,638	3,678	(5,316)
Reduction in provision for prior years' taxes	0	0	0	0	0	0	0	226	0	0	0
Estimated loss on properties to be sold	0	0	0	0	0	0	0	0	0	(300)	(3,000)
Retirement of treasury stock	0	0	0	0	0	0	0	0	(1,037)	(2,968)	0
Credit from charge equivalent to federal income tax	0	0	0	0	0	0	0	0	2,212	2,040	0
Net earnings - 3 months ending 12/30/67	0	0	0	0	0	0	0	1,393	0	0	0
Excess of cost over par value of treasury stock	0	(627)	0	0	0	0	0	0	0	0	0
Ending equity	$88,199	$81,155	$68,295	$56,169	$48,483	$43,918	$36,205	$31,543	$29,495	$24,520	$22,139

Sources: Berkshire Hathaway Annual Reports 1964–1974.

Table 3.18: Berkshire Hathaway, select data and ratios, 1964–1974

	12/28/74	12/29/73	12/30/72	12/31/71	12/31/70	01/03/70	12/28/68	12/30/67	10/01/66	10/02/65	10/03/64
Return on average equity	8.32%	17.21%	19.49%	14.69%	9.88%	19.85%	13.76%	3.63%	10.23%	9.77%	0.79%
Operating earnings ($ thousands)	$8,384	$11,931	$11,198	$6,941	$4,508	$4,235	$2,488	$1,007	$2,763	$2,279	$176
Stockholders' equity per share	$90.04	$82.85	$69.72	$57.34	$49.49	$44.83	$36.74	$32.01	$28.99	$24.10	$19.46
Change in textile revenues	(2.5%)	20.4%	6.7%	5.9%	(39.2%)	(12.1%)	17.8%	(20.9%)	0.1%	(1.4%)	0.0%
Change in textile operating income	(6.2%)	67.2%	627.3%	117.5%	(92.6%)	(7.1%)	2722.2%	(98.9%)	3.5%	788.2%	NM
Receivables to textile revenues	13.4%	15.4%	14.6%	19.6%	15.9%	15.8%	16.4%	19.4%	16.4%	15.1%	14.9%
Inventories to textile revenues	18.4%	21.4%	24.6%	23.2%	34.5%	22.9%	26.8%	29.7%	24.8%	20.8%	23.4%
Textile working capital[1] ($ thousands)			$7,646	$7,825	$10,373	$11,862	$15,640	$13,724	$17,375	$14,440	$16,257
Textile "core" working capital to revenues	13.4%	15.4%	27.6%	30.1%	42.2%	29.3%	34.0%	35.1%	35.2%	29.3%	32.5%

Footnote:
1: Accounts receivables plus inventory less accounts payable.

Sources: Berkshire Hathaway Annual Reports 1964–1974.

Table 3.19: Berkshire Hathaway Insurance Group balance sheets, 1967–1974

($ thousands)	12/28/74	12/29/73	12/30/72	12/31/71	12/31/70	01/03/70	12/28/68	12/30/67
Cash	$10,652	$2,866	$3,044	$4,563	$812	$788	$598	
Bonds, at amortized cost	71,531	74,474	88,148	84,079	51,609	31,835	30,201	
Preferred stocks	2,855	2,298	2,942	999	1,041	1,647	33	
Common stocks	50,670	49,757	17,412	11,676	10,254	8,607	9,151	
Total cash & investments	135,708	129,395	111,547	101,317	63,717	42,876	39,982	
Investment in Blue Chip Stamps	14,371	13,717	11,287	4,128	0			
Property, plant and equipment, net	1,581	1,605	1,674	1,313	1,191	1,191		
Other assets	20,679	13,121	14,976	16,556	9,338	6,344		
Total assets	172,338	157,839	139,484	123,314	74,246	50,412	44,692	
Losses and loss adjustment expenses	72,761	61,676	60,275	52,991	29,759			
Unearned premiums	21,705	21,282	23,839	25,516	17,483			
Other liabilities	7,641	7,179	9,789	9,564	7,170			
Total liabilities	102,107	90,137	93,903	88,071	54,412			
Stockholders' equity	70,231	67,702	45,581	35,243	19,834	13,338	13,453	9,524
Total liabilities and stockholders' equity	$172,338	$157,839	$139,484	$123,314	$74,246	$50,412	$44,692	
Average float (rounded)	$79,100	$73,300	$69,500	$52,500	$32,400	$23,400	$19,900	$17,300

Sources: Berkshire Hathaway Annual Reports 1968–1974 and 1992 (float data).

Table 3.20: Berkshire Hathaway Insurance Group income statements, 1968–1974

($ thousands)	12/28/74	12/29/73	12/30/72	12/31/71	12/31/70	01/03/70	12/28/68
Premiums written, net	$60,997	$50,372	$57,950	$66,456	$45,086	$28,776	$22,620
Premiums earned	60,574	52,929	59,627	60,867	39,173	25,258	22,617
Losses and loss expenses incurred	47,120	32,836	36,987	40,783	26,858	16,361	14,798
Underwriting expenses	20,346	16,774	18,356	18,675	12,645	9,050	7,251
Total losses and expenses	67,466	49,610	55,343	59,458	39,503	25,411	22,049
Pre-tax underwriting gain/(loss)	(6,892)	3,319	4,284	1,409	(330)	(153)	568
Pre-tax net investment income	7,880	7,283	6,644	4,974	2,870	2,025	1,612
Realized gain/(loss) on investments, net of tax	(1,340)	930	929	719	(301)	282	707
Equity in earnings of Blue Chip Stamps	792	1,008	111	0	0	0	0
Net income	$2,529	$9,871	$8,984	$5,944	$1,806	$2,115	$2,497

Sources: Berkshire Hathaway Annual Reports 1969–1974.

Table 3.21: Berkshire Hathaway Insurance Group reconciliation of stockholders' equity, 1967–1974

($ thousands)	12/28/74	12/29/73	12/30/72	12/31/71	12/31/70	01/03/70	12/28/68	12/30/67
Beginning stockholders' equity	$67,702	$45,581	$35,243	$19,834	$13,338	$13,453	$9,524	
Contribution from parent	0	9,750	1,500	0	0	0	0	
Excess of proceeds over par value of capital stock issued	0	1,000	500	6,000	1,500	0	0	
Net income	2,529	9,871	8,984	5,944	1,806	2,115	2,497	
Change in common stock - National Indemnity Company	0	1,500	0	1,500	500	0	0	
Change in common stock - National Fire & Marine	0	0	500	1,000	0	500	0	
Excess of market value over cost on stocks	0	0	(1,146)	965	1,373	(2,538)	1,833	
Increase in beginning unassigned surplus	0	0	0	0	1,317	0	0	
Decrease in liability for unauthorized reinsurance	0	0	0	0	0	32	13	
Change in excess reserves	0	0	0	0	0	331	200	
Increase in non-admitted assets	0	0	0	0	0	(55)	(13)	
Stock dividend	0	0	0	0	0	(500)	(600)	
Ending stockholders' equity	$70,231	$67,702	$45,581	$35,243	$19,834	$13,338	$13,453	$9,524

Sources: Berkshire Hathaway Annual Reports 1969–1974.

Table 3.22: Berkshire Hathaway Insurance Group key ratios and figures, 1968–1974

	12/28/74	12/29/73	12/30/72	12/31/71	12/31/70	01/03/70	12/28/68
Net premiums written to average equity	88%	89%	143%	241%	272%	215%	197%
Loss ratio	77.8%	62.0%	62.0%	67.0%	68.6%	64.8%	65.4%
Expense ratio	33.4%	33.3%	31.7%	28.1%	28.0%	31.4%	32.1%
Combined ratio	111.1%	95.3%	93.7%	95.1%	96.6%	96.2%	97.5%
Return on average equity	3.7%	17.4%	22.2%	21.6%	10.9%	15.8%	
Growth in premiums written, net	21.1%	(13.1%)	(12.8%)	47.4%	56.7%	27.2%	
Growth in premiums earned	14.4%	(11.2%)	(2.0%)	55.4%	55.1%	11.7%	

Sources: Berkshire Hathaway Annual Reports 1969–1974.

Table 3.23: Illinois National Bank & Trust Co. of Rockford, balance sheets, 1968–1974

($ thousands)	1974	1973	1972	1971	1970	1969
Cash and due from banks	$21,544	$26,684	$22,111	$17,833	$15,157	$19,918
US Government Bonds	10,615	11,355	10,615	12,633	15,129	11,228
Obligations of states and political subdivisions	45,858	47,713	50,163	42,884	36,627	36,005
Other securities	3,846	3,358	7,779	5,865	210	210
Subtotal investments	60,319	62,426	68,556	61,382	51,966	47,443
Federal funds sold	5,000					
Loans	70,854	66,022	59,618	54,032	50,841	47,963
Bank premises and equipment	1,009	1,117	1,361	1,523	1,624	1,825
Accrued interest receivable and other assets	2,857	2,156	1,750	1,252	1,739	1,040
Total assets	161,581	158,404	153,397	136,021	121,326	118,189
Demand deposits	53,178	55,716	55,130	51,208	52,478	58,237
Time deposits	85,519	81,450	77,558	64,640	49,095	41,317
Total deposits	138,697	137,166	132,688	115,848	101,573	99,555
Accrued taxes and other expenses	1,005	835	887	814	679	638
Total liabilities	139,702	138,002	133,575	116,662	102,252	100,193
Reserve for loan losses	1,251	1,164	1,025	855	860	800
Total capital accounts	20,628	19,239	18,797	18,505	18,213	17,196
Total liabilities and capital	$161,581	$158,404	$153,397	$136,021	$121,326	$118,189

Sources: Berkshire Hathaway Annual Reports 1969–1974.

Table 3.24: Illinois National Bank & Trust Co. of Rockford, income statements, 1968–1974

($ thousands)	1974	1973	1972	1971	1970	1969
Interest and fees on loans	$6,608	$5,316	$4,134	$4,006	$4,130	$3,820
Income on federal funds sold	361	237	110	109	317	392
Interest and dividends on:						
United States government obligations	942	632	598	708	569	1,003
Obligations of states and political subdivisions	2,798	2,796	2,677	2,094	1,717	1,155
Other Securities	284	343	524	228	13	0
Trust department	434	451	385	336	280	343
Service charges on deposit accounts	139	130	127	137	152	220
Other	560	500	411	307	354	248
Total operating income	12,126	10,403	8,968	7,925	7,531	7,181
Operating expenses:						
Salaries	1,552	1,503	1,367	1,352	1,298	1,159
Pensions, profit sharing, and other employee benefits	247	263	239	138	151	114
Interest on deposits	4,954	4,295	3,419	2,733	2,029	1,695
Interest on federal funds purchased	14	55	3	2	4	13
Net occupancy expense of bank premises	257	418	314	359	358	302
Equipment rentals, depreciation, and maintenance	248	253	264	289	272	260
Provision for loan losses	19	16	37	36	52	62
Other	592	767	645	681	661	558
Total operating expenses	7,884	7,570	6,288	5,588	4,826	4,161

Continued...

… Continued from prior page.

Income before income taxes and securities gains / losses	4,242	2,833	2,680	2,337	2,705	3,020
Applicable income taxes:						
Current			1	121	454	1,061
Deferred			(2)	(12)	30	(22)
Total applicable income taxes	220	61	(0)	109	484	1,039
Income before securities gains or (losses)	4,022	2,772	2,680	2,228	2,221	1,981
Securities gains or (losses)	175	67	156	35	367	(789)
Applicable income taxes	(7)	(34)	(72)	(9)	(179)	417
Securities gains or (losses) net of applicable income taxes	168	33	84	26	189	(372)
Gain on sale of real estate, net of taxes	0	43				
Net income	$4,190	$2,848	$2,764	$2,254	$2,410	$1,608

Sources: Berkshire Hathaway Annual Reports 1969–1974.

Table 3.25: Illinois National Bank & Trust Co. of Rockford, key ratios and figures, 1969–1974

	1974	1973	1972	1971	1970	1969
Average loans ($ thousands)	$68,438	$62,820	$56,825	$52,436	$49,402	$47,479
Average assets ($ thousands)	$159,993	$155,901	$144,709	$128,674	$119,758	$117,749
Average total deposits ($ thousands)	$137,932	$134,927	$124,268	$108,711	$100,564	$99,320
Average equity ($ thousands)	$19,933	$19,018	$18,651	$18,359	$17,704	$17,018
Average loans to average assets	42.8%	40.3%	39.3%	40.8%	41.3%	40.3%
Average assets to average equity	8.03	8.20	7.76	7.01	6.76	6.92
Average capital ratio	12.5%	12.2%	12.9%	14.3%	14.8%	14.5%
Pre-tax operating return on average assets	2.51%	1.78%	1.85%	1.73%	1.85%	1.68%
Pre-tax operating return on average deposits	2.92%	2.05%	2.16%	2.05%	2.21%	1.99%
Pre-tax operating income / average equity	21.3%	14.9%	14.4%	12.7%	15.3%	17.7%
After-tax operating income / average equity	20.2%	14.6%	14.4%	12.1%	12.5%	11.6%
Efficiency ratio	41%	53%	52%	55%	51%	45%
Interest income / average assets	6.87%	5.98%	5.56%	5.55%	5.63%	5.41%
Interest expense / average deposits	3.60%	3.22%	2.75%	2.52%	2.02%	1.72%
Net interest margin	3.27%	2.76%	2.80%	3.04%	3.61%	3.69%
Average loans to average deposits	49.6%	46.6%	45.7%	48.2%	49.1%	47.8%
Provision for loan losses / avg. loans	0.03%	0.03%	0.06%	0.07%	0.10%	0.13%

Sources: Berkshire Hathaway Annual Reports 1969–1974.

Chapter 4
1975–1984

Table 4.1: Decade snapshot: 1974–1984

	1974	1984
Business:	Textiles, Insurance, Banking, Candy, Publishing	Insurance, Newspapers, Furniture Retailing, Candy, Banking, Textiles
Key managers:	Chairman & CEO: Warren E. Buffett; President: Kenneth V. Chace	Chairman & CEO: Warren E. Buffett; Vice Chair: Charles T. Munger
Annual revenues:	$101.5 million	$729 million
Stockholders' equity:	$88.2 million	$1.27 billion
Book value per share:	$90.02	$1,108.77
Float (average):	$79 million	$253 million

Major Capital Allocation Decisions:

1. Purchased Waumbec Mills in Manchester, NH for $1.7 million (1975).

2. Purchased Buffalo News for $35.5 million (1977).

3. Merged Diversified Retailing into Berkshire (1978).

4. Divested Illinois National Bank and Trust (1980).

5. Merged Blue Chip Stamps into Berkshire (1983).

6. Purchased Nebraska Furniture Mart for $60 million (1983).

7. Allocated 75% of $1.3 billion common equity portfolio into stock of GEICO, General Foods, Exxon, Washington Post.

Noteworthy Events:

1. Inflation averages 7.8% per year and peaks at 12.4% in 1980.

Table 4.2: Berkshire Hathaway earnings[1]

($ thousands)	1984	1983	1982	1981	1980	1979	1978	1977	1976	1975	1974
Insurance Group:											
Underwriting	($48,060)	($33,872)	($21,558)	$1,478	$6,737	$3,741	$3,000	$5,802			
Net investment income	68,903	43,810	41,620	38,823	30,927	24,216	19,691	12,804			
Buffalo News	27,328	16,547	(724)	(725)	(1,655)	(2,744)	(1,637)	389			
Nebraska Furniture Mart[2]	11,609	3,049									
See's Candies	26,644	24,526	14,235	12,493	9,223	7,598	7,013	6,598			
Associated Retail Stores	(1,072)	697	914	1,763	2,440	2,775	2,757	2,775			
Blue Chip Stamps - parent[3]	(1,843)	(1,876)	2,492	2,171	4,588	1,425	1,198	566			
Mutual Savings and Loan	1,166	(467)	(2)	766	2,775	4,751	4,638	2,747			
Precision Steel	3,278	2,102	493	1,648	1,352	1,480	2,916	(620)			
Textiles	418	(100)	(1,545)	(2,669)	(508)	1,723	777	813	See note 6 below.		
Wesco Financial - parent	7,831	4,844	2,937	2,145	1,392	1,098					
Illinois National Bank[4]					5,200	5,614	4,710	3,706			
Amortization of goodwill[5]	(1,434)	(563)	90								
Interest on debt	(14,097)	(13,844)	(12,977)	(12,649)	(9,390)	(5,860)	(4,546)	(4,255)			
Shareholder-designated contributions	(3,179)	(3,066)	(891)								
Other	4,529	9,623	2,658	1,992	1,308	996	438	102			
Operating earnings, pre-tax	**82,021**	**51,410**	**27,742**	**47,236**	**54,389**	**46,813**	**40,955**	**31,427**			
Special GEICO distribution	7,896	19,575									
Special General Foods distribution											
Sales of securities and unusual sales of assets	101,376	65,089	21,875	33,150	15,757	9,614	13,395	10,807			
Total earnings - all entities (pre-tax)	191,293	136,074	49,617	80,386	70,146	56,427	54,350	42,234			
Income tax and minority interest	(42,397)	(23,908)	(3,243)	(17,782)	(17,024)	(13,610)	(15,108)	(11,841)			
Total earnings - all entities (after tax)[7]	$148,896	$112,166	$46,374	$62,604	$53,122	$42,817	$39,242	$30,393	$24,966	$6,121	$8,163

Notes:

1. This table presents Berkshire Hathaway's share of earnings, as adjusted for Berkshire's ownership interest in each company.
2. 1983 figures are those for October through December.
3. 1982 and 1983 are not comparable; major assets were transferred in the mid-year 1983 merger of Blue Chip Stamps.
4. The Illinois National Bank was divested as of December 31, 1980.
5. Amortization of goodwill is included in Other for years prior to 1982.
6. Buffett began including a table entitled Sources of Earnings in his 1978 Chairman's letter, which included a comparison to 1977. Since comparable data was not available for these years, I left them blank.
7. The figures for 1974–1976 were taken from the 1978 report, which differ slightly from the amounts reported in these years.

Sources: Berkshire Hathaway Annual Reports 1978–1984.

Introduction

Warren Buffett began his second decade at the helm of Berkshire Hathaway with a company worth four times as much as it was when he acquired control of it in 1965. Monetary value though was not the only differentiator. Instead of a failing textile business, shareholders now owned a large, successful conglomerate consisting of an insurance operation that provided profits and excess cash (float) to invest in marketable securities, a bank, and a newspaper. Plus, through an investment in Blue Chip Stamps, it owned an interest in a candy company and had more float to invest (value that would accrue to Berkshire's full benefit when the two companies merged). This was a Berkshire shaped in Buffett's image using his capital allocation skills and the resources and opportunities available to him at that time. The Berkshire Hathaway that would emerge from this second decade of work would also reflect this image but with a much larger shadow due to its sheer size (see Table 4.1).

Throughout the decade beginning in 1975, Berkshire would expand existing (profitable) operations, buy other operating businesses, and buy pieces of businesses via its investment portfolio. It would be forced to divest of its bank, and intentionally shrink another banking operation to reduce risk. Different businesses helped with Berkshire's growth in different ways. While the textile division was being shrunk to allow Berkshire's diversification into more profitable lines of business, the Insurance Group was a platform for expansion through organic growth and acquisitions.

The decade would also include notable changes in business relationships. Two of the largest investments, Diversified Retailing and Blue Chip Stamps, would be merged into Berkshire, bringing with them important and valuable subsidiaries. Blue Chip would become another platform for building a portfolio of wholly-owned operating businesses (all the while managing down its own dying trading stamp business). Through Blue Chip, Berkshire would come to own another bank, Mutual Savings and Loan Association, a steel warehouse company, another newspaper, and See's Candies. The candy business would shine brightly throughout the decade, though not without some difficulties along the way. The Berkshire that emerged from Buffett's second decade would be the result of the successful allocation of over $1 billion of capital. This result would come in part from great patience and fortitude in the face of the economic recession of the mid-1970s, the large storm that hit the usually strong insurance industry during the latter half of the decade, record interest rates, troubles at the *The Buffalo News*, and other challenges along the way.

Table 4.3: Select information 1975–1984

	1975	1976	1977	1978	1979	1980	1981	1982	1983	1984
BRK book value per share - % change	21.9%	59.3%	31.9%	24.0%	35.7%	19.3%	31.4%	40.0%	32.3%	13.6%
BRK market value per share - % change	2.5%	129.3%	46.8%	14.5%	102.5%	32.8%	31.8%	38.4%	69.0%	(2.7%)
S&P 500 total return	37.2%	23.6%	(7.4%)	6.4%	18.2%	32.3%	(5.0%)	21.4%	22.4%	6.1%
US GDP Growth (real %)	(0.2%)	5.4%	4.6%	5.5%	3.2%	(0.3%)	2.5%	(1.8%)	4.6%	7.2%
10-year Treasury Note (year-end %)	8.0%	6.9%	7.7%	9.0%	10.4%	12.8%	13.7%	10.5%	11.8%	11.5%
US inflation (%)	9.1%	5.8%	6.5%	7.6%	11.3%	13.5%	10.4%	6.2%	3.2%	4.4%
US unemployment (%)	8.5%	7.7%	7.1%	6.1%	5.9%	7.2%	7.6%	9.7%	9.6%	7.5%

Sources: Berkshire Hathaway Annual Reports 2018, 2019 and Federal Reserve Bank of St. Louis.

1975

The beginning of the second decade of Buffett's control of Berkshire Hathaway was a challenging one. The previous year, Buffett had told shareholders that the outlook for 1975 was not encouraging. Now he reported that his forecast was "distressingly accurate." The business produced the lowest return on equity since 1967—a bleak 7.6%. Even worse, profits included a one-time benefit from Federal income tax refunds. True ongoing operating results had been lackluster.

Amid the bad news came indications of better days. The textile industry had shown some degree of rationality in 1975, with industry participants cutting back production rather than competing to the point of massive operating losses like during prior industry slumps. Berkshire continued to increase its investment in Blue Chip Stamps. The big swing factor was insurance underwriting. Underwriting was hard to predict due to the actions of industry participants and the uncertainty of future loss claims; it could make or break any given year. Still, there were some favorable winds at Berkshire's insurance back that hinted of possible underwriting improvements during the year.

Textiles

During the year Berkshire acquired Waumbec Mills and Waumbec Dyeing and Finishing Co. in Manchester, New Hampshire. On April 28, 1975 Berkshire purchased the company for $1.7 million, partially funding the purchase with $1.15 million of promissory notes issued by Berkshire at the parent company level. This followed a decade where Berkshire reduced production or sold off certain textile manufacturing locations. So why buy Waumbec?

Buying a company in a dying industry doesn't make sense on the face of it, but a few factors likely influenced the decision. First, Waumbec was like the Home Fabrics division and focused on the more profitable finished woven products, primarily drapery and apparel. Buffett thought it could complement Berkshire's existing operations.

Next, the purchase appealed to Buffett's instinct to acquire bargains. The purchase price for Waumbec was below book value, reflecting its diminished economic position. That means Berkshire paid less than what the net assets recorded in the books were worth, at least on paper. In the notes to the financial statements in Berkshire's Annual Report for 1975, a disclosure is made. To balance the purchase price against the book value of the company, no net property, plant, and equipment was carried onto the consolidated financials. By extension, no depreciation expense would be incurred either. This seems odd by today's accounting standards, but it was consistent with the accounting treatment at the time.*

Additionally, 1975 was a big year for the textile industry. The recession in 1974 hit textiles hard, but there were huge increases in the latter half of 1975. Many manufacturers reported going from operating two or three days a week to five or six days with three shifts a day.

The below-book value purchase price was a result of Waumbec's weak operating results. Waumbec was operating 55% of its looms at 50% of operating capacity. The business improved in the latter part of 1975, but the period leading up to Berkshire's purchase saw a lot of red ink. In fact, those losses resulted in $2.6 million of unused net operating loss carryovers at the time of purchase—essentially tax credits available to offset any future income from Waumbec.

While the headline textile revenue figure listed in the financial statements gave the appearance of an okay year, digging deeper told a more nuanced story. Berkshire did report an increase in sales of textiles during 1975. But because the current year included results from Waumbec (which hadn't been under Berkshire's ownership the prior year), sales results were worse than at first glance (see Table 4.4). If Berkshire had owned Waumbec all of 1974, revenues would have reflected a 22% decline. The significant decline in revenues notwithstanding, strong profits in the fourth quarter brought the results into the black for the year. This also proved that revenues and profits do not always correlate—and can sometime diverge quite drastically.

---

* Accounting Principles Board Opinion No. 16.

Table 4.4: Textile Division—select data

($ millions)	1975	1974	% Change
Revenues	$32.8	$32.6	1%
Revenues (with Waumbec)	36.0	45.9	(22%)

Sources: Berkshire Hathaway Annual Report, 1975.

Buffett concluded his update on textiles with praise for Ken Chace and his team and said they and Berkshire would look for ways to increase business without undue investment. Buffett considered it unwise to make major investments in new fixed assets in the textile industry due to the "relatively low returns historically earned," a comment which seems to confirm the low purchase price indeed made the Waumbec acquisition appealing.

Insurance

"The property and casualty insurance industry had its worst year in history during 1975. We did our share." So Buffett began his report to shareholders about the insurance segment. Berkshire's insurance companies suffered disproportionately due to weakness in auto and long-tail lines.* Insurance underwriting results suffered due to multiple aspects of one overall trend: inflation. Three aspects were of particular concern:

- A surging general rate of inflation. This caused the costs to deliver on promises (i.e. to repair property and pay for medical costs) to soar above the level expected when the premiums were written.
- Social inflation was a growing problem. Juries were issuing large restitution payments to claimants at a far higher rate than had previously been experienced. To compound matters, these large awards led to more lawsuits and more restitution payments. Buffett summed this up nicely: Juries were "in effect adding coverage [to customers] beyond what was paid for." Insurance companies had to payout the awards and price future policies accordingly.
- Other (weaker) insurance companies who underpriced or under-reserved went out of business. Their losses were effectively subsidized by other insurers through Guaranty Funds—comparable to today's Federal Deposit Insurance Corporation (FDIC) for banks. In the FDIC's case and in the Guaranty Funds' case, industry participants (banks and insurance companies, respectively) basically pay an insurance premium to cover failed firms.

---

* Long-tail lines are insurance contracts that take a long time to play out. An insurance policy covering one year has losses that are known within that 12 months. A reinsurance contract covering a decade would by contrast take that much longer before profitability was known.

Challenges aside, all was not doom and gloom in insurance. The Home and Auto business was now included along with the Home State companies under Home State multiple lines. After a disastrous expansion into Florida, the business receded to its home turf of Chicago. Buffett wrote that adjusted for start-up costs the Texas United Insurance Company made outstanding progress. Cornhusker Casualty, the oldest and largest of the Home State operations, turned in both higher premiums and, more importantly, a combined ratio under 100%.

Expected premium growth for 1976 reflected an anticipated repricing of premiums to match the inflated costs—rather than growth in the number of policies. "Under normal circumstances such a gain in volume would be welcome, but our emotions are mixed at present," Buffett explained.

Overall, the Insurance Group reported a combined ratio of 117.8% (see Table 4.5). Its loss ratio, which had jumped from 62% in 1973 to almost 78% in 1974, creeped up to 81% in 1975. Together with expenses of 36.9% (likely reflecting some of the previously mentioned start-up costs and higher relative fixed expenses on lower premium volume), results were truly horrific. The combined ratio was predicted to remain above 100% in 1976.

Table 4.5: Insurance Group, select information

($ thousands)	1975
Premiums written, net	$58,975
Premiums earned	
Specialized auto and general liability	38,513
Workers' compensation	3,632
Reinsurance	12,407
Home state multiple lines	6,670
	61,222
Underwriting gain (loss), pre-tax	
Specialized auto and general liability	(7,450)
Workers' Compensation[1]	(342)
Reinsurance	(2,651)
Home State multiple lines	(907)
	($11,350)
Combined ratio (statutory)	117.8%
Footnote: 1.Workers' Compensation coverage written by Home State is not broken out per the footnote to the financial statements.	

Note: The data in this table was taken from the segment results section of the Annual Report and differs in some cases with figures listed in earlier reporting periods. I've chosen to use the data from the 1979 report as it is more consistent. Comparative data for prior years is available, but due to inconsistencies it was thought best to omit it here.
Source: Berkshire Hathaway Annual Report 1979.

Even though insurance underwriting and insurance investing are inextricably linked, they are also nonetheless separate. Buffett delegated the day-to-day underwriting to others, while retaining the investing—meaning capital allocation—to himself. This two-pronged approach to operating the insurance businesses and evaluating their results is still in use at Berkshire today.

Berkshire placed little emphasis on year-to-year realized and unrealized gains and losses. Buffett was rather looking for business results, no different than Berkshire's subsidiaries:

> "Our equity investments are heavily concentrated in a few companies which are selected based on favorable economic characteristics, competent and honest management, and a purchase price attractive when measured against the yardstick of value to a private owner."

Like the two-pronged approach to insurance overall, the general investment criteria have remained steadfast.

Banking

Eugene Abegg and Illinois National Bank continued to impress. During 1975, the bank had average loans of about $65 million, yet loan losses were a mere $24,000 (or 0.04% of loans). That record is outstanding—then and now. While one year may be an aberration, the long-term track record spoke for itself. In 1975, the bank earned over 2% on assets, compared to a fourth of that or 0.5% for the largest thirty banks in the country.

A fan of history (especially business history), Buffett gave shareholders a glimpse into the beginnings of Illinois National. Eugene Abegg founded the bank in 1931 with $250,000 in capital and earned $8,782 during its first full year in 1932. Fast forward forty-four years and the bank was earning $3.5 million annually with equity approaching $22 million—a compounded annual rate of return of 10.7%. That is even better than it seems since the bank paid regular dividends to owners over those years.

Signing off the 1975 letter was a reminder of Berkshire's operating philosophy: A "conservatively financed and highly liquid business—possessing extra margins of balance sheet strength consistent with the fiduciary obligations inherent in the banking and insurance industries—which will produce a long-term rate of return on equity capital exceeding that of American industry as a whole." Under Buffett's control, that return on equity capital was 15% compounded annually—a doubling every five years.

1976

After a very difficult 1975, the new year brought a pleasant surprise. Insurance underwriting, led by Phil Liesche of National Indemnity Group, turned in results that exceeded the most optimistic projections. Berkshire's overall operating earnings of $16 million reflected a return on equity of 17.3%, above Berkshire's long-term average of 15% in the Buffett era.

Berkshire repurchased its own shares during 1976 (see Table 4.6). Though the amount repurchased represented less than 1% of Berkshire's outstanding shares, it shed light on Buffett's view of the attractiveness of the stock, which continued to be priced attractively.

Table 4.6: Berkshire Hathaway share repurchases, 1976

Cost	$432,055
Shares repurchased	6,647
Average cost per share	$65.00
Average shares outstanding	976,246
Implied valuation	$63,455,990
Average book value	$104,091,663
Price / book value	0.61

Sources: Berkshire Hathaway Annual Report 1976 and author calculations.

Textiles

There was a dark spot among the good news, and unsurprisingly, it was in textiles. Returns on revenues and on capital were back to trend and inadequate.* The Waumbec Mill, acquired only a year earlier, was not pulling its weight. The entire group continued a long slide into economic oblivion. Still, Buffett believed "reasonable returns on average are possible." He told shareholders that the Textile Group was an important source of employment in New Bedford, Massachusetts and Manchester, New Hampshire. His words come across as conscious of the social ramifications of operating according to strict economic yardsticks that might not consider the people who depended on the plants for their livelihoods. Berkshire, even then, was guarding its reputation.

As the textile business was shrinking, so too were the details of its operations in the financial statements. This was, of course, partly because Berkshire had grown

---

* This was how Buffett summarized the results for the year. Pre-tax earnings fell from $1.3 million in 1975 to $1.1 million in 1976.

significantly in size and scope into many other business lines. Some detail on textile inventories were provided, but revenues were now grouped into "net sales of manufactured products". This was probably due to the acquisition of K&W Products,[*] a small automotive chemical company in California, and it now made sense from a financial reporting standpoint to report its finances with the Textile Group.

Insurance

When assessing the performance of a conglomerate, component results must be analyzed. These parts often have different economic characteristics and performance. This was the case with Berkshire's subsidiaries. While the Textile Group faltered, the Insurance Group flourished. The industry, including Berkshire's Insurance Group, had improved, as shown in Table 4.7.

Table 4.7: Combined ratio, selected groups

	1976	1975
Stockholder-owned property/casualty	103.0%	108.3%
Stockholder-owned auto lines	107.4%	113.5%
Berkshire Hathaway	94.6%	117.8%

Note: The Berkshire Hathaway figures differ slightly from those presented by Buffett in his letter (1976: 98.7%; 1975: 115.4%). Buffett used the statutory figures which immediately expensed deferred premium acquisition costs.
Sources: Berkshire Hathaway Chairman's letter 1976 and author's calculations.

Notably, the combined ratio dipped below 100%.[**] Instead of having a float or capital cost of 17.8% of the premiums it earned, policyholders essentially paid Berkshire 5.4% for the privilege of holding their cash. Some insurers, then and now, are content to operate at levels above 100%, reasoning that the float, or money they get to hold and invest, will make up the difference.[***] Berkshire always strives for superior underwriting results.

---

[*] Buffett had noted the purchase of K&W in his 1975 letter to shareholders. He described its $2 million of revenues as relatively small but noted it had consistent earnings.
[**] A ratio above 100% means an insurer has costs exceeding its premiums.
[***] The magnitude of this effect depends on the general level of interest rates and opportunity cost.

Table 4.8: Insurance Group, select information

($ thousands)	1976	1975
Premiums written, net	$94,773	$58,975
Premiums earned		
Specialized auto and general liability	50,778	38,513
Workers' Compensation	5,815	3,632
Reinsurance	17,220	12,407
Home State multiple lines	11,058	6,670
	84,871	61,222
Underwriting gain (loss), pre-tax		
Specialized auto and general liability	4,768	(7,450)
Workers' compensation[1]	(1,093)	(342)
Reinsurance	(2,879)	(2,651)
Home State multiple lines	(548)	(907)
	$248	($11,350)
Combined ratio (statutory)	94.6%	117.8%

Footnote:
1. Workers' Compensation coverage written by Home State is not broken out per the footnote to the financial statements.

Note: The data in this table was taken from the summary of segment results section of the Annual Report and differs in some cases with figures listed in earlier reporting periods.
Source: Berkshire Hathaway Annual Report 1979.

While direct business, such as the auto and general liability lines, showed a marked improvement during the year as higher premiums covered costs, the reinsurance business fared slightly less well. Reinsurers insure other insurance companies, so their results lag behind those writing the direct policies. Consequently, Berkshire's reinsurance operations continued to feel the effects of a weak 1975 during 1976, with Buffett cautioning shareholders that "the near term outlook still is not good for our reinsurance business."

The acquisition of a small reinsurance operation hinted at bullishness on the long-term prospects of reinsurance. The K&W Products manufacturing company (described earlier) included a sister operation engaged in the reinsurance business and an insurance brokerage. In January, Berkshire acquired Kerkling Reinsurance Corporation, also headquartered in Nebraska.* The company assumed excess business from National Indemnity's reinsurance arm (about $1 million premium volume annually). The $2 million purchase price was equal to book value.

Home State operations were another bright spot. Premiums grew 66% and Berkshire planned to form another Home State operation during the year. The Home

---

* Technically, the acquiring entity was National Fire & Marine Insurance Company.

and Auto business in Chicago moved to a six-month direct bill policy which allowed more frequent repricing (and therefore the ability to correct underpriced policies).

Overall, Berkshire expected a better year in 1977, though concerns about continued economic and social inflation remained. Additionally, the significant industry rebound to profitability during the year was a siren call that competition might again drive down profitability.

Investments

A new table appeared in the Annual Report detailing equity investments (common + preferred) with a cost of over $3 million. The combined portfolio totaled $75 million (at cost*), with Government Employees Insurance Company (GEICO) accounting for nearly a quarter of it at $23.5 million ($19 million in convertible preferred stock and $4 million in common stock). Buffett had continued to follow the company after first learning about it as a student at Columbia Business School and understood what made the company special.** GEICO had strayed beyond its core business of insuring above-average drivers, losses mounted, and the market concluded there was a real risk the company wouldn't make it. Buffett's insight was that the company's core business would allow it to survive. The size of the GEICO investment presaged the starring role the company would ultimately play in Berkshire's future. Another notable investment listed in the table was the $10.6 million investment in *The Washington Post* Company first purchased in 1973.

Berkshire's investment in Blue Chip Stamps was *not* included in the table. Berkshire's $27 million investment was carried on the balance sheet separately since it owned about 33% of the business.*** Berkshire first invested in Blue Chip Stamps in 1971, when it owned 6% of the company.

Banking

Buffett as usual had good things to say about Berkshire's banking operations, and 1976 was no exception. Perennial praise for Eugene Abegg was followed by a financial reporting of its success. The bank continued to earn 2% on assets while maintaining high levels of liquidity and paying out maximum rates of interest to depositors. The only negative factor that was on Buffett's mind concerning the bank was its impending divestiture. New banking regulations required Berkshire to divest its star asset by the end of 1980.

---

* Insurance accounting at the time valued securities at cost. The market value of the portfolio of preferred and common stock was $45 million greater.
** GEICO's advantage stemmed from its direct-to-consumer model that reduced underwriting expenses below that of its competitors who were entrenched in a broker model. GEICO will be discussed in more detail later.
*** This is the equity method of accounting. Berkshire's share of Blue Chip Stamps' equity and equity in net earnings were reported on its balance sheet and income statement, respectively.

1977

Buffett led off the 1977 letter to shareholders with a note on how he viewed capital gains and losses: "While too much attention should not be paid to the figure in any single year, over the longer term the record … is of significance." He wanted to remind shareholders to think like owners. That is, long term.

He also continued his practice of tempering expectations. Buffett cautioned shareholders to view Berkshire's 37% increase in earnings per share as "considerably less impressive than it might appear at first glance" because beginning capital was up 24%. By turning the attention to the *rate* of return on shareholders' equity, not earnings per share, Buffett was calling out a mischievous practice that continues to this day. "We find nothing particularly noteworthy in a management performance combining, say, a 10% increase in equity capital and a 5% increase in earnings per share. After all, even a totally dormant savings account will produce steadily rising interest earnings each year because of compounding," he wrote. Berkshire's results were impressive nonetheless.

Weighed down by its roots as a textile company Berkshire's 1977 results were that much more impressive. Meanwhile, Blue Chip Stamps and the Insurance Group continued to shine.

Berkshire's repurchase of its own shares was again relegated to the footnotes of the financial statements. Perhaps due to the relatively small amount (about ¼ of 1% of outstanding shares), Buffett didn't think it worth mentioning (see Table 4.9). The price paid implied a valuation higher than that of the previous year, but still below book value.

Table 4.9: Berkshire Hathaway share repurchases, 1977

Cost	$229,162
Shares repurchased	2,244
Average cost per share	$102.12
Average shares outstanding	971,800
Implied valuation	$99,242,260
Average book value	$128,540,768
Price / book value	0.77

Sources: Berkshire Hathaway Annual Report 1977 and author calculations.

Textiles

Berkshire remained in textiles despite its shrinking size and dismal prospects. Of its $379 million of identifiable assets at year-end 1977, just $22 million were in the textile division. Still, Buffett put himself in the shoes of a minority shareholder and asked the question: Why was Berkshire continuing to operate the Textile Group when it seemed to present nothing but problems, and where opportunities clearly existed to redirect the capital elsewhere? He then answered himself.

"Our reasons are several: (1) Our mills in both New Bedford and Manchester are among the largest employers in each town, utilizing a labor force of high average age possessing relatively non-transferable skills. Our workers and unions have exhibited unusual understanding and effort in cooperating with management to achieve a cost structure and product mix which might allow us to maintain a viable operation. (2) Management also has been energetic and straightforward in its approach to our textile problems. In particular, Ken Chace's efforts after the change in corporate control took place in 1965 generated capital from the textile division needed to finance the acquisition and expansion of our profitable insurance operation. (3) With hard work and some imagination regarding manufacturing and marketing configurations, it seems reasonable that at least modest profits in the textile division can be achieved in the future."

The fate of textiles was coming, but not for several more years.

Insurance

Berkshire bought National Indemnity and National Fire and Marine for $8.6 million in 1967 when it had annual premium volume of $22 million. A decade later, the Insurance Group had grown to combined premium volume of $159 million.* More impressive was that this was done without the issuance of any shares of Berkshire stock. (In fact, it had repurchased shares during this period.)

Berkshire founded or acquired for cash several insurers during the preceding decade:

- 1970: Cornhusker Casualty Company
- 1971: Lakeland Fire & Casualty Company
- 1972: Texas United Insurance Company

---

* The original figure Buffett quoted in the 1977 Chairman's letter was $151 million. The amount was revised in 1978 after the Diversified Retailing merger.

- 1973: The Insurance Company of Iowa
- 1977: Kansas Fire and Casualty Company

The newest addition to the Berkshire family of insurance companies was Cypress Insurance Company, acquired in late 1977. Cypress, in South Pasadena, California, was writing about $12.5 million in workers' compensation volume annually. Although National Indemnity had its own worker's compensation operation, Cypress and National Indemnity would operate independently by utilizing different marketing strategies. Buffett was not one to make any changes to what he considered a first-class operation.

First class did not mean perfect. Buffett pointed to four mistakes made by Berkshire's existing insurance operations to date:

- The surety operation attempted in 1969
- A money-losing venture in aviation insurance
- The failed expansion attempt of Home and Auto into Florida
- And attempting to build out workers' compensation in California (which was now back in action and proceeding in earnest)

But he did not linger on them. "It is comforting to be in a business where some mistakes can be made and yet a quite satisfactory overall performance can be achieved. In a sense, this is the opposite case from our textile business."

Table 4.10: Insurance Group, select information

($ thousands)	1977	1976	1975
Premiums written, net	$158,704	$94,773	$58,975
Premiums earned			
Specialized auto and general liability	80,690	50,778	38,513
Workers' Compensation	18,916	5,815	3,632
Reinsurance	24,100	17,220	12,407
Home State multiple lines	19,382	11,058	6,670
	143,088	84,871	61,222
Underwriting gain (loss), pre-tax			
Specialized auto and general liability	7,800	4,768	(7,450)
Workers' Compensation[1]	(1,644)	(1,093)	(342)
Reinsurance	(1,251)	(2,879)	(2,651)
Home State multiple lines	896	(548)	(907)
	$5,801	$248	($11,350)
Combined ratio (statutory)	93.2%	94.6%	117.8%

Footnote:
1. Workers' Compensation coverage written by Home State is not broken out per the footnote to the financial statements.

Note: The data in this table was taken from the summary of segment results section of the Annual Report and differs in some cases with figures listed in earlier reporting periods.
Source: Berkshire Hathaway Annual Report 1979.

Buffett appreciated the Insurance Group's generally high performance but was more interested in explaining results and looking ahead than highlighting stellar performance. "The winds in insurance underwriting were squarely behind us." Removed from the disastrous years of the 1974–1975 period, which resulted in competitors and capacity leaving the market, rates were now on the rise, offsetting inflation (now rising at 1% per *month*[*]).

Buffett also foresaw a return to stiff competition in future years as high prices lured others back into the market. "As markets loosen and rates become inadequate, we again will face the challenge of philosophically accepting reduced volume." Berkshire's insurance operations didn't operate in secret. There were no real barriers to entry, hence wild swings as competition waxed and waned. To remain competitive over the long haul, Berkshire would require "unusual managerial discipline" to focus on profitability, not volume.

In 1975, the Reinsurance Group wrote just under $10 million of premiums. Fast forward to 1977 and its volume was $24 million. Although underwriting profitability

---

[*] It should be made clear that it was not just the general price inflation Buffett was counting, but the other social inflation factors due to increasing number of lawsuits resulting in large jury awards.

was not met (and had an underwriting loss in each of the prior three years), it still generated large sums that were available for investment.

Reinsurance is the sharing or offloading of risk. Essentially, insurers pay part of the premiums they collect from policyholders to a reinsurance company, and in exchange, the reinsurance company agrees to share in losses and/or cover losses above certain limits. This kind of business came in spurts and those spurts could come in quite large chunks. The liabilities assumed were often of longer duration.* This meant Berkshire could invest the float for a longer period than say, automobile insurance, which was written on a six- or twelve-month basis and paid out about as quickly.**

Investments

Insurance investments, at cost, grew from $135 million to $253 million over the preceding two years. Fueling this growth was capital gains on investments and net underwriting profit along with large increases in premium volume and the consequential float generated. Chief among these float generators was reinsurance.

The Chairman's letter now detailed equity holdings of the Insurance Group for each holding over $5 million of market value. The combined value of Berkshire's investment in GEICO Common Stock and Convertible Preferred Stock still represented almost a quarter of the $181 million portfolio of equities (see Table 4.11). The remainder was comprised of simple, easy-to-understand businesses including aluminum companies, advertising agencies, and communications/broadcasting.

---

* The economics are such that one upfront premium is paid covering losses that (usually) develop over long periods of time. Losses are usually more weighted toward the present. For example, a reinsurer might payout 20% in each of the first three years followed by three years at 10% with the balance over a decade or more. Reinsurance contracts vary *widely* (this is just an example). Pricing reinsurance policies can be difficult and are fraught with risk.
** Short-tail insurance can be just as valuable if it is steady, which makes it a revolving fund.

Table 4.11: Berkshire Hathaway equity portfolio, 1977 (Insurance Group)

Shares	Company	Market Value ($ thousands)	% Total
934,300	The Washington Post Company Class B	$33,401	18%
1,986,953	GEICO - Convertible Preferred	33,033	18%
592,650	The Interpublic Group of Companies, Inc.	17,187	9%
220,000	Capital Cities Communications, Inc.	13,228	7%
1,294,308	GEICO - Common	10,516	6%
324,580	Kaiser Aluminum & Chemical Corporation	9,981	6%
226,900	Knight-Ridder Newspapers, Inc.	8,736	5%
170,800	Ogilvy & Mather International, Inc.	6,960	4%
1,305,800	Kaiser Industries, Inc.	6,039	3%
	Others	41,992	23%
	Total equities	$181,073	100%

Note: Percentages are rounded and don't add exactly to 100%.
Sources: Berkshire Hathaway Chairman's letter 1977 and author's calculations.

Buffett used Capital Cities* to illustrate a finer point to shareholders about how he thought of Berkshire's part-ownership in companies via ownership of their publicly traded shares. In 1977 Berkshire paid $10.9 million for its stake in Capital Cities. Earnings on those 220,000 shares amounted to about $1.3 million. However, only $40,000 of those earnings (the dividend Capital Cities paid Berkshire), showed up on Berkshire's bottom line.

Because of the way accounting works, Berkshire reported as income just a tiny fraction (the dividend) of the true economic earnings (the $1.3 million). The accounting was obscuring the economic reality. Why, asked Buffett, would Berkshire prefer to seek out a wholly-owned business to buy like Capital Cities when such an investment would cost at least twice as much as an investment in Capital Cities' common stock? "We can obtain a better management result through non-control than control. This is an unorthodox view, but one we believe to be sound." He continued, "excellent business results by corporations will translate over the long term into correspondingly excellent market value and dividend results for owners, minority as well as majority."

Berkshire would continue to use economics as its guide and explain to shareholders the shortfalls of conventional accounting.

---

* Capital Cities would become an important investment for Berkshire, with Buffett joining its board of directors. Capital Cities' star manager, Tom Murphy, would later join Berkshire's board.

Banking

Buffett had nothing but ongoing praise for the now 80-year-old Eugene Abegg and the Illinois National Bank. This time, he punctuated it with some more facts and figures. Since Berkshire purchased the bank in 1969, it had paid Berkshire $20 million in dividends. Berkshire paid $17.7 million for the bank, meaning it had recouped its investment and more in dividends, and still owned an asset generating good returns.

Abegg asked that year that a successor be brought in. Peter Jeffrey was brought in as president and CEO (from Omaha-based American National Bank). Abegg would continue as chairman.

Merger with Diversified Retailing

The benefit of hindsight allows us to see the effects of different accounting methods on the presentation of the same economic results. Since the Diversified Retailing merger was not completed until December 30, 1978, we have two views of the 1977 Berkshire Hathaway financial statements: once from the original 1977 report, and another from the post-merger report for 1978 that contained a comparison to 1977. More detail on this merger will be presented in the following segment. For now it is worth noting a few of these changes, as they apply to 1977.

The merger caused Blue Chip Stamps to become fully consolidated with Berkshire's financials, rather than its equity being presented on one line on the balance sheet as an asset and its earnings similarly on one line on the income statement. In effect, the revised presentation of the financials illustrated to Berkshire shareholders Buffett's notion of look-though earnings (instead of just earnings, shareholders had much more detail on revenues, expenses and other items.). Table 4.12 highlights a few key figures from Berkshire's financial statements for 1977, as originally reported, and as restated the following year.

Table 4.12: Berkshire Hathaway, select financial information

($ millions)	(Original) 1977	(Restated) 1977	Change
Total assets	$379	$572	$193
Total liabilities	237	370	133
Minority interest	0	48	48
Equity	$141.8	$154.6	$12.8
Revenues	$198	$363	$165
Total expenses	182	333	151
Minority interests	0.0	1.9	1.9
Net earnings	$26.7	$30.4	$3.7

Sources: Berkshire Hathaway Annual Reports 1977, 1978; and author's calculations.

From the 1978 financial statements, Diversified Retailing had $27.1 million of equity at the beginning of 1977. Since it earned $3.7 million in 1977,[*] we would have expected Berkshire's equity to reflect a $30.8 million increase (beginning equity plus retained earnings). But it didn't, it increased just $12.8 million. Why?

Part of the reason was that Diversified Retailing had itself repurchased shares prior to combining with Berkshire. These repurchases amounted to approximately $1.2 million, above and beyond those made by Berkshire itself during the year.

But the primary reason was that each company owned a piece of the other. In combining the two companies, the cross-ownership needed to be reconciled and eliminated.[**] Accounting is (most often) logical, but it can be messy.

1978

Late in 1978, Berkshire finally completed the merger with Diversified Retailing and simplified some of the byzantine ownership between the two companies and the major shareholders. It was a long time coming. The merger was originally proposed in 1973, but the deal was first called off due to an SEC investigation. Finally, on December 30, 1978, Berkshire Hathaway and Diversified Retailing Company merged as one.

Diversified Retailing operated on a parallel course to Berkshire throughout the mid-1960s and 1970s. Diversified was a holding company formed on January 31, 1966 by Warren Buffett, Charlie Munger, and their friend and future Berkshire director, David Gottesman. Buffett's investment partnership, Buffett Partnership Limited, owned 80%, and Munger and Gottesman each owned 10%. They planned to use the company to acquire retailers. The first acquisition was Hochschild Kohn, a lower-

---

[*] As adjusted for Berkshire's equity in earnings included in Diversified's reported earnings.

[**] The Diversified shares owned by Berkshire were carried on its books net of tax at approximately $16.8 million. Adjusting for these figures, including the $1.2 million in repurchases, the $12.8 million increase in equity upon combination of the two companies is reconciled.

tier department store in Baltimore purchased for $12 million using $6 million of debt early in 1966. Buffett and his partners quickly realized the many challenges and pitfalls of department store retailing. Hochschild Kohn was sold in December 1969 for $11 million.* An outstanding issue of debentures with restrictive provisions and tax considerations resulted in Diversified retaining the proceeds of the sale.

That capital was ultimately invested in Blue Chip Stamps, and the formation of Reinsurance Corporation of Nebraska in 1970 (later renamed Columbia Insurance Company), which took reinsurance business off the books of National Indemnity.** In 1974, through Columbia, Diversified also bought Southern Casualty Company, which wrote workers' compensation insurance in Louisiana. The major operating business at the time of the Diversified/Berkshire merger was another department store.

Diversified Retailing paid $6 million for Associated Retail Stores, Inc., in April 1967. Berkshire now owned 100% of Associated Retailing, a chain of seventy-five women's apparel stores operating under various names. Buffett, always a fan of business history, gave a brief background: "Associated was launched in Chicago on March 7, 1931 with one store, $3,200, and two extraordinary partners, Ben Rosner and Leo Simon." After Simon died, Rosner operated the business alone and it faced many challenges inherent in retailing. Buffett said, "Ben's combination of merchandising, real estate and cost containment skills has produced an outstanding record of profitability, with returns on capital … often in the 20% after-tax area." Associated accounted for a fraction of Berkshire's consolidated operating earnings, but Buffett cherished his association with Rosner, who was 75-years-old and still going strong.

The Berkshire/Diversified merger was a business marriage and like a traditional marriage, was beneficial to shareholders but not without its complexities. As married couples know, no matter when vows are taken (it could be January 1 or December 31) the Internal Revenue Service views the couple as having been married throughout the whole year. Accounting principles generally work the same way, with one exception. Instead of looking back one year, accounting conventions at the time required the assumption that both companies had been one *since their formation.****

Buffett did his best to explain some of the changes for the shareholders not well-versed in accounting intricacies. For one, shareholders comparing the 1977 Annual Report to figures in the 1978 report for 1977 would have seen very different numbers for revenues, expenses, assets, liabilities, and other items. (Select figures are presented below in Table 4.13; see the table at the end of the 1977 segment for the full presentation.)

---

* The Buffett Partnership letters detail the proceeds as follows: $5,045,205 cash and $6,540,000 notes due over the following year and a half. Buffett said the present value of the notes were about $6 million, hence the $11 million figure.

** To illustrate how close Berkshire and Diversified already were at the time of the merger, National Indemnity handled all of the bookkeeping and administrative functions for the insurance subsidiaries of Diversified.

*** This method, known as the pooling of interests method, was eliminated in 2001.

Table 4.13: Berkshire Hathaway, select parent-level information

($ millions)	1977 Original	1977 Restated
Cash	$4.9	$14.0
Investments	252.8	332.0
Total assets	379.2	572.1
Total liabilities	237.5	417.6
Shareholders' equity	141.8	154.6
Total revenues	$197.9	$363.6
Net income	26.7	30.4

Sources: Berkshire Hathaway Annual Reports 1977 and 1978.

Secondly, Berkshire's ownership investment in Blue Chip was now 58%, and this meant that Blue Chip's accounts would be fully consolidated. Prior to the merger with Diversified Retailing, it was included as one line on the balance sheet and income statement.

The net effect of all this accounting maneuvering was the obfuscation of the financial statements. The merger consolidated many different businesses, some wholly owned and some partly owned. Buffett said this combination "tends to obscure economic reality more than illuminate it. In fact, it represents a form of presentation that we never prepare for internal use during the year and which is *of no value to us in any management activities.*" (Emphasis added)*

For this reason, Buffett included separate financial disclosures on the various segments of the business that shareholders and managers alike would find useful. This was Buffett imagining himself in the shoes of shareholders and providing the information he would want if roles were reversed. The data was presented in the Chairman's letter and focused on the income statement. No balance sheet information was provided.** The table was entitled Sources of Earnings and began in the 1978 report with a comparison to 1977. Presented this way, the information was very useful at assessing the various operating businesses. The Sources of Earnings table (Table 4.2) is reproduced on page 98.

---

* It is primarily for this reason that I was hesitant to present the full, consolidated accounts at the end of the chapter. It was an accounting requirement but since Buffett thought it added no value, it made no sense to reproduce them in this book after this decade (they are very messy indeed). Instead, in subsequent chapters I have attempted to present as much detail as I would have wanted as a shareholder looking at each year. The separate division financials are presented as appropriate or necessary.

** Though not unimportant, the balance sheet was less informative than the sources of earnings table, at least for disaggregating results. Berkshire preferred to use very little debt and typically held it at the parent level. Financial debt represented just 22% of stockholders' equity and only 7.5% of total assets at year-end 1978. Most of the liabilities on the balance sheet were held in the Insurance Group in losses and adjustment expenses, and unpaid premiums.

Importantly, the table stripped away much or all the noise. Items such as capital gains and losses, taxes, and, later, amortization of goodwill, were presented as separate line items. This left the economic results of each business largely unobscured by accounting conventions that Buffett (rightly) thought twisted reality. To this day, Berkshire presents its operating results in a similar fashion, though the categories have been renamed and broadened to accommodate the growing roster of businesses.

Insurance

The Insurance Group once again wrote to an overall combined ratio below 100%. Remember, a ratio below 100% means the operation earned a profit on top of any profits made by investing the float. For the Insurance Group in 1978 this translated into an underwriting profit of $3 million. That was on top of net investment income of almost $20 million and ignores gains on the sale of investments. Buffett called the three years from 1975 to 1978 a bonanza for the industry, with good premium growth and low loss ratios. Indeed, it was a bonanza for Berkshire, as premiums written and earned doubled over that time.

Table 4.14: Insurance Group, select information

($ thousands)	1978	1977	1976
Premiums written, net	$198,313	$158,704	$94,773
Premiums earned			
Specialized auto and general liability	96,126	80,690	50,778
Workers' Compensation	29,893	18,916	5,815
Reinsurance	30,160	24,100	17,220
Home State multiple lines	29,894	19,382	11,058
	186,073	143,088	84,871
Underwriting gain (loss), pre-tax			
Specialized auto and general liability	11,543	7,800	4,768
Workers' Compensation[1]	(3,944)	(1,644)	(1,093)
Reinsurance	(2,443)	(1,251)	(2,879)
Home State multiple lines	(2,155)	896	(548)
	$3,001	$5,801	$248
Combined ratio (statutory)	96.7%	93.2%	94.6%

Footnote:
1. Workers' Compensation coverage written by Home State is not broken out per the footnote to the financial statements.

Note: The data in this table was taken from the summary of segment results section of the Annual Report and differs in some cases with figures listed in earlier reporting periods.
Source: Berkshire Hathaway Annual Report 1979.

There were reasons not to over-celebrate. For one, the Home State operation had a disappointing year which was that much worse against the backdrop of profitability elsewhere. The loss was in part due to both storms that hit the Midwest and subpar underwriting. The Workers' Compensation line also had a difficult year due to continued cost increases related to increasingly large jury awards that its solid premium growth couldn't cover. Reinsurance also reported a loss, but the long-tail nature of its business (and its long-duration float) made the loss less painful than that of the primary insurers.

Buffett's eye and pen were pointed to the future. Such good results for the industry over the prior three years could only mean one thing: a return to lower profitability as competitors entered the market and cut rates. Still, he was optimistic on the longer-term outlook for insurance. Berkshire had excellent managers that possessed the ability and willingness to write policies that were profitable, regardless of volume. Berkshire would continue to buy and build insurance businesses, "since the rewards for success in this field can be exceptional." They most certainly were.

Investments

In addition to Berkshire's significant investment in wholly-owned insurance businesses, it also had a large investment in another insurance company via its equity portfolio. SAFECO, comprising almost 12% of Berkshire's insurance equities portfolio of $221 million at year-end 1978, was Berkshire's third-largest individual equity investment behind GEICO (17%) and *The Washington Post* (20%).

Buffett had high praise for SAFECO calling it "probably the best property and casualty insurance company in the United States ... a much better insurance operation than our own." Berkshire's investment was made below book value, which meant Berkshire acquired its interest below the cost to even build a similar business from scratch. According to Buffett, other less-well-run insurers had been purchased by others for much higher than 100 cents on the dollar. Buffett was content to let SAFECO's management—who had proven themselves highly capable of operating the insurer—run the operation without interruption. When he found good managers, he let them be, as he knew he was not perfect. "Some of our expansion efforts—largely initiated by your Chairman, have been lackluster, others have been expensive failures." Berkshire would be better off economically if Buffett did not let his ego come into play.

Textiles

There is not much to say on textiles as it relates to the business and industry itself. The brutal economics were still at work. The business was fading relative to its own historical record—even more so relative to the diverse and growing stable of businesses now under Berkshire's control. Still, for shareholders reading Buffett's letters, his comments offered clues to Buffett's thought process.

Buffett began by commenting on the low return of 7.6% in textiles. It was produced by $1.3 million of after-tax earnings on $17 million of capital employed in the business. Yet even this calculation was generous: The plant and equipment in the Textile Group was heavily depreciated on the books, though it retained its usefulness. In other words, to replace the equipment would cost much more, and therefore the Textile Group's balance sheet showed a "bargain cost" for its fixed assets. The economics were even worse than at first blush.

Even with this lower-than-economic cost, capital turnover (revenues to capital) was very low, "reflecting required high investment levels in receivables and inventory compared to sales." This in and of itself would not be a problem if it weren't for the low margin on revenues. After all, the revenue/capital ratio multiplied by the profit/revenue ratio equals return on capital. The ratio can be low on one side if it is offset by a higher ratio on the other—but low on both sides equate to mediocrity.

Buffett then listed several remedies to improve the situation: "differentiation of product, lowered manufacturing cost through more efficient equipment or better utilization of people, redirection toward fabrics enjoying stronger market trends, etc." The problem was Berkshire's textile management, as well as everyone else in the industry, was trying those same things. So the textile operation had no competitive advantage. If anything, it had a competitive disadvantage. Buffett summed up the ruthless economics at work: "As long as excess productive capacity exists, prices tend to reflect direct operating costs rather than capital employed."

I believe Buffett uses this ultra-simplified framework for all his business experience. It is just the start of the analysis, of course. How much capital is needed in the business? What are profit margins? The investor then pays a price/capital employed ratio that determines his/her going-in rate of return. Buffett then thinks through how capital levels might change in the future, and what profit margins might do, all through the lens of barriers to entry and competitive advantage. Textiles were a lesson on how hard things could get.

Blue Chip Stamps

It is a fitting time to examine Berkshire's history with Blue Chip Stamps, since the merger of Diversified Retailing and Berkshire Hathaway meant Blue Chip would be consolidated into Berkshire's financials and much of the finer detail would be lost.* Berkshire's share grew from a modest 6% ownership interest in 1971 totaling $4 million to a significant 36.5% ownership interest in 1977 totaling $36 million (see Table 4.15). The Diversified merger brought it to 58% of the company.**

Table 4.15: Berkshire Hathaway history with Blue Chip Stamps

1971: Berkshire owns 6% of Blue Chip at year-end
1972: Berkshire increases its interest to approximately 17%
1973: Blue Chip first mentioned in Chairman's letter; additional disclosure made in Berkshire's footnotes
1974: Berkshire's interest increased to 25.5%; separate section on Blue Chip added the Chairman's letter
1975: Blue Chip mentioned in opening section of Chairman's letter; interest increased to 31.5%
1976: Ownership interest increased to 33%
1977: Ownership interest increased to 36.5%
1978: Merger with Diversified Retailing causes ownership interest to increase to 58%. Blue Chip now fully consolidated with Berkshire's financials

Sources: Berkshire Hathaway Annual Reports 1971–1978.

Over eight years, Blue Chip became an increasingly important asset to Berkshire shareholders. At the time of the merger, Blue Chip's subsidiaries represented 35% of Berkshire's earnings.*** The merged operations had many operational similarities. Like Berkshire Hathaway, Blue Chip was a company undergoing transformation. An examination of select data (see Table 4.16) reveals how Blue Chip changed over a relatively short period. Blue Chip replaced income from its original business line of trading stamps with income from acquisitions unrelated to the dying stamp business. It was the Berkshire Hathaway playbook implemented by the same capital allocators.

---

* Berkshire shareholders could still see the Blue Chip Stamps standalone results by obtaining its filings from the SEC. However, this was much more difficult before the information age.
** According to the 1977 Blue Chip Stamps 10K filing, Buffett beneficially owned 13% of Blue Chip Stamps. This consisted of his personal ownership of 550,090 shares, Susan Buffett's 125,455 shares, and his ownership via Berkshire Hathaway and Diversified Retailing.
*** Pre-tax operating earnings, calculated based on the Sources of Earnings table from the 1978 Berkshire Chairman's letter.

Table 4.16: Blue Chip Stamps, select financial information

($ thousands)	Fiscal year-end: 12/30/1978	Fiscal year-end: 02/27/1971
Balance sheet items:		
Cash	$3,357	$531
Marketable securities & short-term investments	76,494	113,168
Fixed assets, net	40,603	4,213
Investment in Wesco Financial	49,370	0
Total assets	216,872	142,138
Liability for unredeemed trading stamps	66,832	87,429
Long-term debt	18,247	10,840
Shareholders' equity	$114,325	$43,296
Income statement items:		
Stamp service income	$16,531	$118,374
Merchandise promotions and motivation business	3,791	1,719
Candy revenues	73,653	0
Newspaper	44,674	0
Total revenues	143,586	127,567
Net income	$14,280	$8,584

Sources: Blue Chip Stamps 10K Reports 1971, 1975, 1978.

The Blue Chip that existed as of 1971 was the same business it had always been—trading stamps. The company sold trading stamps to 23,000 retail locations across Arizona, California, Nevada and Oregon, which in turn provided them to customers as a promotion. The customers could redeem the stamps for products or cash at any one of Blue Chips' eighty-nine redemption stores.[38] The business was very much like insurance where cash was received ahead of product delivery. Like an insurer, a trading stamp company could make money not only from its products, but by investing the cash it held in the meantime.

The majority of its assets at year-end 1971 were invested in marketable securities. Those assets were funded by the float inherent in the unredeemed trading stamps, which were carried on the balance sheet as a liability. The remainder of the assets were funded by long-term debt and equity. Fast forward to year-end 1978 and Blue Chip's financial picture had changed significantly. A look at the income statement revealed the dramatic decline in trading stamp revenues over the preceding half-decade and the corresponding growth of other, newer subsidiaries. What capital allocation decisions were made to create such a transformation over eight years?

Blue Chip's balance sheet shared characteristics of Berkshire's higher-quality insurance companies, but its operations faced challenges more akin to textiles. Stamp service revenues reached $126 million in 1970, and that would prove to be the high-water mark. Its business faced competition not only from other trading stamp and promotional companies, but from the retailers themselves who introduced discount merchandising. The 1978 Blue Chip Stamps annual report also pointed to the 1973 gasoline shortage, which caused many service stations to eliminate stamps entirely. As Buffett and Munger acquired a greater interest in Blue Chip over time, the two men came to control the capital allocation decisions of the company. They recognized the continued decline in the trading stamp business and worked to reallocate Blue Chip's significant assets and liquidity into higher-returning businesses.

See's Candies

The first such reallocation was the acquisition of See's Candy Shops, Inc. Between January 3, 1972, and March 4, 1972, Blue Chip acquired 93% of See's. The ownership increased to 99% on March 3, 1973. The purchase price was $34.7 million but excess cash on its balance sheet brought the effective purchase price lower.[*]

See's represented Buffett's first time paying a high multiple for a business, and he attributes the decision to Charlie Munger's insights. Munger convinced Buffett it was worth the high multiple since the underlying business was so good. See's was earning over 50% pre-tax on tangible capital. Even after paying three times the underlying capital in the business, Blue Chip earned a satisfactory return. And if See's could expand, which it turned out it could (though slowly), the incremental returns would enhance the initial economics of the purchase. As a bonus, this high-return business had protection against inflation. Since 1972 when Blue Chip bought See's, pre-tax earnings grew from $4.2 million to $12.6 million with very little incremental investment.

---

[*] The See's purchase price is often quoted as $25 million. This is because See's had excess cash on its balance sheet, which reduced the effective price to that amount. (In the 1991 Berkshire Hathaway Annual Report, Buffett quotes the $10 million excess cash figure.)

Table 4.17: See's Candy Shops, Inc., select data

($ millions)	1972
Revenues	$29.0
Pre-tax earnings	4.2
Tangible capital base	8.0
Revenues/capital	$3.63
Pre-tax margin	14.5%
Return on capital - pre-tax	52.5%
Purchase price	$34.7
Excess cash	(10.0)
Effective purchase price	$24.7
Purchase price/tangible capital	3.1x
Blue Chip Stamps earnings yield[1]	17.0%
Footnote:	
1. Blue Chip Stamps' earnings yield represents See's pre-tax return on capital divided by the multiple Blue Chip paid for See's tangible capital. (An alternative method to calculate this would be to divide the pre-tax earnings of See's into the Blue Chip Stamps purchase price.)	

Sources: Blue Chip Stamps Annual Report 1973, Berkshire Hathaway Chairman's letter 1991 and author's calculations.

It did not take long for Buffett to realize the full potential of See's—and the potential pitfalls. In a letter to CEO Chuck Huggins in December 1972,[39] Buffett urged Huggins to create a narrative around the See's brand in order to protect its image. "The surroundings in which our candy is offered affect potential customers' mental—and even gastronomical—impression of our quality," he wrote. Comparing See's to Coors beer, which benefitted from its availability solely in Colorado at the time, Buffett said: "We might be able to tell quite a story about the little kitchen in California that has become the kitchen known 'round the world.'" He thought See's should tightly control all aspects of marketing and distribution and highlight its insistence on fresh ingredients rather than have it displayed alongside inferior products. "It should be very hard to get, available only periodically, and then (to the consumer) apparently only in limited quantities."

Over time, Buffett would come to appreciate See's not only for the business it was, but the education it provided him on recognizing the inherent value in high-quality businesses—and their limitations. It would not be a stretch to say the lessons from See's would shape the future of Berkshire Hathaway. Buffett would become more at ease paying higher multiples for businesses with protected economic positions. He would later credit his experience with See's for allowing him to see the value in Coca-Cola, a major investment made in the next decade. See's would also become a training ground of sorts for Buffett. The high returns on capital enjoyed by See's naturally created a desire for expansion. The numerous attempts and mixed success over the years to expand See's beyond its protected West Coast niche would provide Berkshire's capital allocators with first-hand evidence of the boundaries of economic moats. Considering this educational aspect and the turning point it represented in Buffett's investment philosophy, See's may well have been one of Buffett's best investments.

Wesco Financial Corporation

Blue Chip's next major subsidiary was Wesco Financial Corporation. Blue Chip began acquiring shares in 1973, and by the end of that fiscal year it owned 21.9% of the company. After it sought and obtained approval to increase ownership beyond 25%, Blue Chip purchased an 80.1% stake in Wesco over the next five years. Amassing that stake hadn't come easy. To get there Buffett and Munger convinced Wesco's controlling shareholder, Elizabeth Caspers Peters (daughter of Wesco's founder), to nix a deal to sell to another bank and instead sell to them.*

Wesco was the holding company for a bank, Mutual Savings and Loan Association. As of 1973, Mutual Savings operated out of ten locations across four California counties and primarily provided real estate loans to individuals. It financed its $452 million balance sheet, including a $390 million loan portfolio, mainly with savings deposits.[40]

By 1978 Wesco had opened six new branches in Southern California. Its asset base at year-end 1978 was $646 million,** including $465 million of loans, that were financed by $488 million in savings deposits. Throughout this time, Wesco also owned its headquarters location in Pasadena, which included third-party tenants.[41]

Why was Wesco an attractive investment? Wesco appeared to be a well-run operation with a history of satisfactory returns. It probably helped that it was headquartered in Charlie Munger's figurative backyard in Pasadena, California. Based on Blue Chips' original purchase price for 21.9% of Wesco, the company was valued at just 0.56 times its underlying book value at the time of purchase*** (see Table 4.18). By 1978, the company was earning $11.7 million pre-tax—a 30% return on Blue Chip's aggregate investment.

---

* Buffett and Munger's willingness to purchase shares of Wesco stock at a higher than market price also factored into the SEC investigation of Blue Chip Stamps.
** Included in Wesco's assets was a 21.5% stake in the Detroit International Bridge Company, which owned its namesake bridge into Canada. It is interesting to note the nesting doll-like ownership structure in which Buffett and Munger purchased assets using cash available in various subsidiaries.
*** A consequence of acquiring shares below book value was the amortization into income of the excess of book value acquired on top of the purchase price over a period of 40 years. This contrasts to today's usual situation where an excess of purchase price over the assets acquired is amortized into expense.

Table 4.18: Wesco Financial Corporation, select data

($ thousands)	
Blue Chip 1973 investment	$8,099
Percentage of company owned	21.9%
Implied market value	$36,982
Wesco 1973 average shareholders' equity	$65,785
Price / book	0.56x
Pre-tax earnings, 1972	$8,436
Blue Chip going-in return	22.8%
Return on assets (pre-tax, avg. 5 years)	1.64%

Sources: Blue Chip Stamps Annual Report 1973; Wesco Annual Reports 1970, 1973.

Table 4.19: Blue Chip Stamps' investment and equity in earnings of Wesco Financial Corporation

	Fiscal year-end:						
	12/30/1978	12/31/1977	01/01/1977	02/28/1976	03/01/1975	03/02/1974	03/03/1973
Ownership (# shares)							
Beginning balance	5,703,087	1,840,863	1,527,299	1,527,299	1,058,042	518,860	0
Purchases	0	180,498	313,564	0	469,257	539,182	518,860
3:1 stock split	0	3,681,726	0	0	0	0	0
Ending balance	5,703,087	5,703,087	1,840,863	1,527,299	1,527,299	1,058,042	518,860
Ownership amount	80.1%	80.1%	77.6%	64.4%	64.4%	44.6%	21.9%
Ownership ($ thousands)							
Beginning balance	$43,892	$38,661	$28,588	$26,307	$17,446	$8,099	$0
Purchases	0	1,208	6,306	0	7,025	8,125	8,099
Interim period adjustment[1]	0	0	185	0	0	0	0
Equity in earnings[2]	7,417	5,715	4,459	3,092	2,189	1,455	0
Other[3]	0	0	116	76	457	218	0
Distributions	(1,939)	(1,692)	(993)	(887)	(810)	(451)	0
Ending balance	$49,370	$43,892	$38,661	$28,588	$26,307	$17,446	$8,099

Footnotes:

1. Blue Chip Stamps changed its fiscal year from approximately February 28 to approximately December 31.
2. Net of tax on undistributed portion.
3. Amortization of excess of equity in net assets over cost.

Sources: Blue Chip Stamps Annual Reports 1973–1978.

The Buffalo Evening News

The third major acquisition was *The Buffalo Evening News*.* On April 15, 1977, Blue Chip acquired the paper** for cash (in addition to the assumption of pension liabilities). The purchase was partially financed with a $30 million bank loan which was repaid to $13.5 million by year-end 1977.

The Buffalo News, as it later came to be known, operated a weekday newspaper in Buffalo, New York. At the time, it was a two-newspaper town, with *The News'* chief competitor being *The Courier-Express*. *The Buffalo News* had the highest percentage of circulation among newspapers in Upstate New York with two-thirds of households subscribing.[42] It published six days a week. *The Courier-Express* published the dominant Sunday paper. Buffett's investment thesis was simple: The two-newspaper town was soon destined to become a one-newspaper town, and with *The Buffalo News* being stronger financially, it was more likely to survive. Buying in at book value meant that if such a winner-take-all situation occurred in Buffalo, Blue Chip, Berkshire, and Buffett and Munger would win big.

Buffett got early signs his prediction would come true. *The Buffalo News* made plans for a Sunday edition in November 1977, not long after the purchase. It was soon hit with a lawsuit that lingered until one of the papers went out of business. Though things ultimately worked out in favor of *The News*, at the time the situation was precarious and not at all certain.*** The first eight months Blue Chip owned the paper (April to December 1977), it earned just $751,000. In 1978, it lost $2.9 million. The red ink was destined to flow for a while.

Table 4.20: The Buffalo Evening News—acquisition analysis

($ thousands)	
Cash consideration	$34,000
Pension liabilities assumed	1,433
Total purchase price	$35,433
Underlying net assets	$34,679
Excess of purchase price	$754
Price/book	1.02x

Source: Blue Chip Stamps Annual Report 1977.

---

* The paper had been offered to *The Washington Post* first, which had turned it down (*The Snowball*, p. 463).
** The purchase was technically structured as an asset purchase, whereby Blue Chip Stamps organized a new subsidiary of essentially the same name (The Buffalo Evening News, Inc.) which in turn purchased the paper's assets and assumed certain of its liabilities.
*** *The News* had labor unions which Buffett and Munger knew could put it out of business if they went on strike for any meaningful amount of time. The pair told the unions as much and were successful in avoiding a strike.

After the Diversified Retailing merger with Berkshire Hathaway, Blue Chip's subsidiaries became much more important to Berkshire's overall success. Because of the varying degrees of ownership at each subsidiary level (and there were many), determining the individual impact on the economic success of Berkshire became that much more difficult. This is why a new table appeared in Buffett's 1978 Chairman's letter (see Table 4.2 at the beginning of the chapter). This table showed the operating earnings of each subsidiary business, as adjusted for Berkshire's ownership interest and irrespective of its parent company.* In this way Berkshire's shareholders could assess for themselves how much emphasis and attention to place on each source of Berkshire's earnings. With Buffett and Munger using Blue Chip as a platform for expansion, understanding the impact on Berkshire was important. Buffett was once again putting himself in the shareholders' shoes.**

Like Berkshire, Blue Chip had transformed itself from a dying, single-line business into a diverse enterprise with multiple sources of earnings and valuable assets. Buffett and Munger were using their capital allocation skills to shape Blue Chip in Berkshire's image.

1979

Changes to accounting rules necessitated another lesson on accounting in 1979. The prior year required an update due to the complexities surrounding the merger with Diversified Retailing. This time it was the Insurance Group's accounting that required some explaining. Specifically, the accounting rules regarding marketable securities were changed to record values at market, rather than at the lower of aggregate cost or market. The result was a substantial increase to reported equity.

The resulting change caused the Insurance Group's 1978 equity, as shown on the balance sheet, to increase $61 million to $204 million. Nothing had really changed from an economic perspective. To confuse things even more the accounting change only applied to insurance companies. This meant that Blue Chip Stamps, which was fully consolidated with Berkshire, reported its equity investments the old way, at the lower of aggregate cost or market. The same security owned by Berkshire's insurance companies and Blue Chip would therefore be reported at two different values. Shareholders were therefore given the information on aggregate cost *and* market value of securities in the footnotes to the financial statements regardless of where they were held in Berkshire.

---

* Adjustments were also made to isolate the economic performance of the subsidiaries beyond accounting. For example, amortization of goodwill and interest on debt were removed to separate lines, but these were reconciled to GAAP earnings.

** This is a phrase both Buffett and Munger have used on many occasions, including in their written communications.

Buffett reminded shareholders how he viewed Berkshire's short- and long-term operating performance. He took the view that operating earnings prior to any securities gains and losses was the correct numerator for any calculation. For the denominator, he used the prior year's ending equity with securities valued at cost, not market. The equation looked like this:

Equation 4.1

$$\text{Operating performance} = \frac{\textit{Operating earnings (prior to securities gains or losses)}}{\textit{prior year's ending equity (securities valued at cost)}}$$

The rationale was to provide the most accurate representation of managerial performance, since a decline in equities valued at market would unduly depress the denominator and make performance the next year look artificially high. Conversely, a strong year for capital gains would cause good operating performance to look less impressive than it might otherwise have been due to a larger denominator.

Long term, Buffett looked to include everything: all capital gains/losses, and any one-time or non-recurring items. He would also use securities valued at market for this calculation. Buffett warned against measuring results with earnings per share. "The primary test of managerial performance is the achievement of a high earnings rate on equity capital employed (without undue leverage, accounting gimmickry, etc.) and not the achievement of consistent gains in earnings per share," he wrote. Some real numbers summed up the achievements since 1964: On September 30, 1964 (the then year-end) Berkshire's book value was $19.46 per share. At year-end 1979 that figure (again, with securities valued at market) was $335.85 per share—a compounded annual gain of 20.5%.

Though certainly a good result, Berkshire's 20.5% rate of return was insufficient to produce real gains in purchasing power if inflation continued running double digits and taxes remained at current levels. One must ask the question, what was the alternative? If a 20% return was insufficient, what other investment at the time could have maintained or grown purchasing power in a world of high inflation? Buffett had no solution to this problem, other than to use opportunity cost as his guide.

Sources of Earnings

The new table presented in the Chairman's letter provided shareholders with a wealth of direct and meaningful information on Berkshire's operating performance throughout the year. Buffett was again role-reversing and giving shareholders information he would want if he were in their shoes. What a story it told.* (See Table 4.2 on page 98.)

Textile earnings, once the sole source of Berkshire's earnings, generated less than 4% of the nearly $47 million of earnings before taxes and securities gains (but after interest). The largest source of earnings power was in the Insurance Group. See's Candies, the Illinois National Bank and Trust, and Mutual Savings and Loan were the only subsidiaries after insurance whose earnings contributed 10% or more to Berkshire's pre-tax earnings.

Table 4.21: Berkshire Hathaway summary sources of operating earnings 10% or more, 1979

Insurance underwriting	8.0%
Insurance net investment income	51.7%
Total insurance	59.7%
See's Candies	16.2%
Illinois National Bank	12.0%
Mutual Savings and Loan	10.1%
All others, combined	14.4%
Interest on debt	(12.5%)
Total	100.0%

Note: Totals do not add up to 100% due to rounding.
Sources: Berkshire Hathaway Chairman's letter 1979 and author's calculations.

Sharp-eyed readers would have noticed a new business reported in the table in 1979. Precision Steel Warehouse, Inc., an 80%-owned subsidiary of Blue Chip,** contributed almost $1.5 million to Berkshire's earnings in 1979. In the letter to Blue Chip shareholders included as an appendix to the Berkshire Annual Report, Chairman Charlie Munger reported that Blue Chip purchased its interest in the steel company in February 1979 for $15 million.*** Writing to Blue Chip's shareholders, Munger wrote:

---

* Unless otherwise noted, I am referring to Berkshire's share of pre-tax earnings. In this way, figures are comparable from year-to-year without any distorting effects of taxes.

** Precision Steel was technically owned by Wesco Financial Corporation, the entity that also owned Mutual Savings and which was in turn owned by Blue Chip. From an economic perspective, the holding structure is inconsequential.

*** The table in the 1979 Berkshire Chairman's letter indicated Precision Steel earned $3.25 million pre-tax in 1979. This would equate to a 21.6% pre-tax return (4.6 times earnings) on the $15 million purchase price. The steel business was cyclical, and it's unclear to what degree this was factored into the purchase price.

"A steel service center business may strike some of our shareholders as a peculiar addition to a candy company, even one already joined to a savings and loan business. However, Precision Steel shares an extremely important quality with See's: a company-wide culture of constant concern for customer interests and fair dealing."

Both Munger and Buffett were concerned not about the product per se, but about businesses they understood and that had good economic characteristics. Candy or steel, it did not matter.

The summary table showed Berkshire's creditors they had little to worry about. Earnings covered interest almost nine times over and the $52.6 million of earnings before interest would have been nearly enough to pay off *all* of Berkshire's direct financial debt. To be fair, the earnings figure was a look-through number that accounted for Berkshire's share of all underlying earnings as adjusted for its ownership percentages. A corresponding balance sheet look-through number was not provided. Berkshire's unconsolidated ownership interests had some debt of their own, which, under a proper analysis would be accounted for. The main point is Berkshire's creditors were very safe because they had a debtor with a large and growing stream of earnings on top of a conservatively financed balance sheet.

Textiles and Retailing

Given the gloom associated with textiles, the fact that textiles and retailing were combined under the same heading likely would not be comforting to a manager. Yet Buffett had praise for Ben Rosner, head of Associated Retail Stores, who "continues to pull rabbits out of the hat—big rabbits from a small hat." The praise also gave shareholders a glimpse into Buffett's thinking on earnings. Cash was king. Those earnings produced by Associated Retail were, "realized in cash and not in increased receivables and inventories as in many other retail businesses."

Insurance

Insurance underwriting again turned in a profit, meaning Berkshire's cost of float was negative.* But Berkshire was the exception; the industry reported an underwriting loss that year. Negative cost of float, remember, was a very good thing since it meant

---

* In Buffett's Chairman's letter, he states that the combined ratio *decreased* from 98.2% to 97.1%. The discrepancy to Table 4.22 is the result of the fact that Buffett, I believe, did not include deferred policy acquisition costs (DPAC). DPAC are not detailed in the summary figures in the Annual Report from which I have based my calculation.

Berkshire was getting paid to hold policyholders' money above and beyond any investment income. Still, Berkshire had some variation in its own results.

Table 4.22: Insurance Group, select information

($ thousands)	1979	1978	1977
Premiums written, net	$186,185	$198,313	$158,704
Premiums earned			
Specialized auto and general liability	90,646	96,126	80,690
Workers' compensation	19,350	29,893	18,916
Reinsurance	30,864	30,160	24,100
Home State multiple lines	41,089	29,894	19,382
	181,949	186,073	143,088
Underwriting gain (loss), pre-tax			
Specialized auto and general liability	7,845	11,543	7,800
Workers' compensation[1]	5,130	(3,944)	(1,644)
Reinsurance	(4,338)	(2,443)	(1,251)
Home State multiple lines	(4,895)	(2,155)	896
	$3,742	$3,001	$5,801
Combined ratio (statutory)	97.2%	96.7%	93.2%

Footnote:
1.Workers' Compensation coverage written by Home State is not broken out per the footnote to the financial statements.

The data in this table was taken from the summary of segment results section of the Annual Report and differs in some cases with figures listed in earlier reporting periods.
Source: Berkshire Hathaway Annual Report 1979.

According to Buffett, "really extraordinary results were turned in by National Indemnity." The details proved his words were not an exaggeration. Buffett highlighted the portion of National Indemnity's business operated by Phil Liesche, which underwrote to a profit of $8.4 million on $82 million of earned premiums—a combined ratio just under 90%.* Workers' Compensation premiums earned fell by 35%, yet profitability soared. This result, Buffett said, was, "far, far better than we had any right to expect at the beginning of 1979" and was due in large part to favorable results in California, which finally began pulling its weight after years of struggles.

In Berkshire's other areas of insurance, the numbers were not so good. Home State reported disappointing results in 1979. Part of the problem lay with Cornhusker Casualty Company, which had poor underwriting results on top of other issues that required the attention of Jack Ringwalt. Nonetheless, efforts to expand what Buffett

---

* National Indemnity's business would have fallen primarily within the specialized auto and general liability category but also included business categorized elsewhere.

viewed as a sound long-term business in Home State insurance continued with the formation of a Colorado subsidiary.

Losses were also reported in reinsurance following the trend of the industry overall. Tempering the loss (but only partially) was the meaningful source of float reinsurance provided to Berkshire.

Buffett remained optimistic for the insurance business, even though he expected a tough five-year period ahead with an industry-wide combined ratio in the area of 105%. Part of the problem, he explained, was interest rates. High interest rates were causing managers of insurance businesses to take on less profitable business, since even a modest cost of float (somewhere above 100%) would be a cheaper source of funds than could be obtained elsewhere. Another source of optimism was high gas prices, which caused people to drive less and therefore lowered auto accident frequencies.*

Investments

Though Berkshire preferred equities, bonds were an important part of the investment portfolio. At year-end 1979, bonds on the insurance balance sheet (at amortized cost) amounted to $186 million, compared to equities (at market) of $337 million.

Buffett pointed to accounting conventions as a major contributor to the "extraordinary amount of money" lost in bonds by insurance companies. Because those conventions reported their value at amortized cost, the fluctuations in market values (due to changes in interest rates) were not realized (either in the accounting sense or in the cerebral sense; some managers had no idea that bonds could lose so much value). Instead, some insurance companies were blind to the fact that high interest rates caused the real, economic value of their bond investments to decrease in value. (As the ubiquitous line in financial reporting goes, bond prices move inversely to yield.) Buffett speculated that if managers were forced to recognize the value of their bonds at market value, and not at amortized cost, managers might have "been focused much earlier on the dangers of a very long-term bond contract."

A master at analogy, Buffett used an example to illustrate the inconsistency of insurance company managers. Managers were cutting back on issuing one-year policies reasoning (correctly) that six-month policies would better protect them from the rising prices of delivering on their insurance promises. Yet those same managers took insurance premiums and "sold the money" (i.e. invested it) at a fixed price for thirty or forty years. It was interesting, thought Buffett, that buyers seeking a fixed price contract for any other product or service over the same time would be laughed down, yet the buyer of money could lock in a fixed interest rate for a generation or more.

---

* Fewer accidents meant that (all things being equal) insurance claims were lower and profits higher, leading companies to lower their premiums rates.

Buffett's criticisms were not only for others; he was, in fact, hardest on himself for the mistakes he made in bonds. "You do not adequately protect yourself by being half awake while others are sleeping. It was a mistake to buy fifteen-year bonds, and yet we did." Instead of staying in a tough situation in bonds, he should have realized his mistake and sold at a loss. It was a lesson, he told readers, he should have learned from the textile business, noting "we should have realized the futility of trying to be very clever … in an area where the tide was running heavily against us."

Banking

The Bank Holding Company Act of 1969 set a deadline of December 31, 1980, for Berkshire to divest Illinois National Bank and Trust. Buffett asked shareholders to give Eugene Abegg, its founder and manager, a standing ovation for his achievements. And well-deserved they were. The year 1979 was not only the last under Berkshire Hathaway, but the bank had its best year on record with a return on average assets of 2.3%—three times greater than the average major bank.

To comply with the law, Berkshire was, "investigating the possible sale of between 80% and 100% of the stock of the bank." Buffett informed shareholders that the sale would not be based on price alone. He genuinely cared about the post-Berkshire ownership of Illinois National, and took as much care with its divestment as he had in its original selection. He warned shareholders that such a high-quality asset would not be easy to replace: "You simply can't buy high quality businesses at the sort of price/earnings multiple likely to prevail on our bank sale." More will be said on Illinois National in the summary of 1980.

Financial Reporting; Prospects

In a section entitled Financial Reporting, Buffett informed shareholders that Berkshire now traded on the NASDAQ. All shareholders would be able to hear from Dow Jones, the financial news giant, at the same time when Berkshire reported earnings. Buffett told shareholders that while the quarterly reporting would be light, his annual communications would be comprehensive and fitting to an owner of a business. "Your Chairman has a firm belief that owners are entitled to hear directly from the CEO as to what is going on and how he evaluates the business," just as they would with a private company.

Buffett was unconventional in the transparency he showed in his Chairman's letter to shareholders. Those shareholders were also unconventional. Buffett pointed out that 98% of the shares outstanding at the end of year were held by people who were shareholders at the beginning of the year. This loyalty is notable given that stocks are traded daily on the financial markets and frequently have high turnover ratios.*

Concluding the 1979 Chairman's letter under a section entitled Prospects, Buffett tempered expectations for the coming year. He expected higher operating earnings but predicted the *rate* of increase to decline. He warned that the dollar figures could come in lower depending on the timing of the sale of Illinois National. Nonetheless, he expressed long-term optimism about the businesses under Berkshire's umbrella.

Berkshire's policy to have centralization of capital allocation and decentralization of operating authority was a formula for success because it was highly scalable. This system would not change in the coming years and would lead to even more success. In 1979, it was still the early days.

1980

Operating earnings of $41.9 million were sufficiently above the $36 million reported the prior year, but the *rate* of increase in book value (with securities valued at cost) fell from 18.6% to 17.8%. Berkshire also crossed an important (yet arbitrary) milestone in 1980: year-end assets topped $1 billion.

For the third year in a row, shareholders were treated to a lesson on accounting. This lesson was how the financial results of Berkshire's ownership interests in companies were reported to Berkshire shareholders. The accounting treatment depended on whether Berkshire owned 100%, between 50% and 100% of the business, between 20% and 50%, or less than 20%. In all cases, the only thing that mattered to Buffett was the proportionate economic performance—whether Berkshire owned 100% of a business or one share didn't matter. The accounting was another matter, and Buffett wanted Berkshire's shareholders to understand how it could skew the financial picture.

100% Ownership: This is a wholly-owned subsidiary, and the most straightforward case. Financial results are fully consolidated with the parent company. Its balance sheet items (cash, receivables, inventory, fixed assets, liabilities, etc.) and income statement items (revenues, expenses, etc.) are reported together with the parent company's financials. Such accounting treatment makes sense since the new or subsidiary business becomes a part of the parent, even if its results are detailed separately. This was the case for Berkshire's original textile operation in New Bedford, Massachusetts, and its Waumbec operation in Manchester, New Hampshire.

---

* The turnover ratio measures how many shares trade hands during a particular period of time. It is not uncommon to see over 100% turnover ratios. This means (in theory) the corporation has an entirely new set of owners from one year to the next.

One problem with such accounting arises when a parent company owns many diverse businesses. Remember back to the 1978 discussion of the Berkshire-Diversified Retailing merger. The merger caused the fully consolidated results to become nonsensical, or at best of little value since the accounting obscured reality. Berkshire therefore began providing a separate table to shareholders to help them make sense of the noise.

50%–99% Ownership: When a business owns between 50% and 100% of another business, the minority shareholders (those owning 49% or less) must be considered. In these instances, a 'ia' item can be added to the fully consolidated method of accounting. The solution is to keep the accounts consolidated like the example above (along with the accounts of the majority owner), but to add an entry on the financial statements for minority interests. The financial accounts are lumped together with the parent, and both the equity and equity in earnings attributable to the other shareholders is accounted for with a single line item.*

20%–49% Ownership: With this level of ownership, the accounting treatment is like the minority interest accounting above, only the parent company in question is the minority owner. To use a Berkshire-specific example, Blue Chip Stamps was accounted for in this way until Berkshire's investment crossed the 50% threshold with the Diversified Retailing merger. Prior to that time, the only entry attributable to Blue Chip was an "equity in Blue Chip Stamps" representing Berkshire's proportional ownership in Blue Chip, and a similar entry on the income statement accounting for its share of earnings named "equity in earnings of Blue Chip Stamps."

Less than 20% Ownership: This is where economics and accounting diverge. Accounting rules dictate that only the dividends received from an investee in this class can be counted as income. To use an oversimplified example, if Berkshire owned 19.99% of a company with $100 in net after-tax earnings paying out no dividends, it would record no earnings from this investment. If it instead owned 20% of the same company, it would record an entry for "equity in earnings of XYZ" of $20. It's the same economics; just drastically different accounting.

Berkshire's insurance companies owned significant amounts of stock, many of which fell into that last category. And since many of these investees retained most of their earnings (in other words, paid out little of their earnings as dividends) the income did not appear in Berkshire's financial statements. In fact, Berkshire's share of the income of these investees (called look-through earnings) were larger than the total reported operating earnings of Berkshire. To paint the mental picture, Buffett described a large iceberg mostly hidden below the surface of the water. The substance was there, one just needed to look more closely to see it.

---

* The reverse of the next category of between 20% and 49% ownership.

Buffett warned shareholders that his views were unconventional. He needed them to understand that he focused on the economics, not the accounting. Buffett showed he could immediately increase Berkshire's reported results, even though such an action "tempts us not at all." All he would have to do is sell Berkshire's equity portfolio and use the proceeds to buy long-term tax-free bonds. Such a move would increase accounting earnings by over $30 million (representing over 50% additional after-tax reported earnings). But it would also be detrimental to Berkshire's economic position since its claim on the underlying earnings of companies in the equity portfolio were worth more.* As a controlling shareholder in Berkshire, Buffett could follow the path that made the most sense in pure economic terms, rather than be tempted by the apparent prosperity allowed by accounting.

As it turned out, inflation peaked at 13.5% in 1980. Buffett likened inflation to an implicit tax on capital. When combined with the explicit income tax, an owner of a business (even a very good business) could lose purchasing power. The example Buffett used was a business earning 20% return on equity in a world of 12% inflation. Someone in the 50% tax bracket would, if he or she was paid out all earnings as dividends, end up with a 10% after tax return and *lose* 2 percentage points of purchasing power a year. Since Berkshire was not immune to inflation, Buffett wanted shareholders to be aware of its pernicious effects even if he had no solution to the problem.

Sources of Earnings

Berkshire's pre-tax operating earnings increased 16% to $54 million (see Table 4.2 on page 98). The primary driver was improved results from insurance (presented in more detail below) followed by increases at See's and Blue Chip Stamps. To provide Berkshire shareholders with as much relevant information on their investment as possible, for several years Buffett had included the letters to shareholders from its major investees, Blue Chip Stamps, and Wesco, at the end of Berkshire's report. The letters were penned by Chairmen Charlie Munger and Louis Vincenti, respectively. In 1980 both told the story of Wesco's divestiture of most (fifteen locations) of its Mutual Savings branch network.**

The sale resulted from a desire to mitigate the effects of inflation on a borrow-short-lend-long operation like a bank. The sale of the branch network, save for the bank's headquarters office building and one satellite branch, was, "motivated by the

---

* To use the iceberg analogy from above, the income from the bonds would show up above the surface but be less valuable than a claim on a hidden (but larger) iceberg. A switch to bonds would also entail paying capital gains taxes.
** Blue Chip Stamps owned stock in Wesco, which owned Mutual Savings. So both men were discussing Mutual Savings, an important asset to each company, in their reports to their respective shareholders (which of course had considerable overlap).

margin-of-safety considerations intrinsic in engineering and still appropriate, we think, in financial institutions" to reduce an "earthquake risk," according to Munger's letter to Blue Chip shareholders.

The buyer of the branch network was Brentwood Savings, another local savings and loan institution. The sale consisted of the transfer of $307 million of savings account liabilities, an equal amount of mortgage loans, and the physical assets of the branch offices. It resulted in a net pre-tax gain of $5.9 million to Wesco ($2.8 million pre-tax to Berkshire). Though the transaction would reduce Wesco's average yield on its assets from 9.3% to 7.7%, it would come with a significant decrease in leverage and, importantly, help protect Wesco from the ravaging effects of inflation. The sources of earnings table presented in the Berkshire report took pains to separate the gain on the sale from Wesco's operating results.

Berkshire's investments in non-controlled businesses (those in the less than 20% category) had a combined market value of $530 million and a cost of $325 million. At $13 million, the combined earnings attributed to Berkshire's ownership interest in Aluminum Company of America (ALCOA) and Kaiser Aluminum and Chemical Corp were larger than most of Berkshire's wholly-owned subsidiaries. Those investments made up 10% of Berkshire's equity portfolio (at market) at year-end but their full economic earnings did not show up in financial statements due to conventional accounting rules.

Another much larger non-controlled investee was GEICO. Berkshire's 7.2 million shares represented a 33% interest in the insurer,* and its earnings attributable to Berkshire that one year were $20 million. Berkshire bought the shares for $47 million in 1976 and four years later they were worth $105 million (20% of the portfolio). Buffett used GEICO to show how the stock market frequently provides opportunities to buy great businesses at less than private market values. Buffett said buying a similar ownership interest in $20 million of earnings would cost at least ten times as much. Yet Berkshire was able to acquire its shares in GEICO at a bargain price and was content to let management run the business as they saw fit, including choosing the dividend policy.

One quirk related to Berkshire's investment in GEICO should be noted. Normally a 33% ownership interest would call for the investee accounting treatment, with Berkshire's proportional interest in earnings reported on the income statement. But because of Berkshire's other insurance holdings, it had transferred its right to vote the shares to an independent party. This special order from Washington, D.C., and the New York Insurance Departments, allowed Berkshire to own more of GEICO than it otherwise could have but necessitated an accounting treatment similar to that of a non-controlled business (reporting only its dividends in earnings).

---

* Berkshire had added to its holdings and GEICO also began buying back stock.

Insurance

The insurance industry turned in a year similar to Buffett's prediction. The industry combined ratio was 103.5% in 1980, which meant its float (monies held but ultimately destined to policyholders and others) cost 3.5%. This was not a terrible result given that interest rates at that time were in the double digits. In fact, some managers outside of Berkshire rationalized the writing of business at a combined ratio over 100% for just that reason. That same interest rate environment was causing other, even more irrational behavior within the investment portfolios of some insurers.

An environment of rising interest rates generally has a negative effect on bond prices. This is because a lower price (denominator) is needed to cause the same coupon payment (numerator) to represent a higher ratio or yield. In an equity portfolio, these declines in market price would be reflected as a corresponding decrease in book value. For bonds, they were carried on the books at amortized cost, effectively protected from market swings on paper. An insurer couldn't sell a lower yielding bond (even to trade to a higher yielding issue) without incurring a capital loss. At best, some held on to avoid the potential embarrassment of showing a loss on the income statement. Others were forced to maintain the investments since realizing losses would have reduced an already thin shareholder equity account.[*] The bond portfolios of most insurers were usually multiples of shareholder equity and were typically funded primarily by policyholder premiums. The insurer was thus incentivized to write business at any cost to maintain its float. The rational course when reporting underwriting losses would be to realize the capital losses and move into taxable bonds to capture a higher after-tax yield.

Berkshire was not immune to the above scenario, and Buffett even chided himself for not acting earlier to sell unattractive bond holdings at a loss. Berkshire was protected in two ways. First, its investment portfolio had a higher concentration of equites and a corresponding lower concentration in bonds. Second, Berkshire's insurance businesses wrote far less volume in relation to equity capital than its peers. Its $185 million in premiums written amounted to just 56% of average ending equity of $331 million.[**] Furthermore, its bond portfolio represented just under 50% of equity capital at year-end compared to 300% (or three times) for other insurers. This meant any losses in bonds had less impact on Berkshire's capital. Still, as Buffett noted, "troubles for the industry mean troubles for us."

---

[*] In reality these losses and reductions to capital were already there.
[**] This is based on GAAP equity. A ratio using statutory capital would have been higher but still below that of industry peers.

Table 4.23: Insurance Group, select information

($ thousands)	1980	1979	1978
Premiums written, net	$184,864	$186,185	$198,313
Premiums earned			
Specialized auto and general liability	88,404	90,646	96,126
Workers' compensation	19,890	19,350	29,893
Reinsurance	33,804	30,864	30,160
Home State multiple lines	43,089	41,089	29,894
	185,187	181,949	186,073
Underwriting gain (loss), pre-tax			
Specialized auto and general liability	7,395	7,845	11,543
Workers' compensation[1]	4,870	5,130	(3,944)
Reinsurance	(233)	(4,338)	(2,443)
Home State multiple lines	(5,294)	(4,895)	(2,155)
	$6,738	$3,742	$3,001
Combined ratio (statutory)	96.4%	97.2%	96.7%

Footnote:
1. Workers' Compensation coverage written by Home State is not broken out per the footnote to the financial statements.

The data in this table was taken from the summary of segment results section of the Annual Report and differs in some cases with figures listed in earlier reporting periods.
Sources: Berkshire Hathaway Annual Reports 1979, 1982.

Buffett gave a frank assessment of Berkshire's insurers. National Indemnity continued to produce good results under a self-imposed reduction of premium volume due to insufficient pricing. National Indemnity's reinsurance business reflected the ongoing weaknesses of the primary market and wasn't expected to have much future growth. Buffett said the delay factor in reinsurance caused him to bemoan industry conditions "that were transforming the reinsurance market into amateur night." People were lured by ease of entry into the business, large amounts of upfront cash, and delayed expenses. It set the stage for even larger swings in profitability and required a significant amount of discipline over many years. Even so, the small underwriting loss in reinsurance during 1980 was a very good result considering its associated float (assuming business on the books was appropriately reserved).

With the exception of a good performance in Kansas, Home State insurance operations were poor. Results were so bad in Iowa that the Insurance Company of Iowa, founded in 1973, was shut down and merged into Cornhusker Casualty.

With much negative industry information to report, Buffett apparently forgot to mention that Berkshire's own insurance companies collectively turned in a great year. The combined ratio improved and a record underwriting profit was achieved. This was on top of nearly $31 million of investment income. Nonetheless, Buffett again left off with a prediction for the following year. He anticipated lower volume and poorer underwriting results in 1981, but that Berkshire's results would be above the industry average.

Textiles and Retail Operations

In 1980, the report on Berkshire's textile operations and its Associated Retail operation was moved away from the beginning of the letter. That was because the scope of the textile business was reduced. Buffett informed shareholders that New Bedford's loom capacity was reduced by one-third, and that operations ceased at Waumbec in Manchester, New Hampshire. The rest of the operation was split into independent manufacturing and sales divisions. Even though the Textile Group had, "more than doubled capacity in our most profitable textile segment through a recent purchase of used 130-inch Sauer looms," capital employed in the segment was being reduced.

Though lumped together in the same segment as the faltering textile operations, Buffett praised Associated Retail. He noted that in 1981 Associated Retail would celebrate fifty years in operation, all under the leadership of Ben Rosner.

Illinois National Bank and Trust of Rockford

The news on Berkshire's banking subsidiary, Illinois National, was doubly sad. First, Berkshire was forced to divest of the well-run and highly profitable bank, which was completed on December 31, 1980, to comply with Federal Law. Then its founder, Eugene Abegg, died on July 2, 1980 at the age of 82. Buffett had much praise for Abegg and fondly recalled their eleven-year business relationship.

"As a friend, banker and citizen, he was unsurpassed," said Buffett. Buffett admired both Abegg's under-promise and over-deliver business approach, and his strength of character. "The seller has dozens of opportunities to mislead the buyer …" yet he, "laid all negative factors face up on the table." Yet Abegg hid, or forgot to mention, positive factors that came with Berkshire's purchase when they periodically materialized.

Buffett's praise read like a business obituary (though the business was not dead) and eulogy wrapped together. Abegg started the bank in the 1930s at the request of George Mead (no known relation to the author*), a wealthy industrialist at the time. He ran it for close to fifty years, producing record industry results. When other banks were failing or trying to figure out how to pay depositors after the one-week bank

---

* As an amateur genealogist, I would be most obliged to anyone that could connect my family line to the George Mead referenced here.

holiday of 1933, Abegg had enough cash on hand to pay all depositors in full. His "fiduciary attitude was always dominant," said Buffett. High praise indeed.

The financial divestiture of the bank was complicated but designed in the best interests of both Berkshire's shareholders and those of the bank. The divestiture would not be entirely financially motivated—Buffett wanted to reciprocate the fair treatment received by Abegg in the purchase and operation of the bank with an equally fair sale. Though the mechanism was somewhat complex, the process amounted to an I-cut-you-choose type of split. As the controlling shareholder in the bank and Berkshire, Buffett designed the exchange ratio. Since he designed it, he left himself as the exchanger of last resort.

Berkshire's 1,300 shareholders were left with three options:

- Proportional option: Maintain an equal ownership in Berkshire and the bank post-divestiture, with the only difference being having two stock certificates after the divestiture. Chosen by: Twenty-four shareholders.
- Bank-preferred exchange: Increase ownership in the bank while decreasing ownership proportionally in Berkshire. Chosen by: Thirty-nine shareholders.
- Berkshire-preferred exchange: Reverse of the second option, with ownership increasing in Berkshire and ownership decreasing, up to the entire amount, in the bank. Chosen by: 1,237 shareholders.

The bank was left with sixty-five shareholders, all of whom chose to become a shareholder. Because the divestiture was accomplished via a transaction to existing Berkshire shareholders, its equity on the books of Berkshire was removed in a treasury shares transaction, which gave the appearance of Berkshire repurchasing 41,086 shares for nearly $29 million.

Financing

During 1980, Berkshire sold $60 million of 12.75% notes due August 1, 2005. The bonds contained a sinking fund arrangement that would take effect in 1991. A sinking fund is a technical term for money set aside to repay a debt in regular installments. It's a lot like a monthly mortgage payment of principal and interest. Unlike a conventional mortgage, however, corporate debt often contains unique provisions. In this case, Berkshire would have use of the original $60 million from 1980 until 1991, and during that time would only be required to remit interest payments. In 1991, the loan would start amortizing, meaning the principal would begin to be repaid. Such a provision decreases the risk to a lender. It allows the debt to be repaid over a known period rather than relying on a new loan to repay the full amount once the original loan comes due. Even though Berkshire did not have an immediate use in mind for the proceeds, they were raised in anticipation of opportunities arising. Buffett was thinking into the future, knowing full well that the time to borrow money was when one didn't need it.

1981

Berkshire's after-tax operating earnings of $39.7 million in 1981 produced a 15.2% return on beginning equity capital (at cost). Maintaining such a rate of return would require favorable opportunities to purchase more businesses in whole or in part via the stock market. Given this, Buffett laid out Berkshire's acquisition strategy.

Berkshire was okay with either total ownership of a business or part ownership (in the form of marketable securities). He went so far as to say many of Berkshire's non-controlled investments (stocks) were better than its controlled businesses because of the mispricing opportunities presented by the market from time to time. In either case, no attention was paid to accounting over economics. The economics won out every time, even if the earnings attributable to Berkshire's share never appeared on financial statements. Combined, these unreported-but-economically-real earnings already exceeded Berkshire's reported earnings and were why Buffett took pains to illustrate what was going on.

Four of Berkshire's investees are good examples: GEICO, General Foods, R.J. Reynolds Industries, and *The Washington Post* had combined undistributed earnings attributable to Berkshire totaling $35 million. This was over half of Berkshire's 1981 earnings before interest.* Though very little of that money appeared on Berkshire's financials because of low dividend payout ratios, it would eventually show up as capital gains as the market recognized the accumulating value in the underlying businesses. In the short run, the accounting could skew down the annual return on equity calculation, but over time it would show up in book value for Berkshire's shareholders.**

Buffett looked down on companies that preferred accounting over economics, but he understood why managers made that choice. They were type-A personalities who, "seldom are deficient in animal spirits and often relish increased activity and challenge." These managers, Buffett said, knew exactly where they stood on *Fortune Magazine's* Fortune 500 list of largest companies by revenues. But how many knew their ranking based on profitability? Few, he conjectured. These managers would

---

* I'm using earnings before interest to base the comparison on the underlying earning power of the Berkshire subsidiaries irrespective of the fact that Berkshire financed part of their purchase price with borrowed money.
** We can quantify this. The operating earnings above are $40 million. If $4 million of the undistributed investee earnings of $35 million were paid out it would increase Berkshire's earnings by 10%. Berkshire's reported return on equity would increase by 1.5 percentage points.

buy the proverbial toad they thought they could kiss and turn into a superstar. A few managed such a feat, and Buffett named them: Ben Heineman at Northwest Industries, Henry Singleton at Teledyne, Erwin Zaban at National Service Industries, and especially Tom Murphy at Capital Cities Communications. Murphy got extra praise for being skilled in both acquisitions and operations. Notably, Buffett explicitly excluded himself from such managerial accolades.

The topic of inflation remained a concern as the rate of inflation continued to run near double digits. Buffett said inflation acted like a "gigantic corporate tapeworm," consuming investment dollars regardless of the health of the host. The less prosperous a business, the greater proportion of dollars were consumed. Not only would taxes and inflation combine to reduce individual investors' real purchasing power over time, businesses would be forced to retain earnings. To maintain unit volume over time required continual reinvestment in capital such as receivables, inventories, and fixed assets. One of the worst parts about inflation was its distorting effects on managerial decision-making. Reductions in purchasing power and forced reinvestment were real issues. The problem, it seemed, was that some managers and owners did not make decisions that took inflation and changes in interest rates into account.

Sources of Reported Earnings

The now-familiar table in the Chairman's letter (see Table 4.2 on page 98), gives a broad look at how the budding Berkshire conglomerate fared during 1981. Action was concentrated in two areas: insurance and candy. Insurance dominated 85% of the year's pre-tax operating earnings. Insurance underwriting, which was viewed and managed distinct from investment income, declined but was still profitable. The underwriting profit together with an increase in net investment income was enough to bring the Insurance Group's total contribution to pre-tax operating earnings above that of the prior year. Such a comparison is slightly misleading since Berkshire had used $28.75 million of its $60 million of proceeds raised the prior year to add to the Insurance Group's equity capital.

Table 4.24: Berkshire Hathaway summary sources of operating earnings 10% or more, 1981

Insurance underwriting	3.1%
Insurance net investment income	82.2%
Total insurance	85.3%
See's Candies	26.4%
All others, combined	15.0%
Interest on debt	(26.8%)
Total	100.0%

Note: Totals do not add up to 100% due to rounding.
Sources: Berkshire Hathaway Chairman's letter 1981 and author's calculations.

See's Candies' $12.5 million of pre-tax earnings (Berkshire's share),[*] representing over a quarter of the total, jumps out as the second largest contributor. In his letter to Blue Chip's shareholders, Charlie Munger described See's in more detail. The figures below in Table 4.25 showed a modest annualized increase in pounds. The ability of See's to pass on increases in prices, however, resulted in double-digit growth in revenues and an even greater increase in profits during that time.

Table 4.25: See's Candies, select data

($ and pounds in millions)	1981	1972	% Change	% / Yr.
Pounds sold	24	17	41%	3.9%
Revenues	$113	$31	260%	15.3%
After-tax profits	$11	$2	450%	20.9%

Sources: Blue Chip Stamps Chairman's letter 1981 and author's calculations.

In 1981, profits at See's increased 41%.[**] Such increases were that much more impressive, said Munger, considering the industry was basically stagnant.

Why was this so? Munger, always one to seek out the why behind any result (good or bad), attributed the success of See's to a couple of factors. First, customers preferred its taste and texture over competitors. This was likely the result of its "fanatic insistence on expensive natural quality control and cheerful retail service." Second, See's controlled the distribution of its candy very carefully, owning all its stores and

---

[*] The figure reported for Berkshires share of See's Candies' earnings in 1981 was $13 million. This is an example of the minor discrepancies between the original year and the lookback year in the following years' Annual Report. I have used the 1982 figure for 1981 results as these are presumably more correct having had the benefit of time.

[**] The 41% referenced here is lower than the 44% increase shown in the table in Munger's letter. Munger used the company-level figures. I've used the figures included in the Berkshire Chairman's letter for consistency. The difference arises due to state income taxes paid by Blue Chip Stamps.

handling distribution to those stores itself. See's was therefore rewarded, said Munger, with, "extraordinary sales per square foot … frequently two to three times those of competitors." With such excellent business attributes See's was clearly worth far in excess of the $38.3 million carrying value Blue Chip attributed to it on the books.

The remainder of Berkshire's sources of earnings in 1981 made up just 15% of the total, but some were of interest. After divesting its branch network in 1980, Mutual Savings and Loan lived up to expectations and saw its pre-tax earnings drop from $2.8 million to $0.8 million. *The Buffalo Evening News*, a subsidiary of Blue Chip Stamps, continued to struggle with litigation issues from its competitor and turned in a loss of $0.7 million for Berkshire shareholders. Shareholders would also have noticed the jump in interest expense. A direct result of the $60 million borrowed in 1980, interest expense jumped from $9.4 million to $12.7 million in 1981.

Insurance

Irrational pricing by insurance industry participants in 1981 continued throughout the year and gave Buffett the confidence to predict in his Chairman's letter (written in early 1982), "that 1982 will be the worst year in recent history for insurance underwriting." Industry data (see Table 4.26) showed a correlation between the yearly change in premiums written and the impact on profitability the ensuing year. In an inflationary world, low increases in premiums meant insurers weren't covering their costs; and profitability, expressed in a combined ratio above 100%, was trending the wrong way.

Table 4.26: Select insurance industry data

	1981	1980	1979
Growth in written premiums	3.6%	6.0%	10.3%
Growth in earned premiums	4.1%	7.8%	10.4%
Combined ratio	105.7%	103.1%	100.6%

Source: Best's Aggregates and Averages, as quoted in the 1981 Berkshire Hathaway Annual Report.

Over the preceding three years, premium growth industrywide fell to single digits. Consequently, the combined ratio deteriorated. Based on then-current trends in quarterly data, which were quickly deteriorating, things were expected to get much, much worse. Because of the open book nature of the insurance industry, rates were generally subject to the actions of the least rational competitor. That is, that outfit would attract the most business and others would feel the need to follow. Berkshire, unwilling to write business at an obvious loss, wrote almost 20% less volume in 1981 compared to 1980. (Part of the decline came from shuttering the Iowa Home State operation during 1980.)

Table 4.27: Insurance Group, select information

($ thousands)	1981	1980	1979
Premiums written, net	$148,000	$184,864	$186,185
Premiums earned			
Specialized auto and general liability	73,177	88,404	90,646
Workers' compensation	18,193	19,890	19,350
Reinsurance	29,446	33,804	30,864
Home State multiple lines	38,197	43,089	41,089
	159,013	185,187	181,949
Underwriting gain (loss), pre-tax			
Specialized auto and general liability	3,020	7,395	7,845
Workers' compensation[1]	2,822	4,870	5,130
Reinsurance	(3,720)	(233)	(4,338)
Home State multiple lines	(644)	(5,294)	(4,895)
	$1,478	$6,738	$3,742
Combined ratio (statutory)[2]	101.6%	96.4%	97.2%

Footnotes:
1. Workers' Compensation coverage written by Home State is not broken out per the footnote to the financial statements.
2. The 1981 combined ratio illustrates the divergence between statutory and GAAP combined ratios. When underwriting is near breakeven, apparent inconsistencies can arise when using the statutory combined ratio.

Note: The data in this table was taken from the summary of segment results section of the Annual Report and differs in some cases with figures listed in earlier reporting periods.
Sources: Berkshire Hathaway Annual Report 1979, 1982.

Shareholder Designated Contributions

Berkshire's new charitable giving program was the brainchild of Berkshire Vice Chairman Charlie Munger. It gave Berkshire's shareholders the option to designate contributions to any charity, with the amount based on the number of shares they owned (Berkshire set the per share amount). This option was limited to shareholders who owned shares in book name (that is, directly registered and not through a broker). In the first year 90% of shareholders (95.6% if Buffett's own shares were included) elected to participate. In total, $1.8 million was paid to 675 charities. Berkshire was effectively paying a tax-free dividend to shareholders that was immediately sent to their favorite charity.

1982

Buffett's prediction of a poor year for insurance underwriting came true. This, in addition to two other factors, caused his benchmark return on beginning shareholders' equity to come in at 9.8%. This subpar number was reported in the very first sentence of his 1982 Chairman's letter. The two other factors contributing to the decline were the growth in the equity capital base and higher levels of investment in non-controlled businesses.

Maintaining high rates of growth on Berkshire's capital was more challenging with each passing year. Berkshire's practice of retaining all earnings resulted in capital accumulating much faster than at other businesses that paid a dividend or regularly bought back shares. Accompanying (and in part because of) Berkshire's large and growing investment in non-controlled businesses via the stock market, Berkshire's reported earnings did not fully reflect actual economic earnings. The iceberg Buffett described in a previous letter was growing, but it was doing so largely below the surface.

For this reason, Buffett proposed a change to his preferred yardstick. Instead of looking at the ratio of operating earnings to beginning equity capital (valuing securities at cost), he suggested the annual change in net worth or book value (valuing securities at market).[*] This measure would allow the retained earnings of non-controlled businesses to show their worth, albeit with stock prices gyrating year-to-year around their intrinsic value.

Buffett provided several examples to back up his rationale for changing his yardstick. The four companies mentioned in the prior report (GEICO, General Foods, The Washington Post Co., and R.J. Reynolds Industries) had earnings of $54 million attributable to Berkshire in 1982. Yet only dividends showed up on Berkshire's income statement, so only $14 million of the earnings were included. GEICO only contributed $3.5 million after tax to Berkshire's accounting earnings—an additional $23 million of GEICO's undistributed earnings remained below the surface. A large portion of Berkshire's economic earnings in many other non-controlled businesses in its $921 million equity portfolio were similarly *hidden*.

This new yardstick proposal by Buffett raised the "only 9.8%" return to 40%, since the gain in net worth came to $208 million—a whopping 6.6 times the $31.5 million of accounting operating earnings. Buffett came right out and said what he would have been thinking if he were in shareholders' shoes: "You should be suspicious of such an assertion. Yardsticks seldom are discarded while yielding favorable results," he said. "We generally believe in pre-set, long-lived, and small bullseyes," not, "shoot[ing] the arrow of business performance into a blank canvas and then carefully draw[ing] the

---

[*] The calculation included an adjustment for the taxes that would be due if any gains were realized.

bullseye." Buffett's logic was sound, and for Berkshire it made sense to readjust the performance gauge to make up for the vagaries of financial accounting.

Sources of Reported Earnings

Sticking out like a sore thumb, the $21.6 million pre-tax underwriting loss from the Insurance Group was enough to put a pit in one's stomach. The swing to a loss, though anticipated, was still hard to comprehend. One positive factor within insurance (which will be discussed in more detail below), or at least a mitigating factor to the large underwriting loss, was the $41.6 million of pre-tax net investment income in 1982. It must have been somewhat comforting knowing the insurance business overall was profitable.

Table 4.28: Berkshire Hathaway summary sources of operating earnings 10% or more, 1982

Insurance underwriting	(77.7%)
Insurance net investment income	150.0%
Total insurance	72.3%
See's Candies	51.3%
Wesco Financial - parent	10.6%
All others, combined[1]	12.6%
Interest on debt	(46.8%)
Total	100.0%
Footnote:	
1. Blue Chip Stamps - parent represented 9.0%.	

Sources: Berkshire Hathaway Chairman's letter 1982 and author's calculations.

While still reporting operating losses ($0.7 million pre-tax attributable to Berkshire that year), the success of *The Buffalo News* in attracting Sunday readership presaged good things to come. *The News* had grown Sunday circulation to 367,000. This was an incredible feat given that six years prior it had no Sunday edition. Further, when Sunday was entirely served by *The News'* competitor, *The Courier-Express*, the circulation was just 272,000. In a market with very little household growth, these figures pointed toward the value subscribers found in the paper. The managers Henry Urban, Stan Lipsey, Murray Light, Clyde Pinson, Dave Perona, and Dick Feather, were singled out by name in the Chairman's letter.

Another entry in the same sources of earnings table* would have stuck out. Mutual Savings and Loan, the now one-headquarters-one-branch bank owned through Blue Chip's Wesco subsidiary, had lost money pre-tax (Berkshire's share was $2,000, no zeroes omitted) but had generated an after-tax *profit* of over $1.5 million. What was going on?

Charlie Munger explained this in his report to Blue Chip shareholders. He told shareholders that the peculiar result of pre-tax loss and after-tax gain, was of "less-than-highest quality" since it arose due to tax savings as part of being consolidated for tax purposes with Blue Chip.** Munger also pointed to another quirk. Mutual Savings and Loan's operating earnings, notwithstanding the tax boost, earned just 7.1% on its $46.2 million of beginning shareholders' equity. Because Blue Chip purchased its interest in Mutual Savings and Loan at a discount, its rate of return was 18.1%.***

Mutual Savings and Loan operated a lot like Illinois National Bank and Trust, the bank Berkshire was forced to divest two years prior. Mutual Savings and Loan had a policy of holding high levels of equity in relation to interest-bearing deposits, a high percentage of assets in short-term cash and cash equivalents, and above average amounts of assets in tax-exempt issues yielding more than typical mutual banks' mortgage portfolios. During 1981, deregulation of banks and thrifts unleashed changes and stiff competition that Munger likened to a hurricane. Mutual Savings largely escaped damage because it shed its branches in 1980 and because of its conservative operating philosophy.

Blue Chips' two other major subsidiaries, See's Candies and Precision Steel, had divergent years. See's did well; Precision Steel did poorly. "See's is by far the finest business we have ever purchased," wrote Munger. Its earnings rose 13.4% to $14.2 million in 1982, continuing to benefit from the fanaticism described in the account of 1981 above. Although it still reported a profit, Precision Steel suffered due to a severe recession in the industry on top of an unprofitable precision measuring tool line closed at an after-tax cost of $650,000.

Textile results improved over 1981 (though textiles still lost over $1.5 million pre-tax). The business continued to shrink. Sales were $21.8 million and total assets just $12.9 million, including inventories of $4.4 million (receivables were not separately detailed). The group was literally fading to a footnote.

---

* Buffett's letter included pre-tax earnings both on the company level and for Berkshire's share, in addition to Berkshire's share of after-tax earnings. Table 4.2. presented on page 98 includes only the pre-tax earnings for Berkshire's share.
** Mutual Savings realized a loss on the sale of mortgage-backed securities. This created a tax benefit.
*** Blue Chip carried Wesco on its books at $18.2 million. It also benefitted from a small boost from a positive amortization into income of the discount to purchase price.

Insurance

In every area of business volume was down, and all but one group, workers' compensation, turned in an underwriting loss. The two major killers were National Indemnity's specialized auto and general liability, and the reinsurance business. Berkshire's insurance underwriting deteriorated far more than the overall industry in 1982. As was his style, Buffett did not sugar-coat this fact; he stated it plainly.

Table 4.29: Insurance Group, select information

($ thousands)	1982	1981	1980
Premiums written, net	$149,091	$148,000	$184,864
Premiums earned			
Specialized auto and general liability	69,026	73,177	88,404
Workers' compensation	15,951	18,193	19,890
Reinsurance	27,408	29,446	33,804
Home State multiple lines	37,552	38,197	43,089
Structured settlements and portfolio reinsurance	3,008		
	152,945	159,013	185,187
Underwriting gain (loss), pre-tax			
Specialized auto and general liability	(12,647)	3,020	7,395
Workers' compensation[1]	2,658	2,822	4,870
Reinsurance	(7,524)	(3,720)	(233)
Home State multiple lines	(3,949)	(644)	(5,294)
Structured settlements and portfolio reinsurance	(96)		
	($21,558)	$1,478	$6,738
Combined ratio (statutory)[2]	115.0%	101.6%	96.4%

Footnotes:
1. Workers' Compensation coverage written by Home State is not broken out per the footnote to the financial statements.
2. The 1981 combined ratio illustrates the divergence between statutory and GAAP combined ratios. When underwriting is near breakeven, apparent inconsistencies can arise when using the statutory combined ratio.

Note: The data in this table was taken from the summary of segment results section of the Annual Report and differs in some cases with figures listed in earlier reporting periods.
Sources: Berkshire Hathaway Annual Reports 1979, 1982.

In the reinsurance line, underwriting losses jumped for two reasons. First, storms in the US Southwest during the beginning of 1982 caused immediate claims. The second was adverse loss development.

The nature of reinsurance is that claims stretch out over years, yet management must make an initial estimate of all future costs immediately (regardless of how far in the future they are expected to be incurred). When those prior year loss estimates change, as they did for Berkshire's reinsurance business during 1982, loss development charges are booked in the year the adjustment is made. Adverse loss development occurs when initial estimates of costs are found to be too low.* The long time horizon is good from the standpoint of creating long-lived float, but management's estimates are subject to optimism at best and outright deception at worst, frequently leading to inadequate reserving.

Competitive pressures not only kept rates down industrywide but allowed risk to increase as well. National Indemnity's specialized auto and general liability segment had a massive swing in underwriting profitability. Berkshire self-admittedly accepted some of this business. It tried an undefined attempt to counter the adverse trends which, in retrospect but still without explanation, were "ill-conceived and poorly executed."

The Home State group continued to struggle with profitability. Underwriting was so bad in Minnesota that Berkshire closed Lakeland Fire and Casualty Company, the entity formed in 1971 to conduct business in that state. The workers' compensation group was the only ray of sunshine. It turned in a fourth consecutive year of profits.

Berkshire's 115% combined ratio in 1982 was bad in its own right; it was even worse compared to the 109.5% ratio Buffett estimated for the industry overall. And it would be a bloodbath in just a few more years if trends continued. Buffett called the industry average estimates a best case. Because of the significant discretion management had in estimating future losses, much mischief could be done.

Buffett did not name names but said several other insurers used questionable accounting in 1982 to lessen the blow of the significant losses affecting the industry. Buffett put it bluntly: "In insurance, as elsewhere, the reaction of weak managements to weak operations is often weak accounting." His dig continued with one of the aphorisms he was known for: "It's difficult for an empty sack to stand upright."**

Others thought the weaknesses in pricing would subside and move toward better profitability, just as in other insurance cycles. But not Buffett. He foresaw continued losses in 1983 and 1984. Insurance was a commodity-type business with ease of entry. Its very nature of delayed recognition of the profitability of underwritten business caused over-capacity to arise more often than not. Also, there were no government-imposed prices. Industry participants were free to price as they please.

Such unrestrained competition hadn't always ruled. In decades past, such as between 1950 and 1970, the industry averaged a 99.0% combined ratio. Buffett said the industry then worked with "a legal quasi-administered pricing system fostered by insurance regulators" where competition was not pervasive. If they became

---

* Favorable loss development can occur too, but most often seen is unfavorable or adverse development since optimism pervades estimates.
** Buffett used this in quotes. The quote is attributed to Benjamin Franklin.

unprofitable, all participants would work in a gentlemanly manner to correct them. Insurance companies were in fact prevented by law from undercutting one another on price. That day was gone and the only way to correct the misery was to decrease industry capacity (meaning supply).

Issuance of Equity

The very first sentence under a section entitled Issuance of Equity foretold the future: "Berkshire and Blue Chip are considering a merger in 1983." That should have made readers sit up and pay close attention. Buffett did not expound on the merger itself. Instead he described share-based mergers and acquisitions in general, and the all-too-often value-destroying practices they produce.

Remember the metaphor about mergers being a business marriage? The wise would not go into marriage without a lot of thought and knowledge. Buffett's long explanation of mergers was his way of sharing knowledge. Commenting on Berkshire's policy relating to share-issuances, he said: "Our share issuances follow a simple basic rule: we will not issue shares unless we receive as much intrinsic business value as we give." Don't all other managers act in such a rational manner? No. Quite frequently, Buffett explained, one or a combination of the managers' thirst for deals, or the valuation of either side of a merger, caused value-destructing action for one of the parties involved. Most often, it was the acquirer that engaged in value-destroying practices (usually by issuing undervalued shares or overpaying for a target), but it's possible for either side to destroy value.

Buffett used the example of a family farm. A hypothetical merger of a 120-acre farm with a neighboring sixty-acre farm would result in a 180-acre farm. The merger provides an equal partnership between the two farmers. Yet this calculation sees the owner of the larger farm experience a 25% reduction in ownership (from 100% of 120 acres to 50% of 180 acres, or ninety acres pro rata). This happens all the time in business mergers.

Even if the two farms were of equal size, their relative valuations could cause a value-destroying result. For example, if one of the two farms were selling for half of their worth, the result would be the same as the scenario Buffett described above since the undervalued side would be giving up more than they were getting. Buffett thought managers and directors should ask themselves if they would sell 100% of the business at the same valuation as they were considering selling part of it. This train of thought was identical to that used by Buffett when buying less than 100% of a business, public or private. Start with the valuation of the whole, and then split it into pieces to determine the per-share price one is willing to pay.

The crux of the issue was that CEOs had different incentives than owners. By using stock rather than debt or cash, he (for the vast majority of CEOs at the time were male) would end up with more kingdom to manage at the expense of owners. Such mergers or acquisitions were frequently done on the basis that either future business value would materialize, growth for growth's sake was needed, or for perceived tax reasons (giving some consideration in stock because the manager had to).

Buffett was priming his shareholders for the proposed Blue Chip merger and letting them know he would act in their best interests. He reminded them that the only other such merger under his management of Berkshire that caused the issuance of shares took place in 1978 with the merger of Diversified Retailing.* With the impending Blue Chip merger Buffett promised to, "not equate activity with progress or corporate size with owner-wealth." Since Buffett was Berkshire's largest shareholder, and therefore proportionately affected by all capital allocation decisions, minority partners should have felt ease about having him at the helm.

Businesses Wanted!

Buffett's 1982 Chairman's letter included a short advertisement. This was the first of such advertisements—not for product, but rather for business acquisition prospects— that would remain essentially unchanged over the ensuing decades, save for the size of the business sought. Here are Buffett's criteria, as laid out in 1982:

"We prefer:

1. Large purchases (at least $5 million of after-tax earnings),
2. Demonstrated consistent earning power (future projections are of little interest to us, nor are "turn-around" situations),
3. Businesses earning good returns on equity while employing little or no debt,
4. Management in place (we can't supply it),
5. Simple businesses (if there's lots of technology, we won't understand it),
6. An offering price (we don't want to waste our time or that of the seller by talking, even preliminarily, about a transaction when price is unknown).

We will not engage in unfriendly transactions. We can promise complete confidentiality and a very fast answer as to possible interest—customarily within five minutes. Cash purchases are preferred, but we will consider the issue of stock when it can be done on the basis described in the previous section."

Berkshire would, over time, find several businesses this way.

---

* While technically true, this assertion is not 100% accurate since the spin off of the Illinois National Bank and Trust at year-end 1980 necessitated Buffett setting the price (exchange ratio) of both Berkshire and the bank. And in fact the divestiture was accounted for with a treasury stock transaction.

1983

Buffett's 1983 letter to Berkshire Hathaway shareholders opened with the report, almost in passing, that Berkshire had merged with Blue Chip Stamps, previously its 60%-owned mini-conglomerate. Buffett now had 2,900 owners to report to, up from 1,900, so he summarized the major business principles Berkshire followed pertaining to the manager-owner relationship. These principles would later be codified into Berkshire's Owners' Manual.

The thirteen principles, as laid out in the 1983 Chairman's letter, were as follows (summarized):

1. "Although our form is corporate, our attitude is partnership." Buffett and Munger, "view the company as a conduit through which our shareholders own the assets."
2. Directors are all major shareholders and four out of five have over 50% of family net worth in Berkshire. "We eat our own cooking."
3. Their long-term goal is increase in intrinsic value *per share*—not the overall size of Berkshire.
4. Their preference is to own 100% of businesses, but they would also own parts of businesses and prefer those "that generate cash and consistently earn above-average returns on capital."
5. Buffett and Munger look to economic performance, not accounting. They, "virtually ignore [Berkshire's] consolidated numbers." Despite this, they promise to provide the information they would want if they were a non-controlling shareholder.
6. Like above, they do not care about accounting consequences and want shareholders to know that some economic earnings don't show up (referring to the undistributed earnings of non-control investees).
7. They "rarely use much debt and … will reject interesting opportunities rather than over-leverage our balance sheet."
8. We "will only do with your money what we would do with our own."
9. They measure performance as delivering at least $1 in market value for each $1 retained over a five-year rolling basis.
10. Berkshire will only issue shares, "when we receive as much in business value as we give."
11. Buffett wanted existing and new shareholders to know that they didn't engage in what Buffett called "gin rummy capitalism." They would not sell good businesses regardless of price and would hang on to subpar ones if they promised to generate some cash and if relations with management were good.
12. They promised to be candid and present the business facts as if their positions

were reversed and Buffett and Munger were the shareholders.

13. For competitive reasons, their candor could not extend to what they were buying, thinking of buying, or had bought in the open market.

Nebraska Furniture Mart

Buffett's birthday present to himself in 1983 was a business. After long admiring Nebraska Furniture Mart and its founders, the Blumkin Family, Buffett finally struck a deal to acquire 90% of the business on August 30, 1983. The business was located in his hometown of Omaha, Nebraska.

The description of the family matriarch, Rose Blumkin, or Mrs. B., read almost like an obituary. Yet at 90 years old in 1983, she was still very much alive and active in the business. The business was her life and she spent seven days a week at the store. She had escaped Russia and labored to establish her family in America before saving $500. With that seed capital, she started her home furnishings store in Omaha. Over the ensuing years the hard-working Mrs. B. clashed with competitors, who couldn't match her low prices. One fight ended up in a court battle culminating in the judge buying carpet from her.

Buffett admired Mrs. B's self-taught business-sense (more impressive considering she was illiterate), which she turned around and instilled in her son, Louie, and then in his three sons, Ron, Irv, and Steve. When Berkshire took control, Nebraska Furniture Mart sold over $100 million annually out of one 200,000 square foot store. That was more than any other home furnishings store in the country and more than all Omaha competitors combined.

The Nebraska Furniture Mart purchase, laid out on a one-and-a-half-page contract, called for Berkshire to buy an 80% economic interest in the company. This math contrasts with the 90% majority interest quoted earlier because of a 10% option set aside allowing key members of the management team to buy into the business. The 80% figure assumes this option is acted on.* The rest would remain in the Blumkin family.

What did Buffett see in Nebraska Furniture Mart? To start, it was in his hometown. Also, the store kept growing over time and he could see that Mrs. B's attitude toward pricing was making life hard on her competitors.

---

* The contract laid out the purchase of 90% of the business with 10% retained by Louis Blumkin and his family. Berkshire also made 10% available as an option to allow key members of the management team to buy into the business. The exact figures here are somewhat ambiguous. Table 4.30 calculates the value based on the contractual price and ownership amount. As late as the 1984 Berkshire Hathaway Annual Report, the ownership is stated as 90% but the economic interest as 80%. Ignoring the time value of money and assuming the 10% option was exercised immediately in 1983 (and on the same basis as the purchase price), Berkshire's 80% interest would have cost $49.2 million. These figures are also close to Buffett's statement at the 2014 Annual Meeting Q&A that the 100% basis was $60 million.

Nebraska Furniture Mart benefitted from classic economies of scale. The more it sold, the lower its fixed overhead became as a percentage of revenues. The lower its relative costs, the lower it was willing to charge, on and on in a virtuous, reinforcing cycle. Add in a huge selection of merchandise, and Nebraska Furniture Mart had a recipe for both saving its customers money and delivering superior returns to its owners. Once firmly entrenched, the business had a virtually impregnable moat that protected it from the onslaught of competition.[*]

Table 4.30: Nebraska Furniture Mart, select data and valuation, 1983

($ millions)	
Purchase price	$55.4
Ownership interest	90%
Valuation	$61.5
1983 revenues[1]	$100
1983 pre-tax margin[1]	7%
Tangible assets	$35.0
Pre-tax return on capital	20.0%
BRK price/tangible assets	1.75x
BRK going-in return, pre-tax	11.4%
Footnotes: 1. These are approximate values stated by Buffett in response to a question at the 2014 Annual Meeting.	

Sources: Berkshire Hathaway Annual Reports 1983, 2013; 2014 Annual Meeting Q&A.

Goodwill and its Amortization: The Rules and The Realities

Berkshire's book value grew 32% that year to $975.83 per share. The nineteen-year record, since Buffett took control in 1965, was 22.6% compounded annually. Buffett wanted shareholders to know, loud and clear, that they should not expect similar results in the future. "Those who believe otherwise should pursue a career in sales, but avoid one in mathematics." Buffett said he reported book value because it was a decent proxy for intrinsic business growth, "the measurement that really counts." He also provided a comparative description: Book value tells what is put in the business and intrinsic business value is what can be taken out, which is why it matters more.

---

[*] Writing in his 1988 Chairman's letter Buffett recounted how Dillard's, a large successful department store, entered the Omaha, Nebraska market but without a furniture line, choosing not to even try to compete with Nebraska Furniture Mart.

The explanation came because Buffett thought Berkshire's intrinsic value now exceeded its book value. This was due to Berkshire venturing heavily into marketable securities (some of whose values were not reported at market), and its purchase of higher quality businesses above their book value (necessitating the inclusion of intangible accounts). Despite the accounting depressing book value and the higher quality businesses now part of the company, Berkshire's stock price rarely traded above book value. Sparing those not so well-versed in accounting the gory details, Buffett only alluded to his appendix on goodwill. We will dig in.

Over four pages, Buffett's appendix on goodwill provided those willing to spend the time with a valuable lesson on business. He was quick to point out that it was economic and accounting goodwill he was referring to, not customers' feelings of a company's product or service.

Buffett explained that goodwill arises due to the difference between the purchase price of a business, and the accounting value of its assets. Usually the purchase price is higher than the underlying assets and, therefore, an entry on the asset side of the balance sheet must be made so that the transaction balances out.* To make the lesson more concrete Buffett used See's Candies as an example.

When Blue Chip purchased See's in 1972 for $25 million, it had about $8 million** of net tangible assets*** and earned about $2 million after tax, or 25% on its net tangible assets. The difference between the $25 million and $8 million was placed on the balance sheet as $17 million of goodwill. Prior to November 1970, this goodwill would simply remain on the balance sheet. After 1970, a charge to earnings was required for GAAP purposes (but not for tax purposes) to amortize the balance to zero. Most managements, Berkshire included, chose to do this over the maximum 40 years.

Buffett viewed the amortization charge, which was included in expenses and therefore depressed reported earnings, as an artificial construct. He thought the economic reality of a See's-type of business, one that earned much higher returns on its net tangible assets than other companies with similar resources, should be recognized by analysts and thus needed an accounting correction. The $425,000 charge to earnings that GAAP required Berkshire take every year ($17 million divided by forty years) was not real and could safely be ignored.

All transactions where the purchase price was greater than the underlying tangible assets required recognition and related amortization of goodwill, but not all those

---

* There are instances where the purchase price is below the value of the underlying assets. Blue Chip Stamps' purchase of its interest in Mutual Savings and Loan is such an example. In these cases of a bargain purchase the excess is amortized into income—the reverse of the more typical case and that described here.

** This $8 million figure is inconsistent with Buffett's 1991 Chairman's letter, in which he states See's had $7 million of net tangible assets.

*** Buffett points out here that he considered accounts receivable to be a tangible asset, "a definition proper for business analysts."

businesses were good. An eager management team on the hunt for a deal could overpay for a business and throw shareholders' money down the drain. Only a business with economic goodwill, one with a "consumer franchise…allow[ing] the value of the product to the purchaser, rather than its production cost, to be the major determinant of selling price," deserved such a treatment by analysts. Other such consumer franchises with true economic goodwill included those with a governmental advantage or monopoly, such as a TV station, or the low-cost producer in an industry, like GEICO.

To further complicate matters, the 1983 Berkshire merger with Blue Chip Stamps caused additional goodwill to be added to the equation for See's. Because Berkshire owned just 60% of Blue Chip prior to the merger, the purchase of the remaining 40% (via its increased ownership of Blue Chip) caused $28.4 million of additional goodwill to be added to the balance sheet along with its own amortization schedule against earnings. The goodwill amortization for See's would increase to $1 million annually for the next twenty-eight years and then decline to $0.7 million for the following twelve years as the two pieces of the amortization reached their accounting conclusion. Having two separate amortization schedules for two pieces of the same business was an accounting oddity without an easy solution.

There was another lesson in this side-note discussion of goodwill, and it was related to inflation. Buffett countered the "traditional wisdom—long on tradition, short on wisdom" that tangible assets were the way to protect against inflation. Again, using See's as an example, he imagined the hypothetical doubling of prices and its effect on required investment in net tangible assets. With $8 million of combined net tangible assets (receivables, inventories, fixed assets, etc.), a doubling of prices would cause the owner of See's to ante up an additional $8 million of capital to maintain the same unit volume. A business with the same earnings but requiring $18 million of capital (that is, a business earning a lower rate of return on its capital) would require $18 million from its owners just to stand still. Clearly, the business with lower capital requirements would be worth more to its owners.

Buffett wanted Berkshire's owners to realize the value in true, economic goodwill, because Berkshire would likely move in the direction of acquiring other businesses requiring similar treatment. The value of the goodwill asset on Berkshire's books totaled over $79 million at year-end 1983 and would likely continue to grow. Like the accounting for non-controlled businesses via the stock market, goodwill accounting told a story much different from the underlying economics—and it was the economics about which Berkshire cared most. Berkshire probably wouldn't find another business like See's, which was earning $13 million after tax on $20 million of net tangible assets—but a business even close would be worth paying up for.

Buffett hinted at Berkshire's valuation in the discussion of value-given-vs-value-received as it related to using shares as currency in a transaction. He noted that the true cost of the Blue Chip merger was slightly higher because, "the market value of Berkshire shares given up in the merger was less than their intrinsic business value."

We can estimate the valuation used in the Berkshire/Blue Chip Stamps merger. Using Berkshire's high and low share prices during the third quarter of 1983 (when the merger would have taken place) values Berkshire between $900 million and $1.2 billion (see Table 4.31). The resultant average price-to-book value was 1.35x.

Table 4.31: Berkshire Hathaway implied valuation in Blue Chip Stamps merger

Shares outstanding (year-end 1982)	986,509
BRK share price Q3 1983 (high)	$1,245
BRK share price Q3 1983 (low)	$905
Implied market value (high)	$1,228,203,705
Implied market value (low)	$892,790,645
Book value mid-1983 (estimated)	$784,000,000
Price-to-book value (high)	1.57x
Price-to-book value (low)	1.14x
Average price-to-book value	1.35x

Sources: Berkshire Hathaway Annual Report 1983 and author's calculations.

Sources of Reported Earnings

Due to the merger with Blue Chip in mid-1983, special care was needed in reading the earnings summary table in the Chairman's letter. Since the ownership in Blue Chip increased from 60% to 100%, that change alone was enough to skew Berkshire's share of Blue Chip's (and its subsidiaries') earnings up, all things being equal. Looking at the company-level results instead of the share attributable to Berkshire's ownership solved this issue.[*]

---

[*] The table presented three columns: pre-tax at the company level, pre-tax for Berkshire's share, and after tax for Berkshire's share. Consistency is key in analysis. The value lay in correctly communicating to shareholders how the businesses were doing. A pre-tax, company-level analysis removed the distortions arising from varying tax rates and ownership levels. I have attempted to use the most appropriate comparison at each juncture, here presenting the company-level figures during the year of transition.

Table 4.32: Earnings of Berkshire Hathaway subsidiaries, company-level

($ thousands)	1983	1982
Insurance Group:		
Underwriting	($33,872)	($21,558)
Net investment income	43,810	41,620
Buffalo Evening News	19,352	(1,215)
Nebraska Furniture Mart[1]	3,812	
See's Candies	27,411	23,884
Associated Retail Stores	697	914
Blue Chip Stamps - parent[2]	(1,422)	4,182
Mutual Savings and Loan	(798)	(6)
Precision Steel	3,241	1,035
Textiles	(100)	(1,545)
Wesco Financial - parent	7,493	6,156
Amortization of goodwill[3]	(532)	151
Interest on debt	(15,104)	(14,996)
Shareholder-designated contributions	(3,066)	(891)
Other	10,121	3,371
Operating earnings, pre-tax	61,043	41,102
Special GEICO distribution	21,000	
Sales of securities and unusual sales of assets	67,260	36,651
Total earnings - all entities (pre-tax)	$149,303	$77,753

Footnotes:
1. 1983 figures are those for October through December.
2. 1982 and 1983 are not comparable; major assets were transferred in the mid-year 1983 merger of Blue Chip Stamps.
3. Amortization of goodwill is included in Other for years prior to 1982.

Note: This table presents each company's earnings on a company-level basis. It differs from the presentation elsewhere which adjusts for Berkshire's ownership interest in each company.
Source: Berkshire Hathaway Annual Report 1983.

Leading off the table was insurance underwriting, whose losses had swollen on the heels of industry weakness. Berkshire's results were again worse than the industry average. The Insurance Group was profitable overall thanks only to its net investment income. More will be said about the Insurance Group below. Other notable entries in the table in 1983 were *The Buffalo News*, See's Candies, Blue Chip Stamps, Precision Steel, and a special distribution from GEICO.

The Buffalo News, long mired in a fight with its competitor, *The Courier-Express*, won its long battle[*] and was rewarded with soaring profits. The elimination of a competitor surely helped but other factors also accounted for the success of *The Buffalo News*. First, a stable population in the Buffalo area made citizens highly

---

[*] *The Courier-Express* closed in 1983, making Buffalo a one-paper town as Buffett rightly predicted.

interested in current events. Second, *The Buffalo News* had an earned reputation for editorial quality. Third, by design it provided more news than other papers: about 50% compared to an average in the upper 30% range for competitors. Because of all these things, Sunday circulation (that was previously provided only by the competitor) increased from 314,000 to 376,000. This was even more impressive against a backdrop of little to no population growth.

Never one to bask in the glow of good news, Buffett pointed out two extraordinary factors leading to the large swing in the profitability of *The Buffalo News* that year. Because of the substantial losses incurred in prior years, the business owed a "subnormal" amount of state income taxes. Additionally, there was a large drop in the cost of newsprint, a critical cost.

Continuing to examine Table 4.32 from 1983, we can see that Blue Chip Stamps reported a loss compared to a sizable profit the year before. The two years weren't comparable because major assets were transferred in the merger. When the merger took place, Blue Chip's subsidiaries became direct subsidiaries of Berkshire and accounts not associated with any entity would have transferred too. It's unclear why Blue Chip remained as a reporting line and why it continued to lose money to the tune of $2 million per year (the footnotes did not mention it). Such a large swing in profitability, while notable, probably wasn't overly concerning given the circumstances.

Precision Steel's profitability was depressed in 1982 due to weak industry factors and a business line venture into the measuring tool business that did not work out. In 1983 its profits rose threefold compared to that low base. Charlie Munger told Wesco shareholders, and Berkshire's as the report was shared with them, about the mistake. (Munger replaced Louis Vincenti as chairman after Vincenti was forced to retire because of health reasons.) Overall, Munger thought that Precision Steel would do well in 1984.

See's Candies

Berkshire owned 100% of See's after the Blue Chip/Berkshire merger. While an exceptional business, See's faced its share of challenges. These were twofold: raw material costs rising faster than inflation and difficulty growing unit volume. Raw material costs were not a problem at the time, but they could become one given See's "fanatical" (Munger's word) adherence to quality. Buffett told shareholders See's would only buy the finest ingredients, regardless of price. "We regard product quality as sacred," he said.

The second problem, pounds sold per store, was mainly an industry phenomenon, as per capita consumption of chocolate slowly declined. The increased prices at See's, a recession, and an already high market share probably all played a role. Poundage growth was hard to come by. Pounds sold declined 0.8% on a same-store basis during 1983. Cumulatively, volumes had declined 8% since 1979. Although revenues were up due to a combination of price increases (related to and on top of inflation) and new stores, focus was rightly placed on pounds sold per store. Cutting right to the key economic variable for See's and other retailers, Buffett told shareholders that "we regard the most important measure of retail trends to be units sold per store rather than dollar volume." More will be said in the discussion of 1984 results, which contain a history of revenues, operating profits, poundage, and number of stores for See's.

Insurance

Bleak prospects and irrational competition dogged Berkshire's insurers and the industry. The 1982 revised figure for the industry combined ratio came in at 109.7%. The estimate for 1983: 111%. Berkshire's own combined ratio in 1983 was an atrocious 122.8% (see Table 4.33). Noting the delayed nature of the business, Buffett placed the blame on his own shoulders. Prior to hiring Mike Goldberg to manage the Insurance Group, Buffett had made mistakes that finally materialized in 1983. Those mistakes included placing the wrong personnel in key operational positions, as well as direct and indirect mispricing of business.

Table 4.33: Insurance Group, select information

($ thousands)	1983	1982	1981
Premiums written, net	$149,849	$149,091	$148,000
Premiums earned			
Specialized auto and general liability	68,148	69,026	73,177
Workers' compensation	18,849	15,951	18,193
Reinsurance	26,889	27,408	29,446
Home State multiple lines	35,328	37,552	38,197
Structured settlements and portfolio reinsurance	3,266	3,008	
	152,480	152,945	159,013
Underwriting gain (loss), pre-tax			
Specialized auto and general liability	(14,880)	(12,647)	3,020
Workers' compensation[1]	(1,091)	2,658	2,822
Reinsurance	(8,387)	(7,524)	(3,720)
Home State multiple lines	(8,834)	(3,949)	(644)
Structured settlements and portfolio reinsurance	(680)	(96)	
	($33,872)	($21,558)	$1,478
Combined ratio (statutory)[2]	122.8%	115.0%	101.6%

Footnotes:
1. Workers' Compensation coverage written by Home State is not broken out per the footnote to the financial statements.
2. The 1981 combined ratio illustrates the divergence between statutory and GAAP combined ratios. When underwriting is near breakeven, apparent inconsistencies can arise when using the statutory combined ratio.

Note: The data in this table was taken from the summary of segment results section of the Annual Report and differs in some cases with figures listed in earlier reporting periods.
Sources: Berkshire Hathaway Annual Reports 1982, 1984.

Buffett praised his managers, whom he said swam a good race against strong industry tides that year. He singled out National Indemnity's Roland Miller for delivering improved results while competitors had opposite performance. He also identified Tom Rowley, who had joined Berkshire a year prior, to run Continental Divide Insurance, a Colorado Home State operation.

Against the backdrop of weak industry results and underwriting losses across all of Berkshire's insurance segments, Buffett was optimistic for the reinsurance segment. That segment had reported losses in each year dating back to 1975. Still, it had an ability to generate large float and, importantly, a way to monetize Berkshire's financial conservatism. The long period between buying reinsurance and when it might be needed meant a counterparty to a reinsurer wanted to know the reinsurer would be around when collection time came. Berkshire fit this mold perfectly. Its premier financial strength could be marketed as a differentiator.

Putting this unparalleled financial strength to use, Berkshire entered the structured settlements business. In exchange for an upfront premium (which the insurer could invest) that converted a lump sum settlement into a stream of cash flows, this long-tail line of insurance paid out claims over many years. For some claimants dependent on receiving lifetime financial security, the viability of the insurer paying the claims is all important.

Insurance—GEICO

Berkshire's one-third interest in GEICO was proportionally larger than Berkshire's other insurance interests combined. Objectively speaking, it was better too. If proportionally divided based on ownership, Berkshire's share of GEICO's premium volume would have been $270 million in 1983. GEICO's combined ratio of 96% was by all accounts stellar. Such a financial result was reflected in the market value of the business. Berkshire's stake cost $47 million and had a market value of $398 million at year-end 1983. Buffett had nothing but admiration for the trio responsible: managers Jack Byrne and Bill Snyder, and GEICO's investment manager, Lou Simpson.

The summary of earnings table included a $21 million entry for a special GEICO distribution. This was a de facto dividend from GEICO, accomplished via a tender offer that maintained Berkshire's ownership interest. Since it was treated as a dividend rather than a sale, Berkshire got away with paying an effective income tax rate of just 6.9%, compared to the 28% due if the transaction was recognized as a capital gain.

Stock Splits and Stock Activity

Calls to split Berkshire's stock intensified as the price crossed the $1,000 mark for the first time. Buffett thought that splitting Berkshire's stock was the wrong thing to do. Berkshire's communications practices were designed to cultivate a rational base of owners that sensibly considered the prospects of the underlying business and priced the stock accordingly. He preferred owners who cared about business results, and not the ever-fluctuating price of a stock. A high stock price discouraged frequent trading. In a simple example, Buffett asked rhetorically whether an owner of one Berkshire share valued at $1,300 (where the stock then traded) would be better off if Berkshire split 100 for one and he owned more shares equaling the same value. Buffett very clearly liked rational owners over ones "preferring paper to value."

It was not just the optical illusion of such artificially constructed stock splits that Buffett disliked. It also laid a cost on owners. If taken as a group, a company's owners were paying upwards of 2% of the market value of a business just for the privilege of moving in and out. Academia praised such liquidity as did those who profited from the turnover (stockbrokers, and exchanges, etc.). Buffett disagreed. More shares would equal more fees since those fees were often based on the number of shares traded. "Splitting the stock would increase that cost, downgrade the quality of our shareholder population, and encourage a market price less consistently related to intrinsic business value. We see no offsetting advantages." As logical as Buffett's arguments were, and the clear disadvantages of a split, calls for splitting Berkshire's stock would continue.

1984

Continuing his practice of leading with the bad news first, Buffett opened his 1984 Chairman's letter to shareholders saying that the nearly $153 million gain in net worth during the year was mediocre. Such an amount of money was (and still is) quite a large sum; the problem was it represented just a 13.6% increase on the prior year's book value. This was far short of the 22.1% compounded annual gain over the previous twenty years. "Economic gains must be evaluated by comparison with the capital that produces them," wrote Buffett.

Berkshire Hathaway's equity capital crossed the $1 billion threshold during 1983. This was partly due to the merger with Blue Chip Stamps. Maintaining high rates of return on that capital would get more difficult every year. To achieve even a 15% annual gain would require adding $3.9 billion to book value over the ensuing decade, assuming no dividends were paid. Such a rate of return seemed modest, but it represented a doubling every five years—not an easy feat for *any* business, let alone one Berkshire's size.

Accomplishing high rates of growth on Berkshire's equity base would, "require a few big ideas—small ones just won't do." Rather than try to lay out a detailed plan of action, Buffett continually searched and waited for ideas to come. The question was when? "[O]ur experience has been that they pop up occasionally," he said. "How's that for a strategic plan?" Buffett was not being curt, just realistic. Rather than try to force ideas to happen, and therefore potentially make a mistake, patience would be the default course of action. Later in the letter, in discussing Berkshire's equity portfolio, Buffett commented, "we find doing nothing the most difficult task of all."

Sources of Reported Earnings

Berkshire's operating results were best viewed on a company-level pre-tax basis considering the merger with Blue Chip Stamps the prior year. This view also stripped out the goodwill amortization charges required by accounting standards and placed them on a single line.

Table 4.34: Earnings of Berkshire Hathaway subsidiaries, company-level

($ thousands)	1984	1983
Insurance Group:		
Underwriting	($48,060)	($33,872)
Net investment income	68,903	43,810
Buffalo News	27,328	19,352
Nebraska Furniture Mart[1]	14,511	3,812
See's Candies	26,644	27,411
Associated Retail Stores	(1,072)	697
Blue Chip Stamps - parent[2]	(1,843)	(1,422)
Mutual Savings and Loan	1,456	(798)
Precision Steel	4,092	3,241
Textiles	418	(100)
Wesco Financial - parent	9,777	7,493
Amortization of goodwill[3]	(1,434)	(532)
Interest on debt	(14,734)	(15,104)
Shareholder-designated contributions	(3,179)	(3,066)
Other	4,932	10,121
Operating earnings, pre-tax	87,739	61,043
Special GEICO distribution[4]		19,575
Special General Foods distribution	8,111	
Sales of securities and unusual sales of assets	104,699	67,260
Total earnings - all entities (pre-tax)	200,549	147,878

Footnotes:
1. 1983 figures are for October through December.
2. 1982 and 1983 are not comparable; major assets were transferred in the mid-year 1983 merger of Blue Chip Stamps.
3. Amortization of goodwill is included in Other for years prior to 1982.
4. The accounting of the GEICO special dividend was changed during 1984.

Note: This table presents each company's earnings on a company-level basis. It differs from the presentation elsewhere which adjusts for Berkshire's ownership interest in each company.
Source: Berkshire Hathaway Annual Report 1984.

Front and center was insurance underwriting (discussed in more detail later), again posting a miserable result. Weak industry conditions, coupled with self-inflicted wounds, were causing the red ink to continue flowing in Berkshire's underwriting. Net investment income had again saved the day to bring the Insurance Group out of the red.

Related to insurance, the special GEICO distribution reported in 1983 again garnered attention in 1984. Though the distribution was technically accomplished via a share repurchase, it had functioned more like a dividend since Berkshire's ownership interest remained unchanged. This is how Berkshire had viewed it, as had the Omaha office of its auditor, Peat, Marwick, Mitchell & Co. However, in 1984, the New York office of the auditor reversed course. It said the transaction should be viewed as a repurchase, with some of the proceeds being recorded against (that is, reducing) the carrying value of the stock on Berkshire's books. There were no tax consequences and the economics remained unchanged, but the accounting did. Berkshire expressly disagreed with the auditors' conclusion but went along with it rather than incur a qualified opinion of the financial statements.

The GEICO special distribution might have gone unrevised had it not been for a very similar transaction with General Foods in 1984. With General Foods, the share repurchases had been over time, whereas with GEICO it was a one-time event. The total amount received from General Foods was $21.8 million and Berkshire's ownership interest remained at exactly 8.75%. The difference between the reported amount of $8.1 million and the total amount received was recorded as a capital gain.

Buffett was a fan of the type of share repurchases conducted by GEICO, General Foods, and others, since the shares were selling below intrinsic value at the time of repurchase. Share repurchases below intrinsic value increased underlying value to continuing shareholders, but also shrunk the size of the business that the manager operated. Managers not focused on their owners (shareholders) would seldom conduct such transactions or would blindly repurchase shares without considering valuation. These managers were short-sighted, thought Buffett. The obvious reward for conducting value-add share repurchases was a gain in per share intrinsic value for continuing shareholders. The less obvious and longer-term reward was a share price that reflected the sound management of the company. Buffett preferred to partner with "shareholder-conscious managers."

Nebraska Furniture Mart

Nebraska Furniture Mart was still earning an excellent return on capital for shareholders, but it provided just as much value to customers through lower prices for high-quality merchandise.

How did it do this? In short, it sold a lot of merchandise through one location and relentlessly controlled expenses. Nebraska Furniture Mart operated on a gross profit margin* in the mid-20% range. By comparison Levitz Furniture, the industry leader at the time, had a gross profit margin of 44.4%. Levitz's operating expenses (all the other costs that go into running a store such as payroll, advertising, and upkeep of the buildings) amounted to 35.6% compared to Nebraska Furniture Mart's costs of 16.5%. Buffett estimated that Nebraska Furniture Mart saved its customers over $30 million each year due to its lean operating structure. All of this is that much more impressive since Buffett considered the Levitz operation well managed.

---

* The amount left over on a sale after paying for the goods sold, but before other operating expenses.

What was the secret? Buffett compared the Blumkin family to Ben Franklin and Horatio Alger and said they applied themselves with enthusiasm and energy, stayed within their circle of competence, and always acted honestly. Buffett saw the best of himself and Berkshire in the Blumkin Family.

See's Candies

Table 4.35: See's Candies, select data

($ and lbs in thousands)							
Year	Revenues	Profit[1]	Pounds sold	# Stores		Price / lb	Profit / lb
1984	$135,946	$13,380	24,759	214		$5.49	$0.54
1983	133,531	13,699	24,651	207		5.42	0.56
1982	123,662	11,875	24,216	202		5.11	0.49
1981	112,578	10,779	24,052	199		4.68	0.45
1980	97,715	7,547	24,065	191		4.06	0.31
1979	87,314	6,330	23,985	188		3.64	0.26
1978	73,653	6,178	22,407	182		3.29	0.28
1977	62,886	6,154	20,921	179		3.01	0.29
1976	56,333	5,569	20,553	173		2.74	0.27
1975	50,492	5,132	19,134	172		2.64	0.27
1974	41,248	3,021	17,883	170		2.31	0.17
1973	35,050	1,940	17,813	169		1.97	0.11
1972	$31,337	$2,083	16,954	167		$1.85	$0.12
1. Operating profit after tax.				Total gain:		197%	340%
				Compounded:		9.5%	13.1%

Sources: Berkshire Hathaway Annual Report 1984 and author's calculations.

If Nebraska Furniture Mart earned Buffett's high praise, See's really got his blood pumping. According to the 1984 Annual Report, identifiable assets for See's averaged $63 million and after-tax profits of $13.4 million equated to a return of 21%. On tangible assets of $28.2 million, the return was even higher: 47%. The actual economic return of See's was even better considering not all aspects of the business were part of the accounting. The report only listed tangible assets; it did not account for the spontaneous liabilities associated with conducting business, such as accounts payable. Since others provided part of the capital to operate the business, the company did not need to fund it. Given this assumption and the use of a seasonal line of credit to fund short-term inventory, the returns on net tangible assets, or equity, were likely well above 100% for the candy company.

Still, the business wasn't perfect. The boxed-chocolate industry suffered from marginal profitability and slow growth. The latter ailment also beset See's. Same-store sales fell 1.1% in 1984, though total poundage was up 0.6% because of store growth. If pounds sold only grew through physical store expansion, the per-pound selling cost would, by definition, increase—a result that could not go on forever.

Despite these problems See's had clear pricing power. Over the thirteen years that Berkshire (via Blue Chip) had owned See's, it was able to increase its per-pound selling price by 9.5% per year, and its per-pound profits by 13%. Over that same period the price level increased, on average, 7.9% per year.

Given the success of See's against the backdrop of weak industry conditions, the natural question is how? Buffett said it was the company's relentless focus on quality. Competitors, he said in his letter, would, "add preservatives or freeze the finished product in order to smooth the production cycle and thereby lower unit costs. We reject such techniques … ." See's was willing to put up with the headaches that came with trying to produce and deliver product in a short window of time during the holiday season using nothing but the freshest ingredients.

The month prior to Christmas accounted for 40% of the volume and 75% of the profit for the year. Easter and Valentine's Day also did well but the remainder of the year was spent treading water. The success of See's seemed to stem from the company's willingness to think and act long term and to accept short-term pain in exchange for long-term profitability. It focused on the customer and built its business around it, rather than trying to smooth out operations and manage the business from an accounting viewpoint first. See's was an excellent cash cow for Berkshire—one that would continue to deliver profits to Omaha for redeployment into the ever-growing Berkshire empire.

The Buffalo News

The Buffalo News delivered a $27.3 million pre-tax profit to Berkshire in 1984. Compared to what it earned in 1983,* this represented an almost $8 million or 41% increase. Competition, or the lack thereof now that *The Courier-Express* folded, was a major contributor to the success of *The Buffalo News*. So too were its customer-centric policies which were, somewhat unexpectedly at first glance, very similar to See's.

Coming out on top in a winner-takes-all contest helped tremendously, but the paper deserved its success. Like See's, it delivered (no pun intended) more value to its customers than the competition. Buffett summed up its strategy this way: "Since high standards are not imposed by the marketplace, management must impose its own." This was no different than the self-imposed quality standards at See's, which paid for the highest-quality ingredients, almost regardless of cost.

---

* At a company level, pre-tax. *The Buffalo News* was owned via Blue Chip Stamps, so a comparison of Berkshire's proportional share of the paper would not have made sense.

The newspaper's news hole, meaning its ratio of news to total printed pages, was 50.9% in 1984. This compared to more typical levels between 35% to 40% at similar papers. *The News* was willing to incur the additional cost of newsprint paper as well as more newsroom staff than competitors. It was rewarded with higher readership, which was in turn valued by advertisers.

Two other related factors played an important role in the paper's success. For one, the readership of the paper was concentrated into the Buffalo, New York area. This translated into high value to advertisers. Paid advertising by a grocery store that was viewed by a reader 100 miles away, for example, would be wasted. In fact, the term used for such an occurrence was wasted circulation.

The penetration ratio was another success factor. Since *The Buffalo News* reached a very high percentage of Buffalo residents, advertisers wanting to reach those subscribers could easily do so. The paper's penetration ratio and the relevance of readership to potential advertisers can be thought of visually as two overlapping circles. The wider the circles, the greater the penetration ratio; the more overlap between the two circles, the more shared customers between the paper and its paid advertisers.

Insurance

Berkshire's underwriting loss in 1984 resulted in a what Buffett called a humbling combined ratio of 136%[*] (see Table 4.36). The industry, by comparison, wrote at a ratio of 117.7% and was not increasing premiums fast enough to make up for increases in underlying costs. This was the third year in a row that Berkshire's experience was worse than the industry.

---

[*] This ratio was calculated directly from the reported financial statements. Buffett calculates a ratio of 134% which excluded structured settlements and the assumption of loss reserves. The two figures are close enough; both reflect a terrible underwriting experience.

Table 4.36: Insurance Group, select information

($ thousands)	1984	1983	1982
Premiums written, net	$133,558	$149,849	$149,091
Premiums earned			
Specialized auto and general liability	64,003	68,148	69,026
Workers' compensation	22,665	18,849	15,951
Reinsurance	16,066	26,889	27,408
Home State multiple lines	32,598	35,328	37,552
Structured settlements and portfolio reinsurance	4,910	3,266	3,008
	140,242	152,480	152,945
Underwriting gain (loss), pre-tax			
Specialized auto and general liability	(16,049)	(14,880)	(12,647)
Workers' compensation[1]	(12,560)	(1,091)	2,658
Reinsurance	(12,703)	(8,387)	(7,524)
Home State multiple lines	(4,101)	(8,834)	(3,949)
Structured settlements and portfolio reinsurance	(2,647)	(680)	(96)
	($48,060)	(33,872)	($21,558)
Combined ratio (statutory)	135.9%	122.8%	115.0%

Footnote:
1. Workers' Compensation coverage written by Home State is not broken out per the footnote to the financial statements.

Note: The data in this table was taken from the summary of segment results section of the Annual Report and differs in some cases with figures listed in earlier reporting periods.
Sources: Berkshire Hathaway Annual Reports 1982, 1984.

The poor industry performance and even poorer Berkshire results did not dissuade Buffett. That year, Berkshire added capital to its reinsurance unit, Columbia Insurance Company, to continue growing the structured settlements business. He expected a lot of competition but satisfactory returns. Berkshire would continue to use its financial strength to its advantage, and only write business that made sense.

The financial strength was hard to see precisely on Berkshire's consolidated financials. Prior to 1981, Berkshire had presented separate condensed group financial statements that provided some additional detail on balance sheet items such as the investment portfolio, plant and equipment, loss liabilities, unearned premiums, and other items. From these it was clear exactly how much shareholders' equity was attributable to the Insurance Group. Detail on the income statement items largely remained in subsequent reports, but a holistic balance sheet was not provided.

Even without the specific detail it was clear Berkshire remained heavily weighted toward insurance.*

Making some assumptions,** we can estimate that Berkshire's written volume in 1984 would have represented just 17% of equity capital—a ratio far below the capacity of an insurer*** and an indication as to how much Buffett and his managers had put the brakes on operations during the period of weak pricing.

GEICO dwarfed Berkshire's Insurance Group. Looking through to Berkshire's share of GEICO's premiums (Berkshire owned 36% of GEICO at this time), Berkshire's share of its premium volume in 1984 was $320 million. Buffett praised its managers, Jack Byrne, Bill Snyder, and Lou Simpson for creating and sustaining a "major, sustainable competitive advantage" in an industry where such an advantage was almost unheard of. He heaped additional praise on Simpson, who, "has the rare combination of temperamental and intellectual characteristics that produce outstanding long-term investment performance."

As good as GEICO was—and it was (and is) a very good business—its advantage stopped at its core business. It was natural for a management team to build on its success and expand into adjacent areas. Yet attempts to do so had largely failed, and this refocused GEICO's management back on the core automobile insurance business.

Errors in Loss Reserving

The business lesson for 1984 was on a topic central to insurance, Berkshire's largest and most important division. It also shed some light onto what created the large underwriting losses of the last several years and why management couldn't immediately stem the red ink. Central to the insurance business are estimates of its future losses. Because they are just that, estimates, they are subject to error at best. At worst they can lead to lying and fraud.

In a normal business, profits or losses are known fairly rapidly. A box of chocolates that cost $4 to produce and sell and that was sold for $5 would clearly generate a profit of $1. An insurer, on the other hand, takes in its revenues first (whether earned or unearned) and must estimate upfront what its future costs will be over the life of the insurance contract. It not only doesn't know how *much* it will cost, but it might not even know *when* the cost will come.

---

* Without more detailed information, what could be gleaned from the 1984 Annual Report was that the insurance segment represented $1.6 billion of the $2.0 billion of identifiable assets at year-end. Clearly a large chunk of the $1.3 billion of consolidated Berkshire equity was attributable to the insurance companies, though the specific amount was unknown.

** If we assume that equity was 50% of total assets, an assumption made based on the known 1980 ratio, Berkshire's insurance companies would have had roughly $800 million of equity at year-end 1984.

*** Ratios above 100% were not uncommon, according to later Berkshire Annual Reports.

In short-tail lines of insurance, like automobile insurance, policies are written for six months to a year and claims are paid out accordingly. There may be a slight delay in when a claim happens and when it is reported (these are referred to as incurred but not reported losses or IBNR), but generally the insurer knows very quickly.

In long-tail lines of business, such as with Berkshire's reinsurance or specialty units, claims might take years or even decades to come to light. Results from year to year understandably move around, though provided the insurer sets premiums at a level that reflects its costs *over time*, it will ultimately report a profit.

Insurers track their guesses for future profitability of the business they write in what are known as loss development tables.* As time goes on and claims are paid out, the true profitability emerges. This can take some time and the road can be bumpy. Buffett's 1984 letter contained a table of the five years ended in 1984 that listed underwriting results both as originally reported and as corrected one year later. The table showed one year of favorable loss development (1980) followed by three years of results that deteriorated in hindsight. The question mark left in the table suggested the loss in 1984 was anyone's guess. Berkshire tried to be conservative in its underwriting, but the track record suggested results would only worsen.

Table 4.37: Insurance underwriting profit/(loss)

($ thousands)	Original report	One year later
1984	($45,413)	?
1983	(33,192)	(50,974)
1982	(21,462)	(25,066)
1981	1,478	(1,118)
1980	6,738	14,887

Note: Excludes structure settlement and loss-reserve assumption business.
Source: Berkshire Hathaway Chairman's letter 1984.

Not only was Berkshire suffering from current industry weakness, but the business it wrote in years past was haunting it. Accounting and insurance reporting conventions dictate that as loss estimates for prior years worsen, revisions are included with the current year's underwriting results. For example, consider a $100 policy written in year one, with an expected profit of $5. Now consider that in the next year that profit was revised to a loss of $5. The $5 profit would remain in the first year (the insurer wouldn't restate its earnings) but instead a $10 loss would be booked to losses in year two. It was simply the nature of the business and its accounting

---

* Berkshire's 10K reports began including loss development tables for the 2001 reporting period. Until then, shareholders could only glean information from the aggregate loss development figure presented in the footnotes to the financial statements.

conventions and made for a bumpy ride. To add insult to injury, an optimistic insurer who overestimated profit paid more tax than would have otherwise been necessary. These overpayments eventually correct themselves but there is no interest received on the amount overpaid.

Buffett was more than embarrassed by the missed estimates. He felt he had let shareholders down and said so in his letter. He wrote that his error in reporting "is a source of particular chagrin to me because (1) I like for you to be able to count on what I say; (2) our insurance managers and I undoubtedly acted with less urgency than we would have had we understood the full extent of our losses."

Revisions in 1984 to prior year estimates totaled $17.8 million, or 12.7% of premiums earned that year. These revisions stemmed primarily from the reinsurance segment, which itself was subject to the estimates provided by the primary insurers whose business they took on. Most of the remainder of the change in loss reserves was due to workers' compensation, which was another long-tail type of insurance whose ultimate profitability took time to materialize.

The insurance business had another quirk which made trust and track records important. The revisionary-type scenario above is simply a part of the business. Any one year or a few years might be poor, so an insurer with a long-term track record of overly optimistic reserving would find itself nearly out of business. In such a case, its management could forestall that day of reckoning by continuing to write new business—even at a rate that would ensure a loss. Since premiums generate cash upfront to pay claims later, unscrupulous managements could bring the ship right up to the edge of a cliff before falling straight off. As Buffett put it: "insurance is different: you can be broke but flush."

Buffett openly worried about the effect of these "walking dead" type companies, and their effect on Berkshire. Not only would Berkshire suffer once as a competitor when those companies drove down premium rates, but again via state guarantee-type arrangements which bailed out policyholders of failed firms. He urged regulators to more strictly police the industry to mitigate the damage from such events.

Washington Public Power Supply System

From late 1983 through mid-1984, Berkshire's Insurance Group purchased large quantities of bonds in Washington Public Power Supply System (WPPSS). Specifically, Berkshire's $139 million investment was in Projects 1, 2 and 3. This distinction was important as Projects 4 and 5 were abandoned and $2.2 billion of related bonds languished in default. The default was what presented the opportunity to Berkshire.

There was acknowledged risk that the investment could prove unsatisfactory, but both Buffett and Charlie Munger judged the risk appropriate. The default issues with Projects 4 and 5 meant they could pay a lower price (and therefore receive a higher yield) for the investment in Projects 1, 2, and 3 compared to other bonds available at the time. Those projects also had important differences in credit quality. Berkshire's $139 million investment earned $22.7 million after tax, equating to a 16.3% unleveraged return. He said a similar-earning business might fetch between $250 million and $300 million.

The description of the investment read like that of an equity investment, but the WPPSS investment was in its bonds, an important distinction. Buffett wrote that a "bond-as-a-business" mindset "may strike you as a bit quirky. However, we believe that many staggering errors by investors could have been avoided if they had viewed bond investment with a businessman's perspective." Focusing on the underlying business—the ultimate source of interest payments to bondholders *and* any residual earnings accruing to equity holders—led to more rational thinking.

The bond-as-a-business investment was a large one. Just like Berkshire's equity investments, it did not make inconsequential investments in attractive bond investments. The $139 million investment represented almost 12% of Berkshire's 1984 average equity and 7% of its average assets. If these WPPSS bonds defaulted like Projects 4 and 5, Berkshire would take a large hit. Buffett and Munger were willing to make such "intelligent-but-with-some-chance-of-looking-like-an-idiot" investments because they thought the odds were in their favor. Controlling 47% of Berkshire's stock between them also helped.

Berkshire's financial strength played a role in allowing it to take calculated risks in pursuit of superior returns. In writing far less business than it otherwise was capable, financial strength often penalized Berkshire's results. In cases such as WPPSS, Berkshire could make the investment without much fear of backlash from insurance regulators because it possessed a large margin of safety in its capital position. Other insurers often wrote as much as their balance sheets would allow. This handicapped them since their capital position was "not strong enough to withstand a big error, no matter how attractive an investment opportunity might appear when analyzed on the basis of probabilities." The result was that these insurers had to invest much more conservatively, hurting their long-term investment results.

The WPPSS bonds were an attractive security in an asset class that did not generally interest Berkshire. Even though inflation had diminished substantially, it was always lurking just around the corner. Owners of businesses would be hurt by inflation, to be sure, but bondholders would be in a far worse position that could potentially wipe out their advantageous capital position.

Mutual Savings

Charlie Munger's Chairman's letter to Wesco shareholders (again included in the Berkshire Annual Report) provided readers with an education on banking. His comments on the thrift (savings and loan) industry contrasted Mutual Savings' conservative operating practices to a world where competitors were increasingly taking on significant risks.

For Berkshire shareholders who had become familiar with the banking business via their investment in the now-divested Illinois National Bank, Mutual Savings would seem familiar. Munger said Mutual Savings had three major characteristics. It:

1. Maintained a high level of shareholders' equity compared to total assets and savings account liabilities;
2. Held a large proportion of cash and marketable securities to offset those liabilities;
3. And had a low-yielding mortgage portfolio, primarily a result of its branch divestiture in 1980.

Though the average yield on its mortgage portfolio was below the bank's cost of funds paid to depositors, it had remained profitable every year due to its large marketable securities portfolio. Just like Berkshire's Insurance Group, Mutual Savings was waiting for the right terms and conditions on which to do additional business.

The summary data on Mutual Savings provided in the Berkshire Annual Report illustrated its conservatism. Its assets were funded by a stable source of deposits and backed by a large amount of shareholders' equity and liquid resources.*

Table 4.38: Mutual Savings and Loan, select data, 1984

(*$ millions*)	
Cash and marketable securities	89
Loan portfolio	95
Total assets	295
Savings account liabilities	228
Shareholders' equity	62
Loan portfolio (% total assets)	32%
Loan portfolio (% deposits)	42%
Shareholders' equity (% total assets)	21%

Sources: Berkshire Hathaway Annual Report 1984 and author's calculations.

---

* It is not uncommon to see banks with loans equal to 80% of assets and over 100% of deposits.

Banking then and now, almost by definition, involved borrowing short and lending long. A bank took its depositors' money, most of which was usually on demand, and lent it on terms to borrowers to purchase homes, finance businesses, and for other needs. The mismatch between the typically lower short-term interest rates paid to depositors and the typically higher rates received from borrowers (the spread) is how a bank makes money. Such an arrangement carried a small risk that interest rates would increase rapidly and cause the cost of money (the interest rate paid) to exceed the rate at which it was lent out.

Savings and loan institutions (also known as thrifts) such as Mutual Savings benefitted from quasi-governmental protections over other traditional banking operations. These protections gave them a slight edge over traditional banks and reduced competition. When regulations changed allowing free competition for deposits (i.e. no limit on interest rates paid), some banks (and more acutely thrifts) found themselves paying higher rates to depositors than those earned from lending—a disastrous backward result.

Mutual Savings was staying far away from more lenient lending practices. In addition to the cost of money (interest paid to depositors), a banking institution also faced costs from losses on bad loans. Just like the insurance business, those losses can take time, sometimes years, to materialize. Munger described "a sort of Gresham's law" where "bad loan practice drives out good," and where some institutions, attempting to cover rising interest costs, began lending to increasingly riskier borrowers.

Munger knew it was only a matter of time before trouble arose. He decried the actions of competitors not just because it hurt Mutual Savings, but because competitors were profiting from using the government's credit. Since depositors benefitted from government guarantees on their savings if the institution failed, they were indifferent to how their money was used. Losses above a bank's equity capital would ultimately accrue, in the case of the thrift industry, to the Federal Savings and Loan Insurance Corporation (FSLIC), the government arm that insured their deposits.

Munger used an automobile insurance example to illustrate Mutual Savings' position: Mutual Savings was like the sober and careful driver who drove few miles but had to pay an insurance premium based on the risk attributes of a larger pool of drivers. Those other drivers drove a high number of miles and led other-than-sober lives. Through the premiums it paid for deposit insurance, Mutual Savings was subsidizing the rest of the industry. Munger praised Federal Home Loan Bank Board Chairman Edwin R. Gray for taking on the unenviable task of reining in the risky behaviors of less conservative industry participants.

Mutual Savings' unwillingness to participate in risking lending practices had caused a decline in business, but there was some good news. In accounting terms Mutual Savings' loan portfolio declined by 11% to $95 million. However, during the year it agreed to forward purchase a $30 million pool of government-guaranteed mortgages that yielded 15% on its $19 million purchase price.* In coming years, the loan portfolio yield of Mutual Savings would start covering its funding cost as these higher-yielding mortgages became part of the mix. The commitment to purchase these mortgages in the future was the economic equivalent of making a loan during 1984. Munger told Wesco shareholders that in substance its mortgage portfolio had *increased* by 7%.

Dividend Policy

Buffett repeatedly told shareholders why he disliked dividends. He used a long section in his 1984 Chairman's letter to illustrate why in detail. Buffett considered capital allocation crucial and thought "managers and owners should think hard about the circumstances under which earnings should be retained and under which they should be distributed." He did not like the fixed percentage-of-earnings dividend payout ratios that other managements blindly targeted without any thought to alternative uses for that capital. Instead, opportunity cost should be front of mind and attention paid to economic reality.

The key was getting managers to think like owners and compare *all* investment opportunities—even if they lay outside of the manager's own business. Some managers displayed contradictory behavior. On the one hand they might tell an under-earning subsidiary to give the parent company its earnings, which were then reinvested into a high-earning one (a rational decision on its own). The problem was those managers would then turn around and have earnings retained at the parent level, even though there were higher-earning opportunities elsewhere.

The other consideration relating to dividend policy was inflation. In an inflationary environment, a capital-intensive business required reinvestment to maintain its unit volume. Even if a business showed a bottom line profit, the economic reality could be such that a portion, or even 100%, of those profits weren't economically real.** A business that paid out in dividends more than its economic earnings would face oblivion as its competitive position and/or financial strength eroded. As an example, recall the textile companies from the first part of this book. A business that faced higher costs due to inflation and did not have the capital on hand to pay was no different than the textile companies in the early part of the twentieth century that paid out dividends when they should have used that cash to replenish depreciated equipment.***

---

* The higher effective yield arises due to the discount paid relative to the face value of the mortgages. It is just like buying a bond at a discount.

** The terms Buffett used were ersatz and restricted.

*** Consider another example. You are in a business selling one item annually. You have $90,000 invested in the business, which represents the entire cost of that one item. You sell the item for $100,000, netting a $10,000

Those textile companies eventually suffered mightily, and so too would the owner of a capital-intensive business operating in an inflationary environment.

Buffett said Berkshire's own dividend policy would be to retain all earnings. Berkshire met the test of creating one dollar of market value for every dollar retained and would have done shareholders a disservice by instituting a dividend. Looking forward, he even teased a future use of those retained earnings: He thought the insurance industry was set for a rebound in 1985, and a financially strong competitor like Berkshire stood to do well with available cash to invest.

Buffett's 1984 letter concluded with two advertisements. One was the same business-wanted advertisement as prior letters looking for acquisition candidates. The other was an invitation for his shareholder-partners to the annual meeting in Omaha where a purchase at Nebraska Furniture Mart could "save far more than enough to pay for your trip." After twenty years under Buffett's leadership, Berkshire had become a far more diversified and profitable business, and one where shareholders might have—dare it be said—fun.

Decade in Review

The changes that occurred during Warren Buffett's second decade at the helm of Berkshire Hathaway can be summed up in two words: size and scope. Its equity capital grew by a factor of more than fourteen, from $88.2 million to almost $1.3 billion. Its insurance operations grew both organically and from investments in multiple Home State operations, workers' compensation, and reinsurance. Berkshire grew its stable of wholly-owned businesses into diverse industries such as steel products and newspapers, and through Blue Chip Stamps and its marketable securities portfolio, into many diverse enterprises.

The question of just where all that additional equity capital came from can be summed up in a few categories:

---

profit. The next year the cost of the item, because of inflation, increases to $100,000. You must now take your entire profit from the prior year of $10,000 plus your original capital of $90,000 just to buy the item to sell the next year. Even if your profit on the next year's sale went up by the same amount, you'd still be left with a permanent and required investment into the business that had to come from profit (or borrowed money or additional equity).

Table 4.39: Reconciliation of shareholders' equity, 1965–1984

($ millions)	1965–74	1975–84	1965–84
Beginning of period shareholders' equity	$22	$88	$22
Net income - operations	57	366	423
Net income - realized gains	7	199	207
Unrealized appreciation of investments	0	486	486
Mergers/divestitures	0	133	133
Dividends/treasury stock	(3)	0	(3)
Other/misc.	4	0	4
End of period shareholders' equity	$88	$1,272	$1,272
Change in equity during period	$66	$1,184	$1,250

Sources: Berkshire Hathaway Annual Reports and author's calculations.

Table 4.40: Contribution toward change in equity during period

	1965–74	1975–84	1965–84
Net income - operations	86%	31%	34%
Net income - realized gains	11%	17%	17%
Unrealized appreciation of investments	0%	41%	39%
Mergers/divestitures	0%	11%	11%
Dividends/treasury stock	(4%)	0%	(0%)
Other/misc.	7%	0%	0%
Total	100%	100%	100%

Note: The 1965–84 category does not add to 100% due to rounding.
Sources: Berkshire Hathaway Annual Reports and author's calculations.

Table 4.40 illustrates the degree to which Berkshire's investment portfolio became the driver of growth. Berkshire took advantage of chances to buy businesses outright but found more opportunity to buy pieces of good businesses via investments in their publicly traded stock. Accounting considerations were relegated to the background in favor of economic reality, though pains were taken to reconcile the two in communications with shareholders. Even Berkshire's largest division, insurance, found itself shadowed by the investment portfolio (which, to be fair, funded a large portion of it). By the end of the decade Berkshire's share of GEICO's premium volume eclipsed that of its own group of insurance businesses. The mergers/divestitures net row above aggregates three distinct and important transactions:

1. In 1977, Berkshire merged with Diversified Retailing, which resulted in a net of about $9 million added to Berkshire's equity capital.*

---

* This figure does not include the $3.7 million of additional net income added that year due to the merger. It is included in the Net income – operations line.

2. In late 1980, Berkshire divested of the Illinois National Bank and Trust. That transaction (effectively accomplished via a treasury stock transaction) reduced Berkshire's equity by approximately $29 million.

3. In 1983, Berkshire merged with Blue Chip Stamps, adding a net of about $154 million to Berkshire's equity.

The result for shareholders was that book value per share increased from $90.02 at year-end 1974 to $1,108.77 at year-end 1984—a compounded annual rate of return of 28.5%. Importantly, this result was on a *per share* basis. There had been some dilution to shareholders as shares outstanding grew from 980,000 to 1,147,000 (1.6% per annum) over the preceding ten years, but by and large Buffett had not enlarged his managerial kingdom at the expense of shareholders. On the contrary, during the Diversified, Illinois National, and Blue Chip transactions, he went out of his way to ensure fairness to his shareholder partners.

A powerful tailwind pushed Berkshire's stock price upward over the decade. The market rewarded the high growth rate of underlying intrinsic value (proxied by the change in book value) with an increasingly higher price-to-book value. Steadfast investors owning Berkshire for the entire decade were rewarded with a return of 40% *per year*.

Figure 4.1: Berkshire Hathaway stock price, 1975–1984

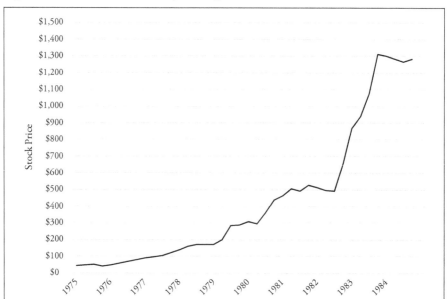

Sources: *Of Permanent Value* (Kilpatrick), Berkshire Hathaway Annual Reports 1975–1984, and author's calculations.

Figure 4.2: Berkshire Hathaway price to book ratio, 1975–1984

Sources: *Of Permanent Value* (Kilpatrick), Berkshire Hathaway Annual Reports 1975–1984, and author's calculations.

The fuel for this remarkable growth was largely Berkshire's Insurance Group. Growth over the preceding decade was impressive, even after pulling back toward the end of the decade because of industry weakness. Yet the financials understated Berkshire's massive push into insurance, as its 36% investment in GEICO was responsible for an additional $336 million in premiums on a look-through basis.[*]

Table 4.41: Berkshire Hathaway, select data

	1984	1974
Written insurance premiums	$134	$61
Earned insurance premiums	140	61
Float, average	253	79
Cash and investments	$1,714	$140
Investment income	84	8

Sources: Berkshire Hathaway Annual Reports 1974, 1984.

---

[*] A look-through analysis takes a company-level figure, in this case premiums but most often earnings, and adjusts for the level of ownership.

Berkshire's investment portfolio grew steadily, funded through funds generated via float, retained earnings, and additional capital contributed to the insurance companies. The composition of the portfolio at the beginning and end of this decade highlights Buffett's propensity for holding companies for a long time and his increasing tendency to concentrate bets. Of the $1.3 billion common stock portfolio at year-end 1984, almost one-third was GEICO. The top four positions (GEICO, General Foods, Exxon, and *The Washington Post*) represented 75% of the entire portfolio in 1984. The top four positions in 1974 represented 48% of the portfolio. *The Washington Post*, which represented a quarter of the portfolio in 1974, was the only investment in the top four that extended over the entire decade and had dropped to fourth place. Berkshire was much more concentrated at the end of the decade than at the beginning.

Table 4.42: Berkshire Hathaway common stock portfolio, select detail

($ thousands)	1984	% of total	1974	% of total
Affiliated Publications	$32,908	2.6%	$1,023	2.9%
American Broadcasting Companies, Inc.	46,738	3.7%		
California Water Service Co.			3,151	9.1%
Exxon Corporation	175,307	13.8%		
GEICO Corporation	397,300	31.3%		
General Foods Corporation	226,137	17.8%		
Handy & Harmon	38,662	3.0%	1,337	3.8%
Interpublic Group, Co.	28,149	2.2%	2,772	8.0%
Munsingwear, Inc.			2,094	6.0%
National Presto Industries			2,592	7.4%
Northwest Industries	27,242	2.1%		
Ogilvy & Mather International			1,550	4.5%
Omaha National Corporation			1,066	3.1%
Sperry & Hutchinson Company			1,758	5.1%
Time, Inc.	109,162	8.6%		
Washington Post Company - Class B	149,955	11.8%	8,000	23.0%
All others	37,326	2.9%	9,458	27.2%
Total common stocks	$1,268,886	100.0%	$34,802	100.0%

Notes:

1. Totals do not add to 100% due to rounding.

2. 1974 & 1984: Market values.

3. 1974: Detail on investments greater than $1 million in value. All others represents 36 companies.

4. 1984: Detail taken from the Chairman's letter in the Berkshire Hathaway Annual Report.

Sources: Berkshire Hathaway 10K filing 1974, Berkshire Hathaway Annual Report 1984, and author's calculations.

Buffett was comfortable with this level of investment concentration because he had conviction, and because Berkshire's financial strength allowed for it. The float generated by the Insurance Group was technically the result of the assumption of liabilities to finance additional asset purchases. But these liabilities had no due date and could be controlled for the most part by writing additional business. Berkshire's financial debt at year-end 1984 was low, and at $127 million, it represented just 10% of shareholders' equity. What's more, it consisted of long-term notes with varying maturities stretching over twenty years into the future.

Berkshire's diverse sources of earnings power also contributed to its ability and willingness to concentrate its investment portfolio. Berkshire could count on cash coming in the door from the recently acquired Nebraska Furniture Mart, its now-profitable Buffalo News, See's Candies, and the various businesses under the Wesco umbrella. Pre-tax operating earnings from its non-insurance businesses after deducting interest (but excluding amortization of goodwill and the discretionary shareholder-designated contributions) amounted to $66 million in 1984. This figure was also outside of the $69 million of pre-tax net investment income largely attributable to the insurance segment.

The Berkshire that emerged from Buffett's two decades of polishing, painting, and refining was radically changed from the money-losing textile operation he inherited in 1965. Shareholders owned, through Berkshire, investments in many diverse business operations—some in whole, some in part. They could look forward to communications that did not just report troubles but opportunities. Berkshire going into Buffett's third decade of control had *prospects*.

Lessons: 1975–1984

1. Even good businesses can experience challenges. Buffett and Munger faced many problems from the Insurance Group during the decade and oversaw massive underwriting losses toward the end of it. Even See's Candies, a wonderful business by all accounts, had its problems dealing with certain input costs.
2. Competition can be brutal and sometimes irrational. The actions of competitors in the insurance industry and their lack of understanding about the true, long-term cost of doing business, caused industry premiums to be inadequate. Not only did those specific competitors suffer but others, including Berkshire, suffered as well. In a completely different business, *The Buffalo News*, the paper almost failed because of competition. There was no room for two competing papers, but the competitor did not go down without a protracted legal fight.
3. Inflation wreaks havoc on *all* businesses, and especially those with high capital requirements. It causes some earnings to be illusory or, to use Buffett's words,

ersatz or restricted. It forces capital to be reinvested in a business just to stand still and maintain unit volume. Sometimes inflation can be other than just monetary, such as the social inflation in jury awards.

4. Mergers/divestitures are okay if done at an appropriate valuation. What truly matters to shareholders is not the size of a company, but its growth in *intrinsic value per share*. Managers can destroy value by issuing undervalued shares to complete acquisitions.

5. Economics vs. accounting. Owners' wealth is built over the long run by focusing on economic realities. Accounting is only the starting point of the analysis, and it oftentimes "obscures rather than illuminates," according to Buffett. In Berkshire's case, this was an acute problem since significant value resided in the look-through earnings of its investees via its marketable securities portfolio.

Table 4.43: Berkshire Hathaway consolidated balance sheets, 1974–1984

($ thousands)	1974	1975	1976	Original 1977	Restated 1977	1978	1979	1980	1981	Original 1982	Restated 1982	1983	1984
Current assets													
Cash	$4,231	$6,045	$3,437	$4,921	$13,996	$13,001	$14,924	$9,993	$7,232	$7,392	$7,762	$6,161	$3,682
Bonds, at amortized cost					132,929	157,651	185,564	187,802	206,078	189,330	189,330	208,245	303,928
Marketable equity securities (including preferred)	82,639	94,936	104,705	145,960	163,294	283,185	411,358	525,947	641,269	920,909	979,024	1,232,150	1,235,903
Preferred stock	2,855	2,558	22,287	23,232									
Common stock	50,670	39,341	53,108	83,657									
Invested cash, U.S. Treasury Bills and other short-term investments, at cost which approximates market					35,730	61,056	18,172	50,546	63,529	51,814	58,765	75,343	170,039
Total investments, other than affiliates	136,164	136,836	180,100	252,849	331,953	501,892	615,094	764,295	910,876	1,162,053	1,227,119	1,515,738	1,709,870
Investments in affiliates:													
The Illinois National Bank & Trust Co. of Rockford					25,839	27,146	28,785						
Wesco Financial Corporation					43,892	49,370	56,750	63,040	68,874	75,858			
Investment in Mutual Savings and Loan Association											23,758	27,004	32,927
Other unconsolidated subsidiaries					1,627	1,477	1,377	1,187					
Total investments in affiliates					71,358	77,993	86,912	64,227	68,874	75,858	23,758	27,004	32,927
Accounts receivable from customers, agents and others					38,009	45,283	52,231	49,861	49,901	109,768	113,770	72,813	88,489
Inventories					23,776	23,029	25,704	23,802	22,120	20,670	26,039	37,516	41,332
Accounts receivable, net - textiles	4,378	6,567	8,102	9,169									
Accounts receivable, net - other	13,513	13,143	15,628	22,035									
Inventories - textiles	6,000	8,136	8,976	9,766									
Inventories - other		0	326	242									

Continued...

...Continued from prior page

($ thousands)	1974	1975	1976	Original 1977	Restated 1977	1978	1979	1980	1981	Original 1982	Restated 1982	1983	1984
Property, plant, and equipment, net:													
Textiles	2,333	2,196											
Manufacturing			3,415	3,417									
Insurance	1,581	1,526	1,636	2,164									
Property, plant, and equipment, net					47,106	47,877	49,793	51,484	51,472	54,070	63,020	69,749	67,919
Investment in bank subsidiary	22,417	23,424	24,732	25,839									
Common Stock of Blue Chip Stamps	16,924	18,777	27,304	35,774									
Investment in other subsidiaries	1,187	1,120	880	1,612									
Goodwill											13,823	79,327	77,269
Deferred insurance premium acquisition costs	4,400	2,950	6,820	9,810	10,852	13,846	13,652	14,163	12,313	10,264			
Other assets	3,087	5,021	1,685	1,645	35,093	34,691	33,955	32,756	35,123	45,549	57,993	48,084	13,715
Total assets	216,214	225,741	283,041	379,241	572,143	757,612	892,265	1,010,581	1,157,911	1,485,624	1,533,284	1,856,392	2,035,203

($ thousands)	1974	1975	1976	Original 1977	Restated 1977	1978	1979	1980	1981	Original 1982	Restated 1982	1983	1984
Current liabilities													
Losses and loss adjustment expenses	72,761	73,033	85,152	133,592	139,461	180,870	197,697	199,128	190,970	193,477	193,477	212,706	243,298
Unearned premiums	21,705	22,344	36,737	52,191	57,128	69,368	73,604	73,281	62,269	58,414	58,414	55,783	49,099
Funds held under reinsurance treaties	2,857	2,939	3,783										
Amounts due for purchase of securities	294	680	839										
Accounts payable and accrued expenses	4,435	5,790	7,259										
Liability for unredeemed trading stamps					66,209	66,832	67,524	64,053	64,262	60,240	60,240	60,669	58,957

Continued...

...Continued from prior page

($ thousands)	1974	1975	1976	Original 1977	Restated 1977	1978	1979	1980	1981	Original 1982	Restated 1982	1983	1984
Accounts payable, accrued expenses, and other				17,216	35,466	33,983	38,792	43,462	51,915	48,340	50,552	58,094	73,346
Income taxes - current	164	179	3,346	1,524	6,492	10,768	10,411	7,919	13,759	21,868	22,007	8,511	11,432
Income taxes - deferred	3,044	2,519	4,677	6,588	7,793	36,034	52,079	63,329	87,089	149,987	149,987	194,462	177,907
Notes payable to bank				2,000	2,000								
7.50% debentures due 1987	556	506	464										
Promissory notes and debentures				4,343									
8.00% senior notes due 1993	20,000	20,000	20,000	20,000									
Sundry installment promissory notes	1,274	3,602	4,522										
Term loan payable to bank					13,500	13,500							
Senior notes payable					27,000	27,000							
Other notes and debentures payable					14,604	16,571							
Long-term debt							55,099	104,344	97,768	137,581	169,947	128,984	127,104
Total financial debt	*21,830*	*24,108*	*24,987*	*26,343*	*55,104*	*57,071*	*55,099*	*104,344*	*97,768*	*137,581*	*169,947*	*128,984*	*127,104*
Minority shareholders' interest	924	1,258	968	0	47,926	48,520	52,097	59,851	70,416	88,234	101,177	17,990	22,299
Other					0	0	0	0	0	0	0	0	0
Total liabilities	128,015	132,851	167,748	237,452	417,579	503,446	547,303	615,367	638,448	758,141	805,801	737,199	763,442
Shares Issued	*980*	*980*	*980*	*980*	*1,214*	*1,214*	*1,214*	*1,214*	*1,214*	*1,214*	*1,214*	*1,375*	*1,375*
Less: Treasury Shares	*0*	*0*	*(7)*	*(9)*	*(184)*	*(187)*	*(187)*	*(228)*	*(228)*	*(228)*	*(228)*	*(228)*	*(228)*
Shares outstanding (000's)	*980*	*980*	*973*	*971*	*1,031*	*1,027*	*1,027*	*986*	*987*	*987*	*987*	*1,147*	*1,147*
Total stockholders' equity	88,199	92,890	115,293	141,788	154,564	254,166	344,962	395,214	519,463	727,483	727,483	1,119,193	1,271,761
Total liabilities and stockholders' equity	$216,214	$225,741	$283,041	$379,241	$572,143	$757,612	$892,265	$1,010,581	$1,157,911	$1,485,624	$1,533,284	$1,856,392	$2,035,203

Note: The year 1977 was restated due to the merger with Diversified Retailing; 1983 was restated due to the merger with Blue Chip Stamps. Buffett's distaste for the presentation of Berkshire's consolidated financial statements is only compounded by trying to show them over multiple years.

Sources: Berkshire Hathaway Annual Reports, 1975–1984.

Table 4.44: Berkshire Hathaway consolidated statements of income

($ thousands)	1984	1983	Restated 1982	Original 1982	1981	1980	1979	1978	Restated 1977	Original 1977	1976	1975	1974
Insurance premiums earned	$140,242	$152,480	$152,945	$152,945	$159,013	$185,187	$181,949	$186,073	$143,087	$136,890	$80,780	$58,336	$60,574
Net sales and operating revenues of manufacturing, merchandising and service operations	500,219	381,674	306,564	267,622	263,374	259,200	247,952	235,576	203,752				
Net sales of textile products										48,189	47,174	32,833	32,592
Net sales of manufactured products													
Interest and dividend income	84,161	85,903	58,003	52,416	49,189	38,966	30,440	24,293	16,796	12,549	10,820	8,918	8,030
Real estate income				6,408	7,120	8,804	8,784	7,417		288	294	287	286
Equity in earnings excluding realized investment gain of Wesco Financial Corporation													
Equity in earnings excluding realized investment gain of Mutual Savings and Loan Association	4,557	3,669	3,960										
Total revenues	729,179	623,726	521,472	479,391	478,696	492,157	469,125	453,359	363,635	197,917	139,068	100,375	101,482
Insurance losses and loss adjustment expenses	141,550	134,109	121,996	121,996	103,417	118,230	120,337	132,263	96,869	91,585	55,376	47,238	47,120
Cost of products and services sold	296,770	214,362	177,508	146,081	155,661	160,261	158,710	151,521	130,647				
Cost of textile products sold										43,736	41,573	28,234	27,429
Cost of manufactured products sold													
Insurance underwriting expenses	46,752	52,243	52,508	52,508	54,119	60,219	57,870	50,810	40,417	39,122	24,694	21,745	20,346
Selling, administrative and other expenses	138,875	122,023	110,021	104,109	93,756	84,188	79,839	71,172	60,698	5,869	4,949	4,192	3,641
Interest expense										2,075	2,028	1,845	1,718
Interest expense and financing costs	14,734	15,104	14,995	11,828	11,486	9,185	5,729	5,058	4,789				
Total expenses	638,681	537,841	477,028	436,522	418,439	432,083	422,485	410,824	333,420	182,387	128,622	103,255	100,254

Continued...

...*Continued from prior page*

($ thousands)	1974	1975	1976	Original 1977	Restated 1977	1978	1979	1980	1981	Original 1982	Restated 1982	1983	1984
Earnings from consolidated operations including minority interest, before applicable income taxes, equity in earnings of unconsolidated subsidiaries and realized investment gain					30,215	42,535	46,640	60,074	60,257	42,869	44,444	85,885	90,498
Earnings (loss) from insurance underwriting and manufacturing operations before applicable income taxes	1,228	(2,880)	10,446	15,530									
Income tax expense applicable to above					9,487	10,735	9,796	13,943	12,091	2,386	2,524	10,353	16,420
Income tax credit (expense) applicable to operating loss (earnings)	2,010	4,141	(1,489)	(2,914)									
Earnings from continuing operations including minority interests, before equity in earnings of unconsolidated subsidiaries and realized investment gain					20,728	31,800	36,844	46,131	48,166	40,483	41,920	75,532	74,078
Minority interest in above					3,489	6,058	5,883	7,647	8,443	8,986	10,423	7,337	3,877
Earnings before equity in earnings of unconsolidated subsidiaries and realized investment gain					17,239	25,742	30,961	38,484	39,723	31,497	31,497	68,195	70,201
Earnings before equity in net earnings of other companies and realized investment gains (losses)...	3,239	1,261	8,957	12,615									
Equity in net earnings of bank subsidiary	4,093	3,450	3,750	3,550	3,550								

Continued...

...Continued from prior page

($ thousands)	1974	1975	1976	Original 1977	Restated 1977	1978	1979	1980	1981	Original 1982	Restated 1982	1983	1984
Equity in net earnings of Blue Chip Stamps	1,052	2,003	3,366	5,739									
Equity in net earnings of Wesco Financial Corp.					2,683								
Earnings before realized investment gains (losses)	8,384	6,714	16,073	21,904	23,472	25,742	30,961	38,484	39,723	31,497	31,497	68,195	70,201
Realized investment gains (losses)	(1,908)	(2,888)	9,962	6,870	13,310								
Applicable income tax (expense) credit	568	866	(3,200)	(2,050)	(4,448)								
Applicable minority interest					(1,941)								
Net realized investment gains (losses)	(1,340)	(2,022)	6,762	4,820	6,921								
Equity in earnings before securities losses of unconsolidated banking subsidiary, divested as of Dec. 31, 1980						4,242	4,960	4,731					
Earnings before realized investment gains						29,984	35,921	43,215	39,723	31,497	31,497	68,195	70,201
Realized investment gains, continuing operations						9,258	6,896	10,790	22,881	14,877	14,877	45,298	78,694
Equity in securities losses of unconsolidated banking subsidiary								(883)					
Net earnings	$7,043	$4,692	$22,835	$26,724	$30,393	$39,242	$42,817	$53,122	$62,604	$46,374	$46,374	$113,493	$148,895

Note: The year 1977 was restated due to the merger with Diversified Retailing; 1983 was restated due to the merger with Blue Chip Stamps. Buffett's distaste for the presentation of Berkshire's consolidated financial statements is only compounded by trying to show them over multiple years.

Sources: Berkshire Hathaway Annual Reports, 1974–1984.

Table 4.45: Berkshire Hathaway consolidated reconcilliation of shareholders' equity, 1974–1984

($ thousands)	1984	Restated 1983	Restated 1982	Original 1982	1981	1980	1979	1978	Restated 1977	Original 1977	1976	1975	1974
Prior year equity	$1,119,193	$727,483	$519,463	$519,463	$395,214	$344,962	$254,166	$154,564	115,293	$115,293	$92,890	$88,199	$81,155
Current year net income / (loss)	148,895	113,493	46,374	46,374	62,604	53,122	42,817	39,242	30,393	26,724	22,835	4,692	7,043
Change in common		805							1,173				
Change in paid in capital		153,860							3,517				
Treasury stock	(280)				180	(28,967)		(574)	(1,476)	(229)	(432)		
Change in treasury stock due to restatement with Diversified Retailing									(9,389)				
Change in retained earnings due to restatement with Diversified Retailing									15,053				
Change in equity due to accounting change, marketable securities								60,934					
Change in unrealized appreciation of securities, net of tax	3,673	123,832	161,646	161,646	61,465	26,097	47,979						
Ending Equity	$1,271,761	$1,119,193	$727,483	$727,483	$519,463	$395,214	$344,962	$254,166	$154,564	$141,788	$115,293	$92,890	$88,199

Sources: Berkshire Hathaway Annual Reports, 1974–1984.

Table 4.46: Berkshire Hathaway Insurance Group balance sheets, 1974–1984

($ thousands)	1974	1975	1976	1977	Restated 1977	1978	Restated 1978	1979	1980	1981	1982	1983	1984
Cash and Treasuries	$10,652	$15,914	$17,585	$23,167	$26,695	$45,638	$45,638	$12,182	$30,950				
Cash, Treasuries, and other short-term investments										$536,748	$793,569	$793,569	$793,569
Bonds, at amortized cost	71,531	78,761	89,216	127,324	132,929	157,651	157,651	185,564	187,802				
Marketable equity securities, at cost					108,107	133,766							
Marketable equity securities, at market							220,929	336,680	424,530				
Preferred stocks	2,855	2,558	22,287	23,232									
Common stocks	50,670	39,341	53,108	86,657									
Total cash and investments	135,708	136,574	182,196	260,381	267,731	337,055	424,218	534,426	643,282				
Investment in Blue Chip Stamps	14,371	15,401	17,740	21,679	26,862	31,442	31,442	35,355	32,272				
Property, plant and equipment, net	1,581	1,526	1,636	2,164	2,164	2,757	2,757	3,383	3,388				
Other assets	20,679	20,558	22,812	29,008	36,487	46,011	46,011	50,257	50,731				
Total assets	172,338	174,059	224,384	313,231	333,244	417,265	504,428	623,421	729,673				
Identifiable assets at year-end (from footnotes)	172,338	164,443	261,752	377,954	377,954	470,023	470,023	585,103	693,859	825,635	1,059,670	1,322,160	1,615,274
Losses and loss adjustment expenses	72,761	73,033	85,152	133,592	139,461	180,870	180,870	197,698	199,128				
Unearned premiums	21,705	22,344	36,737	52,191	57,128	69,368	69,368	73,604	73,281				
Other liabilities	7,641	7,734	14,033	17,579	18,157	23,876	50,025	69,272	78,951				
Total Liabilities	102,107	103,111	135,922	203,361	214,746	274,114	300,263	340,574	351,360				
Shareholders' equity	$70,231	$70,947	$88,463	$109,870	$118,498	$143,151	$204,165	$282,847	$378,313				
Average float (rounded)	$79,100	$87,600	$102,600	$139,000	$139,000	$190,400	$190,400	$227,300	$237,000	$228,400	$220,600	$231,300	$253,200

Sources: Berkshire Hathaway Annual Reports, 1974–1984; 1992 (float data).

Table 4.47: Berkshire Hathaway Insurance Group statements of income, 1974–1984

($ thousands)	1984	1983	1982	1981	1980	1979	Restated 1978	1978	Restated 1977	1977	1976	1975	1974
Premiums written, net	$133,558	$149,849	$149,091	$148,000	$184,864	$186,185	$198,313	$198,313	$158,704	$151,083	$94,773	$58,975	$60,997
Premiums earned	140,242	152,480	152,945	159,013	185,187	181,950	186,073	186,073	143,088	136,890	80,780	58,336	60,574
Losses and loss expenses incurred	141,550	134,109	121,996	103,416	118,230	120,338	132,263	132,263	96,869	91,585	55,376	47,238	47,120
Underwriting expenses	46,752	52,243	52,508	54,119	60,219	57,870	50,809	50,809	40,418	39,122	24,694	21,745	20,346
Total losses and expenses	188,302	186,352	174,504	157,535	178,449	178,208	183,072	183,072	137,287	130,707	80,071	68,983	67,466
Pre-tax underwriting gain / (loss)	(48,060)	(33,872)	(21,559)	1,478	6,738	3,742	3,001	3,001	5,801	6,184	709	(10,647)	(6,892)
Pre-tax net investment income	68,903	43,810	41,620	38,823	30,939	24,224	19,705	19,705	12,804	12,282	10,438	8,441	7,880
Operating profit before taxes, continuing operations	20,843	9,938	20,061	40,301	37,677	27,966	22,706	22,706	18,605	18,465	11,147	(2,206)	988
Realized gain (loss) on investments, net of tax					10,588	6,241	8,873	8,873	4,917	4,820	7,043	(2,022)	(1,340)
Equity in earnings of Blue Chip Stamps					4,488	3,960	3,230	3,230	3,852	3,134	1,637	1,141	792
Net Income					$47,899	$32,763	$30,128	$30,128	$24,614	$23,407	$18,515	$716	$2,529

Sources: Berkshire Hathaway Annual Reports, 1974–1984.

Table 4.48: Berkshire Hathaway Insurance Group select ratios, 1974–1984

($ thousands)	1984	1983	1982	1981	1980	1979	Restated 1978	1978	Restated 1977	1977	1976	1975	1974
Net premiums written to average equity	100.9%	88.0%	79.8%	65.0%	55.9%	76.5%	122.9%	151.6%	153.4%	152.4%	118.9%	83.5%	86.9%
Loss ratio					63.8%	66.1%	71.1%	71.1%	67.7%	66.9%	68.6%	81.0%	77.8%
Expense ratio	35.0%	34.9%	35.2%	36.6%	32.6%	31.1%	25.6%	25.6%	25.5%	25.9%	26.1%	36.9%	33.4%
Combined ratio	135.9%	122.8%	115.0%	101.6%	96.4%	97.2%	96.7%	96.7%	93.2%	92.8%	94.6%	117.8%	111.1%
Return on average equity					14.5%	13.5%	18.7%	23.0%	21.6%	23.6%	23.2%	1.0%	3.6%
Growth in premiums written, net	(10.9%)	0.5%	0.7%	(19.9%)	(0.7%)	(6.1%)	25.0%	25.0%	67.5%	59.4%	60.7%	(3.3%)	21.1%
Growth in premiums earned	(8.0%)	(0.3%)	(3.8%)	(14.1%)	1.8%	(2.2%)	30.0%	30.0%	77.1%	69.5%	38.5%	(3.7%)	14.4%

Sources: Berkshire Hathaway Annual Reports, 1974–1984, and author's calculations.

Table 4.49: Insurance Group select information, 1974–1984

($ thousands)	1984	1983	1982	1981	1980	1979	1978	1977	1976	1975
Premiums written, net	$133,558	$149,849	$149,091	$148,000	$184,864	$186,185	$198,313	$158,704	$94,773	$58,975
Premiums earned										
Specialized auto and general liability	64,003	68,148	69,026	73,177	88,404	90,646	96,126	80,690	50,778	38,513
Workers' Compensation	22,665	18,849	15,951	18,193	19,890	19,350	29,893	18,916	5,815	3,632
Reinsurance	16,066	26,889	27,408	29,446	33,804	30,864	30,160	24,100	17,220	12,407
Home State multiple lines	32,598	35,328	37,552	38,197	43,089	41,089	29,894	19,382	11,058	6,670
Structured settlements and portfolio reinsurance	4,910	3,266	3,008							
	140,242	152,480	152,945	159,013	185,187	181,949	186,073	143,088	84,871	61,222
Investment income	69,291	44,249	41,791	39,019	31,111	24,407	19,944	13,061	10,975	8,806
Insurance segment revenues	209,533	196,729	194,736	198,032	216,298	206,356	206,017	156,149	95,846	70,028
Underwriting gain (loss), pre-tax										
Specialized auto and general liability	(16,049)	(14,880)	(12,647)	3,020	7,395	7,845	11,543	7,800	4,768	(7,450)
Workers' Compensation*	(12,560)	(1,091)	2,658	2,822	4,870	5,130	(3,944)	(1,644)	(1,093)	(342)
Reinsurance	(12,703)	(8,387)	(7,524)	(3,720)	(233)	(4,338)	(2,443)	(1,251)	(2,879)	(2,651)
Home State multiple lines	(4,101)	(8,834)	(3,949)	(644)	(5,294)	(4,895)	(2,155)	896	(548)	(907)
Structured settlements and portfolio reinsurance	(2,647)	(680)	(96)							
	(48,060)	(33,872)	(21,558)	1,478	6,738	3,742	3,001	5,801	248	(11,350)
Net investment income	68,903	43,810	41,620	38,823	30,939	24,224	19,705	12,805	10,841	8,723
Insurance segment operating profit (loss) before taxes	$20,843	$9,938	$20,062	$40,301	$37,677	$27,966	$22,706	$18,606	$11,089	($2,627)
Combined ratio (statutory)	135.9%	122.8%	115.0%	101.6%	96.4%	97.2%	96.7%	93.2%	94.6%	117.8%

Notes:

Workers' Compensation coverage written by Home State is not broken out per the footnote to the financial statements.

The data in this table was taken from the summary of segment results section of the Annual Report and differs in some cases with figures listed in earlier reporting periods.

Sources: Berkshire Hathaway Annual Reports, 1979, 1982, 1984.

Table 4.50: The Illinois National Bank & Trust Co. of Rockford consolidated balance sheets, 1968–1979

($ thousands)	1979	1978	1977	1976	1975	1974	1973	1972	1971	1970	1969	1968
Cash and due from banks	$27,602	$20,232	$20,973	$10,868	$18,797	$21,544	$26,684	$22,111	$17,833	$15,157	$19,918	$23,244
US Government Bonds		42,938	42,120	30,499	39,758	10,615	11,355	10,615	12,633	15,129	11,228	26,922
Obligations of states and political subdivisions		63,577	58,696	54,002	46,959	45,858	47,713	50,163	42,884	36,627	36,005	17,803
Other securities		5,394	6,054	6,629	4,053	3,846	3,358	7,779	5,865			
Federal Reserve Bank stock		300	300	300	300					210	210	210
Federal funds sold		3,000	7,000	32,000		5,000						
Investments	104,103	115,209	114,169	123,430	91,071	65,319	62,426	68,556	61,382	51,966	47,443	44,936
Loans, gross	84,377	76,122	62,268	56,188	58,081	70,134	66,022	59,618	54,032	50,841	47,963	46,995
Reserve for loan losses							(1,164)	(1,025)	(855)	(860)	(800)	(599)
Loans, net	84,377	76,122	62,268	56,188	58,081	70,134	64,859	58,593	53,177	49,980	47,163	46,396
Bank premises and equipment	1,820	1,106	1,022	896	967	1,009	1,117	1,361	1,523	1,624	1,825	1,237
Accrued interest receivable and other assets	3,097	3,146	2,720	2,010	2,555	2,857	2,156	1,750	1,252	1,739	1,040	896
Total assets	220,999	215,815	201,152	193,393	171,471	160,861	157,241	152,372	135,167	120,466	117,389	116,709
Demand deposits		58,133	56,978	54,875	53,478	53,178	55,716	55,130	51,208	52,478	58,237	57,677
Time deposits		127,002	117,890	113,462	93,501	85,519	81,450	77,558	64,640	49,095	41,317	41,408
Total deposits	187,223	185,134	174,868	168,337	146,979	138,697	137,166	132,688	115,848	101,573	99,555	99,085
Borrowed funds[1]	3,367	2,357			1,000							
Accrued taxes and other expenses	2,821	2,413	1,717	1,628	1,411	1,223	835	887	814	679	638	783
Total liabilities	193,411	189,904	176,585	169,965	149,390	139,920	138,002	133,575	116,662	102,252	100,193	99,869
Total capital accounts	27,588	25,910	24,567	23,428	22,081	20,942	19,239	18,797	18,505	18,213	17,196	16,841
Total liabilities and capital	$220,999	$215,815	$201,152	$193,393	$171,471	$160,861	$157,241	$152,372	$135,167	$120,466	$117,389	$116,709

Footnote: 1. Amount in 1975 consists of Fed Funds.

Note: Prior to 1974 loans were presented on a gross basis as an asset, with the loss reserve presented separately as a liability. I have adjusted these years to conform to the subsequent presentation; therefore, the total assets figure differs from that presented in the financial statements.

Sources: Berkshire Hathaway Annual Reports, 1968–1979.

Table 4.51: The Illinois National Bank & Trust Co. of Rockford consolidated statements of income, 1968–1979

($ thousands)	1979	1978	1977	1976	1975	1974	1973	1972	1971	1970	1969	1968
Interest and fees on loans		$6,480	$5,480	$5,093	$5,712	$6,608	$5,316	$4,134	$4,006	$4,130	$3,820	$3,431
Income on federal funds sold		298	288	225	214	361	237	110	109	317	392	320
Interest and dividends on:												
United States government obligations and agencies		3,270	2,271	2,491	1,615	942	632	598	708	569	1,003	1,420
Obligations of states and political subdivisions		4,032	3,848	3,255	2,853	2,798	2,796	2,677	2,094	1,717	1,155	532
Time deposits with other banks					204							
Federal Reserve Bank stock		18	18	18	18							
Other Securities		484	577	501	253	284	343	524	228	13		
Total interest income	18,196	14,582	12,481	11,583	10,868	10,993	9,324	8,044	7,145	6,745	6,371	5,702
Interest on deposits		7,387	6,600	5,880	5,191	4,954	4,295	3,419	2,733	2,029	1,695	1,493
Interest on federal funds purchased		2	2	4	4	14	55	3	2	4	13	3
Interest on borrowed funds		36										
Interest expense	9,605	7,425	6,602	5,884	5,195	4,968	4,351	3,422	2,734	2,032	1,707	1,496
Net interest income	8,591	7,157	5,879	5,700	5,673	6,024	4,973	4,622	4,410	4,713	4,663	4,206
Provision for loan losses	108	60	16	12	12	19	16	37	36	52	62	66
Net interest income after provision for loan losses	8,483	7,097	5,863	5,688	5,662	6,005	4,957	4,585	4,375	4,661	4,602	4,141
Trust department		710	637	547	503	434	451	385	336	280	343	339
Service charges on deposit accounts		76	116	149	134	139	130	127	137	152	220	199
Other		376	577	635	583	560	500	411	307	354	248	250
Other income	1,208	1,162	1,330	1,331	1,220	1,133	1,080	924	780	786	811	789
Salaries					1,643	1,552	1,503	1,367	1,352	1,298	1,159	1,073
Pensions, profit sharing, and other employee benefits					293	247	263	239	138	151	114	137
Salaries and employee benefits		2,174	2,097	2,025	1,936	1,798	1,766	1,605	1,489	1,450	1,273	1,210
Net occupancy expense of bank premises		311	269	259	247	257	418	314	359	358	302	325
Equipment rentals, depreciation, and maintenance		212	215	233	246	248	253	264	289	272	260	235
Other		739	812	838	766	592	767	645	681	661	558	497
Total non-interest expense	3,944	3,436	3,393	3,355	3,195	2,896	3,204	2,829	2,818	2,742	2,392	2,267
Earnings before income taxes and securities gains (losses)	5,747	4,822	3,800	3,663	3,686	4,242	2,833	2,680	2,337	2,705	3,020	2,662
Income taxes	601	459	429	108	172	220	61	0	109	484	1,039	1,110
Earnings before securities gains (losses)	5,146	4,363	3,371	3,555	3,514	4,022	2,772	2,680	2,228	2,221	1,981	1,551
Securities gains or (losses) net of applicable income taxes[1]	(68)	(20)	269	292	52	168	34	84	26	189	(372)	110
Net income[2]	$5,078	$4,343	$3,640	$3,847	$3,567	$4,190	$2,806	$2,764	$2,254	$2,410	$1,608	$1,661

Footnotes: 1. 1973: Included is $43 gain on sale of real estate, net of tax. 2. 1970: Net income is presented before a $633 tax benefit from parent.

Sources: Berkshire Hathaway Annual Reports, 1968–1979.

Table 4.52: The Illinois National Bank & Trust Co. of Rockford select data and ratios, 1968–1979

($ thousands)	1969	1970	1971	1972	1973	1974	1975	1976	1977	1978	1979
Average loans	$46,780	$48,572	$51,579	$55,885	$61,726	$70,134	$64,107	$57,135	$59,228	$69,195	$80,249
Average assets	$117,049	$118,927	$127,816	$143,770	$154,806	$160,861	$166,166	$182,432	$197,272	$208,483	$218,407
Average total deposits	$99,320	$100,564	$108,711	$124,268	$134,927	$138,697	$142,838	$157,658	$171,603	$180,001	$186,179
Average equity	$17,018	$17,704	$18,359	$18,651	$19,018	$20,942	$21,511	$22,754	$23,998	$25,239	$26,749
Average loans to average assets	40.0%	40.8%	40.4%	38.9%	39.9%	43.6%	38.6%	31.3%	30.0%	33.2%	36.7%
Average loans to average deposits	47.1%	48.3%	47.4%	45.0%	45.7%	50.6%	44.9%	36.2%	34.5%	38.4%	43.1%
Average capital ratio	14.5%	14.9%	14.4%	13.0%	12.3%	13.0%	12.9%	12.5%	12.2%	12.1%	12.2%
Pre-tax operating return on average assets	2.58%	2.27%	1.83%	1.86%	1.83%	2.64%	2.22%	2.01%	1.93%	2.31%	2.63%
Pre-tax operating return on average deposits	3.04%	2.69%	2.15%	2.16%	2.10%	3.06%	2.58%	2.32%	2.21%	2.68%	3.09%
Pre-tax operating income / average equity	17.7%	15.3%	12.7%	14.4%	14.9%	20.3%	17.1%	16.1%	15.8%	19.1%	21.5%
After-tax operating income / average equity	11.6%	12.5%	12.1%	14.4%	14.6%	19.2%	16.3%	15.6%	14.0%	17.3%	19.2%
Efficiency ratio[1]	44%	50%	54%	51%	53%	40%	46%	48%	47%	41%	40%
Interest income / average assets	5.44%	5.67%	5.59%	5.59%	6.02%	6.83%	6.54%	6.35%	6.33%	6.99%	8.33%
Interest expense / average deposits[2]	1.72%	2.02%	2.52%	2.75%	3.22%	3.58%	3.62%	3.72%	3.85%	4.10%	5.08%
Net interest margin	3.72%	3.65%	3.07%	2.84%	2.80%	3.25%	2.92%	2.63%	2.48%	2.90%	3.25%
Provision for loan losses / avg. loans	0.13%	0.11%	0.07%	0.07%	0.03%	0.03%	0.02%	0.02%	0.03%	0.09%	0.13%
After-tax operating return on average assets	1.69%	1.87%	1.74%	1.86%	1.79%	2.50%	2.11%	1.95%	1.71%	2.09%	2.36%

Footnotes:
1. Efficiency ratio is the ratio of non-interest expense divided by the sum of net interest income and non-interest income.
2. Average deposits includes borrowed funds in the years applicable.

Sources: Berkshire Hathaway Annual Reports 1968–1979.

Chapter 5
1985–1994

Table 5.1: Decade snapshot: 1984–1994

	1984	1994
Business:	Insurance, newspapers, furniture retailing, candy, banking, textiles	Insurance, newspapers, furniture retailing, candy, jewelry, encyclopedias, home cleaning systems, shoes, misc. manufacturing, significant stakes in several public companies
Key managers:	Chairman & CEO: Warren E. Buffett; Vice Chair: Charles T. Munger	Chairman & CEO: Warren E. Buffett; Vice Chair: Charles T. Munger
Annual revenues:	$729 million	$3.8 billion
Stockholders' equity:	$1.27 billion	$11.9 billion
Book value per share:	$1,108.77	$10,083
Float (average):	$253 million	$3.06 billion

Major Capital Allocation Decisions:

1. Shut down textile operations (1985).

2. Contributed additional equity to Insurance Group (various).

3. Invested $517.5 million into Capital Cities/ABC (1985).

4. Acquired Scott Fetzer for $410 million (1986).

5. Purchased Fechheimer (1986).

6. Purchased $700 million issue of Salomon Brothers Convertible Preferred Stock (1987).

7. Acquired Borsheim's (1989).

8. Purchased Coca-Cola shares for $1.3 billion (1988–94).

9. Purchased convertible preferred stock issues from Gillette ($600 million); USAir ($358 million); Champion International ($300 million) (1989).

10. Issued $900 million Zero Coupon debt (1989).

11. Acquired H.H. Brown Shoe (1991).

12. Repaid a significant amount of debt (1991–92).

13. Acquired Lowell Shoe (1992).

14. Acquired Dexter Shoe for $433 million, issuing 25,303 shares (1993).

15. Exited savings and loan business (Wesco/Mutual Savings; 1993).

Noteworthy Events:

1. Berkshire enters the super catastrophe (super-cat) business in a big way (1990).

2. Ken Chace retires from Berkshire Board, replaced by Susan Buffett (1990).

3. Malcolm G. Chace, Jr. retires from Berkshire Board, replaced by son, Malcolm "Kim" Chace III.

4. Rose "Mrs. B." Blumkin turns 100 years old (1993).

Table 5.2: Berkshire Hathaway Earnings

($ thousands)	1994	1993	1992	1991	1990	1989	1988	1987	1986	1985	1984
Insurance Group:											
Underwriting	$129,926	$30,876	($108,961)	($119,593)	($26,647)	($24,400)	($11,081)	($55,429)	($55,844)	($44,230)	($48,060)
Net investment income	419,422	375,946	355,067	331,846	327,048	243,599	231,250	152,483	107,143	95,217	68,903
Buffalo News	54,238	50,962	47,863	37,113	43,954	46,047	42,429	39,410	34,736	29,921	27,328
Fechheimer[1]	14,260	13,442	13,698	12,947	12,450	12,621	14,152	13,332	8,400		
Finance businesses	21,568	22,695									
Kirby	42,349	39,147	35,653	35,726	27,445	26,114	26,891	22,408	20,218		
Nebraska Furniture Mart	17,356	21,540	17,110	14,384	17,248	17,070	18,439	16,837	17,685	12,686	14,511
Scott Fetzer – Manufacturing Group	39,435	38,196	31,954	26,123	30,378	33,165	28,542	30,591	25,358		
See's Candies	47,539	41,150	42,357	42,390	39,580	34,235	32,473	31,693	30,347	28,989	26,644
Shoe Group[2]	85,503	44,025	27,883	13,616							
Wesco – other than insurance[3]	24,662	19,915	15,153	12,230	12,441	13,008	16,133	6,209	5,542	16,018	15,325
World Book			29,044	22,483	31,896	25,583	27,890	25,745	21,978		
Purchase-price accounting & goodwill charges	(22,595)	(17,033)	(12,087)	(10,134)	(9,427)	(9,127)	(9,148)	(8,408)	(12,588)	(1,475)	(1,434)
Interest expense[4]	(60,111)	(56,545)	(98,643)	(89,250)	(76,374)	(42,389)	(35,613)	(11,474)	(23,891)	(14,415)	(14,734)
Shareholder-designated contributions	(10,419)	(9,448)	(7,634)	(6,772)	(5,824)	(5,867)	(4,966)	(4,938)	(3,997)	(4,006)	(3,179)
Other[5]	36,232	28,428	72,223	77,399	58,309	23,755	41,059	22,460	20,770	6,744	2,435
Operating earnings - pre-tax	**839,365**	**643,296**	**460,680**	**400,508**	**482,477**	**393,414**	**418,450**	**280,919**	**195,857**	**125,449**	**87,739**
Special Gen. Foods distribution										4,127	
Special Washington Post distribution										14,877	8,111
Continued...											

...Continued from prior page

Sales of securities and unusual sales of assets	91,332	546,422	89,937	192,478	33,989	223,810	131,671	27,319	216,242	468,903	104,699
Decline in value of USAir Preferred Stock		(268,500)									
Total earnings - all entities (pre-tax)	662,197	1,189,718	550,617	592,986	516,466	617,224	550,121	308,238	412,099	613,356	200,549
Income tax and minority interest[6]	(167,399)	(501,597)	(143,332)	(153,078)	(122,373)	(169,747)	(150,851)	(73,686)	(129,738)	(177,541)	(51,653)
Total earnings - all entities (after tax)	$494,798	$688,121	$407,285	$439,908	$394,093	$447,477	$399,270	$234,552	$282,361	$435,815	$148,896

Footnotes:
1. Fechheimer was acquired on June 3, 1986.
2. H.H. Brown acquired July 1, 1991; includes Lowell and Dexter beginning in 1993. Dexter acquired on November 7, 1993.
3. Includes Wesco-Parent, Mutual Savings and Loan, and Precision Steel.
4. Excludes interest expense of Scott Fetzer Financial Group; includes prepayment penalties.
5. Other includes Associated Retail, Textiles, and Blue Chip Stamps-Parent.
6. Imputed from the difference between the reported pre-tax and after-tax earnings figures.

Note: This table presents the company-level pre-tax operating earnings for each company. The presentation in the discussion of the prior decade used Berkshire's share of pre-tax earnings. Readers comparing the year 1984 as presented in this table with the presentation from the prior decade will notice a difference in the earnings for entities in which Berkshire did not have 100% ownership.

Sources: Berkshire Hathaway Annual Reports 1985–1994 and author's calculations.

Introduction

F ocusing just on the third decade of Warren Buffett's control of Berkshire Hathaway we find a company hitting its stride. Up until 1985, Buffett and his business partner, Berkshire Vice Chairman Charlie Munger, had something of a weight around their ankles in the form of the company's former identity, namely the textile division. Even with this anchor, they achieved an incredible amount in the prior decade, reallocating capital to more profitable businesses. In 1985, Berkshire freed itself from its past by closing the textile division. This really allowed the wind to fill its sails.

The magnitude of the changes Berkshire Hathaway experienced during the 1985–1994 decade were incredible. Revenues grew from $729 million in 1984 to $3.8 billion at year-end 1994. Shareholders' equity, while somewhat augmented by issuing stock, increased almost tenfold to $11.9 billion and resulted in a similar magnitude change in per share book value. Many capital allocation decisions created that change. They fell into two broad categories: allocation of capital into new wholly-owned subsidiaries, and the purchase of part ownership interests in very good public companies.

Berkshire acquired several simple yet highly profitable new businesses during this decade. Major additions included Scott Fetzer, a mini conglomerate whose largest divisions, World Book Encyclopedias and Kirby vacuum cleaners, were well-known to the general public. Unexpectedly, Berkshire also moved into the shoe industry in a big way.

Under the direction of expert capital allocators Buffett and Munger, Berkshire acquired large stakes in several well-known public companies and in some cases joined the boards. The company issued and redeemed a significant amount of debt during this time, and also issued shares in connection with a sizable acquisition. The 1985–1994 decade was one where Berkshire Hathaway moved swiftly to implement its leaders' understanding of good businesses, and in particular the potential for value creation in its insurance operations.

Table 5.3: Select information 1985–1994

	1985	1986	1987	1988	1989	1990	1991	1992	1993	1994
BRK book value per share - % change	48.2%	26.1%	19.5%	20.1%	44.4%	7.4%	39.6%	20.3%	14.3%	13.9%
BRK market value per share - % change	93.7%	14.2%	4.6%	59.3%	84.6%	(23.1%)	35.6%	29.8%	38.9%	25.0%
S&P 500 total return	31.6%	18.6%	5.1%	16.6%	31.7%	(3.1%)	30.5%	7.6%	10.1%	1.3%
US GDP Growth (real %)	4.2%	3.5%	3.5%	4.2%	3.7%	1.9%	(0.1%)	3.5%	2.8%	4.0%
10-year Treasury Note (year-end %)	9.3%	7.1%	9.0%	9.1%	7.8%	8.1%	7.1%	6.8%	5.8%	7.8%
US inflation (%)	3.5%	1.9%	3.6%	4.1%	4.8%	5.4%	4.2%	3.0%	3.0%	2.6%
US unemployment (%)	7.2%	7.0%	6.2%	5.5%	5.3%	5.6%	6.9%	7.5%	6.9%	6.1%

Sources: Berkshire Hathaway Annual Reports 2018, 2019 and Federal Reserve Bank of St. Louis.

1985

Having labored through some difficult years in the past, the year 1985 was a good one for Berkshire Hathaway. Not just because of the record 48.2% gain in net worth. Its insurance businesses, though still struggling with underwriting losses, were moving in the right direction (as was the industry). And the insurance business was bolstered by new volume acquired via a quota-share arrangement. Berkshire also received a windfall from its General Foods investment when that company was taken over in a leveraged buyout.

Not one to bask in glory no matter how richly deserved, Buffett tempered the results with some history and math. Increasing Berkshire's net worth by 15% per annum over the next decade would require Berkshire to earn profits of $5.7 billion. Only fifteen companies in the US managed such a feat over the preceding decade. Although "our scope is not circumscribed by history, structure, or concept ... we will also need a full measure of good fortune to average our hoped-for 15%."

Tempering expectations was classic Buffett, but it was especially appropriate in 1985. Berkshire's stock usually sold at a slight discount to intrinsic value, but recently it had started trading at a premium. This would be a boon to exiting shareholders, but not new ones. For their results to match Berkshire's underlying results, that premium would have to remain. If it shrunk to its historical below-intrinsic value level then good business results at Berkshire could translate into less-than-satisfactory results for those new shareholders. Buffett would continue to subtly influence the share price via Berkshire's candid disclosures.

Shutdown of the Textile Business

Reflecting on the past, Buffett considered buying control of Berkshire a colossal mistake. It led his original partnership investors (himself included) to give up a fraction of the ownership of much better businesses acquired though Berkshire, rather than buy them through another entity. And that was to say nothing of the now two decades of frustrations watching an industry decline into oblivion. As Buffett put it, the unpleasant job of shuttering the remnants of Berkshire's past was largely completed by July 1985. He was sympathetic to the managers and employees associated with the textile operations, but in the end economics won out. Berkshire couldn't remain in a competitively disadvantaged business that required ongoing capital investment at subpar returns.

The figures were unambiguous: Over the nine years prior to Buffett's involvement, Berkshire Hathaway was entirely engaged in textile manufacturing. During that time it lost $10 million on a total of $530 million of revenues. By comparison, See's Candies earned $2 million on revenues of $31 million the first year it was purchased. Although textiles did deliver some profits in the 1960s, they were not adequate compared to the capital required to produce them. As the years wore on the division's profits only worsened, and as the competitive disadvantages accrued, it became obvious that the business was not viable.

Buffett praised the division's managers, Ken Chace and Garry Morrison as "resourceful, energetic, and imaginative" in their efforts to operate the Textile Group profitably. He even put those managers on the same level as those running a gem like See's. The textile business failed not because of them, but despite their monumental efforts. They were simply dealt a bad hand. Berkshire's employees and their unions were praised, too, for accepting below-average wages and understanding the economic position of their employer. Even after the decision to liquidate the mills was made, both management and the employee base performed superbly, said Buffett.

Buffett summed up his predicament in allowing the mills to operate at subpar levels for so long:

"I won't close down businesses of sub-normal profitability merely to add a fraction of a point to our corporate rate of return. However, I also feel it inappropriate for even an exceptionally profitable company to fund an operation once it appears to have unending losses in prospect. Adam Smith would disagree with my first proposition, and Karl Marx would disagree with my second; the middle ground is the only position that leaves me comfortable."

His statement reflected the owner-related business principle of not participating in "gin rummy capitalism" contained at the beginning of the Annual Report. Berkshire would buy for keeps, and as a rule would not sell underperforming units in an effort to redeploy the capital into higher earning assets. Buffett communicated his position to shareholders in the past by reminding them that Berkshire's textile workers were largely older and possessed almost no skills outside of textile manufacturing. Many were also foreign-born and spoke very little English and would have been severely hurt by closure of the mills. Many were hurt with the 1985 mill closure, but Buffett could at least point to efforts to cushion the blow.

The problem was that the textile business, especially in New England, was not economically viable. The liquidation of the mills' assets told the story:

Table 5.4: Berkshire Hathaway Textile division, select data

Employees	1,000
Space occupied *(sq. ft.)*	750,000
Select data on textile equipment ($ thousands):	
Original cost	$13,000
Balance sheet value	866
Cost to replace in 1985	30,000 to 50,000
Liquidation proceeds	163

Source: Berkshire Hathaway Chairman's letter 1985.

Equipment of enormous importance in prior years was rendered economically useless over time by the onslaught of competitive pressures. In the end it was sold for almost nothing.

A commodity-type business like Berkshire's textile operation faced illusory investment options. Each opportunity for investment, say a new machine that promised to reduce costs, was rational from the standpoint of the individual firm. But when *all* companies in the industry made such decisions the advantages disappeared. Buffett summed it up as akin to standing on one's tiptoes watching a parade. It helps for a fleeting moment—until everyone else does the same. Then you see no better and have achy legs.

Considering the situation of Berkshire's textile operations in 1985, it was quite clear that the industry was, at best, difficult. Yet some textile mills remained. Burlington Industries was the largest US textile company from the time Buffett took over Berkshire until it closed the division. In 1964, Burlington had revenues of $1.2 billion compared to Berkshire's $50 million. In the twenty-one years that followed Burlington made $3 billion of capital expenditures. Revenues in 1985 were just $2.8 billion. It was a devastating result that led Burlington's share price to essentially remain unchanged at $60 over that period. Considering the consumer price index had risen threefold over that time, Burlington shareholders who stayed on for the ride saw their real purchasing power shrink commensurately.*

Berkshire's shareholders would surely have faced the same agonizing decline if it weren't for the arrival of Warren Buffett and his capital allocation skills. Instead of oblivion, Berkshire's shareholders saw a newcomer harness the textile business's dying breaths to create a profitable enterprise with a diversified stream of earnings. With the aid of Chace, Morrison, and the employees of the textile operations, Berkshire slowly reduced its investment in textiles. Monies raised by selling off plant and equipment, and shrinking investments in receivables and inventories, were recycled into more profitable investments in operating businesses, such as National Indemnity and Illinois National Bank, and into marketable securities.

The liquidation of the textile operations in 1985 and 1986 was the end of an era. What began as an association with the country's first mill operators and continued for almost two centuries in various forms, ended with a money-losing fire sale. Although its original business of textiles was no longer part of the picture, the story of those who built Berkshire Hathaway would always have a place in history because of Warren Buffett.

Three Very Good Businesses (and a Few Thoughts About Incentive Compensation)

As the textile business faded into history the businesses it spawned flourished. Buffett used some figures on Nebraska Furniture Mart, See's, and *The Buffalo News* to opine on incentive compensation. It was also an excellent lesson on business economics and the importance of thinking through facts and figures carefully.

The three businesses just mentioned earned $72 million pre-tax for Berkshire Hathaway in 1985 and represented about half of pre-tax operating earnings (prior to interest expense) for that year. Those businesses were earning about $8 million fifteen years earlier, before Berkshire purchased any of them. Buffett cautioned against seeing such an increase as automatically good. That record was good, but there was information missing. To properly appreciate the economic characteristics of a business and whether growth is good, it must properly be compared to the capital required to produce those earnings.

For *The Buffalo News*, See's, and Nebraska Furniture Mart, the incremental return on capital investment was highly satisfactory, said Buffett, being understated as usual.

---

* Burlington Industries would ultimately find itself filing for bankruptcy in late 2001. Berkshire actually bid for it at auction, but the deal fell through and its business was split apart and sold. It remains today, at least in name, as part of the International Textile Group, which purchased its assets out of bankruptcy in 2003.

Doing some simple math illustrated the excellent economics of those businesses: The rate of return pre-tax was 160% (see Table 5.5). This result stands out when compared to other businesses Berkshire could have purchased. "The average American business has required about $5 of additional capital to generate an additional $1 of annual pre-tax earnings," he said. Such a rate of return of 20% pre-tax was not a poor result—but it wasn't 160% either.

Table 5.5: The Buffalo News, See's, and Nebraska Furniture Mart incremental return on capital analysis

($ millions)	
Pre-tax earnings, 1985	$72
Pre-tax earnings, 1970	8
Increase	64
Incremental capital required	$40
Incremental return on capital	160%

Source: Berkshire Hathaway Chairman's letter 1985.

The only problem, if it could be called one, was the businesses possessed such low reinvestment requirements that they could hardly reinvest their earnings. In fifteen years, those businesses found opportunities to invest just $40 million.* Berkshire would have invested another $40 million if it could find anything close to the 160% incremental return seen over the previous fifteen years. Instead, they shipped the excess cash off to Omaha for reallocation into other investment opportunities.

Nebraska Furniture Mart was a low-cost operation with one location. This allowed it to set prices below its competitors and still earn a good result for its owners. See's, though still an excellent business, continued to face the industry headwind of declining per capita consumption of boxed chocolates. Declining pounds meant per-pound cost pressures, which were difficult to fully compensate through price increases. *The Buffalo News*, with exceptional penetration rates near 80%, had little room for future growth within its territory. It could expand advertising with preprints (advertisers supplying inserts vs. on-page advertisements) but those were less profitable and subject to competition. The common thread with all three was exceptional management.

Buffett was not opposed to paying large sums for above-average performance, but he disliked compensation for average performance. He thought managers whose companies increased earnings at the same pace as capital invested in the business deserved no applause. These average managers (and those compensating them) focused blindly on increased dollar earnings. What mattered more was the *rate* of change.

---

* Above and beyond depreciation expense.

An ordinary savings account provided an ultra-simplified example. An account earning 8% would quadruple its annual earnings in eighteen years. The manager of the account would have done nothing but sit back and let the interest accumulate and compound. The above-average manager found ways to increase value. Value enhancement might come in the form of increasing the rate of return on capital through better margins, or perhaps by conducting the same level of operations with less capital. It could also come in the form of expanding a difficult-to-grow business while maintaining good rates of return on capital.

Another way to make money doing nothing was with fixed-price options for company shares. Managers who issued themselves such options were incented to retain earnings even if it made more sense to payout some or all of them to shareholders. The larger the pie at the end of their option period, the bigger their payout. This really got Buffett's blood boiling.

Buffett wanted managers to think and act like owners. He said owners would understand that there was a cost to capital and that rates of return mattered more than simply increasing earnings. He also thought options should only be issued to those responsible for the overall performance of the business. Though Berkshire didn't issue options, he thought it entirely appropriate for the manager of a well-performing subsidiary to receive a large bonus even though Berkshire overall performed poorly in comparison. Conversely, a well-performing Berkshire would not automatically mean a big check if the individual unit performed poorly. Many other corporations acted against this rational approach. Their owners paid for it quite literally by giving up a portion of their interest to the managers.

Insurance Operations

The insurance industry presented another perplexing year in 1985. Despite an estimated 20.9% increase in premium volumes, combined ratios remained elevated. The 1985 estimated industry combined ratio of 118%, and Berkshire's own overall ratio of 105%[*] was because losses remained high. Part of the problem was the persistent social inflation where judges and juries awarded far more than insurers had priced into policies. The real issue, though, was the addition of reserves, which reflected the sins of prior years' underwriting.

---

[*] This figure is calculated on the statutory basis and is based on the summary of insurance underwriting activities. It includes structured settlements and portfolio reinsurance. The Annual Report calculates the ratio using underwriting expenses to premiums earned (the GAAP basis calculation) to arrive at a ratio of 114%. The large difference arises due to the fact that the $497.4 million of premiums written were 57% greater than the $317.1 million premiums earned.

Table 5.6: Insurance Group, select information

($ millions)	1985 Amount	%	1984 Amount	%
Primary Group				
Premiums written	$269.1		$118.1	
Premiums earned	184.3	100.0%	119.3	100.0%
Losses and loss expenses	140.0	76.0%	110.5	92.6%
Underwriting expenses	52.5	28.5%	41.6	34.9%
Total losses and expenses	192.5	104.4%	152.1	127.5%
Underwriting gain/(loss) - pre-tax	(8.1)		(32.9)	
Unfavorable (favorable) loss development included in losses and loss expenses	*0.1*	*0.0%*	*8.1*	*6.8%*
Statutory combined ratio		95.5%		127.9%
Reinsurance Group				
Premiums written	$178.5		$10.5	
Premiums earned	82.9	100.0%	16.1	100.0%
Losses and loss expenses	85.7	103.4%	23.7	147.6%
Underwriting expenses	27.2	32.8%	4.9	30.5%
Total losses and expenses	112.9	136.2%	28.6	178.2%
Underwriting gain/(loss) - pre-tax	(30.0)		(12.6)	
Unfavorable (favorable) loss development included in losses and loss expenses	*19.4*	*23.5%*	*9.7*	*60.2%*
Statutory combined ratio		118.6%		194.2%
Structured settlements and portfolio reinsurance				
Underwriting gain/(loss) - pre-tax	(6.1)		(2.6)	
Total Insurance Group underwriting gain/ (loss) pre-tax	($44.2)		($48.1)	
Insurance Group overall statutory combined ratio		104.7%		135.9%

Notes:

1. Totals may not add due to rounding.

2. The loss and expense ratios are shown as they were reported in the Annual Reports, which is on a GAAP basis. The GAAP basis ratios are calculated with underwriting expenses divided by earned premiums. This contrasts to the statutory basis calculation, where the ratio uses written premiums. In both the GAAP and statutory calculations, losses and loss adjustment expenses are divided by earned premiums.

Sources: Berkshire Hathaway Annual Reports 1985, 1987; and author's calculations.

Due to the nature of the insurance business, which requires estimating all future costs today for policies that may cover risks stretching far into the future, operating results are subject to much less precision than normal businesses. When an insurance company determines that estimated losses for prior years are inaccurate (usually they are too low), it must record a charge to the current years' operating results. Innocently named reserve development, these adjustments are really mistakes. These mistakes are a part of the business, though they sometimes tempt unscrupulous managers to fiddle with the estimates.

In Berkshire's case in 1985, its Insurance Group began the year with an estimate for future claims (termed unpaid losses and loss expense) of $243.3 million. During 1985, with hindsight, Berkshire determined it had underestimated losses it really incurred for business written prior to 1985 by $22.9 million. This amount was then included in the current years' income statement under item losses and loss adjustment expenses.

Details in the footnotes revealed some important information about the adverse loss development. The segment attributed to the Primary Group (Berkshire's collection of primary or direct operations), recorded a $63,000 prior-year adjustment. Although the segment still wrote at a loss, the losses were all tracking as expected through 1985. The story of the 1985 adverse loss development was largely in the reinsurance segment, which booked charges of $19.4 million—a massive 41% of the balance attributable to reinsurance at the beginning of the year.

About two-thirds of the loss reported from the Reinsurance Group* in 1985 was the result of adverse loss development on policies written in prior years (the other third represented losses on business written in 1985). Such a loss was large but not uncommon. The reinsurance business is typically long-tail (requiring many years for actual profitability to materialize) and subject to the primary insurance company's estimates, making revisions of prior year loss estimates common. It is also a contributing factor to the number of entrants to the business when business is seemingly good. Since losses take many years to materialize, the feedback loop is also long and pricing errors can go undetected and uncorrected for many years.

The insurance industry in general has a unique capacity feature, one that can exacerbate the problems of reinsurance. Most commodity industries (indeed most businesses) take time to react to demand and/or pricing and bring additional capacity online. This is because plants must be designed and built, equipment ordered, and personnel hired. Conversely in insurance, capacity can materialize instantly since it is of a financial nature. This feature also leads to quick changes in the other direction. When times are tough—such as a major hurricane or earthquake that leads to industry losses—insurers and their capital backers pull back.

---

* Other than structured settlements and portfolio reinsurance.

This pull back of industry capacity was when Berkshire shone brightest. The year 1985 was one such year of tight capacity, in which others, having suffered through years of losses, lost the ability or willingness to write new business. Berkshire, on the other hand, lived for such years. In 1985, Berkshire's Insurance Group wrote 372% more premium volume compared to 1984 and it earned 226% greater premiums. The winds were finally favorable, but if history was any guide they wouldn't last long.

The increased pricing caused by tight supply in 1985 caused new entrants and reentrants into the market. In 1985, fifteen insurers raised over $3 billion to capture the better industry pricing, according to Buffett. Buffett knew it would only be a matter of time before this new capital pushed prices down below the cost of doing business, and the cycle would start all over again. There was a bright spot in the darkening cloud Buffett painted, one uniquely suited for Berkshire.

Berkshire had built a unique advantage through a combination of its excellent track record, good reputation, and significant capital base. The latest cycle reminded some insurance buyers that premiums only paid for an IOU, and that if the insurer or reinsurer went belly up payment wasn't guaranteed. (Most consumer-type insurance contracts have some industry protections, but others, like reinsurance contracts, do not.) Berkshire's unparalleled financial strength meant that buyers of insurance or reinsurance knew their backer would be around if and when it came time to pay.

Fireman's Fund Quota-Share Contract

A major new source of insurance business presented itself during 1985 when Jack Byrne, CEO of GEICO, departed to run Fireman's Fund, another insurer. Berkshire struck an arrangement to participate in 7% of virtually all* of the business of Fireman's Fund for four years. Directly and through some subsidiaries (including a newly formed subsidiary at Wesco), Berkshire would be remitted premiums and pay claims promptly. It would be as if Berkshire created a brand-new insurance company of its own overnight, complete with favorable float characteristics (which it could invest as it saw fit, unlike a direct investment in equity) and a well-seasoned manager in Byrne.

The business from Fireman's Fund would be managed by Berkshire's National Indemnity Company and a newly formed Wesco Financial Insurance Company (Wes-FIC). National Indemnity would write five-sevenths of the business while Wes-FIC would take the remaining two-sevenths. Since Fireman's Fund was doing about $3 billion of business, that meant the 7% share for Berkshire represented over $200 million of premium volume.

Even though Berkshire had a majority ownership in Wesco and could direct its activities, it deferred to the Peters and Caspers families (descendants of Wesco's

---

* The arrangement did not include the reinsurance Fireman's Fund wrote for unaffiliated companies.

founder who still held a minority position) in deciding whether to enter the reinsurance business with Fireman's Fund. This was an unusual degree of deference for a majority owner to show, but it was also a very shrewd, quiet, advertisement to demonstrate to others how Berkshire treated its financial partners. This reputation would pay off in the future with other acquisitions.

Investments

Practically jumping off the page (see Table 5.2. on page 205) was a large $469 million gain on sales of securities during 1985. Buffett tempered the enthusiasm for this by likening it to the day of a college graduation where nothing more is learned yet the degree is suddenly bestowed. Like the college degree, Berkshire's large securities gains in 1985 were the result of years of behind the scenes accumulation.

A significant part of that year's realized gains was due to a $338 million pre-tax gain from the sale of General Foods. Buffett was content to let Berkshire own General Foods (which it purchased in 1980) indefinitely, owing to the combination of good business economics and management quality. However, the stock was successfully targeted as a takeover by Philip Morris, and Berkshire found itself with cash instead.

In addition to the large capital gain realized on the sale of its General Foods stock, Berkshire recognized a $4.1 million special distribution (which occurred prior to the takeover). It also recorded a $14.9 million special distribution from The Washington Post Company. Both were structured as share repurchases but acted (and were taxed by the IRS) as dividends owing to the exact same pre- and post-sale ownership percentages. These were like the GEICO special distributions/buyback arrangements done in prior years.

Berkshire's investment portfolio continued to show high degrees of concentration. At year-end 1985 the portfolio had a market value of just under $1.2 billion, with a cost of $275 million. The biggest change in the portfolio over the preceding 12 months was the elimination of the $152 million (year-end 1984 value) position in Exxon Corporation.

GEICO, the largest holding by far, reflected Buffett's degree of confidence in the insurer. The GEICO investment had a cost basis of just $46 million and a market value at the end of 1985 representing 50% of the total portfolio. That Buffett was willing to maintain 50% of the portfolio in one company and 85% in just four reflected his belief in concentration. It also reflected the relative scarcity of great investment opportunities.

The Washington Post provided a good example of how investors' attitudes had changed from pessimistic to optimistic. *The Washington Post*, valued by the stock market at around $100 million when Berkshire first purchased its $10 million stake in

1973, was now worth twenty times that much. The increase reflected the managerial skill of Katherine "Kay" Graham and her willingness (with Buffett's urging) to repurchase shares when they were depressed. It also reflected a growing sense of optimism for stocks in general.

Table 5.7: Berkshire Hathaway common stock portfolio, select detail

($ thousands)	1985	% of total	1984	% of total
Affiliated Publications	$55,710	4.6%	$32,908	2.6%
American Broadcasting Companies, Inc.	108,997	9.1%	46,738	3.7%
Beatrice Companies, Inc.	108,142	9.0%		
Exxon Corporation			175,307	13.8%
GEICO Corporation	595,950	49.7%	397,300	31.3%
General Foods Corporation			226,137	17.8%
Handy & Harmon	43,718	3.6%	38,662	3.0%
Interpublic Group, Co.			28,149	2.2%
Northwest Industries			27,242	2.1%
Time, Inc.	52,669	4.4%	109,162	8.6%
Washington Post Company - Class B	205,172	17.1%	149,955	11.8%
All others	27,963	2.3%	37,326	2.9%
Total common stocks	$1,198,321	100.0%	$1,268,886	100.0%
Reporting threshold	$25,000		Unknown	

Note: Totals may not add due to rounding.
Sources: Berkshire Hathaway Chairman letters 1984, 1985; and author's calculations.

The bond portfolio is also worth a note, especially Washington Public Power Supply System (WPPSS) bonds. Of the roughly $400 million of tax-exempt bonds held in the insurance subsidiaries, almost half, or $194 million at amortized cost, were WPPSS bonds. The WPPSS bonds alone provided Berkshire with around $30 million of tax-exempt interest annually, amounting to one-third of Berkshire's $95 million investment income that year.*

Capital Cities/ABC, Inc.

The news Buffett couldn't wait to tell shareholders in his letter (both literally as it had to be disclosed, but more so because it was exciting news) was Berkshire's investment in Capital Cities/ABC, Inc. ("Cap Cities"). Berkshire purchased 3 million shares of Cap Cities at the beginning of 1986. The $517.5 million purchase was made to assist Cap Cities in financing its $3.5 billion purchase of ABC. The deal was a white knight

---

* The footnotes to the financial statements report that total tax-exempt interest income in 1985 was $36.6 million. The footnotes also disclose that $16.8 million of tax was saved because of the tax-exempt status.

situation that helped Cap Cities avoid the destructive tendencies of the leveraged buyout trend of the 1980s. It also brought Berkshire together with Thomas Murphy and Dan Burke, two managers Buffett highly admired. "I've been on the record for many years about the management of Cap Cities: I think it is the best of any publicly-owned company in the country."

Berkshire provided Murphy and Burke with an extraordinary agreement that spoke to Buffett's confidence in them. Provided that either Murphy or Burke occupied the CEO role, Cap Cities would have an irrevocable proxy to vote Berkshire's 18.7% interest in the company for ten years. Why do this? Handing Berkshire's vote to Cap Cities would allow the managers to focus on running the business and not lose any sleep looking over their shoulder and wondering what their new owner might do in the future. The move amounted to providing the management of a public company an advantage of a private company: the ability to think and act long term rather than appease an ever-changing roster of shareholders.

Miscellaneous

Reflecting its growing equity base, Berkshire raised the threshold of businesses it was looking for in its recurring businesses-wanted advertisement to $10 million of pre-tax earnings. The equity base was now over $1.8 billion at year-end 1985. Berkshire and its subsidiaries would continue to seek and close "tuck-in" acquisitions* (smaller acquisitions of businesses folded into existing units) that made sense but Buffett wanted to focus on the big fish.

The Illinois National Bank, which had been divested by Berkshire at the very end of 1980—by law and not by choice—was sold in 1985 to Americorp Financial. Having cut the cake and let shareholders choose first, Buffett was pleased that any slice (shareholders could choose all-Berkshire, all-bank, or a combination of the two) had been reasonably equitable.

Overall, the year 1985 was a good one for Berkshire. Its existing businesses, including its primary line of business, insurance, were doing well. It also found profitable new investment opportunities in Cap Cities, and a new major subsidiary in Scott Fetzer, a nesting-doll of a business which had subsidiaries and subsidiaries of subsidiaries that would join the Berkshire family in early 1986. The closure of the textile business was bittersweet but necessary. Berkshire was moving firmly and swiftly into the future.

---

* Later termed "bolt-on" acquisitions.

1986

Results for 1986 for the most part did not disappoint. The acquisition of Scott Fetzer in January and later, in June, of Fechheimer Brothers, pushed consolidated revenues past the $2 billion mark, up from under $1 billion just a year earlier. Insurance, Berkshire's largest line of business, improved and GEICO, its major insurance investee, continued to prosper. Berkshire did face some headwinds in 1986. A rising stock market helped Berkshire's investment portfolio but also left fewer investment opportunities since companies became more fully priced. A major tax law change in 1986 affected Berkshire's businesses and its investees in different—and not always positive—ways.

Buffett took pains to point out that Berkshire's growth (book value increased $492.5 million or 26.1% in 1986) was of a very high quality. Some companies grew their businesses by issuing new shares, which gave management a larger business to manage but left shareholders, on a per share basis, worse off. Berkshire, by contrast, had grown by 10,600% (or 23.3% compounded annually) over the twenty-two years under Buffett's management, all while diluting shareholders' ownership interests by less than 1% per year.

As Buffett saw it, he and Charlie Munger had a two-pronged job description. One was attracting and motivating managers who ran the various subsidiaries. One of Buffett's favorite ways to praise managers was naming them in his Chairman's letter: the first page of the 1986 letter praised the Blumkin family of Nebraska Furniture Mart, Mike Goldberg who ran the Insurance Group, Chuck Huggins at See's, Stan Lipsey at the *The Buffalo News*, and two newcomers: the Heldmans who ran Fechheimer, and Ralph Schey at Scott Fetzer.

The other part of that two-pronged job description was capital allocation. Because Berkshire's businesses were so good—they used very little capital and generated gobs more—and because Berkshire retained all its earnings, Buffett's job was a "considerably more important challenge than at most companies." Shareholders used to reading his Chairman's letters knew that he was not showing off. It was simply basic math. As Buffett put it: "In a company adding only, say, 5% to net worth annually, capital-allocation decisions, though still important, will change the company economics far more slowly." Berkshire was like a ship (and a very fast moving one at that) with a very sensitive rudder. One wrong move, a twitch even, could send the ship off in the wrong direction. For that reason, Buffett preferred to patiently wait for the right opportunities. Finding few in 1986 (Scott Fetzer closed in 1986 but was really a decision made in the prior year), Berkshire's "main capital allocation moves in 1986 were to pay off debt and stockpile funds."

Looking at Berkshire's consolidated balance sheet for year-end 1986 we can see just how conservatively financed it was. About half (55%) of Berkshire's $4.44 billion in assets were funded with equity (including minority equity stakes), the most permanent of funding sources. The liabilities section, because of Berkshire's insurance businesses, was somewhat obscured. The $2.02 billion in liabilities were surely real, but their nature was unique. The insurance float that Buffett so loved was made up of the liabilities owed to policyholders for premiums not yet earned by the insurer or claims not yet paid. These liabilities were of a higher quality because they had no due date and were regenerated each time the Insurance Group wrote additional business.

At $414 million at year-end 1986, the deferred income tax line item funded over 9% of Berkshire's assets. Like insurance float, deferred tax liabilities benefitted Berkshire because there was no contractual due date. The liabilities arose largely from significant investment portfolio appreciation, in addition to other tax-to-GAAP timing differences. In the case of taxes due on unrealized appreciation of investments, the tax was only due to the government if or when the security was sold. In this way, Berkshire could put more funds to work than it otherwise could have if it had sold the investments and paid the taxes every year. Deferred taxes were, as Buffett would later write, an "interest-free loan from the government" and would become an important, though not well understood, source of funds in future years. Berkshire, like most other companies, also had an interest-free funding source from the spontaneously generated working liabilities such as accounts payable and accruals, but these were a more normal part of doing business and largely not controllable.

The only true debt on Berkshire's 1986 year-end balance sheet was $95 million of long-term borrowings. After paying a premium to retire an obligation from 1980,[*] Berkshire only had about $17 million of term debt at the parent level. Its subsidiaries, including its newest acquisition, Scott Fetzer (which came to Berkshire with debt of its own), had a total of about $78 million of debt at year-end. To put this in perspective, Berkshire could pay off the entire $95 million using just seven months of 1986 after-tax operating earnings.[**]

Scott & Fetzer Company

On January 6, 1986, Berkshire Hathaway acquired Scott & Fetzer Company, a small conglomeration of seventeen businesses based in Cleveland, Ohio. The addition of Scott Fetzer's $700 million in revenues nearly doubled Berkshire's revenue base.

Scott Fetzer came to Berkshire after a few zigs and zags. The company had been in play for several years, having been pursued by corporate raiders. After a failed attempt to take the company private via an employee stock ownership plan, Buffett wrote its CEO, Ralph Schey, expressing interest in purchasing the company. Buffett and

---

[*] Berkshire paid a $5.4 million premium to retire the $60 million, 12.75% 1980 debentures.
[**] After appropriately adding back amortization and purchase-price accounting charges, and shareholder-designated contributions.

Munger met with Schey for dinner in Chicago and Berkshire signed an acquisition contract a week later.

Scott Fetzer had a rich history. Its namesake founders, George Scott and Carl Fetzer, founded the company in 1914 in Cleveland, Ohio as a machine shop. Scott and Fetzer were soon joined by Jim Kirby, inventor of the Kirby vacuum cleaner, and over the ensuing years acquisitions fueled the company's growth.

The largest of Scott Fetzer's subsidiaries in 1986 was World Book, Inc. World book represented 40% of Scott Fetzer's business and had pre-tax earnings of $22 million under Berkshire's first year of ownership. With twice the unit sales of its nearest competitor and more than the top four competitors combined, World Book dominated the industry. Like Nebraska Furniture Mart, this scale allowed World Book to sell its product for less than competitors and still maintain excellent economics for its owner. The encyclopedias were expensive as a set, but on a per page basis cost just 5 cents. Additionally, the books were well edited and consumer focused. Longer entries started simply and built on themselves using increasingly complex words so kids could understand them (the company ranked over 44,000 words by difficulty). Selling World Book was a calling for over half of its salespeople who were teachers or former teachers (and to a lesser extent librarians).

The other major standalone Scott Fetzer subsidiary—almost as big as World Book with pre-tax earnings of $20.2 million in 1986—was Kirby. Kirby sold high-priced but long-lasting vacuum cleaners. It had been doing so since the company was founded by its namesake founder, Jim Kirby, in 1906. Although Kirby and its sister company, World Book, were very different, they shared one important trait. Both Kirby and World Book were sold via the direct sales model, at the time often referred to as door-to-door.

Other Scott Fetzer companies, though not of the same size or scale as World Book or Kirby, nonetheless possessed similar economic characteristics. They were basic, almost boring businesses, such as Campbell Hausfeld air compressors and Wayne burners and water pumps. They also included Adalet, France, Halex, Meriam, and Northland, which made products and components for industrial use or small parts that would ultimately end up in finished products sold to consumers. The basic-but-critical nature of many of the products, combined with their low relative prices compared to the price of the end product meant the businesses were able to generate strong returns on capital. These businesses collectively earned $25.4 million in 1986.

Scott Fetzer also came with a small finance organization.* Both World Book and Kirby were supported by subsidiaries which allowed customers to buy on credit. These receivables and installment loans were in turn partly financed by term debt. Buffett considered a conservative amount of debt appropriate for such an operation, which

---

* Berkshire reported these earnings in its Other category.

was akin to a small bank that paid a rate of interest for interest-bearing accounts and earned a spread on what it charged customers for loans.

Buffett was thrilled by the acquisition and called it "a prototype—understandable, large, well-managed, a good earner." Judging by the financial results Scott Fetzer was indeed a good earner. Over the ten years ending in 1984 (the last full year available), Scott Fetzer earned an average pre-tax return on capital of 22.5%. If adjusted for excess cash on the balance sheet,* this figure rises to 28.2%. Scott Fetzer's past success had resulted in the company carrying cash and short-term investments of upwards of 50% of shareholders' equity. Upon purchase, Scott Fetzer paid Berkshire a $125 million dividend. This reduced Berkshire's $410 million purchase price (including $90 million of assumed debt) to $285 million. Even after paying a modest multiple for Scott Fetzer's underlying capital, Berkshire would earn a 25% pre-tax return on its investment in 1986.

Table 5.8: Scott & Fetzer, key metrics and acquisition data

	1986	1984	1983	1982	1981	1980	1979
Revenues ($ thousands)	$677,240	$695,382	$615,396	$544,859	$592,589	$570,191	$697,401
Revenues/average capital[1]	$3.20	$3.26	$2.97	$2.64	$2.92	$2.53	$3.06
EBIT margin	11%	10%	8%	8%	8%	5%	9%
Return on capital - pre-tax	34%	33%	25%	20%	25%	13%	28%
Berkshire's purchase multiple[2]	1.35x						
Berkshire's going-in return, pre-tax	25.1%						

Footnotes:
1. Average capital used for 1979–1984. Capital adjusted for cash and investments in excess of 5% of revenues.
2. Berkshire's purchase price was $410 million including assumed debt of $90 million. I've reduced the purchase price by the $125 million Scott Fetzer distributed to Berkshire in 1986, which represented excess cash on the balance sheet at the time of purchase.

Note: Scott Fetzer did not file a public report its 1985 because it was acquired by Berkshire.

Sources: Berkshire Hathaway Annual Report 1986, Scott Fetzer Annual Reports 1980–1984, and author's calculations.

---

* I've considered cash and short-term investments in excess of 5% of revenues to be excess cash. I've used a higher percentage than the typical 2.5% due to the fact that Scott Fetzer had two financial subsidiaries supporting World Book and Kirby sales.

The Fechheimer Bros. Co.

Berkshire's second acquisition of the year was Fechheimer Bros. Co., which closed on June 3. The company came to Berkshire as a direct result of Buffett's annual advertisement in his Chairman's letters. As Buffett told the story, early in 1985 he received a letter from Bob Heldman in Cincinnati informing him that the company he chaired passed Buffett's test.

Fechheimer passed the simple test with flying colors. Founded in 1842, it manufactured and distributed uniforms. Though a simple business, Fechheimer was highly profitable. The underlying business was earning 50% or more on capital per year.* Like Scott Fetzer and many other companies of the 1980s, Fechheimer had gone through the unpleasant experience of being owned by those seeking short-term profits. In 1981, the company was the subject of a leveraged buyout transaction that saw management, including Bob Heldman and his brother George, president of the company, retain an interest in the business. Having ridden the wave for the typical five-to-seven year holding period, the venture capitalists wanted out. The Heldmans' father Warren, who had originally gotten the family involved in the business in 1941, sought a permanent home for Fechheimer.

They found that home in Berkshire Hathaway.

A short history of leveraged buyouts provides an important backdrop to 1986. The 1980s was marked by a boom and bust cycle in private equity that included a wave of leveraged buyouts. In a typical takeover, a corporate raider buys enough stock to gain control. In a leveraged buyout, a company's own executives are often doing the buying. The deals are often financed with high yield but risky bonds called junk bonds. These kinds of buyouts are hostile. In 1986, a third of mergers and acquisitions were of this type.[43] Fechheimer was not the only company Berkshire owned or invested in that was affected. The deal with Cap Cities helped it avoid a leveraged buyout and Berkshire received a windfall when General Foods was taken over in a leveraged buyout.

In Fechheimer, Berkshire received an excellent business at a fair price. Fechheimer's underlying business was earning 50% or more on capital and Berkshire's purchase multiple gave it a 26% pre-tax return. Like Nebraska Furniture Mart, Fechheimer was run by a devoted multigenerational family.

---

* That Fechheimer had historically earned this return on capital is an assumption based on the analysis of the 1986 data, and the company's earnings subsequent to Berkshire's purchase of the company. These facts, and Buffett's preference for demonstrated earnings power, point to the high probability the business was stable prior to 1986.

Table 5.9: Fechheimer, acquisition analysis

($ thousands)	1986
Acquisition price	$46,000
Percentage of company	84%
Implied valuation	54,762
Pre-tax earnings (June 3 - Dec. 31)	$8,400
Annualized	14,400
Capital employed	$26,704
Pre-tax return on capital	54%
Berkshire's purchase multiple	2.05x
Berkshire's going-in return, pre-tax	26%

Sources: Berkshire Hathaway Annual Report 1986 and author's calculations.

Sources of Reported Earnings

The changes in Berkshire's sources of earnings was evident in the now-familiar table in the 1986 Chairman's letter (refer to Table 5.2 on page 204).

To say the addition of Scott Fetzer was a milestone for Berkshire would be an understatement. Scott Fetzer, coupled with improvements in the operating earnings of other Berkshire subsidiaries in 1986, pushed consolidated pre-tax operating earnings to almost $196 million, up more than 56% from 1985.

Ten years into its ownership of *The Buffalo News*, and with its competitor *The Courier-Express* gone, Berkshire's paper was thriving: pre-tax earnings reached $35 million—equal to the entire 1977 purchase price. Under the leadership of Stan Lipsey, the paper was controlling its costs while continuing to provide readers with a 50% news hole. Probably because of this commitment to above-average content, its Sunday paper penetration ratio now topped 83%—even higher than the 63% *The Courier-Express* achieved during its long period of Sunday dominance.

Buffett praised the amazing Blumkin family at Nebraska Furniture Mart who "continue to perform business miracles." Operating out of a single store (though with an expanded warehouse), Nebraska Furniture Mart was generating $132 million of annual revenues. With little organic growth in population locally in Omaha, customers were coming from far and wide to take advantage of its everyday rock-bottom prices.

See's Candies operated in a tough environment and nonetheless increased earnings almost 5% to $30 million. Buffett thought profits should stay at about their present level owing to stagnant same-store poundage. Though See's was able to increase prices minimally and did increase overall poundage by 2%, this was done only by adding stores. See's was (and is) an excellent business with high returns on capital, but this excellence came at the cost of little-to-no unit growth.

Insurance

The Insurance Group's headline $55.8 million pre-tax underwriting loss appeared to run counter to Buffett's prediction of better industry conditions in 1986. Looking more closely at the results between the Primary Group and the Reinsurance Group revealed a slightly different story.

Table 5.10: Insurance Group, select information

($ millions)	1986 Amount	1986 %	1985 Amount	1985 %
Primary Group				
Premiums written	$594.6		$269.1	
Premiums earned	463.1	100.0%	184.3	100.0%
Losses and loss expenses	347.5	75.0%	140.0	76.0%
Underwriting expenses	112.1	24.2%	52.5	28.5%
Total losses and expenses	459.6	99.2%	192.5	104.4%
Underwriting gain/(loss) - pre-tax	3.5		(8.1)	
Unfavorable (favorable) loss development included in losses and loss expenses	16.0	3.5%	0.1	0.0%
Statutory combined ratio		93.9%		95.5%
Reinsurance Group				
Premiums written	$398.4		$178.5	
Premiums earned	344.4	100.0%	82.9	100.0%
Losses and loss expenses	282.6	82.0%	85.7	103.4%
Underwriting expenses	111.2	32.3%	27.2	32.8%
Total losses and expenses	393.7	114.3%	112.9	136.2%
Underwriting gain/(loss) - pre-tax	(49.4)		(30.0)	
Unfavorable (favorable) loss development included in losses and loss expenses	21.0	6.1%	19.4	23.5%
Statutory combined ratio		110.0%		118.6%
Structured settlements and portfolio reinsurance				
Underwriting gain/(loss) - pre-tax	(10.0)		(6.1)	
Total Insurance Group underwriting gain/(loss) pre-tax	($55.8)		($44.2)	
Insurance Group overall statutory combined ratio		101.8%		104.7%

Notes:

1. Totals may not add due to rounding.

2. The loss and expense ratios are shown as they were reported in the Annual Reports, which is on a GAAP basis. The GAAP basis ratios are calculated with underwriting expenses divided by earned premiums. This contrasts to the statutory basis calculation, where the ratio uses written premiums. In both the GAAP and statutory calculations, losses and loss adjustment expenses are divided by earned premiums.

Sources: Berkshire Hathaway Annual Report 1987 and author's calculations.

For the first time since 1981, the Primary Group reported a pre-tax underwriting gain. This was a result of strength in specialized auto and general liability reflecting tighter market conditions (read: higher premiums were obtainable). Workers' compensation and Home State again wrote to losses, but these were not enough to prevent an overall profit of $3.5 million and a combined ratio of 93.9%.

The industry increased premiums by over 22% in both 1985 and 1986. As a result, the industry combined ratio had declined markedly from a high of almost 118% in 1984 to an estimated 108.5% in 1986. Though over 100%, indicating underwriting cost industry participants money, it was in the range of 107%–112% and that was enough to produce breakeven results after considering the earnings from float.[*]

Industry tightness and the higher pricing that went along with it factored into the overall doubling of premiums written in Berkshire's primary segment, to $595 million. Earned premiums grew even more: about two-and-a-half times, to $463 million. The only significant black mark on the primary insurers' results was $16 million of adverse loss development included in 1986 results. Representing 7.5% of beginning reserves, the adjustment was, "outside of the more respectable plus-or-minus 5% range" that the Annual Report quoted as a target. Buffett called attention to this fact in the Chairman's letter, "If the psychological rules that applied to Pinocchio apply to me, my nose would now draw crowds."

The story of the Reinsurance Group in 1986 was one of generally improving results on a fast-growing book of business. Premiums written and earned were up 222% and 415% respectively. This was largely driven by the 7% quota-share arrangement with Fireman's Fund. The combined ratio was not ideal at 110% and resulted in a $49.4 million pre-tax underwriting loss. But it was better than the 119% ratio recorded in 1985, and far better than the 194% recorded in 1984. The reinsurance business could stand higher combined ratios, though probably not much higher than the 1986 result. Remember, the long-tail nature of reinsurance means premiums are held longer before being paid as claims, providing more time to earn investment income. A 110% combined ratio implied a 10% loss from underwriting results. Making up anything more than this from investments would be difficult.

According to Buffett's estimates, Berkshire was the fastest-growing large insurer between 1984 and 1986. This contrasted starkly to having been the slowest-growing insurer in the few preceding years. The vacillations were not intentional but market driven. Berkshire was the industry's most steadfast participant, said Buffett—at the right price. Berkshire was willing to write almost any business if it thought the price was right, and the risks manageable and appropriately sized to its capital base. Prior

---

[*] Berkshire's investment income easily covered its underwriting loss because its premium volume was far lower than competitors.

to 1985, it had found the market unreasonable and therefore wrote less business; when the industry tightened, Berkshire wrote more business.

For an employee at one of Berkshire's insurance subsidiaries, these swings might have caused apprehensions about job security. To properly incentivize writing only profitable business, Berkshire instituted a no-layoff policy at its insurers. Other insurers paid more attention to volume, either explicitly or via misaligned incentives that caused employees to reason they needed to book business at any cost. Berkshire thought it better to incur a slightly higher expense ratio now rather than a much worse loss ratio in the future. This overall approach focused attention solely on long-term profitability.

GEICO had an outstanding year in 1986, and because Berkshire had a 41% ownership interest in the insurer, it shared in its success. Berkshire's share of GEICO's premiums in 1986 was over $500 million, almost equal to Berkshire's primary insurers combined. GEICO's rock-bottom operating costs created a moat protecting it against competitors and Buffett loved moats. He called what GEICO had built a "valuable and much-sought-after business castle" and said GEICO's book of business was "one of the best in the world of insurance, far better indeed than Berkshire's own book."

GEICO wrote 16% more volume in 1986 than the year before. Better yet, it did so at a 96.9 combined ratio.[*] All the while it was repurchasing its own shares, ending 1986 with 5.5% fewer shares than the beginning of the year. The 6,850,000 shares Berkshire carried on its books at a cost of $45.7 million had a market value at year-end 1986 of almost $675 million.

But excellent economics driven by low-cost operations was not GEICO's only advantage. GEICO had another asset worthy of Buffett's praise in GEICO Vice Chairman Lou Simpson, the individual responsible for its investments. Simpson had an investment track record that rivaled Buffett's. Buffett even joked that it was only because of his controlling interest in Berkshire that he was comfortable sharing Simpson's record in his Chairman's letter.

Investments

At year-end 1986 Berkshire boasted a $1.87 billion common stock portfolio and a bond portfolio of $1.27 billion largely held within the Insurance Group.[**] Consistent with its owner-mindset, Berkshire continued to maintain a highly concentrated common stock portfolio:

---

[*] Statutory ratio after policyholder dividends (GEICO 1986 Annual Report).
[**] Equity securities were held at market value in the insurance subsidiaries and at the lower of cost or market elsewhere. The difference between cost and market was trivial in 1986. The bond portfolio was held at cost of $1.12 billion and had a market value of $1.27 billion at year-end.

Table 5.11: Berkshire Hathaway common stock portfolio, select detail

($ thousands)	1986	% of total	1985	% of total
Affiliated Publications			$55,710	4.6%
American Broadcasting Companies, Inc.			108,997	9.1%
Beatrice Companies, Inc.			108,142	9.0%
Capital Cities/ABC, Inc.	$801,694	42.8%		
GEICO Corporation	674,725	36.0%	595,950	49.7%
Handy & Harmon	46,989	2.5%	43,718	3.6%
Lear Siegler, Inc.	44,587	2.4%		
Time, Inc.			52,669	4.4%
Washington Post Company-Class B	269,531	14.4%	205,172	17.1%
All others	36,507	1.9%	27,963	2.3%
Total common stocks	$1,874,033	100.0%	$1,198,321	100.0%
Reporting threshold	$25,000		$25,000	

Note: Totals may not add due to rounding.
Sources: Berkshire Hathaway Chairman letters 1985, 1986.

Buffett told shareholders that he viewed Berkshire's three largest investments as permanent holdings and that he would probably not sell them even if they were to become overvalued. He thought a "'til-death-do-us-part policy" would set the right tone and allow the managers of those companies to operate without the fear of a large change in ownership. Buffett was communicating his long-term ownership philosophy outside of Berkshire's wholly-owned subsidiaries to those of its major investees, and it was done in self-interest. *

The bond portfolio exhibited similar concentration. The Washington Public Power Supply System (WPPSS) Projects 1, 2, and 3 bonds were valued at $310 million, or 24% of the bond portfolio. From these Berkshire received $31.7 million in annual tax-exempt interest. In 1986, Berkshire purchased an additional $700 million of tax-exempt bonds with maturities ranging from eight to twelve years. But these purchases were made not so much for their superior investment potential as the most palatable of options available. Buffett liked the prospects of neither stocks nor bonds in 1986, but Berkshire had to hold marketable securities of some kind in its insurance companies and invest them. (He even called the bonds "mediocre investments" and "least objectionable.") Of the $118 million of interest and dividend income earned in 1986, nearly $72 million was from issues exempt from federal tax.

---

* Buffett said that the Lear Siegler, Inc. investment was an arbitrage position.

NHP, Inc.

Buffett chose to highlight NHP, Inc., one of the smaller equity investments that did not make the cut for the table in the Chairman's letter. At year-end, Berkshire had a $23.7 million stake in NHP, representing 45% of the company. Highlighting this small investment showed his penchant for storytelling, as well as the relative dearth of great investment ideas at that time. NHP was an unusual corporation formed to develop and manage affordable housing for low- and moderate-income tenants. It was the product of a political creation, and as such law required that one of its subsidiaries have three directors appointed by the president of the United States and confirmed by the Senate. At the time of Berkshire's investment, NHP managed around 500 properties in forty states, the District of Columbia, and Puerto Rico, or 80,000 total housing units. NHP was owned by Berkshire, Weyerhauser (22% stake) and a group led by NHP's CEO, Ron Heller, in addition to about sixty major corporations with interests no greater than 2%.

Taxation

On October 22, 1986, President Reagan signed into law The Tax Reform Act of 1986. This law significantly altered the US tax code. There were positives and negatives, but the net effect for Berkshire was negative:

- For owners of Berkshire stock wishing to sell (and assuming business value tracked Berkshire's intrinsic value with corresponding increases in share price), the new 28% capital gain rate would leave fewer net proceeds than the old 20% rate.
- Corporate capital gains tax rates increased from 28% to 34%, effective in 1987. Importantly, GAAP reporting still used the old 28% rate at present, meaning $73 million would disappear from Berkshire's net worth when the financial accounting caught up with the new tax changes.
- Dividend and interest income received by insurance companies would be taxed at a higher effective rate, a significant negative. Previously only 15% of dividends received from domestic corporations would be taxed; that proportion now increased to 20%. Additionally, for property/casualty insurance companies, the remaining 80% would be taxed at 15%. Finally, interest on bonds purchased by property/casualty companies after August 7, 1986 would be only 85% tax-exempt.

There were also a few positives:

- The tax rate on corporate ordinary income was going down from 46% to 34%, a net positive for Berkshire and most of its investees.
- A fresh start provision offset some of the negatives affecting insurance. This provision effectively gave Berkshire a double deduction as a one-time benefit by offsetting changes in loss reserve deductions for tax purposes.

The tax law affected property/casualty insurers acutely, and Buffett estimated it would reduce the earning power of Berkshire's Insurance Group by at least 10%. Because many insurers had different tax situations (due to prior loss carry forwards, or because they were part of other companies), each would respond to the changes differently.

The law also affected Berkshire's non-insurance companies in other ways. Buffett posed the question: What really happens when tax rates change? That is, do corporations pass along the increases or decreases to consumers via prices, or are they absorbed by the corporation with corresponding increases or decreases in profitability? Buffett said the answer depended on the type of business. He laid out three:

1. A utility-type organization: Would largely be required by regulators to pass along any changes.
2. Price-competitive businesses: Though not publicly regulated, the free market caused prices to adjust in response to tax changes.
3. Unregulated businesses with strong franchises (or moats) protecting them: In these cases, such as with See's, *The Buffalo News*, and many of Berkshire's other investees (owned in whole or in part), pricing power shielded the businesses from market-driven price adjustments.

The 1986 Tax Act also repealed the General Utilities Doctrine. The Doctrine formerly protected owners from double taxation (once at the corporate level and again at the personal level) during corporate liquidations. It did not affect Berkshire directly since Berkshire was long past the point of considering liquidating, but it would impact other companies such as oil and gas, some media companies, and real estate businesses, where the operating economics were meaningfully altered because of the change. This meant prospective investments must be evaluated more carefully.

Miscellaneous

Jokingly starting this next section with a tiny-sized font, Buffett informed shareholders that Berkshire bought a corporate jet in 1986. Falling on his sword and admitting he changed his mind on what he had previously bemoaned as an unnecessary luxury, he said he experienced a counter-revelation. The jet made travel a lot easier, but costlier. Buffett did note he bought the jet used, as depreciation affects planes and cars proportionally. Later dubbed "The Indefensible", Buffett was perhaps eased into such a purchase by the fact that Scott Fetzer owned a plane.[44]

Owner Earnings

Buffett excused shareholders from reading his accounting update if they so chose, removing it to an appendix to his Chairman's letter. Entitled, Purchase-Price Accounting Adjustments and the "Cash Flow" Fallacy, it used Scott Fetzer's before-and-after financial statements (prior to and after Berkshire's purchase) to illustrate his concept of owner earnings. Under two columns labeled O (old) and N (new), he asked the hypothetical question: which company was worth more? O showing higher earnings, or N showing lower earnings. The answer, of course, was that they were the same Scott Fetzer, only manipulated for accounting changes required due to Berkshire having purchased it.

The figures for Scott Fetzer are unimportant, but understanding the changes that occur when one company buys another illustrates how economics diverges from accounting. When an acquisition like this occurs, assets and liabilities are appraised at current market values. If inventory was carried on the books at a low price, it is marked up to what it would cost at the time of the acquisition. Similar revisions occur with real estate. Liabilities too, if they do not reflect current values, are revised (though they are often very accurate). If there is anything left over between the purchase price and the net asset value it is placed on the balance sheet as goodwill.

The net effect of these accounting revisions is often higher-valued assets. This affects future accounting in three ways:

1. Higher-cost inventory means reported profits are lower.
2. Higher-valued real estate (except land, which is not depreciated) causes higher depreciation expense.
3. Goodwill amortization (at the time it was amortized for both tax and GAAP purposes) is expensed and lowers profits.

The net effect is a new company on paper with greater assets and lower earnings. To an owner, however, the cash flows and intrinsic values were identical. The economics are the same; only the accounting changed.

Buffett's owner earnings formula was simple and intuitive:

Owner earnings = Reported earnings + depreciation, depletion, amortization, and any other non-cash charges – any capitalized expenditures and related working capital needs required to maintain unit volume.

As could be seen in the Scott Fetzer example, earnings charges for amortization created simply by adding and then expensing a new goodwill asset were not real business expenses. But depreciation, and the deduction for capital expenditures were very real. Buffett bemoaned the use of the newly trendy cash flow or EBITDA (earnings before interest, taxes, depreciation, and amortization) figures being used by Wall Street, since they improperly (and intentionally) omitted capital spending in an attempt to justify certain transactions. Buffett later lamented this accounting mechanism. In 1989, he said it would "induce lenders to finance even sillier transactions" and called it a "sawed off yardstick" as it was delusional and ignored depreciation.*

Thus 1986 ended with a Berkshire Hathaway sticking—quite profitably it might be added—with sound business principles, logic, and patience.

1987

With the benefit of hindsight, we can view the 1987 results through a different lens. Included at the end of the 1988 Annual Report were separate unaudited financial statements that distinguished between Berkshire's main operating activities and included a comparison to 1987. This breakdown better informed shareholders of the economic characteristics of each business line and more fully told the story of Berkshire's $464 million or 19.5% increase in book value during the year.

The first of these categories was the Insurance Group, Berkshire's primary economic engine, which held the majority of its assets (including most of its marketable securities portfolio), liabilities, and equity. Next was the Manufacturing, Publishing, and Retailing Businesses, which aggregated such operating subsidiaries as *The Buffalo News*, Nebraska Furniture Mart, See's Candies, Fechheimer, Precision Steel, and the many Scott Fetzer subsidiary businesses. The Finance-Type Businesses

---

* To be clear, it was primarily depreciation Buffett focused on (and to a lesser extent amortization). EBIT, or earnings before interest and taxes, accounted for depreciation and amortization expense and is not derided by Buffett like EBITDA.

category included Wesco's Mutual Savings and Loan, as well as the Scott Fetzer Financial Group. Lastly, the Non-Operating Activities segment held everything that did not fit into the other categories, including general corporate overhead for Berkshire headquarters and parent-company debt. Importantly, the Non-Operating Activities segment also included goodwill and property account adjustments, and their related amortization, which were separated from the business acquisitions that created them. GAAP accounting conventions included such amortization with each business, which obscured the underlying business results.

Insurance Group

Looking at the Insurance Group it is quickly apparent that its twelve individual subsidiaries constituted the bulk of Berkshire Hathaway's operating activities. Even after the Scott Fetzer acquisition in 1986, which added a host of operating businesses (and very good ones at that), Berkshire Hathaway was still primarily an insurance company. The Insurance Group accounted for 77% of Berkshire's year-end 1987 consolidated assets and a full 84% of its equity.

Table 5.12: Insurance Group, select information

($ millions)	1987 Amount	1987 %	1986 Amount	1986 %
Primary Group				
Premiums written	$412.7		$594.6	
Premiums earned	441.6	100.0%	463.1	100.0%
Losses and loss expenses	338.6	76.7%	347.5	75.0%
Underwriting expenses	105.8	24.0%	112.1	24.2%
Total losses and expenses	444.4	100.6%	459.6	99.2%
Underwriting gain/(loss) - pre-tax	(2.7)		3.5	
Unfavorable (favorable) loss development included in losses and loss expenses	(9.4)	(2.1%)	16.0	3.5%
Statutory combined ratio		102.3%		93.9%
Reinsurance Group				
Premiums written	$328.0		$398.4	
Premiums earned	372.8	100.0%	344.4	100.0%
Losses and loss expenses	287.6	77.2%	282.6	82.0%
Underwriting expenses	112.9	30.3%	111.2	32.3%
Total losses and expenses	400.5	107.4%	393.7	114.3%
Underwriting gain/(loss) - pre-tax	(27.7)		(49.4)	
Unfavorable (favorable) loss development included in losses and loss expenses	4.5	1.2%	21.0	6.1%
Statutory combined ratio		111.6%		110.0%
Structured settlements and portfolio reinsurance				
Underwriting gain/(loss) - pre-tax	(25.0)		(10.0)	
Total Insurance Group underwriting gain/(loss) pre-tax	**($55.4)**		**($55.8)**	
Insurance Group overall statutory combined ratio		109.3%		101.8%

Notes:

1. Totals may not add due to rounding.

2. The loss and expense ratios are shown as they were reported in the Annual Reports, which is on a GAAP basis. The GAAP basis ratios are calculated with underwriting expenses divided by earned premiums. This contrasts to the statutory basis calculation, where the ratio uses written premiums. In both the GAAP and statutory calculations, losses and loss adjustment expenses are divided by earned premiums.

Sources: Berkshire Hathaway Annual Report 1987 and author's calculations.

The 1987 insurance underwriting results looked very similar to the prior year with a pre-tax underwriting loss of $55.4 million compared to $55.8 million in 1986. But important differences existed beneath the surface. Written premiums, which are assigned to the year in which they are written but earned over time, fell by 25%.

Earned premiums, because of the aforementioned lag relating to when premiums are actually earned, were essentially flat. Berkshire's combined ratio* increased slightly from 103% to 105%. This was very similar to the industry overall, but Berkshire's business model meant it generated more float.

In fact, Berkshire's average float in 1987 increased from $800 million to $1.3 billion. Importantly, it cost just 4.4% compared to government bonds that yielded 9%.** Higher float directly contributed to the $153 million pre-tax net investment income in 1987, a $45 million increase.

There were also important differences within each insurance segment. The Primary Group, which wrote policies directly to those incurring the insured risks, wrote to a combined ratio of 102.3%, compared to 93.9% the year before. The results for 1987 were slightly worse than it seemed, however, when we consider that the $2.7 million pre-tax underwriting loss was after $9.4 million of favorable loss development. Although a positive factor in itself, the inclusion of favorable loss development meant that business written in 1987 was technically not as profitable as the headline 102.3% might suggest, though its true profitability would take time to pan out.

The 1987 results for Berkshire's Reinsurance Group, which through that time excluded structured settlements and portfolio reinsurance, were markedly improved. Coming down from a high of 194% in 1985 the combined ratio for the segment registered at 112% in 1987. This nearly halved the pre-tax underwriting loss compared to the year before and included just 1.2 percentage points of unfavorable loss development.

The last category of the Insurance Group, which would be combined with the reinsurance segment beginning in 1990, was structured settlements and portfolio reinsurance. These activities, while strictly insurance, were more akin to incurring debt with a roughly known coupon rate. These activities contributed $25 million to the pre-tax underwriting loss from insurance in 1987. While we cannot know for sure, we must assume the area was a profitable one for Berkshire because it remained in the business.

Given the improving underwriting and increased float and related investment income, the Insurance Group could have been considered on the upswing. Quick to temper expectations, Buffett told shareholders "the party is over." Looking forward, Buffett saw the mediocre 8.7% increase in industry written premiums as inadequate to cover his estimate of the minimum of 10% year-over-year volume increases required to cover the ever-increasing costs of social inflation. Breaking 1987 down into quarterly figures, Best's (an industry publication), showed year-over-year volume increases for

---

* I am using the figures supplied by Buffett in his 1987 Chairman's letter since they exclude structured settlements and financial reinsurance.
** Source for the float and cost of float information is the 1994 Chairman's letter.

the industry falling to below 6% in the second half of 1987. Industry capacity, lured by improving profitability, was already sowing the seeds of its own demise.

Berkshire had seen this story play out before and had been warning shareholders of its arrival for several years. Opportunity and ease of entry led to increased premium volume, but not long-term financial gain. Buffett was a long-term pessimist for the industry overall but a long-term optimist for Berkshire's insurance operations. In doing so, he reminded shareholders of Benjamin Disraeli's observation: "What we learn from history is that we do not learn from history."

Berkshire, though, was different and could rise above the pack in two ways. First, through capital strength. Though buyers of coverage in short-tail lines such as auto or homeowners would not pay much attention to Berkshire's balance sheet, those buying long term or larger insurance protection would understandably care more deeply about its counterparty's ability to pay when times got tough.* This financial flexibility also gave Berkshire the ability to invest in assets that carried expectations of higher returns over the long run. It could hold higher concentrations of stocks compared to bonds, or even own whole businesses within the insurance companies. The tight capital ratios maintained by other insurers sometimes prevented them from holding higher levels of stocks or illiquid investments.

The second factor providing Berkshire an edge over its competition was its total indifference to volume. Because of its financial flexibility and the industry's characteristic of ease of entry, Berkshire could stand by until industry conditions were favorable. Buffett had seen the ill effects of other companies focused on volume over profitability and instituted a culture focused on profitability above all else. As discussed in the segment on 1986, he even maintained a policy of no layoffs to ensure managers and employees would not be tempted to make decisions based on short-term gains.

Manufacturing, Publishing, and Retailing

Berkshire's small but growing non-insurance operating business segment represented 8% of its total consolidated assets and 6% of its equity. Berkshire would not formalize the category until the 1988 Annual Report, however the Chairman's letter for 1987 included clues to its formalization as a separate business unit, at least in Buffett and Munger's minds.

Buffett dubbed the largest of these non-insurance businesses the "Sainted Seven." They included: *The Buffalo News*, Fechheimer, Kirby, Nebraska Furniture Mart, Scott

---

* A measure of balance sheet utilization is premiums written to average equity. The notes to the 1987 financial statements disclose a statutory premiums-to-surplus ratio of 0.27:1 (or 27%) compared to an industry ratio of approximately 1.9:1 (or 191%).

Fetzer Manufacturing Group, See's Candies, and World Book. They were excellent businesses with excellent leaders. Human nature leads most business leaders to tell others that his/her managers are wonderful but Berkshire's operating managers truly deserved their high praise.

This group of "Sainted Seven" businesses earned $180 million before interest and taxes in 1987, and $178 million after $2 million of interest expense.* Though the tiny amount of interest expense was information enough to judge the businesses as conservatively financed, there is more to the story. Earnings had to be compared to the capital that was required to produce the earnings to fully assess the economic performance. As it was, this group required just $175 million, which put their after-tax return on equity capital at a mouth-watering 57%.

But that was not the whole story. The $175 million figure was the historical cost basis of those companies' capital, an important distinction. Because Berkshire paid a premium to acquire them, the accounting required adjustments to certain accounts and the addition of goodwill. These were not insignificant: Berkshire paid approximately $222 million more than that $175 million. Buffett thought that the operating managers should not be judged on the higher figure, since his agreeing to pay a higher price than the underlying capital didn't magically give those managers additional capital to employ. Having paid that premium, Buffett could rightly be judged by the lower 25% after-tax return.

The first-class problem that came with owning such wonderful businesses was that of reinvestment. The businesses earned high returns on capital but could not profitably reinvest much more capital at such high rates, though they tried. As a result, excess cash was usually sent to Omaha to find the best use for it. Buffett and Munger could reinvest it in other subsidiaries with growth potential (the Insurance Group was a recipient of numerous capital injections over the years), purchase other operating businesses, or buy marketable securities. The important thing was that the operating managers had a relief-valve for excess capital that mitigated making subpar investment decisions, and they were incented to grow only if that growth was profitable.

The 1987 Chairman's letter gave a quick update on each of the major operating units within the Manufacturing, Publishing, and Retailing segment. Buffett noted that his brevity was not a lack of recognition for good work, but that much had already been said in the past, and little had changed. As he wrote, "Experience ... indicates that the best business returns are usually achieved by companies that are doing something quite similar today to what they were doing five or ten years ago." Buffett therefore kept his updates brief:

---

* The "Sainted Seven" made up almost all of the Manufacturing, Publishing, and Retailing businesses. In total, the group earned $181.9 million on $207.3 million of capital ($168.5 million equity plus $38.8 million term debt and other borrowings).

- Nebraska Furniture Mart was humming along nicely, with sales at its one store up 8% to $143 million.
- *The Buffalo News* continued to dominate its market and maintain high penetration rates, driven by local reporting. Its commitment to a 50% news hole would remain unchanged even if margins declined and profits fell, which they were expected to do given skyrocketing newsprint costs.
- Fechheimer, with three generations consistently driving the simple uniform business, increased profits to a record $13.3 million pre-tax.
- See's sold a record 25 million pounds of candy and had flat same-store sales. Flat same-store sales was praiseworthy compared to six years of declines amid ever-shrinking consumption by consumers.
- Scott Fetzer increased pre-tax earnings by 10%, all the while decreasing average capital employed.

Clearly these businesses and their managers deserved the loud informed applause Buffett gave.

Finance-Type Businesses

The two businesses making up this segment in 1987 were Wesco's Mutual Savings and Loan, and Scott Fetzer Financial Group (part of Scott Fetzer). The latter was a separate operating subsidiary under the Scott Fetzer umbrella setup to finance consumer purchases of such products as World Book and Kirby. While Mutual Savings was in fact a bank, Scott Fetzer Financial Group operated as one. Both were highly leveraged as measured by an assets-to-equity ratio. However, unlike Mutual Savings, which primarily used savings accounts and other deposits to fund itself, Scott Fetzer Financial financed its assets with term debt.

Viewing this segment as a bank we can observe that at year-end 1987 it had equity amounting to 15.5% of its total assets. This was akin to a bank's capital ratio, and at that level would be considered well-capitalized. Another standard metric by which banks are measured is return on average assets, which measures operating performance. An estimate[*] of the 1986 return on assets for Berkshire's Finance-Type Businesses of 2.6% would have ranked it among the very best banks.

---

[*] The 1987 report does include a separate set of accounts for Mutual Savings and Scott Fetzer Financial. However, the combined figures differ somewhat from those presented in the Finance-Type Businesses segment in the 1988 Annual Report.

Non-Operating Activities

The Non-Operating Activities segment was the proverbial kitchen sink. It held accounts including acquisition-created property adjustment and goodwill. These two items alone totaled about $210 million and accounted for almost 60% of the assets reported in the segment. The income statement of the segment suffered from the related amortization charges. While the segment did hold some real assets, such as cash and marketable securities, it was clear the breakout was meant more as a cleanup to reconcile to the GAAP financials rather than to provide substantive analytical value.[*]

Investments

Primarily held within the Insurance Group, Berkshire's marketable securities were viewed as a separate entity from underwriting activities. The latter were managed by the various operating managers, while the former was entirely under the direction of the chairman and vice chairman. Buffett's evolving attitude toward owning great businesses for the long term started to show when he elevated several equity investments to the level of a permanent operating-company status. To be sure, they were subject to sale if the Insurance Group needed the funds to pay claims. However, he thought of three of Berkshire's partial ownership positions as essentially no different than wholly-owned ones. Buffett summed it up succinctly: "Eventually our economic fate will be determined by the economic fate of the business we own, whether our ownership is partial or total."

These three permanent holdings were the relatively recently acquired 3,000,000 shares of Capital Cities/ABC, Inc., the 6,850,000 shares of GEICO, and the 1,727,765 shares of The Washington Post Company. Together they had a market value of over $2.1 billion at year-end 1987 and represented most of the $2.3 billion total equity portfolio.

The attitude of permanence for the select few marketable securities investments could not overcome two distinct advantages a wholly-owned business afforded Berkshire. One was capital allocation. Though it seldom did in practice, Berkshire could direct the operating subsidiaries as it saw fit, including reallocating excess capital elsewhere. The second advantage of control was taxes. Berkshire could reallocate capital within and across subsidiaries without any tax consequences. With investments below an 80% ownership position, such as in the case of its marketable securities portfolio, Berkshire was subject to double taxation of dividends and a higher capital gains rate.

---

[*] To the extent that this 'kitchen sink' accounting concentrated and highlighted the various accounting-created adjustments, it did add value to readers of Berkshire's financial statements.

If the three permanent holdings of common stock Berkshire held at the end of 1987 were de facto operating subsidiaries, then that left the $222 million other equities as everything else. To place over 44% in one company (Cap Cities/ABC), and over 90% in its top three holdings reflected a significant degree of concentration by Wall Street standards. But it also reflected the paucity of investment opportunities available at that time. Some of that $222 million remainder was invested in short-term arbitrage positions (taking advantage of short-term pricing differentials, usually upon an announced merger or acquisition), but otherwise Buffett found stocks unattractive. The October 19, 1987, Black Monday crash that led stocks to tumble over 22% was dramatic, to be sure. It was one of the worst stock market crashes in the history of Wall Street. But the quick rebound and already-high levels of the market still left the index up 2.3% for the year and Berkshire unable to find a bargain.

The fixed maturity portfolio (read: bonds) was no different. Considering the possibility of inflation and the United States' enormous trade deficit, Buffett wrote that he and Berkshire would "continue to have an aversion to long-term bonds," and even posed the possibility that medium-term bonds would be similarly disadvantaged. Instead, like the equity portfolio, Berkshire concentrated its $2 billion* bond portfolio. A full $240 million of that was the Washington Public Power Supply System (WPPSS) tax-exempt bonds.

Almost 35% of the fixed maturity portfolio** was comprised of the carrying value of a new investment in Salomon, Inc. The 9% convertible preferred stock investment worth $700 million received much fanfare from the business press.*** Though the investment into one of Wall Street's leading investment banks would later haunt him, at the time Buffett viewed it as a medium-term fixed-income investment with an "interesting conversion possibility." (The issue was convertible after three years into Salomon common stock at $38 per share.) Another large part of the fixed maturity portfolio was $104 million of Texaco bonds. The short-maturity bonds were purchased after Texaco had filed for bankruptcy. Owing to the Insurance Group's strong capital position, Berkshire was able to make the investment into the significantly marked down bonds where another insurer could not.

---

* The fixed maturity portfolio was held at $1.94 billion amortized cost on the balance sheet, but had a market value of $2.05 billion at year-end 1987.
** Calculated on the basis of the $674 million carried within Berkshire's accounts. The remaining $26 million was held at Mutual Savings, which was not consolidated with the Berkshire parent (Mutual Savings was held on an equity basis on Berkshire's books).
*** More will be said later on Salomon. The investment received so much attention probably because Buffett had so often criticized Wall Streets' behaviors and excesses. Both Buffett and Munger joined Salomon's board after Berkshire's investment.

Wesco, K&W and Harry Bottle

Included as a regular part of the Berkshire report was Charlie Munger's Wesco Chairman's letter. In it, he continued to urge Wesco (and Berkshire) shareholders not to think of Wesco as a miniature Berkshire Hathaway. Its Mutual Savings subsidiary was mediocre, Munger wrote, because of tough industry conditions. These conditions stemmed from less-well-behaved participants using the government's credit to attract deposits and then turn around and lend them in a risky manner. A $1.9 million after-tax charge Mutual Savings took in 1987 to write off prepayments of its deposit insurance premiums (presumably now economically worthless) reflected Munger's pessimism. Mutual Savings did have some bright spots in its well-located headquarters building and its 31 building lots under development. All in all, Munger thought Mutual Savings could average 10% per year on the after-tax proceeds which could be realized from its liquidation.*

Moving to Wesco's better operating subsidiaries, Munger described the 100-year flood that hit Precision Steel that year. Actual flood damage caused a $672,000 loss after a severe rainstorm in August 1987. Munger was a frequent critic of aggressive accounting, including of managers who repeatedly excluded such one-time items from earnings discussions. But he had no hesitation excluding this one-off mishap from a natural disaster.

Wesco-Financial, Wesco's newly formed insurance subsidiary, received another $45 million from the parent entity to take advantage of the Fireman's Fund's increasing volume. In 1987, premiums earned by Wes-FIC amounted to over $73 million and afforded Wesco with use of the related float.

In more good news, a $9 million venture capital-type investment in a resuscitated Bowery Savings Bank was sold for an after-tax gain of $5 million after a friendly takeover. The risk-reward bet** had paid off handsomely. Some investors in the project are now-familiar names: the Tisch family, the family behind the Loews Corporation, and Richard Rosenthal, a former Salomon partner who died in a tragic plane crash that year.[45]

A final anecdote completed Buffett's 1987 Chairman's letter. He wrote of the déjà vu experience of working with Harry Bottle. Bottle earned his reputation with Buffett when he quickly turned around an investment Buffett Partnership Limited

---

* Too detailed to discuss in any great length, Mutual Savings had, up until 1968, taken significant bad debt write-offs for tax purposes. This had the effect of reducing Wesco's tax basis to the point that in 1987, as the footnote to the Wesco financial statements stated, it was limited to distributing $5 million of retained earnings before incurring additional tax. If its $47 million of bad debt reserves (counted as equity for GAAP purposes) were taxed at the then-current capital gains rate of 22% this would reduce Mutual Savings' liquidating value by over $10 million. Thus, Munger was implying that Mutual savings might earn somewhere around $4.5 million long term after tax on equity.
** Munger described this in the 1986 letter.

had in Beatrice, Nebraska-based Dempster Mill in 1962. Twenty-four years later Munger tapped Bottle to turnaround Wesco's K&W Products subsidiary. The small automotive compound manufacturer struggled under its previous CEO, who lost focus. Munger "made him CEO, and sat back to await the inevitable," wrote Buffett. Very soon Bottle had cut receivables and inventories by 20% while growing profits more than 300%. Bottle clearly deserved his reputation for turnarounds, which left Buffett to muse that he'd be first on the list to call if another situation arose. For now, though, Berkshire and its subsidiaries were in good shape.

1988

The resiliency of the Berkshire Hathaway model under the leadership of Warren Buffett and Charlie Munger shone through in 1988. While Berkshire found a couple of new investment opportunities that year, the investment climate was largely against them. Nonetheless, Berkshire's momentum carried it forward to a 20.0% gain in book value. That was due to past capital allocation decisions and the dedication and ongoing commitment of Berkshire's managers and employees. The compounded annual rate of return for the twenty-four years under Buffett's leadership was 23.0%—a doubling almost every three years.

Repeating the past record would be very difficult, if not impossible. The major problem Berkshire faced was its past success. Such high rates of historical return had grown shareholders' equity from a mere $22 million in 1964 to over $3.4 billion in 1988. Even just 15% growth would necessitate earning $10.3 billion over the ensuing decade. Berkshire had great businesses, such as the "Sainted Seven" non-insurance operating subsidiaries (*The Buffalo News*, Fechheimer, Kirby, Nebraska Furniture Mart, Scott Fetzer Manufacturing Group, See's, and World Book), but these could only do so much.

Berkshire faced other strong headwinds. The stock market had become more fully-priced and was thus less attractive. In a similar vein, plentiful credit drove up prices of entire businesses and corporate tax rates were less favorable than the past due to a series of tax overhauls starting in 1986. Finally, Berkshire's permanent investments (its significant ownership interests in Capital Cities/ABC, GEICO, and *The Washington Post*) faced more difficult industry operating conditions.

Accounting Changes

Major changes to Generally Accepted Accounting Principles (GAAP) mandated the full consolidation of subsidiaries on Berkshire's balance sheet and income statements in 1988. Mutual Savings and Scott Fetzer Financial (the entity that provided financing to World Book and Kirby customers) had been included on an equity basis. The results were condensed into net profit and equity, and Berkshire's ownership interest in each was included on the income statement and balance sheets, respectively. Now everything would be broken out, with appropriate minority interests deducted in separate line items. This was not unlike the treatment for many of Berkshire's other operating subsidiaries, such as the 84%-owned Fechheimer, or the 90%-owned Nebraska Furniture Mart. The change would affect the comparative periods in Berkshire's 1988 financial statements, but not the economic reality.

Possibly due to the above-mentioned accounting changes, Berkshire presented a supplement in the Annual Report beginning in 1988. It broke down its business lines into groupings more closely aligned with economic reality:

- Insurance Group
- Manufacturing, Publishing, and Retailing businesses
- Finance-Type Businesses (Mutual Savings and Scott Fetzer Financial)
- Non-Operating Activities

Buffett had long said that Berkshire's consolidated parent-level financial statements were of little analytical value to shareholders. For this reason, he presented significant detail in the Chairman's letters for each segment to aid shareholders' analysis of Berkshire. Buffett said the number and diversity of Berkshire's subsidiaries made this segmented data essential to answer three key questions:

1. How much is the company worth?
2. Is the company likely to meet its future obligations?
3. How well are managers doing with the hand they are dealt?

These were the questions Buffett asked, and he believed shareholders would also want answers. The supplemental data aided analysis without overloading shareholders with details. Buffett and Munger had always had easy access to this data. Putting themselves in shareholders' shoes (something they did often), they realized shareholders would also want this information.

Sources of Reported Earnings

From the summary table provided in the Chairman's letter (refer to Table 5.2. on page 204) it was quickly apparent that 1988 was a highly satisfactory year for Berkshire. The Insurance Group, which we will analyze later, posted improved underwriting and net investment income also increased noticeably. Most non-insurance businesses performed very well in 1988.

Manufacturing, Publishing, and Retailing

The overall results for the Manufacturing, Publishing, and Retailing Segment were a $202.3 million pre-tax profit which translated into $121.7 million of after-tax earnings for Berkshire. Pre-tax return on tangible capital was an astounding 89.2%. The group generated a 107.2% and 66.8% pre- and after-tax return on average tangible equity,* respectively, while employing just 18% leverage from borrowed funds.

Led by the still-hard-charging 95-year old Rose Blumkin, Nebraska Furniture Mart turned in even higher profits of $18 million pre-tax (up 10%). The store had just opened a detached 20,000 square foot Clearance Center to continue to provide rock-bottom prices to customers. Dillard's, a large, nationwide department store, entered the Omaha market that year without its customary furniture department. This was a testament to the power Nebraska Furniture Mart had in Omaha. Buffett relayed comments that went further. Paying Nebraska Furniture Mart and the Blumkin's a high honor, Chairman William Dillard said, "We don't want to compete with them. We think they are about the best there is." High praise indeed.

The Buffalo News, led by Stan Lipsey, delivered a record pre-tax profit of $42.2 million (up 8%), all while continuing to provide readers with an above-average 50% news hole. The expected decline in operating margins hadn't occurred. Chuck Huggins led See's to sell a record 25.1 million pounds (increasing pre-tax profits 2% to $33 million) against a backdrop of tough industry conditions. More impressive, a full 90% of the candy company's profits were earned in the month of December.

At Fechheimer, the uniform manufacturer, Buffett displayed his trust in the Heldman family by allowing them to make "a fairly good-sized acquisition" that year without either Buffett or Munger's permission. Their trust was well-earned and the Heldman's delivered, with pre-tax profits improving 6% to $14 million in 1988. Buffett heaped much praise on Ralph Schey at Scott Fetzer. In addition to operating Scott Fetzer's nineteen subsidiaries, Schey was on the boards of many non-profit institutions in the Ohio region. Though the Scott Fetzer Manufacturing Group (everything other than World Book, Kirby, and the Scott Fetzer finance businesses) saw pre-tax earnings decline 7% to $29 million, Scott Fetzer's two largest subsidiaries (broken out separately) did well. World Book improved pre-tax earnings by 8% to $28 million and Kirby improved them by 20% to $27 million.

---

* Consistent with the segment presentation, these are the company-level metrics which do not include purchase-price accounting adjustments.

Insurance

A.M Best estimated written premiums for the insurance industry grew just 3.9% in 1988. This was below the 10% threshold Buffett estimated it needed to maintain profitability amid social and general inflation. As a result, the industry's combined ratio ticked up from 104.6% to 105.4%, and Buffett estimated it would get worse considering insurance industry executives' tendency to under reserve.

Public anger over insurance rates made an already-challenging industry even more challenging. The commodity-type business economics of insurance made it difficult to raise prices and resulted in poor results. A new California law compounded these challenges. Proposition 103 required prior approval before insurance companies could issue rates. Soon after passing, it was suspended pending court review. Proposition 103 was the result of outraged consumers trying to keep down insurance costs. Though Berkshire typically walked away from subpar rates anyway, its major investee, GEICO, wrote about 10% of its business in California. More worrisome for GEICO, and perhaps for Berkshire overall, would be if other states saw similar ballot or legislative initiatives.

In another negative for Berkshire's insurance operations, its four-year 7% quota-share with Fireman's Fund expired in late 1989. As a result Berkshire would have to return an estimated $85 million of unearned premiums, reducing its float. The returned premiums would flow through the premiums written account as a negative figure but wasn't expected to significantly impact profits.

Table 5.13: Insurance Group, select information

($ millions)	1988 Amount	%	1987 Amount	%
Primary Group				
Premiums written	$218.8		$412.7	
Premiums earned	292.3	100.0%	441.6	100.0%
Losses and loss expenses	196.2	67.1%	338.6	76.7%
Underwriting expenses	78.7	26.9%	105.8	24.0%
Total losses and expenses	274.8	94.0%	444.4	100.6%
Underwriting gain/(loss) - pre-tax	17.5		(2.7)	
Unfavorable (favorable) loss development included in losses and loss expenses	(29.1)	(10.0%)	(9.4)	(2.1%)
Statutory combined ratio		103.1%		102.3%
Reinsurance Group				
Premiums written	$203.3		$328.0	
Premiums earned	229.3	100.0%	372.8	100.0%
Losses and loss expenses	170.5	74.3%	287.6	77.2%
Underwriting expenses	73.3	32.0%	112.9	30.3%
Total losses and expenses	243.8	106.3%	400.5	107.4%
Underwriting gain/(loss) - pre-tax	(14.5)		(27.7)	
Unfavorable (favorable) loss development included in losses and loss expenses	0.0	0.0%	4.5	1.2%
Statutory combined ratio		110.4%		111.6%
Structured settlements and portfolio reinsurance				
Underwriting gain/(loss) - pre-tax	(14.1)		(25.0)	
Total Insurance Group underwriting gain/(loss) pre-tax	**($11.1)**		**($55.4)**	
Insurance Group overall statutory combined ratio		107.4%		109.3%

Notes:

1. Totals may not add due to rounding.

2. The loss and expense ratios are shown as they were reported in the Annual Reports, which is on a GAAP basis. The GAAP basis ratios are calculated with underwriting expenses divided by earned premiums. This contrasts to the statutory basis calculation, where the ratio uses written premiums. In both the GAAP and statutory calculations, losses and loss adjustment expenses are divided by earned premiums.

Sources: Berkshire Hathaway Annual Reports 1987, 1988; and author's calculations.

Overall pre-tax underwriting losses shrunk 80% from $55 million in 1987 to just $11 million in 1988. The Primary Group, where premiums written and earned fell 47% and 34% respectively, nonetheless turned in a combined ratio of 103.1%. The 1988 result benefited from $29.1 million of favorable loss development, the second year in a row that occurred.

Within the Reinsurance Group, premiums were similarly off by 38% both on a written and earned basis. The segment's combined ratio of 110.4% was another improvement over prior years and included no impact from loss development. Structured settlements, separated from reinsurance for the time being, contributed $14.1 million of pre-tax loss to the overall $11.1 million Insurance Group pre-tax loss.

Commenting on the significant decline in premium volume Buffett wrote, "So be it." Berkshire would continue to write business solely on profitability, results fall as they may. It would wait patiently, ready for the deluge of insurance business that would someday come its way. Berkshire's 1988 insurance experience of significantly reduced written and earned premiums combined with improved underwriting results and significantly higher investment income, made it, in the words of Nassim Taleb, anti-fragile. Berkshire positioned itself so that no matter what happened in the industry, it benefitted. When pricing made sense and volume was there, its capital base and AAA Standard and Poor's credit rating (the highest level possible) enabled it to write huge amounts of premiums; when rates were inadequate, it let business fall off and continued to benefit from previously sound underwriting practices and float.

Float grew from $1.46 billion in 1987 to $1.54 billion in 1988. This highlights the fact that growth in float is only partially dependent upon premium volume. Float can grow while premiums fall if premiums and incurred losses are held longer.

Finance-Type Businesses

The Finance-Type Businesses (Mutual Savings and Scott Fetzer Financial Group) did well in 1988. Largely due to the absence of the one-time Federal Savings and Loan Insurance Corporation write-offs, in addition to strong volume at World Book and Kirby, pre-tax profit rose 47% to $13.5 million. This translated into an after-tax return on equity of 13.4%.[*]

Investments

Buffett considered five investment categories Berkshire's Insurance Group could choose from: (1) long-term common stock commitments, (2) medium-term fixed income securities, (3) long-term fixed income, (4) short-term cash equivalents, and (5) short-term arbitrage.[**]

---

[*] Return on assets was 2.0% with a 14.9% capital ratio.

[**] There are two types of arbitrage under this category that Buffett employed over the years. Riskless arbitrage profited from small discrepancies in the price of the same security (or similar securities in credit markets) in two different markets. Risk arbitrage, or merger arbitrage, on the other hand, was buying in anticipation of a pending merger. Mergers sometimes fell through causing stock prices to fall, hence the term risk arbitrage.

In 1988, Berkshire made two major commitments to the first option. One was The Coca-Cola Company and the other was Federal Home Loan Mortgage Corporation, better known as Freddie Mac. Coca-Cola cost $592 million for 14.2 million shares and Freddie Mac cost $72 million for 2.4 million shares of Preferred Stock. The latter was considered the "financial equivalent to a common stock" since it had a claim on residual earnings and so was included in the table.* It was also the maximum allowed by law, representing 4% of the company. The investment rationale was described by Munger in his letter to Wesco shareholders (the Freddie Mac shares were held at Wesco in the Mutual Savings subsidiary) and is discussed below.

Table 5.14: Berkshire Hathaway common stock portfolio, select detail

($ thousands)	1988
Capital Cities/ABC, Inc.	$1,086,750
The Coca-Cola Company	632,448
Federal Home Loan Mortgage Corp.[1]	121,200
GEICO Corporation	849,400
Washington Post Company - Class B	364,126
Reporting threshold	$100,000

Footnote:
1. Nominally a preferred stock, Buffett said it was financially equivalent to a common stock.

Note: Buffett's Chairman's letter only included select investments and did not inlcude a total. I have elected not to take data from the footnotes of the Annual Report since Buffett's classifications historically differed slightly from GAAP reporting.
Source: Berkshire Hathaway Chairman's letter 1988.

The Coca-Cola investment was another permanent holding, though Buffett did not say so. He only hinted at it. (Berkshire was feverishly buying all the shares of Coke it could get. Buying continued into 1989.) Given the backdrop of an expensive stock market, finding Coca-Cola at an attractive valuation suggested the market did not yet fully appreciate its excellent business attributes. Those attributes included a basic business selling syrup to bottlers who turned around and sold it to consumers.** Population growth coupled with increasing per capita incomes meant Coke had a long runway. Coke's unmatched distribution system put its products in front of consumers worldwide, and those consumers increasingly guzzled the company's products. Coca-Cola was like See's in its high margins and low capital requirements.

---

* The security was called participating preferred.
** Coca-Cola over the years has gone through periods where it owns bottlers and at other times has divested of them.

Perhaps most importantly, Coca-Cola had an attribute See's lacked: reinvestment opportunities. Growth at high incremental rates of return meant Berkshire's seemingly-low going-in return (or said another way the high price) would quickly become more favorable. In hindsight Berkshire's purchase of Coca-Cola looked like a bargain. Coca-Cola was one of "only a handful of businesses about which we have strong long-term convictions," Buffett said, adding that its management had both integrity and ability and loved the business. This praise was akin to that of Berkshire's permanent holdings of Capital Cities/ABC, GEICO, and *The Washington Post*.

Table 5.15: Coca Cola Company, key data and analysis

	1988	1987	1986	1985	1984
Revenues *($ millions)*	$8,338	$7,658	$6,977	$5,879	$5,442
Revenues/average capital	$1.43	$1.33	$1.46	$1.42	$1.45
EBIT margin	19%	17%	13%	14%	16%
Return on capital - pre-tax	27%	23%	19%	19%	23%
Return on equity	33%	28%	29%	25%	22%
Berkshire's purchase multiple	4.60x				
Berkshire's going-in return	7.2%				

Sources: The Coca-Cola Company Annual Report 1988 and author's calculations.

Berkshire also chose investment option number five: arbitrage. Berkshire's $282 million RJR Nabisco investment was an arbitrage commitment.* The commitment, which had a market value of $305 million at year-end 1988, and which was eliminated shortly thereafter at the beginning of 1989 at a "better-than-expected" profit of $64 million, came about after an announced tender offer from the takeover specialist Kohlberg, Kravis, Roberts & Co. The takeover company had a long history of completing its deals and Buffett admired its managers. Buffett would have liked to purchase more RJR Nabisco stock, but Salomon was involved in the transaction and Buffett and Munger were on its board. Thus their "directorships cost Berkshire significant money." Salomon would also soon cost Buffett much time, headache, and even risk to his well-earned reputation.

Wesco

Buffett's 1988 Chairman's letter urged shareholders to read Charlie Munger's Wesco letter, which he said contained "the best description of the events that produced the present savings-and-loan crisis." The unfolding crisis centered on the savings

---

* Because it was considered an arbitrage investment Buffett did not include it in his table in the Chairman's letter. It was, however, included along with Berkshire's other equity investments in the financial statements.

and loan or thrift industry. Thrifts were simple banks designed to take in customers' deposits and re-loan them out as safe consumer loans such as home mortgages and car loans. They were *supposed* to provide the basic function of moving excess money from savers to qualified borrowers. As a result, they were given special government-mandated privileges to conduct business. Abuses of these privileges led to the downfall of the system.

A history buff, Munger excitedly described the story of the Federal Savings Loan Insurance Company. The FSLIC operated much like the Federal Deposit Insurance Company (FDIC). Wesco's Mutual Savings and other such banks paid premiums to the FSLIC to insure depositors against losing their deposits if banking institutions failed. Thrifts were supposed to run on boring business models, such as keeping a required 60% of assets in housing-related loans or securities. To help the thrifts carry on their business and attract deposits to fund their loans, legislation gave them a 0.25% advantage over traditional banks (in other words, they could pay a higher rate of interest on savings accounts). Unchecked interest rate competition between all types of banks had been allowed before the Great Depression but was stopped afterward as lawmakers thought it had allowed insolvent banks to attract capital.

Despite this funding advantage, the thrifts still faced the built-in risk that interest rates would rise sharply and cause fixed-rate assets to yield less than the bank's variable-rate funding sources. Under Louis Vincenti and then Charlie Munger's leadership, Mutual Savings had seen this risk and sought to avoid it. Others attempted to grow their way out through ever-increasing amounts of loans funded by ever-increasing deposits. When their balance sheets became stretched, meaning assets grew faster than equity and the ratio of equity to assets fell, they petitioned and received legislation to decrease required equity levels.

Much changed during the 1980s that caused trouble for thrifts. Inflation and the related rising interest rates led to large losses. The thrifts first lost their funding advantage through competition to money market funds, and then in 1986 to other banks when the Congress eliminated interest rate caps and allowed deposit competition among banks and thrifts. To make things worse, the managers of the thrifts had every incentive to push the envelope into riskier assets since the government was effectively subsidizing the interest rate costs by providing deposit insurance.[*]

The result was a "runaway-feedback mode" of the negative sort, said Munger. He described it as a new form of Gresham's law (bad behavior drives out good) where "bad lending drives out good". Accounting allowed losses to be delayed or temporarily covered, the system incented growth to average higher-yielding new assets with lower-yielding existing portfolios, and insolvency caused managers who had nothing

---

[*] Depositors did not really care if their institution went bankrupt because the FDIC (and/or the government) would ensure the safety of their deposits (to a certain threshold).

on the line personally to risk it all like a desperate gambler trying to make up losses by doubling down. The system naturally attracted risk takers, crooks, and other "helpers" such as brokers paid to bring in the deposits necessary to fund the expansion of assets. These brokers were shopping around with the government's credit, to borrow a phrase from Munger.

Munger derided the United States League of Savings Institutions, an industry lobbying association, which "combined a blind loyalty to silly ideas with a blind loyalty to member associations." In a portent of what was to come, Munger wrote: "If the League does not act more responsibly in the future, Mutual Savings will resign." Munger thought the FSLIC was doomed and that its insolvency would result in a combination of some or all of: higher deposit premiums, higher equity requirements, curtailed investment options for thrifts, limits on growth of deposits, tougher accounting, quicker closure of questionable institutions, more regulation and oversight by Congress, a moratorium on new charters, and/or new overall state and federal banking laws. He saw the need for such reforms but knew it was probably wishful thinking given the politics of the situation.

Finding investment opportunity when others face adversity is a defining characteristic of Berkshire Hathaway. In 1988, this was on display with Mutual Savings' investment in Freddie Mac, a hybrid operated by the Federal Home Loan Bank Board and owned by private investors.

Freddie Mac's business was simple: It purchased housing mortgage loans from originators and packaged them into securities that it guaranteed and sold. It earned a fee and spread while avoiding interest rate risk. This was an essential financial function for the economy and its owners could earn returns on equity north of 25%.

Munger laid out his and Buffett's investment thesis. (They were willing to do so because they had hit the maximum they could otherwise legally purchase.) Munger wrote that given Freddie Mac's connection with government its securities were perceived as having government backing. This gave Freddie Mac an enormous advantage. Between 1985 and 1988, this advantage was reflected in a return on equity ranging from the high twenties to 30%—an indication of a very good business. Perhaps due to its recency and vividness, some thought the same bureaucrats that ruined the FSLIC would cause Freddie Mac to suffer through mismanagement or through unfair dealings with owners. But the institutions and regulators were different. Munger considered the risk unlikely, at least for the time being. He also thought that investors generally had a lack of familiarity with Freddie Mac. The fact that the shares were trading around $50 per share, compared to the $30 per share purchase price, was an indication of a correct investment thesis, at least for the time being.

Financing

Comments* on a new $250 million issue of debt that closed in early 1988 demonstrated the subtle-yet-powerful logical reasoning of Buffett and Munger. Counterintuitively, at first glance, Berkshire borrowed the $250 million with nothing in mind to do with the money. This meant the loan was costing Berkshire money up front. Berkshire borrowed at 10% and then invested it at 6.5% while waiting for good opportunities to come along. The cost of this waiting: about $160,000 a week.** Why would Berkshire borrow money when the only prudent investment was *below* its cost?

"Unlike many in the business world we prefer to finance in anticipation of need rather than in reaction to it," Buffett wrote." The rationale was clear cut: A business's assets and liabilities can be managed separately, so why not focus on maximizing each independently to get the highest-possible return on assets and the lowest-possible cost of liabilities? Reason tells us that the best time to buy assets or acquire companies and the best time to borrow money rarely coincided exactly and are often exactly opposite, Buffett said. Therefore "action on the liability side should sometimes be taken independent of any action on the asset side." Though expensive on the surface, Buffett said if Berkshire found the right sort of business within five years, the wait would have been worth the interest paid on the debt.

New York Stock Exchange Listing

Berkshire's shares began trading on the NYSE on November 29, 1988, after the exchange agreed to allow Berkshire to be measured in 10-share round lots instead of the usual 100.*** In a letter sent to shareholders in August that year and reiterated in his Chairman's letter, Buffett told shareholders that the primary reason for the listing was *not* to maximize Berkshire's share price. Instead, he and Munger wished to reduce transaction costs for shareholders. The listing allowed shareholders to buy or sell without the hidden "tax" of high commissions and wide bid-ask spreads. Providing this environment would let shareholders prosper alongside business results, not suffer share price gyrations unnecessarily. In short, they wished it to operate more like a private business, with infrequent turnover of shareholders and a share price that tracked intrinsic value more closely.

---

* Buffett discussed this in the 1987 Annual Report.
** This 3.5% spread is against the short-term rate. Comparing Berkshire's 10% coupon to the 30-year Treasury Bond at the time the spread was probably less than 2%. This reflected Berkshire's capital strength and its S&P rating of AA+.
*** Buffett noted that a 10-share Berkshire round lot would have a greater value than any 100-share round lot of a NYSE-listed company. Shares were then trading around $5,000. The exchange rules required at least 2,000 shareholders of a company have a 100-share round lot to qualify for listing.

The NYSE listing also brought with it a requirement to add another independent director, since only Malcolm Chace, Jr. met the test. To meet the requirement, Berkshire added Walter Scott, Jr., CEO of Peter Kiewit Sons', Inc., an Omaha-based construction company, to the board.[*]

David L. Dodd

Buffett concluded his 1988 letter to shareholders with a eulogy of sorts to David Dodd. Dodd, the behind-the-scenes investment partner of Benjamin Graham and co-author of *Security Analysis* died that year at 93 years old. Buffett fondly remembered Dodd's friendship and tutelage, and praised his teaching of "simple, sound, useful, and enduring" investment principles. Paying Dodd the highest compliment, Buffett wrote that Berkshire's "prosperity is the fruit of their [Dodd and Graham's] intellectual tree."

1989

The year 1989 marked a quarter-century of Berkshire under Buffett's management. The milestone was a cause for reflection and mild celebration. Buffett, characteristically, let others do the celebrating and instead focused on his mistakes over the past twenty-five years. First though, a review of the more recent past was in order.

Berkshire's gain in book value during the year amounted to a whopping $1.5 billion, or 44.4%. This brought the compounded annual rate of return over the past twenty-five years to 23.8%. Buffett used science to explain why such a result could not repeat: "In a finite world, high growth rates must self-destruct," he wrote, explaining this was especially true at Berkshire which had a large and ballooning equity capital base of $5 billion. "A high growth rate eventually forges its own anchor." The outlier year in 1989 was because of (to borrow a term from Charlie Munger) a "lollapalooza", or a confluence of factors working in the same direction.

Berkshire's marketable securities portfolio caused the bulk of the 1989 gain. Secondary were excellent results from wholly-owned subsidiaries. Within the investment portfolio two factors were at play: First was the growth in intrinsic business value of the holdings due to good management and secondly, a catch-up factor where the market correctly reappraised upward its estimate of those companies' values. Such catch-ups were one-time events, and future gains would come from the lower-but-still-satisfactory increases in intrinsic business value. Berkshire's equity portfolio was $5.3 billion at year-end and amounted to 56% of total assets and over 100% of shareholders' equity. The growing size of Berkshire's equity portfolio meant that just a 10% decline in its quoted market value could cause book value to decline in any given year.

---

[*] Berkshire's headquarters in Omaha remains in the Kiewit building.

Taxes

Berkshire's common stock portfolio had a $5.3 billion carrying value at year-end 1989 and $3.6 billion of it was unrealized gains (increases in market value over cost that had yet to be sold). Like other forms of income, the government taxed gains on the sale of assets (known as capital gains). However, the tax was only due when the asset was sold. This led to an interesting economic benefit for the holder of the asset akin to an interest-free loan from the US Treasury.*

Here's how it worked: Due to the power of compounding without interruption, an asset held for a long period of time (assuming its value increased) would grow at a higher compounded annual rate of return by paying one tax at the end versus lots of little taxes in between. This is somewhat counterintuitive since one would think that a tax paid every year would be the same as one paid at the end. But it is not. The accrued tax incurred, but not paid, appreciates and a portion of this subsequent gain is shared with the owner. The net result of a tax deferred over many years is a much higher rate of return.**

At year-end 1989, Berkshire included a liability on its balance sheet for the $1.1 billion that it would owe if it sold all its investments and realized the gains heretofore left accruing. Buffett posed and answered two questions:

1. Q: Was the tax the same as any other liability, such as a trade payable or debt due a creditor?
   A: It was different since the holder could defer payment indefinitely and choose the period in which the gain was realized.
2. Q: Was the liability a "meaningless accounting fiction"?
   A: No, since the tax was very real, but deferred.

Berkshire intended to hold its investments in its permanent holdings for a long period of time, so it would continue to benefit from this interest-free loan.

---

* Deferring tax also aids the government since its ultimate tax is higher than it otherwise would have been, the only difference is it has to wait to receive it.
** An example will illustrate. A $100 investment earning 10% compound interest for 25 years without interruption will grow to $1,083. Paying a hypothetical 35% tax results in a net gain of $738 for a net return of 8.3% per year. Paying a tax of 35% each year reduces the annual compounding rate to 6.5%. Such a rate of return grows $100 to $483 by the end of 25 years—a significant difference.

Sources of Reported Earnings

Berkshire's large common stock portfolio is relevant to the discussion of its operating earnings and intrinsic value, as shown in the table of operating earnings (refer to Table 5.2 on page 204). Net investment income of $244 million dwarfed every other operating subsidiary and made up a large portion of the $393 million of pre-tax operating earnings for Berkshire. Importantly, this did not include any gains on the sale of investments, which were reported separately.

But this was only part of the story.

In addition to the interest and dividend income coming from the portfolio, Berkshire's common stock investees retained a large portion of their earnings for reinvestment. The five major holdings making up the bulk of the portfolio (Capital Cities/ABC, Coca-Cola, Freddie Mac, GEICO, and *The Washington Post*) netted Berkshire $45 million in dividends after tax. The retained earnings amounted to around $212 million pre-tax. If these so-called look-through earnings* were added to Berkshire's after-tax operating earnings of $300 million its operating earnings after tax might be in the area of $500 million—that's 66% higher than reported.

Insurance

The Insurance Group did not have a great year on the surface:

- On a consolidated basis, premiums written and earned each slid over 30% after similar declines the prior year.
- Total earned premiums in 1989 were just $394 million—a decline of more than 52% from the peak of $825 million in 1986 and 1987.

Judged by these metrics, the year would have been considered a disappointment. But remember, Berkshire's Insurance Group measured itself on profitability. On that score, the group performed better.

---

* Buffett's formula for look-through earnings took the share of the operating earnings retained by its investees and subtracted the tax that would have been due if those investees paid out all their operating earnings as dividends. Buffett frequently pointed to the fact that capital gains in any particular year were meaningless but that, over long periods of time, were important to Berkshire. As such, capital gains were ignored in the calculation.

Table 5.16: Insurance Group, select information

($ millions)	1989 Amount	%	1988 Amount	%
Primary Group				
Premiums written	$169.7		$218.8	
Premiums earned	188.9	100.0%	292.3	100.0%
Losses and loss expenses	125.9	66.6%	196.2	67.1%
Underwriting expenses	58.8	31.1%	78.7	26.9%
Total losses and expenses	184.7	97.8%	274.8	94.0%
Underwriting gain/(loss) - pre-tax	4.2		17.5	
Unfavorable (favorable) loss development included in losses and loss expenses	*(20.0)*	*(10.6%)*	*(29.1)*	*(10.0%)*
Statutory combined ratio		101.3%		103.1%
Reinsurance Group				
Premiums written	$66.0		$203.3	
Premiums earned	146.8	100.0%	229.3	100.0%
Losses and loss expenses	109.4	74.5%	170.5	74.3%
Underwriting expenses	48.6	33.1%	73.3	32.0%
Total losses and expenses	158.0	107.6%	243.8	106.3%
Underwriting gain/(loss) - pre-tax	(11.2)		(14.5)	
Unfavorable (favorable) loss development included in losses and loss expenses	*0.2*	*0.1%*	*0.0*	*0.0%*
Statutory combined ratio		148.2%		110.4%
Structured settlements and portfolio reinsurance				
Underwriting gain/(loss) - pre-tax	(17.4)		(14.1)	
Total Insurance Group underwriting gain/(loss) pre-tax	**($24.4)**		**($11.1)**	
Insurance Group overall statutory combined ratio		115.4%		107.4%

Notes:

1. Totals may not add due to rounding.

2. The loss and expense ratios are shown as they were reported in the Annual Reports, which is on a GAAP basis. The GAAP basis ratios are calculated with underwriting expenses divided by earned premiums. This contrasts to the statutory basis calculation, where the ratio uses written premiums. In both the GAAP and statutory calculations, losses and loss adjustment expenses are divided by earned premiums.

Sources: Berkshire Hathaway Annual Report 1988, 1990; and author's calculations.

The Primary Group underwrote to a 101.3% combined ratio. Digging deeper, favorable loss experience of $20 million was responsible for 11 percentage points of the combined ratio, meaning Berkshire's results for 1989 reflected a still-weak industry backstop. Because of the precipitous decline in premium volume written the expense ratio was higher than prior years. A large portion of that decline was attributed[*] to the New York City-based Commercial Casualty and Professional Liability and Special Risks Divisions. Peaking at $93 million in 1987, business premium volume was just $20.2 million in 1989 due to inadequate pricing.

The Reinsurance Group (still excluding structured settlements and portfolio reinsurance) saw its 1989 combined ratio jump from 110% to 148%. The $11.2 million pre-tax underwriting loss was even more impressive compared to the $15 million from a year earlier considering that premiums written fell off a cliff and were down 68% to $66 million. Even the longest of payout tails wouldn't overcome that bad result, but it would have been worse if not for earned premiums falling slower than written premiums, as underwriting expenses could be reduced only so far in a short period. Earned premiums fell by *just* 35% due to strong volumes in prior years from the 7% quota-share arrangement with Fireman's Fund, which expired in mid-September 1989. Though Berkshire returned approximately $55 million in unearned premiums (net of ceding commissions), it remained liable for future losses that would not be complete until many years later.

A large contributor to the underwriting loss result for the overall Insurance Group was a $17.4 million loss from structured settlements and portfolio reinsurance. Due to their differing float characteristics (as has been noted in discussions of prior years), this line was not comparable to Berkshire's other lines of insurance underwriting activities.

Insurance generated an overall profit for Berkshire of almost $220 million in 1989 because of the significant investment income produced by float, now over $1.5 billion. While that float would have to be replenished via new written premiums to continue to be a profitable source of funds, Berkshire's strategy of focusing on profitable underwriting front and center was clearly working. Berkshire's large marketable securities portfolio will be discussed separately later as it was and is considered distinct from underwriting activities.

Considering a 2.1% estimated increase in industry premiums in 1989, industry combined ratios were forecast to remain elevated. History suggested a natural reversion to better pricing and stronger underwriting profitability, but this wasn't automatic. In the past the industry operated in a cartel-like environment where regulators and others largely abided by the same rates. Now the industry was a more commoditized marketplace. Industry profitability would not automatically come back. Instead low industry pricing would cause losses, followed by participants and capacity leaving and a return to tighter conditions with more favorable pricing. The timing of this sequence of events was unknown.

---

[*] According to the notes to the financial statements.

Berkshire's willingness to write large volumes of business acted as an industry stabilizer. When pricing was right, Berkshire would be willing to write as much as $250 million of coverage that it would retain itself. Virtually no other insurer could match Berkshire in this area. Capital restrictions, or the possibility of looking foolish, prevented others from writing business despite satisfactory long-term expectations. Conversely, Berkshire was "willing to *look* foolish as long as we don't feel we have *acted* foolishly," said Buffett. After two unusual and disrupting events in 1989, Hurricane Hugo and a California earthquake, Berkshire wrote a substantial amount of catastrophe coverage at what it deemed appropriate prices.

Borsheims

A new non-insurance subsidiary joined Berkshire in 1989. Borsheims is an Omaha-based jewelry store with more than a few connections to Nebraska Furniture Mart, Berkshire's Omaha-based furniture retailer. Long admired by Buffett, Borsheims was operated by Louis and Rebecca Friedman, who purchased the store in 1948. They came to Omaha from Russia in 1922, escaping through Latvia with only their "extraordinary combination of brains, integrity, and enthusiasm for work."

If the Friedman's story sounded similar to that of Rose Blumkin, who had escaped Russia through Manchuria about the same time, it was no coincidence. Rebecca Friedman was Rose's sister. And like Nebraska Furniture Mart, Borsheims flourished by operating under the same "sell cheap and tell the truth" credo. Though worlds apart in terms of product, Borsheims and Nebraska Furniture Mart were economic cousins. Each operation had the same fundamentals:

1. One location with a massive amount of inventory across various price ranges;
2. Daily attention to detail by top management (featuring generations of each family);
3. High turnover;
4. Astute buying;
5. And low expenses for its industry.

With four generations of Friedmans in the business, Buffett wrote that "Charlie and I will stay on the sidelines where we belong" and let them run the business.

Borsheims was too small in terms of purchase price and annual revenues to be detailed in the Berkshire Annual Report. If not for Buffett's commentary a reader of Berkshire's financials would not know of the new subsidiary.

Manufacturing, Publishing, and Retailing Businesses

Buffett's prior bestowal upon this group of businesses the title of "Sainted Seven" posed a small literary problem with the addition of Borsheims in 1989. Perhaps eager to move on or simply unable to find a new moniker, he now dubbed the group, "The Sainted Seven Plus One." So much for originality. Buffett compared this so-called divine assemblage to the 1927 all-star line-up of the New York Yankees. Pre-tax earnings of $204.8 million increased 1.2% from 1988 and produced a pre-tax return on tangible capital of 78.6% and a 56.5% after-tax return on average tangible equity capital without any net leverage (cash was greater than funded debt).

Borsheims, the Omaha-based jewelry store and newest of the Saints, met all expectations with sales twice what they were four years prior and four times ten years prior.* The jeweler had one store with over 4,000 customers on a busy day. Rebecca Friedman, her son, Ike, and their family, sold a high volume of goods at great value, all the while delivering a good economic result for its new owner, Berkshire. Because of high volumes and careful overhead cost control, costs for Borsheims were about one-third of other jewelry stores.

At See's Candies, poundage grew 8% to 27 million pounds as a result of additional advertising. Even more impressive, same-store sales, which had been stagnant, finally began to grow. With 225 stores and the close attention of Chuck Huggins, See's delivered to Berkshire strong profits of $34 million (up 5%).

Nebraska Furniture Mart created some distressing news for shareholders. It wasn't the fact that pre-tax earnings declined slightly to $17 million. That still produced an excellent economic result. Instead, it was that Mrs. B., after a spat with her family members over a flagging carpet department, had quit. But at 96 years old she did not retire. She started a competing business across the street selling furniture and carpet. Buffett would later bemoan that he did not have Mrs. B. sign a non-compete agreement. Only at Berkshire would an executive nearing 100-years-old pose a competitive threat upon departure. Mrs. B.'s short departure gave the next generations a spot in the limelight.** The carpet department (the source of the split) had a 75% market share of the carpet business in the Omaha region, up from 68% in 1988 and over six times its nearest competitor.

The Buffalo News, led by Editor Murray Light and Publisher Stan Lipsey, continued to amaze. Amid a declining population in the Erie County area, the primary distribution area of the paper, Sunday readership increased to an average

---

* The level of revenues were still not disclosed.
** Mrs. B. would eventually return to Nebraska Furniture Mart, though the incident did cost Berkshire about $5 million—the amount Buffett paid Mrs. B. for her new location, which became part of Nebraska Furniture Mart. Source: *The Snowball p. 503.*

of 292,700 copies compared to the 207,500 copies sold by its former competitor *The Courier-Express* during earlier, more populous times. While many other major papers saw profits decline, *The Buffalo News* delivered a seventh consecutive year of profits, with pre-tax earnings rising 9% to $46 million.

Fechheimer's pre-tax earnings fell 11% to $12.6 million due to integration issues related to its 1988 acquisition. The result still represented an excellent return on invested capital and illustrated one of the benefits of owning wonderful businesses. Even when they encounter the occasional issue, their previously high rates of return on capital allow a buffer against missteps.

Even with its challenges, Scott Fetzer continued to increase earnings and its return on invested capital remained excellent. In 1989, it was the lesser known businesses that carried the day. Pre-tax earnings at Kirby fell 3% to $26.1 million, and at World Book 8% to $25.6 million. Part of the decline at World Book was due to a decentralization of its single Chicago location into four locations. At Kirby, although unit sales were up strongly—international sales doubled in the last two years and quintupled in the last four—the company was gearing up to introduce a new 1990s model vacuum cleaner. This required additional operating expenses and an investment of $11.2 million in capital expenditures in 1989, compared to depreciation of just $3.3 million.

In 1989, the Manufacturing, Publishing, and Retailing segment recorded total revenues of $1.5 billion and delivered pre-tax earnings of almost $205 million. Though largely unchanged from the $202 million of pre-tax earnings in 1988, the group generated a return on average equity of 92% pre-tax and 57% after-tax, all while employing little debt. That the group did not grow was okay. These were an excellent collection of businesses, but ones without the ability to reinvest large sums. Redeployment of excess capital was Buffett's job and fortunately, as will be discussed in the investment section, he found an outlet for some of the surplus cash.

Finance-Type Businesses

Mutual Savings continued to contribute modestly to Berkshire's results. Combined with the Scott Fetzer Finance Group, the two entities reported net earnings after tax of $10.7 million in 1989. This was good for a 2.1% return on assets and a 14.7% return on equity.

Non-Operating Activities

A cursory glance at the dumping ground that was the Non-Operating Activities (the all other segment) reveals a large decrease in equity, to a deficit of almost $260 million. This was partly due to the accumulated effects of required accounting charges for intangible assets, but largely because of an additional $517 million of parent-level debt (including a zero-coupon convertible issue discussed below). The capital was contributed to operating units, including the Insurance Group. It nonetheless remained unassigned and reduced equity of the Non-Operating Activities segment since there was no corresponding increase in assets.

Investments

Despite an elevated level of the overall stock market in 1989, Buffett continued to add to Berkshire's shares of Coca-Cola. But the market hadn't fully caught on. By year-end, Berkshire held 23.4 million shares with a cost of just over $1 billion and a market value of about $1.8 billion. Buffett chided himself on taking over fifty years to recognize the excellent qualities of Coke, whose products he had sold in the 1930s as one of his first entrepreneurial ventures.[46]

The truth was that Buffett was somewhat slow to recognize the value being unleashed by CEO Roberto Goizueta, and President Don Keough. Coke had drifted somewhat in the 1970s, taking its focus away from its core syrup business. Now Goizueta and Keough were at the helm and the "mesh of marketing and finance is perfect and the result is a shareholder's dream." As discussed in the section on 1988, Buffett saw a ubiquitous product combined with virtually exploding international sales sold by a business with low capital requirements. He decided to load up on shares of Coke.

Table 5.17: Berkshire Hathaway common stock portfolio, select detail

($ thousands)	1989
Capital Cities/ABC, Inc.	$1,692,375
The Coca-Cola Company	1,803,787
Federal Home Loan Mortgage Corp.[1]	161,100
GEICO Corporation	1,044,625
Washington Post Company - Class B	486,366
Reporting threshold	$100,000
Footnote: 1. Nominally a preferred stock, Buffett said it was financially equivalent to a common stock.	

Source: Berkshire Hathaway Chairman's letter 1989.

Berkshire went so far as to advertise in the Annual Reports its special interest in purchasing convertible preferred issues as a long-term investment. In 1989, Berkshire filled its appetite almost completely* by spending $600 million on a Gillette issue

---

* After the investments in 1989 Buffett's usual advertisement for businesses to purchase, which included the desire to purchase controlling blocks of stock or preferred, said that Berkshire, "was now close to the maximum position we feel appropriate" for preferred.

(razors), $358 million on a USAir Group issue (airline), and $300 million on a Champion International Group issue (paper producer).

Buffett thought well of each management team and considered Gillette's long-term prospects favorable enough to join its board of directors. But he could not see as clearly the future of these companies, so Berkshire structured the investments differently. Each of the preferred issues carried approximately the same terms. Contractual dividend rates, which were cumulative, ranged from 8.75% to 9.25%. Each issue required mandatory redemption in ten years, and each was convertible into common shares at prices modestly above their then-current market prices. The issues were structured to provide the investees with a long-term and interested capital partner, with a mediocre downside possibility for Berkshire if they didn't work out, and upside potential if the underlying companies did very well. Munger put it well in his letter to Wesco shareholders (Wesco also invested in a smaller portion of the same issues) saying "we regard these investments in the aggregate as sound but not exciting."

Zero-Coupon Securities

Augmenting its already-strong capital position still further, Berkshire issued $902.6 million of Zero-Coupon Convertible Subordinated Debentures in September 1989.

The nomenclature and workings of zero-coupon bonds is less foreign than at first glance. Berkshire's issue was no different than US Savings Bonds issued at a lower price than the common $25 face amount. Most savers are familiar with these instruments, and while the US Treasury does not call them zero-coupon bonds, they are in fact just the same. Most bonds require regular interest payments, usually semiannually. A zero-coupon bond, or savings bond, requires none as the investor (or Berkshire bondholder) pays a purchase price that is lower than the face value at maturity.

Berkshire's zero-coupon bonds were issued at 44.314% of face value, bringing in $400 million minus $9.5 million in fees. Instead of paying periodic interest, Berkshire would be required to pay back the full $900 million in fifteen years when it came due. For Berkshire, this was the mathematical equivalent of a 5.5% interest rate. Better still, the imputed interest was tax deductible each year since it was technically accruing.*

Berkshire's zero-coupon issue also came with a conversion privilege. Each $10,000-denominated bond could be converted into 0.4515 shares of Berkshire Hathaway stock. At a cost of $4,431 (the 44.314% issue price) the conversion implied a $9,815 share price for Berkshire (see Table 5.18), which was a 15% premium to its price at the time of purchase.

---

* This deductibility was fair from the standpoint of the US Treasury since holders of the debt paid tax every year on the accrued-but-not-received interest payments.

This conversion price, with a little manipulation, can give us a window into Buffett's thinking regarding Berkshire's valuation at that time:

Table 5.18: Berkshire Hathaway implied valuation, 1989

Bond face value	$10,000
Issue price	44.314%
Cost	$4,431
Conversion rate	0.4515
Implied value per share	$9,814
BRK shares outstanding	1,146,000
Implied BRK market value	$11,246,790,698
Berkshire shareholders' equity	$4,925,126,000
Conversion price/book value	2.28x

Sources: Berkshire Hathaway Annual Report 1989 and author's calculations.

The effective conversion price implied Buffett was willing to issue shares in Berkshire at a price-to-book value of about 2.3x. Buffett had thus positioned Berkshire for the use of $390 million of capital that would do one of two things: cost it less than 5.5% after considering the favorable effects of interest deductibility; or at a valuation that did not dilute existing shareholders.* It was a win-win, and classic Buffett.**

But that is not always the case. Buffett observed abuses of similar-type instruments. Wall Street, he wrote, classically took a good idea and went too far. Since it was "impossible to default on a promise to pay nothing" (remember, there were no interim payments due, only the one balloon payment at the end), an issuer could technically not miss a payment. Some on Wall Street used these features to fund the leveraged-buyout boom (buying a company almost entirely using debt) with zero-coupon securities and their cousin, pay-in-kind (or PIK) bonds.***

Acquiring a company using a significant amount of debt is risky. It was now possible for a company to borrow far more than it economically could be expected to repay, considering its debt servicing capacity and capital expenditure needs. Cash was not needed immediately for payments, so Wall Street coined the term EBDIT, or earnings before depreciation, interest, and taxes (a similar moniker to today's EBITDA, with the A being amortization). Wall Street reasoned that if the interest was not due, it didn't need to be counted. A company with $100 million of earnings

---

* If Berkshire's intrinsic value was below 2.3x book value (which it most certainly was), issuing shares at that valuation meant bondholders that chose to convert were buying in at an expensive price.

** Another important attribute of the issue was the fact, according to the footnotes to the financial statements, that there were "no materially restrictive covenants".

*** PIK bonds were payments of interest in more bonds rather than cash and functioned just like zero-coupon bonds.

could incur debt with $90 million of interest due currently and an additional $60 million of annual PIK interest that would accrue but not be paid in cash (a total of $150 million year one). That company would remain operational despite more debt service than income.

Such "models of modern finance" were rightly considered delusional to Buffett and Munger, who thought that not only were the zero-coupon-type accruals of interest very real expenses, but so was the depreciation that was ignored. Summing up the whole debacle quite elegantly, Buffett wrote: "A base business cannot be transformed into a golden business by tricks of accounting or capital structure." His warning was precise as it was brief: "Financial alchemy" doesn't work.*

Wesco

Wesco made headlines with the public resignation of Mutual Savings and Loan from the League of Savings. Both Buffett and Munger decided to resign after becoming disgusted with the League's behavior. The League lobbied on behalf of savings and loan institutions who purchased some of the same zero-coupon issues described above from shaky borrowers, just to record the earned-but-not-received interest.

The one-page letter, signed by Munger and released to the press "as one small measure of protest ... for such attention as may ensue," lambasted the League for its behavior. The letter dismissed the idea that such trade associations were expected to behave only in ways that are not counter to their members' interests, even if it meant endorsing egregious behavior like the "micky-mouse accounting" of "institutions dominated by crooks and fools." Munger thought a responsible association should attempt to clean up the mess which it had created, and which he estimated would cost taxpayers over $100 billion. Instead, he wrote, the association "persists in prescribing continuation of loose accounting principles, inadequate capital and, in effect inadequate management," rather than become a constructive player in the reform. Wesco would continue alone until some sort of resolution occurred.

In the meantime, Wesco had some bright spots. Not the least of which was Precision Steel, and a new operating subsidiary, New America Electrical Corporation, 80% of which was purchased for $8.2 million at the end of 1988.

Wes-FIC, the insurer set up to hold the business of Fireman's Fund, whose share arrangement had ceased as of the latter part of 1989, continued writing some business of its own, though just $438,000 in direct premiums in 1989. More promising was

---

* Leaving aside the inclination of the Wall Street enablers, it is simply amazing that managements and boards of directors would push the envelope so far. Some of the reasons why they do it are their competitive natures and agency-type misalignment of incentives that create the opportunity for abuse. These systems that put gain before risk go entirely against the Berkshire attitude, which is encapsulated from a quote in the 1987 Chairman's letter: "We do not wish it to be only likely that we can meet our obligations; we wish that to be certain."

a new agreement, effective January 1, 1990, to reinsure half of Berkshire's Cypress Insurance Company, one of its workers' compensation insurance businesses.

Mistakes of the First Twenty-Five Years

Reflecting on a quarter-century at the helm of Berkshire Hathaway, Buffett devoted two entire pages of his Chairman's letter to a "condensed version" of his mistakes and the lessons he learned.

1. Mistake number one: Purchasing control of Berkshire to begin with (which may come as a surprise to readers). He was "enticed to buy because the price looked cheap" but quickly realized that such a price reflected the difficult business conditions.
   - The lesson: "time is the friend of the wonderful business, the enemy of the mediocre."
2. Mistake number two: Buying several mediocre businesses at seemingly low prices.
   - The lesson: "It's far better to buy a wonderful company at a fair price than a fair company at a wonderful price."
3. Mistake number three: An unseen force Buffett termed the institutional imperative. This was a tendency for managers to make irrational decisions and misspend shareholders' money by blindly following others in the business community. This was quite contrary to what was taught in business schools.
   - The lesson: Manage Berkshire to minimize the influence of institutional imperatives and "attempt to concentrate our investments in companies that appear alert to the problem."
4. Mistake number four: Berkshire often partnered with managers such as Chuck Huggins, Ralph Schey, and the Blumkin's who were liked, trusted and admired, and who led successful companies. But not always.
   - The lesson: While above-average managers would not cure a below-average business, he preferred such individuals to others—even if it meant slightly lower results for Berkshire. "We've never succeeded in making a good deal with a bad person."
5. Mistake number five: One oft-forgotten category of mistakes were those of omission. Contrary to mistakes of commission, which are explicit, those of omission are the decisions or investments that should have been made.
   - The lesson: Buffett admitted to taking a pass when good deals were served up on a platter and said "the cost of this thumb-sucking has been huge."

In summation, Buffett said Berkshire used "consistently-conservative financial policies" that "may appear to have been a mistake, but in [his] view were not." He wrote that Berkshire probably could have increased the 23.8% compounded annual return it had achieved by borrowing more money, but he was uncomfortable with even a 1% chance of failure. Even at 99:1 odds, he and Munger would not have been comfortable with the risks.

Ending his discussion on mistakes was a subtle reassurance to shareholders that despite his personal fortune of $4.2 billion (placing him second on the Forbes 400 list of wealthiest Americans[47]), Buffett was not done painting his picture: "Charlie and I have never been in a big hurry: We enjoy the process far more than the proceeds—though we have learned to live with those also."

The First 25 Years—1965 to 1989

Figure 5.19: Selected financial data at five-year intervals (reproduced from the 1989 Annual Report)

($ thousands, except per share amounts)	1989	1984	1979	1974	1969	1964
Revenues:						
Sales and service revenues	$1,526,459	$496,971	$286,493	$32,592	$40,427	$49,983
Insurance premiums earned	394,279	140,242	181,949	60,574	25,258	0
Investment income, insurance group	250,723	69,281	24,747	7,916	2,017	0
Realized investment gain (loss)	223,810	114,136	10,769	(1,908)	5,722	0
Total revenues	2,483,892	861,388	560,381	100,384	73,424	49,983
Earnings (loss):						
Before realized investment gain	299,902	70,201	35,921	8,383	3,863	(2,824)
Realized investment gain (loss)	147,575	78,694	6,896	(1,340)	4,090	0
Net earnings (loss)	447,477	148,895	42,817	7,043	7,953	(2,824)
Earnings (loss) per share:						
Before realized investment gain (loss)	262.46	61.21	34.97	8.56	3.92	(2.41)
Realized investment gain (loss)	127.55	68.61	6.71	(1.37)	4.15	0.00
Net earnings (loss)	390.01	129.82	41.68	7.19	8.07	(2.41)
Year-end data:						
Total assets	9,459,594	2,297,516	1,433,863	216,214	95,746	27,887
Term debt and other borrowings	1,007,516	127,104	134,416	21,830	7,419	2,500
Shareholders' equity	4,925,126	1,271,761	344,962	88,199	43,918	22,139
Common shares outstanding (thousands)	1,146	1,147	1,027	980	980	1,138
Shareholders' equity per outstanding share	$4,296.01	$1,108.77	$335.85	$90.04	$44.83	$19.46

Source: Berkshire Hathaway Annual Report 1989.

Having just covered the mistakes of the first twenty-five years, it is worth taking a moment to put into perspective the incredible change in Berkshire during Warren Buffett's control. The table above (Table 5.19) tells a compelling story. While change in any individual year was smaller or focused on a few things, taken as a whole those changes collectively transformed Berkshire Hathaway into an economic powerhouse.

It is also instructive to take a closer look at how that 23.8% compounded annual rate of return on book value was created.* Beginning with just $22 million of equity capital in a self-described subpar textile business, Berkshire Hathaway was transformed completely. Over twenty-five years, shareholders' equity grew to $4.9 billion. The sources of that increase were, roughly:

- 48% from unrealized gains on marketable securities;
- 30% from operating activities: the wholly-owned subsidiaries, plus dividends and interest from investees;
- 19% from realized gains on marketable securities;
- And 3% from the addition of Diversified Retailing and Blue Chip Stamps during the 1975–1984 decade. (A very small change was due to dividends, treasury stock transactions, and miscellaneous.)

Table 5.20: Reconciliation of shareholders' equity, 1965–1989

($ millions)	
1964 ending shareholders' equity	$22
Net income - operations 1965–1989	1,493
Net income - realized gains 1965–1989	936
Unrealized appreciation of investments	2,341
Mergers/divestitures	133
Dividends/treasury stock	(4)
Other/misc.	4
1989 ending shareholders' equity	$4,925

Sources: Berkshire Hathaway Annual Reports and author's calculations.

Taking apart the twenty-five years, we can see how Berkshire earned its gains over that time. The first ten-year period (1964–1974) was largely driven by operating

---

* Examining the table at the beginning of this section more closely, the calculated rate of annual book value and per share book value growth (24.1%) appears to differ from Buffett's calculation of 23.8%. The difference arises due to two factors: one being the miniscule 0.03% per annum growth in shares outstanding (essentially nothing, an amazing feat), and the other is because of the extra three months one must include in 1964. Berkshire's 1964 figure was actual as of September 30. Using the precise timeframe of twenty-five years, three months, we arrive at Buffett's calculation of 23.83%, rounded to 23.8%.

activities. During the next decade (1975–1984) the contribution of operations to book value growth shrunk to one-third of the total change, with over half coming from a combination of realized gains and unrealized gains on appreciation of investments. It was in this decade that saw a meaningful portion of the change in net worth come from the addition of Diversified Retailing and Blue Chip Stamps, both of which merged with Berkshire.

The change during the five-year period from 1985–1989, while shorter than a decade, nonetheless illustrates the continued shift toward the importance of the marketable securities portfolio. During that five-year span almost three-quarters of the change in Berkshire's book value came from realized or unrealized appreciation of investments, with unrealized appreciation accounting for a full half of the change.

Table 5.21: Reconciliation of shareholders' equity, 1965–1989

($ millions)	1965–74	1975–84	1985–89	1965–89
Beginning of period shareholders' equity	$22	$88	$1,272	$22
Net income - operations	57	366	1,070	1,493
Net income - realized gains	7	199	729	936
Unrealized appreciation of investments	0	486	1,855	2,341
Mergers/divestitures	0	133	0	133
Dividends/treasury stock	(3)	0	(1)	(4)
Other/misc.	4	0	0	4
End of period shareholders' equity	$88	$1,272	$4,925	$4,925
Change in equity during period	$66	$1,184	$3,652	$4,903

Sources: Berkshire Hathaway Annual Reports and author's calculations.

Table 5.22: Reconciliation of shareholders' equity, 1965–1989

	1965–74	1975–84	1985–89	1965–89
Net income - operations	86%	31%	29%	30%
Net income - realized gains	11%	17%	20%	19%
Unrealized appreciation of investments	0%	41%	51%	48%
Mergers/divestitures	0%	11%	0%	3%
Dividends/treasury stock	(4%)	0%	(0%)	(0%)
Other/misc.	7%	0%	0%	0%
Total	100%	100%	100%	100%

Sources: Berkshire Hathaway Annual Reports and author's calculations.

1990

While the first twenty-five years of Berkshire Hathaway under Warren Buffett's control ended on a high note, it began lackluster, and the next twenty-five followed that pattern. Book value grew just 7.3% in 1990. The Berkshire of the bygone era was a textile business with dim prospects, while that of 1990 featured a conglomerate with much potential. The off year in 1990 was largely caused by Berkshire's significant common equity portfolio, which made up over half of its average assets and fluctuated along with changes in the overall stock market. While the current rate of book value growth was well below Buffett's goal of 15% per annum, Berkshire's businesses continued to be exceptional, with most of those businesses making good progress during the year.

Look-Through Earnings

The annual change in Berkshire's book and market values could swing wildly from year to year and diverge significantly from each other (see Table 5.23).

Table 5.23: Berkshire Hathaway change in book and market values

	1990	1989
Change in book value	7.4%	44.4%
Change in market value	(23.1%)	84.6%
Difference (book-market)	30.5pts	(40.2pts)

Source: Berkshire Hathaway Annual Report 2018.

This was because accounting obscured important information about Berkshire's economic earning power. Capital Cities/ABC was an extreme case. In 1990, Berkshire owned 17% of the company. Berkshire's share of its 1990 earnings was over $83 million, yet Berkshire only recorded income of $600,000. Why? Because Cap Cities paid Berkshire $600,000 in dividends, and accounting conventions only counted those—completely ignoring roughly $82 million that Cap Cities retained for reinvestment on Berkshire's behalf. Many of Berkshire's other investees had similar, though not so extreme, disparities. If those companies continued to do well their underlying earning power would *eventually* translate into corresponding gains in market value.

The solution for this accounting problem was look-through earnings (see Table 5.24). Look-through earnings accounted for retained earnings and adjusted for the taxes that would have been due if paid as dividends. The total for 1990: $591 million. It was an approximate figure to be sure, though one more closely-aligned to economic reality.*

---

* Securities gains and losses were ignored in the calculation. These were not unimportant but were erratic by nature. Any gains or losses (over an appropriate period of time) would (or should) reflect the undistributed earnings of investees and show up as capital gains.

Table 5.24: Berkshire Hathaway look-through earnings, 1990

($ millions)	
Operating earnings retained by investees (BRK share)	$250
Less: taxes owed if paid out as dividends	(30)
Net operating earnings attributable to BRK	220
Berkshire Hathaway after-tax operating earnings	371
Total look-through earnings	$591

Source: Berkshire Hathaway Annual Report 1990.

Manufacturing, Publishing, and Retailing

Berkshire's non-insurance economic engine continued to impress. Taken as a whole, the group contributed $216.8 million pre-tax to Berkshire's earnings in 1990, representing a pre-tax return on average tangible capital of 73% and equity of over 83%. The after-tax return on tangible equity was an equally impressive 51% and, importantly, was achieved with no net debt.* Such high returns on capital were scarce, and there were few incremental growth opportunities available within the subsidiaries themselves. As a result, most funds were sent to Omaha for reinvestment. In fact, over 80% of the Manufacturing, Publishing, and Retailing businesses' earnings were sent to the parent company over the prior five years.

Amid weak economic conditions (the US entered a recession in 1990 marked by hundreds of bank failures), Borsheims turned in revenue growth of 18%.** From one store (which Buffett estimated to be the largest after Tiffany's New York City location) the Friedman family continued to operate from a simple and effective playbook. They maintained rock bottom operating costs, which produced a positive feedback loop from low prices driving additional demand. This kept operating costs as a percentage of revenue low. It was the Nebraska Furniture Mart playbook, only for jewelry. Such low prices attracted shoppers from far beyond Omaha. The store had grown outside its physical footprint with a mail-order service that shipped assortments of pieces valued at upwards of $100,000 to all over the country, counting on people's honesty to pay for them or return them. This seemingly risky business had yet to produce a loss from customer dishonesty.***

Nebraska Furniture Mart continued its relentless progress. Revenues grew 4% to $159 million in 1990 by attracting shoppers from far and wide. Profits ticked up 1% to $17 million. Nebraska Furniture Mart ranked number three in popularity in Des Moines, Iowa, which was 130 miles away (the equivalent of driving from Washington

---

* Leverage in a traditional sense (debt to shareholders' equity) was just 0.13:1 or 13%.
** Still no specific information was provided on the earnings from Borsheims.
*** Buffett said customers did not need to be known to Borsheims but always came well recommended.

D.C. to Philadelphia). It outranked seventeen stores closer to Des Moines. Its low prices, like those of its sister company Borsheims, created an "irresistible magnet" that lured shoppers from far outside a traditional market radius and allowed Nebraska Furniture Mart to maintain even lower prices by avoiding opening additional stores.

Taking advantage of Nebraska Furniture Mart's popularity, See's had a cart in the Omaha store. In what Buffett termed a "counter-revelation" against his dislike of the term "synergy," this cart did more business than some California-based standalone stores. These successes, coupled with a 5% price increase, led See's to increase pre-tax profits nearly 16% to $39.6 million. This was despite a Christmas season that fell slightly below the mark.

Reporting on *The Buffalo News*, Buffett wrote that, "the business showed far more vulnerability to the early stages of a recession than has been the case in the past." He openly questioned whether the paper's 5% decline in pre-tax profits to $44 million was temporary, or an indication of a permanent situation. The relative weakness was also a window into the impact alternative advertising channels were having at two of Berkshire's major investees, Capital Cities/ABC and *The Washington Post*. Berkshire and *The Buffalo News* remained committed to its customers, however. Buffett wrote that it would not deviate from providing the quality of news that led it to success in the first place. "Regardless of earnings pressures, we will maintain at least a 50% news hole. Cutting product quality is not a proper response to adversity."

At Fechheimer, pre-tax profits grew just 4%, to $12.9 million. Fechheimer continued to have excellent prospects. It moderated or solved some of the issues that its large 1988 acquisition had thrown up. Still, amid a recessionary environment, the fact that it grew revenues and profits was a meaningful achievement.

Scott Fetzer, under the leadership of Ralph Schey, turned in a result that would have placed it near the top of the Fortune 500 based on return on equity. Pre-tax earnings came in at $101.9 million.* Scott Fetzer's finance businesses earned a record $12.2 million pre-tax in 1990. Pre-tax earnings from its World Book unit increased 25% to $31.9 million despite lower unit sales.** At Scott Fetzer's Kirby unit, the new Generation 3 vacuum cleaner was an unqualified success. Costs associated with the new product introduction kept earnings down temporarily, but increased unit volumes and strong international demand portended strong results for 1991. Campbell Hausfeld, a Scott Fetzer subsidiary and producer of small- and medium-sized air compressors, earned a mention in the 1990 Chairman's letter for its particularly fine year.***

---

* No comparative data is available because the earnings from the Scott Fetzer finance businesses are not broken out. We only have the data Buffett provided.

** This was attributed to the success of decentralization efforts, which had hurt earnings in 1989.

*** Revenues reached $109 million with over 30% coming from products introduced over the preceding five years.

Insurance

Weakness in pricing continued to be the story in insurance, though Berkshire did find a way to put its reputation and capital base to profitable use in 1990.

Table 5.25: Insurance Group, select information

($ millions)	1990 Amount	%	1989 Amount	%
Primary Group				
Premiums written	$139.1		$169.7	
Premiums earned	154.0	100.0%	188.9	100.0%
Losses and loss expenses	102.0	66.2%	125.9	66.6%
Underwriting expenses	51.5	33.4%	58.8	31.1%
Total losses and expenses	153.5	99.7%	184.7	97.8%
Underwriting gain/(loss) - pre-tax	0.5		4.2	
Unfavorable (favorable) loss development included in losses and loss expenses	*(18.3)*	*(11.9%)*	*(20.0)*	*(10.6%)*
Statutory combined ratio		103.3%		101.3%
Reinsurance Group				
Premiums written	$435.2		$66.0	
Premiums earned	437.5	100.0%	146.8	100.0%
Losses and loss expenses	432.2	98.8%	109.4	74.5%
Underwriting expenses	32.5	7.4%	48.6	33.1%
Total losses and expenses	464.7	106.2%	158.0	107.6%
Underwriting gain/(loss) - pre-tax	(27.2)		(11.2)	
Unfavorable (favorable) loss development included in losses and loss expenses	*0.0*	*0.0%*	*0.2*	*0.1%*
Statutory combined ratio		106.3%		148.2%
Structured settlements and portfolio reinsurance				
Underwriting gain/(loss) - pre-tax[1]	NR		(17.4)	
Total Insurance Group underwriting gain/(loss) pre-tax	**($26.7)**		**($24.4)**	
Insurance Group overall statutory combined ratio		104.9%		115.4%

Footnote:
1. In 1990, Berkshire began including structured settlements and portfolio reinsurance with reinsurance.

Notes:
1. Totals may not add due to rounding.
2. The loss and expense ratios are shown as they were reported in the Annual Reports, which is on a GAAP basis. The GAAP basis ratios are calculated with underwriting expenses divided by earned premiums. This contrasts to the statutory basis calculation, where the ratio uses written premiums. In both the GAAP and statutory calculations, losses and loss adjustment expenses are divided by earned premiums.
Sources: Berkshire Hathaway Annual Reports 1990, 1992; and author's calculations.

Berkshire's Primary Group wrote and earned almost 20% lower volume, totaling $139 million for premiums written and $154 million for premiums earned. The primary businesses continued to ignore volume for its own sake and remained focused on profitable underwriting. In one such example, premium volume in the New York City office fell from a high of $93 million in 1987 to just $18 million in 1990. The combined ratio for the primary businesses, at 103.3%, benefited from a fourth consecutive year of favorable loss development. Expecting a trend like that to continue was dangerous since it could be decades before all cases were settled.

The real story in the Insurance Group in 1990 was the reinsurance division. Having written just $66 million in 1989, the Reinsurance Group wrote $384 million in 1990—multiples of the year before.* The large increase in premiums was driven by $378 million of 1990 volume related to insuring large risks. Considering the volatility inherent in such business, Buffett took pains to explain the logic.

He said that while volume in other lines "continues to be small but satisfactory," Berkshire was pursuing business in the super cat (short for super catastrophe) area of reinsurance. This line of business reinsured other insurance companies for large losses from natural disasters, typically above a pre-determined threshold of loss for the primary insurer (no different than a deductible). The advantage Berkshire brought to this arena was both its willingness to write large policies and its financial strength. The latter was less important to consumers but all-important to large buyers of reinsurance. For the right price Berkshire was willing to concentrate risk rather than lay it off. Profits were expected over time, but they came at the expense of volatility. For this segment alone, the combined ratio could be zero in some years, or as high as 300% when earthquakes, hurricanes, and other natural events struck. Measured over a period of a decade, Buffett thought that Berkshire's overall results would be better than insurers who preferred to lay off the risk to others in exchange for smoother sailing. He summed it up nicely: "Charlie and I always have preferred a lumpy 15% return to a smooth 12%."

Buffett's basic framework, and how he thought insurers should be measured, was the cost of float. This was determined based on a ratio of underwriting loss to average float. In this way the cost of float (assuming a combined ratio over 100%) was akin to the cost of debt. Comparing the cost of float to an interest rate benchmark would provide a gauge for the quality of float generated. Most insurers could still produce a breakeven result with a cost of float between 7% and 11%. Under long-tail situations where a long time period elapsed from premium collection to the payout of losses, a higher combined ratio of 115% or more could be profitable.

---

* The reader should note that beginning in 1990 Berkshire began consolidating the structured settlements and portfolio reinsurance segment with the overall reinsurance segment. The $66 million figure is the original 1989 presentation. By contrast, the 1990 presentation for 1989 results show volume of $126 million.

Berkshire first entered the insurance industry with the purchase of National Indemnity in 1967. Between 1967 and 1990, Berkshire underwrote to a profit in half of those years (see Table 5.26). This meant its cost of float was negative.* In seven additional years, its cost of float was below that of long-term US government bonds, meaning the Insurance Group was borrowing at a cost lower than the US government. In the remaining five years, Berkshire's cost of float was higher than the long-term government bond. The worst year was 1984 with a differential of 7.4 percentage points. In short, Berkshire generated a large and growing amount of float at an attractive cost. In 1990, Berkshire's $1.6 billion of float cost it just 1.6%, far below the 8.2% cost incurred by the US government.

Table 5.26: Berkshire Hathaway Insurance Group
Float and cost of float compared to U.S. Government Bonds

	Underwriting Loss ($ mil.)	Average float ($ mil.)	Approximate cost of Funds	Year-end Yield on Long-Term Gov't Bonds
1967	profit	$17.3	less than zero	5.5%
1968	profit	19.9	less than zero	5.9%
1969	profit	23.4	less than zero	6.8%
1970	$0.37	32.4	1.14%	6.3%
1971	profit	52.5	less than zero	5.8%
1972	profit	69.5	less than zero	5.8%
1973	profit	73.3	less than zero	7.3%
1974	7.36	79.1	9.30%	8.1%
1975	11.35	87.6	12.96%	8.0%
1976	profit	102.6	less than zero	7.3%
1977	profit	139.0	less than zero	8.0%
1978	profit	190.4	less than zero	8.9%
1979	profit	227.3	less than zero	10.1%
1980	profit	237.0	less than zero	11.9%
1981	profit	228.4	less than zero	13.6%
1982	21.56	220.6	9.77%	10.6%
1983	33.87	231.3	14.64%	11.8%
1984	48.06	253.2	18.98%	11.6%
1985	44.23	390.2	11.34%	9.3%
1986	55.84	797.5	7.00%	7.6%
1987	55.43	1,266.7	4.38%	9.0%
1988	11.08	1,497.7	0.74%	9.0%
1989	24.40	1,541.3	1.58%	8.0%
1990	26.65	1,637.3	1.63%	8.2%

Source: Berkshire Hathaway Annual Report 1990.

---

* Despite the unfavorable-seeming nomenclature, a negative cost of float was a good thing. It meant Berkshire was being paid to hold its customers' funds. This is akin to a negative interest rate in which the creditor pays the borrower.

Keying shareholders into his thoughts on valuation, Buffett wrote that the Insurance Group's intrinsic value was "worth far more than its carrying value." Even though its variability in results caused the intrinsic value of Berkshire's insurance operations to be harder to value than the non-insurance businesses, it was, he said, the one with the greatest potential.

Investments

Given the Berkshire philosophy of viewing common stock investments as equivalent to ownership of entire businesses, it comes as no surprise to see little activity in its holdings. That was the case in 1990. As Buffett put it: "Lethargy bordering on sloth remains the cornerstone of our investment style. This year we neither bought nor sold a share of five of our six major holdings." This meant there was no trading activity for Capital Cities/ABC, Coca-Cola ("the most valuable franchise in the world," according to Buffett), Freddie Mac, GEICO, or *The Washington Post*. The only real activity in the equity portfolio in 1990 was purchasing Wells Fargo shares.

While Berkshire began buying shares the year before, it was not disclosed anywhere in the Annual Report, since very few shares were acquired in 1989. By the end of 1990, Berkshire had acquired 5,000,000 shares at an average cost of under $58 per share, or about $290 million.* This was equivalent to three times pre-tax earnings or five times after-tax earnings. Berkshire's ownership was equal to 10% of Wells Fargo. The way Buffett described it reflected his attitude toward buying a portion of any business public or private. Berkshire's Wells Fargo stake was "roughly equivalent to [Berkshire] buying 100% of a $5 billion bank." Wells Fargo had about $56 billion of assets at the time. While Buffett and Munger were not big fans of the banking business due to the risks inherent in a highly leveraged enterprise, the quality of Wells Fargo and its manager, Carl Reichardt, coupled with the attractiveness of its share price, presented a worthwhile investment opportunity.

Wells Fargo stock had recently fallen over 50% in a short period due to concerns that a real estate bust tied to the recession would cause large losses at West Coast banks. Buffett's rational logic explained his reasoning for why Wells Fargo would fare just fine amid the landscape of bank failures nationwide:

"Consider some mathematics: Wells Fargo currently earns well over $1 billion pre-tax annually, after expensing more than $300 million for loan losses. If 10% of all $48 billion of the bank's loans—not just its real estate loans—were hit

---

* With Berkshire's ownership of 10% of the bank Berkshire's $290 million purchase price equated to a $2.9 billion value for the entire bank. That value was equal to Wells Fargo's 1989 ending shareholders' equity (source: Wells Fargo Annual Report, 1989).

by problems in 1991, and these produced losses (including foregone interest) averaging 30% of principal, the company would roughly break even."

Such a low-level possibility event, wrote Buffett, would cause Wells Fargo to report no profit that year, and then go on earning 20% on growing equity.

The fixed-maturity portion of Berkshire's investment portfolio saw few changes in 1990. Berkshire increased its holdings of RJR Nabisco bonds to $440 million but avoided other below-investment-grade issues. Even though the logic of acquiring junk bonds as a portfolio was sound if purchased at the right price, Wall Street had characteristically taken the idea too far. There was a key difference between the bonds of former investment grade companies, such as RJR Nabisco, which were downgraded, and those that originated as junk bonds. The former had managers who worked to regain the company's investment grade status while the latter had no benchmark to guide their behavior. Though he was writing about the savings and loan industry, Charlie Mungers' label of "knaves and fools" would have done well for a description of some of the junk-bond company managers and their Wall Street brethren pushing them at the time. (Buffett used a similar term: financiopath.)

There was some mixed news on Berkshire's four major convertible preferred stock issues:

- The $700 million Salomon issue and the $300 million Champion International issue were performing as expected.
- The USAir issue was likely worth substantially less than the $358 million purchase price. The airline was struggling due to continued industry weakness and integration problems with another airline it purchased.
- Berkshire's $600 million of Gillette Company convertible preferred, though worth somewhat more than it had paid, was about to go away. The issue had been called, and as a result Berkshire would receive 12 million shares of Gillette on April 1, 1991.* Berkshire would give up over $50 million of annual preferred stock dividends, but it would continue to hold a nearly equal asset in its claim to 11% of Gillette's earning power.

Wesco

The savings and loan crisis was a slow-moving financial disaster that began in 1986 and ended a decade later with about a third of savings and loan institutions out of business. With additional time to study the issue, Munger used ten pages of his

---

* Callable preferred stock is a type of preferred stock where the issuer has the right to call in or redeem the stock at a fixed number of common shares at a certain date.

Wesco Chairman's letter to provide excellent observations as to why Wesco didn't fall for the tactics that led to bank failures.* Munger wrote out of "overwhelming disgust with the present scene" and was inspired by a long association to an eccentric fellow (Buffett), who "encourages this kind of writing."

Munger said the cause of the savings and loan crisis was a confluence of events. One issue was government-provided deposit insurance, which effectively allowed bankers to use the government's credit to obtain low-cost funding. Related to that was a structural weakness in that short-term sources of funds were used to finance long-term assets, creating interest-rate risk. A weak regulatory structure allowed a bank to shop for its regulator and this caused a lowest-common-denominator effect where the weakest banks were attracted to the easiest regulator.

Then came deregulation of interest rates and low-overhead money market funds. This caused a higher cost of funds for all banks (thrifts and commercial banks). That in turn produced the natural effect of riskier lending as banks needed higher-yielding assets to cover their higher costs. Some banks even went so far as to advertise a willingness to fund a portion of consumers' vacations, among other risky lending activities. Banks were not alone in risky lending. The 1980s heralded the invention of large-scale original-issue junk bonds pushed by the likes of Michael Milken. Before the 1980s, few people issued junk bonds. They became common in the early 1980s as a way for young companies with no credit to issue bonds and get early funding. This practice came to a temporary halt at the end of the 1980s as default rates rose, though it did return in future decades.

Munger's analysis started with a question. "How then does bad lending occur so often?" he asked. The answer, he said, was because humans are social animals with "predictable irrationalities." This leads them to follow the crowd and copy bad behavior. The effect of such folly was predictable: "many bank insolvencies will come." He was right. By 1995, over 1,000 banks were out of business.

Munger offered a possible solution, or at least mitigation of the above deficiencies. One solution was significantly reducing deposit insurance. Quite the opposite of shoring up the weak deposit system, Munger wrote that additional deposit insurance might weaken it, since it raised banks' costs above those of money market funds, which paid no deposit insurance. His other ideas included the elimination of money market funds via legislation, or bringing back interest rate controls, both of which were technically possible but unlikely. Still other ideas, which could be used alone or in combination, were forcing weak banks to close or merge with local or non-local banks. Banks that closed should do so before they became insolvent. (Munger thought it bonkers that regulators would wait until the very end, at which point large losses to the deposit insurer were almost guaranteed.)

---

* I am using this term loosely to encompass all bank-like companies, such as thrifts and commercial banks.

Another option Munger proffered up would affect the accounting of banks and their brethren. He thought discussions of accounting were not focused on the right area. Discussions centered on how to delay loan write-offs via accounting maneuvers. Munger felt this created poor incentives for bank managers to front-end interest and fee income from loans, especially with new classes of risky loans having as-yet-to-be-determined loss characteristics. This encouraged lending to riskier borrowers since income could be booked immediately that might ultimately have to be reversed. Munger called this "reality denial" and believed much more conservatism was needed to begin with. Munger's system would be more like insurance, in which future losses would be estimated upfront using logical and conservative methods and then corrected as time went on.* He thought offering a carrot in the form of tax savings, in addition to the regulatory sticks, would incent the right behavior on the part of managers and boards of directors.

Toward the end of the 1990 Berkshire Hathaway Chairman's letter was the familiar advertisement seeking acquisition candidates. Buffett augmented his usual plea by including as an appendix a two-page letter written to an owner considering selling to Berkshire (the business was not named). Entitled Some Thoughts on Selling Your Business, Buffett's letter went through the advantages of selling to Berkshire. It was also candid: "You would be no richer after the sale than now … A sale would [only] change the form of your wealth" from 100% of one business to cash and investments in other businesses.

The letter offered some insight into Buffett's thinking on acquiring family-built companies. Although Berkshire would "adapt to [the sellers'] methods rather than vice versa," he had a few stipulations. One was that he preferred the selling family maintain a 20% ownership interest. This put Berkshire's ownership at the 80% level needed for tax purposes. More important, it maintained the proper alignment of incentives so Berkshire could be hands-off. "The areas I get involved in are capital allocation and selection and compensation of the top man," he wrote. The latter was another key policy that helped avoid ballooning compensation costs given that just about all other decisions would be made at the operating company level.

Finally, Buffett informed shareholders that Ken Chace had decided to step down from the board. Buffett's wife, Susan, would be nominated to succeed him. An informed board member, she had the second-largest ownership stake in Berkshire after her husband and shared his views on succession and preserving the Berkshire culture he so painstakingly put into place.

---

* Munger anticipated the Current Expected Credit Loss or CECL (pronounced "Cecil") framework issued by FASB in 2016.

1991

Berkshire Hathaway's book value shot up 39.6% in 1991. Like the previous year (which saw an increase of just 7.4%), the current year was heavily influenced by Berkshire's large investment portfolio. Of the $2.1 billion gain in book value in 1991, over three-quarters of it (or $1.6 billion) was due to appreciation of just two stocks: the recently purchased 7% interest in Coca-Cola and newly converted shares in Gillette. Against a backdrop of a general recession in the United States in 1991, Berkshire's operating companies did well, though less well than the year before. Pre-tax operating earnings fell 17% to $401 million. Berkshire also found a new operating company to buy in H.H. Brown Shoe.

Also, Warren Buffett reluctantly found a second job running (and saving) Salomon, Inc. The story of Buffett's interlude running Salomon is a cautionary one and well worth the effort to study in full.[48]

Berkshire first purchased a $700 million convertible preferred stock issue from Salomon in 1987, which put Buffett and Charlie Munger on its board to represent Berkshire's 12% voting interest. Several years went by without a problem. Then, in mid-1991, news came to light that one of Salomon's employees had broken the law by abusing Salomon's privilege as a primary dealer in US Treasury securities when he improperly used customers' accounts.[*] The fact that Salomon had committed the transgression wasn't the real sin. The real problem was CEO John Gutfreund knew about it and did not tell the government.

The series of events which followed are like a Greek tragedy. The Salomon employee set the scene by committing the crime more than once during the beginning of 1991. Salomon's management made it a tragedy by not reporting the wrongdoing to Salomon's regulator, the New York Federal Reserve Bank. The General Counsel took the matter to his boss, CEO John Gutfreund, who did nothing, precipitating his own downfall. Gutfreund believed it would either go away or at worst result in nothing more than a slap on the wrist. This was a fatal error of judgement.

Instead, the situation blew up as Gutfreund not only failed to inform the government of Salomon's violations of the law, but also didn't inform Salomon's board, including Buffett and Munger. What happened next was a run on Salomon as its creditors rightly assumed it could fail if the government stopped doing business with it. Gutfreund found himself out of a job and Buffett found himself chairman of a teetering investment bank. He explained it this way:

---

[*] Primary dealers were the wholesalers of government securities. The government conferred upon a few investment banks the privilege of making a market, buying securities for their own and customers' accounts, effectively channeling them into the economy. The banks earned a spread for this service, in exchange for abiding by strict rules designed to minimize abuse of their monopoly-like status.

"In 1989, when I—a happy consumer of five cans of Cherry Coke daily—announced our purchase of $1 billion worth of Coca-Cola stock, I described the move as a rather extreme example of putting our money where my mouth was. On August 18 of [1991] when I was elected Interim Chairman of Salomon Inc., it was a different story. I put my mouth where my money was."

What followed was a heroic, nearly ten-month-long rescue mission that stretched into 1992. Buffett feared that many innocent Salomon employees would lose their jobs. He feared for the entire financial system given Salomon's deep ties to the financial world. He also feared for his own reputation. So Buffett pleaded with government officials to maintain Salomon's status as a dealer in Treasuries and not shut down the bank. At the very last hour, he was successful. If Buffett had been unsuccessful, the firm surely would have failed. Instead, Buffett risked his well-earned reputation to save Salomon and then handed off the reins to Deryck Maughan, an insider with deep knowledge who could credibly claim innocence since he was stationed at the firm's Tokyo office at the time.[*]

The Salomon episode would later burnish Buffett's reputation, not just because he had saved the firm. His forthrightness and honesty, including waiving attorney-client privilege during investigations, set a high bar and showed how a crisis should be managed (made easier of course because he had no hand in the making of it). At every Berkshire Hathaway Annual Meeting, Buffett plays a clip of himself testifying at a Congressional hearing.[**] "Lose money for the firm and I will be understanding. Lose a shred of reputation for the firm and I will be ruthless," is Buffett's now-famous message. It is a message worth repeating.

The other Salomon lesson was that Berkshire could operate fine without him. The Salomon stint did not impact Berkshire to any significant degree because Berkshire's managers were capable and in control. Still, Buffett was quick to point out the word interim in his new Salomon "Interim Chairman" title. "Berkshire", he wrote shareholders, "is my first love and one that will never fade."

Sources of Reported Earnings

Look-through earnings declined by 14%, from $602 million in 1990 to $516 million in 1991.[***] Both Berkshire's operating income and its share of investees earnings

---

[*] Salomon ended up paying a $290 million fine. In 1997, Salomon was sold to Travelers for $9 billion, with Berkshire's stake amounting to $1.7 billion.

[**] This clip is easily found online.

[***] The attentive reader will notice a discrepancy between the $591 million figure reported in the section on 1990 and this amount. The figure reported here came from Buffett's Chairman's letter. His data were likely more precise looking back from the vantage point of early 1992 (when the 1991 letter was written).

contributed to the decline. Media companies Cap Cities/ABC and *The Washington Post* suffered due to changing industry economics. Wells Fargo posted a loss that hurt investee look-through earnings, but which was offset by dividends received (and counted toward Berkshire's operating earnings). Berkshire's largest operating division, insurance, recorded significantly lower but still excellent profits. Pre-tax operating earnings from insurance, including underwriting and investment income, dropped from $300 million in 1990 to $212 million in 1991 because of a large underwriting loss.

Table 5.27: Berkshire Hathaway look-through earnings, 1990–1991 (reproduced from the 1991 Chairman's letter)

Berkshire's major investees	Berkshire's ownership of company at year-end		Berkshire's share of undistributed operating earnings *($ millions)*	
	1991	1990	1991	1990
Capital Cities/ABC, Inc.	18.1%	17.9%	$61	$85
The Coca-Cola Company	7.0%	7.0%	69	58
Federal Home Loan Mortgage Corp.[1]	3.4%	3.0%	15	10
The Gillette Company[2]	11.0%	0.0%	23	0
GEICO Corp.	48.2%	46.1%	69	76
The Washington Post Company	14.6%	14.6%	10	18
Wells Fargo & Company[3]	9.6%	9.7%	(17)	19
Berkshire's share of undistributed earnings of major investees			230	266
Hypothetical tax on these undistributed investee earnings			(30)	(35)
Reported operating earnings of Berkshire			316	371
Total look-through earnings of Berkshire			$516	$602

Footnotes:
1. Net of minority interest at Wesco.
2. Earnings for the nine months after Berkshire converted its preferred stock on April 1.
3. Earnings calculated on average ownership for the year.

Note: Amounts are after tax.
Source: Berkshire Hathaway Annual Report 1991.

A Change in Media Economics and Some Valuation Math

In a section of his Chairman's letter so entitled, Buffett illustrated quite simply how media companies, such as Cap Cities/ABC, *The Washington Post*, and *The Buffalo News*, had weaker performance than in years past. The discussion also included Buffett's thinking on the three types of businesses in the business universe.

Type one: The most valuable business, regardless of industry, was an economic franchise. Not to be confused with the more commonly known lease-a-concept business operation, Buffett defined a business franchise as one that: "(1) is needed or desired; (2) is thought by its customers to have no close substitute and; (3) is not subject to price regulation." Such businesses, which included media companies prior to 1991 and might have included them then, had pricing power and earned high returns on capital. Also, they were largely immune to inept management.

Type two: A good business. Buffett was realizing that media companies were becoming less franchise-like and more akin to a good business. The only way for a business to earn high returns on capital was to be the low-cost operator. This was usually the result of an above-average manager. Media companies' valuations suffered as their operations faced a slide in quality. As a franchise, many media companies regularly grew earnings 6% per year without the need for additional capital. This pricing power provided solid earnings and returns on capital. But media businesses were losing their ability to price aggressively and be managed loosely as competition intensified and the companies lost some of their franchise strength.

Quite understandably, investors priced them to suit: Assuming a 10% discount rate and 6% perpetual growth, such a business would rationally be worth twenty-five times earnings.* But when that cost-free growth disappeared due to the shift in economics favoring alternative forms of advertising, such a business would only be worth ten times earnings. Such normal businesses could still be good investments, but they would require additional capital to grow. Buffett was trying to explain that growth was not some ethereal concept to be plugged into a model without thought. It took knowledge of how underlying operations worked.

A business was usually restricted due to capital requirements. Growth could not be had unless more capital was put up through retained earnings, additional equity, or borrowing (or a combination of the three). Absent additional capital, Buffett said a "'bob around' pattern is indeed the lot of most businesses." Berkshire shareholders could look to Scott Fetzer, or more broadly the Manufacturing, Publishing, and Retailing segment, to see that high returns on capital did not automatically come

---

* The formula I am alluding to is the "Gordon growth model" which, very simply is Value = Earnings / (Discount rate – Growth rate).

with growth. Buffett had noted in his 1990 letter that 80% of the Manufacturing, Publishing, and Retailing businesses' earnings were paid out as dividends to Omaha. This was okay since the underlying returns on capital were satisfactory. It just meant searching elsewhere for a place to allocate the excess capital above and beyond those businesses' needs.

Type three: Buffett did not discuss the third type of business, essentially everything other than a franchise or a good business. He presumed shareholders could figure that out for themselves. High-cost commodity operations* and/or those requiring a lot of capital with no attendant growth would fall into this last category. Of those there were many. Perhaps Buffett didn't want to discuss the poster child for such a business—Berkshire's own textile businesses of the prior decade.

Insurance

The 30,000-foot view of the operating earnings summary showed the Insurance Group posting a large loss from underwriting, but positive earnings overall due to investment income. Insurance earnings were down significantly but they were nonetheless excellent in context. The underwriting loss provided a cost of float of 6.3%, lower than the long-term Government Bond rate of 7.4%, and float grew 16% to an average of $1.9 billion. The Insurance Group was following a basic recipe for success: more float at an attractive cost.

---

* Commodity here is not necessarily referring to businesses in the physical commodity industries (such as metals, coal, etc.) but also includes basic, easily copied businesses with no competitive advantages whatsoever.

Table 5.28: Insurance Group, select information

($ millions)	1991 Amount	%	1990 Amount	%
Primary Group				
Premiums written	$135.5		$139.1	
Premiums earned	141.0	100.0%	154.0	100.0%
Losses and loss expenses	95.2	67.5%	102.0	66.2%
Underwriting expenses	48.3	34.3%	51.5	33.4%
Total losses and expenses	143.5	101.8%	153.5	99.7%
Underwriting gain/(loss) - pre-tax	(2.5)		0.5	
Unfavorable (favorable) loss development included in losses and loss expenses	(23.8)	(16.9%)	(18.3)	(11.9%)
Statutory combined ratio		103.2%		103.3%
Reinsurance Group				
Premiums written	$667.0		$435.2	
Premiums earned	635.4	100.0%	437.5	100.0%
Losses and loss expenses	731.9	115.2%	432.2	98.8%
Underwriting expenses	20.6	3.2%	32.5	7.4%
Total losses and expenses	752.5	118.4%	464.7	106.2%
Underwriting gain/(loss) - pre-tax	(117.1)		(27.2)	
Unfavorable (favorable) loss development included in losses and loss expenses	(30.0)	(4.7%)	0.0	0.0%
Statutory combined ratio		118.3%		106.3%
Total Insurance Group underwriting gain/(loss) pre-tax	**($119.6)**		**($26.7)**	
Insurance Group overall statutory combined ratio		115.1%		104.9%

Notes:

1. Totals may not add due to rounding.

2. The loss and expense ratios are shown as they were reported in the Annual Reports, which is on a GAAP basis. The GAAP basis ratios are calculated with underwriting expenses divided by earned premiums. This contrasts to the statutory basis calculation, where the ratio uses written premiums. In both the GAAP and statutory calculations, losses and loss adjustment expenses are divided by earned premiums.

3. In 1990, Berkshire began including structured settlements and portfolio reinsurance with reinsurance.

Sources: Berkshire Hathaway Annual Report 1992 and author's calculations.

It is important to understand the impact of the type of premiums written by the Insurance Group and the related accounting conventions. Berkshire was moving into the greener pastures of super cat insurance, using its superior capital strength and willingness to write large policies to its advantage. The super cat business had the benefit of producing a lot of float, but it also came with risk and volatility in reported earnings. Such lines could cause a $100 million profit in a good year or a $200 million loss in a bad one. Berkshire priced the business to pay out 90% of premiums over the long term, which it thought would produce a profit over time.

Accounting for super cats and other long-tail types of insurance was even more difficult than the primary or direct lines—and even those weren't easy. The nuances were important for shareholders to understand. Even in a good year where no super cat events occurred and Berkshire earned all its large $100 million annual premium volume, it was economically accruing risk and future losses that would—someday—be paid out as claims. Accounting conventions, however, did not allow for reserving for such near-certain future losses, and so reported results could swing wildly.

Super cats were not the only possibilities for accounting confusion. The notes to the financial statements provided important accounting disclosures as there was potential for readers to be misled. Even though Berkshire had recorded yet another year of favorable loss development, including a full $30.6 million relating to the quota-share reinsurance contracts previously shared with Fireman's Fund and others, there was still a chance for unfavorable development in future years. Berkshire was not immune to unfavorable surprises, but on balance its financial statements usually exhibited elements of conservatism.

One important disclosure for readers to be aware of was deferred charge amortization for retroactive reinsurance contracts. A retroactive reinsurance contract provides insurance for known loss events that are expected to extend into the future, but which a primary or other reinsurer wishes to lay off.* Since claims come in the future (sometimes far into the future) and float is available for a long time to generate income to offset future losses, reinsurers appropriately accept premiums lower than the expected future payouts.**

The accounting for retroactive reinsurance contracts can cause some confusion if not properly understood. The day a contract is booked the reinsurer receives an upfront cash premium. Since the earned premium is offset by losses larger than the premium received, the losses are split into two buckets. One is equal to the premium just received and expensed immediately as an incurred loss. Second, the day-one excess of loss over the premium received is placed on the balance sheet as an asset. While somewhat counterintuitive at first, this accounting generally makes sense. In theory this new deferred charge asset will be amortized away via the expense account, offset by earnings from the investment income generated by the upfront cash received, hopefully with a small profit leftover. While this theory is sound, it has the effect of causing apparent underwriting losses in future periods as the deferred charge asset is

---

* Perhaps because they need to free-up space to write more business, or perhaps because the timing and amount of such losses aren't known for sure.
** Reflecting the time value of money.

expensed without any offsetting premium being earned.* (Remember, the entirety of the premium is earned day one, with the economics of the transaction based partly on the ability to generate investment income.)

In 1991, Berkshire disclosed $26.2 million of underwriting loss associated with such deferred charges on retroactive reinsurance. In addition, a $22.8 million underwriting loss was booked with respect to structured settlements. Structured settlements were also based on time-value-of-money concepts and caused similar accounting issues like retroactive reinsurance. In short, the favorable economics of these contracts (holding cash for a long time) could be overshadowed by what looked like losses (amortization of the asset) due to the accounting.**

Manufacturing, Publishing, and Retailing

The manufacturing, publishing, and retailing businesses reported pre-tax earnings of $214.5 million, down 1% from the prior year. Revenues grew 4.6% to $1.65 billion but also contained revenues from acquisitions, including H.H. Brown mid-year. Flat earnings seem unimpressive until translated into a pre-tax return on tangible capital of 57.2%. That result is impressive on its own, no doubt. But it fell from 73% in 1990. The cause? A recession and Berkshire's continued acquisition of very good but slightly less spectacular businesses. After-tax return on equity fell from 51.1% to 39.3%.

Berkshire's history with See's Candies illustrates the economics of a wonderful business. When Blue Chip Stamps purchased See's in 1972 it was already a very good business. Its pre-tax return on capital was north of 50%. Nineteen years later in 1991, See's was doing even better. Pre-tax earnings had grown tenfold while the capital needed to operate the business had only tripled. The result: an explosion of profitability with a pre-tax return on capital in the triple-digits. A truly mouthwatering result.

With such large numbers it was easy to conclude the growth of See's was a success; it was not as apparent with other businesses. Buffett laid out his analysis: "For an increase in profits to be evaluated properly, it must be compared with the incremental capital investment required to produce it." Using this framework, See's required an investment of $17 million to increase earnings by $38 million—a wonderful return by any standard.

---

* The contracts were also imperfect, with adjustments made along the way as both the magnitude and timing of the loss experience was determined.
** Given the clear time-value-of-money concepts at work here some had proposed allowing discounting of reinsurance contracts, which would have had the effect of eliminating the need for the deferred charge asset and its related amortization. Buffett thought it sound logic but inappropriate due to the clear risk of abuse of such a system. (Some state insurance regulators did allow discounting.)

Table 5.29: See's Candies, select data

($ millions)	1991	1972	Change
Revenues	$196.0	$29.0	6.8x
Pre-tax earnings	42.4	4.2	10.1x
Tangible capital	25.0	8.0	3.1x
Incremental earnings	$38.2		
Incremental capital	17.0		
Incremental return on capital	225%		
Revenues/capital	$7.84	$3.63	
Return on capital, pre-tax	170%	53%	

Source: Berkshire Hathaway Annual Report 1991.

How was this possible, especially given the frequent commentary by Buffett and Munger that the industry was very tough? The answer was the company's untapped pricing power. Said another way, its customers were not overly price sensitive. This was evident in the fact that 1991 results were better, even in the face of a new tax on snack food. Same-store poundage fell 5% but pre-tax earnings increased 7% to $42.4 million. Lower cost inflation helped to cause that result, but See's was still an excellent business.

The $410 million of earnings distributed to Blue Chip/Berkshire Hathaway by See's over the prior two decades was sweet, but the company brought something else that was perhaps more valuable. The lessons learned from See's made Berkshire significant money by teaching Buffett and Munger the advantages of owning great businesses.

H.H. Brown Shoe

Berkshire's latest acquisition* was H.H. Brown Shoe Co., the leading North American manufacturer of work shoes and boots at the time. Buffett reported that the Massachusetts-based business earned fine margins on sales and assets. It was founded by Ray Heffernan and later run by his son-in-law, Frank Rooney. After Heffernan's death, the family decided to look for a home for the business and found one in Berkshire. Like many other Berkshire subsidiaries, Rooney had no monetary need to work but continued to do so because he loved the business.

The H.H Brown acquisition put Berkshire on a path back to manufacturing, this time in the shoe business. New England was a hotbed for shoe manufacturing. In the

---

* The purchase price was not disclosed. The footnotes to the financial statements disclose that $161 million was paid for business acquisitions, but this would not have been entirely attributable to H.H. Brown. Nebraska Furniture Mart purchased a business during the year, and other, smaller "tuck-in" acquisitions may have occurred that were not disclosed.

1970s, there were 1,100 shoe manufacturing plants in the US, but by 1985 only about 500 remained. The decline in American shoe manufacturing employment was in full force in 1991. This may sound ominous and the factors just described probably played a part in the price Berkshire was willing to pay.[49]

H.H. Brown's unusual compensation program warmed Buffett's heart. Company managers were paid an annual salary of just $7,800, with the remaining compensation coming from a percentage of profits, after a capital charge. "These managers, therefore, truly stand in the shoes of owners," wrote Buffett. The business joined Berkshire on July 1, 1991 and earned $13.6 million pre-tax for Berkshire that year.

Nebraska Furniture Mart increased revenues 4% to $171 million amidst a sluggish retail environment. Pre-tax profits, however, decreased 17% to $13.9 million as the company lowered its prices (which were already very low), "in order to protect and reinforce its image as a low-cost supplier." It also purchased a small business in Lincoln, Nebraska, though details were not provided.

The Buffalo News saw pre-tax profit decline 15.6% to $36.6 million as demand for print advertising fell off a cliff. Berkshire disclosed in a footnote that it thought profits would continue to decline as a result of increased competition from direct mail and a continued decline in newspaper advertising. Additionally, the footnote disclosed a $2 million buyout offer made to printers and pressman early in 1992.

At World Book, profits fell almost 30% to $22.2 million, though this was compared to a record high year in 1990. Profits fell 12% compared to a more normal year like 1989. The decline was partly attributable to the recession and in larger part due to a costly change in a marketing strategy.

Despite the recession, which caused sales and profits to falter at some other Berkshire subsidiaries, the Kirby unit did well in 1991. Driven primarily by the introduction of the new Generation 3 vacuum cleaner, revenues increased 2% to $192 million. With lower start-up costs compared to 1990 (when the new model was released) pre-tax profit ballooned almost 31% to $37 million.

The story was similar at Fechheimer. As a result of growth in retail operations, a new fire-protection line, and higher sales of marching band uniforms, revenues increased 6% to $100 million and pre-tax profit increased 4% to $12.2 million. Integration-related problems experienced in prior years abated and Fechheimer managers were cautiously optimistic going into 1992—the company's 150th anniversary.

Investments

There were a few things to note in Berkshire's investment portfolio for 1991, including its first significant foreign investment. In 1991 Berkshire acquired 31.2 million shares of Guinness PLC, maker of the famous namesake stout beer, for just under $265 million. Berkshire's stakes in its remaining six permanent investments did not change in 1991 in terms of number of shares held.

Berkshire found some fixed income replacements for its recently converted Gillette preferred stake into common stock, and its RJR Nabisco preferred, which was also eliminated due to an exchange offer. Berkshire increased its holdings of preferred shares in ACF Industries, a railcar manufacturer, to $94 million at cost, and established a position in American Express preferred stock, purchased for $300 million but valued at $263 million at year-end.* It also purchased $40 million of First Empire State preferred. The bank was run by Bob Wilmers, whom Buffett greatly admired. Reflecting a "risk that the industry will remain unprofitable for virtually all participants in it," Berkshire wrote down the value of its USAir preferred stock by 35% to $232.7 million. Overall the fixed-income portfolio had treated Berkshire well by earning more than comparable fixed-income portfolios.

Characteristically, Buffett did not let an opportunity go by for airing his mistakes. Over more than half a page in his letter he chided himself for missing an investment opportunity in Fannie Mae, a similar entity to that of Freddie Mac. He wrote that such mistakes of omission never showed up anywhere, but that they were still costly. Buffett estimated this mistake cost Berkshire about $1.4 billion.

Miscellaneous

Malcolm G. Chace, Jr., retired in 1991. At 88 years old, Chace had a long history with Berkshire that began in 1931 at Berkshire Fine Spinning Associates and continued to his chairmanship of Berkshire in 1957. It was Chace that made it possible for Buffett to buy into Berkshire in the first place. Chace's son, Malcolm "Kim" Chace III, was nominated to replace his father.

Berkshire began paying off some of its high-cost debt in 1991, including a $22 million partial redemption of a 9.75% issue and $50 million of a 10% debenture (both at the Berkshire-parent level). With interest rates at their lowest since the mid-1970s (the 10-year Treasury fell below 7% at the end of 1991), more debt reduction was slated for 1992. This included the remaining $100 million portion of the 10% debenture and $36 million of subsidiary-level debt with interest rates close to 10%. Given Berkshire's high levels of liquidity and few great prospects for investments, such capital allocation moves made sense.

---

* The table presented in the Chairman's letter noted that the value had been determined by Buffett and Munger. This write-down likely reflected the large drop in AMEX's stock price during 1991. The preferred was subject to a mandatory conversion after three years.

1992

In 1992, Berkshire Hathaway's increase in per share book value comfortably exceeded Buffett's 15% target threshold, rising 20.3% and adding $1.5 billion to the equity account. But this high growth rate affected Berkshire's balance sheet equity and the per share rate of increase slightly differently. More than 98% of the growth came from Berkshire's usual operating company and investing activities; the balance came from the issuance of 2,162 shares after Berkshire called its convertible debentures and some holders elected to convert.*

These new shares priced Berkshire Hathaway at a market value of about $13.5 billion (see Table 5.30). Using Berkshire's average equity during the year, that valuation was equal to 1.7x book value—not an unreasonably high or low valuation. Viewed another way, the $13.5 billion price tag would provide owners with a 4.5% earnings yield against Buffett's own estimate of owner earnings. For a company regularly exceeding a 15% growth rate such a valuation would not have been unreasonable.**

Table 5.30: Berkshire Hathaway implied valuation

Issue price	$11,719
BRK shares outstanding	1,152,547
Implied market value *($ millions)*	13,507
1991 average book value *($ millions)*	8,138
Price/book value	1.66x
Estimated owner earnings *($ millions)*	604
Earnings yield	4.5%

Sources: Berkshire Hathaway Annual Report 1992 and author's calculations.

After ten months, Buffett concluded his Salomon interlude. Buffett praised the managers responsible for the remarkable turnaround: CEO Deryck Maughan, Bob Denham, Don Howard, and John Macfarlane. He also praised Ron Olson, Charlie Munger's partner at the law firm Munger, Tolles & Olson, who helped manage the complex maneuvering through different financial and regulatory agencies. Buffett said he was delighted to be back full-time running Berkshire.

His delight turned to exhilaration with the acquisition of several new businesses in 1992. One was the purchase of 82% of Central States Indemnity, an Omaha-based insurer of credit card payments for the disabled or unemployed. Central States was writing $90 million of premiums and earning profits of about $10 million.*** One of

---

* An additional 3,944 shares were issued after year-end 1992 relating to the same debentures.
** Berkshire's shares traded in a range of $8,850 to $11,750 that year.
*** Based on the data, that would be an excellent 88.8% combined ratio.

Berkshire's newer acquisitions, H.H. Brown Shoe, acquired Lowell Shoe Company during the year. Berkshire's other subsidiaries found four other add-on acquisitions. Buffett called such add-ons low-risk, high-return propositions since they "enlarge the domain of managers we already know to be outstanding." This is a strategy Berkshire has continued to successfully employ to this day. It was not unlike increasing the ownership positions of existing marketable securities holdings.

Insurance

Judged by cost of float, Berkshire's Insurance Group did well in 1992. Its nearly $2.3 billion of average float, up almost 21% from 1991, cost it just 4.8%* compared to the Long-Term US Government Bond rate of 7.4%.

Understanding these gains and losses requires a close look at what was happening in 1992. In August, Hurricane Andrew (a category five hurricane) hit the East Coast of the US and caused large damages. Buffett thought that about four points of the industry's estimated combined ratio of 115% in 1992 could be attributed to that storm. Berkshire fared better than most. Berkshire sustained about $125 million of losses from Hurricane Andrew, but since it took in almost the same amount in premiums, the result for the super cat business line was breakeven. GEICO sustained after-tax losses of $50 million from the storm, which translated into about $25 million on a look-through basis for Berkshire (which now owned 50% of GEICO as a result of continued buybacks; Berkshire's original investment remained unchanged).

---

* For the close-eyed reader, the 115.1% statutory combined ratio resulted in a lower cost of float due to the significant growth in average float. If float did not grow as it did in 1992 the cost of float would have been higher.

Table 5.31: Insurance Group, select information

($ millions)	1992 Amount	1992 %	1991 Amount	1991 %
Primary Group				
Premiums written	$132.4		$135.5	
Premiums earned	152.8	100.0%	141.0	100.0%
Losses and loss expenses	98.0	64.1%	95.2	67.5%
Underwriting expenses	46.8	30.6%	48.3	34.3%
Total losses and expenses	144.8	94.8%	143.5	101.8%
Underwriting gain/(loss) - pre-tax	8.0		(2.5)	
Unfavorable (favorable) loss development included in losses and loss expenses	(36.4)	(23.8%)	(23.8)	(16.9%)
Statutory combined ratio		99.5%		103.2%
Reinsurance Group				
Premiums written	$607.2		$667.0	
Premiums earned	511.5	100.0%	635.4	100.0%
Losses and loss expenses	589.7	115.3%	731.9	115.2%
Underwriting expenses	38.8	7.6%	20.6	3.2%
Total losses and expenses	628.5	122.9%	752.5	118.4%
Underwriting gain/(loss) - pre-tax	(117.0)		(117.1)	
Unfavorable (favorable) loss development included in losses and loss expenses	0.0	0.0%	(30.0)	(4.7%)
Statutory combined ratio		121.7%		118.3%
Total Insurance Group underwriting gain/(loss) pre-tax	**($109.0)**		**($119.6)**	
Insurance Group overall statutory combined ratio		115.1%		115.1%

Notes:

1. Totals may not add due to rounding.

2. The loss and expense ratios are shown as they were reported in the Annual Reports, which is on a GAAP basis. The GAAP basis ratios are calculated with underwriting expenses divided by earned premiums. This contrasts to the statutory basis calculation, where the ratio uses written premiums. In both the GAAP and statutory calculations, losses and loss adjustment expenses are divided by earned premiums.

3. In 1990, Berkshire began including structured settlements and portfolio reinsurance with reinsurance.

Sources: Berkshire Hathaway Annual Report 1992 and author's calculations.

In the Primary Group, results for 1992 were generally favorable. Earned premiums increased 9% to $153 million, reflecting some minor thawing in the competitive environment. Even better, underwriting returned to profitability with an $8 million underwriting gain compared to a $2.5 million loss the previous year. Other data points included:

- Motor vehicle/general liability earned premiums declined 5% to $85 million.
- The commercial casualty/professional liability/specialty risk group (which had seen its premiums fall to $14 million in 1991 from a high of $93 million in 1987) earned $27 million of premiums.
- The Home State group earned generally flat volume of $41 million in 1992 compared to the two prior years.

The year benefitted from both the higher volume of specialty risk earned and from over $36 million of favorable loss development—a considerable 23.8% of earned premiums.* The footnotes to the financial statements again cautioned readers not to get too comfortable with what was now the sixth year of favorable loss development.

Taken as a whole, the Reinsurance Group in 1992 wrote to a combined ratio of 121.7%. It was a year that saw losses continue at an elevated level on lower written and earned premium volume. Even with 20% lower earned premium volume, continued growth in long-tail lines such as retroactive reinsurance, and others, led to growth in float. Buffett praised Ajit Jain ("simply the best in this business") for steadfastly holding to Berkshire's high underwriting standards. Berkshire rejected 98% of business offered to it—an impressive display of discipline.

It's worth noting an important accounting treatment with respect to super cat-type policies. With other insurance policies, premiums were recorded over the life of the policy. By contrast, Berkshire recognized super cat premiums as earned revenues when either a loss event occurred or when the policy expired. It did this because the likelihood of a super cat policy causing losses was greater at the end of the year. Of the ten largest insured losses as of 1992, nine occurred in the later part of the year. Consequently, quarterly results were essentially meaningless.

Manufacturing, Publishing, and Retailing

Coming out of the recession of the year before, and with new businesses included in the category, the businesses in the manufacturing, publishing, and retailing segment reported pre-tax earnings up 17.6% to $252.2 million on revenues that increased 7.2% to $1.8 billion. Pre-tax return on tangible capital remained very strong at 55.6% (down 1.6 percentage points). After-tax return on tangible equity remained attractive at 36.9%. These businesses were splendid, but they would never achieve the heights of returns achieved just a few years before.

Over a handful of short paragraphs in his Chairman's letter, Buffett summarized the fascinating ongoing story that was the life of Rose "Mrs. B" Blumkin, now 99 years

---

* The loss development amounted to 6.4% of beginning reserves. This figure was still above a 5% threshold cited in earlier years as acceptable.

old. Remember that Mrs. B feuded with her children and grandchildren in 1989 over the Nebraska Furniture Mart carpet department. The company was doing fine without her (pre-tax earnings rebounded 19% to $17.1 million in 1992), but Mrs. B missed her work. Not one to slow down, she purchased a building across the street from Nebraska Furniture Mart and set up shop again. Mrs. B made amends with her family and offered to sign a non-compete agreement. The price tag to buy her new business was $5 million.[50] "Mrs. B. belongs in the Guinness Book of World Records on many counts. Signing a non-compete at age 99 merely adds one more," Buffett wrote reverently.

Scott Fetzer earned $110 million pre-tax on just $116 million of equity capital. Scott Fetzer was a perfect example of the type of growth Buffett valued. What impressed Buffett was growth while maintaining high rates of return on capital and employing very little debt. In Scott Fetzer's case, the business was simultaneously growing while shrinking its use of capital. In other words, return on capital was improving. This made it possible for Scott Fetzer to distribute over 100% of its earnings to Berkshire since its acquisition seven years before. It also earned Ralph Schey Buffett's accolades.

An analysis of Scott Fetzer contains a glimpse into the small unofficial bank Berkshire was building. While the Scott Fetzer parent company used scarce amounts of borrowed money, its finance subsidiary wasn't shy about borrowing. Why the difference? Why wasn't Berkshire using some of its excess liquidity to eliminate or substantially reduce this debt? Viewed along the lines of a regular operating business, the capital structure was risky. But considered as the economic equivalent of a bank with financial assets funded by financial liabilities, it was appropriate. The assets of Scott Fetzer Financial Group were comprised largely of interest-bearing receivables it purchased from Kirby and World Book. Since the sales were complete only credit risk remained, and as such it was appropriate to borrow to finance them.

Kirby sales were essentially flat (down 1%) due to weakness in foreign unit sales, though pricing and expense management helped pre-tax earnings grow 19% to $17.1 million. World Book had a 21% decline in revenues and pre-tax earnings grew almost 30% to $29 million. The unit discontinued its unprofitable syndication business and reduced certain reserves for sales draws, both of which were one-time items.

At See's, poundage fell 4% but was offset by a 5% price increase. A new 8.5% sales tax on snack foods in California, which had since been repealed, likely affected pre-tax earnings at See's, which were unchanged from the year before at $42.4 million.

Fechheimer added ten stores, bringing its total to fifty-three. This growth accounted for a 10% increase in revenues during 1992. The result was a 6% increase in pre-tax earnings to $13.7 million.

Rebounding from the recent recession, pre-tax profits of *The Buffalo News* ballooned almost 30% to $47.9 million. Increased levels of advertising and a 20% reduction in the cost of newsprint (offset by a $2.9 million charge for an employee buyout) led to these results.

Investments

Berkshire's equity portfolio saw some modest changes in 1992. The now-familiar names were all there—Cap Cities/ABC, Coca-Cola, Freddie Mac, GEICO, Gillette, Guinness, *The Washington Post*, and Wells Fargo. Berkshire added moderately to Guinness and Wells Fargo and doubled its stake in Freddie Mac. There was one newcomer: General Dynamics, a defense contractor, originally purchased as an arbitrage opportunity. General Dynamics was run by Bill Anders, one of the first men to orbit the Moon on Apollo 8. It turned out Anders was a good capital allocator and Berkshire ended the year with 14% of the company as a new long-term investment.

Buffett sought to clarify the "fuzzy thinking" that he believed led investors to choose between growth and value investing. The two terms had become (and largely continue to be) one of the key ways investment funds are marketed. Buffett correctly saw them as connected: "In our opinion, the two approaches are joined at the hip: Growth is *always* a component in the calculation of value, constituting a variable whose importance can range from negligible to enormous and whose impact can be negative as well as positive."

Readers of shareholder letters from the average public company can come away with the misconception that growth is always good.* What's missed by those managers and investors who seek out and reward such thinking is that bigger doesn't always equal better. Growth is good *only* when it comes at satisfactory rates of return on incremental capital employed. Opportunity cost, or alternative uses of capital, should also factor into the analysis. It is a mistake to buy a company just because it is growing, or to avoid one because it isn't. What really matters is price relative to value. Growth (like the above quote states) is simply one component of the equation.

Within its fixed income portfolio Berkshire added to its holdings of ACF Industries debentures. A portion of the Washington Public Power Supply System bonds were called, reducing its stake in that company. And Berkshire sold its entire stake in RJR Nabisco. Investing wisdom accompanied the news of these changes. Buffett wrote that the secondary market (where existing shares of stock and bonds are traded) as contrasted to the primary or new issue market, was the better arena for investors. First-issue shares were (and are) usually priced much more rationally in the primary market due to the control that issuers and their investment banks have over timing. In the secondary market, an investor can benefit from taking advantage of Mr. Market. They may even find that "shares worth *x* in business value have sold

---

* Usually the focus is on revenues or earnings when it should be the rate of return on capital. Negative growth (i.e. shrinking) a company with a poor return on capital can *add* value. Berkshire did this by shrinking its early textile business to release the capital trapped in a poor business, which was then reinvested elsewhere at a higher rate of return.

in the market for ½ *x* or less." Berkshire's negotiated purchases of preferred stock, including the convertible preferred issue from Gillette, proved this rule. Buffett said Berkshire had done well in those investments, but perhaps not as well as if he had taken his own advice.

Two New Accounting Rules and a Plea for One More

In keeping with his intent to educate and inform, Buffett's 1992 Chairman's letter included important accounting updates. In a section entitled Two New Accounting Rules and a Plea for One More, he provided three lessons.

Lesson one: a new rule related to deferred taxes. The new rule, which Buffett thought reasonable, required accruing deferred tax at one uniform rate, then 34%. Prior to this change, which would take effect in 1993, Berkshire used a two-tiered system where $6.4 billion of its unrealized appreciation on investments was taxed at a 34% rate and the $1.2 billion balance at the older 28% rate. The result of the new rule would be a $70 million increase to the tax liability and a corresponding decrease to equity.

Lesson two: Businesses must now recognize present value liabilities related to post-retirement healthcare benefits. Prior to 1993, GAAP had only required companies to record the present value of their pension liabilities, but Buffett said it illogically ignored liabilities for health benefits extending past the time of employment. The change would have little effect on Berkshire because its future obligations to its 22,000 employees were negligible. This was no accident. Buffett and Munger avoided acquiring businesses burdened with post-retirement healthcare obligations; they also tended to avoid buying the stocks of companies with such liabilities. This new accounting rule would force the recognition of a previously ignored economic reality that such obligations were a real, if not precisely quantifiable, liability.

Lesson three: how to value stock options. The crux of the matter was that companies did not account for the issuance of stock options as an expense on their books. Stock options are difficult to value and are non-cash in nature, so executives and others argued that they should not be included on a company's books. Buffett, as usual, cut through the fog and opined: "If options aren't a form of compensation what are they? If compensation isn't an expense, what is it? And, if expenses shouldn't go into the calculation of earnings, where in the world should they go?"

This third lesson, though not associated with an accounting change, got more ink than the first two combined. And rightly so. Buffett wrote that accountants and regulators should be shamed by letting companies and their executives strong-arm them into such egregious accounting. Since the issuance of equity directly affected an investor's return from their investment, it was an extremely important issue for the accounting profession to tackle, imprecise and messy as it might be. This was a battle Buffett would long fight until the expensing of options was made mandatory in the mid-2000s.[51]

While Berkshire did not use stock options, it did have an outstanding issue of 5.5% zero-coupon convertible debentures issued in September 1989, which were called that year.* Buffett did not like the prospect of Berkshire shareholders not knowing exactly what their ownership interest was at any given time. "Berkshire shareholders are disadvantaged by having a conversion option outstanding." The terms of the debenture looked less favorable to Berkshire after interest rates declined and book value nearly doubled in that short time.

Miscellaneous

Wrapping up his 1992 letter to shareholders, Buffett relayed what he called two pieces of regrettable news. His long-time assistant, Gladys Kaiser, who had been with him twenty-five years, was retiring after the 1993 Annual Meeting. Additionally, Verne McKenzie was stepping down as CFO, leaving the post to his understudy, Marc Hamburg.**

His usual invitation to Omaha for the Annual Meeting followed. As did the customary plea to shop at Nebraska Furniture Mart and Borsheims during the visit.

1993

The year 1993 could be described as a prototypical year for Berkshire Hathaway. It found one large acquisition candidate, largely left its investment portfolio intact, maintained its insurance underwriting discipline in the face of continued so-so pricing, and polished around the edges of its various other businesses.

Berkshire's gain in book value was 14.3% during the year, falling just below Buffett's stated goal of 15% per year.*** Berkshire's net worth increased by $1.5 billion and was affected by several non-operating items. Two factors were positive and two were negative.

The two negative factors were related to a change in Generally Accepted Accounting Principles (GAAP). They pertained to accruing for deferred taxes on unrealized appreciation of securities gains. The first, discussed in the 1992 segment, called for all unrealized gains (and losses, if applicable) to be netted against the 34%

---

* Called for payment on January 4, 1993.
** McKenzie was slowing down not stopping, remaining connected to Berkshire via a consulting arrangement.
*** Buffett stated in his letter to shareholders that intrinsic value also increased by 14% in 1993, roughly matching the increase in book value. Shares appreciated by 39% that year.

corporate tax that would be due if/when sold, rather than the previous bifurcating practice depending on when the securities were purchased. The second related factor was a 1% increase in the tax rate to 35% that went into effect in late 1993, which meant accruing additional tax. The tax itself was straightforward. The accounting, however, necessitated that both one-time charges be deducted from earnings, even though the unrealized appreciation never was.* Taken together these amounted to approximately $145 million of charges that reduced Berkshire's net worth.

Offsetting these charges were two positive factors. One was a change in the way common equity securities were valued on Berkshire's balance sheet. Beginning in 1993, all common stocks would be valued at market, in contrast to being carried at cost. The change increased Berkshire's reported net worth by $172 million in 1993. The increase in net worth from this change would have been much larger had it not been for the fact that Berkshire's Insurance Group already valued its common stock holdings at market, an accounting convention that began in 1979. The accounting fixed a peculiarity that valued the same security differently depending on which subsidiary held the asset.**

The second factor positively affecting Berkshire's net worth was the issuance of shares. Some 3,944 shares were issued in January relating to the conversion of the convertible debentures called for redemption (some investors elected for shares, the remaining for cash).*** Another 25,203 shares were issued in connection with the 1993 acquisition of Dexter Shoe, discussed below. Thus Berkshire's net worth increased by about $478 million due to the issuance of 29,147 shares. Because they were issued at a price above book value, their issuance increased per share book value. More shares meant a higher benchmark to meet the 15% annualized return target. Instead of $1.8 billion, Berkshire would need to increase its book value by $1.85 billion by the year 2000 to meet its goal.

Dexter Shoe

One of Berkshire's largest acquisitions this decade was Dexter Shoe based in Dexter, Maine. Harold Alfond founded the business in 1956 with $10,000 of initial capital and grew it into one of the largest American footwear manufacturers and retailers with the help of his nephew, Peter Lunder. By 1993, Dexter was selling over 7.5 million pairs of shoes from seventy-seven retail locations. Though some were manufactured

---

* Here's an illustration of what happened. Suppose Berkshire had an unrealized gain of $1 million. Under the old system a $280,000 tax (the previous tax rate of 28%) was accrued as a deferred tax liability and the balance of $720,000 was recorded as a direct increase to shareholders' equity. The income statement was not affected at all. To correct for the new 35% tax rate (assuming the unrealized gain remained $1 million), an additional 7% tax or $70,000 was included as an expense on the income statement which then increased the deferred tax liability (since it wasn't paid) and a corresponding decrease to shareholders' equity was recorded.

** The change also pertained to other securities with characteristics of common stocks.

*** Some investors converted prior to year-end 1992 while others did so just after year-end. In total 6,106 shares were issued in relation to the debentures.

in Puerto Rico, most were manufactured in Maine. This countered the prevailing wisdom that imports made such arrangements uncompetitive.* Dexter's shoes were sold in familiar retailers including Nordstrom and J.C. Penney.

Berkshire paid $433 million for Dexter,** exchanging 25,203 shares for the business. Buffett held out the Dexter acquisition as an example to others of the Berkshire system. The deal came together because of Frank Rooney, manager of H.H. Brown Shoe, who knew Alfond and Dexter Shoe well. Alfond made a deal with Buffett for an all-share purchase, rather than cash. It highlighted some of the advantages Berkshire could provide a seller. In addition to saving on taxes by using shares instead of cash, Alfond traded "a 100% interest in a single terrific business for a smaller interest in a large group of terrific businesses." Where Rose Blumkin had declined such an offer ten years earlier for Nebraska Furniture Mart (instead opting for cash), Alfond took Buffett up on what amounted to a tax-free diversification for Alfond and his family's business holdings.

The Dexter acquisition provided a great example of Berkshire's strategic planning—or lack thereof. "Five years ago we had no thought of getting into shoes. Now we have 7,200 employees in that industry," Buffett said. It proved the wisdom of always being ready for action. Berkshire expected the Shoe Group (H.H. Brown, Lowell Shoe, Dexter) to earn around $85 million pre-tax on revenues of $550 million in the coming year.

Insurance Operations

Berkshire's main economic engine was insurance. Insurance comprised $16.2 billion of Berkshire's $19.5 billion of identifiable assets at year-end 1993 and showed no signs of slowing down. Though patience and a willingness to walk away from business was still the rule, Berkshire saw a large opportunity to put its superior financial strength to use in marketing super cat and other reinsurance products where staying power counted. This did not mean that reinsurance was immune to competition. Almost $5 billion of capital had recently been raised to form new entities to compete in the reinsurance space. What it did mean was Berkshire had the financial strength and prowess to weather business cycles and eventually come out ahead.

Berkshire's Insurance Group was proudly holding its own in 1993. As a whole the Insurance Group wrote and earned about the same volume in 1993 as it did in 1992: $737 million and $651 million, respectively (see Table 5.32). It also marked the first overall underwriting profit—$30 million pre-tax—since 1981. Better still both the primary and reinsurance segments wrote to combined ratios below 100%.

---

* Imports would later wreak havoc on the domestic footwear industry and Buffett would regret issuing shares for Dexter.

** The footnotes to the financial statements indicate $428.4 million in new shares were issued, and $4.7 million of Treasury shares (25,203 shares in total) were used to fund the acquisition.

Table 5.32: Insurance Group, select information

($ millions)	1993 Amount	%	1992 Amount	%
Primary Group				
Premiums written	$208.4		$132.4	
Premiums earned	208.3	100.0%	152.8	100.0%
Losses and loss expenses	99.8	47.9%	98.0	64.1%
Underwriting expenses	95.8	46.0%	46.8	30.6%
Total losses and expenses	195.6	93.9%	144.8	94.8%
Underwriting gain/(loss) - pre-tax	12.7		8.0	
Unfavorable (favorable) loss development included in losses and loss expenses	(41.7)	(20.0%)	(36.4)	(23.8%)
Statutory combined ratio		93.9%		99.5%
Reinsurance Group				
Premiums written	$528.7		$607.2	
Premiums earned	442.4	100.0%	511.5	100.0%
Losses and loss expenses	350.9	79.3%	589.7	115.3%
Underwriting expenses	74.2	16.8%	38.8	7.6%
Total losses and expenses	425.1	96.1%	628.5	122.9%
Underwriting gain/(loss) - pre-tax	17.3		(117.0)	
Unfavorable (favorable) loss development included in losses and loss expenses	0.0	0.0%	0.0	0.0%
Statutory combined ratio		93.4%		121.7%
Total Insurance Group underwriting gain/(loss) pre-tax	**$30.0**		**($109.0)**	
Insurance Group overall statutory combined ratio		92.2%		115.1%

Notes:

1. Totals may not add due to rounding.

2. The loss and expense ratios are shown as they were reported in the Annual Reports, which is on a GAAP basis. The GAAP basis ratios are calculated with underwriting expenses divided by earned premiums. This contrasts to the statutory basis calculation, where the ratio uses written premiums. In both the GAAP and statutory calculations, losses and loss adjustment expenses are divided by earned premiums.

3. In 1990, Berkshire began including structured settlements and portfolio reinsurance with reinsurance.

Sources: Berkshire Hathaway Annual Reports 1992, 1994; and author's calculations.

Examining the larger segment, the Reinsurance Group wrote to a 93.4% combined ratio and turned in a $17.3 million pre-tax underwriting gain. The bulk of premiums earned came from the larger super cat policies and quota-share arrangements with other insurers.

Over the prior three years Berkshire all but walked away from retroactive reinsurance and structured settlements due to unfavorable pricing. Premiums earned in these lines fell 88% between 1991 and 1993, from $363 million to $44 million. The underwriting loss from these business activities was $64.3 million in 1993. These losses were almost entirely due to the amortization of deferred charges and did not accurately reflect economic results since Berkshire continued to benefit from the use of float. Remember, float from these long-tail policies was usually considerable in relation to premium volume and its benefits were seen in insurance investment income, not underwriting.

In contrast, the Primary Group had premium growth in 1993 and earned a $13 million underwriting profit. Premiums earned and written were both $208 million, up 57% and 36% respectively. Part of the reason for the increase was Central States Indemnity, Co., the newest addition to the team acquired the year before, which turned in a $5 million underwriting gain on premiums of $69 million. Reflecting overly conservative loss reserving, the segment again benefitted from favorable loss development. The favorable loss development represented 20% of premiums earned and 7.4% of the amount of reserves at the start of the year.* This favorable development was largely attributable to National Indemnity's traditional commercial auto business. The Home State companies, seemingly needing a new name, expanded beyond their borders and planned additional expansion in the coming years. Headwinds were likely coming, however, as industry capacity remained abundant.

Manufacturing, Publishing, and Retailing

The new Shoe Group, together with the other businesses in the manufacturing, publishing, and retailing segment, continued to churn out excellent results for Berkshire. Pre-tax earnings grew 8% to $272.5 million on revenues up 10.6% to $2 billion. Pre-tax return on tangible capital, however, fell from 55.6% in 1992 to 48.2% in 1993. Likewise, after-tax return on tangible equity fell from 36.9% to 31.3%, achieved basically without debt (cash exceeded debt by three times). Returns were declining from the stratosphere but remained highly satisfactory.

Nebraska Furniture Mart was reunited with its matriarch, Mrs. B, who turned 100 years old in 1993 and showed no signs of slowing down. Nebraska Furniture Mart turned Mrs. B's location across the street into an outlet store and planned a 100,000 square feet expansion for an appliance and electronics superstore. Pre-tax profits swelled 26% to a record $22 million.

At World Book revenues continued to slide substantially, falling 19% to $47.3 million. Pre-tax earnings fell 31% to $20 million as electronic competition from CD-

---

* Such an adjustment, while favorable, is large enough to be considered a mistake.

ROMs weighed on its paper-based product. Though the company could not say whether the decline would reverse, World Book was not waiting to find out. It was working on its own electronic version to compete with the likes of Microsoft and others trying to take market share.

The Buffalo News saw a modest increase in revenues from increased advertising and circulation. Its pre-tax profits grew 6% to $51 million. The story was largely the same at Kirby (pre-tax profits up 10% to $39 million), See's (down 3% to $41 million) and most of the other units in the manufacturing, publishing, and retailing segment. Revenues and earnings "bobbed around" but were not specifically noteworthy. A new mail order program at See's was put in place to try to mitigate the inch-by-inch decline in poundage experienced almost every year since Blue Chip purchased it.

Wesco

Surprisingly, Buffett's Chairman's letter did not discuss a relatively major event at Mutual Savings. During 1993, Wesco exited the savings and loan business by transferring its savings account liabilities (offset by a mortgage portfolio and cash) to CenFed Bank, headquartered in Pasadena, California. Munger wrote Wesco shareholders that he and Wesco's management cared about what happened to Mutual Savings customers and CenFed, as it was known, was chosen since it "was considered likely to serve depositors safely and well."

Wesco formed a new holding company for its real estate including its headquarters (the bottom floor of which was now a CenFed branch), the remaining ocean-side lots, and some troubled loans that would slowly be liquidated. It stayed in the housing finance business. Wesco held on to 7.2 million shares of Freddie Mac, the lower-cost competitor to the now-extinct Mutual Savings thrift. The Freddie Mac shares, which cost $72 million, now had a market value of almost $360 million (these were included with Berkshire's total of almost 14 million shares).

Finance Businesses

The shutdown of Mutual Savings caused some important changes to the Finance Businesses supplemental segment now included at the end of the Berkshire Annual Report. Whereas in 1992 the segment included Mutual Savings and Scott Fetzer Financial Group, in 1993 Mutual Savings was replaced by Berkshire Hathaway Credit Corporation. Very little was disclosed about this new entity. What could be gathered from the footnotes to the financial statements is this: it held high-quality, short-term mortgage-backed securities funded by investment agreement borrowings that were structured to match the duration of the assets. It was as if Berkshire had formed its own mini bank without depositors or the strings associated with operating a regulated bank. The Freddie Mac shares retained by Wesco were now included in the Insurance Group segment along with Berkshire's own shares of the mortgage company.

Investments

As Berkshire's marketable securities portfolio grew (now $12.5 billion at year-end), the threshold for reporting also grew. In 1993, the cutoff was $250 million but there was not much to report. This was as it should be, said Buffett. It was hard to find outstanding businesses to purchase, and an owner of a small part of a good company should, like his or her counterpart owning the entirety of a business, hold on "with the same tenacity." The lower investment portfolio turnover compared to years past was in part due to Berkshire's growing size, which limited the investable universe, and in part due to Buffett's increasing appreciation for high-quality businesses.

Long holding periods also confer meaningful compounding advantages through the way taxation works. Buffett's extreme example was a doubling of a dollar for twenty years with a 35% tax rate on the investment. Paying tax annually would result in over $22,370 at the end of two decades. Counterintuitively, allowing the compounding to take place and paying one 35% tax at the end would result in a far better outcome: A result of over $680,000—all due to the power of deferring taxes.

Berkshire's portfolio contained significant unrealized capital gains. At year-end 1993, its marketable securities portfolio had over $8.2 billion in unrealized appreciation—a 300% gain. The most extreme examples were GEICO and *The Washington Post*. Berkshire's GEICO stake had appreciated thirty-eight times its original cost to $1.7 billion; *The Washington Post* Company over forty-five times to $440 million.

Table 5.33: Berkshire Hathaway equity portfolio, 1993

($ millions)	Cost	Market	Unrealized Gain/(Loss)
Capital Cities/ABC, Inc.	$345	$1,239	$894
The Coca-Cola Company	1,024	4,168	3,144
Freddie Mac	308	681	374
GEICO Corp.	46	1,760	1,714
General Dynamics Corp.	95	401	306
The Gillette Company	600	1,431	831
Guinness PLC	333	271	(62)
The Washington Post Company	10	440	430
Wells Fargo & Company	424	879	455
Other	1,134	1,271	136
Total	$4,318	$12,540	$8,222

Sources: Berkshire Hathaway Annual Report 1993 and author's calculations.

Despite the headwinds faced in some parts of its business such as insurance, Berkshire in 1993 was proving the resiliency of a financially strong business operated for the long term.

1994 Annual Meeting

Looking back, we have the benefit of hindsight. Now, thanks to technology we also can sit in on the Annual Meetings, which were filmed for the first time in April 1994 and made available to the public in 2018.[52] A few interesting discussion topics from that first recorded meeting are worth noting.

One was the degree to which Buffett and Munger thought about public companies as private ones. Buffett's shareholder letters around this time started discussing Berkshire's rising share price, which had never been split and which had recently crossed the $10,000 per share mark. At the 1994 Annual Meeting, the question about share price was asked by a shareholder. Charlie Munger, as usual, cut right to the chase: "I think the idea of carving ownerships in an enterprise into little, tiny $20 pieces is almost insane .... I don't see why there shouldn't be a minimum as a condition of joining some enterprise ... we'd all feel that way if we were organizing a private enterprise." Even in the early 1990s, a share of a private company or partnership very likely required more than $10,000.*

Other questions touched on how Buffett went about finding and valuing businesses. He thought just about anyone could do what he and Munger did by reading annual

---

* The focus on stock price is evidence, in my mind, of a focus on quantity over quality. Shareholders somehow feel better owning more shares, even if the economics haven't changed at all.

reports and other communications from companies and their competitors. Buffett said they simply looked at a company's products, distribution systems, and finances. Then they tried to determine if they could assess what the economics of the business and industry would look like ten or twenty years out. He said 95% of the businesses he looked at wouldn't make the cut due to their falling outside of his circle of competence or for other reasons. Another important insight was to ignore noise, including that from pundits and others about the general economy. Charlie Munger said it was best to be "agnostic about macro factors and therefore devote all your time to thinking about individual businesses and individual situations."

One key component to valuing businesses was growth. Buffett thought that this was a concept misunderstood by others, including managers and analysts. What mattered, he said, was the amount of cash that could be taken out of a business from now until forever, discounted back to the present. Growth was simply a variable, not something always positive, as others seemed to insinuate. If physical or unit growth required additional capital to grow that was okay, so long as the rate of return on capital was satisfactory. "There's a huge difference in the business that grows and requires a lot of capital to do so, and the business that grows, and doesn't require capital," he said in response to a question. As a conglomerate, Berkshire was structured so it could take the cash generated from slow or no-growth businesses with good returns on capital, such as Scott Fetzer, and put it to use elsewhere.

Another theme of questions was on management compensation. The answers illustrated the fact that even though Berkshire's arrangements were usually very simple, much thought was put into them. The trick was to structure compensation so it aligned managers with owners. Buffett and Munger suggested a few guiding principles:

- It didn't make sense for an operating manager to be compensated on Berkshire as a whole, since only Buffett and Munger controlled that outcome.
- The aim was a system that was symmetrical, meaning a manager was rewarded for good performance but suffered if poor performance was delivered.
- The arrangement should be structured based on the economics of the business, since all businesses were different.

In short, management compensation was best when it aligned the interests of managers to that of owners, regardless of the situation.

By any standard of executive compensation, Warren Buffett and Charlie Munger were paid almost nothing. Their $100,000 salaries remain unchanged to this day. Considering their track record, they could have easily justified seven- or eight-figure salaries like their Fortune 500 contemporaries. But they chose not to, and it sends a strong message. They were already rich, each had most of their net worth in Berkshire, and they loved their work—the perfect example of management alignment.

1994

The effects of Berkshire's size were starting to show. A $1.45 billion increase in net worth during the year equated to just 13.9% growth and resulted in Berkshire's equity climbing to almost $12 billion at year-end 1994. Buffett had been warning shareholders for years that size was forging an anchor to future returns. However, past results far above the 15% goalpost seemed to contradict him.[*]

While Berkshire's growing size was beginning to bring down its rate of return, its methods were largely unchanged. Buffett would continue to learn and improve but Berkshire, he wrote shareholders that year, would "stick with the approach that got us here." Importantly, Berkshire would not relax its standards. "A fat wallet, however, is the enemy of superior investment results," he quipped.

Insurance

Berkshire's float—specifically the cost of it if forced to choose—was probably *the* most significant aspect of Berkshire's growth over time. Berkshire's float at year-end 1994 averaged over $3 billion. Better still, its cost (as measured by the underwriting gain/loss in relation to average float) registered negative for the second year in a row. Negative is a good thing in this case, since it meant the Insurance Group wrote to a profit and its cost compared to a government bond[**] was less than zero.

Profits of $129 million in 1994 produced an 86% combined ratio. The 1967 National Indemnity acquisition was beginning to look like a bargain.

---

[*] See the table at the beginning of the Annual Report listing the change in Berkshire's book value against that of the S&P 500.

[**] At the time long-term bonds were yielding close to 8%.

Table 5.34: Insurance Group, select information

($ millions)	1994 Amount	%	1993 Amount	%
Primary Group				
Premiums written	$225.7		$208.4	
Premiums earned	234.8	100.0%	208.3	100.0%
Losses and loss expenses	88.4	37.6%	99.8	47.9%
Underwriting expenses	98.1	41.8%	95.8	46.0%
Total losses and expenses	186.5	79.4%	195.6	93.9%
Underwriting gain/(loss) - pre-tax	48.3		12.7	
Unfavorable (favorable) loss development included in losses and loss expenses	*(53.9)*	*(23.0%)*	*(41.7)*	*(20.0%)*
Statutory combined ratio		81.1%		93.9%
Reinsurance Group				
Premiums written	$689.8		$528.7	
Premiums earned	688.4	100.0%	442.4	100.0%
Losses and loss expenses	476.9	69.3%	350.9	79.3%
Underwriting expenses	130.8	19.0%	74.2	16.8%
Total losses and expenses	607.7	88.3%	425.1	96.1%
Underwriting gain/(loss) - pre-tax	80.7		17.3	
Unfavorable (favorable) loss development included in losses and loss expenses	*37.0*	*14.1%*	*0.0*	*0.0%*
Statutory combined ratio		88.2%		93.4%
Total Insurance Group underwriting gain/(loss) pre-tax	**$129.0**		**$30.0**	
Insurance Group overall statutory combined ratio		86.1%		92.2%

Notes:

1. Totals may not add due to rounding.

2. The loss and expense ratios are shown as they were reported in the Annual Reports, which is on a GAAP basis. The GAAP basis ratios are calculated with underwriting expenses divided by earned premiums. This contrasts to the statutory basis calculation, where the ratio uses written premiums. In both the GAAP and statutory calculations, losses and loss adjustment expenses are divided by earned premiums.

3. In 1990, Berkshire began including structured settlements and portfolio reinsurance with reinsurance.

Sources: Berkshire Hathaway Annual Report 1994 and author's calculations.

One reason for the extreme profitability had to do with Berkshire's new super cat business, into which it was moving more heavily to put its superior capital strength to work. While it could be profitable in the long run, such business was prone to down periods. Berkshire just hadn't seen many of them yet. With the exception of an earthquake in California, Berkshire experienced an absence of large insured losses in 1994. This meant most super cat premiums went right to the bottom line and put the loss experience above trend. Such outsize profits could not continue indefinitely, and very well could have started in the other direction.

In 1994, Berkshire's Reinsurance Group wrote and earned just under $700 million of premium volume. Catastrophe excess of loss reinsurance contracts (super cat), which had grown three-fold to $447 million, contributed to the 56% overall increase in reinsurance premiums. Earned premiums declined in other areas including quota-share, structured settlements, and retroactive reinsurance. As noted earlier, profits from the super cat business were a major reason behind reinsurance underwriting profits swelling from $17 million in 1993 to $81 million in 1994. Profits would have been even higher had it not been for $37 million of adverse loss development.[*]

The Primary Group also grew premiums written and earned. The segment turned in a combined ratio of 81% on $235 million of earned premiums (up 13%), although some markets remained soft. Favorable loss development in traditional commercial auto and commercial casualty/professional liability/special risks led to 23 percentage points of positive adjustment. While a favorable adjustment added to reported profitability and could be termed conservative, the change reflected the imprecise nature of reserve estimation. Such a large adjustment in either direction corresponded to meaningful past underwriting errors.[**]

Manufacturing, Publishing, and Retailing

The addition of Dexter for a full year (compared to two months in 1993) was a big contributor to the 20% increase in revenues (to $2.4 billion) and 23% increase in pre-tax profit (to $336 million) for the Manufacturing, Publishing, and Retailing segment. Pre-tax return on average invested capital remained strong at 49.3%, up from 48.2%. After-tax return on tangible equity improved from 31.3% to 32.4% without the use of leverage.

The Shoe Group completed a small acquisition of eleven stores located in Maryland, Pennsylvania, and Virginia and added a new computerized distribution center which was expected to increase operating efficiencies. One fact from the summary table (see Table 5.2 on page 204) of the Chairman's letter stands out. In 1993, Buffett stated that the Shoe Group, made up of H.H. Brown, Dexter, and Lowell, would probably

---

[*] The footnotes to the Annual Report do include a reconciliation of unpaid losses and loss adjustment expenses for just the property/casualty segment. This table showed a $60 million unfavorable development in 1994, $11 million in 1993, and $29 million in 1992. On beginning net unpaid losses and loss adjustment expense balances of around $2.5 billion, these figures were essentially breakeven.

[**] A proper comparison would use beginning net loss reserves not premiums earned. In either case it was likely still outside of a tolerable range.

earn about $85 million in the coming year. The actual result: $85.5 million. This was probably a coincidence, but it also demonstrated that the businesses Berkshire was buying were simple and understandable with somewhat predicable futures.

See's, long beset by declines in poundage, saw an impressive 5.3% increase in pounds sold from increased mail-order business and larger orders. Revenues increased 7.5% to $216 million and pre-tax income rose 15.6% to $48 million. Its operating margin remained a mouthwatering 21.6%.

World Book continued to see declines in unit volume of physical book sets but was optimistic that some offset would be seen in increases of sales of CD-ROM sets and upgrades. Though revenues declined 3.8% to $191 million, pre-tax income rose over 25% to $24.4 million, largely due to a $3.3 million charge taken in 1993.

The Home Cleaning Systems segment, led by Kirby, improved unit sales marginally in the domestic US market but increased them 14% internationally. This resulted in a 7% increase in revenues and pre-tax income, to $208 million and $43.9 million, respectively.

Listed under Home Furnishings, Nebraska Furniture Mart, with its new 100,000 square foot Mega Mart in service, increased revenues 17.6% to $245 million. Owing to its strategy of maintaining extremely low prices and because of a $2.3 million charge to write off unused fixed assets, pre-tax operating income declined 20% to $16.9 million. Its operating margin, already low historically, dropped to 6.9% that year from around 10% in prior years. Against such paper-thin margins, it was no wonder Nebraska Furniture Mart's competitors stayed far away from Omaha.

The Buffalo News continued to be an exceptional business even though it was operating in a tougher environment than previous years. In 1994 it saw pre-tax income increase 6.5% to $53.7 million on revenues that increased 3.7% to $151 million. Judging by the financial results, business was okay. The retail price of the paper increased from 35 cents to 50 cents, and this price increase was more than enough to offset the continual decline in circulation. Going into 1995, newsprint cost increased almost 40%, enough to temper expectations for the coming year.

At Fechheimer, Berkshire's uniform subsidiary, the company scored a big win with a contract to supply all the New York City Fire Department with uniforms and safety accessories for three years. As a result, sales increased almost 24%. However, operating profit increased just 6% to $14 million due to start-up costs associated with building out the related distribution infrastructure needed for the NYC contract. In addition, a new computer system and problems with recent retail store acquisitions held down profits.*

---

* It is striking the honesty and candor which is included in the Annual Reports, including the footnotes. The fact that its recent store acquisitions were experiencing problems could easily have been omitted.

Investments

Berkshire's equity portfolio saw a few changes in 1994. Gannett, Co., Inc., a newspaper holding company, and PNC Bank were new. Berkshire also enlarged its holdings of Coca-Cola by about 7 million shares to 100 million shares* and its American Express holdings increased to almost 28 million shares with a cost of $723 million.** American Express was a company Buffett was very familiar with, having purchased 5% of the company for $13 million in the mid-1960s for his investment partnership. He continued to follow the company and remarked that a long-term familiarity with a company is often helpful in evaluating it. Such familiarity with businesses was built over many years and was the result of reading hundreds of annual reports per year. Such wide and deep reading provided the proper reference points to compare various investment alternatives and was a critical component to Berkshire's success.

Table 5.35: Berkshire Hathaway common stock portfolio, select data

($ millions)	1994
American Express Company	$819
Capital Cities/ABC, Inc.	1,705
The Coca-Cola Company	5,150
Federal Home Loan Mortgage Corp.	644
Gannett Co., Inc.	365
GEICO Corporation	1,678
The Gillette Company	1,797
PNC Bank Corporation	411
Washington Post Company	419
Wells Fargo & Company	985

Notes:
1. Buffett's Chairman's letter only included select investments and did not include a total. I elected not to take data from the footnotes of the Annual Report since Buffett's classifications historically differed slightly from GAAP reporting.
2. The reporting threshold was $300 million of market value.
Source: Berkshire Hathaway Chairman's letter 1994.

The summary earnings table in the Annual Report (see Table 5.2 on page 204) contained a glaring item. Deteriorating conditions at USAir culminated in the company deferring the preferred dividend, so Berkshire wrote down its investment in its preferred stock by $268.5 million to $89.5 million. Buffett was quick to chastise himself both in his letter to shareholders and at the Annual Meeting. The original $358 million

---

* This was Berkshire's final purchase of Coca-Cola shares, which represented 7.8% of the company's then outstanding shares. The $1.299 billion cost basis remains as of 2020.
** Buffett described the AMEX holding as "enlarged" even though it was not named in the table in the 1993 report. Berkshire also owned convertible preferred stock in AMEX which was not included in the table.

purchase of the preferred stock issue was an unforced error that came about solely due to bad analysis on Buffett's part. He "simply failed to focus on the problems that would inevitably beset a carrier whose costs were both high and extremely difficult to lower."

USAir was run by a competent and able manager, but the company was battling basic economics. Its labor costs, driven by unions, were out of line (a "relic of a regulated market" he told shareholders at the Annual Meeting) with lower-cost competitors. Buffett felt stuck with the investment due to its size and structure. Preferred stocks are ahead of common shares but behind any bonds. Unlike common shares, preferred shares have similar characteristics of fixed, coupon-paying securities such as bonds, but are between the two in terms of claims on a company's assets. USAir's bondholders would have a priority claim on its assets if the company went bankrupt, and if a recognized expert in investing did not want the preferred stock its sale price might have to be extremely low. Instead, Berkshire wrote it down and continued to hold onto it, though both Buffett and Munger also decided to step down from the USAir board.

Another mistake Buffett pointed out was the sale of 10 million shares of Cap Cities during the year. He thought it a mistake since after he sold it, the investment continued to appreciate. The $222.5 million forgone gain on those shares (Buffett did the math for shareholders) wasn't the mistake, it was that this was the second time he'd sold Cap Cities shares and seen them continue to go up. The business was one he understood well and knew had favorable long-term prospects, yet he sold part of it anyway. Buffett was probably being a little too hard on himself. Responding to a question at the Annual Meeting, he noted that Berkshire tendered the shares to lead the way on an offer from Cap Cities to buy back shares. Berkshire had participated in similar situations in the past (GEICO, General Foods) and perhaps felt somewhat obligated. Berkshire retained 20 million shares in Cap Cities and Buffett would cling to these for some time.

Book Value and Intrinsic Value

Buffett had at times more subtly and at other times more explicitly commented on Berkshire Hathaway's intrinsic value. In 1994, he was more explicit. In his letter and at the shareholders' meeting, he guided investors to Berkshire's approximate true worth.* He also attempted to unlink intrinsic value from a strict book value-based approach. Buffett assured shareholders he was not doing this to pump up Berkshire's stock price. Rather, he and Munger preferred to see the stock rise and fall in lockstep with intrinsic value, such that shareholders would obtain an investment result in line with Berkshire's business performance.

---

* In the 1994 Annual Report, he stated that Berkshire's book value gain of 13.9% approximated the gain in intrinsic value.

Buffett used Scott Fetzer to demonstrate. When Berkshire bought the business in 1986, it paid a premium of 1.8 times Scott Fetzer's underlying equity capital.* Through 1994, and without the use of leverage,** Scott Fetzer paid out more in dividends than it earned, which reduced its book value. Yet during that time, earnings steadily increased from $40 million in 1986 to $79.3 million in 1994. One can see why Buffett would heap such praise on Scott Fetzer's manager, Ralph Schey. He took a business earning $40 million a year to one earning close to double that, all while releasing capital employed in the business. It was an amazing achievement.

Schey unquestionably had a genuine passion for his business. He also had an incentive to find ways of increasing returns and sending cash to Omaha as that was how he was compensated. The key underlying idea was to align management with owners, and one of the most important areas to incentivize was the use of capital. While Berkshire's compensation arrangements with managers varied widely depending on the economic characteristics of the business under consideration, all were focused on capital and return on capital. Buffett disclosed that Scott Fetzer (and others) were charged a high rate*** for incremental capital used in the business. Importantly, bonus arrangements also "credit them at an equally high rate for the capital [managers] release." Put very simply, Buffett said it reflected a "money's-not-free-approach."

The lesson did not end there. The difference between the purchase price of a business and the original book value (the plug number) was goodwill, which at that time was amortized over a forty-year period. Between 1986 and 1994 this goodwill asset had been amortized from $142.6 million to $54.2 million. Berkshire's carrying value for Scott Fetzer was half of what it paid for it, yet the business was earning close to double what it was when Berkshire purchased it. Clearly accounting book value was not the definitive guide to business value, as this vividly demonstrated.

---

* The attentive reader will note the difference between the figure of $410 million used in the section on 1986 and the $315.2 million used here. This analysis focuses on Scott Fetzer's equity capital, while the latter considered total capital (debt plus equity). They are two different ways of looking at the same company.
** Aside from the finance subsidiary.
*** Disclosed as between 14% and 20% at the Annual Meeting Q&A. Buffett also stated that short-term uses of parent-company capital by subsidiaries were charged a rate based on LIBOR, but that generally it was kept very simple.

Table 5.36: Scott Fetzer, book value and carrying value

($ millions)	Scott Fetzer Book Value	Berkshire's Carrying Value
Beginning book value, 1986	$172.6	$172.6
Purchase premium over beginning book value		142.6
Berkshire's purchase price, 1986		315.2
Cumulative earnings, 1986–94	555.4	555.4
Cumulative dividends, 1986–94	(634.0)	(634.0)
Ending book value, 1994	94.0	94.0
Cumulative purchase-premium charges (1986–94)		(88.4)
Ending carrying value, 1994		$148.2

Source: Berkshire Hathaway Annual Report 1994.

The Scott Fetzer example provided a more tangible framework for Buffett's comments on the divergence of book value and intrinsic value. It directly related to Berkshire's activities in buying equities, and it also applied to Berkshire itself. Though not precise, the concept of intrinsic value is all-important in investing. Berkshire's Annual Report sought to supply all the figures necessary to estimate its intrinsic value through candid and meaningful disclosures, including additional unaudited reports when GAAP wasn't fully up to the task.

Buffett was hinting that Berkshire's valuation was getting too high. Berkshire's look-through earnings increased between 1990 and 1994, but the market placed an outsize valuation on those earnings (see Table 5.37). We can observe this effect in the price-to-book value increasing from around 1.5x between 1990 and 1992, to 2x in 1994.

Table 5.37: Berkshire Hathaway look-through earnings and valuation, 1990–1994

($ millions)	1994	1993	1992	1991	1990
Berkshire's share of undistributed earnings of major investees	492	422	298	230	266
Hypothetical tax on these undistributed investee earnings	(68)	(59)	(42)	(30)	(35)
Reported operating earnings of Berkshire	606	478	348	316	371
Total look-through earnings of Berkshire	$1,030	$841	$604	$516	$602
Market value of Berkshire at year-end	$24,031	$19,231	$13,501	$10,371	$7,650
Price/book value at year-end	2.02x	1.84x	1.52x	1.41x	1.45x
Change in book value	14%	17%	21%	40%	
Change in market value	25%	42%	30%	36%	

Notes:
1. Earnings are after tax.
2. Earnings for major investees are calculated based on average ownership for the year.
Sources: Berkshire Hathaway Annual Reports 1991, 1993, 1994; and author's calculations.

Guiding shareholders to Berkshire's intrinsic value cultivated and enhanced its shareholder base. The goal was to encourage a partnership feel despite Berkshire's large (and growing) size. Once lost, a long-term oriented shareholder base was hard to regain. One of the ways Berkshire sought to repel buyers of stock keen on turnover was to not split its stock, which crossed the $20,000 mark in 1994.

Preferred Stock Authorization

Berkshire's proxy statement for 1994 included a proposal to allow it to issue preferred stock for future acquisitions. Buffett told shareholders that the request was in response to the realization that it could be useful in future acquisitions. Even after taking pains to make clear that the shares wouldn't be used to harm shareholder interests, enough shareholders voted against it that he took some time at the beginning of the 1995 Annual Meeting to discuss the matter and expand upon his reasoning. He said he wanted to ensure Berkshire had the right "currency" available for an acquisition if a seller decided they wanted something other than either cash or Berkshire stock. A preferred issue, whether straight preferred, adjustable preferred, or convertible preferred, could provide what a seller wanted without Berkshire giving up more in intrinsic value than it received.

Buffett thought there wasn't a downside to the proposal, but the way some shareholders voted prior to the Annual Meeting indicated that his explanation in the Annual Report did not convince shareholders of this fact. It was simply a matter of form, he said, and it did not matter what the accounting treatment might be for Berkshire.* So long as the value-for-value test was met, Berkshire was willing to issue any form of security, with this preferred authorization giving the advantage of flexibility, including a possible tax-free transaction with a prospective seller. "If we do something stupid with this," he told shareholders at the Annual Meeting, "we would do something [stupid] with cash" or stock.

Berkshire shareholders then approved the issuance of up to 1 million shares of preferred stock, sending a clear message they trusted Buffett and Munger's judgement.

Decade in Review

That one man had headed a company for three decades was a relatively unusual statistic. What that man achieved during that time (with some help) put him in a

---

* Buffett noted that other companies care more about the accounting treatment, and would, presumably, give up more in intrinsic value than they received just to avoid having to explain the situation to shareholders. Berkshire focused on the economics of transactions first and foremost, and knew its shareholder body was "intelligent enough to understand the economic reality of a transaction."

league of his own. The Berkshire Hathaway that existed at year-end 1994 was very different from just a decade before, but it was unrecognizable from that which existed at the beginning of 1965. A few key figures tell the story.

Table 5.38: Reconciliation of shareholders' equity, 1965–1994

($ millions)	1965–74	1975–84	1985–94	1965–94
Beginning of period shareholders' equity	$22	$88	$1,272	$22
Net income - operations	57	366	2,869	3,292
Net income - realized gains	7	199	1,354	1,561
Unrealized appreciation of investments	0	486	5,877	6,363
Mergers/divestitures	0	133	433	566
Dividends/treasury stock	(3)	0	69	66
Other/misc.	4	0	0	4
End of period shareholders' equity	$88	$1,272	$11,875	$11,875
Change in equity during period	$66	$1,184	$10,602	$11,852

Note: Figures may not add due to rounding.
Sources: Berkshire Hathaway Annual Reports and author's calculations.

Table 5.39: Contribution toward change in equity during period

	1965–74	1975–84	1985–94	1965–94
Net income - operations	86%	31%	27%	28%
Net income - realized gains	11%	17%	13%	13%
Unrealized appreciation of investments	0%	41%	55%	54%
Mergers/divestitures	0%	11%	4%	5%
Dividends/treasury stock	(4%)	0%	1%	1%
Other/misc.	7%	0%	0%	0%
Total	100%	100%	100%	100%

Note: Figures may not add due to rounding.
Sources: Berkshire Hathaway Annual Reports and author's calculations.

Shareholder equity ballooned each decade, as did net income from operations. But this ballooning net income from operations was not the reason for the huge jump in shareholder equity. Berkshire's operations between 1985 and 1994 contributed an additional $2.9 billion to equity, both from existing subsidiaries and new ones acquired during this time—many dollars but only slightly more than a quarter of the total increase. In fact, as a percentage of the change, net income from operations shrunk with each decade and net income from realized gains remained mostly unchanged. The main driver of growth, as we can see when we look at Table 5.39 of major contributors to growth, was the result of investment outside of direct operating subsidiaries, meaning the investment portfolio.

Berkshire's investment portfolio, specifically its common stock portfolio, produced over $1.3 billion of after-tax securities gains during the 1985–94 period. On top of that, another $5.9 billion remained on the books as unrealized gains.[*] Thus a combined $7.2 billion—or 68% of the total change in shareholders' equity during the decade—came from the successful allocation of capital to businesses not controlled or managed by Berkshire Hathaway. That unrealized gains grew so much reflected Berkshire's evolution toward investing in higher-quality businesses and holding them longer.

Insurance fueled a lot of this growth. Here Berkshire had two very important sources of value: insurance underwriting and float. Remember that float is money held by Berkshire but owed, ultimately, to policyholders and others. A large portion went into the marketable securities portfolio, which enabled the multibillion-dollar gains in that area. It also provided capital for business acquisitions and allowed Berkshire to operate with very little borrowed money in the traditional sense.

Part and parcel with float, and in fact its source, was insurance underwriting. Berkshire started the decade with an imperfect understanding of the value of its insurance subsidiaries, recognizing its float-generating capacities but making pricing mistakes along the way. Those mistakes led to a cumulative $285 million pre-tax loss from underwriting activities over ten years, an expensive but ultimately valuable education. As the decade went on Berkshire finetuned its underwriting skills and held fast to its belief that policies should only be written with the expectation of a profit.

Later in the decade Berkshire moved more heavily into reinsurance, and specifically into the super catastrophe or super cat world. Berkshire found it could use its large capital position to its advantage by writing large policies for sophisticated buyers, which were usually other reinsurers.[**] By the end of 1994, Berkshire was one of the largest reinsurers in the world, and probably the largest single-risk writer.

The super cat business, and related lines, also produced large amounts of float for Berkshire against relatively small premium volume (compared to short-tail lines). This contributed to average float growth each year despite a significant decline in premium volume mid-decade. Berkshire came to understand that the stability of its float—the fact that it could be replenished as a revolving fund—would almost equate it to that of equity capital, and Buffett even alluded to its being a big part of Berkshire's intrinsic value.

---

[*] These unrealized gains were after taking into account taxes that would have been owed upon sale.

[**] Table 5.47 on page 328 contains data on premiums written to average equity. Berkshire's ratio in the single digits was an indication of its superior financial strength and capacity to write business.

Table 5.40: Berkshire Hathaway Insurance Group
Float and cost of float compared to U.S. Government Bonds

	Underwriting Loss ($ millions)	Average float ($ millions)	Approximate cost of Funds	Year-end Yield on Long-Term Gov't Bonds
1967	profit	$17.3	less than zero	5.5%
1968	profit	19.9	less than zero	5.9%
1969	profit	23.4	less than zero	6.8%
1970	$0.37	32.4	1.1%	6.3%
1971	profit	52.5	less than zero	5.8%
1972	profit	69.5	less than zero	5.8%
1973	profit	73.3	less than zero	7.3%
1974	7.36	79.1	9.3%	8.1%
1975	11.35	87.6	13.0%	8.0%
1976	profit	102.6	less than zero	7.3%
1977	profit	139.0	less than zero	8.0%
1978	profit	190.4	less than zero	8.9%
1979	profit	227.3	less than zero	10.1%
1980	profit	237.0	less than zero	11.9%
1981	profit	228.4	less than zero	13.6%
1982	21.56	220.6	9.8%	10.6%
1983	33.87	231.3	14.6%	11.8%
1984	48.06	253.2	19.0%	11.6%
1985	44.23	390.2	11.3%	9.3%
1986	55.84	797.5	7.0%	7.6%
1987	55.43	1,266.7	4.4%	9.0%
1988	11.08	1,497.7	0.7%	9.0%
1989	24.40	1,541.3	1.6%	8.0%
1990	26.65	1,637.3	1.6%	8.2%
1991	119.59	1,895.0	6.3%	7.4%
1992	108.96	2,290.4	4.8%	7.4%
1993	profit	2,624.7	less than zero	6.4%
1994	profit	3,056.6	less than zero	7.9%

Source: Berkshire Hathaway Annual Report 1994.

During the decade, Berkshire partnered with many additional managers that it trusted and admired. Through the acquisition of entire businesses such as Scott Fetzer, Fechheimer, Borsheims, H.H. Brown Shoe, Dexter Shoe, and others, Berkshire brought many new family members into the Berkshire fold. One other way in which Berkshire partnered with managers was through its publicly owned holdings. Buffett and Munger came to view Berkshire's investments in companies such as Coca-Cola, GEICO, Washington Post, Cap Cities/ABC, and others, as permanent holdings, and wrote glowingly of management at those companies.

Berkshire did have some stumbles along the way, but they were minor relative to its size then and now. One was selling part of its stake in Capital Cities/ABC (a multi-part mistake in fact, since Buffett had previously sold some before). Another mistake was the purchase of USAir preferred stock. Buffett wrote that he missed the basic economic situation completely, and Berkshire ended the decade with its investment written down to 25 cents on the dollar.

Berkshire's purchase of Salomon preferred was a mistake in hindsight. Not only was Salomon a company in which Buffett and Munger admittedly did not have a great understanding of where the industry would end up in a decade or two, but it cost Buffett a lot of time. During a ten-month stint as CEO of Salomon, he risked his reputation to save the company and Berkshire's $700 million investment.

The market finally recognized Berkshire's track record and its ability to compound book value at high rates. Berkshire's book value per share increased from $1,600 to $20,000 in this decade—a gain of 24.7% per year. Underlying book value increased at 25% per year, with the small 0.3% difference resulting from the net change in average shares outstanding. Like the prior decade, an outsize increase in the stock price came from a higher price-to-book ratio on top of underlying intrinsic value growth. This added an additional 5.5% per year to the share price and took the average price-to-book ratio over 2.0x by year-end 1994.* Part of the premium price-to-book ratio can be explained by interest rates. The 10-year Treasury rate fell from 11.5% at the beginning of the decade to under 5.5% by the end of 1993; rates increased to 7.8% at the end of 1994. When the market got ahead of itself and priced Berkshire over 2x book value, Buffett stepped in to subtly nudge onlookers toward a proper valuation, something almost unheard of.

---

* The amount was a whopping 7.2% *per year* when using period-end figures.

Figure 5.1: Berkshire Hathaway stock price, 1985–1994

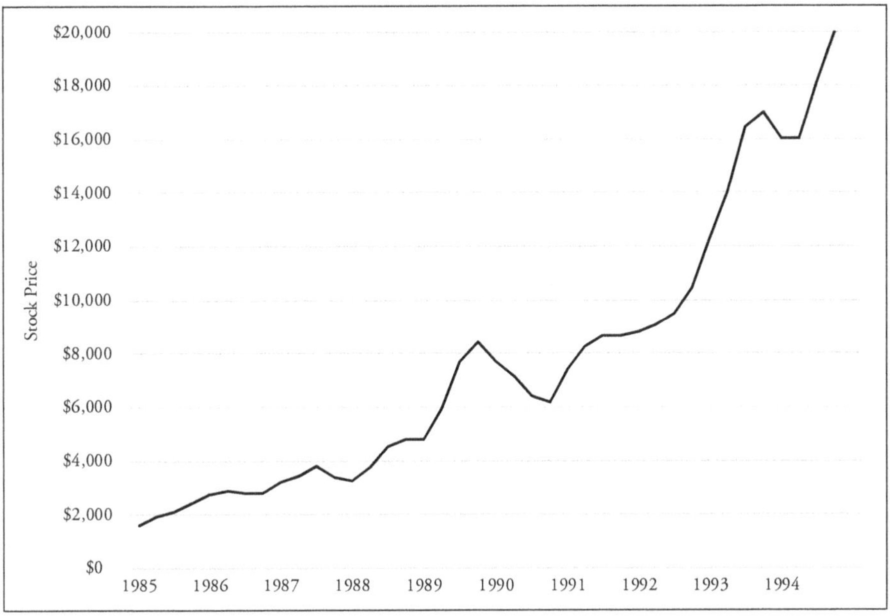

Sources: *Of Permanent Value* (Kilpatrick), Berkshire Hathaway Annual Reports 1985–1994, and author's calculations.

Figure 5.2: Berkshire Hathaway price to book ratio, 1985–1994

Sources: *Of Permanent Value* (Kilpatrick), Berkshire Hathaway Annual Reports 1985–1994, and author's calculations.

At the end of 1994, Berkshire Hathaway, like its equity portfolio, was a compounding machine with two capital allocators, Warren Buffett and Charlie Munger, who were not slowing down. Notably, this was the decade where Berkshire made the final split with the textile industry by liquidating its remaining mills. Berkshire had come a long way over the preceding three decades—and much more was to come.

Lessons: 1985–1994

1. Businesses don't need to be complicated to be great and have excellent returns on capital. The 1986 acquisition of Scott Fetzer, with its World Book, Kirby, and other simple operating subsidiaries was a wonderful purchase for Berkshire. Scott Fetzer distributed to Berkshire hundreds of millions of dollars (more than its purchase price in fact), doubled its earning power and, best of all, was essentially debt free. Fechheimer, a uniform business; the Shoe Group; Borsheims, jewelry; and others, demonstrated the money to be made in simple industries.

2. Simple businesses need superb managers who always keep their eye on the ball. Many of Berkshire's operating subsidiaries were not, to use Buffett's term, franchise businesses. See's, Nebraska Furniture Mart, Borsheims, and others, were all in tough industries. Their managers loved what they did, knew the businesses inside and out, and focused relentlessly, which allowed for some spectacular business results.

3. Businesses can thrive inside of a conglomerate structure, and they can do better for owners given greater capital allocation choices. Many of the wholly-owned businesses inside of Berkshire earned great returns on capital but could not reinvest that capital to any meaningful degree. Berkshire solved this problem by allowing those businesses to distribute excess cash to Omaha for redeployment into other Berkshire subsidiaries, or outside of Berkshire via its investments.

4. Economies of scale are powerful, and feedback loops are important. Berkshire first saw the advantages of a high-volume, low-margin business in Nebraska Furniture Mart. The idea applied equally to Borsheims and the jewelry business. A wide selection at low prices attracts shoppers, and the large volume of resulting sales allow for continued low prices and rates of overhead far below competitors.

5. Float, the money held by insurers but owed to claimants and others, can grow significantly while remaining at an attractive cost relative to long-term government bonds.

Table 5.41: Berkshire Hathaway, select parent-level financial information

($ thousands, except per share data)	1994	1993	1992	1991	1990	1989	1988	1987	1986	1985
Revenues:										
Sales and service revenues	$2,351,918	$1,962,862	$1,774,436	$1,651,134	$1,580,074	$1,526,459	$1,407,642	$1,326,829	$1,219,252	$504,872
Insurance premiums earned	923,180	650,726	664,293	776,413	591,540	394,279	584,235	824,895	823,884	317,059
Interest and dividend income	426,094	354,028	364,895	347,293	317,095	331,452	314,251	237,319	181,992	144,722
Income from investment in Salomon, Inc	30,058	63,000	63,000	63,000	63,000	0	0	0	0	0
Income from finance businesses	24,885	22,226	20,696	19,475	13,498					
Sundry						7,892	27,094	13,901	6,316	1,930
Realized investment gain	91,332	546,422	89,937	192,478	33,989	223,810	131,671	28,838	220,764	495,055
Total revenues	$3,847,467	$3,599,264	$2,977,257	$3,049,793	$2,599,196	$2,483,892	$2,464,893	$2,431,782	$2,452,208	$1,463,638
Earnings:										
Before realized investment gain and cumulative effect of accounting change[1]	$433,659	$402,403	$347,726	$315,753	$370,745	$299,902	$313,441	$214,746	$131,464	$92,948
Realized investment gain	61,139	356,702	59,559	124,155	23,348	147,575	85,829	19,806	150,897	342,867
Cumulative effect of change in accounting for income taxes	0	(70,984)	0	0	0	0	0	0	0	0
Net earnings	$494,798	$688,121	$407,285	$439,908	$394,093	$447,477	$399,270	$234,552	$282,361	$435,815
Year-end data:										
Total assets	$21,338,182	$19,520,469	$17,131,998	$14,461,902	$10,670,423	$9,459,594	$6,816,848	$5,863,235	$4,931,354	$3,480,789
Borrowings under investment agreements and other debt[2]	810,719	972,389	1,154,697	1,100,464	1,082,265	1,007,516	480,009	289,886	260,170	117,879
Shareholders' equity	11,874,882	10,428,374	8,896,331	7,379,918	5,287,454	4,925,126	3,410,108	2,841,659	2,377,797	1,885,330
Common shares outstanding (000's)	1,178	1,178	1,149	1,146	1,146	1,146	1,146	1,147	1,147	1,147
Shareholders' equity per outstanding share	10,083	8,854	7,745	6,437	4,612	4,296	2,975	2,477	2,073	1,644

Footnotes:

1. 1994: Includes $172,579 USAir write-down ($146.52/sh). 1993: Includes $75,348 charge due to the change in federal income tax rate.
2. Excludes borrowings of finance businesses.

Note: Data taken from 1994 (1990–1994) and 1989 (1985–1989) Annual Reports to maintain consistency with the reporting for each five-year period. Slight differences exist for any particular year depending on the report year.

Sources: Berkshire Hathaway Annual Reports 1989, 1994.

Table 5.42: Berkshire Hathaway consolidated reconciliation of shareholders' equity, 1985–1994

($ thousands)	1994	1993	1992	1991	1990	1989	1988	1987	1986	1985
Prior Year Equity	$10,428,374	$8,896,331	$7,379,918	$5,287,454	$4,925,126	$3,410,108	$2,841,659	$2,377,797	$1,885,330	$1,271,761
Current Year Net Income / (Loss)	494,798	688,121	407,285	439,908	394,093	447,477	399,270	234,552	282,361	435,815
Change in Common[1]		20	11							
Change in Paid In Capital[2]		473,810	24,887							
Treasury Stock[3]		4,659				0	(1,355)			
Cumulative effect of adoption on 12/31/93 of SFAS 115		171,775								
Change in unrealized appreciation of securities, net of tax	951,710	193,658	1,084,230	1,652,556	(31,765)	1,067,541	170,534	229,310	210,106	177,754
Ending Equity	$11,874,882	$10,428,374	$8,896,331	$7,379,918	$5,287,454	$4,925,126	$3,410,108	$2,841,659	$2,377,797	$1,885,330

Footnotes:

1. 1992: 2,162 shares issued upon conversion of Zero Coupon Convertible Subordinated Notes.
   1993: 3,944 shares issued in conversion of Zero Coupon notes.
2. 1992: $24,887 from conversion of Zero Coupon notes.
   1993: $45,457 from conversion of Zero Coupon notes; $428,353 in connection with 25,203 shares issued for Dexter Shoe acquisition.
3. 1988: Value of Berkshire stock received in connection with termination of pension plans.
   1993: Issued from Treasury in connection with Dexter Shoe acquisition.

Sources: Berkshire Hathaway Annual Reports 1985–1994.

Table 5.43: Insurance Group, select information

($ millions)	1994 Amount	1994 %	1993 Amount	1993 %	1992 Amount	1992 %	1991 Amount	1991 %	1990 Amount	1990 %
Primary Group										
Premiums written	$225.7		$208.4		$132.4		$135.5		$139.1	
Premiums earned	234.8	100.0%	208.3	100.0%	152.8	100.0%	141.0	100.0%	154.0	100.0%
Losses and loss expenses	88.4	37.6%	99.8	47.9%	98.0	64.1%	95.2	67.5%	102.0	66.2%
Underwriting expenses	98.1	41.8%	95.8	46.0%	46.8	30.6%	48.3	34.3%	51.5	33.4%
Total losses and expenses	186.5	79.4%	195.6	93.9%	144.8	94.8%	143.5	101.8%	153.5	99.7%
Underwriting gain/(loss) - pre-tax	48.3		12.7		8.0		(2.5)		0.5	
Unfavorable (favorable) loss development included in losses and loss expenses	*(53.9)*	*(23.0%)*	*(41.7)*	*(20.0%)*	*(36.4)*	*(23.8%)*	*(23.8)*	*(16.9%)*	*(18.3)*	*(11.9%)*
Statutory combined ratio		81.1%		93.9%		99.5%		103.2%		103.3%
Reinsurance Group										
Premiums written	$689.8		$528.7		$607.2		$667.0		$435.2	
Premiums earned	688.4	100.0%	442.4	100.0%	511.5	100.0%	635.4	100.0%	437.5	100.0%
Losses and loss expenses	476.9	69.3%	350.9	79.3%	589.7	115.3%	731.9	115.2%	432.2	98.8%
Underwriting expenses	130.8	19.0%	74.2	16.8%	38.8	7.6%	20.6	3.2%	32.5	7.4%
Total losses and expenses	607.7	88.3%	425.1	96.1%	628.5	122.9%	752.5	118.4%	464.7	106.2%
Underwriting gain/(loss) - pre-tax	80.7		17.3		(117.0)		(117.1)		(27.2)	
Unfavorable (favorable) loss development included in losses and loss expenses	*37.0*	*14.1%*	*0.0*	*0.0%*	*0.0*	*0.0%*	*(30.0)*	*(4.7%)*	*0.0*	*0.0%*
Statutory combined ratio		88.2%		93.4%		121.7%		118.3%		106.3%
Structured settlements and portfolio reinsurance										
Underwriting gain/(loss) - pre-tax	*In above*		*In above*		*In above*		*In above*		*In above*	
Total Insurance Group underwriting gain/(loss) pre-tax	**$129.0**		**$30.0**		**($109.0)**		**($119.6)**		**($26.7)**	
Insurance Group overall statutory combined ratio		86.1%		92.2%		115.1%		115.1%		104.9%

1. Totals may not add due to rounding.

2. The loss and expense ratios are shown as they were reported in the Annual Reports, which is on a GAAP basis. The GAAP basis ratios are calculated with underwriting expenses divided by earned premiums. This contrasts to the statutory basis calculation, where the ratio uses written premiums. In both the GAAP and statutory calculations, losses and loss adjustment expenses are divided by earned premiums.

3. In 1990, Berkshire began including structured settlements and portfolio reinsurance with reinsurance.

Sources: Berkshire Hathaway Annual Reports 1985–1994 and author's calculations.

Table 5.44: Insurance Group, select information

($ millions)	1989 Amount	%	1988 Amount	%	1987 Amount	%	1986 Amount	%	1985 Amount	%	1984 Amount	%
Primary Group												
Premiums written	$169.7		$218.8		$412.7		$594.6		$269.1		$118.1	
Premiums earned	188.9	100.0%	292.3	100.0%	441.6	100.0%	463.1	100.0%	184.3	100.0%	119.3	100.0%
Losses and loss expenses	125.9	66.6%	196.2	67.1%	338.6	76.7%	347.5	75.0%	140.0	76.0%	110.5	92.6%
Underwriting expenses	58.8	31.1%	78.7	26.9%	105.8	24.0%	112.1	24.2%	52.5	28.5%	41.6	34.9%
Total losses and expenses	184.7	97.8%	274.8	94.0%	444.4	100.6%	459.6	99.2%	192.5	104.4%	152.1	127.5%
Underwriting gain/(loss) - pre-tax	4.2		17.5		(2.7)		3.5		(8.1)		(32.9)	
Unfavorable (favorable) loss development included in losses and loss expenses	(20.0)	(10.6%)	(29.1)	(10.0%)	(9.4)	(2.1%)	16.0	3.5%	0.1	0.0%	8.1	6.8%
Statutory combined ratio		101.3%		103.1%		102.3%		93.9%		95.5%		127.9%
Reinsurance Group												
Premiums written	$66.0		$203.3		$328.0		$398.4		$178.5		$10.5	
Premiums earned	146.8	100.0%	229.3	100.0%	372.8	100.0%	344.4	100.0%	82.9	100.0%	16.1	100.0%
Losses and loss expenses	109.4	74.5%	170.5	74.3%	287.6	77.2%	282.6	82.0%	85.7	103.4%	23.7	147.6%
Underwriting expenses	48.6	33.1%	73.3	32.0%	112.9	30.3%	111.2	32.3%	27.2	32.8%	4.9	30.5%
Total losses and expenses	158.0	107.6%	243.8	106.3%	400.5	107.4%	393.7	114.3%	112.9	136.2%	28.6	178.2%
Underwriting gain/(loss) - pre-tax	(11.2)		(14.5)		(27.7)		(49.4)		(30.0)		(12.6)	
Unfavorable (favorable) loss development included in losses and loss expenses	0.2	0.1%	0.0	0.0%	4.5	1.2%	21.0	6.1%	19.4	23.5%	9.7	60.2%
Statutory combined ratio		148.2%		110.4%		111.6%		110.0%		118.6%		194.2%
Structured settlements and portfolio reinsurance												
Underwriting gain/(loss) - pre-tax	(17.4)		(14.1)		(25.0)		(10.0)		(6.1)		(2.6)	
Total Insurance Group underwriting gain/(loss) pre-tax	($24.4)		($11.1)		($55.4)		($55.8)		($44.2)		($48.1)	
Insurance Group overall statutory combined ratio		115.4%		107.4%		109.3%		101.8%		104.7%		135.9%

1. Totals may not add due to rounding.

2. The loss and expense ratios are shown as they were reported in the Annual Reports, which is on a GAAP basis. The GAAP basis ratios are calculated with underwriting expenses divided by earned premiums. This contrasts to the statutory basis calculation, where the ratio uses written premiums. In both the GAAP and statutory calculations, losses and loss adjustment expenses are divided by earned premiums.

3. In 1990, Berkshire began including structured settlements and portfolio reinsurance with reinsurance.

Sources: Berkshire Hathaway Annual Reports 1985–1994 and author's calculations.

Table 5.45: Insurance Group, income statements, 1986–1994

($ millions)	1994	1993	1992	1991	1990	1989	1988	1987	1986
Premiums written	$915.5	$737.1	$739.6	$802.5	$574.3	$296.1	$484.7	$751.3	$1,009.4
Premiums earned	$923.2	$650.7	$664.3	$776.4	$591.5	$394.3	$584.2	$824.9	$823.9
Losses and loss expenses	564.3	450.7	687.6	827.2	534.2	309.4	437.7	661.1	655.8
Underwriting expenses	229.0	169.1	85.7	68.8	83.9	109.3	157.6	219.2	224.0
Total losses and expenses	793.3	619.8	773.3	896.0	618.1	418.7	595.3	880.3	879.7
Underwriting gain (loss) pre-tax	129.9	30.9	(109.0)	(119.6)	(26.6)	(24.4)	(11.1)	(55.4)	(55.8)
Net investment income	419.4	375.4	355.1	331.8	327.0	243.9	231.2	152.5	107.1
Realized investment gain	92.0	555.9	52.6	110.8	15.8	220.6	127.9	26.3	147.5
Other than temporary decline in value of investment in USAir Group, Inc. Preferred Stock	(261.0)								
Earnings before income taxes	380.3	962.2	298.7	323.0	316.2	440.1	348.0	123.4	198.8
Income tax expense (benefit)	51.7	254.4	25.4	38.4	34.1	88.9	63.7	(13.2)	(16.6)
	328.6	707.8	273.3	284.6	282.1	351.2	284.3	136.6	215.4
Minority interest	4.3	4.1	2.6	2.8	3.0	4.0	3.6	1.9	1.3
Net earnings	$324.3	$703.7	$270.7	$281.8	$279.1	$347.2	$280.7	$134.7	$214.1
Net investment income detail:									
Dividends	$362.4	$306.7	$287.5	$244.7	$244.7	$149.9	$86.0	$31.2	$16.8
Interest	92.2	77.9	74.0	98.7	91.2	100.8	145.9	121.8	90.0
Equity in net loss of Salomon, Inc.	(31.7)								
Investment expenses	(3.5)	(9.2)	(6.4)	(11.6)	(8.9)	(6.8)	(0.7)	(0.5)	0.4
Total net investment income	$419.4	$375.4	$355.1	$331.8	$327.0	$243.9	$231.2	$152.5	$107.1

Sources: Berkshire Hathaway Annual Reports 1988–1994.

Table 5.46: Insurance Group, balance sheets, 1987–1994

($ millions)	1994	1993	1992	1991	1990	1989	1988	1987
Assets								
Investments:								
Fixed maturities[1]								
Wash. Pub. Power Supply System			$58.8	$158.6	$188.9	$194.0	$247.0	$235.7
RJR Nabisco				98.9	187.7	136.5		
Other			479.2	367.0	377.4	409.4	802.9	1,004.8
Bonds	$1,099.0	$715.9						
Preferred Stocks:								
Champion International			279.0	279.0	279.0	279.0		
Salomon Inc.			650.0	650.0	637.0	624.0	624.0	624.0
USAir			348.0	348.0	348.0	348.0		
Gillette					600.0	600.0		
Other			10.6	0.5	0.7	0.7	10.5	15.7
Preferred stocks	410.4	650.9						
Equity securities at market:								
Capital Cities/ABC, Inc.	1,662.4	1,208.0	1,497.9	1,278.8	1,354.4	1,664.2	1,068.6	1,017.8
Coca-Cola Company	5,137.6	4,157.3	3,901.1	3,738.0	2,166.0	1,799.2	632.4	
GEICO	1,678.3	1,759.6	2,226.2	1,363.2	1,110.6	1,044.6	849.4	756.9
Gillette	1,797.0	1,431.0	1,365.0	1,347.0	600.0			
Wells Fargo & Company	957.8	854.6	471.5	279.3	278.7	60.6		
Salomon, Inc.	972.2	673.6						
FHLMC			435.2	13.1				
General Dynamics			450.8					
Guinness, PLC			299.5	296.8				

Continued…

...continued from prior page.

	1994	1993	1992	1991	1990	1989	1988	1987
Washington Post			396.9	336.0	342.1	486.4	364.1	323.1
Other	3,890.4	2,873.6	86.9	91.9	232.9	63.1	498.6	215.1
Preferred Stocks:								
American Express Company			290.5	247.5				
First Empire State Corp.			68.0	50.0				
Other			53.2	31.1	72.6	23.5	8.6	4.4
Total investments	17,605.1	14,324.5	13,368.3	10,974.7	8,176.0	7,733.2	5,106.3	4,197.4
Cash and cash equivalents	90.3	1,368.0	471.2	458.5	115.6	45.4	121.6	109.1
Deferred costs	468.2	490.6	529.2	552.5	364.2	15.0	45.5	57.2
Receivables			188.1	414.1	222.2	71.0	139.7	131.2
Other	301.9	290.4	8.0	2.8	2.3	2.3	3.3	24.6
	$18,465.5	$16,473.5	$14,564.8	$12,402.6	$8,880.3	$7,866.9	$5,416.3	$4,519.7
Liabilities								
Losses and loss adjustment expenses	$3,430.0	$3,155.9	$2,978.5	$2,849.1	$2,050.3	$1,436.3	$1,407.2	$1,260.4
Unearned premiums	307.2	315.8	227.8	152.5	126.4	143.6	241.8	341.3
Funds held under reinsurance assumed	307.3	215.8						
Accounts payable, accruals and other	255.0	233.6	379.9	222.1	226.0	201.0	85.4	55.7
Income taxes, principally deferred	3,209.3	2,944.5	2,476.3	1,908.2	1,099.0	1,136.2	565.3	471.9
	7,508.8	6,865.6	6,062.5	5,131.9	3,501.7	2,917.1	2,299.7	2,129.4
Equity								
Minority shareholders'	136.5	124.9	70.4	56.5	39.8	35.2	25.0	21.2
Berkshire shareholders'	10,820.2	9,483.0	8,431.9	7,214.2	5,338.8	4,914.6	3,091.7	2,369.1
	10,956.7	9,607.9	8,502.3	7,270.7	5,378.6	4,949.8	3,116.6	2,390.2
	$18,465.5	$16,473.5	$14,564.8	$12,402.6	$8,880.3	$7,866.9	$5,416.3	$4,519.7

Footnote:
1. Fixed maturities at market in 1994 and amortized cost prior.

Sources: Berkshire Hathaway Annual Reports 1988–1994.

Table 5.47: Insurance Group, key ratios and figures, 1986–1994

Ratios and key figures	1994	1993	1992	1991	1990	1989	1988	1987	1986
Loss ratio	61.1%	69.3%	103.5%	106.5%	90.3%	78.5%	74.9%	80.1%	79.6%
Expense ratio (against written premiums)	25.0%	22.9%	11.6%	8.6%	14.6%	36.9%	32.5%	29.2%	22.2%
Combined ratio (statutory)	86.1%	92.2%	115.1%	115.1%	104.9%	115.4%	107.4%	109.3%	101.8%
Change in premiums written	24.2%	(0.3%)	(7.8%)	39.7%	94.0%	(38.9%)	(35.5%)	(25.6%)	
Change in premiums earned	41.9%	(2.0%)	(14.4%)	31.3%	50.0%	(32.5%)	(29.2%)	0.1%	
Premiums written / average equity	8.9%	8.1%	9.4%	12.7%	11.1%	7.3%	17.6%		

Sources: Berkshire Hathaway Annual Reports 1988–1994.

Table 5.48: Manufacturing, Publishing, and Retailing Businesses: Balance sheets, 1987–1994

($ millions)	1994	1993	1992	1991	1990	1989	1988	1987
Assets								
Cash and cash equivalents	$77.0	$90.4	$62.7	$67.3	$28.9	$25.6	$43.4	$36.2
Accounts receivable	308.8	275.9	230.9	211.3	184.0	175.6	150.4	142.0
Inventories	398.2	351.0	253.7	227.0	174.1	165.7	133.8	122.5
Properties and equipment	219.6	195.9	163.9	154.7	149.1	141.9	130.4	130.6
Other	29.8	36.1	29.9	18.7	19.7	18.4	15.7	22.0
Total assets	$1,033.4	$949.3	$741.1	$679.0	$555.8	$526.8	$473.6	$453.2
Liabilities								
Accounts payable, accruals and other	$293.4	$257.2	$223.3	$211.2	$198.0	$214.2	$179.3	$193.6
Income taxes	30.5	38.5	40.6	37.0	38.4	37.9	47.7	52.3
Term debt and other borrowings	21.7	24.7	28.1	40.9	36.1	38.0	37.7	38.8
Total liabilities	345.6	320.4	292.0	289.1	272.5	290.1	264.7	284.7
Equity								
Minority shareholders' equity	40.1	35.8	33.2	31.1	28.2	25.2	19.0	14.5
Berkshire shareholders' equity	647.7	593.1	415.9	358.8	255.1	211.5	189.8	154.1
Total equity	687.8	628.9	449.1	389.9	283.3	236.7	208.8	168.5
Total liabilities and equity	$1,033.4	$949.3	$741.1	$679.0	$555.8	$526.8	$473.6	$453.2

Footnote:
1. Fixed maturities at market in 1994 and amortized cost prior.

Sources: Berkshire Hathaway Annual Reports 1988–1994.

Table 5.49: Manufacturing, Publishing, and Retailing Businesses: Income statements, 1986–1994

($ millions)	1994	1993	1992	1991	1990	1989	1988	1987	1986
Revenues:									
Sales and service revenues	$2,352.0	$1,962.9	$1,774.4	$1,651.1	$1,580.1	$1,526.4	$1,407.6	$1,326.8	$1,219.3
Interest income	9.0	8.0	7.5	8.5	6.7	8.4	6.7	6.8	7.9
Sundry income				2.1	1.4	2.6	2.5	0.7	0.8
	2,361.0	1,970.9	1,781.9	1,661.7	1,588.2	1,537.4	1,416.8	1,334.3	1,228.0
Costs and expenses:									
Costs of products and services sold	1,442.9	1,172.5	1,043.6	933.7	865.6	838.7	747.8	699.7	641.9
Selling, general and administrative expenses	578.5	522.2	481.5	508.6	499.3	487.7	461.8	446.0	413.1
Interest on debt	3.7	3.7	4.6	4.9	6.5	6.2	4.9	6.7	6.1
	2,025.1	1,698.4	1,529.7	1,447.2	1,371.4	1,332.6	1,214.5	1,152.4	1,061.1
Earnings from operations before income taxes	335.9	272.5	252.2	214.5	216.8	204.8	202.3	181.9	167.0
Income tax expense	122.3	103.7	97.4	82.3	83.9	78.9	76.2	79.6	83.2
	213.6	168.8	154.8	132.2	132.9	125.9	126.1	102.3	83.8
Minority interest	4.9	4.5	4.2	4.6	5.4	5.0	4.4	3.5	3.0
Net earnings	$208.7	$164.3	$150.6	$127.6	$127.5	$120.9	$121.7	$98.8	$80.8

Sources: Berkshire Hathaway Annual Reports 1988–1994.

Table 5.50: Manufacturing, Publishing, and Retailing Businesses: Key ratios and figures, 1986–1994

	1994	1993	1992	1991	1990	1989	1988	1987	1986
Change in revenues	19.8%	10.6%	7.2%	4.6%	3.3%	8.5%	6.2%	8.7%	
Change in pre-tax profit (operating income)	23.3%	8.0%	17.6%	(1.1%)	5.9%	1.2%	11.2%	8.9%	
Gross margin	38.7%	40.3%	41.2%	43.4%	45.2%	45.1%	46.9%	47.3%	47.4%
Pre-tax margin	14.2%	13.8%	14.2%	12.9%	13.7%	13.3%	14.3%	13.6%	13.6%
Return on invested capital (avg.) pre-tax	49.3%	48.2%	55.6%	57.2%	73.0%	78.6%	89.2%		
Return on invested capital (avg.) after-tax	31.3%	29.9%	34.1%	35.2%	44.7%	48.3%	55.6%		
Return on average equity - pre-tax	51.0%	50.6%	60.1%	63.7%	83.4%	91.9%	107.2%		
Return on average equity - after tax	32.4%	31.3%	36.9%	39.3%	51.1%	56.5%	66.8%		
Debt/equity	3.2%	3.9%	6.3%	10.5%	12.7%	16.1%	18.1%	23.0%	

Sources: Berkshire Hathaway Annual Reports 1988–1994; and author's calculations.

Table 5.51: Finance Businesses: Balance sheets, 1987–1994

($ millions)	1994	1993	1992	1991	1990	1989	1988	1987
Assets								
Cash and cash equivalents	$16.0	$37.0	$64.4	$32.7	$72.9	$40.0	$63.2	$77.0
Fixed maturity investments[1]	538.9	667.1	68.9	143.7	58.2	48.0	78.5	130.9
Equity investments			71.7	71.7	108.5	108.5	108.6	33.7
Collateralized loans receivable			101.9	100.9	107.4	153.8	137.0	139.4
Installment and other receivables	173.2	179.8	181.1	177.7	169.7	173.2	152.8	164.7
Deferred tax assets	6.2	4.2						
Other	1.5	1.6	31.2	36.2	32.3	30.1	27.9	12.3
	$735.8	$889.7	$519.2	$562.9	$549.0	$553.6	$568.0	$558.1
Liabilities								
Borrowings under investment agreements and other debt	$601.6	$772.7						
Savings accounts			$250.9	$289.0	$286.4	$293.1	$288.5	$287.1
Accounts payable, accruals, and other	31.5	52.1	27.8	26.2	22.2	18.4	32.8	12.7
Annuity reserves	41.0	5.4						
Term debt and other borrowings			145.1	154.6	157.1	159.6	150.2	157.7
Income taxes			0.7	1.5	1.3	1.5	1.8	2.8
	674.1	830.2	424.5	471.3	467.0	472.6	473.3	460.4
Equity								
Minority shareholders'			12.5	11.8	10.1	9.7	9.9	11.3
Berkshire shareholders'	61.7	59.5	82.2	79.8	71.9	71.3	84.8	86.5
	61.7	59.5	94.7	91.6	82.0	81.0	94.7	97.7
Total	$735.8	$889.7	$519.2	$562.9	$549.0	$553.6	$568.0	$558.1

Footnote:
1. Equity securities at market; at cost prior to 1993.

Sources: Berkshire Hathaway Annual Reports 1988–1994.

Table 5.52: Finance Businesses: Income statements, 1986–1994

($ millions)	1994	1993	1992	1991	1990	1989	1988	1987	1986
Revenues									
Interest and fees on loans and financed receivables	$37.8	$43.6	$49.7	$53.2	$51.9	$49.4	$50.2	$47.9	$40.8
Interest and dividends on investment securities	35.4	21.0	16.4	18.3	18.3	19.2	20.9	22.7	19.6
Annuity premiums earned	36.0	5.6							
Sundry income				1.3	0.3	0.3	0.6	1.8	2.5
	109.2	70.2	66.1	72.8	70.5	68.9	71.7	72.3	62.9
Expenses									
Interest on savings accounts				18.3	22.0	21.5	20.8	20.9	22.4
Interest on debt				14.3	14.3	13.9	14.1	15.1	9.2
Interest expense	35.5	25.2	25.9	32.6	36.3	35.4	34.9	36.0	31.6
Annuity benefits and underwriting expenses	37.7	5.6							
General and administrative[1]	13.9	16.2	20.4	20.7	20.7	20.8	23.3	29.5	20.5
	87.1	47.0	46.3	53.3	57.0	56.2	58.2	65.5	52.1
Earnings from operations before income taxes	22.1	23.2	19.8	19.5	13.5	12.7	13.5	6.8	10.8
Income tax expense	7.5	7.7	6.4	4.6	1.7	1.2	2.0	0.5	1.2
	14.6	15.5	13.4	14.9	11.8	11.5	11.5	6.3	9.5
Minority interest	0	0.8	0.7	0.9	0.8	0.8	1.0	0.4	0.4
Earnings before investment gain	14.6	14.7	12.7	14.0	11.0	10.7	10.5	5.9	9.1
Realized gain on divestment of preferred				4.5					
Net earnings	$14.6	$14.7	$12.7	$18.5	$11.0	$10.7	$10.5	$5.9	$9.1

Footnote:

1. Includes $3.6 write-off of prepaid FSLIC insurance premiums in 1987.

Sources: Berkshire Hathaway Annual Reports 1988–1994.

Table 5.53: Finance Businesses: Key ratios, 1986–1994

	1994	1993	1992	1991	1990	1989	1988	1987
Total assets / total equity	11.9	15.0	6.3	7.1	7.6	7.8	6.7	6.5
Capital ratio (inverse of above)	8.4%	6.7%	15.8%	14.2%	13.1%	12.9%	14.9%	15.5%
Return on average assets (after tax)	1.80%	2.20%	2.48%	2.68%	2.14%	2.05%	2.04%	
Return on average equity (after tax)	24.1%	21.9%	16.5%	19.6%	16.5%	14.7%	13.4%	

Sources: Berkshire Hathaway Annual Reports 1988–1994 and author's calculations.

Table 5.54: Non-operating activities: Balance sheets, 1987–1994

($ millions)	1994	1993	1992	1991	1990	1989	1988	1987
Assets								
Cash and cash equivalents	$106.2	$358.9	$595.3	$205.6	$29.9	$96.0	$38.5	$10.5
Investments:								
Fixed maturities:								
Bonds	286.8	0	127.1	211.2	326.9	75.0	2.3	10.6
Preferred stocks	75.8	81.0	81.0	81.0	81.0	81.0	50.0	50.0
Equity securities	113.0	232.5	38.1	38.1	20.1	11.5	28.3	11.5
Unamortized goodwill and property account adjustments	520.4	541.8	277.7	257.2	210.1	220.0	201.3	210.3
Deferred tax assets	8.0	7.7						
Other	186.3	174.9	28.5	47.9	40.8	73.7	63.6	63.8
	$1,296.5	$1,396.8	$1,147.7	$841.0	$708.8	$557.2	$384.1	$356.7
Liabilities								
Accounts payable, accruals, and other	$62.2	$62.8	$16.5	$34.5	$33.8	$31.6	$28.1	$18.2
Income taxes	67.3	59.4	10.5	(3.3)	(7.8)	(24.7)	7.6	2.8
Borrowings under investment agreements and other debt	799.0	960.2	1,141.0	1,065.0	1,046.2	809.9	292.1	93.4
	928.5	1,082.4	1,168.0	1,096.2	1,072.2	816.8	327.8	114.4
Equity								
Minority shareholders'	22.7	21.6	13.4	17.7	15.0	12.7	12.6	10.3
Berkshire shareholders' equity	345.3	292.8	(33.7)	(272.9)	(378.4)	(272.3)	43.7	232.0
Total equity	368.0	314.4	(20.3)	(255.2)	(363.4)	(259.6)	56.3	242.3
	$1,296.5	$1,396.8	$1,147.7	$841.0	$708.8	$557.2	$384.1	$356.7

Sources: Berkshire Hathaway Annual Reports 1988–1994.

Table 5.55: Non-operating activities: Income statements, 1986–1994

($ millions)	1994	1993	1992	1991	1990	1989	1988	1987	1986
Revenues									
Interest and dividend income	$31.1	$24.3	$58.9	$60.1	$41.1	$7.2	$7.4	$7.0	$6.1
Realized investment gain (loss)	(0.7)	(9.4)	37.3	69.5	18.2	3.8	0	0	0
Sundry income	0	0	0	4.4	2.0	5.5	28.5	14.8	6.9
	30.4	14.9	96.2	134.0	61.3	16.5	35.9	21.8	13.0
Expenses									
Corporate administration	5.0	4.9	4.2	5.6	4.1	3.4	3.8	3.4	2.7
Shareholder-designated contributions	10.4	9.4	7.6	6.8	5.8	5.9	5.0	4.9	4.0
Amortization of goodwill and property account adjustments	22.5	17.1	12.0	10.0	9.5	9.4	9.6	8.4	12.6
Interest on debt	59.4	54.0	94.5	84.5	71.3	37.3	30.7	4.9	18.5
Other (income) expense	1.7	(2.3)	(2.0)	0.9	0.6	0.9	0.5	1.8	2.9
Other than temporary decline in value of investment in USAir Group, Inc. Preferred Stock	7.5								
	106.5	83.1	116.3	107.8	91.3	56.9	49.6	23.4	40.7
Loss before income taxes	(76.1)	(68.2)	(20.1)	26.2	(30.0)	(40.4)	(13.7)	(1.6)	(27.7)
Income tax expense (benefit)[1]	(22.8)	125.8	8.9	12.7	(7.6)	(9.8)	(1.2)	2.6	(6.5)
	(53.3)	(194.0)	(29.0)	13.5	(22.4)	(30.6)	(12.5)	(4.2)	(21.2)
Minority interest	(0.5)	0.6	(2.3)	1.5	1.1	0.6	1.1	0.7	0.4
Net loss	($52.8)	($194.6)	($26.7)	$12.0	($23.5)	($31.2)	($13.6)	($4.9)	($21.6)

Footnote:
1. Includes prepayment penalty of $5.355 in 1986 relating to called 12.75% debentures.

Sources: Berkshire Hathaway Annual Reports 1988–1994.

Chapter 6
1995–2004

Table 6.1: Decade snapshot: 1994–2004

	1994	2004
Business:	Insurance, newspapers, furniture retailing, candy, jewelry, encyclopedias, home cleaning systems, shoes, miscellaneous manufacturing, significant stakes in several public companies	Insurance, utilities, flight services, building products, furniture retailing, candy, jewelry, encyclopedias, home cleaning systems, shoes, newspapers, various finance businesses, miscellaneous manufacturing, significant stakes in several public companies
Key managers:	Chairman & CEO: Warren E. Buffett; Vice Chair: Charles T. Munger	Chairman & CEO: Warren E. Buffett; Vice Chair: Charles T. Munger
Annual revenues:	$3.8 billion	$74.4 billion
Stockholders' equity:	$11.9 billion	$85.9 billion
Book value per share:	$10,083	$55,824
Float (average):	$3.1 billion	$45.2 billion

Major capital allocation decisions:
1. Purchased remaining half of GEICO for $2.3 billion (1996).
2. Issued $565 million of Class-B shares (1996).
3. Acquired FlightSafety for $1.5 billion in stock (1996).
4. Issued $500 million convertible preferred stock (1996).
5. Purchased $4.6 billion US Treasury Strips, 111.2 million ounces of silver (1997).
6. Acquired International Dairy Queen with $587.8 million cash/stock (1998).
7. Acquired Executive Jet for $700 million in cash/stock (1998).
8. Acquired General Reinsurance for $22 billion in stock (1998).
9. Acquired majority economic interest in MidAmerican Energy for $1.24 billion cash (2000).
10. Acquired Justin Industries for $570 million cash (2000).
11. Acquired Benjamin Moore for $1 billion cash (2000).
12. Acquired 87% of Shaw Industries for $2 billion (2000).
13. Acquired Johns Manville for $1.8 billion cash (2000).
14. Acquired Fruit of the Loom for $835 million cash (2001).
15. Invested additional $402 million convertible preferred and $1.27 billion trust preferred in MidAmerican to assist with Northern Natural and Kern River acquisitions.
16. Purchased Clayton Homes for $1.7 billion (2003).
17. Borrowed $2 billion to re-lend to Clayton (2003).
18. Acquired McLane from Walmart for $1.5 billion cash (2003).
19. Borrowed additional $1.6 billion to re-lend to Clayton (2004).

Noteworthy events:
1. On March 10, 2000, the NASDAQ hit its all-time high of 5,132 while Berkshire shares traded at their lowest level since 1997.
2. Berkshire adds new board members: William Gates III, David Gottesman, Charlotte Guyman, Donald Keough, and Thomas Murphy.
3. The September 11, 2001 terrorist attacks shake the insurance world and close stock markets until September 17.

Table 6.2: Berkshire Hathaway earnings

($ millions)	2004	2003	2002	2001	2000	1999	1998	1997	1996	1995	1994
Insurance Group:											
Underwriting - General Re	$3	$145	($1,393)	($3,671)	($1,254)	($1,184)	*Not detailed in presentation*				
Underwriting - Berkshire Hathaway Reinsurance Group	417	1,047	534	(647)	(162)	(256)					
Underwriting - Super-Cat	*Consolidated into Berkshire Reinsurance Group*						154	283	167		
Underwriting - Other Reinsurance							(175)	(155)	(175)		
Underwriting - Reinsurance[1]	420	1,192	(859)	(4,318)	(1,416)	(1,440)	(21)	128	(8)		
Underwriting - GEICO	970	452	416	221	(224)	24	269	281	171	*Not detailed*	
Underwriting - Other Primary	161	74	32	30	25	22	17	53	59		
Total Underwriting	1,551	1,718	(411)	(4,067)	(1,615)	(1,394)	265	462	222	21	130
Net Investment Income	2,824	3,223	3,050	2,824	2,773	2,482	974	882	726	502	419
Apparel[2]	325	289	229	(33)							
Building Products[3]	643	559	516	461	34						
Finance and Financial Products Businesses	584	619	1,016	519	530	125	205	28	23	21	22
Flight Services[4]	191	72	225	186	213	225	181	140	3		
McLane Company	228	150									
MidAmerican Energy[5]	237	429	613	565	197						
Home Furnishings[6]	*Consolidated into Retail Operations*					79	72	57	44	30	17
Jewelry[7]						51	39	32	28	34	
Retail Operations[8]	163	165	166	175	175	130	111	89	72	64	17
Shaw Industries[9]	466	436	424	292							

Continued...

…Continued from prior page

($ millions)	2004	2003	2002	2001	2000	1999	1998	1997	1996	1995	1994
Kirby									59	50	42
World Book				*Consolidated back into Scott Fetzer*					13	9	25
Scott Fetzer Manufacturing Group									51	34	40
Scott Fetzer (excluding finance operation)[10]	*Consolidated into Other Businesses*		129	129	122	147	137	119	122	93	107
Buffalo News						55	53	56	50	47	54
Shoe Group			*Consolidated into Other Businesses*			17	33	49	62	58	86
International Dairy Queen						56	58				
See's Candies						74	62	59	52	50	48
Other Businesses - original presentation			256	212	221						
Other Businesses[11]	465	486	385	341	343	349	343	283	286	249	294
Purchase-price premium charges[12]	*In Other*	(177)	(119)	(726)	(881)	(739)	(123)	(101)	(76)	(27)	(23)
Interest expense[13]	(92)	(94)	(86)	(92)	(92)	(109)	(100)	(107)	(94)	(56)	(60)
Shareholder-designated contributions[14]	*Discontinued*		(17)	(17)	(17)	(17)	(17)	(15)	(13)	(12)	(10)
Other[15]	(138)	24	19	25	39	33	60	60	73	54	50
Operating earnings - pre-tax	**7,447**	**7,899**	**6,010**	**453**	**1,699**	**1,085**	**1,899**	**1,721**	**1,221**	**815**	**839**
Sales of securities and unusual sales of assets	3,489	4,121	603	1,320	3,955	1,365	2,415	1,106	2,485	194	91
Decline in Value of USAir Preferred Stock											(269)
Total Earnings - all entities (pre-tax)	**10,936**	**12,020**	**6,613**	**1,773**	**5,654**	**2,450**	**4,314**	**2,827**	**3,706**	**1,009**	**662**
Income tax and minority interest[16]	(3,628)	(3,869)	(2,327)	(978)	(2,326)	(893)	(1,484)	(926)	(1,217)	(284)	(167)
Total Earnings - all entities (after tax)	**$7,308**	**$8,151**	**$4,286**	**$795**	**$3,328**	**$1,557**	**$2,830**	**$1,901**	**$2,489**	**$725**	**$495**

Continued…

...Continued from prior page

Footnotes:

1. Underwriting - Reinsurance: In 1999 the presentation was changed to combine Super Cat and Other Reinsurance into one category. The data above is from the notes to the financial statements from 2000.

2. Apparel: Includes Fruit of the Loom from April 30, 2002 and Garan from September 4, 2002. Also included, beginning in 2002, is the H.H. Brown Shoe Group, now containing Dexter, and Fechheimer.

3. Building Products: Includes Acme Brick from August 1, 2000; Benjamin Moore from December 18, 2000; Johns Manville from December 18, 2000; 80% owned through 2001; 80% owned thereafter. Figures from 2003 and 2004 come from the 2004 presentation, and are not comparable to those of prior years. Prior to 2003, the Sources of Reported Earnings table included Berkshire's share of MidAmerican's net income plus the interest income Berkshire earned from lending to MidAmerican. Berkshire's equity in the earnings of MidAmerican were $429 million in 2003, $359 million in 2002, and $134 million in 2001.

4. Flight Services: FlightSafety acquired on December 23, 1996. Beginning in 1998 includes Executive Jet (acquired August 7, 1998).

5. MidAmerican Energy: MidAmerican Energy 76% owned through 2001; 80% owned thereafter. Figures from 2003 and 2004 come from the 2004 presentation, and are not comparable to those of prior years. Prior to 2003, the Sources of Reported Earnings table included Berkshire's share of MidAmerican's net income plus the interest income Berkshire earned from lending to MidAmerican. Berkshire's equity in the earnings of MidAmerican were $429 million in 2003, $359 million in 2002, and $134 million in 2001.

6. Home Furnishings: Includes RC Willey beginning June 29, 1995; Star Furniture from July 1, 1997.

7. Jewelry: Includes Helzberg's beginning April 30, 1995. Jewelry was included in Other in prior years.

8. Retail Operations: Beginning in 2000, Home Furnishings and Jewelry were combined into Retail Operations.

9. Shaw Industries: Shaw Industries acquired on January 8, 2001.

10. Scott Fetzer (excluding finance operation): Prior to 1997, Kirby and World Book were segregated from other Scott Fetzer businesses.

11. Other Businesses: Beginning in 2000, The Buffalo News, the Shoe Group, International Dairy Queen, and See's were combined into Other Businesses. That presentation also re-allocated $8 million from Other to this category for 1999 (shown above in the original 1999 presentation). CTB and Pamper Chef are included in this category beginning with their acquisitions in 2002. Beginning in 2003 Scott Fetzer began being included in this category.

12. Purchase-price price premium charges: Beginning in 2002, accounting rules changed such that goodwill was no longer amortized. In 2004, these charges were included in the Other category.

13. Interest expense: Excludes interest expense of Finance Businesses.

14. Shareholder-designated contributions: Shareholder-designated contributions were discontinued in 2003.

15. Other: Beginning in 1997, Fechheimer included in Other category. Beginning in 2001, it is included in the Other Businesses category. Other category includes General Re for 10 days in 1998. Other category in 2004 includes amortization charges.

16. Income tax and minority interest: Imputed from the difference between the reported pre-tax and after-tax earnings figures.

Note: In 2003, the Chairman's letter stopped containing the Sources of Reported Earnings table. For the years 2003 and 2004 I have used pre-tax data from the Operating Businesses segment of the 2004 Annual Report. Most categories are comparable to Buffett's tables; however, a major difference is the reporting of earnings from MidAmerican. I have used the figures Buffett presented up to 2002, and the figures from the aforementioned table in the Annual Report for years 2003 and 2004. Thus, the data from 2000–2002, and 2003–2004 are not comparable.

Sources: Berkshire Hathaway Annual Reports 1995–2004.

Introduction

The 1995–2004 decade was marked by compounding growth. Not only did the headline figures such as revenues, earnings, and shareholders' equity expand, but the sheer number of acquisitions increased noticeably.

Berkshire's 1996 acquisition of the second half of GEICO and the 1998 acquisition of General Reinsurance supercharged its insurance operations. These two acquisitions were the final two cornerstones of the Insurance Group, which would see average float balloon to over $45 billion during the decade.

Insurance was certainly a dominating force at Berkshire, but its many non-insurance acquisitions further diversified its earnings streams. A number of these new acquisitions, such as within the jewelry and furniture retailing segments, resulted from existing industry relationships Berkshire subsidiaries had with non-competitor peers. Some acquisition opportunities manifested suddenly after past troubles caused a need for new ownership. Other times, acquisitions occurred after financial buyers (such as private equity groups only interested in short-term profits) caused the businesses to falter, and which were revitalized under Berkshire's protective umbrella and conservative financing. Some acquisitions during this period, most notably MidAmerican and MiTek, came with additional outlets for cash after they made their own acquisitions.

All these acquisitions added to the family tree that was Berkshire but did not alter the overall structure of the company. The Berkshire Hathaway that ended the decade, like the one that began, was a conglomerate with many diverse businesses. At the end of the decade, it was just a larger and more rounded-out conglomerate. Insurance was the main engine, followed by its wholly-owned businesses and important long-term investments in marketable securities. In order to comply with SEC regulations, Berkshire increased its directorship with five new members to its board of directors.

In some ways, Berkshire's size finally began catching up with it. Interest rates continued to decline during this period, making idle cash that much more painful to hold and driving up valuations in controlled businesses and marketable securities. The dotcom boom that started in the mid-1990s and continued into the first years of the new millennium did have one silver lining. While others were busy bidding up businesses with no cash flow or long-term prospects, Berkshire picked up numerous old-line businesses with long histories of producing cash. Yet even with these acquisitions Berkshire ended the decade with over $40 billion of cash and no immediate place to put it to profitable use.

Table 6.3: Select information 1995–2004

	1995	1996	1997	1998	1999	2000	2001	2002	2003	2004
BRK book value per share - % change	43.1%	31.8%	34.1%	48.3%	0.5%	6.5%	(6.2%)	10.0%	21.0%	10.5%
BRK market value per share - % change	57.4%	6.2%	34.9%	52.2%	(19.9%)	26.6%	6.5%	(3.8%)	15.8%	4.3%
S&P 500 total return	37.6%	23.0%	33.4%	28.6%	21.0%	(9.1%)	(11.9%)	(22.1%)	28.7%	10.9%
US GDP Growth (real %)	2.7%	3.8%	4.4%	4.5%	4.8%	4.1%	1.0%	1.7%	2.9%	3.8%
10-year Treasury Note (year-end %)	5.7%	6.3%	5.8%	4.7%	6.3%	5.2%	5.1%	4.0%	4.3%	4.2%
US inflation (%)	2.8%	2.9%	2.3%	1.5%	2.2%	3.4%	2.8%	1.6%	2.3%	2.7%
US unemployment (%)	5.6%	5.4%	4.9%	4.5%	4.2%	4.0%	4.7%	5.8%	6.0%	5.5%

Sources: Berkshire Hathaway Annual Reports 2018, 2019 and Federal Reserve Bank of St. Louis.

1995

The year 1995 represented the start of Buffett's fourth decade at the helm of Berkshire Hathaway. Often time executives think about retiring, or at least reducing their workload. Buffett reached the typical retirement age of sixty-five that August, and Munger was already seventy-one, so it was a fair question whether Berkshire's two capital allocators would soon slow down. While both were outwardly showing some signs of aging, their minds were not—if anything, they were getting *better*. As Charlie Munger would say at the Annual Meeting in March 1996, Buffett (though this also applied to Munger himself) was a "learning machine." Berkshire would benefit enormously by having top managers without any preconceived notions of retirement, allowing their knowledge to compound just like the capital under their control.

Defying Buffett's predictions (again) that Berkshire's size would be an anchor for future returns, headline figures for 1995 showed an enormous increase in net worth. After adjusting for shares issued in connection with two acquisitions, per-share book value increased an eye-popping 43.1%* compared to the S&P's increase of 37.6%. More exciting were three acquisitions that doubled Berkshire's revenue and significantly added to its long-term earning power.

During 1995, Berkshire acquired two non-insurance companies (Helzberg Diamond Shops and RC Willey Home Furnishings) using Berkshire shares and half of an insurance company (GEICO, of which it already owned 51%) using cash.

---

* The headline increase in net worth was 45%. That return was diluted by the issuance of shares.

The GEICO acquisition technically closed January 2, 1996, so 1995 was filled with discussions about the upcoming event.

Helzberg Diamonds

The Helzberg acquisition closed on April 30, 1995. Founded in Kansas City, Missouri, Helzberg grew from one location in 1915 to 134 stores in twenty-three states by the mid-1990s. In 1994, the company had $282 million of revenues, which was an almost thirty-fold increase from the $10 million in revenues it had in 1974. Proving Buffett's point that the best strategic plan was no plan, the company arrived on Buffett's radar accidentally when Barnett Helzberg, the company's CEO and the grandson of its founder, saw Buffett on a street corner in New York City and approached him.

Helzberg was comparable to Borsheims in that both sold jewelry at rates per square foot far above their competitors, and both had low overhead compared to their competition. But the businesses were different in other respects. For one, Helzberg operated a chain of stores that were predominantly in malls or strip malls. Borsheims was a one-store location that had over $50 million of inventory, a huge selection that couldn't be replicated over dozens of locations. As Buffett put it, "Borsheims can't be Helzbergs, and Helzbergs can't be Borsheims." But both were good businesses. It is interesting to note how good returns on capital can be produced in two different ways in the same industry.

Helzberg's success stemmed from its rock-bottom operating costs and prime locations in busy shopping malls nationwide. The average Helzberg store had $2 million of annual sales, far more than its competitors. Helzberg's higher sales also produced lower expense ratios compared to competitors. Helzberg was a quintessential Berkshire/Buffett acquisition of a good company with great management. For the selling family, it was a tax-free way to diversify their holdings.

RC Willey

Berkshire's other 1995 acquisition, also completed via a stock transaction, was RC Willey Home Furnishings. The RC Willey acquisition came about through Irv Blumkin of Nebraska Furniture Mart. Irv Blumkin, Rose Blumkin's grandson, knew RC Willey CEO Bill Child and had spoken to both Child and Buffett about the merits of a partnership. Like the Helzberg family, the Child family wished to diversify and take care of estate planning while continuing to run the family business. Berkshire was a perfect fit.

As with Helzberg and Borsheims, some differences existed between RC Willey and its sister company Nebraska Furniture Mart, which Berkshire purchased in 1983.

Nebraska Furniture Mart, like Borsheims, was Omaha-based and operated out of a campus of adjacent buildings. Both RC Willey and Nebraska Furniture Mart had similar sales volume (RC Willey had $257 million in revenues in 1995), but unlike Nebraska Furniture Mart, RC Willey operated out of five (soon to be six) Utah-based locations. Both Nebraska Furniture Mart and RC Willey were also retailers, a business Buffett knew to be very difficult. Both were run by managers with long track records of success, a key criterion for Buffett, who told shareholders: "Buying a retailer without good management is like buying the Eiffel Tower without an elevator." Also, just as Nebraska Furniture Mart had a lock on the Omaha market, RC Willey had over 50% of the furniture business in Utah.

The acquisition was funded by a combination of Berkshire stock and cash. The exact price was not disclosed.

GEICO

The third and largest acquisition of the year was the second half of GEICO, which legally closed on the second day of 1996. Shareholders were very familiar with GEICO, which had been on Berkshire's books as a marketable security since 1976. Berkshire's ownership grew from 33% to 51% in that time owing entirely to GEICO's frequent share repurchases. In 1995, the opportunity arose to buy the remaining half of the business.

Compared to the $46 million it cost Berkshire to buy the first part of GEICO, the $2.3 billion price tag for the remaining portion was enormous. This implied a roughly $4.8 billion valuation for the whole company, or about 2.5 times its year-end 1995 book value of $1.87 billion. The price tag was large, but not exorbitant. GEICO had $3 billion of float, and its long history of profitable underwriting meant the float would be profitable and had a high probability of growing. This proved true. At the 1996 Annual Meeting a discussion on float and GEICO suggested Berkshire got a bargain.

Is Float Better Than Equity?

In response to a question on the intrinsic value of Berkshire's insurance companies, Buffett offered insight into his and Munger's thinking on float. It was and is somewhat counterintuitive, but upon reflection is astoundingly simple and brilliant. Buffett, always one to use extremes to prove a point, posed a rhetorical question: "Would I trade that [Berkshire's float] for $7 billion [of equity] and not have to pay tax on the gain … but then have to stay out of the insurance business forever?" His answer was no. "We wouldn't even think about it very long." Buffett was saying he would not take a genie-in-a-bottle arrangement to magically transform a $7 billion liability into $7 billion of equity.

This should have caused everyone to sit on the edge of their seats.

The reason Buffett would not take such a hypothetical arrangement was that he expected the float to grow over time and at an attractive cost. Berkshire's insurance businesses were gems due to one simple fact. An insurance operation is valuable *only* if its float does not cost it money, or at worst costs what it would cost the government to borrow funds, which is cheaper than the cost a corporation would have to pay. Berkshire's insurance businesses were arranged over time, and not without some bumps and lessons along the way, to deliver cost-free float.* Float, a liability to the company, was more akin to equity than it first appeared. If float could grow over time, it would be that much more valuable.

This assertion that a liability could be considered equity can be a hard concept to grasp. It helps to think about what pure traditional equity is. Is not the equity owners put or retain in a company a liability due them at some unspecified future date? Does it not come without the requirement to pay interest? Why not then define equity as funds held by a company that have no explicit repayment terms and no explicit cost or interest rate? Following this logic, it stands to reason that the right kind of float could be considered equity—or in some cases better than equity if it generated an underwriting profit over time. Furthermore, such quasi-equity did not dilute shareholders ownership like a pure equity investment would.

Berkshire's float, and especially GEICO's, was money owed to policyholders in one form or another but that, because of its revolving nature, could not be called in its entirety like a loan. In other words, individual policies would be paid daily, but new premiums would be written collectively that could reasonably be expected to maintain the overall level of float. Considering Berkshire had a recent history of writing profitable business and growing float even under poor pricing conditions, this was an easy argument to make.

If we assume that GEICO's float would, at worst, break even and not grow,** it could appropriately be considered quasi-equity. Adding this quasi-equity to its book equity, we arrive at a purchase multiple of 1x book value (see Table 6.4). We can also use an earnings approach as a check. This framework results in an initial pre-tax earnings yield that may seem low. Considering this did not account for any expected growth, nor any look-through earnings from the investment portfolio, it is worthwhile validation of the $4.7 billion valuation for GEICO that Berkshire paid to acquire the rest of the company.

---

* Just to be sure the reader is clear, cost-free float means, at worst, a breakeven underwriting result over time.
** Buffett stated at the 1996 Annual Meeting that GEICO's float was almost certain to grow.

Table 6.4: GEICO acquisition analysis

Balance sheet approach	
($ billions)	
Price paid for 49%	$2.33
Implied value of 100%	4.76
Book value (12/31/95)	1.87
Price/book value	2.55x
Float	3.00
Book value + float	4.87
Float-adjusted price/book value	0.98x
Earnings approach	
($ millions)	
Premium volume	$3,000
Assumed combined ratio	96%
Pre-tax underwriting gain	120
Net investment income (1995)	227
Total pre-tax earning power	347
Implied acquisition valuation	4,755
Pre-tax earnings yield	7.3%

Sources: Berkshire Hathaway Annual Report 1995 and author's calculations.

Insurance

Underscoring the good year Berkshire had in 1995 was a third straight year of underwriting profit and yet another year of growth in float. All told, Berkshire's insurance operations generated a pre-tax underwriting profit of $21 million, and float increased 18% to $3.6 billion.

Table 6.5: Berkshire Hathaway—Insurance Underwriting

($ millions)	1995	1994
GEICO Corporation		
Premiums written	$2,856	$2,545
Premiums earned	2,787	2,473
Underwriting gain/(loss) - pre-tax	$92	$79
Berkshire Hathaway Reinsurance Group		
Premiums written	$777	$690
Premiums earned	718	688
Underwriting gain/(loss) - pre-tax	($21)	$81
Berkshire Hathaway Primary Group		
Premiums written	$247	$226
Premiums earned	240	235
Underwriting gain/(loss) - pre-tax	$41	$48
Total underwriting gain/(loss)	$21	$130
Year-end average float - total	3,607	3,057
Cost of float	(0.6%)	(4.3%)
Aggregate adverse (favorable) loss development	$56	$60

Note: Totals and ratios do not include GEICO. GEICO included for comparative purposes.
Sources: Berkshire Hathaway Annual Reports 1994–1995 and author's calculations.

It is worth highlighting the conservatism embedded in Berkshire's insurance operations, not only on an operating basis (i.e. its unwillingness to accept improperly-priced risks), but also on an accounting basis. For more attentive readers, the financial statements contained clues to the margin of safety built into Berkshire's accounting. Berkshire's reported results were better than the headline underwriting gains would suggest due to accounting practices that did not factor in the time value of money. In its structured settlements business and certain reinsurance contracts, payments would be made years, or in some cases decades, in the future. This meant Berkshire benefitted from the use of the funds over time. However, the accounting required that all future expected losses (except for structured settlements, which were discounted) be booked on an undiscounted basis—that is, upfront. It was the economics that mattered most, not the accounting. If any grey area existed, Berkshire would err on the side of conservatism, even if it made results look worse.*

Conservatism and smoothness are sometimes lumped together, but they shouldn't be. Buffett liked conservatism and was also okay with lumpiness (or uneven results). Berkshire's entrance into the super cat business brought large policies and large (but infrequent) losses. Berkshire at this time was willing to underwrite a $1 billion policy,

---

* Buffett said he and Munger would always attempt to explain to shareholders any major points.

though it was rejected. The largest policy it wrote was $400 million. Large policies would create volatility but were also a competitive advantage that led to superior long-term results. Competitors preferred a smoother ride that ensured the safety of their jobs.

The Reinsurance Group wrote and earned higher premiums in 1995, but pricing began to soften as competitors flush with capital looked for business. Unfavorable loss development added $30 million to losses. Accounting charges from deferred charge amortization and discount accretion of structured settlements were also responsible for reinsurance swinging to a loss of $21 million from an underwriting profit of $81 million in 1994.

Berkshire's more traditional (and less lumpy) Primary Group performed magnificently. National Indemnity wrote to an 84.2% combined ratio, Home State operations turned in an 81.4% ratio, and Central States Indemnity grew volume 23% and underwriting profit by 59%. Buffett had nothing but praise for Ajit Jain, Don Wurster, Rod Eldred, Brad Kinstler, and John Kizer—all of whom Buffett pointed out were under forty-five years old.

GEICO, not yet part of Berkshire, turned in strong results in 1995 that rivaled Berkshire's entire existing insurance operations.

Manufacturing, Publishing, and Retailing

Berkshire's non-insurance operating subsidiaries had a few stumbles during 1995, and Buffett was quick to point them out. "Just tell me the bad news; the good news will take care of itself," was the philosophy Buffett attributed to Munger and what he followed in reporting to shareholders. The shoe businesses, *The Buffalo News*, and World Book all had different problems during the year, which led pre-tax earnings for the manufacturing, publishing, and retailing businesses to fall 1% to $332 million. Worse, pre-tax return on tangible invested capital fell eleven points to 38% because of higher average capital employed. After-tax return on equity was 26% (-6%).

In the Shoe Group, comprised of H.H. Brown, Dexter, and Lowell Shoe, pre-tax operating earnings fell 32% to $58.4 million. Buffett told shareholders he thought the problem was cyclical, not secular, and he expected operations would, "climb back to top-grade earnings in the future." If it was any consolation, Buffett reported that competitors in the industry "made only marginal profits or worse."

Including *The Buffalo News* in the troubled category was no surprise to shareholders. Prior reports detailed the long and winding road from losses to profits to current challenges. The paper was still a good business, but it could no longer be considered an economically superior business like some of Berkshire's other gems. Pre-tax earnings declined 14% from the year before as cost pressures weighed on results. These included newsprint costs up 40% in one year, employee buyouts, and changes to depreciation schedules. Still, the business was pulling its weight with $47 million in pre-tax earnings. Not bad for a business that cost $35 million.

World Book was also not a surprise in this group of bad-news-first companies. Its print encyclopedias continued to struggle against fierce competition from CD-ROMs. Earnings that year plummeted 64% to $8.8 million as the business worked to remain viable in an electronic age, including shifting toward direct distribution channels. If any of the managers at these units were worried, Buffett provided some reassurance to them: "[T]here is not one of them we would replace." Going one step further at the Annual Meeting, he assured shareholders World Book would not be sold.

See's operating profits continued to churn higher even as the growing slate of businesses meant it received less attention. In 1995, revenue at See's grew 8.1% to $234 million as the company pushed into wholesale and mail orders. Long beset by physical volume declines, pounds of candy increased 7.1%. Same-store sales, an important metric indicating demand from individual stores, was not disclosed. Operating profit increased 6% to $50 million—an incredible 21.1% operating profit margin and a return on tangible equity likely in the triple digits.*

Together with the results from insurance, Berkshire's consolidated pre-tax operating income declined a little less than 3% in 1995, to $815 million. This was not a bad result, but it wasn't great either. Buffett's comment that there's "no reason to do handsprings over 1995's gains" is borne out by this operating result. In fact, most of the 43.1% gain in per share book value was a result of the rising tide of the stock market pushing up the value of Berkshire's investment portfolio, not intrinsic business growth.

Convertible Preferred Stocks

Berkshire's goal with its five preferred stock investments was to do better than fixed-income securities available elsewhere. On average, it had done reasonably well. The superior performance of the Gillette issue saved the day and balanced out mistakes made with other investments in this class.

The 8.25% convertible preferred issue from Gillette had cost Berkshire $600 million. At the end of 1995, it was valued at over $2.5 billion owing to the performance of the common shares. This was a very good result, yet a more profitable path was possible. Berkshire would have earned $555 million more if it had purchased all common stock instead of the convertible issue.

---

* While equity capital was not disclosed specifically for See's, we know from the footnotes that it had $69.4 million of beginning identifiable assets and, though not detailed, a large remaining balance of goodwill was included in those assets.

On the negative side of the ledger, the Salomon preferred came with its infamous and relatively recent episode of management distraction and a serious risk of loss. The biggest mistake, though, was the USAir preferred. The airline's prospects looked better in 1995 than they did the year before, but Berkshire was not yet out of the woods.

An important aspect to the USAir preferred is worth mention. The security was structured with a cumulative dividend provision. USAir had stopped paying the dividend owing to its operating troubles, but those skipped dividends were still owed to Berkshire and were compounding at a rate of 5% over the prime rate. The company would have to come out of its woes to pay the monies it owed, but at least Berkshire had some protection as a creditor.*

1996

Few CEOs would state that they thought it a good thing that their company's stock price changed little during the year, yet this is exactly what Warren Buffett told shareholders in his 1996 Chairman's letter. Buffett and Munger wanted Berkshire's share price to closely track its underlying intrinsic value. During 1995, that relationship became unhinged and Berkshire's stock price got ahead of its underlying intrinsic value. A year later, its intrinsic value increased significantly and caught up with a slower-advancing share price.

How Berkshire's business results led to that correction is the story of 1996, but first it is worth examining the numbers behind the ratio. Beginning in the prior year's Annual Report, Buffett began supplying a table they believed would help people trying to estimate Berkshire's intrinsic value. The table showcased the two-column method of valuing Berkshire (see Table 6.6). It supplied readers with historical data on investments per share and pre-tax earnings per share, excluding all investment income. We can make some reasonable assumptions with that data to come up with an estimate of Berkshire's intrinsic value and, perhaps more important for this exercise, view the change in the price/value relationship.

The logical investment framework behind the two-column method is that Berkshire's value stems from its investment portfolio and a capitalized multiple of its operating earnings. It is important to note that, especially as it pertains to investments per share, Berkshire's capital structure was conservatively financed. Investments per share could have easily been funded via debt. Yet, at both year-end 1995 and 1996 Berkshire's borrowings amounted to under 10% of equity capital. Its assets were funded by float, but float was growing and profitable. It was therefore appropriate to ascribe investments per share to value per share. At year-end 1996, investments per share totaled $28,500, compared to $22,088 at year-end 1995.

---

* If the issue were non-cumulative preferred USAir would not have been required to make the missed payments.

The assumptions behind the capitalized value of operating earnings also deserve some careful thought. Since all assets are in some way tied to the opportunity cost of risk-free investments, it is appropriate to look to the long-term US Treasury rate (in this case the 30-year bond) for comparison. Between year-end 1995 and 1996 this benchmark averaged around 6.50%. Using a 10% discount rate might be appropriate here since it provides a margin above the risk-free rate.* The discount rate is important when valuing cash flows. It is the rate at which future cash flows are brought back to the present. Because of the time value of money (a dollar today is worth more than a dollar in the future), the further into the future cash flows are, and the greater the uncertainty they will materialize, must be considered.** Here we'll use a 10% discount rate for simplicity, which implies a multiple of ten times. Based on this framework Berkshire's pre-tax operating earnings per share of $421.39 and $258.20 were worth about $4,214 and $2,582 at year-end 1996 and 1995, respectively. Adding the per share values of investments and operating earnings we find that Berkshire's per share intrinsic value increased by approximately 33% during 1996. Because the share price increased just 6% during that time, Berkshire's price-to-estimated-value decreased from a rich 1.30 times to 1.04 times—just about parity.***

Table 6.6: Berkshire Hathaway intrinsic value estimation

Per share:	1996	1995
Investments	$28,500	$22,088
Pre-tax operating earnings (ex. investment income)	421	258
Estimated value (investments + 10x operating earnings)	32,714	24,670
Year-end share price	34,100	32,100
Year-end book value per share	19,011	14,025
Price/estimated value	1.04x	1.30x
Price/book	1.79x	2.29x
Value/book	1.72x	1.76x
Change in estimated value	33%	
Change in share price	6%	

Sources: Berkshire Hathaway Annual Reports 1995, 1996; and author's calculations.

---

* As strong as Berkshire was, it was never as risk free as the US government, which could print money.
** If a company gets bigger by investing in projects that earn less than their cost of capital, they destroy value. Even though a company's cost of equity capital is impossible to precisely define, projects earning a rate below an investor's discount rate mean the company is not increasing value for that investor. The discount rate incorporates the benchmark set by the risk-free rate and a margin capturing risk. A higher discount rate means future cash flows are not worth as much in the present, and vice versa. Growth factors into the equation by offsetting the effect of discounting (assuming such growth does not destroy value).
*** As a check on this valuation exercise we can also impute the earnings yield the $1.5 billion of look-through earnings provides on a roughly $33 billion above valuation. The result of approximately 4.5% would imply a 5.5% growth rate (assuming a 10% discount rate), which would not be out of line with Berkshire's growth rates at the time, especially considering the value inherent in the recent GEICO acquisition.

The valuation exercise above also lends itself to the discussion of the issuance of new B-shares during 1996. At the time, Buffett and Munger said the shares were not undervalued and their issuance would not decrease Berkshire's per-share intrinsic value. Since the shares were issued at a price just over the year-end 1995 share price (which was at a price-to-estimated-value of 1.30 times), the assertion holds.

FlightSafety International

Berkshire's 1996 share count was also affected by the issuance of shares to acquire FlightSafety International, a new operating subsidiary that trained pilots using flight simulators. Berkshire paid a total of approximately $1.5 billion for the company and funded it with 51% cash and the remainder in A- and B-shares (see Table 6.7). Altogether 17,728 A-shares and 112,655 B-shares were issued to acquire FlightSafety.

The FlightSafety acquisition came to Berkshire via Richard Server, a shareholder of both Berkshire and FlightSafety who was familiar with Buffett's annual advertisement for seeking acquisitions.

FlightSafety was the result of a lifetime of work by then 79-year-old founder, Al Ueltschi. Ueltschi was an aviator who once piloted for Charles Lindbergh. The company manufactured and operated high-technology flight simulators for pilots of various types of aircraft. The flight simulators were indispensable to aircraft operators since they trained pilots in a realistic environment at a fraction of the cost, and perhaps more importantly, without the risk of operating an actual aircraft.

FlightSafety represented a shift in Berkshire's acquisition philosophy. The business was a capital-intensive operation with forty-one locations and 175 simulators. The simulators cost up to $19 million apiece to manufacture. Furthermore, they became outdated each time new aircraft were introduced into the market.

Balancing out the capital-intensive nature of the business was a huge moat—something Berkshire admired and sought in acquisitions. Since competitors would have to invest tens of millions of dollars for a single simulator, the price of entry was steep. This provided a potential competitive advantage. FlightSafety's long history also gave it a knowledge base to build simulators, supply its customers with numerous machines in numerous locations, and work with aircraft manufacturers to more quickly introduce machines for new aircraft. This deep well of knowledge earned it a joint venture with Boeing and a government contract through Raytheon.

Analyzing Berkshire's acquisition of FlightSafety, we can conclude it was a fair price for a good company. Berkshire's effective purchase price (deducting excess investments on the balance sheet) resulted in a going-in pre-tax return of 8.7%. This seems very low at first glance—and it is. But Berkshire would benefit from FlightSafety's historical returns on capital and the moat protecting those returns. Any future growth the company might achieve, if anywhere near its historical returns on capital, would more than make up for the low initial return. On top of this, the company came with a passionate founder/manager. That he was 79 years old only endeared him to Buffett even more. "An observer might conclude from our hiring practices that Charlie and I were traumatized early in life by an EEOC bulletin on age discrimination. The real explanation, however, is self-interest: It's difficult to teach a new dog old tricks," Buffett wrote. Like Mrs. B at Nebraska Furniture Mart, Ueltschi was still at the top of his game.

Table 6.7: FlightSafety International acquisition analysis

	1995	1994	1993
Revenues *($ millions)*	$326	$301	$297
Revenues/average capital	$0.76	$0.76	$0.79
EBIT margin	36%	36%	34%
Pre-tax return on capital	27%	27%	27%
Purchase price (equity)	$1,500		
Assumed debt	40		
Less: excess investments	(194)		
Effective purchase price	1,346		
Purchase multiple	3.15x		
BRK going-in pre-tax return	8.7%		

Sources: Berkshire Hathaway Annual Report 1996; FlightSafety International Annual Reports 1993, 1995; and author's calculations.

Kansas Bankers Surety

Berkshire's other, much smaller, acquisition of 1996 provides another lesson in business moats. Kansas Bankers Surety, per its name, wrote insurance policies for banks. It provided directors and officers insurance, excess deposit insurance for depositors above the FDIC limit and other related areas of coverage. Due to its relatively small size, KBS was tucked into Wesco's Insurance operations.* The business was run by Don Towle and had just 13 employees.[53]

The lesson in Kansas Bankers Surety was that its relatively small size and limited opportunities for growth were the source of its competitive advantage. This sounds counterintuitive but is straightforward after some examination. The business required intimate relationships with hundreds of bankers, a process that takes time to build. With a limited number of clients and relatively slow turnover in bank executives, gaining an edge on Kansas Bankers Surety was hard. It was in a class of wonderful businesses that had a natural size limit but which generated a lot of surplus cash flow. Berkshire was more than happy to be a home to such a business.

---

* In his 1996 Chairman's letter, Buffett said he offered $75 million for the company; Charlie Munger's comments in his Wesco letter put the figure at about $80 million.

Insurance

Berkshire's insurance operations fell into two broad categories: The Reinsurance Group included the super catastrophe lines (or super cat), the relatively plain vanilla reinsurance business of taking on the risk entered into by primary insurers, in addition to the structured settlements business. The Primary Group encompassed everything from National Indemnity's specialized auto line and Home State companies to the workers' compensation business. GEICO, now a wholly-owned subsidiary of Berkshire, fell squarely into the primary category. Owing to its size (GEICO's operations were more than ten times that of Berkshire's other primary lines combined), GEICO was reported separately.

Berkshire's Insurance Group, now led by GEICO, was hitting on all cylinders. The overall result for the group was a pre-tax underwriting gain of $222 million on earned premiums of $4.1 billion. Aided by GEICO, Berkshire's float nearly doubled, from $3.6 billion in 1995 to $6.7 billion in 1996.

Table 6.8: Berkshire Hathaway—Insurance Underwriting

($ millions)	1996	1995
GEICO Corporation		
Premiums written	$3,122	$2,856
Premiums earned	3,092	2,787
Underwriting gain/(loss) - pre-tax	$171	$92
Berkshire Hathaway Reinsurance Group		
Premiums written	$716	$777
Premiums earned	758	718
Underwriting gain/(loss) - pre-tax	($8)	($21)
Berkshire Hathaway Primary Group		
Premiums written	$268	$247
Premiums earned	268	240
Underwriting gain/(loss) - pre-tax	$59	$41
Total underwriting gain/(loss)	$222	$21
Year-end average float - total	6,702	3,607
Cost of float	(3.3%)	(0.6%)
Aggregate adverse (favorable) loss development	($90)	$56

Note: Data for GEICO in 1995 provided for comparative purposes. GEICO's results are not included in the totals.

Sources: Berkshire Hathaway Annual Reports 1995, 1998; and author's calculations.

Insurance – Reinsurance

Berkshire earned $758 million in reinsurance premiums in 1996 and wrote to a 101% combined ratio.* The segment was greatly aided by the super cat business, which turned in an underwriting profit of $167 million on earned premiums of $268 million. This was the third straight year of significant super cat underwriting gains, which prompted Buffett to warn that the ride would be bumpy despite expected satisfactory results long term. "What you must understand, however, is that a truly terrible year in the super cat business is not a possibility—it's a certainty. The only question is when it will come." He even advised shareholders to reduce their estimates for Berkshire's earnings during years of above-average profitability when calculating Berkshire's intrinsic value.

While the policies Berkshire wrote in 1996 were large, they were not unreasonable compared to its capital position. Buffett thought a worst-case, after-tax loss from a "true mega-catastrophe" to be around $600 million—less than 3% of Berkshire's book value and easily absorbed by earnings from its other businesses. Berkshire could do better than its peers over time by striving to underwrite each deal profitably and letting results fall where they may, rather than attempting for a smooth outcome each year. Indeed, Berkshire's reinsurance business model could be described as profiting from the desire of other insurers to smooth their underwriting experiences in an uncertain world.

Berkshire had three major competitive advantages in the super cat business.

1. *The marketplace*: Berkshire had a reputation of having the capital to pay its claimants and paying them fast, even under the very worst of circumstances.
2. *Price and timing*: Berkshire would always have a great willingness to write business at the right price. When times became tough other reinsurers might pull back from the marketplace. Berkshire's reputation was now such that it was earning "stand-by" fees from other reinsurers. This gave the other reinsurers comfort that Berkshire would write them a policy if others wouldn't.
3. *Large policies*: Berkshire had the ability and willingness to write large policies. Buffett, and Berkshire's insurance whiz, Ajit Jain, stood ready to commit to evaluate risks, price coverage, and respond to its customers very quickly.

Perhaps demonstrating how open the insurance business really was, Buffett wrote that Berkshire tried "to price our super cat exposures so that about 90% of total premiums end up being eventually paid out in losses and expenses." Berkshire's advantage was that

---

* For consistency with other years the GAAP combined ratio is used going forward. The relative stability of premiums written and earned means the GAAP and SAP ratios would be very close.

it was willing to walk away from risks it didn't understand. Others relied on computer models that offered a false sense of comfort. Some direct writers were unknowingly the biggest super cat writers. Companies writing business in certain geographic areas, such as on Long Island, might have the most risk. A single large hurricane could cause wind damage to an entire portfolio of claimants diverse in all ways except their geographic exposure to one large, infrequently occurring risk. "They don't think of themselves as being in the super-cat business … [but] they are very exposed."

The other half of Berkshire's reinsurance operations, making up $490 million of earned premiums in 1996, was the property and casualty excess-of-loss and quota-share business. This line was more straightforward and less volatile than the super cat business. Though the segment turned in an underwriting loss of $101 million in 1996, and similar-sized losses in prior years, these were long-tail-type policies that produced the significant float for Berkshire. When priced appropriately, they would produce satisfactory results over time.

Insurance – Primary Group

Berkshire's legacy primary lines, its bread-and-butter insurance businesses, produced excellent results. On $268 million of earned premiums, the group turned in a combined ratio of 78.2%,* good for an underwriting profit of $59 million. Buffett singled out the managers responsible for producing this achievement for Berkshire: Don Wurster at National Indemnity, Rod Eldred of the Home State operation, John Kizer at Central States Indemnity, and Brad Kinstler, who ran the workers' compensation group and expanded it into six new states during 1996.

Insurance – GEICO

Berkshire's new gem, GEICO, run by Tony Nicely on the underwriting side and Lou Simpson on the investment side, also received well-earned praise. Buffett was clearly excited about its prospects. There was nothing complicated about GEICO, but its advantages were huge. GEICO's competitive advantage stemmed from being the low-cost operator and using a direct-to-consumer business model among competitors entrenched in a broker model. In 1996, GEICO's customers referred one million others to the company, which produced better than 50% of its new business. The savings on acquisition expenses were then passed on to customers, in a virtuous cycle.

Employees at GEICO, from Nicely down, focused on two metrics: growth in voluntary policies in force** and the profitability of seasoned business (business on

---

* GAAP basis.

** The word "voluntary" is important. These were the policies GEICO sought out and which formed the basis

the books for more than a year). It was a very simple operating philosophy. Bring in more customers and make sure those that stayed were profitable. This incentive structure formed the basis of all bonuses at GEICO.

The two-part structure was carefully designed to maximize the benefit for GEICO's owners, now Berkshire Hathaway shareholders. By focusing on the profitability of seasoned business, the underwriting part of the equation sought to ensure GEICO was pricing its product appropriately for the long-term and rejecting unprofitable risks. Because it excluded customer acquisition expenses associated with bringing in new business, which hurt profitability in the short-term, the structure incentivized actions that built long-term value. This allowed for liberal spending to drive future results of the business.

As simple as this incentive structure was, GEICO's competitors, and especially public companies, followed other paths. Beholden to the short-term-thinking of Wall Street, these companies often put near-term earnings first and sometimes starved their marketing budgets. GEICO's path from being the sixth or seventh largest auto insurer in the country to being one of the largest was the result of its long-term strategy.

It is worth noting that Simpson, GEICO's long-time investment manager, remained on to manage GEICO's investment portfolio after the merger. This said a lot about how highly Buffett viewed Simpson's investment prowess. With every other insurance acquisition, Buffett had taken over the investment part of the equation and left the managers to focus on the underwriting side.

In 1996, GEICO's first year under the Berkshire roof wholly owned, it wrote to a 94.5% combined ratio, producing an underwriting gain of $171 million pre-tax.

Manufacturing, Publishing, and Retailing

The manufacturing, publishing and retail segment continued impressive operations. Earning $378 million pre-tax in 1996, the group produced a pre-tax return on invested capital of 30%.* In isolation it represented a great result, but it marked a sharp decline from the 38% return earned in 1995 and the 49% result in 1994. Deteriorating profitability in the Shoe Group over the past few years explained part of the decline. The addition of capital-intensive FlightSafety explained the drop in 1996.** Most of

---

for its superior profitability. Involuntary policies, by contrast, came from "risk pools" that every participating company was forced to take part of to insure those that could not find insurance but whose state laws required them to be insured.

* As a reminder, these figures are the non-GAAP results published at the back of the Annual Report and exclude purchase price adjustments and amortization of goodwill, etc.

** Invested capital (debt + equity) for the MPR businesses increased 46% between 1995 and 1996. FlightSafety employed about $450 million in capital at year-end 1995.

the businesses in this category continued to contribute as they had in the past. A few business units are worth highlighting.

While the going was still tough at World Book, the business had made some progress. It was now the only direct-seller of encyclopedias after Encyclopedia Britannica stopped its business line. World Book also partnered with IBM and invested heavily in a new CD-ROM product. Pre-tax operating earnings at the unit grew 43% to $12.6 million but remained below the $25 million profit earned in 1994.

Operating earnings at *The Buffalo News* grew 7.7% to $50.4 million. The gain was partly because the prior year had higher one-time charges due to employee severance costs and certain depreciation adjustments. The current year benefitted from lower newsprint costs, which came back down after skyrocketing in 1995.

The Shoe Group saw profits increase 5.5% to $61.6 million, but they remained far below the $86 million earned just two years before. Management successfully capitalized on opportunities to market and distribute product and lower overhead costs. More profits were expected in the coming year.

Helzberg, Berkshire's newest jewelry acquisition, stumbled during 1996 and brought jewelry profits down 18% to $28 million. Increased expenses in anticipation of a large revenue increase that never materialized caused the disappointment. Buffett said CEO Jeff Comment was "addressing the expense problem in a decisive manner" and that he expected increased earnings in 1997.

USAir – Update

The saga of Berkshire's investment in USAir preferred stock continued. Only this time it was news to the upside. Despite the many mistakes Buffett admitted making with the investment, there was one bright spot. The preferred stock included an unusual provision stipulating penalty dividends 5 percentage points over the prime rate for payments that were in arrears. Since USAir had skipped two years of preferred dividend payments due to operating troubles, this provision was triggered. The regular 9.25% dividend was now closer to 14% for the last two years.

This penalty provision gave USAir an incentive to pay the amount in arrears. Buffett praised company CEO Stephen Wolf for working to right the ship. While he asserted that USAir "still has basic cost problems that must be solved," Wolf's actions saved Berkshire's investment such that Buffett now thought it worth its $358 million par value.

Not one to bask in glory, Buffett admitted to twice trying to unload the USAir stock, first in 1995 and again in early 1996. Both efforts failed. Buffett told shareholders after the second attempt, "You're lucky: I again failed in my attempt to snatch defeat from the jaws of victory."

The Walt Disney Company

In March 1996, The Walt Disney Company acquired Capital Cities/ABC in a cash and stock transaction. The deal was borne of a meeting between Michael Eisner of Disney and Tom Murphy of Cap Cities/ABC at a Sun Valley retreat. While Buffett attributed the meeting to his influence, he later said that he thought the deal would have eventually materialized on its own. Berkshire received a total of $2.5 billion, of which $1.2 billion was in Walt Disney stock, which Berkshire retained, and the remainder in cash. The event caused a $2.2 billion realized gain.

Salomon Debt Issue

During 1996, Salomon Brothers, Berkshire's go-to investment bank, sold an unusual security for Berkshire. The security was a $500 million, five-year debt issue that was convertible into shares of Salomon stock owned by Berkshire. Responding to a question about the issue at the 1997 Annual Meeting Buffett noted that, "it's a way of taking the capital out of that block of stock at a low-interest cost to use elsewhere, while retaining a limited portion of the upside in the Salomon stock." With stocks generally trading at elevated levels,* Berkshire was again taking advantage of favorable financing opportunities independent of any immediate need for capital.

Investment Lessons

Buffett provided some explicit words of wisdom for investors in his Chairman's letter and at the Annual Meeting. He stressed the advantages of a low-cost index fund, which he thought would over time beat "the great majority of investment professionals." Addressing attendees at the Annual Meeting, he said investing is "the only field in the world … where the amateur, as long as he recognizes he's an amateur, will do better than the professional."

Buffett frequently pointed to his own shortcomings and limitations with respect to investing. He thought investors wanting to strike out on their own and construct their own portfolios should clearly define their circle of competence and stick to it. "You don't have to be an expert on every company, or even many," he wrote shareholders. "Your goal as an investor should simply be to purchase, at a rational price, a part interest in an easily-understandable business whose earnings are virtually certain to be materially higher, five, ten and twenty years from now." These companies were rare so investors should load up when they found one. Buffett

---

* In Buffett's 1996 Chairman's letter, he wrote that there was an overpayment risk in virtually all stocks.

pointed to Berkshire's own look-through earnings, which had risen in tandem over time with Berkshire's stock price, as an example of his counsel in action.

The best part about investing was that it was cumulative. Buffett had studied many businesses for years, even using FlightSafety as an example of one he read about for twenty years before learning enough to purchase it. All it took to be knowledgeable about many businesses and industries was time and an interest in continual learning. Compounding knowledge would lead to compounding money.

*Class B Common Stock Issuance**

Up until 1996 Berkshire Hathaway had only one class of common equity. Buffett's unwillingness to split the stock to cultivate and maintain a certain shareholder base meant its shares were priced significantly higher than the average issue. Companies typically split shares to keep prices in the "affordable" range of $20 to $100.** Berkshire's shares had never been split and its per share price—over $33,000—reflected that fact. This caused some problems for shareholders wishing to make gifts, but the problems were surmountable.*** The 1996 proposal to issue Class B shares was a defensive move on Berkshire's part: It was partly to protect potential investors, and partly to protect Berkshire's reputation.

Berkshire had successfully foiled many plans to create a unit trust stocked solely with Berkshire shares by appealing to the promotors of the trusts. Now it seemed someone was ignoring those pleas and at least one trust might be created.**** The potential unit trust would buy Berkshire shares on the open market and then sell shares in the trust to prospective investors wishing to buy less than whole shares of Berkshire common stock. Buffett and Munger thought such a proposal would harm investors in two ways. First, through the fees that would cause the investment to lag that of true Berkshire shares. Second, the incentive to grow those fees would cause the promoter to market the trust by promoting the high rate of return which had been achieved in the past, but which Buffett said was not repeatable. There was also the issue of supply and demand. The unit trust would have a fixed number of shares. Heavy promotion might cause the price to exceed the value of the underlying Berkshire shares. Investors would do worse than the underlying Berkshire shares as the discrepancy corrected itself over time.

---

* Unless otherwise noted, all references to per share figures are on an A-share equivalent basis.
** Like cutting a pizza into additional slices, stock splits increase the number of shares outstanding without affecting the underlying value of a business. In other words, it's largely cosmetic.
*** Without giving advice on the matter, Buffett had previously told shareholders of a way to set up a family corporation that could own the stock, and whose own shares could then be gifted to children, etc.
**** Such a unit trust was not illegal nor was Berkshire's permission required. While some may have sought this scheme as a way to effectively split the stock for convenience, others were doubtless attracted by the possibility of profit.

The high expectations of such a Berkshire unit trust investment could also harm Berkshire and Buffett's reputation. If purchasers of such a trust bought in at a high price relative to the underlying Berkshire stock, its performance would surely be disappointing over time. Even if Berkshire were not to blame, which it wouldn't have been, the negative association would remain.

To thwart the promotors, Berkshire devised a plan to create a sub-class of shares that would represent direct ownership, but at slightly disadvantageous terms. The newly created B shares would be priced at 1/30th of that of an A share (the original share class) but they would have voting rights of just 1/200th of the A shares. Further, only the A-shares would be eligible for the charitable contribution program. In this way, there would be a slight advantage to owning the A-shares, but the newer B-share investors would still be owners of the company.

Berkshire went even further to temper expectations and take the idea of a unit trust off the table. Guided by basic economics, Berkshire stated that it would issue as many shares as investors wanted. This would eliminate any possibility of outsized demand from temporary excitement since Berkshire would just issue new shares to satisfy demand. Additionally, the A-shares would be convertible at the option of the holder into 30 B-shares, but the privilege would not go the opposite way. If B-shares traded higher than the equivalent A-shares for some reason, arbitrage would ensure the differential would not become too great. (An investor could buy A-shares, convert them to B-shares, and then sell them at a higher price. The parts would be more valuable than the whole.)

Lastly, Berkshire publicly stated (including in the prospectus offering) that both Buffett and Munger did not think Berkshire was undervalued at the issue price and that they were not interested in purchasing shares at that price. Some shareholders thought this meant Berkshire was overvalued. Buffett made clear that should not be inferred. He said saying that Berkshire was not undervalued was not the same as saying it was overvalued. Based on Berkshire's book value at the end of 1995, the new shares would have valued the company at over twice book value.

When the actual issuance was completed, the expected $100 million offering was oversubscribed. Berkshire ultimately ended up issuing 517,500 new B-class shares, which brought in just under $565 million. With no immediate plans for the money, Berkshire put it into the pool of capital available for other opportunities. Munger put the new shares in context. At about 1% dilution, he said the creation of the B-shares was a non-event.

Berkshire shareholders, not surprisingly, voted at the 1996 Annual Meeting to approve the B-share issuance. The Berkshire unit trust idea never resurfaced, and Berkshire's reputation and shareholders were unharmed.

The complete language of the offering—vastly different than anything typically found on Wall Street—is worth reading in its entirety:

WARREN BUFFETT, AS BERKSHIRE'S CHAIRMAN, AND CHARLES MUNGER, AS BERKSHIRE'S VICE CHAIRMAN, WANT YOU TO KNOW THE FOLLOWING (AND URGE YOU TO IGNORE ANYONE TELLING YOU THAT THESE STATEMENTS ARE "BOILERPLATE" OR UNIMPORTANT):

1. Mr. Buffett and Mr. Munger believe that Berkshire's Class A Common Stock is not undervalued at the market price stated above. Neither Mr. Buffett nor Mr. Munger would currently buy Berkshire shares at that price, nor would they recommend that their families or friends do so.

2. Berkshire's historical rate of growth in per-share book value is NOT indicative of possible future growth. Because of the large size of Berkshire's capital base (approximately $17 billion at December 31, 1995), Berkshire's book value per share cannot increase in the future at a rate even close to its past rate.

3. In recent years the market price of Berkshire shares has increased at a rate exceeding the growth in per-share intrinsic value. Market overperformance of that kind cannot persist indefinitely. Inevitably, there will also occur periods of underperformance, perhaps substantial in degree.

4. Berkshire has attempted to assess the current demand for Class B shares and has tailored the size of this offering to fully satisfy that demand. Therefore, buyers hoping to capture quick profits are almost certain to be disappointed. Shares should be purchased only by investors who expect to remain holders for many years.

1997

With stock markets continuing their upward trend, Buffett likened Berkshire's 34.1% per share increase in book value to a rising tide. He said Berkshire was the duck and even though its gain beat the S&P (by 0.7 percentage points) it was more attributable to luck than business acumen. That is not to say Berkshire did not make important gains during 1997. Buffett estimated intrinsic valued increased in tandem with book value.

Using the two-column method and our arbitrary though consistent 10x multiplier on pre-tax operating earnings, we can calculate that Berkshire's intrinsic value grew about 38%, which is close to the 34% increase in book value (see Table 6.9).

Table 6.9: Berkshire Hathaway intrinsic value estimation

Per A-share	1997	1996
Investments	$38,043	$28,500
Pre-tax operating earnings (ex. investment income)	718	421
Estimated value (investments + 10x operating earnings)	$45,221	$32,714
Year-end share price	$46,000	$34,100
Year-end book value per share	25,488	19,011
Price/estimated value	1.02x	1.04x
Price/book	1.80x	1.79x
Value/book	1.77x	1.72x
Change in estimated value	38%	
Change in share price	35%	

Sources: Berkshire Hathaway Annual Reports 1996, 1997; and author's calculations.

Buffett made sure to temper any enthusiasm. Berkshire's super cat business again experienced no major claims and GEICO had an unusually good year. Additionally, a rising stock market was making it harder to find good values there. He said prices were high and "if we swing, we will be locked into low returns." Buffett knew the value in waiting for the "fat pitch" but found some things during 1997 to keep himself out of trouble.

Unusual Commitments

For Buffett, keeping himself out of trouble meant finding market inefficiencies to exploit. This involved three unusual investments: oil contracts, zero-coupon US government bonds, and silver. The first was an investment in futures positions for 14 million barrels of oil. This was the remainder of a contract established in 1994 and 1995. The total profit from 45.7 million barrels of oil for those years created $62 million of profit for Berkshire.

The second was the purchase of $4.6 billion (at amortized cost) of US Treasury zero-coupon obligations. Paying no interest, they were a significant bet on a downward move in interest rates. The bet risked looking foolish if rates rose, but the odds were judged favorable. At year-end 1997, this bet was working out to the tune of almost $600 million.

The third investment was in silver and proved the remarkable power of staying true to simple economic concepts. In this case, supply and demand. Berkshire had a position of 111.2 million ounces of silver at year-end 1997. Buffett and Munger invested in silver because they thought that the world's supply and demand equation had gotten out of whack, and that a higher price would be necessary to resolve the discrepancy. Buffett stressed that inflation played no part in the calculation.

The logic was this: The world at that time used about 800 million ounces of silver each year. With 500 million ounces being produced, and another 150 million ounces being reclaimed annually, a 150 million-ounce shortfall existed. Since inventories were low, the demand would soon outstrip supply and cause a rise in price.

There was an important nuance to this investment, and it highlighted the concept of inelasticity. Very simply, elasticity in economics refers to the degree to which a given thing is price sensitive. Since the supply of silver came largely as a by-product of mining other metals, its supply was price inelastic. This meant that no one was out there prospecting simply for silver. Supply of silver was based on the fundamentals of other metals; more demand did not induce additional supply. The demand side also had some inelasticity. Silver was used in photography and jewelry, but demand for silver was not overly sensitive to price. Combine these factors and it created a situation that clearly favored an upward price-shift eventually. (Like other investments, Buffett knew the *if* but not the *when*.)

Charlie Munger pithily dismissed the investment at the 1998 Annual Meeting as being something that Buffett patiently studied for decades only to invest 2% of Berkshire's assets. In other words, it was not something to be excited about because it wasn't going to move the needle at Berkshire. Compared to Berkshire's multibillion-dollar investments in Coke, Gillette, and others, it really was a non-event. Still, for our purposes the investment is interesting and instructive.

Insurance

Aided by several positive factors, the Insurance Group hit it out of the park in 1997. Insurance earned almost $4.8 billion of premiums and wrote to an underwriting gain of $462 million before tax.

Table 6.10: Berkshire Hathaway—Insurance Underwriting

($ millions)	1997	1996
GEICO Corporation		
Premiums written	$3,588	$3,122
Premiums earned	3,482	3,092
Underwriting gain/(loss) - pre-tax	$281	$171
Berkshire Hathaway Reinsurance Group		
Premiums written	$955	$716
Premiums earned	967	758
Underwriting gain/(loss) - pre-tax	$128	($8)
Berkshire Hathaway Primary Group		
Premiums written	$309	$268
Premiums earned	313	268
Underwriting gain/(loss) - pre-tax	$53	$59
Total underwriting gain/(loss)	$462	$222
Year-end average float - total	7,093	6,702
Cost of float	(6.5%)	(3.3%)
Aggregate adverse (favorable) loss development	($131)	($90)

Sources: Berkshire Hathaway Annual Report 1998 and author's calculations.

Insurance – Reinsurance Group

With no super catastrophes in 1997, $283 million out of $310 million of catastrophe excess-of-loss premiums fell to the bottom line as profit. But the possibility of losses materializing in any given year were meaningful, and they were certain to occur at some point in the future. With an enlarged capital base and appetite for new deals, Berkshire was willing to suffer a $1 billion loss without any discomfort. Berkshire had confidence in its pricing of risks and knew that over time the odds would be in its favor. Losses in other property/casualty lines of $73 million, and $82 million in losses from retroactive reinsurance and structured settlements brought the Reinsurance Group gain down to $128 million.

While the lack of loss experience (catastrophes and ensuing expensive damage claims) in super cat was a near-term positive, it did bring unwelcome consequences. The insurance industry had long suffered from the ebbs and flows of capital coming into the industry during times of small losses, only to retreat when large losses came. The budding threat was now a new financial instrument dubbed catastrophe bonds.

Buffett disliked catastrophe bonds, but not because they represented competition. He disliked them primarily because he thought they would likely be sold to unsophisticated buyers. Buffett defined them as "investors," using quotes to suggest they were not informed buyers. The word bond would induce prospective buyers to associate them with the safety inherent in traditional bonds, such as those sold by corporations or governments, when in fact they were really an instrument designed to circumvent state laws preventing unlicensed insurance activity. He also called them an Orwellian misnomer because they were not like a bond at all. They were more like a mispriced layer of insurance.

Whereas a true bond requires the issuer to repay the debt using income and is usually backed by assets, these were more like reinsurance and put the greater risk on the purchaser. This is how it worked: Investors put up money to back a pool of risks. If no risks materialized, the investor would receive a payment. Unlike a traditional bond, however, if a loss event did occur, the bond capital was used to make the issuer whole—leaving the bond holders empty handed. Like other times of capital influx, lower volumes were expected in the years ahead.

Insurance – GEICO

GEICO, already a shining gem, shone brighter than ever in 1997. After a record-setting 10% growth in 1996, GEICO, led by Tony Nicely, rocketed to 16% growth of in-force business in 1997. GEICO turned in an underwriting profit of $281 million, up 64% from the previous year. The resulting 91.9% combined ratio reflected GEICO's low-cost operation and generally favorable conditions industrywide. Using the same two-pronged compensation arrangement focused on growth in policies-in-force and the profitability of seasoned business, 10,500 GEICO employees shared a $71 million bonus pool that amounted to almost 27% of base salaries.

For GEICO an underwriting gain of over 8%, while not unwelcome, was too high. Targeting a 4% gain (meaning a combined ratio of 96%), GEICO planned to cut its rates in the coming year. GEICO would do better over time passing the benefits of its low-cost operation back to customers to drive future growth. It planned to spend over $100 million on advertising in the coming year to capture some of the $115 billion market—huge potential to grow GEICO's 3% market share.

Insurance – Primary Group

Berkshire's other primary lines wrote to a 15% underwriting profit during 1997. Premiums earned increased 17% from the prior year and reflected the progress of the many smaller-but-excellent insurance subsidiaries in that group.

Manufacturing, Publishing, and Retailing

Berkshire's financial reports reflected its growth. Insurance (including investment income) made up 78% of pre-tax operating earnings (up from 65% in 1994) so it was natural that more information was added to each segment as time progressed. The businesses in the non-insurance segment, by contrast, increasingly made up a smaller portion of the growing conglomerate. Consequently, certain businesses were lumped together for reporting purposes, but that didn't make them any less valuable. Together these businesses earned 32.8% on average invested capital (up from 29.6%).

Both Kirby and World Book were combined into one line along with the Scott Fetzer Manufacturing Group. Together, Scott Fetzer made up just 7% of Berkshire's consolidated pre-tax operating earnings in 1997. The Scott Fetzer finance operation remained a separate line item. The newly reconstituted Scott Fetzer (excluding finance) reported a 2% decline in pre-tax earnings to $119 million.

Most of the other non-insurance operating businesses did better in 1997 than in 1996. An exception was the Shoe Group. Reflecting overall industry weakness, sales volume declined 12% at Dexter, which was struggling against a tough retail environment that included imports. The company planned a new marketing strategy using global advertising. Pre-tax earnings from the Shoe Group declined 21% to $49 million.

See's was the bright star that never seemed to dim. In 1997, the business grew revenues 8.2% to $269 million. Long struggling with declines in pounds sold, the year saw a 5.5% increase in poundage. The reason is unclear. Perhaps it was the legions of shareholders returning home with memories of their candy indulgences during the Annual Meeting who helped increase quantity and mail order volume at See's. In any event, See's was finding ways to increase its unit volumes while continuing to implement annual price increases.

It is interesting to compare FlightSafety, Berkshire's first admittedly capital-intensive acquisition, to See's (see Table 6.11). Looking solely at operating margins, one might conclude by the 7.5 percentage point difference that FlightSafety was the better business. Here the lesson of capital intensity comes into play. While FlightSafety generated a larger profit margin on revenues, its capital requirements were similarly large.* FlightSafety had nineteen times the assets of See's but generated only 50% more revenues. The greater operating margin at FlightSafety did not make up for the company's low level of revenues compared to its capital employed in the business. As a result, See's enjoyed a spectacular 65% return on assets compared to just 7% at FlightSafety.

---

* Using data from the table of identifiable assets in the Annual Report. We are ignoring goodwill for simplicity.

See's did not possess the ability to reinvest that FlightSafety enjoyed. This illustrated one of the many tradeoffs in business. See's generated excellent returns on capital but had no place to put the earnings except distributing them to Berkshire. FlightSafety, by contrast, could reinvest larger sums but at lower rates of return. Berkshire welcomed, and needed, both businesses.*

Table 6.11: Comparison of FlightSafety and See's Candies, select 1997 data

	FlightSafety	See's Candies
($ millions)		
Revenues	$411	$269
Identifiable assets	1,679	88
Operating margin	29%	21%
Revenues/assets	0.24	3.06
Return on assets	7%	65%

Sources: Berkshire Hathaway Annual Report 1997 and author's calculations.

Star Furniture and International Dairy Queen

Another year, another acquisition. In 1997 Berkshire agreed to acquire Star Furniture and Dairy Queen, though the latter closed in early 1998. Buffett recounted how Irv Blumkin of Nebraska Furniture Mart, and later Bill Child of RC Willey, had both identified Star as a well-run furniture store. When Melvyn Wolff and his sister, Shirley Toomin, decided to sell the family business, they reached out to Salomon Brothers who in turn introduced them to Buffett. Not long after, a deal was made to purchase the twelve-store, Texas-based furniture business. The price was not disclosed.**

International Dairy Queen was a bread-and-butter (burgers and fries, really) operation that fit well with the Berkshire family of businesses. When Berkshire Hathaway agreed to purchase the company in 1997 it had 5,792 Dairy Queen locations. It sold hamburgers, fries, and ice cream, among other similar offerings, and operated in twenty-three countries. The International Dairy Queen parent also operated 409 Orange Julius and forty-three Karmelkorn franchise locations that sold other treats. In addition, there were 190 treat centers, that combined some or all three of those brands. Most locations were franchised.

---

* A business like FlightSafety could reinvest its own profits, and if it needed more, Berkshire's conglomerate structure allowed profits from a business like See's with little reinvestment opportunities to be transferred easily and without tax consequences.

** While we cannot be certain there weren't other tuck-in acquisitions during the year, the notes to the financial statements disclose "common stock issued in connection with acquisition of business" of $73 million. This figure probably would not have been inappropriate for Star.

Dairy Queen had a troubled history. After some years of operation that saw a jumbled mess of varying franchise agreements and too much debt, a Minneapolis group purchased the business in 1970. In 1997, one of the two owners died and his estate sought to sell the business.

The International Dairy Queen deal was structured similar to the FlightSafety acquisition. A combination of cash and Berkshire stock was offered, with the cash portion slightly richer to entice sellers to choose that over stock.* Despite this nudge, only 45% of Dairy Queen shareholders chose cash. The total purchase price was $587.8 million, and the merger closed on January 7, 1998 (see Table 6.12). Like Berkshire's other acquisitions during this period, it paid a premium price for a company earning very good returns on capital.

Table 6.12: International Dairy Queen acquisition analysis

($ millions)	1996	1995	1994
Revenues	$412	$372	$341
Revenues/avg. capital	$2.39	$2.27	$2.31
Pre-tax margin	13%	14%	15%
Pre-tax return on capital	32%	32%	34%
Purchase price[1]	$588		
Assumed debt	4		
Effective purchase price[2]	$591		
Purchase multiple	3.44x		
BRK going-in pre-tax return	9.3%		

Footnote:
1. Cash on the balance sheet at year-end 1996 was $38 million, which would suggest excess cash. The effect on the economics of the transaction would have been very modest.
2. Total does not add due to rounding.

Sources: Berkshire Hathaway Annual Report 1997, 1998; International Dairy Queen Annual Report 1996; and author's calculations.

International Dairy Queen was a different economic model from McDonalds, a stock Berkshire previously owned and sold.** While both companies were (and are) franchisors, McDonalds owned and operated about one-third of its locations and owned the underlying real estate of most locations. By contrast, International Dairy Queen operated a few of its locations but was mostly a franchisor. That arrangement made for a relatively small investment in capital compared to McDonalds. International Dairy Queen treated its franchisees fairly with a franchise fee of 4% of revenues, which was at the low end of the spectrum for the industry.

---

* Those electing cash would receive $27 per share, where those electing stock were offered $26 per share.
** Buffett made it clear the sale of McDonalds stock wasn't connected to Berkshire's purchase of IDQ.

Under a section of his 1997 letter entitled, A Confession, Buffett wrote that the International Dairy Queen and FlightSafety-type acquisitions made with Berkshire shares had cost shareholders money. He was clear that such value-detracting moves were not due to the underlying companies, but instead because Berkshire's existing group of businesses were so great. He used a baseball analogy to demonstrate his point. Trading any player for a .350 hitter was a good idea in most cases. Except when it was at the expense of a .380 hitter.[*] His point was that Berkshire already had a star roster filled with wonderful businesses. Issuing Berkshire stock in any future acquisition meant trading away a small percentage of the ownership of these wonderful businesses. For this reason, Buffett wrote that "you can be sure Charlie and I will be very reluctant to issue shares in the future."

Even though it was flagged as a mistake, Buffett did not say Berkshire would stop issuing shares. Instead, Berkshire would offer splits such as that used in the International Dairy Queen acquisition that encouraged cash over stock. The stock-type deals would remain, but as an option in the cases where sellers desired stock as a currency.

Investments

While usually changing at the speed of molasses, the Berkshire investment portfolio was not immune to some fluctuations. The inevitables, a word Buffett coined in 1996 to describe those companies destined to do very well over time, were still there: Berkshire had 49 million shares of American Express, 200 million shares of Coke,[**] 1.7 million shares of *The Washington Post*, and 6.7 million shares of Well Fargo. In addition, Berkshire still held its 64 million shares of Freddie Mac and 48 million shares of Gillette.

All told, the $7.2 billion cost common stock portfolio had a market value of $36.2 billion at year-end 1997, with Coke making up almost 37% of it. The next largest was American Express at 12%. The listed securities (those with a market value over $750 million) totaled eight in name and represented almost 88% of the portfolio.

---

[*] For the non-sports types, batting averages are expressed as a three-decimal number. A 1.000 average would mean a perfect batter. A 0.400 was the more realistic ideal hit only rarely in baseball history. A 0.350 hitter was a very good hitter, while a 0.380 hitter could be described as great.

[**] Coke split its shares 2:1 in May 1996.

Table 6.13: Berkshire Hathaway common stock portfolio, select detail

($ millions, at market value)	1997	% total
American Express Company	$4,414	12%
The Coca-Cola Company	13,338	37%
The Walt Disney Company	2,135	6%
Federal Home Loan Mortgage Corp.	2,683	7%
The Gillette Company	4,821	13%
Travelers Group, Inc.	1,279	4%
Washington Post Company	841	2%
Wells Fargo & Company	2,271	6%
Others	4,467	12%
	$36,248	100%

Notes:

1. Figures may not add due to rounding.

2. The reporting threshold was $750 million.

Sources: Berkshire Hathaway Chairman's letter 1997 and author's calculations.

Included in the top eight was a new name: Travelers Group, Inc. Berkshire's 23.7 million shares of Travelers were as a result of the merger of Salomon with Travelers that netted Berkshire common and preferred stock. The architect of the Travelers deal was Sandy Weill, whom Buffett praised as a great manager with a proven record. Such comments provided an answer for why Berkshire continued with the investment.[*]

Responding to a question at the Annual Meeting about Coke, Buffett provided some remarkably candid insights into his and Munger's thinking on the investment. The question was whether and how to include the periodic gains reported by the company via its sales of bottlers. Buffett said he completely ignored such gains and instead focused on two variables. "The two important elements in [valuing] Coke are unit case sales and shares outstanding," he said. Looking forward a decade or two, if one thought (which presumably he did) that Coke would be selling "multiples of its present volume" and the number of outstanding shares were expected to go down (the company was a repurchaser of its own shares), it was "as far as you needed to go" in analysis. Of course, there was more to that conclusion, including the knowledge of the superiority of Coke's worldwide distribution system. At the end of the day, those two variables remained and told a compelling story. No wonder Coke made up over one-third of the portfolio.

---

[*] For those technically-minded readers, Berkshire's 1996 issue of exchangeable notes (a preferred issue convertible into shares of Salomon that Berkshire held) remained after the transaction. The ratio of shares exchangeable was revised to reflect the Salomon-to-Travelers share price. Additionally, Berkshire was required to book against unrealized investment gains a charge reflecting the excess of the value of Travelers stock over the accreted value of the Notes, since the Exchange Notes had more value in exchange owing to the appreciation of the underlying stock. At year-end 1997 this contingent value, the amount charged against unrealized appreciation, amounted to $342.6 million.

In addition to disposing of the McDonalds investment, Berkshire also trimmed its holdings in certain larger positions including Walt Disney (down 12% to 21.6 million shares), Freddie Mac (down 0.5% to 64 million shares), and Wells Fargo (down 8% to 6.7 million shares). In total, about 5% of the beginning value of the portfolio was sold and shifted into fixed maturity investments, including increased holdings in Treasuries and other government securities. One noteworthy category of bonds largely missing from the mix were corporates. At year-end 1997, the portfolio contained just a $35 million allocation, largely unchanged from 1996.

On the whole, Berkshire's 1997 investment portfolio was comprised of $10.3 billion of fixed maturity investments and $36.2 billion of equity securities. The resulting stock/bond split was 78/22. This compared to the 1996 portfolio with $6.4 billion in bonds and $27.8 billion in equities, a split of 81/19. Buffett thought the equity market was at such a level that little-to-no margin of safety existed at current prices. *If* interest rates remained where they were or fell, and *if* returns on equity remained high (as they were in late 1997 and early 1998) then markets would not be overvalued. Judging by Berkshire's actions, Buffett seemed to be leaning toward a judgement of overvaluation.

1998

"Normally, a gain of 48.3% would call for handsprings—but not this year," Buffett wrote to shareholders in his 1998 Chairman's letter. After several years of such talk (Berkshire delivered average annual gains in per-share book value of 39% over the prior four years compared to 31% for the S&P 500), shareholders might again dismiss this as Buffett being Buffett. But this year really was different. Berkshire did find sensible things to do during 1998, especially against a backdrop of an evermore expensive stock market, but the per-share gains in book value were not as good as they looked.

The gain in 1998 was mostly due to issuing shares to make business acquisitions. For someone who had written just a year earlier that it was a mistake to issue shares in prior acquisitions, 1998 was a veritable spending spree with shares. So why did Berkshire do it? Presumably, Buffett and Munger thought their simple test had been met: In these cases, Berkshire received as much in value as they gave by issuing new shares. During the year Berkshire acquired three new businesses: the International Dairy Queen merger at the beginning of January (discussed in the 1997 section), Executive Jet, and Berkshire's largest acquisition to date, General Reinsurance (sometimes referred to as General Re). Because these deals all involved issuing above-book-value shares of Berkshire, the transactions instantly increased per-share book value figures. What wasn't instantaneous was a change in per-share intrinsic value if equal intrinsic value was given as received.*

Berkshire's per-share intrinsic value did increase during the year, but it was well short of the gain in book value per share and therefore not a cause for celebration. Continuing to use the two-column method (see Table 6.14), Berkshire's intrinsic value increased an estimated 16%—far short of the change in book value. Two items in the 1998 analysis deserve extra attention. One is the fact just discussed that Berkshire's book value increased along with the issuance of shares. If we presume a 1:1 exchange of value, this had the effect of decreasing the proper price/book multiple necessary to arrive at Berkshire's intrinsic value.** This decline was probably less than the change shown in the table due to the second factor: General Re reported a loss in 1998 which depressed Berkshire's operating earnings. Had Berkshire not acquired General Re operating earnings would have increased slightly.***

Table 6.14: Berkshire Hathaway intrinsic value estimation

Per A-share	1998	1997
Investments	$47,647	$38,043
Pre-tax operating earnings (ex. investment income)	474	718
Estimated value (investments + 10x operating earnings)	$52,392	$45,221
Year-end share price	$70,000	$46,000
Year-end book value per share	37,801	25,488
Price/estimated value	1.34x	1.02x
Price/book	1.85x	1.80x
Value/book	1.39x	1.77x
Change in estimated value	16%	
Change in share price	52%	

Sources: Berkshire Hathaway Annual Reports 1997, 1998; and author's calculations.

---

* A simple example might illustrate the effect of such above-book-value issuances of shares. If I sold you a silver dollar containing $1.50 worth of silver metal for $1.50, I would show a 50% increase in book value (the $1.50 you gave me compared to the $1 face value of the coin). Yet, I would not have gained anything in value since the coin I originally possessed had the same $1.50 value. Berkshire's shares were the silver dollar in the preceding example and the transaction merely shed light on the underlying value exchange.

** Continuing the silver dollar example, the proper valuation for the $1 silver dollar worth $1.50 was 1.5:1. If it were exchanged for $1.50 then the valuation would clearly drop to 1:1 even though no actual diminution of intrinsic value would have occurred.

*** Assuming 1998 pre-tax operating earnings equal to those of 1997, the estimated value/book ratio would increase to 1.45x. With the addition of General Re at year-end 1998, Buffett told readers of his Chairman's letter that he had intentionally omitted the look-through earnings segment. "Neither a historical nor a pro-forma calculation of a 1998 number seems relevant."

General Reinsurance Corporation

Berkshire completed the $22 billion acquisition of General Re on December 21, 1998. Issuing 272,200 A-equivalent shares for the company, it was by far Berkshire's largest acquisition to date.

General Reinsurance was, as its name suggested, a reinsurance business. The name General Re was technically the parent company that conducted professional property and casualty reinsurance under the names of General Reinsurance Corporation and National Reinsurance Corporation, the largest such outfit in the United States. General Re also owned an 82% interest in Cologne Re, a major international reinsurer and the oldest in the world. Through Cologne Re, General Re also reinsured life and health insurers.[*]

Why was Berkshire interested in acquiring General Re? The answer required a word previously anathema to both Buffett and Munger: synergy.[**] The reasons were laid out in the press release announcing the acquisition:

1. Many investments: General Re would almost double Berkshire's investment portfolio with its $24 billion, or $80,000 per A-share (equivalent) issued.
2. Expansion of General Re's ability to write business: Earnings volatility would not factor into underwriting decision-making as was the case when it was a public company.
3. The ability to expand internationally.
4. Tax considerations: Berkshire's large base of taxable earnings outside of reinsurance would allow General Re to maximize the value of its investment portfolio.
5. Abundance of capital: Berkshire's large capital base would allow General Re to operate unconstrained and write any business that made sense.

The merger was summed up as follows: "These synergies will be coupled with General Re's pristine worldwide reputation, long-standing client relationships and powerful underwriting, risk management and distribution capabilities. This

---

[*] Here is a more robust description of General Re, taken from the 1998 Berkshire Hathaway Annual Report: "In addition, General Re writes excess and surplus lines insurance through General Star Management Company, provides alternative risk solutions through Genesis Underwriting Management Company, provides reinsurance brokerage services through Herbert Clough, Inc., manages aviation insurance risks through United States Aviation Underwriters, Inc., and acts as a business development consultant and reinsurance intermediary through Ardent Risk Services, Inc. General Re also operates as a dealer in the swap and derivatives market through General Re Financial Products Corporation, and provides specialized investment services to the insurance industry through General Re-New England Asset Management, Inc."

[**] Both men were skeptical of the reasons many managements gave for pursuing acquisitions. Acquisitions often relied on projected savings or other efficiencies that usually failed to materialize. In this case, there were real benefits that could be realized by combining the two companies.

combination virtually assures both Berkshire and General Re shareholders that they will have a better future than if the two companies operated separately."

General Re was like Berkshire's home-grown reinsurance business in that it was paid for absorbing the volatility of other insurers. It was unlike Berkshire's existing insurance business in that it was publicly held. Publicly held companies are praised for their smoothness, which goes against the nature of reinsurance. Under Berkshire's umbrella, General Re could take on more volatility (assuming it was properly priced) and live up to its potential. Hidden risks would soon come to light, but this potential was the basis of the acquisition.

Buffett also thought highly of General Re's management team. CEO Ron Ferguson was offered a position on Berkshire's board of directors, but he declined. Like Berkshire's other acquisitions, Ferguson would be left alone to run his business, although General Re's investment portfolio would now be under Buffett's direction. Cologne Re would remain as it was prior to the Berkshire acquisition, with its portfolio managed as before.

Some figures illuminate the size of General Re's operations. As evident in the $22 billion price tag its business was large (see Table 6.16). Compared to the Berkshire Hathaway Reinsurance Group, which wrote just under $1 billion in premium volume during 1998 and earned slightly less, General Re was huge. In 1998 General Re wrote and earned about $6.1 billion of premium volume across three main reporting lines. The largest, at about $2.7 billion or 44% of its premiums, was the North American property/casualty segment. International property/casualty followed at $2.1 billion or 35%, and the Life/Health division wrote and earned about $1.3 billion or 21% of General Re's volume.

General Re's $370 million underwriting loss in 1998 was the one apparent blemish. This translated into a combined ratio of 106.1%. The company's long-term track record of success told a better story. Over the prior fifty years, General Re stood out for its nearly breakeven combined ratio of 100.4%,[54] though this included the most recent five- and ten-year track record averaging 101%.

General Re brought with it approximately $14 billion of float. This tripled Berkshire's float in one year's time to $22.8 billion at year-end 1998. To acquire this float Berkshire paid a premium of 1.57x (the $22 billion price tag vs the $14 billion of float) for General Re. Float, as Buffett noted many times, could be very valuable, especially if it grew and/or came at a low or negative cost. But General Re's large float came with a near-breakeven cost and Buffett did not expect it to grow very much. There were the synergies laid out in the press release, but could these facts alone justify the purchase price? Paying up for a business like GEICO, with its profitable and rapidly growing float made sense, but why pay such a premium for what seemed to be average-quality float?

The answer might lie with the valuation of the Berkshire currency at the time—in other words, Berkshire's share price. The merger was completed late in 1998, but the price was established mid-year based on an average closing price over a 10-day period.* At the time, Berkshire was trading at over $80,000 per A-share. Even conservatively estimating Berkshire's intrinsic value using the year-end 1998 figures, which includes General Re (book value grew between mid-year and year-end), it appears the shares issued in the merger were overvalued by as much as 54%.** Adjusting for this overvaluation, we can conclude the price paid for General Re was not as rich as at first glance. This is consistent with Buffett's comments that as much intrinsic value was given as gained.

Table 6.15: General Re acquisition analysis, 1998

Acquisition price *($ millions)*	$22,000
Shares issued	272,200
Implied BRK.A share price	$80,823
BRK.A estimated intrinsic value 12/31/98[1]	$52,392
Implied price/intrinsic value per share	1.54x
General Re float *($ millions)*	$14,000
Adjusted acquisition price *($ millions)*[2]	$14,261
Price/float multiple[3]	1.02x

Footnotes:
1. Using the two-column method based on per-share investments of $47,647 and ten times per-share operating earnings of $474.45, which includes General Re. The valuation is almost identical to a multiple of 1.75x applied to Berkshire's pre-merger book value on June 30, 1998.
2. Adjusted for the implied price/intrinsic value multiple.
3. The multiple increases to 1.07x using the higher per share operating earnings from 1997.

Sources: Berkshire Hathaway Annual Report 1998 and author's calculations.

One last item is noteworthy with respect to General Re. The acquisition brought analyst attention to Berkshire because of General Re's institutional shareholder base.[55] One of those analysts was Alice Schroeder, who later wrote *The Snowball*, the only authorized biography of Buffett. Schroeder, then an analyst at PaineWebber, wrote a research report[56] on Berkshire that Buffett praised greatly. The analyst attention would also provide a benefit for Berkshire, or at least Buffett, in that they could field calls from institutions or others about Berkshire. Since Berkshire had no investor relations department and Buffett wanted a level playing field between all investors (i.e. no special meetings with him even for large shareholders), the few analysts that now covered Berkshire were a plus.

---

* According to the notes to Berkshire's financial statements.
** Using a price/book multiple of 1.75x (a multiple in-line with our previous estimates of value) applied to Berkshire's pre-merger June 30, 1998 book value results in approximately the same valuation used here.

Table 6.16: Berkshire Hathaway—Insurance Underwriting

($ millions)	1998	1997
GEICO Corporation		
Premiums written	$4,182	$3,588
Premiums earned	4,033	3,482
Underwriting gain/(loss) - pre-tax	$269	$281
General Re		
Premiums written	$6,084	
Premiums earned	6,095	
Underwriting gain/(loss) - pre-tax	($370)	
Berkshire Hathaway Reinsurance Group		
Premiums written	$986	$955
Premiums earned	939	967
Underwriting gain/(loss) - pre-tax	($21)	$128
Berkshire Hathaway Primary Group		
Premiums written		$309
Premiums earned	328	313
Underwriting gain/(loss) - pre-tax	$17	$53
Total underwriting gain/(loss)	$265	$462
Year-end average float - total	15,070	7,093
Cost of float	(1.8%)	(6.5%)
Aggregate adverse (favorable) loss development	($195)	($131)

Notes:

1. Totals and ratios do not include General Re as it was only owned for ten days in 1998.

2. Berkshire Hathaway Primary Group written premiums were not detailed beginning in 1998.

Sources: Berkshire Hathaway Annual Report 1998 and author's calculations.

Berkshire Hathaway Reinsurance Group

Berkshire's existing reinsurance operations swung to a $21 million loss on earned premiums of $939 million (down 3%). Super cat premiums declined 8% to $286 million but another year of low loss events left a $155 million profit. Losses from other property/casualty business totaled $86 million, and retroactive reinsurance and structured settlements recorded underwriting losses of $90 million.

GEICO

"GEICO, once again, simply shot the lights out." Those were Buffett's words of praise in his 1998 Chairman's letter. Even after reducing pricing on average 3.3% to lower its underwriting profit to its target level of 4%, favorable weather conditions and lower accident severity led GEICO to deliver big for Berkshire. Premiums written were up 16% over 1997 and GEICO's underwriting profit of $269 million (or 6.7% of premiums) remained too high. Additional price cuts would be necessary in 1999.

GEICO brought in 1.3 million new voluntary auto policies during the year, which took total policies-in-force to over 3.5 million. The growth in new policies, together with the outsized underwriting profit, produced great results for Berkshire and for GEICO's 9,313 associates. GEICO paid out a record $103 million, or almost one-third of base salaries in bonuses, to its employees. This was the highest on record for the company. Not slowing down one bit, GEICO planned to spend $190 million on advertising in the coming year to spur growth. The campaign was working: market share had risen from 3% to 3.5% in 1998.

Berkshire Hathaway Primary Group

Berkshire's other slate of insurance businesses continued slow yet below-the-radar success in 1998. The group earned $328 million in premiums and turned in a combined ratio of 94.8%. This myriad group that had formed Berkshire's foundation now accounted for just a fraction of its total volume given the General Re acquisition. As small as they were individually or even collectively, they were still an important contributor to Berkshire. This was especially true given their ability to generate negative cost float.

Since the General Re acquisition did not close until very late in 1998, its 1998 underwriting loss did not materially affect Berkshire's consolidated insurance results. In all, including the ten days of General Re's results, and largely due to GEICO, Berkshire's Insurance Group reported a pre-tax underwriting gain of $265 million—another year of cherished negative cost float.

Investments

The General Re merger moved Berkshire's investment portfolio even heavier into bonds, a direction Berkshire was purposely heading. Changes in 1997 took Berkshire's bond allocation from 19% of its $47 billion portfolio to 22%. General Re maintained a higher concentration of bonds, and Berkshire requested that it dispose of its 250-stock equity portfolio prior to the merger. Post-acquisition, Berkshire's investment portfolio grew to $61 billion, with a 35% allocation to bonds.

There were some important changes in the composition of the bond portfolio year-over-year. Most notable were higher exposures to foreign governments and a more meaningful investment in corporate bonds.

Table 6.17: Berkshire Hathaway fixed maturity portfolio

(At market value, in millions)	1998		1997	
US Treasuries, governments, agencies	$2,528	*12%*	$6,490	*63%*
States, municipalities and political subdivisions	9,647	*45%*	2,209	*21%*
Obligations of foreign governments	2,864	*13%*	0	*0%*
Corporate bonds	4,609	*22%*	35	*0%*
Redeemable preferred stocks	355	*2%*	1,280	*12%*
Mortgage-backed securities	1,243	*6%*	284	*3%*
Total	$21,246	*100%*	$10,298	*100%*

Note: Totals may not add due to rounding.
Sources: Berkshire Hathaway Annual Report 1998 and author's calculations.

There were also some meaningful changes to the equity portfolio during 1998. The elimination of McDonalds was discussed earlier, which in hindsight Buffett regretted selling. Buffett also reduced or eliminated smaller positions and added to American Express, buying an additional 1.08 million shares.

With stock markets reaching new heights in general,* and tech-fever raging, Buffett and Munger received several questions at the next Annual Meeting about investing in dot-coms. Why, some asked, if Buffett so admired companies such as Intel and Microsoft, hadn't Berkshire invested in technology? Buffett reiterated his philosophy: he and Charlie looked for businesses about which they could be fairly certain of their ten to fifteen-year prospects. Technology companies didn't pass through that filter.

Buffett said that in 1998, just 400 companies in the United States earned $200 million a year after tax. Yet there were many internet companies with no such earnings being valued on the same basis as some long-established (and profitable) enterprises. The math just didn't work out, he said. "In the end, they have to succeed as businesses."

This sound explanation did not stop other shareholders from prodding Buffett about his reluctance to change his ways. Fortunately for Berkshire shareholders, both he and Munger were comfortable owning basic boring businesses. Afterall, a dollar earned in a technology operation was worth the same as one from an old-fashioned business. Change may be exciting for speculators and good for the citizenry at large, but it was a threat to long-term investment returns.

Executive Jet

The newest non-insurance subsidiary joined Berkshire in August 1998. Executive Jet was the third company acquired with the issuance of shares in 1998 following

---

* Buffett noted at the 1999 Annual Meeting that the Fortune 500 was valued by the market at around $10 trillion yet earned just $334 billion. Doing the math this equated to an earnings yield of 3.34%. On the basis of a P/E ratio, this was a multiple of thirty times.

General Re and International Dairy Queen. The purchase price of $700 million required half to be paid with Berkshire shares. Unfortunately, we cannot readily determine the valuation Berkshire placed on Executive Jet because its results were not detailed separately.

Executive Jet was a simple business. The company sold fractional interests in various aircraft, which were then managed by the company for use by its multiple owners. These fractionally owned aircraft supplemented a fleet of company-owned aircraft that Executive Jet could have available on short notice. The company was founded by Rich Santulli, who Buffett credited with creating the fractional ownership industry in 1986.

Although both Executive Jet and FlightSafety were classified into the same Flight Services category, the businesses had important differences. Whereas FlightSafety was a capital-intensive business requiring significant upfront investment in simulators, Executive Jet was a capital-light operation. An aircraft's owners—whether a single-owner or multiple owners—put up the capital to buy the plane. Owners also paid Executive Jet a monthly management fee and a fee to cover hours flown.

Owing to the capital-light nature of the business, and its advantages over direct ownership of single planes, Buffett was enthusiastic about the business. He had started using the service prior to owning the company. After buying Executive Jet, he even sold The Indefensible, Berkshire's own corporate plane. The company had real growth prospects, and adding more owners and planes would drive costs down as dead head time (planes flying empty to pick up passengers) was reduced. In addition, more planes across the country meant shorter wait times for customers. Already the company accounted for 31% of all corporate jets ordered in the entire world. Executive jet was half of the Flight Services category (FlightSafety and Executive Jet). This category earned $181 million and represented 10% of Berkshire's 1998 pre-tax operating income.

Manufacturing, Service, and Retailing

If there was any question about the diminished relative importance of other businesses in this category, the word publishing was replaced by service in the segment header beginning in 1998. Flight Services was mostly in a league of its own among Berkshire's non-insurance businesses with its 10% of pre-tax operating earnings. (The only other non-insurance business to earn as much was the collective of Berkshire's Finance and Financial Products businesses.) Within the now Manufacturing, *Service*, and Retailing businesses only Scott Fetzer (excluding its finance operations) came close, at 7% of Berkshire's total. Scott Fetzer earned $137 million pre-tax, up 15% from the year before.* Its after-tax profits of $96.5 million was an astounding 86% return on its $112 million of net worth. Also worth mentioning, not for its size but its 22% increase in earnings, were the jewelry businesses, which earned $39 million. *The Buffalo News* had another tough year and earned $53 million, down 5%, and See's increased its earnings by 5% to $62 million.

Finance and Financial Products

The inclusion of General Re's finance subsidiary in Berkshire's Finance and Financial Products segment brought Berkshire's operations in this area back to the forefront, and with it a Wall Street-esque look to the balance sheet due to its complexity. Previously the balance sheet primarily comprised borrowed funds, annuity liabilities, and equity, which financed interest-bearing receivables and investments. It now included securities marked to market, trading securities, and repo securities,** among others. While some of this complexity would wind down over time, as it stood the segment had a portfolio containing huge notional amounts of securities.

The interest rate and currency swap agreements were largest, at over half a trillion dollars ($514,935 *million*) of notional value. The balance sheet had $88 billion of options written and $90 billion of options purchased, in addition to significant futures and forwards contracts. While all of this netted against each other to a more modest $6.2 billion of trading account assets/liabilities, it posed significant hidden risk for General Re and for Berkshire.

Accounting Lessons

Buffett took no less than three pages in the 1998 Chairman's letter to rail against the accounting abuses committed by corporate America. Using General Re as an example, he wrote that the acquisition "put a spotlight on an egregious flaw in accounting." Namely, that Berkshire would replace General Re's option plan with an economically equivalent cash plan. Since options had not been counted in the income statement, Buffett told readers that the proxy statement describing the merger contained a $63 million adjustment to correct for this fact.

Buffett said that he and Munger made similar revisions to the earnings of the public companies they followed. It wasn't uncommon for the adjustments to reach

---

* Only three of Scott Fetzer's many businesses were mentioned in relation to its results, Kirby, Campbell Hausfeld, and World Book. Campbell Hausfeld manufactured air compressors and other related items. Its growth began to overshadow World Book, which continued to struggle with revenues but did generate improved international results according to the footnotes.

** Usually overnight loans secured by government securities.

a very meaningful 5% or 10% of earnings. In some cases, such adjustments were the difference between purchasing a stock or passing on a purchase.*

Restructuring charges were another sore spot. Companies would lump in all sorts of adjustments into one quarter, which would then be explained away and ignored by analysts. Even more egregious, such maneuvers sowed the seeds for future so-called earnings when charges were reversed. Such accounting machinations were the result of a hyper-competitive environment with CEOs eager to please Wall Street and auditors that blessed such arrangements. Not surprisingly, both Buffett and Munger thought such practices despicable.

Buffett lauded SEC Chairman Arthur Levitt for going after such abuses and urged shareholders to read a recent speech on the subject.[57] As for Berkshire, Buffett would tell it as it is. Regular readers of his shareholder letters would know that Buffett was telling the truth. If anything, Buffett took too many pains to point out his and Berkshire's shortcomings. Perhaps Berkshire was the better for it.

1999

The underperformance that Buffett had long predicted finally came true in 1999. Berkshire's gain in book value per share (Buffett's preferred, if only rough proxy) increased just 0.5% compared to an increase of 21% for the S&P 500. Buffett told shareholders the 20.5% underperformance was the worst of his career and that he deserved a D for capital allocation. Still, Berkshire did have some bright spots during the year, including the completion of an acquisition and the arrangement of two more.

The poor performance stemmed from a couple of different spots. The first was a lackluster performance by the marketable securities portfolio. Poor operating performance at the underlying companies caused their stock prices to decline, in turn impacting Berkshire's book value.** The price declines were also likely exacerbated by the internet fever still gripping the country. The Nasdaq Composite rose fivefold between 1995 and 2000, but only for companies investing in technology stock. Berkshire had made no such investments. Additionally, mistakes at General Re, Berkshire's new reinsurance subsidiary, led to a large underwriting loss that caused a corresponding pre-tax operating loss (excluding investment income).

---

* Accounting now appropriately includes stock options as an expense on the income statement, although it is imperfect.
** Unrealized gains and losses, remember, flowed through book value as a component of equity, after recognizing the effect of taxes on the gain/loss.

Insurance

Berkshire reported its first loss from insurance underwriting since 1992. General Re contributed most of the $1.4 billion pre-tax loss, but weakness in other areas played a part. Berkshire's 5.8% cost of float approximated long-term US government bond rates at the time.

Table 6.18: Berkshire Hathaway—Insurance Underwriting

($ millions)	1999	1998
GEICO Corporation		
Premiums written	$4,953	$4,182
Premiums earned	4,757	4,033
Underwriting gain/(loss) - pre-tax	$24	$269
General Re		
Premiums written	$7,043	$6,084
Premiums earned	6,905	6,095
Underwriting gain/(loss) - pre-tax	($1,184)	($370)
Berkshire Hathaway Reinsurance Group		
Premiums written	$2,410	$986
Premiums earned	2,382	939
Underwriting gain/(loss) - pre-tax	($256)	($21)
Berkshire Hathaway Primary Group		
Premiums earned	$262	$328
Underwriting gain/(loss) - pre-tax	$22	$17
Total underwriting gain/(loss)	($1,394)	$265
Year-end average float - total	24,026	15,070
Cost of float	5.8%	(1.8%)
Aggregate adverse (favorable) loss development	($192)	($195)

Notes:
1. Totals and ratios for 1998 do not include General Re as it was only owned for ten days.
2. Berkshire Hathaway Primary Group written premiums were not detailed.
Sources: Berkshire Hathaway Annual Report 1998–1999 and author's calculations.

General Re

During 1999, mistakes of the past finally caught up with General Re. The reinsurer had significantly underpriced its business in both domestic and international markets. Buffett hinted that the culprit might have been the compensation structure at General Re and its major subsidiary, Cologne Re. Those structures were changed. At both companies "incentive compensation plans are now directly tied to the variables of float growth and cost of float, the same variables that determine value for owners." Yet even with perfect hindsight Buffett said he'd make the same deal to acquire General Re.

Just how bad were the 1999 results at General Re? On earned premiums of $6.9 billion General Re recorded an underwriting loss of $1.2 billion—a combined ratio of 117.1%. General Re's results fell into three main components:

- North American property/casualty: A pre-tax underwriting loss of $584 million on $2.8 billion of earned premiums (combined ratio of 120.6%). *Reason for the loss*: inadequate premium rates, higher losses, and unfavorable loss development.
- International property/casualty: A pre-tax loss of $473 million on $2.3 billion of earned premiums (combined ratio of 120.2%). *Reason for the loss*: losses on a motion picture insurance contract, catastrophe losses resulting from European winter storms, earthquakes in Taiwan and Turkey, and a hailstorm in Australia.
- Global life/health: A pre-tax underwriting loss of $127 million on earned premiums of $1.7 billion (a combined ratio of 107.4%).

While the Global life/health line at General Re was the relative bright spot during 1999 in terms of financial results, it bore the stain of a past mistake. Its 1998 underwriting loss* was largely the result of the "Unicover affair." According to an industry article written in 2014 by future CEO Tad Montross,[58] participants in Unicover (a pool of life insurers) "sold dollar bills for 50 cents" via their hugely underpriced reinsurance of the policies. At the Annual Meeting, Buffett praised General Re for being one of the first to record the expected future loss, whereas some others had punted the loss recognition into future years. In a rare lapse, General Re had strayed from its circle of competence and was hurt, but Buffett thought it learned its lesson.

Berkshire Hathaway Reinsurance Group

Berkshire's home-grown reinsurance operation, created and run by Ajit Jain, also posted an underwriting loss during 1999. Here things were a little different as the loss largely reflected the expectations of volatility of results over time in reinsurance. The group continued to write large covers, and in 1999 it wrote $2.4 billion of premiums (and earned just about the same), including $1.25 billion from a single contract. The group's overall underwriting loss of $256 million pre-tax included a $220 million loss from a single aggregate excess contract (a type of reinsurance contract that produces

---

* $290 million on $1.3 billion of premiums.

a lot of float, but with one large upfront loss) during the fourth quarter of the year. Other non-catastrophe losses totaled $135 million and retroactive reinsurance reported a loss of $97 million. With a profit of $196 million, the super cat business reported yet another year of gains.

Berkshire Hathaway Primary Group

The direct or primary lines continued their understated success. Though premium volume slipped 20% to $262 million, the group wrote to an underwriting profit of $22 million, up 29%. In his letter to shareholders, Buffett praised Ron Eldred, Brad Kinstler, John Kizer, Don Towle, and Don Wurster for collectively earning $192 million in pre-tax underwriting profit over the preceding five years.

GEICO

GEICO was still Berkshire's shining star, even if not as bright as the prior two years. Those years saw outsized profitability industrywide driven by lower accident rates and few-to-no catastrophe losses. Accordingly, GEICO's combined ratios of 91.9% and 93.3% in 1997 and 1998, respectively, were too low. In 1999, it returned to earth at 99.5%.

Part of the reason for the return to a normal combined ratio was the effects of higher claims and reduced pricing on the loss ratio. The other part of the equation was GEICO's discretionary spending on advertising for customer acquisition. GEICO might only need to spend $50 million to maintain its policy count, but it instead spent $242 million to grow its business in 1999 and expected to spend up to $350 million in 2000. Buffett said CEO Tony Nicely's "foot is going to stay on the advertising pedal (and my foot will be on his)." Buffett was willing to commit $1 billion a year to advertising if it would result in new business at an attractive cost. They didn't, in part because media rates were up, and each additional dollar of advertising had a diminishing return.

GEICO added 1.65 million new voluntary auto policies in 1999, bringing the in-force count to over 4.3 million. Its premium volume grew accordingly and so did its float, up 10% from 1998 to $3.4 billion.

It was around this time that GEICO introduced the gecko, as GEICO was often mispronounced gecko. The tiny, green, happy creature told people: "My job is to save people money. I love my job." His job was also to attract new customers, which made GEICO a lot of money. A closer look at GEICO's 1999 underwriting gain shows this. Included in underwriting expenses are all costs associated with running the business (including advertising); excluded is losses and loss expenses. At 19.3% of premiums earned, underwriting expenses were about the same as the year before—but they would have been another four points lower without such heavy advertising.

At other auto insurers, and especially publicly traded ones, growth spending might be held back to report higher profits. GEICO, Berkshire, and Buffett were squarely focused on the future. This meant trading current reported profits for a chance to capture a greater slice of the overall market (GEICO's share was 4.1%)—a cycle that would repeat successfully in the future.

Jordan's Furniture

Jordan's Furniture found a new home at Berkshire Hathaway on November 13, 1999, in an all-cash transaction. Berkshire now owned what Buffett considered the four best furniture retailers in the country. The other three: Nebraska Furniture Mart, RC Willey in Utah, and Star Furniture in Texas, had all told Buffett about Jordan's. Buffett hinted about this in previous Annual Reports without naming Jordan's. Now he could talk about it freely.

Buffett said Jordan's had the highest sales per square foot in the country and was the largest furniture retailer in Massachusetts and New Hampshire. Jordan's was operated by Barry and Eliot Tatelman. Their grandfather started the family business in 1927. Jordan's grew by turning shopping into an entertainment experience with soda, cookies, ice cream, and even an IMAX movie theater on site at some locations to augment the shopping experience. In later years, they would again lead the way by adding indoor ropes courses, therefore attracting families for every reason but furniture shopping.

Upon selling the family business to Berkshire, the Tatelmans provided bonuses to long-time employees. They used $9 million of the sale proceeds to give each employee 50 cents for each hour they had been with the company.

Each of Berkshire's furniture stores was the dominant furniture retailer in its geographic market. Together they were a furniture retailing powerhouse with revenues nearing $1 billion annually. Including Jordan's from the time it joined Berkshire in late 1999, Berkshire's furniture group reported $917 million in revenues for the year and $79 million of pre-tax operating profit. Neither the purchase price nor Jordan's earnings were publicly disclosed.

Manufacturing, Service, and Retailing

Viewed as one business, the Manufacturing, Service, and Retailing businesses earned $444 million pre-tax in 1999, which represented a return on capital of 26.7% (down 4.4 points). After-tax and with modest leverage it translated into a respectable 21.5% return on average equity. Most businesses performed well in 1999, but others struggled.

The Shoe Group again reported a decline in pre-tax operating profit, down 52% to $17 million. Dexter was to blame. Its US-produced product was badly impacted by imports. Over 90% of shoes came from outside of the US, where they had the advantage of low-cost labor. To compete, Dexter was making more shoes overseas.

See's Candies again found success in its wholesale and mail-order program, bringing total poundage up 7.2% over the prior year. Sales topped $306 million (up 6%) and a strong operating margin of 24% (up 2.5 percentage points) led to a 19% gain in pre-tax earnings to $74 million.

As profitable as See's was, the business faced few growth prospects. Speaking at the Annual Meeting the following year, Buffett noted how See's, and candy in general, really wasn't that portable. See's found ways to increase its physical volume slightly, but there weren't huge opportunities for growth like other businesses. For some reason candy didn't travel well. Soda and shaving blades did, but See's couldn't just open a store in a faraway state and expect to have the same results. It was tried more than once.

Berkshire's jewelry operations increased pre-tax earnings by 31% to $51 million as costs at Helzberg were brought under control. Scott Fetzer's earnings increased 7% to $147 million.

The Aviation Services segment, comprised of FlightSafety and Executive Jet, collectively earned $225 million in 1999, up 24% from the year before. Part of the increase in earnings was because Executive Jet was acquired in August 1998, so it wasn't a true comparison. The other factor was the ability of the businesses, particularly FlightSafety, to invest in profitable growth.

FlightSafety was a capital-intensive business but had a high operating margin that translated into satisfactory returns on capital. (Its pre-tax return on capital was consistently in the mid-20% range prior to Berkshire acquiring it.) Each flight simulator required up to a $15 million capital investment and could only be used by one person at a time. Together FlightSafety and Executive Jet spent $323 million on capital expenditures in 1999, compared to depreciation of just $77 million. The sky was the limit for these two Berkshire subsidiaries.

Investments

Berkshire's equity portfolio returned low single digits* against the backdrop of the S&P 500 marching forward 21% during the year. Another way to view this performance is via look-through earnings. We can make an approximation based

---

* At year-end 1998, Berkshire had an equity portfolio of $39.8 billion, representing a cost of $10.9 billion and unrealized gains totaling $28.9 billion. At year-end 1999, the portfolio shrunk slightly to $39.5 billion with an unrealized gain of $28.2 billion. But, during the year it also increased its investment to $11.3 billion and realized net gains of $1.4 billion. The net result was a gain of $749 million. Translated into a percentage, this represented a change of just 1.9%.

on the $476 million in dividends reported by the Insurance Group. This probably represented the bulk of dividends Berkshire earned as most of its marketable securities were held in the insurance subsidiaries. On top of that, Berkshire's major investees had look-through earnings of $707 million. Together this amounted to $1.2 billion or 3% of the average portfolio value.

Berkshire's bond portfolio also contributed to the lackluster performance of its investment portfolio. At year-end 1999, unrealized losses on the $30 billion bond portfolio had grown by $1.1 billion. A sharp rise in interest rates was the culprit (the 10-year Treasury increased from 4.7% to 6.5% from December 1998 to December 1999).

Fortune Magazine Article

Included with the 1999 Annual Report was an article Buffett penned for *Fortune* magazine in November 1999.[59] In it, he laid out his case for why the market was setting itself up for disappointment. While not predicting an immediate decline, Buffett hinted toward the market being overvalued. He cited a survey of investors at that time who expected annualized returns of over 22% percent for lower-experienced investors, and as high as almost 13% for more experienced ones who had more insight into markets. He said both were probably too optimistic.

To make his point, Buffett used what he always did: logic. Looking at the Fortune 500 overall, the companies earned $334 billion in 1998. The market value of those same 500 companies as of early 1999 was about $10 trillion. This meant that if one hypothetically owned the entirety of those companies they would be earning a return of something like 3.3%, pre-tax. And this wasn't counting the frictional costs of moving in-and-out of stocks as investors did, which Buffett estimated to be about $100 billion a year.

In early 1999, the 10-year US Treasury Note yielded between 1 and 2 percentage points higher than that 3.3%. Why would investors rationally own a group of risky companies when they could buy a risk-free government security? Likely because investors thought stocks would keep going up, as they had in the past. A more rationally sounding (though not entirely rational) argument was the belief that either interest rates would decline, or corporate profits would increase. Only under those two circumstances would the stock valuations in 1999 make sense.

Buffett believed many company valuations were out of touch with reality.* He discussed valuations at the 2000 Annual Meeting, travelling back in time to make his point. "The first investment primer that I know of, and it was pretty good advice, was delivered in about 600 B.C. by Aesop. And Aesop, you'll remember, said, 'A bird in

---

* Buffett used corporate profits as a percentage of GDP as a key data point. In 1999 they were around 6% compared to the historical range of 4% to 6.5%. Buffett thought a 6% return over the coming decade was the most investors could expect; and that was including an expected 2% inflation rate.

the hand is worth two in the bush.'" He meant that investing involves deciding based on the projected value of a business in the future. Value in this case is calculated by estimating how many birds (how much cash) are in the bush. The value of that cash is further based on when it emerges and the interest rate at that time.

Some companies were valued by the market as high as $500 billion yet produced very little actual earnings. If such a company wasn't going to pay an owner $50 billion that year (assuming a 10% required rate of return) then it had to pay out that much more the next year. Assuming no payment in year one, a $55 billion payout, in perpetuity, was required starting the following year. Wait another year and that annual payout rose to $60.5 billion, and so on to justify the 10% rate of return. Recalling Aesop again, Buffett said that every year one waited to take out a bird (cash), that many more birds (cash) were required in the future. And how certain are you there are that many birds available to take?

This short lesson was important because it explained the rationale behind preferring companies earning cash today since the longer one waited it became that much more important to grow the future stream of cash. It also highlighted the importance of certainty. If you weren't going to get cash immediately, how much worse was it that the future cash flows were uncertain because of the risks to changing business economics? Lastly, the preceding example using a hypothetical $500 billion market cap company would have been the rare elephant, given the requirement to earn something like $80 billion a year pre-tax to get that $50 billion after tax. Since such companies didn't then exist (and even now in 2020 are rare), valuations were clearly incorporating some unrealistic expectations.

As painful as 1999 was from a business perspective (with book value up just half a percentage point), Berkshire Hathaway's stock price also took a big hit. Shares traded between a low of $52,000 and a high of $81,100. Considering Berkshire ended the year with $47,000 of per-share investments, the market was almost entirely discounting Berkshire's significant operating businesses. Even though operating earnings fell, Berkshire remained a wonderful, growing collection of businesses. Its long-term growth in per share book value over the preceding thirty-five years that Buffett had been in control remained at an astounding 24% compounded annually.

Year 2000 Issue

The big worry as the calendar turned to the new millennium was the so-called year 2000 issue, or Y2K. The problem lay with computers and their ability to handle the turn of the millennium with respect to dates. No one knew if, for example, January 1, 2000, would register as January 1, 1900. Such a mistake could cause havoc with systems as some calculations would be a hundred years off, spelling disaster for timing and payment systems, for one.

Berkshire incurred roughly $60 million in costs (not all in 1999) getting ready for the date change. Even though everyone knew the year was coming, some, including governments, were far behind in their preparations and testing. In the end, it was all hype.

Berkshire entered the new century and the new millennium with old-world businesses in hand—and a readiness to acquire more.

2000

At the turn of the millennium Berkshire's two capital allocators faced unrelenting pressure to change their ways.* With internet mania fueling the dot-com boom, Berkshire was decidedly old world and proud of it. Experienced managers Warren Buffett and Charlie Munger, now both in their seventies, stayed within their circle of competence. They, and Berkshire's shareholders, were rewarded for this patience. The year 2000 brought some exciting acquisitions along with some spots of trouble.

Checkbook in hand, Berkshire went on a spending spree. It paid close to $8 billion for eight acquisitions, completing two agreed to in 1999 (MidAmerican and CORT, discussed below) and arranging another six. To make things better, almost 97% of the amount spent was in cash and Berkshire incurred no debt in the process. Despite this frenzy of acquisition activity, Berkshire remained flush with investable funds, and ready for more (and larger) acquisitions.

Finding eight new operating subsidiaries to acquire in just over a year was most assuredly cause for a change in Buffett's self-graded D from 1999—though not the A a star pupil would flaunt to parents. Buffett characterized 2000 as only decent due to some struggles in its existing businesses. GEICO had the rare off year, weaknesses remained at General Re, and Dexter struggled mightily against foreign competition. To make matters worse, Buffett thought Berkshire's equities portfolio was fully priced, meaning its value would likely not rise beyond underlying gains in intrinsic business value.

Acquisitions

"Our acquisition technique at Berkshire is simplicity itself: We answer the phone," Buffett wrote to shareholders. He wasn't kidding. Buffett and Munger had long talked about their strategy of not having a strategy, and the year 2000 was proof it

---

* Buffett and Munger faced continued pressure externally and internally to adapt to the times. Shareholders at prior Annual Meetings had asked why, if they were so smart, couldn't Buffett and Munger figure out internet companies and pick winners. The calls from shareholders were likely amplified by the fact that Berkshire's stock price also took a hit, falling about 50% from a high of about $81,000 in March 1999 to a low of $41,000 by March 2000.

was working. Like business results in general, acquisitions were necessarily lumpy and could not be anticipated or rushed along.

Did Berkshire's capital allocators cave and purchase some fallen internet companies? Quite the opposite. Buffett reported that Berkshire had "embraced the 21st century by entering such cutting-edge industries as brick, carpet, insulation and paint. Try to control your excitement." Though these businesses were the very antithesis of internet companies, the dot-com boom and subsequent bust did play a role in Berkshire acquiring them. Two factors led to this flurry of acquisition activity.

One was the prospect of a near-term economic slowdown. Other people were reluctant to commit in the face of uncertainty. Berkshire was buying to keep and had its eye on the horizon. The second factor was that Berkshire paid with cash and analyzed businesses on an all-equity basis. Other purchasers relied on financing from the junk bond market, which had dried up.

1. MidAmerican Energy

Acquisition Date: March 14, 2000
Description: Provider of electric service in the Midwest US and the
United Kingdom
Purchase Price: $1.24 billion for 76% of the company

MidAmerican was more than an energy business; it was a conglomeration of numerous energy subsidiaries. Like its new conglomerate parent, MidAmerican had a long history and decentralized operations.

MidAmerican's lineage is too long to discuss here, but its history just prior to joining Berkshire is worth mentioning. MidAmerican Energy Holdings Company was the result of the 1998 acquisition of a company of the same name by CalEnergy, an Omaha-based utility company. The new company was renamed MidAmerican Energy Holdings Company and reincorporated in Iowa. MidAmerican's Chairman and CEO David Sokol, and his right-hand man, President Gregory Abel, along with investor and board member, Walter Scott, Jr., used this base to acquire other energy assets.

The MidAmerican deal came about via Walter Scott, Jr., who also sat on Berkshire's board of directors. MidAmerican's talented and entrepreneurial management team impressed Buffett, and he thought investing in MidAmerican might make sense at the right price. Buffett was cited in a press release saying, "We buy good companies with outstanding management and good growth potential at a fair price, and we're willing to wait longer than some investors for that potential to be realized. This investment is right in our sweet spot."[60]

Buffett did not detail his exact thought process in determining the attractiveness of the MidAmerican investment, but there are a few factors that likely weighed into his decision:

- *History as a low-cost operator*: In addition to achieving the highest returns available under regulatory frameworks, the low-cost operator could protect and reinforce its competitive position by keeping rates low for its customers. This in turn could gain favor from regulators, allowing additional investment.
- *Deregulation*: This opened certain markets to allow customers to buy energy from the producer of their choice.* A low-cost operator would have additional opportunities for expansion, aided by its ability to improve the assets it acquired.
- *A strong balance sheet*: MidAmerican's investment-grade credit rating allowed it to lower its cost of debt and thereby improve its ability to keep costs low for customers. It was a virtuous cycle.

Even with the prospect of wider deregulation, MidAmerican remained an operator in regulated markets, most notably in the Midwest United States. During 1999, 66% of MidAmerican's revenues were generated in regulated electric markets, 25% from regulated gas, and 9% from nonregulated businesses.[61] Energy companies within the regulated markets enjoyed protected returns on capital that were typically in the low double-digit area. For example, MidAmerican's Iowa operations were allowed a 12% return on equity.**[62]

The downside of a regulated return was offset by the ability to invest large sums of capital. MidAmerican offered Berkshire Hathaway a place to direct the substantial excess earnings from its other businesses into long-term projects with a near-certain rate of return. At a time when Berkshire was finding little else to do with a growing amount of cash, MidAmerican was a fitting solution.

One final attribute of MidAmerican relates to taxes. Here Berkshire could benefit in two ways. One was via a consolidated tax return. Berkshire's vast collection of highly profitable operating businesses generated a significant tax bill that could potentially be offset by MidAmerican's tax position, which sometimes included tax credits. A standalone energy business might not have the ability to use favorable tax positions immediately if its taxable income was not high enough.

---

* It's important to understand that deregulation was not a uniform definition and was different across markets and energy types (electric vs. gas, etc.). It could also be full or partial. Broadly speaking, it was the energy production market that was deregulated with distribution remaining more tightly controlled.

** An added feature was the ability to earn a higher return so long as part was shared with customers. For example, if MidAmerican earned a return between 12% and 14%, half of those earnings were required to be returned to customers.

The second tax-related attribute of MidAmerican was deferred taxes. MidAmerican had substantial investments in fixed assets. The acceleration of depreciation allowed for tax purposes resulted in the company paying less tax than the income statement indicated. MidAmerican's ability to defer taxes was like the interest-free loan Berkshire created via its holdings of appreciated securities. It allowed the company to have a higher effective compounding rate on its equity capital than even the regulated rate of return would suggest. (It should be noted that regulators would take these tax advantages into account, which allowed the tax advantage to be passed along to customers. MidAmerican's unregulated businesses would benefit from it, however.)

A regulatory restriction barring simultaneous control of regulated and non-regulated entities,* required a unique ownership structure for the MidAmerican deal. Berkshire paid $1.24 billion for common stock and non-dividend paying convertible preferred stock, giving it a 76% economic interest in MidAmerican (see Table 6.19). Its voting interest, however, was just 9.7%. Additionally, Berkshire invested $455 million in an 11% fixed-income security and committed to invest another $345 million under the same arrangement. Because of this arrangement, Berkshire reported MidAmerican's results on one line on its income statement and balance sheet. Instead of reporting all its sales, expenses, and other costs, MidAmerican was carried on the balance sheet in the amount of Berkshire's investment and on the income statement as Berkshire's share of its net income.**

What were Buffett's financial expectations surrounding the MidAmerican acquisition? We cannot know for sure, though the regulated return limits and the 11% fixed income security provide some clues. Using financial information for 1999, the last year before Berkshire purchased its ownership interest in the company, MidAmerican's pre-tax return on capital was 11%.*** Was this a coincidence? Perhaps.

The analysis was probably much simpler. MidAmerican provided Berkshire a platform to invest large sums at low double-digit returns. An added bonus was the tax benefit from joining Berkshire's conglomerate holding structure. Considering its position as a low-cost operator and its monopolistic position in certain markets, the company had a strong likelihood of earning similar returns far into the future. In other words, MidAmerican was protected by a moat.

---

* The Public Utility Holding Company Act of 1935.
** Readers will remember a similar accounting treatment existed for Berkshire's first insurance investments, Blue Chip Stamps, and The Illinois National Bank.
*** The pre-tax return on capital for 1998 was 10%.

Table 6.19: MidAmerican Energy—acquisition analysis

($ millions)	1999	1998	1997
Revenues	$4,411	$2,683	$2,271
Earnings before interest and taxes	783	619	448
Interest expense	426	347	251
Earnings before taxes	357	272	197
Total shareholders' equity	$995	$827	$765
Long-term debt, preferred, minority interests	6,226	6,037	4,892
Total capital	7,221	6,864	5,657
BRK equity acquisition price (100% basis)[1]	$1,632		
BRK implied total purchase price[2]	7,858		
Pre-tax return on average total capital	11.1%		
BRK going-in purchase multiple[3]	1.09x		
BRK going-in pre-tax return on capital	10.2%		

Footnotes:
1. Berkshire paid $1.24 billion for 76% of MidAmerican.
2. This figure takes the existing debt and adds to it the price paid for the equity (100% basis).
3. BRK implied total purchase price / total capital.

Sources: MidAmerican Energy Holdings 10K reports, 1998, 1999; Berkshire Hathaway Annual Report 2000; and author's calculations.

2. CORT Business Services

Acquisition Date: February 18, 2000
Description: Renting furniture to businesses and apartment owners via its 117 showrooms
Purchase Price: $386 million

The CORT Business Services acquisition began in 1999 but closed in 2000 (see Table 6.20). The opportunity materialized after an unfriendly takeover by one of its competitors failed to go through.[63] Buffett liked the "fine though unglamorous business," its CEO Paul Arnold, and the price (established via the failed deal amount).

Berkshire purchased CORT via Wesco, its 80%-owned subsidiary. Wesco's Chairman, remember, was Charlie Munger. Munger summed up the deal succinctly in his 2000 letter to Wesco shareholders: "Thus, in essence, Wesco paid $386 million for $54.3 million in pre-tax operating earnings." Berkshire paid a premium over the company's underlying capital, but its going-in return was satisfactory at 11%. Additionally, it had the prospect of earning good returns on incremental capital going forward if CORT could continue to grow. In short, it appears Wesco and Berkshire acquired a good company for a fair price.

Table 6.20: CORT Business Services—acquisition analysis

($ millions)	1998	1997	1996
Revenues	$319	$287	$234
Revenues/avg. capital[1]	$1.81	$1.89	$1.87
EBIT margin[1]	17%	17%	16%
Pre-tax return on capital	31%	31%	29%
Purchase price (equity)	$386		
Assumed debt	91		
Effective purchase price	$477		
Purchase multiple	2.71x		
BRK going-in pre-tax return	11.4%		
Footnote: 1. Adjustments were made to account for acquired goodwill and its related amortization.			

Sources: Berkshire Hathaway Annual Report 2000; Wesco Annual Report 2000; CORT Annual Reports 1996–1998; and author's calculations.

3. U.S. Liability

Acquisition Date: August 8, 2000
Description: Insurance
Purchase Price: Undisclosed (half cash, half stock)

Augmenting Berkshire's already-large slate of insurance businesses, US Investment Corporation (USIC) was the parent company of U.S. Liability, "a medium-sized, highly-respected writer of unusual risks," wrote Buffett. USIC also came with two smaller sister companies, Mount Vernon Fire, and U.S. Underwriters Insurance Company.[64] The deal came about via General Re CEO Ron Ferguson, who introduced Buffett to USIC CEO Bob Berry. Berry's family had owned U.S. Liability for forty-nine years, though the company was now run by Tom Nerney, a manager Buffett praised for having "achieved a rare combination of excellent growth and unusual profitability."

4. Ben Bridge Jeweler

Acquisition Date: July 3, 2000
Description: A sixty-five-store chain of upscale jewelry stores in shopping malls in the West
Purchase Price: Undisclosed (half cash, half stock)

The Ben Bridge acquisition had many similarities to other successful Berkshire acquisitions, including expanding a business Berkshire was already in (in this case jewelry), being introduced to Berkshire by the home-grown recruitment system (this time Barnett Helzberg) and managers who Buffett admired and trusted to run the business without interference (cousins Ed and Jon Bridge).

Buffett liked the 89-year-old company's truly remarkable record of same-store sales growth over the preceding seven years.* Like Helzberg, Ben Bridge operated out of multiple locations, versus the one-store operation of fellow Berkshire jewelry retailer, Borsheims. Similar to the Tatelman brothers of Jordan's Furniture, the Bridges gave some of their sale proceeds to employees.

5. Justin Industries

Acquisition Date: August 1, 2000
Description: Maker of western boots and bricks for construction
Purchase Price: $570 million

Justin was a somewhat unusual company with its two unrelated business lines, but it was right at home within Berkshire. H.J. Justin started the business in 1879 doing boot repairs. His sons expanded the business to twenty-six states, Canada, Mexico, and Cuba, until 1948, when John Justin, Jr. purchased the business from his father and uncles. In 1968, Justin Industries was formed to hold the boot business and a new, unrelated sister company, Acme Brick. Justin later added Nocona Boot, Chippewa Shoe Company, and Tony Lama Boots.

John Justin, Jr. unfortunately passed away in February 2001, shortly after Berkshire acquired it. Justin left two managers in charge: Harrold Melton who ran Acme, and Randy Watson, in charge of Justin Boot.

Acme produced over a billion bricks a year in twenty-two plants and accounted for 11.7% of US brick production. Rare for a maker of bricks, Acme had a 75% name recognition rate in Texas, compared to 16% for the runner-up. This differential in brand name extended to its dominance in its local market. Because bricks are necessarily a low value-per-pound item (low cost and very heavy), its natural market was limited to a certain radius around each plant by the economics of shipping heavy items. Acme's brick business was subject to economic cycles, but its local economies of scale, and basic necessary business would lead to long-term returns on capital that were satisfactory and protected.

It appeared most of the value in Justin Industries resided in Acme Brick. The brick business grew from 52% of revenues in 1995 to 68% by 1999,[65] and over that time accounted for over 100% of pre-tax operating profits. By contrast, the footwear business struggled over the same period. Footwear profits slowly vanished and losses

---

* Buffett's letter cites same store growth of 9%, 11%, 13%, 10%, 12%, 21%, and 7%.

mounted as management tried to compete against brutal competition. It was a familiar story to Berkshire's existing footwear businesses.

We can see the relative stability in Justin's financial statements during the five years ended in 1999. Its revenues grew just 10% during that period and it maintained steady margins and returns on capital.* If we assume Justin would earn an average of $1.50 of revenues per dollar of invested capital at a pre-tax margin of 9.25% (about its five-year average), the company-level return would amount to 13.9%. With its purchase price of 1.75 times the company's enterprise value, Berkshire could expect to earn a going-in pre-tax return on invested capital of around 8%, close to its going-in return when it made the acquisition.

Table 6.21: Justin Industries—acquisition analysis

($ millions)	1999	1998	1997	1996	1995
Revenues	$510	$455	$440	$448	$461
Revenues/avg. capital	$1.52	$1.47	$1.51	$1.55	$1.59
EBIT margin	9%	9%	10%	9%	10%
Pre-tax return on capital	13%	14%	15%	14%	16%
Purchase price (equity)	$570				
Assumed debt	40				
Effective purchase price	$610				
Purchase multiple	1.75x				
BRK going-in pre-tax return	7.6%				

Sources: Berkshire Hathaway Annual Report 2000; Justin Industries Annual Reports 1995–1999; and author's calculations.

Looking at the brick business more closely reveals the true margin of safety in the Justin acquisition. As discussed above, the business had all the attributes of a moat along with its associated protected returns on capital. While the data is imperfect, it reveals a growing business with solid and stable margins and attractive return on assets. Justin's overall results were dragged down by the low or nonexistent profits from footwear, and this hid the true value of the acquisition.

Table 6.22: Justin Industries—Acme Brick analysis

($ millions)	1999	1998	1997	1996	1995
Revenues	$346	$293	$265	$261	$240
Identifiable assets	255	197	181	172	150
Operating profit	67	49	43	44	42
EBIT margin	19%	17%	16%	17%	18%
Pre-tax return on assets	26%	25%	24%	26%	28%

Sources: Berkshire Hathaway Annual Report 2000; Justin Industries Annual Reports 1995–1999; and author's calculations.

---

* To be sure, this was a relatively stable period in the United States economically.

6. Shaw Industries

Acquisition Date: January 8, 2001
Description: Maker of carpet, rugs, and other floor coverings
Purchase Price: $2.3 billion for 87.3% of the company

Flooring is higher tech than bricks, but not much. Shaw had just the kind of attributes Berkshire looked for: a business with a dominant market share—one third of the US flooring market—and increasing profitability in a fundamental business.[66] It was also a business with increasing economies of scale and one with invested family owners. A key feature of the deal was a requirement that Chairman Robert Shaw, President Julian Saul, and their families retain 5% of the company.

Shaw was started by Robert Shaw's father in 1946 as the Star Dye Company. Julian Saul joined Shaw in 1998 when his family's carpet company, Queen Carpet, was acquired by Shaw Industries.[67] By the time of the Shaw and Queen combination, Shaw had over a quarter of the market share of the US carpet market and Queen controlled 8%.[68]

With $4 billion of revenues, Shaw became Berkshire's largest (by revenues) non-insurance subsidiary. Reflecting on this in his characteristic humor, Buffett told shareholders: "Now, if people walk all over us, we won't mind." Buffett said the Shaw deal came about when Robert Shaw, Saul, and an unnamed CEO of a potential suitor for Shaw Industries, came to see him about writing an insurance policy. Shaw had a potential merger partner with asbestos liabilities from prior years which it desired to lay off on an insurer. Berkshire was unwilling to assume an open-ended risk and the insurance deal fell through—but the meeting planted the seeds for the acquisition soon after.

What did Buffett see in Shaw, and what was Berkshire getting for its money? To start, revenues grew 43% between 1995 and 1999. Part of that growth, to be sure, came from acquisitions, including the 1998 acquisition of Queen, and from strong housing starts in the US. Its pre-tax margin (as adjusted for certain non-recurring items*) doubled between 1995 and 1999, and its pre-tax return on capital almost tripled in that same period. These are evidence of the company achieving economies of scale.**

Shaw's 1999 operating results translated into a return on tangible capital of 36%. If these returns could be sustained, Berkshire would see its going-in pre-tax return continue to grow from a base of 15%. Even if we assume 1999 was a high year and

---

* Buffett had written unfavorably about managements that always pointed to non-recurring items. Here I've added them back as I believe they do in fact skew the true, long-term earnings power of the business.

** Other clues were that working capital fell 9% to $582 million and investment in fixed assets grew just 19% or about half of the increase in revenues.

that Shaw's normalized return on capital was its five-year average of 20%, Berkshire's resulting earnings yield would be 7.8%. In either case, Berkshire's purchase price would be pulled upward over time if the business continued to grow while earning good returns on the capital it employed.

Table 6.23: Shaw Industries—acquisition analysis

($ millions)	1999	1998	1997	1996	1995
Revenues	$4,108	$3,542	$3,576	$3,202	$2,870
Revenues/avg. capital[1]	$3.18	$2.68	$2.73	$2.54	$2.34
EBIT margin[1,2]	11%	8%	5%	5%	6%
Pre-tax return on capital	36%	21%	15%	14%	13%
Purchase price (equity)	$2,291				
Assumed debt	824				
Effective purchase price	$3,115				
Purchase multiple	2.45x				
BRK going-in pre-tax return	14.6%				

Footnotes:
1. Adjustments were made to account for acquired goodwill and its related amortization.
2. Operating income adjusted to remove the effects of non-recurring items and equity in income from joint venture.

Sources: Berkshire Hathaway Annual Report 2000; Shaw Industries Annual Reports 1997–1999; and author's calculations.

7. Benjamin Moore Paint

Acquisition Date: December 8, 2000
Description: Paint
Purchase Price: $1 billion cash

Benjamin Moore added to the slate of low-tech housing-related companies joining the Berkshire family. The 117-year-old business operated via a system of independent dealers, commonly found within hardware stores.

The deal came about in July 2000 when a director of the company, Bob Mundheim, who was also general counsel at Salomon, broached the subject of a possible deal with Buffett. Buffett said he liked the business and its management, Richard Roob and Yvan Dupay. He and Munger "made a $1 billion cash offer on the spot." Other financial details of the company were not disclosed.

8. Johns Manville Corp.

Acquisition Date: February 27, 2001
Description: Manufactures and sells insulation and building products in
North America, Europe, and China
Purchase Price: $1.8 billion

Johns Manville took a long and a winding road to its acquisition by Berkshire. The insulation products manufactured and sold by Johns Manville previously contained asbestos and were subsequently found to have caused many health problems. Litigation led to the company's bankruptcy in 1982. To compensate victims, the bankruptcy court set up a trust for the victims and used a controlling interest in the company as the major asset.

The trust now sought a buyer to diversify its holdings. When a leveraged buyout (LBO) firm could not find financing, Berkshire made a quick all-cash no-financing-strings-attached offer. Buffett convinced Jerry Henry, Johns Manville's retiring CEO, to stay in his post. Henry ultimately retired in mid-2004.[69]

Johns Manville's returns on capital were good but cyclical. This is not surprising considering how closely it was tied to a notoriously cycle-prone industry. Between 1993 and 1999 its return on capital averaged 18%, which included a low of 4% in 1993. The premium Berkshire paid for Johns Manville was double the company's underlying capital. Berkshire could still earn a satisfactory return for itself if Johns Manville continued to average the same results through future business cycles.

Table 6.24: Johns Manville—acquisition analysis

($ millions)	1999	1998	1997	1996	1995
Revenues	$2,162	$1,781	$1,648	$1,552	$1,392
Revenues/avg. capital[1]	$1.94	$1.71	$1.77	$1.22	$0.88
EBIT margin[1]	17%	16%	14%	12%	14%
Pre-tax return on capital	33%	28%	24%	15%	13%
Purchase price (equity)	$1,800				
Assumed debt	513				
Effective purchase price	$2,313				
Purchase multiple	2.08x				
BRK going-in pre-tax return	16.0%				
Footnote:					
1. Adjustments were made to account for acquired goodwill and its related amortization.					

Sources: Berkshire Hathaway Annual Report 2000; Johns Manville Annual Reports 1997–1999; and author's calculations.

Insurance

Berkshire's Insurance Group posted an underwriting loss of $1.6 billion that produced a cost of float of 6.1%. As we will see in a moment, this cost was not as bad as it seemed. Compared to an average 10-year US Treasury rate of around 5.5%, it was higher than Buffett preferred. Apart from the Primary Group, each of Berkshire's main insurance operating segments posted a pre-tax underwriting loss, and General Re's was by far the worst.

Table 6.25: Berkshire Hathaway—Insurance Underwriting

($ millions)	2000	1999
GEICO Corporation		
Premiums written	$5,778	$4,953
Premiums earned	5,610	4,757
Underwriting gain/(loss) - pre-tax	($224)	$24
General Re		
Premiums written	$8,696	$7,043
Premiums earned	8,696	6,905
Underwriting gain/(loss) - pre-tax	($1,254)	($1,184)
Berkshire Hathaway Reinsurance Group		
Premiums written	$4,724	$2,410
Premiums earned	4,712	2,382
Underwriting gain/(loss) - pre-tax	($162)	($256)
Berkshire Hathaway Primary Group		
Premiums earned	$325	$262
Underwriting gain/(loss) - pre-tax	$25	$22
Total underwriting gain/(loss)	($1,615)	($1,394)
Year-end average float - total	26,585	24,026
Cost of float	6.1%	5.8%
Aggregate adverse (favorable) loss development	$211	($192)

Notes:

1. The results for 2000 at General Re include five quarters. In 2000 General Re International and Global Life/Health changed its reporting from a one-quarter lag. The total underwriting loss for 12 months was $1,156 million (2001 presentation).

2. Berkshire Hathaway Primary Group written premiums were not detailed.

Sources: Berkshire Hathaway Annual Report 1999, 2001; and author's calculations.

General Re

General Re posted a $1.25 billion underwriting loss. It represented a cost of float of over 8% on the unit's average float of $15 billion. Pricing mistakes of the past still affected General Re, and it would take time to reprice certain policies. Correcting for those past underwriting mistakes required booking a charge in the current year to cover the adverse loss development of policies written in the past. Progress was being made by top managers, Ron Ferguson, Joe Brandon, and Tad Montross, to get underwriting discipline under control.

In General Re's North American property/casualty line, earned premiums rose 19.5% to $3.39 billion, but its underwriting loss grew 7% to $656 million.[*] Despite the year-over-year loss widening, results were considered better because underwriting discipline began producing improvements and because of a large aggregate excess reinsurance contract. This contract was responsible for a large part of the increase in premiums but also $239 million of the net underwriting loss due to accounting rules.

The economics of excess reinsurance contracts is such that a large premium is paid upfront, and claims are paid (usually) over a long period of time. The result is a large amount of float, which compensates the reinsurer for assuming an expected payout above the premium amount. Such an economic arrangement is not unlike that of a loan. The way the accounting works for these contracts is the premium is booked upfront in addition to all future expected losses; the difference (usually a negative number) is booked as an underwriting loss.[**]

Table 6.26: Accounting and economics of General Re's North American property/casualty unit excess reinsurance contract, 2000

Accounting treatment	
($ millions)	
Upfront premium	$404
All expected future losses	(643)
Underwriting loss	($239)
Economics	
Interest cost if a loan over:	
5 years	9.7%
10 years	4.8%
15 years	3.1%

Sources: Berkshire Hathaway Annual Report 2000 and author's calculations.

---

[*] Note that these figures are from the 2001 presentation and the underwriting loss is $30 million greater than the original 2000 presentation.

[**] Making some generalized assumptions, we can view the economics of the transaction, which is not unlike that of a loan. If Berkshire had use of the $404 million premium for five years and it could pay back the $643 million in year five, it would cost it 10% per year; a ten-year payout would result in a cost of 5% (see Table 6.26). In practice, the timing of payouts could stretch decades, which would affect the cost.

Berkshire had a total of $482 million of such excess reinsurance losses in 2000 ($239 million at Gen Re, the remainder at Berkshire Hathaway Reinsurance Group, or BHRG). This represented over one-third (34.4%) of the underwriting loss for the year in reinsurance. Given the accounting treatment, Buffett thought it appropriate to adjust for these types of contracts when analyzing Berkshire's cost of float. This adjustment changed Berkshire's cost of float to more like 4.5%, said Buffett. Better than 6%, but not zero.

The other type of reinsurance contract Berkshire wrote (General Re and Berkshire Reinsurance) was retroactive reinsurance, where accounting and economic treatments were more closely aligned. The economics of retroactive reinsurance contracts are very similar to an excess contract, with premiums booked upfront. However, instead of being booked as an immediate underwriting loss, the difference between the lower premium amount and the higher expected loss is booked as an asset. This asset is then amortized into earnings as an incurred loss expense over time.[*]

Both excess reinsurance and retroactive reinsurance were considered good lines of business for Berkshire, even if they were not of the gold standard negative cost-type. Buffett welcomed such "pain-today, gain-tomorrow" business so long as the policies were priced appropriately, and he thought it important that shareholders understand the economics and accounting of such business.

Returning to General Re, the notes to the financial statements did not sugar coat the results in International property/casualty. "Underwriting results for General Re's International property/casualty segment for 2000 remained very bad." It suffered another year of motion picture losses, which added 4 points to the ratio. The only good news was that the aforementioned contract had ended. Berkshire's summary of the carnage in General Re's International property/casualty segment:

- 2000: $416 million loss on $2.48 billion of earned premiums; combined ratio of 117%.[**]
- Comparison from 1999: $473 million loss on $2.34 billion of earned premiums; combined ratio of 120%.

General Re Global life/health earned just 2.8% more business in 2000 and its underwriting results remained unsatisfactory. On premiums earned of $1.77 billion, the group lost $84 million, a combined ratio of 104.7%.[***]

---

[*] Since the losses were incurred in prior years, they are booked as prior year losses and cause apparent unfavorable loss development. It is somewhat counterintuitive to place an asset on the books from the assumption of a liability, but it makes more sense from an economic perspective since it roughly reflects the time value of money inherent in float. In theory, the earnings from the premium received would equal the charge against the deferred charge asset (or perhaps produce a small gain).

[**] Twelve-month figure presented for comparability. The 15-month result was a loss of $518 million.

[***] Twelve-month figure presented for comparability. The 15-month result was a loss of $80 million.

Both General Re Global life/health and the International property/casualty segments reported an extra quarter of earnings in 2000. The fifteen months of results, which were not considered to be material to Berkshire's overall results, was done to bring reporting in-line with other segments. The two groups had previously been reporting on a one-quarter lag, and in 2000 that lag was corrected.

Berkshire Hathaway Reinsurance Group

Buffett heaped well-deserved praise on Berkshire Hathaway Reinsurance Group (BHRG) head Ajit Jain. During 2000, volume at Jain's group nearly doubled to $4.7 billion. The growth came mainly from a single $2.44 billion contract that retroactively covered a major UK company (not disclosed). Jain also wrote a contract for the Texas Rangers covering its star, Alex Rodriguez, in case he became permanently disabled. Berkshire covered disability for many sports figures. Another contract covered the payout of a $1 billion ($170 million present value) prize for Grab. com. The underwriting loss from retroactive reinsurance was $191 million.

Like General Re, BHRG wrote excess-of-loss reinsurance contracts that produced first-year losses with no offsetting accounting treatment. In 2000, such losses were $154 million,* which accounted for the bulk of the $162 million underwriting loss from the group. Its catastrophe business again experienced favorable results and posted a profit of $183 million.

BHRG had become a remarkable operation under Jain's leadership. Supporting nearly $5 billion in premium volume was just 2.4 percentage points of overhead (the underwriting expenses line). The rest was 101.3 points of losses and loss expenses. Due to the nature of its business writing a few very large contracts, overhead rates fell to low single digits beginning in 1999 as premiums swelled. Before that, the group's overhead ran closer to 20 points, which was about the same as General Re's rate between 1998 and 2000.

Berkshire Hathaway Primary Group

Within the more mundane (but no less exciting from an economic standpoint) Primary Group, premiums expanded 24% to $325 million and pre-tax underwriting profits rose 14% to $25 million. The increases were primarily due to the inclusion of U.S. Liability.

---

* This figure was revised from the $167 million presented in the 2000 financials, which also had the BHRG combined underwriting loss at $175 million. I've used the 2001 presentation here.

GEICO

GEICO had the rare off year after many years of very good results. One of the reasons was self-inflicted. Buffett said he was wrong in the enthusiasm he displayed in 1999 about investing heavily in advertising. The law of diminishing returns hit GEICO hard. In some cases, the company ran three advertisements per hour, with the third most likely having very little effect on new business compared to the first. Additionally, GEICO's growing market share meant it had already picked the low-hanging fruit. Other customers would take longer to convert.

Due to these factors, GEICO entered a new phase of its operations where growth would be slower. This new phase was already evident in 2000. GEICO previously focused on preferred customers, or good drivers that were low risks to insure. The non-preferred market was dominated by drivers with blemishes on their driving records including traffic violations and sometimes driving under the influence (DUI). With the non-preferred business, lapse ratios (where people did not pay their premiums) were higher, meaning fewer renewals. So even though GEICO added almost a million and a half new voluntary policies during the year, its policies-in-force count grew by only about 20% of that amount.

The major factor in GEICO's underwriting loss was competition. The dominant player in the auto insurance industry in the US was (and still is) State Farm. With 19% of the market, State Farm let its pricing slip and tolerated higher loss ratios. This put pressure on industry rates. GEICO played the long game and focused on underwriting profitably. Its higher market share and increased pricing translated into 18% premium growth, but this wasn't sufficient to cover all costs.

One poor year and a 6.1% cost of float wasn't enough to tarnish GEICO's reputation or its prospects. It still had the low-cost business model and plenty of room to grow and catch up with State Farm.

Manufacturing, Service, and Retailing

Berkshire's financial reporting again shifted to accommodate the newer, larger businesses joining the family. *The Buffalo News*, the Shoe Group, Dairy Queen, and See's Candies now found themselves lumped together with Berkshire's many smaller businesses in the other businesses category. This was necessary to make room for a new building products reporting line to accommodate Acme Building Brands,* Benjamin Moore and Johns Manville (when that acquisition closed in 2001). These businesses reported pre-tax earnings of $906 million. That represented strong growth

---

* Justin Industries' footwear business, Justin Brands, was reported under footwear in Other.

compared to the year before but included new businesses. A more comparable metric is pre-tax return on capital, which fell six percentage points to 20.7%.[*]

Buffett was not one to bury problems. In his letter to shareholders he touched on the Shoe Group, which struggled mightily against foreign competition. Dexter played its part in dragging the Shoe Group's pre-tax operating profit down from $85 million in 1994 to $17 million in 1999 (the last year before the group was consolidated into other business). Berkshire now had overwhelming evidence that Dexter was worth less than it had paid for the company. As a result, it recorded a $219 million goodwill impairment charge late in 2000. In retrospect, acquiring Dexter was a mistake—a mistake compounded by the fact that Dexter was purchased with Berkshire shares. Buffett would continually chide himself for underestimating the powerful economic forces at work. "We may regain some economic goodwill at Dexter in the future, but we clearly have none at present," Buffett wrote. Other US shoe manufacturers probably shared this sentiment.

Earnings from the two Flight Services businesses dipped 5% that year to $213 million but still represented 13% of Berkshire's consolidated pre-tax operating earnings. FlightSafety, the pilot training business, spent $272 million on simulators during 2000. That figure was far above the $70 million figure Buffett cited at the Annual Meeting as the company's annual depreciation expense;[**] the larger number represented physical growth of the business. FlightSafety's 83-year-old founder, Al Ueltschi—like Buffett—was not slowing down.

Executive Jet's monthly management fees and hourly usage fees grew by 49% during the year, which was on top of 46% growth the year before. The business was growing as fast as it could, taking up 7% of the world's output of jets. But building out its business, including an expansion into Europe, was expensive. This weighed on profits and was the reason behind the overall decline in earnings for Flight Services.

With soaring growth, Executive Jet was at the same time careful. Buffett said Founder and CEO Rich Santulli insisted on "unusually high amounts of pilot training" (good news for FlightSafety). Executive Jet's pilots flew just one aircraft model and received an average of twenty-three days a year of training, making them among the best. Citing a competitors' crash the year before in Aspen, Colorado, Charlie Munger told shareholders that Executive Jet's pilots had refused to fly into the airport due to weather conditions. The competitor was pressured by its customer to make the landing, which ended in tragedy.

---

[*] Justin Industries was likely the main reason for the significant decline since its return on capital was in the low double digits.

[**] Total Flight Services depreciation was $90 million, which would leave $20 million as Executive Jets' depreciation.

Operating profit from Scott Fetzer's twenty non-finance businesses declined 17% to $122 million. The big hitters were Kirby, Campbell Hausfeld, and World Book, which comprised 60% of its revenues and 65% of operating profits. Continued struggles at World Book and an unusually strong year at its generator business the year before due to the Y2K scare hurt comparable results in 2000.

Buffett devoted a section of his Annual Report to praise Ralph Schey, who retired at the end of 2000. Since Berkshire purchased Scott Fetzer in 1985, it had sent $1.03 billion to Omaha against a net purchase price of $230 million. Those funds were the seed capital for some of Berkshire's subsequent purchases. He attributed billions of dollars of value to Schey's contributions to Berkshire. Buffett wrote that he and Munger welcomed Schey to the Berkshire Hall of Fame.

Finance and Financial Products

The Finance and Financial Products businesses had quietly grown sizable and received a boost in 1998 with the addition of General Re's finance-related business. At year-end 2000, it had $16.8 billion of assets supported by $1.77 billion of equity capital. It looked very much like a bank leveraged almost ten times (such leverage was ordinary for a bank). Pre-tax earnings jumped from $125 million in 1999 to $530 million in 2000.* It housed everything from Scott Fetzer's finance arm to the structured settlements and annuities business, to General Re's securities business, but relatively little was disclosed about it. Shareholders understandably wondered about the unit.

At the Annual Meeting the following year, Buffett reassured shareholders about the relative risk of the unit, though he really did not reveal much. The more basic operations, he said, such as the structured settlements business, were straightforward, "quite predictable and a very easy business to understand."

Moving up the complexity scale, the segment also contained a trading business outside the normal investment category. Buffett described this as "arbitrage or semi-arbitrage of various types of fixed-income securities." That line of business was run by Mark Byrne (son of long-time GEICO manager Jack Byrne), whom Buffett and Munger praised as smart and trustworthy.

Buffett said the derivatives business within General Re was admittedly outside of their comfort zone, which led them to begin winding down the business. In 2000, Gen Re Securities still had a huge number of derivatives contracts on the books that would take a lot of time—and ultimately a lot of red ink—to dispose.**

---

* There are minor discrepancies between these figures, which come from the Chairman's letter, and those presented in the supplemental statements. Discrepancies exist between the 2000 and 2001 presentations too, which are minor.

** At the time there were some 17,000 contracts representing over $650 billion of notional value.

Investments

Turning to Berkshire's main investment business, run by Buffett (with Munger's input), almost all of its Fannie Mae and Freddie Mac shares were sold. The investments were jettisoned after Berkshire's chief capital allocators sensed their risk profiles had changed.*[70] They would later be proven right after the companies were found to have overstated their earnings. They would also play a part in the 2008–09 financial crisis close to a decade later.

Poking around the edges, Buffett said Berkshire "established 15% positions in several mid-sized companies, bought the high-yield bonds of a few issuers … and added to our holdings of high-grade mortgage-backed securities. There are no 'bargains' among our current holdings: We're content with what we own but far from excited from it."

With little exciting investment news to share, Buffett devoted a couple pages of his Chairman's letter to expanding on the Aesop analogy he first discussed at the prior years' Annual Meeting. He said investing was as simple as the Aesop's proverb that a bird in the hand was worth two in the bush—with one minor qualification. The qualification was *when*, and what was the risk-free rate? If you can answer these three questions, he said, you "rank the attractiveness of all possible uses of capital throughout the universe." Those questions were:

1. How certain are you that there are indeed birds (cash) in the bush?
2. When will they emerge and how many will there be?
3. What is the risk-free interest rate?

The answers to these questions were the foundation of Berkshire's investment program. It was no coincidence that certainty was placed at the head of the list. Buffett said others had strayed into speculation and forgot to pay attention to this framework. They were instead more concerned about movements in share prices that often traded far ahead of what the fundamentals would suggest was reasonable.

A comment by Charlie Munger at the 2001 Annual Meeting was instructive, as it sheds light on his and Buffett's correct thinking about buying internet companies around the time of the dot-com bubble. He recalled that both he and Buffett had worked at Buffett's grandfather's grocery store in Omaha as youngsters. Munger noted that the business, which included delivering goods to customers, "barely supported one family". Buffett made explicit what Munger was referring to: Webvan, an internet-based grocery delivery business, ran into the same costs that Buffett & Son did generations earlier delivering groceries.

---

* The companies were moving away from the fee-guaranty business into holding the mortgages. They owned some mortgages before the crisis too.

The internet hype roped many into a speculative frenzy based on the false belief that technology would somehow eliminate costs and shower profits on all. Buffett and Munger looked beneath to the basic economics and saw otherwise. They saw that ordering groceries would go from paper to computer entry, but the costs of buying the product and distributing it to customers would not change. "There was a lot of money transferred … from the gullible to the promoters [of internet stocks] … It's been a huge trap for the public," Buffett said.

Berkshire vs. S&P 500

Though Berkshire beat its preferred benchmark the S&P 500 by 15.6% in 2000, its book value increased just 6.5%. That was because of a 9.1% decline in the S&P that year. Buffett told shareholders he thought Berkshire's gain in intrinsic value (the metric that really counted) moderately exceeded the gain in book value.

With 1999 and 2000 containing pre-tax operating losses before considering investment income, the two-column method (investments per share plus some multiple of pre-tax operating earnings per share, excluding investment income) for determining Berkshire's intrinsic value became a bit more complicated (see Table 6.27). Buffett even omitted the table in his 2000 Annual Report. Estimating Berkshire's value required working directly from the financial statements, and it also called for some assumptions on insurance profitability.

Table 6.27: Berkshire Hathaway intrinsic value estimation

Per A-share:	2000	1999
Investments	$50,507	$47,339
Pre-tax operating earnings (ex. investment income; adjusted to breakeven insurance underwriting)	846	550
Estimated value (investments + 10x operating earnings)	58,966	52,844
Year-end share price	71,000	56,100
Year-end book value per share	40,442	37,987
Price/estimated value	1.20x	1.06x
Price/book	1.76x	1.48x
Value/book	1.46x	1.39x
Change in estimated value	12%	
Change in share price	27%	

Sources: Berkshire Hathaway Annual Reports, 1999, 2000; and author's calculations.

The first part of this estimate, investments per share, is relatively straightforward. Berkshire's balance sheet provides the amounts for cash and investments excluding the Finance Businesses.*

---

* I am assuming that the cash and investments in the Finance Business are required for its operation. Including

Pre-tax operating earnings is a little more complicated. A quick calculation results in a per-share loss.* Capitalizing a loss would lead to a larger negative value, which would reduce the intrinsic value calculation. Yet we know that Buffett would not tolerate large ongoing losses from insurance underwriting, and we know that the operating businesses had meaningful value. If we make the relatively conservative assumption that insurance underwriting would breakeven, the per-share operating earnings from the non-insurance businesses can be capitalized.

We can use the same methodology for 1999, which showed a similar pre-tax loss due to insurance underwriting. The change in intrinsic value from 1999 to 2000, using the same method, is 12%—a figure consistent with Buffett's moderately higher change.

Berkshire's goal of attaining a 15% average annual rate of return was getting harder year by year, owing to Berkshire's growing size. Buffett told shareholders at the Annual Meeting that very few large companies would achieve such a record over the next decade. Berkshire would do its best, using opportunity cost as its guide. Buffett summed up the strategy very well at the 2001 Annual Meeting:

> "I think our method is a pretty good one. I mean, I think the idea of having a group of good businesses to throw off cash in aggregate, in a big way, that themselves grow, that are run by terrific people, and then adding onto those, sometimes at a slow rate, but every now and then at a good clip, more businesses of the same kind, and not increasing the outstanding shares, I think that's about as good a business model as you can have for a company our size. But what it produces, we'll have to see."

There is nothing more to add.

2001

In its race to outpace the S&P 500, Berkshire Hathaway had only fallen short of the benchmark a few times.** Those years, it at least finished with some sort of increase to book value per share. That changed in 2001 when book value per share declined 6.2% against a decline of 11.9% for the S&P. The string of advances was broken only by a truly terrible catastrophe—the terrorist attacks of September 11, 2001. Like the United States itself, Berkshire was injured but resilient in the face of adversity.

---

them and the operating earnings would be double counting. A case could be made to exclude some amount of cash for the operating businesses as well, however, this would probably be small and not worth the effort given our roughly right vs. exactly wrong approach here.

* The loss was about $193 per share.

** The years Berkshire's book value change had fallen behind the S&P 500 were: 1967, 1975, 1980, and 1999.

Buffett reminded shareholders that relative performance was the name of the game. Berkshire had outperformed the S&P by 5.7%. "If you expect—as Charlie Munger, Berkshire's Vice Chairman, and I do—that owning the S&P 500 will produce reasonably satisfactory results over time, it follows that, for long-term investors, gaining small advantages annually over that index *must* prove rewarding."* Some disagreed with Buffett, but he was stalwart, reminding shareholders his goal of relative performance would not change.

Part of Berkshire's poor performance during 2001 was self-inflicted. Buffett admitted as much. General Re had taken on terrorism-related risks without being properly compensated. Buffett chided himself for knowing General Re was exposed to some of those risks, but he said "on September 11th, this error caught up with us."

On the non-insurance front, Berkshire's businesses were also affected by the attacks and the economy. Buffett thought the country had entered a recession, even though economists hadn't announced it. Officials later dated the early 2000s recession between March and November 2001. Still, Berkshire added non-insurance subsidiaries during the year, completing the previously announced Shaw and Johns Manville acquisitions, and closing and initiating several others. The long-term strategy at Berkshire of continually searching for good investment opportunities was unchanged, even in the face the shock of September 11th. Three of them are listed below:

MiTek

Acquisition Date: July 31, 2001
Description: Building products company
Purchase Price: $400 million in cash for 90%

MiTek made connector plates for roofing trusses, as well as other building-related materials. It also had a proprietary software system it leased to customers.[71] The business came to Buffett's attention the prior year when Gene Toombs, its CEO, sent him a letter along with a hunk of metal (a connector plate).

Prior to Berkshire's purchase, MiTek was owned by Rexam PLC, a UK company.** MiTek was headquartered in Chesterfield, Missouri. The remaining 10% of the company was purchased by fifty-five of its managers, each of whom put up their own cash*** to participate. No detailed financial information was available for MiTek because it was part of a group within Rexam.

---

* Emphasis original.
** Because MiTek's financial performance was reported alongside another subsidiary its specific results and the economics behind Berkshire's purchase cannot be determined.
*** Buffett wrote that the minimum investment was $100,000, and he said that "many borrowed money so they could participate". There were no options granted.

XTRA

Acquisition Date: September 11, 2001
Description: Trailer leasing business
Purchase Price: About $578 million

Buffett said the deal came from his friend, Julian Robertson, whose investment fund, Tiger Fund, owned shares in the company. Even though Berkshire's offer contained an out that would have allowed it to back away considering the events of the day, Berkshire completed the acquisition.

XTRA purchased trailers which were then leased to trucking companies and others moving freight. Its dependence on economic activity made it a cyclical business and therefore like many of Berkshire's other businesses, which overall earned good returns. Owing to the nature of the business it was placed among the Finance and Financial Products businesses.

As a financial-related business, XTRA's balance sheet contained a meaningful amount of debt. The company also earned good returns on total capital. Berkshire's purchase price represented a premium of about 60% over the company's underlying equity capital. Considering the purchase from the standpoint of a 100% cash-financed business, the effective purchase price yielded 12%.[*]

Table 6.28: XTRA Corporation—acquisition analysis

($ millions)	2000	1999	1998
Revenues	$477	$464	$461
Revenues/average capital[1]	$0.41	$0.39	$0.37
EBIT margin[1]	34%	33%	35%
Pre-tax return on capital	14%	13%	13%
Purchase price (equity)	$578		
Assumed debt	788		
Effective purchase price	$1,366		
Purchase multiple	1.17x		
BRK going-in pre-tax return	12.0%		
Footnotes: 1. Adjustments were made for an asset write-down ($25 million) and restructuring costs ($13 million) in 1999.			

Sources: Berkshire Hathaway Annual Report 2001, XTRA Corporation Annual Reports 1998–2000, and author's calculations.

---

[*] Because of the effects of leverage, the going-in return on equity was closer to 18% pre-tax and 11% after tax.

Larson-Juhl

Acquisition Date: February 8, 2002
Description: Manufacturer and distributor of quality custom framing products
Purchase Price: Approximately $225 million

Continuing to add to its low-tech, non-insurance businesses, Berkshire in 2001 agreed to purchase Albecca, Inc., which conducted business as Larson-Juhl. The company serviced a network of 18,000 framing shops in the US and also did business in Canada and Europe.

The company was owned by Craig Ponzio, who had worked in manufacturing in college. Ponzio bought the company in 1981 and went on to increase its revenues 100-fold to $300 million. The business was now run by CEO Steve McKenzie.

Larson-Juhl's economics were very simple. The company serviced many smaller framing shops with very small volumes of business each year. What was important to those shops was a wide selection of inventory available but without the large carrying costs. With its tens of thousands of customers, Larson-Juhl could carry such inventory economically, even though each individual shop might place orders infrequently. This meant 85% of the time Larson-Juhl could have an order to a framing shop the next day. This network and a service organization that called on customers half a dozen times a year created a moat around the business.

Buffett said the deal came together quickly, having first come to his attention on December 3, 2001. He called it a fat pitch, meaning one which took less than fifteen minutes to size up over the phone and ninety minutes to work out in person. Buffett foresaw opportunities for bolt-on acquisitions (small acquisitions by Larson-Juhl that would fit into its existing operations) in the future.

Insurance

The main story of 2001 was insurance. The September 11th attacks caused the largest insured losses in history and Berkshire took its share. Buffett took the unusual step of issuing a press release on September 12, 2001. He said estimating losses from the terrorist attacks would take a very long time to determine but he thought Berkshire would incur about 3% to 5% of the industry's losses.

In a subsequent unusual move, Buffett included commentary in Berkshire's third quarter earnings release, which estimated the loss at about $2.275 billion. In that same press release, Buffett chided General Re for breaking all three of the rules of operating a successful insurance company. Paraphrasing, those rules were:

1. Only accept risks one is capable of evaluating
2. Limit aggregated exposure (i.e. diversify risks)
3. Avoid doing business with bad actors.

Breaking those rules cost CEO Ron Ferguson his job.* Buffett replaced him with Joe Brandon and praised Brandon and his new lieutenant, President Tad Montross, as talented leaders who would clean up General Re. While Berkshire Hathaway Reinsurance had lost money on September 11, Buffett noted that that unit, led by Ajit Jain, had adhered to all three rules of successful underwriting.

The Insurance Group as a unit turned in an underwriting loss of $4.1 billion on $18 billion of earned premiums. Berkshire's cost of float was a staggering 12.8%. That average float grew 19% to $35.5 billion at year-end 2001 was not necessarily a good thing. Remember that a component of float is unpaid losses. Berkshire's float during 2001 grew in large part by incurring losses for which it wasn't compensated. Float at an overall cost in the double digits would not be tolerated for long at Berkshire.

---

* In Alice Schroeders's book, *The Snowball*, she recounts how Buffett was not pleased with Ferguson's performance leading up to this point. Ferguson didn't like the "one foot bars" Buffett and Ajit Jain looked for, instead preferring, apparently, the intellectually tough challenges. Schroeder wrote that Buffett saw what was actually happening was that General Re's customers were dictating terms to General Re, instead of the other way around.

Table 6.29: Berkshire Hathaway—Insurance Underwriting

($ millions)	2001	2000
GEICO Corporation		
Premiums written	$6,176	$5,778
Premiums earned	6,060	5,610
Underwriting gain/(loss) - pre-tax	$221	($224)
General Re		
Premiums written	$8,730	$8,696
Premiums earned	8,353	8,696
Underwriting gain/(loss) - pre-tax	($3,671)	($1,254)
Berkshire Hathaway Reinsurance Group		
Premiums written	$3,254	$4,724
Premiums earned	2,991	4,712
Underwriting gain/(loss) - pre-tax	($647)	($162)
Berkshire Hathaway Primary Group		
Premiums earned	$501	$325
Underwriting gain/(loss) - pre-tax	$30	$25
Total underwriting gain/(loss)	($4,067)	($1,615)
Year-end average float - total	31,690	26,585
Cost of float	12.8%	6.1%
Aggregate adverse (favorable) loss development	$1,165	$211

Notes:

1. The results for 2000 at General Re include five quarters. In 2000 General Re International and Global Life/Health changed its reporting from a one-quarter lag.

2. Berkshire Hathaway Primary Group written premiums were not detailed.

Sources: Berkshire Hathaway Annual Report 2001 and author's calculations.

General Re

Since Berkshire had purchased General Re in late 1998, the business had cumulatively lost nearly $6.5 billion from underwriting. In fact, in each year since 1998 the losses had only grown. The $3.7 billion loss for 2001 was a terrible underwriting result. Having written coverage for which it wasn't paid (terrorism insurance), General Re lost $1.9 billion from the attacks alone. The segment also took an $800 million loss to correct prior years' underwriting miscalculations.

The bulk of the loss at General Re came from its North American property/casualty segment, a $2.84 billion loss on $3.97 billion of earned premiums. This was not a case of long-tail contracts or any effect of accounting, but simply poor underwriting. A full $1.54 billion of the loss came from September 11th. It was the North American property/casualty segment that recorded the $800 million addition to its loss reserves during the year.

The international property/casualty segment at General Re also experienced very poor results. Some stemmed from September 11th. On earned premiums of $2.4 billion (up slightly from $2.5 billion), the unit lost $746 million. The international segment recorded a net $313 million of September 11th-related losses, as well as a $143 million loss from coverage of a steel plant in the UK which had exploded. An additional blunder at General Re was its Argentinian business, which was in peril owing to an economic and political crisis there.

General Re's global life/health business continued to be the less dark segment. During 2001, the unit increased premiums 10.4% to $1.99 billion. It reported an underwriting loss of $82 million, including $15 million of September 11th losses.

Berkshire Hathaway Reinsurance Group (BHRG)

While Ajit Jain's group contained some terrorism-related losses from September 11th, they were not nearly as bad as at General Re. On $2.99 billion of earned premiums (down from $4.7 billion) BHRG reported a $647 million pre-tax underwriting loss. Of that, $530 million or 82% was related to September 11th. BHRG's results also included $371 million in losses from retroactive reinsurance contracts, which were the type that came with deferred charges relating to the asset put on the books at inception. While it's possible some of the loss was due to incorrect underwriting, it's more likely the bulk of that $371 million came from accounting charges.*

Buffett expanded on his thinking regarding the economics of retroactive reinsurance policies at the 2002 Annual Meeting. It didn't matter, he said, what type of claims they were. Buffett used the example of asbestos versus auto claims. What really mattered was the speed of the claims. Since Berkshire always capped its limits, even if it paid up to the capped limit (but over a long period of time), the economics would still be favorable owing to the large amount of float. From purely a financial standpoint, Berkshire's insurance companies (especially the reinsurers) were entities that incurred debt of a slightly different nature. Unlike traditional debt, insurance liabilities had irregular and unknown payments and the possibility of paying less than full face value. Each insurer played an important role in society, which in turn provided it the opportunity to generate float.

Deferred charges relating to retroactive policies masked good performance elsewhere at BHRG. Other catastrophe and non-retroactive reinsurance business earned a profit of $254 million, which partially offset the September 11th losses. With its core catastrophe and non-retro business profitable, Buffett praised Ajit Jain in

---

* The notes to the financial statements in 2001 disclosed that Berkshire anticipated $400 million of deferred charge amortization in 2002. The balance of the unamortized charges grew from $2.6 billion in 2000 to $3.1 billion in 2001.

his letter to shareholders commenting, "never on even a single occasion have I seen him break any of our three underwriting rules." Jain's team, now with eighteen other individuals, would occasionally book a loss, as would be expected, but they would not, Buffett wrote, book foolish losses.

While General Re was in restructuring mode under close supervision by Buffett, BHRG used its position as a leader with unparalleled financial strength to write considerable business. Right after the attacks, Jain's group wrote billions of dollars' worth of premiums for coverage relating to terrorism and all risk was retained for Berkshire's account. This time, Berkshire was paid appropriately for the risk and its coverage contained both caps on exposure and exclusions relating to nuclear, chemical, or biological-type attacks. These latter exposures were so large that they could conceivably wipe out all the capital in the insurance industry, therefore the only natural insurer of such risks was the government.

Berkshire Hathaway Primary Group

Berkshire's steady group of direct writers of insurance reported equally steady gains during 2001. On earned premiums of $501 million, the group reported an underwriting profit of $30 million. While they likely had some terrorism-related losses, none were disclosed.

GEICO

GEICO bounced back from its rare off year with a $221 million underwriting gain in 2001, the best performance within the Insurance Group. Earned premiums rose 8% to $6.1 billion. Its reversal back to a positive underwriting experience was driven primarily from lower losses, which fell 2.9 points to 77% of earned premiums. This was partly due to a mild winter with fewer accidents.

GEICO still had difficulty turning advertising dollars into new customers. It spent $219 million on advertising in 2001 while treading water on the new policy front. Its largest share of customers, the preferred group (the segment on which GEICO had built its business) represented 81% of policyholders and grew just 1.6%. The non-preferred standard and non-standard group fell by over 10% during the year, resulting in a 0.8% decline in overall policies in force.

GEICO's float grew 8% to $4.25 billion despite the overall decline in policies in force. And there were signs soon after year-end pointing to growth in policies in force resuming at GEICO.

Manufacturing, Service, and Retailing

Note: In 2001, Berkshire stopped reporting separate financials for the MSR businesses, so data for their collective earnings and return on capital aren't available. Data reappeared in the 2003 Chairman's letter with an earnings lookback to 2002. Rather than attempt to fill in the gaps, we'll proceed with a look at the individual business units.

The addition of so many new businesses necessitated another change in grouping Berkshire's results. The Building Products line, new in 2000, listed just $34 million in pre-tax profit that year. In 2001, it swelled to $461 million as Benjamin Moore, Johns Manville, and MiTek contributed results.

Shaw received its own reporting line because of its size. In 2001, it earned $292 million pre-tax on $4 billion of revenues. Revenues declined $100 million reflecting lower volumes and were attributed to the September 11th-initiated recession in homebuilding. Shortly after year-end 2001, Berkshire acquired the remaining 12.7% of Shaw it did not own. Berkshire paid 4,740 in A share-equivalents, or about $324 million.*

The September 11th terrorist attacks directly impacted the Flight Services businesses. Executive Jet would need to incur additional costs relating to new safety and security rules. There was also a slowdown in fractional jet services usage and a lower level of training at FlightSafety. Executive Jet still had its competitive advantage, which stemmed from its 300-plane fleet of jets available on short-notice to ferry customers around the country and Europe. FlightSafety also remained committed to the long term, investing $67 million more than its annual depreciation expense to expand capacity.

Retail Operations, comprised of the home furnishings and jewelry businesses, earned $175 million, unchanged from the year before. This flat result represented weakness since it included a full year from Ben Bridge, a small acquisition by Nebraska Furniture Mart, and a new RC Willey store in Nevada. Same-store sales from the jewelry businesses declined 8%.

Scott Fetzer managed to increase earnings 6% to $129 million through continued cost discipline. This was even more impressive in the face of continued declines in sales of Kirby units overseas and at World Book generally.

---

* This implied a valuation of $2.55 billion for the entire company and an 11% pre-tax return on the $292 million of pre-tax income.

Utilities

Perhaps one of the most noticeable changes, aside from the large losses in insurance, was MidAmerican. In 2000, Berkshire reported $197 million in pre-tax earnings for MidAmerican. In 2001 this figure jumped to $565 million.* Why? Two major factors were an increase in operating earnings and the fact that GAAP stopped requiring goodwill amortization (affecting MidAmerican to the tune of $94 million in 2000).**

Finance and Financial Products

The Finance and Financial Products business again reported strong pre-tax results ($519 million pre-tax vs. $530 the year before), but this was becoming Buffett's show more than ever.*** The core businesses of Scott Fetzer's finance arm and the annuity business remained. General Re Securities, like its parent, had fallen from grace. General Re's derivatives business was now in run-off mode; Berkshire was doing its best to get out of the business, but it would take a long time.

Investments

As in prior years, Berkshire's investment portfolio changed at a glacial pace in 2001. Buffett's letter to shareholders used such descriptive phrases "as few changes," "restrained enthusiasm," and "lukewarm feelings about the prospects" to describe his and Munger's feelings toward investments and the market overall. They were content to hold on to most of what Berkshire already owned, since the long-term prospects for American Express, Coca-Cola, Gillette, Washington Post, and Wells Fargo remained favorable. But they thought their own portfolio in aggregate was not undervalued.

Two new investments did join the summary chart in Buffett's letter in 2001, having crossed the $500 million threshold established as a cutoff. Berkshire's nearly 16 million shares in H&R Block, Inc., a tax preparation service company, had a market value of $715 million at year-end 2001 and cost Berkshire $255 million. While new to the table, Berkshire had owned shares in the company since the last quarter of 2000.[72] Another investment crossing the threshold was Moody's Corporation. Moody's was a credit-rating agency that graded companies' debt instruments for investors. Berkshire

---

* I am using the figure from the 2002 Annual Report here, since it would have been more accurate. The original figure presented in the 2001 Chairman's letter was $600 million.

** The after-tax, after-minority interest figures are instructive here. In 2001, Berkshire's share, including the interest-income it earned from the preferred stock, totaled $230 million, up from $109 million in 2000. Additionally, on Berkshire's audited income statement only the equity in net earnings of MidAmerican are shown (interest income is shown elsewhere). These figures were $165 million and $105 million for 2001 and 2000, respectively.

*** Buffett told shareholders earlier that the growth in that business was largely due to his activities.

owned 24 million shares in the company and had first purchased it at the same time as the H&R Block stake.[73]

Berkshire put its money where Buffett's mouth was in terms of lower expectations on its investment performance. The expected rate of return on its pension plan was reduced to 6.5% in 2001 from 8.3% that it expected in 2000. This caused a higher expense and greater liability, all things being equal, since a shortfall between expected returns in the market and cash contributed by Berkshire would widen.

Berkshire made a significant fixed income investment in 2001. Early in the year it committed to be part of a joint venture to loan money on a secured basis to FINOVA Group. FINOVA was a troubled finance company that failed. Its prepackaged bankruptcy had been approved in August 2001. While the deal did close, it was not before being terminated and renegotiated. Berkshire chose to terminate the deal based on a clause allowing Berkshire to do so if the markets closed, which they did after the September 11th attacks. Unlike the XTRA deal, which contained a similar clause but went unexercised, FINOVA was materially affected by the event. FINOVA's assets contained loans relating to aircraft assets that were significantly diminished by September 11th. Its receivables were also affected negatively.

The deal called for Berkshire and Leucadia National Corporation to form a joint venture. The joint venture, dubbed "Berkadia," purchased the failed company. As part of the deal, Berkadia would borrow $5.6 billion to re-lend (with a 2% spread) to FINOVA for its own finance activities. This debt in turn was guaranteed by Berkshire and Leucadia. Berkshire provided a 90% primary guaranty matching its economic interest in the loan. Berkadia also received 50% of FINOVA's common shares, which were in turn owned 50/50 by the joint venture.* True to Berkshire's style, it would be the Leucadia part of the partnership that would manage the investment, not Berkshire.

Goodwill

In June 2001, the Financial Accounting Standards Board (FASB) changed the way goodwill was presented in company financial statements. Prior to this change, goodwill was amortized over a period of forty years. Starting in mid-2001 it would remain on the books forever, until and unless it was found to be impaired. Such an impairment was available under the old system as well, and Berkshire had made such a charge in 2000 when it wrote off the goodwill associated with Dexter.**

A consequence of this accounting change was to bring the accounting closer to the economic reality that Berkshire had always considered more appropriate. For

---

* The common shares were completely written off during the third quarter of 2001 due to operating losses.
** It is important to note that this change was for GAAP purposes. Goodwill remained a tax deduction, typically for up to fifteen years.

years Buffett had presented his Summary of Reported Earnings table in a way that separated accounting charges from the underlying business results that he and Munger considered most important. The new accounting, begun in July 2001, affected acquisitions made after that date. For acquisitions made prior, it would begin in 2002.

If the acquisitions Berkshire made during the year were not proof enough of its unwavering long-term optimism, its existing operating subsidiaries were undeterred as well. Buffett pointed to RC Willey, which had made an unusual investment* in Idaho and then turned to do the same thing in Las Vegas to much success. Nebraska Furniture Mart began constructing a 450,000 square foot store in Kansas City, which would open in 2003.

Berkshire was bruised but not broken by the trying year. Like the country itself, Berkshire learned its lessons and moved forward to strengthen into a better version of the company it was pre-September 11th.

2002

September 11th and the 2001 recession were in the near past, but you wouldn't know it looking at Berkshire's results in 2002. Knowing where and how it erred, Berkshire almost immediately began writing large amounts of reinsurance. Save for General Re, each of the four major parts of the Insurance Group turned in favorable results. During the year it completed and initiated billions of dollars of additional investment and its marketable securities portfolio outdid the market even though valuations remained elevated. These factors came together to produce a 10% increase in per share book value—fully 32.1 percentage points higher than the S&P 500. As Buffett put it in the opening sentences of his 2002 letter to shareholders: "In all respects 2002 was a banner year."

Insurance

After poor results for three years, Berkshire had a 1% cost of float in 2002 (compared to 12.8% the prior year). On earned premiums of $19.2 billion, Berkshire posted a pre-tax underwriting loss of $411 million. This result was mostly due to no large catastrophe losses. Float grew by $5.7 billion to end the year at $41.2 billion. The real story, though, was many stories—meaning the individual businesses in Berkshire's insurance operating segment. General Re began the process of remolding itself into the reinsurer Buffett had thought he purchased at the outset, Ajit Jain's group at

---

* RC Willey, remember, opened a store outside of Mormon Utah, continuing its closed-on-Sunday policy. This, coupled with the fact that Bill Child insisted on funding the store himself in case it failed, made the investment unusual.

Berkshire Hathaway Reinsurance Group outdid itself again, GEICO "shot the lights out," and the Primary Group had an outstanding year.

Table 6.30: Berkshire Hathaway—Insurance Underwriting

($ millions)	2002	2001
GEICO Corporation		
Premiums written	$6,963	$6,176
Premiums earned	6,670	6,060
Underwriting gain/(loss) - pre-tax	$416	$221
General Re		
Premiums written	$8,521	$8,730
Premiums earned	8,500	8,353
Underwriting gain/(loss) - pre-tax	($1,393)	($3,671)
Berkshire Hathaway Reinsurance Group		
Premiums written		$3,254
Premiums earned	3,300	2,991
Underwriting gain/(loss) - pre-tax	$534	($647)
Berkshire Hathaway Primary Group		
Premiums earned	$712	$501
Underwriting gain/(loss) - pre-tax	$32	$30
Total underwriting gain/(loss)	($411)	($4,067)
Year-end average float - total	38,366	31,690
Cost of float	1.1%	12.8%
Aggregate adverse (favorable) loss development	$1,540	$1,165

Notes:
1. Berkshire Hathaway Primary Group written premiums were not detailed.
2. Berkshire Hathaway Reinsurance Group written premiums stopped being reported in 2002.
Sources: Berkshire Hathaway Annual Report 2001–2002 and author's calculations.

General Re

With Joe Brandon and Tad Montross now in control at General Re, Buffett thought the company was "well positioned to deliver huge amounts of no-cost float to Berkshire" without the hidden risks of yesteryear. Both Brandon and Montross focused on profitability of underwriting above all else—long the formula of Berkshire's other insurance businesses. The pair increased premium rates on new business, which served to offset the lower volume of business written across General Re's units.

Even though General Re's combined ratio came in at 116.4% on $8.5 billion of premiums (a loss of $1.4 billion), the underlying business was transformed in short order. This was evident in its underwriting loss, which fell 62% from 2001. The bulk of the loss stemmed from a $1 billion underwriting loss in the North American property/casualty segment, which in turn reflected $990 million of additional loss reserves and followed $800 million in 2001. Continued upward revisions to prior year loss reserves represented real liabilities and clearly frustrated Buffett.

The large loss reserve adjustment swamped a $66 million gain attributable to the 2002 accident year, and followed a $115 million reduction in reserves related to September 11th, which had been estimated too conservatively. Proving Buffett's hunch that September 11th claims would take a long time to sort out, the North American segment paid out just $241 million of the estimated $1.54 billion net loss attributable to the terrorist attacks.*

The underlying positives were a nice reversal for General Re. But like all things related to reinsurance the ultimate results would not be known for years. Berkshire estimated that just 15% of reinsurance claims in any year were reported the year they occurred. A full 50% of the General Re North American property/casualty net loss reserves of $14.9 billion were of the incurred-but-not-reported (IBNR) category. In other words, future information could move the figure in any direction.

The International property/casualty segment at General Re turned in an underwriting loss of $319 million on written premiums of $2.65 billion. Premiums earned grew 10% in dollar terms and were aided by the group's participation in a Lloyd's of London syndicate program where General Re International took over 90% of written business. Like the North American segment, the International segment recorded a loss to correct prior loss reserves, this time to the tune of $240 million. The group also recorded $107 million in losses relating to floods and storms in Europe.

General Re Global life/health saw its underwriting loss improve to $55 million on earned premiums of $1.89 billion. This was a slight improvement from the $82 million loss on $1.99 billion of earned premiums the year before. Its underwriting results were characterized as poor, reflecting losses from exited lines of business.

Berkshire Hathaway Reinsurance Group

"Ajit Jain made so much money I don't even want to tell you about it," Buffett quipped at the 2003 Annual Meeting. BHRG turned in an underwriting gain of $534 million before tax, a dramatic reversal from the previous year's $647 million loss and the most of any insurance division. To do this, BHRG overcame accounting charges and was aided by no major super cat losses.

---

* The $1.54 billion figure was the amount of underwriting loss Berkshire attributed to the September 11th attacks in the General Re North American segment in 2001. After the $115 million adjustment in reserves in 2002 this net loss from September 11th would have been $1.425 billion.

For the first time, the Annual Report broke down BHRG's sub-segments in table form to clearly show its various lines of business. Due to a lack of catastrophes during the year, the catastrophe and individual risk line turned in a pre-tax underwriting gain of $1 billion on $1.3 billion of premiums earned. The catastrophe segment also benefitted from $85 million of reduced reserves relating to the September 11th terrorist attacks. Like General Re, BHRG overestimated its losses and an accounting adjustment corrected for the new estimate. Catastrophe was the type of business prone to large fluctuations in results, but over time was expected to earn a reasonable profit. The profit in 2002 was clearly on the upside. Buffett told shareholders to adjust their assessments of Berkshire's earnings power downward because of it.

It was not uncommon for reinsurers to lay off their own risk. To do this, they would purchase reinsurance to cover the risks they assumed in reinsuring primary companies. Berkshire Hathaway Reinsurance rarely did this. Berkshire was wary of the ability of collecting on others' promises many years into the future and had seen supposedly strong reinsurers go out of business.[*] Berkshire was willing to take the volatility in periodic results in exchange for better results over the long term—and it had the necessary capital to hold all its volume.

The retroactive reinsurance segment of BHRG reported a loss of $446 million on earned premiums of just $407 million. It was this segment of BHRG's operations that had significant accounting peculiarities. Even though the economics were in Berkshire's favor—receiving large premiums up front followed by (usually) long periods of payments out the door—the accounting caused results to look poor. The premiums earned in 2002 were swamped by $428 million amortization of deferred charges relating to premiums earned in prior years.

The favorable economics are illustrated in the $7.5 billion of year-end float from retroactive reinsurance.[**] Berkshire could put this sum to work for its own benefit while concurrently paying claims as they came in. Amortization of the deferred charge asset related to writing those premiums would remain no matter how much in premiums showed up on the topline. Berkshire estimated that 2003 would see $400 million of such charges from contracts already on the books in 2002.

BHRG's quota-share business grew almost sixfold in 2002. The quota-share business, which was a way of participating in a percentage of the business of another insurer, earned premiums of $1.29 billion and reported a loss of $86 million on that volume. Seeing favorable underwriting conditions, the group participated in new Lloyd's of London syndicates and booked a contract with a major US-based insurer. BHRG also earned $60 million on $321 million of earned premiums in its Other segment.

---

* Buffett told the story in his 2002 Chairman's letter of how GEICO once took in $72,000 of premiums for risks "deadbeat reinsurers" ceased paying. This episode had cost GEICO over $90 million so far, including $19 million in 2002 alone. "So much for 'cheap' reinsurance," he wrote.
** This was about half of the $13.4 billion of year-end float attributable to BHRG.

It is worth taking a moment to discuss Lloyd's of London, which has been noted several times. Lloyd's of London was not a single entity, but rather a marketplace for insurance transactions.* Insurers could come together to form syndicates, or risk-sharing pools. Lloyds was like a clearinghouse with known rules and ways of conducting business.

Berkshire Hathaway Primary Group

The primary lines turned in another year of profit and grew float 38% to $943 million. While most of this segment continued to do well, the workers' compensation business in the Home State Group suffered.** Buffett said its reserving severely missed the mark. Placing profitability over growth, he said: "Until we figure out how to get this business right, we will keep it small."

GEICO

Buffett had a maxim: there are no positive surprises in insurance. This was perhaps off mark with GEICO. GEICO had another great year in 2002 and Buffett summed it up succinctly:

> "At GEICO, everything went so well in 2002 that we should pinch ourselves. Growth was substantial, profits were outstanding, policyholder retention was up, and sales productivity jumped significantly. These trends continued in early 2003."

GEICO's 10% growth in earned premiums reflected its growth in voluntary auto policies.*** Its loss ratio also benefitted from a milder winter, which edged down 2.9 percentage points to 77% of earned premiums. Its combined ratio came in at 93.8%—a 6.2% pre-tax underwriting margin. Outstanding indeed.

Acquisitions

During 2002, Berkshire closed five substantial acquisitions in addition to numerous bolt-on acquisitions to operating subsidiaries. Two of the five closed transactions

---

* The entity was technically incorporated by the English Parliament in 1871 but functions like a marketplace.
** There was no cause attributed to the "poor results" of workers' compensation; however, Munger long lamented the issues surrounding that business, especially in California. Claimants would come forward with all types of non-physical and emotional ailments which wreaked havoc on the system.
*** Voluntary policies-in-force grew 9.6%. This included a 7% increase in the preferred segment and a 17.4% increase in the non-preferred segment.

were Albecca (doing business as Larson-Juhl and discussed in 2001) and Fruit of the Loom (discussed below). Two others, with a combined pre-tax profit of $60 million, were CTB and Garan. CTB made agriculture equipment for the poultry, hog, egg production, and grain industries. Garan manufactured children's apparel and is best known for Garanimals, its largest line. Buffett said each company earned decent returns on capital, but no details were disclosed.

Berkshire acquired The Pampered Chef on October 31, 2002, the same day it closed on Garan. Doris Christopher started The Pampered Chef in her basement in 1980 with $3,000 borrowed from her life insurance policy. The company sold kitchenware and equipment at home parties. At the time of Berkshire's purchase, the company was doing $700 million of sales a year through its 67,000 kitchen consultants.

Buffett told shareholders it took about ten seconds for him to decide Berkshire wanted to partner with Christopher and the CEO she had brought in to run the company, Sheila O'Connell Cooper. The purchase price wasn't disclosed.

Fruit of the Loom

The well-known underwear maker was the latest low-tech business to find its way onto Berkshire's radar. How Fruit of the Loom became a Berkshire subsidiary was a little out of the ordinary. The company faced bankruptcy after stumbling with operating and financing issues. Berkshire first purchased its bonds and bank debt at 50% of face value, which equated to a 15% current return and amounted to 10% of Fruit of the Loom's senior debt. An unusual feature of the bankruptcy allowing for interest payments on senior debt during the bankruptcy process attracted Buffett. The investment was originally intended to be nothing more than a junk bond investment, one of very few such outlays during that time.

Two things led to Fruit of the Loom's bankruptcy. First, the company ran up debt of over $1.2 billion. This compared to revenues under $2 billion (and falling), and just $130 million of gross profit. Buffett said such metrics pointed to "a company that, in a financial sense, was out of control." A second major issue, which both precipitated the debt problem and exacerbated it, was bloated costs and other operating issues.

Buffett saw the potential for it to regain its status as a low-cost producer of a basic needed product. It had a 40%+ market share in the men's and boy's market. Buffett believed the company could once again be a good business once it shed its debt burden and costs were brought back in line.

The man to do that job was Fruit of the Loom's former CEO John Holland, who returned on the scene to fix the mess the prior management team made. It was telling that the only major contingency in Berkshire's offer to the bankruptcy court was that Holland remain as CEO.

Berkshire offered the bankruptcy court $835 million, which included the assumption of certain liabilities.* Unlike its other deals, the offer to buy Fruit of the Loom came with no strings attached save for Holland running the company. Neither Berkshire's ability to finance the deal, or even war could derail the transaction from closing (many contracts have what's called force majeure clauses that allow termination for major events such as war or other unforeseeable circumstances). The deal closed on April 30, 2002.

It's not entirely clear what sort of financial returns Berkshire could expect from Fruit of the Loom. It appears the purchase price roughly equated to book value.** If the rescued Fruit of the Loom could earn returns on capital near what it had during Holland's heyday Berkshire could likely expect satisfactory returns upwards of 15%.***

The Fruit of the Loom story has another historical element. During the 1950s while Buffett was working for Graham-Newman, Fruit of the Loom crossed his path. Union Underwear Company (which produced a product under the Fruit of the Loom brand name) had been sold at a mouth-watering price to a company Buffett owned shares in, the Philadelphia and Reading Coal and Iron Company. Philadelphia and Reading purchased Union Underwear, which subsequently purchased control of the Fruit of the Loom brand name and grew pre-tax earnings to over $200 million.

Both the 1955 and 2001 deals were assisted by Graham-Newman partner, Mickey Newman. Mickey was the son of Graham-Newman partner, Jerome Newman, and had assisted Buffett during the 2001 bankruptcy proceedings by sharing his historical knowledge of the company and introducing Buffett to John Holland. Newman attended the 2002 Berkshire Annual Meeting and received applause from shareholders for his work on their behalf.

Another related historical note is appropriate. In December of 2001, H.H. Brown acquired the inventory and trademarks of Acme Boot. Acme had also been purchased by Philadelphia and Reading in 1956. Unlike Fruit of the Loom, Acme had fallen from its former graces. What had been a company with $7 million in annual revenues was sold for a tenth of that amount in 2001.

Berkshire also made two additional acquisitions through MidAmerican. MidAmerican contracted to buy Northern Natural Gas, a 16,600-mile pipeline supplying gas to Midwestern states. The business was originally headquartered in Omaha. It ultimately ended up with the infamous Enron Company in Texas. Enron's

---

* The Q2 2002 Berkshire quarterly report indicates the cash purchase price was $730 million. It's possible this lower figure incorporates one or both of the assumed liabilities and working capital adjustments.

** The purchase agreement stipulated a net working capital figure of $540 million. In addition Fruit of the Loom as of its 2000 10K filing had $277 million of net fixed assets (this assumes Berkshire acquired the majority of the company's fixed assets).

*** This is a very rough approximation. One source (Kilpatrick, 2015) states that Buffett indicated the company might earn $130 million to $140 million pre-tax. This would equate to a 15% pre-tax return and is consistent with returns on capital in the mid-1990s under Holland's direction.

bankruptcy led to the business being held by Dynegy, an Enron creditor that took the pipeline as collateral. It was then quickly sold to MidAmerican over the course of a weekend. The other MidAmerican purchase in 2002 was Kern River. Kern River was also a pipeline business, this time supplying gas to Southern California. MidAmerican now supplied 8% of the gas used annually in the United States.

Berkshire injected additional capital into MidAmerican to fund the Northern Natural and Kern River purchases. Remember that Berkshire could not control MidAmerican, so its original purchase was structured in such a way to give it a majority economic interest but a much lower voting interest. To remain a non-controlling shareholder of MidAmerican and in compliance with the Public Utilities Company Holding Act, Berkshire purchased an additional $402 million of convertible preferred stock and $1.27 billion of trust preferred securities. As a result of the additional investments, Berkshire's fully diluted economic interest in MidAmerican rose to 80.2% at year-end.

Interestingly, MidAmerican was not just an energy company. It had an "accidental" business called HomeServices, a residential real estate brokerage. Residential real estate and energy were very different, but so were the myriad businesses at Berkshire. HomeServices had grown to be the second largest residential broker in the country and did $37 billion of transactions in 2002 alone. This was double its volume just a year earlier. The business was cyclical, but had low capital requirements and plenty of room for growth under the leadership of CEO Ron Peltier.

Mid American's pre-tax earnings grew 8% to $613 million, in part due to acquisitions.

Manufacturing, Service, and Retailing*

Berkshire's other non-insurance businesses had good results in 2002, especially when considering the recent recession. General weakness in the consumer market prevailed but Berkshire's jewelry and furniture businesses held their own. Pre-tax earnings in the Retail Operations segment, which included jewelry and furniture, dropped just 5% to $166 million.

Shaw, the newly acquired carpet manufacturer, increased earnings by 45% to $424 million. Just 1% of the increase was attributable to prices, while the rest was because the company judiciously controlled expenses, leading to margin improvement.

The Chairman's letter grouped Acme Brick, Benjamin Moore, Johns Manville, MiTek and Shaw into a home and construction–related businesses category for discussion purposes. As a group these businesses earned $941 million in 2002.

---

* As a reminder, Berkshire stopped reporting separate financial statements for the Manufacturing, Service, and Retailing businesses in 2001. The reporting began again in 2003.

The Apparel segment reported pre-tax profits of $229 million. These weren't comparable to the $33 million loss the year before since the current year included results from Fruit of the Loom, Garan, and H.H. Brown. Scott Fetzer's pre-tax earnings were unchanged at $129 million.

Results in the Flight Services segment were worse than they appeared. The reported 21% increase in pre-tax earnings to $225 million included a $60 million gain from exiting a joint venture with Boeing. Operations continued to struggle with post-September 11th challenges that included reduced training (reflecting fewer overall flights) and costs to expand fractional jet service into Europe.

Finance and Financial Products

Within the Finance and Financial Products businesses category, pre-tax earnings grew from $519 million in 2001 to $1 billion in 2002. Considering that included a $173 million loss related to winding down General Re Securities, contributions from elsewhere were significant. A large part came from Buffett himself, who conducted undisclosed arbitrage-related activities in highly rated fixed income securities. Another boost came from Berkshire's earnings in its stake in Value Capital, a limited partnership run by former GEICO CEO Jack Byrne's son, Mark.

Viewed in two broad categories—insurance underwriting and non-insurance businesses—the progress made at Berkshire in 2002 was readily apparent. From an underwriting loss of $2.66 billion (after-tax and after minority interests) in 2001, Berkshire's Insurance Group improved to a $292 million loss in 2002. On the non-insurance front earnings jumped from $1.3 billion to $2.2 billion (again after tax) due largely to the addition of several new operating businesses. Berkshire was putting its cash to use productively and returning its core business of insurance to the top of the industry.*

Investments

Charlie Munger's favorite shareholder meeting quip of "nothing to add" seems appropriate with respect to Berkshire's equity investments in 2002. M&T Bank made the $500 million cutoff to be included in the Chairman's letter table for the first time, though it was not a new investment. American Express, Coke, Gillette, and Wells Fargo remained untouched. The only change was in the other category with about $600 million of additional investment (at cost). Berkshire's equity portfolio remained

---

* Berkshire's after-tax operating earnings (before investment gains but including investment income, corporate interest expense, purchase-price adjustments, and other) rose to $3.9 billion from a loss of $47 million in 2001.

concentrated, with 69% of its $28 billion year-end market value in the four returning companies just mentioned above.

It seemed Berkshire's equity portfolio would remain in a holding pattern for some time. Buffett told shareholders that, "unless, however, we see a very high probability of at least a 10% pre-tax return (which translate to 6.5%-7% after corporate tax), we will sit on the sidelines." Asked about this 10% target at the next year's Annual Meeting Buffett said it was nothing scientific, only a somewhat arbitrary point below which it would feel sloppy. He and Munger would rather endure low rates earned on cash (then historically low at around 1.25%) and wait for opportunities to earn higher rates.

While equity markers weren't accommodating, credit markets offered an opportunity for Berkshire to put some of its surplus cash to work at attractive rates of return. A significant decline in the prices of junk bonds began in 2001 and continued into 2002. This improved the risk/reward scenario. As noted earlier, the Fruit of the Loom investment started as a junk bond investment. Berkshire purchased $8 billion of additional junk bonds in 2002 in various energy and telecommunications companies. One notable purchase was $169 million (cost) of euro-denominated Amazon.com junk bonds trading at 57% of par, purchased after the company announced it would expense stock options, a practice that was optional at the time.[74] The action gave Buffett confidence in the business and its management.

Derivatives

As much as Buffett disliked the accounting of stock options, he thought derivatives as a class represented a true risk to the real economy. Buffett railed against the widespread use of derivatives and their potential to cause unintended harm, devoting two pages of his Chairman's letter to it. Derivatives, as the word implies, are contracts that derive value from the performance of an underlying entity such as an asset, index or interest rate. Buffett called them time bombs and saw their potential to aggregate risk, rather than disperse it. Once concentrated into a few counterparties, those would then pose systemic risks to the financial system and the broader economy. Derivatives "carry dangers that, while now latent, are potentially lethal."

In December 2001, Enron's bankruptcy filing shined a light on the dangers of derivatives. Enron had created a market for energy-based derivatives. When the market collapsed, Enron shareholders lost $74 billion. Less than a decade later, their dangers would again be on display during the real estate crisis, in that case due to mortgage-backed securities.[75]

The problem was not the efficacy of derivatives to shift risk among parties on a microlevel, but their aggregated effects. One entity taking the risk of another at times made sense, such as a manufacturer hedging a key input so that costs are known and fixed prices can be established. The issue arose on a macro level where certain intermediaries collected many of these micro transactions. These intermediaries would then seek to hedge their own risks with the use of still more derivative transactions, thinking themselves protected. This is the type of behavior that General Re Securities undertook, eventually finding itself with over 14,000 contracts with 672 counterparties.*

Disaster could (and did) strike when a key counterparty failed, or several down the line failed to keep their promises. This could cause a chain reaction that wiped out many once-strong institutions. Think of Enron.

Another related pernicious effect of derivatives was on accounting and compensation. Buffett and Munger had first-hand knowledge from their time at Salomon, and then at General Re, of how hard some derivatives were to value. With sometimes thin trading, many derivatives were "marked to model," meaning accountants couldn't use market data to establish their value and instead relied on a calculation of value. Oftentimes these models were constructed by the same people compensated for their results. Accountants, to their shame, sometimes failed to question them. Optimism seeped in, of course, and some contracts had a profit attached to it on both sides of the transaction, which clearly could not be the case. Further, since many contracts spanned years or decades, the results of bad bets would be felt long after the traders who booked them received their own paychecks.

Berkshire began winding down General Re's derivatives book at the start of 2002, realizing losses in the process.

SQUARZ Notes

Berkshire issued a first-of-its-kind security during 2002. It was done with the help of Byron Trott, a Goldman Sachs banker who would play an increasingly larger role in Berkshire's acquisitions and financing over the coming years. Christened SQUARZ, the $400 million issue carried a negative interest rate in exchange for the right to purchase shares in Berkshire at a premium (see Table 6.31).

The issue was broken up into $10,000 par value notes due in November 2007. Each required the holder to pay Berkshire 3.75% annually for the right to a 3.00% coupon and the ability to convert the notes into 0.1116 BRK A shares.** Thus, Berkshire was paid 0.75%, net annually. What did the terms of the SQUARZ notes say about Berkshire's prospects as judged by each side of the transaction?

Those purchasing the notes would benefit only if Berkshire shares increased at a steady clip over the ensuing five years. But the rate of return would be lower than

---

* The footnotes to the 2002 Annual Report estimated that if all of the counterparties to General Re's derivative book defaulted, the loss to Berkshire would be roughly $4.9 billion.
** The holder could also elect the equivalent number of B shares, or 3.3480.

the underlying change in share price because of the large upfront premium to both the underlying share price and book value. If the share price declined, holders could elect to receive their cash back at maturity—after paying Berkshire for the privilege.

The advantages of the SQUARZ notes lay almost entirely with Berkshire, yet investors nonetheless found them attractive, perhaps due to Berkshire's historical rates of return. Berkshire had the benefit of:

1. Upfront use of the cash
2. Annual interest income from the negative interest rate
3. Low effective cost if the notes were converted into shares

Buffett was effectively monetizing his modest outlook for Berkshire's future returns.

Table 6.31: Berkshire Hathaway SQUARZ Notes—select data

Price-to-book ratio 2002-Q2	1.75x
Implied price-to-book ratio at issuance	2.24x
Annual return to warrant holder if BRK:	
Increased by 15%/year over five years	8.71%
Increased by 10%/year over five years	3.95%

Sources: Berkshire Hathaway Annual Report 2002 and author's calculations.

Accounting Lessons

Buffett's 2002 Chairman's letter purported to be the first to include a negative pro forma adjustment to earnings. He was poking fun at a very serious problem gripping the accounting and business world. Some companies of the day touted adjusted numbers that sought to exclude one-time or non-recurring items.[*] These appeared to make sense on the surface, but over time they served to divert the reader from what was happening. Buffett's jab in his letter was a downward revision (since others adjusted upward without fail) to correct for Berkshire's benefit from no catastrophe losses in 2002 and some outsize gains Buffett booked in the financial products business.

His lessons for investors were simple and founded on a base of sound skepticism. Lesson one was be wary of company's displaying weak accounting. He used three examples:

1. Companies not expensing stock options, which was still optional at the time;
2. Overly optimistic pension assumptions;
3. And companies and managements touting EBITDA (earnings before interest taxes, depreciation and amortization).

---

[*] This practice continues but generally ebbs and flows with the markets' and regulators' scrutiny.

The "D" in EBITDA, depreciation, particularly bothered Buffett. He said ignoring depreciation was akin to ignoring some other real expense. Just because depreciation was considered non-cash, since no cash went out the door after the initial capital outlay, it was still an expense. Further, it was the worst kind of expense since money went out the door day one and was only recouped over time as the expense was charged against earnings. He knew from first-hand experience that companies not spending their average depreciation would fall behind in real terms.

The second lesson was to be skeptical of unintelligible footnotes. He thought such fuzzy disclosures indicate untrustworthy management. If a reader couldn't understand them, it was probably not their fault—and it could be because the CEO didn't want them to.

His third lesson was to have a healthy level of skepticism. It's worth repeating in its entirety:

> "Finally, be suspicious of companies that trumpet earnings projections and growth expectations. Businesses seldom operate in a tranquil, no-surprise environment, and earnings simply don't advance smoothly (except, of course, in the offering books of investment bankers).
>
> Charlie and I not only don't know today what our businesses will earn *next year*—we don't even know what they will earn *next quarter*. We are suspicious of those CEOs who regularly claim they do know the future—and we become downright incredulous if they consistently reach their declared targets. Managers that always promise to 'make the numbers' will at some point be tempted to make up the numbers."

Business results fall where they may, Buffett would always tell the unvarnished truth.

2003

Berkshire's gain in book value per share fell behind the S&P 500 for the first time in three years. While Berkshire's 21% gain was itself highly satisfactory, the 7.7% lag nonetheless represented the fifth time since 1965 that it had fallen short of the market. Part of the reason had to do with the changing nature of the company. Berkshire's fortunes were less tied to its marketable securities portfolio[*] after it completed a slew of acquisitions. A higher proportion of capital invested in operating businesses would cause performance to lag in an up market like 2003 but lead to outperformance during market downturns. Capital allocation decisions and operating performance in

---

[*] Buffett's letter pointed to the fact that the equity portfolio (including preferred stocks) had fallen from 114% of Berkshire's net worth in the 1980s to 50% in 2000–2003.

2003 were far from disappointing. On the contrary, Berkshire added important non-insurance subsidiaries to its roster and the Insurance Group turned in underwriting results fit for praise.

Insurance

"Last year was a standout," wrote Buffett of 2003 Insurance Group performance. The group turned in an underwriting profit of $1.7 billion and float grew to a record $44 billion. All four of its main insurance segments contributed. Berkshire Hathaway Reinsurance Group continued its tradition of over-achieving, General Re was fixed, GEICO continued to impress, and Berkshire Hathaway Primary Group remained stellar.

Table 6.32: Berkshire Hathaway—Insurance Underwriting

($ millions)	2003	2002
GEICO Corporation		
Premiums written	$8,081	$6,963
Premiums earned	7,784	6,670
Underwriting gain/(loss) - pre-tax	$452	$416
General Re		
Premiums written	$8,021	$8,521
Premiums earned	8,245	8,500
Underwriting gain/(loss) - pre-tax	$145	($1,393)
Berkshire Hathaway Reinsurance Group		
Premiums earned	$4,430	$3,300
Underwriting gain/(loss) - pre-tax	$1,047	$534
Berkshire Hathaway Primary Group		
Premiums earned	$1,034	$712
Underwriting gain/(loss) - pre-tax	$74	$32
Total underwriting gain/(loss)	$1,718	($411)
Year-end average float - total	42,722	38,366
Cost of float	(4.0%)	1.1%
Aggregate adverse (favorable) loss development	$480	$1,540

Notes:

1. Berkshire Hathaway Primary Group written premiums were not detailed.

2. Berkshire Hathaway Reinsurance Group written premiums stopped being reported in 2002.

Sources: Berkshire Hathaway Annual Reports 2002–2003 and author's calculations.

Berkshire Hathaway Reinsurance Group

Ajit Jain's group at BHRG again impressed during 2003. Its total underwriting gain of $1 billion on $4.4 billion of earned premiums was in large part due to a lack of catastrophes.

The catastrophe and individual risk segment (the segment holding the catastrophe risks) earned $1.1 billion on its $1.3 billion earned premiums for the year. Its maximum probable loss from a single event was $6.7 billion. Such a loss would swamp several years of gains. But its operating philosophy was sound with expectations of modest profits over the long term, catastrophes included. Individual risks also contributed to profits in 2003. Jain's group found easy bars to step over. One was a Pepsi promotion where Berkshire insured a $1 billion prize (no one won).* Such "mammoth and unusual risks" were bread-and-butter for BHRG.

The retroactive reinsurance segment reported a $387 million loss on $526 million of earned premiums. This was a good result considering amortization of deferred charges hit losses to the tune of $400 million a year regardless of premium volume.** Even with low levels of earned premiums and reported losses, the retroactive reinsurance segment remained a money-generator for Berkshire. This segment alone accounted for $7.7 billion of the nearly $14 billion of float attributable to BHRG.

Buried in the footnotes in 2003 was an unusual $41 million gain attributed to the BHRG retroactive segment relating to a "commutation of contracts written in prior years in exchange for payments of $710 million." What was going on here? While retroactive reinsurance contracts are typically long-term arrangements, they are sometimes prematurely terminated. The $710 million represented a payment by Berkshire to the original ceding company, essentially giving them back some of their original premium. The $41 million was the accounting gain relating to over-reserving expected losses from those contracts. The net effect was a reduction in float for Berkshire as the premium was returned.

Other activities at BHRG in 2003 included $2.6 billion of earned premiums and $326 million of underwriting profit on traditional multi-line business, with a large part coming from Lloyd's of London syndicates.

General Re

The fixers of General Re, CEO Joe Brandon and President Tad Montross, received Buffett's praise for restoring underwriting discipline to Berkshire's problem child. The

---

* The present value was $250 million. Though details are not known on the premium BHRG received, a similar contest a few years prior for Grab.com purportedly was a 10-to-1 premium for 100-to-1 odds (*The Snowball*, p. 689).
** The $400 million figure comes from the 2002 Annual Report. Unamortized deferred charges were $2.8 billion at year-end 2003.

company was still beset by some unfavorable prior-year loss estimates. Nonetheless, General Re managed to eke out a $145 million underwriting gain on $8.2 billion of earned premiums.

General Re's North American segment, which recovered its underwriting to a $67 million profit on $3.4 billion of earned premiums, improved most. This was up from a staggering loss of $1 billion on $4 billion of earned premiums in 2002. The segment was able to this via a combination of increased pricing (which was partially responsible for the lower premium volume) and a lack of major catastrophes during 2003. Its current year gains (underwriting attributable to just 2003) were $200 million, but those were offset by $133 million of adjustments relating to prior year losses. Included in those prior year loss adjustments were increases to director and officers' insurance liabilities resulting from the fallout from the scandals of the early 2000s. Director and officers insurance provides protection to executives for claims arising from their governance and management of companies. Claims for misconduct in prior years (and the related adjustments insurance companies make to account for them) happen after the fact since most claims come to light only after a major scandal or bankruptcy.

One drag on General Re's North American underwriting results in 2003 was a change to the discount rate used to value workers' compensation claims. Berkshire changed its discount rate of 4.5% for claims prior to 2003 and began using a 1% rate. This reflected conservatism on the part of Berkshire. This weighted those liabilities closer to the present, which necessitated a $74 million charge in 2003.

The International segment of General Re improved similarly in 2003. While premiums earned increased about 6% to $1.9 billion, they only did so as a result of the weakness in the US dollar. Absent such currency-related tailwinds, premium volume declined over 8%. A $20 million pre-tax underwriting gain was a marked improvement from the $319 million loss booked in 2002 and came after a $104 million addition to loss reserves.

Berkshire disclosed more details on General Re's activities in the Faraday or London market, which was previously and subsequently included as part of International. General Re participated in 61% of the Faraday Syndicate 435 business in 2001, 97% in 2002, and 100% in 2003. This additional information showed that most losses were outside of Faraday. The segment was responsible for $200 million of losses between 2001 and 2003, inclusive (with $178 million of that coming in 2001), which was just a fraction of the $921 million of pre-tax loss from the segmented International property/casualty results over that same time period.

The General Re Global life/health segment reported a $58 million gain in 2003. Most of the gains were in its international business.

GEICO

GEICO had excellent results in 2003—even by its own high standards. Preferred policyholder count grew 8.2% and non-preferred grew 21.4%, for a 10.9% overall growth rate. Premiums grew 16.7% to $7.8 billion on the heels of the unit growth and a 2% average premium rate increase.

Such high growth rates necessitated expansion, and in 2003 the company announced an expansion into Buffalo, New York. It was no coincidence that it was in the same city as Berkshire's newspaper, *The Buffalo News*. Stan Lipsey, the paper's publisher, was instrumental in the expansion, which would eventually add 2,500 new jobs.

Even with its ever-increasing need for more employees and space, GEICO kept costs down and profits up. GEICO boosted advertising during the year and still achieved a combined ratio of 94.2%. Moreover, growth in premiums and policies reflected an increasing market share. From the time CEO Tony Nicely took over in 1992 to 2003, GEICO more than doubled its market share from 2.1% to 5%.

Berkshire Hathaway Primary Group

The Primary Group turned in an underwriting profit of $74 million on premiums of $1 billion. Its float grew 41% to $1.3 billion. How could Buffett and Munger be anything but very pleased with this group of managers? It seemed every year the group turned in higher premiums, higher profits, and more float. Buffett's comment in his letter to shareholders in 2003 sums up the group nicely: "These men, though operating in unexciting ways, produce truly exciting results."

Acquisitions

During the year, Berkshire agreed to acquire two companies: Clayton Homes, a leading producer and financer of manufactured homes, and McLane, a distributor of goods to convenience stores and related outlets.

Clayton Homes

The Clayton acquisition came about in a most unusual way—even for Berkshire. Buffett long hosted groups of students who flocked to Omaha to hear him speak. On one such visit he received an autobiography of Clayton founder, Jim Clayton, from a group of Tennessee students. Buffett had some familiarity with Tennessee-based Clayton Homes, but he had not studied the company to any great extent.

Clayton was a big business. It had twenty manufacturing plants, 300 company-owned stores, over 500 independent retailers, and eighty-nine housing communities. It also had a financial services arm that played an integral role in the company's success.

Buffett's newly piqued interest combined with industry turmoil led Berkshire to make an offer for Clayton. Some of Clayton's competitors engaged in poor lending practices to sell homes or make loans to unqualified consumers. Such practices continued longer than they otherwise would have because most loans were securitized. Securitization is a process where many loans are packaged together and sold to investors. Those investors then take on the risk of borrowers defaulting from the manufacturer-originators. Once credit problems began to materialize, the ability to securitize dried up and affected Clayton's ability to obtain financing and in turn lend to its own customers.

Clayton's board of directors recognized Berkshire's ability to provide financing and agreed to sell to Berkshire. Berkshire paid $1.7 billion for Clayton. The deal closed on August 7, 2003.

When Berkshire completed the acquisition of Clayton Homes, it placed its operations in the Finance and Financial Products category. At first this seems quite odd. That is until the extent and importance of its financing business becomes apparent. The basic business model worked like this: A manufacturer like Clayton produced a home and marketed it through a distribution channel that could include its own stores or other retailers. Clayton had a mix of both. The home was either purchased for cash or, (more likely) with financing provided by an unrelated third party or a financing arm of the manufacturer.

Over time, lenders incented to make loans and manufacturers incented to sell homes loosened their standards and began pushing homes and loans on unsuspecting customers with poor credit. To increase their volume of business, the financing was often securitized. The original packagers of the loans, incented to produce volume irrespective of repayment capacity, ultimately underwrote many bad loans. The resulting defaults then caused the securitization market to dry up, which affected everyone in the industry, including Clayton.*

When this happened, Clayton had no way to recoup its cash for additional loans. Berkshire's purchase solved that problem by providing almost unlimited financing to Clayton. Berkshire borrowed money and re-lent it to Clayton at a 1% spread. But why not just give Clayton the money since Berkshire had ample cash and it was now entirely owned by Berkshire? Buffett said Berkshire had a philosophy of "every tub on its own bottom." He went on to explain. "We believe that any subsidiary lending money should pay an appropriate rate for the funds needed to carry its receivables and should not be subsidized by its parent. Otherwise, having a rich daddy can lead

---

* One cannot help but think that the issues plaguing the manufactured home industry during this time was but a small precursor to the main event that was the housing crisis later in the decade.

to sloppy decisions." At year-end 2003, Clayton had just over $2 billion of such loans on its books to finance customers' purchases.

Clayton's financing arrangements contain two lessons. One, financing interest-bearing receivables* with debt is entirely appropriate. It was like a mini bank inside Berkshire that funded its interest-bearing assets with interest-bearing liabilities to take a spread. This was not the first of its kind at Berkshire. Scott Fetzer had a financing subsidiary that financed the purchase of World Book Encyclopedias and Kirby vacuum cleaners this way.

A second lesson from Clayton's financing was the role of credit risk and incentives. With Clayton under Berkshire's umbrella, it could retain all its loans from its customers. This meant it would ultimately bear the cost of underwriting bad loans and had an incentive to do good by its customers.** The securitization model in which the industry previously operated failed in large part because lenders did not care about short-term outcomes. Requiring lenders to keep some of each loan would play a key role in re-shaping the US credit system after the Great Recession of 2009 where many subprime loans were resold in packages as mortgage-backed securities.

Berkshire's purchase price of $1.7 billion suggests it paid a fair price for Clayton's straightforward business model and its history of consistent financial returns. However, its pre-tax return on capital appears to have been at a low in 2002 as a result of the cyclical nature of its business. Berkshire could see an upside benefit if Clayton could achieve its historical average return of 21%. It could also benefit by providing financing to Clayton and avoiding expensive securitized financing.

Table 6.33: Clayton Homes—acquisition analysis

($ millions)	2002	2001	2000	1999	1998	1997	1996	1995	1994	1993
Total revenues	$1,199	$1,151	$1,293	$1,344	$1,128	$1,022	$929	$758	$628	$476
Revenues/avg. capital	$0.91	$0.95	$1.19	$1.24	$1.18	$1.40	$1.46	$1.35	$1.23	$0.98
EBIT margin	17%	15%	18%	19%	19%	18%	18%	17%	17%	18%
Pre-tax return on capital	15%	14%	21%	23%	23%	26%	26%	23%	21%	17%
Purchase price (equity)	$1,700									
Assumed debt	93									
Effective purchase price	$1,793									
Purchase multiple	1.36x									
BRK going-in pre-tax return	11.2%									

Sources: Berkshire Hathaway Annual Report 2003, Clayton Homes Annual Report 2002, and author's calculations.

---

* This term is used broadly to include longer-term receivables and notes such as the mortgages Clayton held on its customers' homes.

** Clayton incented its dealers to make good loans (requiring adequate down payments and checking repayment capacity) by charging any losses to that dealer. It forced long-term thinking. Such long-term thinking was in the customers' best interest as well.

McLane

Berkshire's second major acquisition of 2003 was McLane. McLane came to Buffett's attention via Byron Trott, the Goldman Sachs banker who had worked on the SQUARZ debt issue.

McLane was a subsidiary of Walmart that had grown from Walmart's need to distribute products to many stores. The business then expanded to include non-Walmart stores such as convenience stores, drug stores, wholesale clubs, restaurants, and theaters. Not surprisingly Walmart accounted for 35% of McLane's revenues. McLane conflicted with Walmart's competitors because of its growth, leading Walmart to sell the subsidiary.

Berkshire paid Walmart $1.5 billion for McLane, with the transaction closing on May 23, 2003 (see Table 6.34). The business was simple and understandable and fit right in with Berkshire's other non-insurance businesses. From an earning power standpoint, McLane's business was not all that unusual. Its profit margins compared to other Berkshire subsidiaries, however, were.

McLane was a no-value-add type operation. It simply moved products from one location to another. Consequently, it commanded slim margins. So slim that it earned just 1% pre-tax on a massive $23 billion of revenues. This was a figure greater than all of Berkshire's non-insurance subsidiaries *combined*. While it was profits not revenues that mattered, accounting conventions required that businesses be reported based on their revenues. As a result, McLane would have to remain a separate reporting item in all Berkshire's financial reports going forward.

McLane's thin profit margins are a good lesson on the importance of focusing on the right variables in business analysis. Profit margins would seem to be a good indicator of the desirability of a business, and indeed they do carry some important information. As McLane proves, however, a small profit margin can translate into a satisfactory return on capital, provided enough turnover.[*]

Table 6.34: McLane—acquisition analysis

($ millions)	
Revenues	$23,000
Pre-tax margin	1%
Pre-tax income	$230
Berkshire's purchase price	$1,500
BRK going-in pre-tax return	15.3%

Sources: Berkshire Hathaway Annual Report 2003 and author's calculations.

---

[*] The notes to the financial statements disclose that McLane's 2002 revenues and pre-tax earnings were $21.9 billion and $220 million, respectively.

Non-Insurance Businesses

As Berkshire's stable of businesses grew in number it became challenging to report results to shareholders in a useful and intelligible way. Or as Buffett put it: "without turning out something as long as the World Book." In 2003, the long-familiar Sources of Reported Earnings was omitted from the Chairman's letter.* In its place Buffett reported on Berkshire's four major operating sectors:

1. Insurance
2. Regulated Utility Businesses
3. Finance and Financial Products
4. Manufacturing, Service, and Retailing**

Buffett said his goal was to give shareholders the facts he and Munger would want if roles were reversed, without providing data inessential to calculating Berkshire's intrinsic value.*** He also cautioned shareholders to be careful in their analysis and to "remember that the company should be viewed as an unfolding movie, not as a still photograph. Those who focused in the past on only the snapshot of the day sometimes reached erroneous conclusions." With Berkshire's policy of retaining all its earnings, the reinvestment factor was an important part of the valuation exercise.

Regulated Utility Businesses

Since the Insurance Group was presented above we will start with the utility businesses, all under the umbrella of MidAmerican. MidAmerican's $1.1 billion of earnings before interest and taxes (EBIT) broke down as follows:

- $289 million, UK utilities
- $269 million, Iowa-based utility businesses
- $261 million, pipelines
- $113 million, Home Services
- $144 million, other income

---

* I have attempted to recreate this table for 2003 and 2004 using data from the Annual Report for continuity of the table at the beginning of the chapter.

** I have attempted to align the analysis in this book with Buffett's clues as to the most intelligible way of viewing Berkshire, while at the same time bringing certain interesting or important topics to the attention of the reader.

*** At the 2004 Annual Meeting, Buffett noted Berkshire's $130 billion market cap and how it wasn't "too important to get keen insights into some business making a relatively small amount of money…you have to look at them in aggregate."

MidAmerican's 2003 EBIT increased 36% and its net earnings of $416 million were up 9% from the year before. These increases were largely due to the new pipelines funded with additional capital contributions. MidAmerican owed $10.3 billion to others and $1.6 billion to Berkshire Hathaway. Including interest income, Berkshire's earnings from MidAmerican were $429 million (up from $359 million the year before).

Finance and Financial Products

The Finance and Financial Products segment had the feeling of a drawer of financial odds and ends. All were important businesses and capital allocation activities. Because of the bank-like nature of these activities, they were largely supported by borrowings.

One of the largest businesses was trading, which earned $379 million in 2003 and was supported by $7.8 billion of interest-bearing liabilities at year-end. This was an operation managed entirely by Buffett and consisting of "a few opportunistic strategies in AAA fixed-income securities. Though far from foolproof, these transactions involve no credit risk and are conducted in exceptionally liquid securities." In other words, an arbitrage operation.

The flipside to Buffett's operation was Gen Re Securities, where the derivative business continued to lose money as it was wound down. Gen Re Securities lost $99 million pre-tax during 2003 as outstanding contracts shrunk almost 50% from the year before.[*] Such a slow unwinding illustrated a major risk of derivatives. Berkshire was trying to exit during a time of market tranquility. What would happen if markets wouldn't (or couldn't) work in an orderly fashion? That question would be answered in just a few years.

Another investment included in this segment was Berkshire's investment in Value Capital, a fund run by Mark Byrne. Buffett noted that though the fund had close to $20 billion of debt, the operation was sound and Berkshire did not guarantee the debt. At year-end 2003, Berkshire had a net investment of $634 million in Value Capital after receiving a $30 million distribution.

The more natural components of this segment were the trailer leasing business, XTRA, which was reported under Leasing Operations, and the life and annuity business. The segment also contained the Berkadia operation, which was nearly complete at year-end 2003.[**] As was noted earlier, Clayton's entire operations were included in the Finance and Financial Products segment due to the size of its financing operation even though it also manufactured and sold housing units.

All told the Finance and Financial Products segment earned $666 million pre-tax in 2003, compared to $775 million in 2002. These figures were before $1.2 billion and $578 million of pre-tax capital gains in 2003 and 2002, respectively.

---

[*] Outstanding contracts shrunk to 7,580 among 453 counterparties.
[**] The FINOVA-related debt was entirely repaid in February 2004.

Manufacturing, Service, and Retailing

As the years went on Buffett's Sources of Reported Earnings table had been consolidating certain businesses with others. Home Furnishings and Jewelry became Retail Operations; Scott Fetzer's non-finance businesses were re-consolidated back into that category; and *The Buffalo News*, the Shoe Group, Dairy Queen, and See's Candies were lumped into Other Businesses. Beginning in 2002, the table disappeared but the commentary and the Annual Report footnotes still contained line items for Apparel, Building Products, Flight Services, McLane, and Shaw Industries.

These businesses could be viewed as one sector because of their similarities, though detail was provided for many businesses where needed or important. Each business in this group was closer to a typical business that required working capital, fixed assets, and some limited amounts of debt, than the Insurance or Utilities sectors. To aid analysis, Buffett now presented a summary balance sheet and earnings statement for the MSR Group that was like the supplemental disclosure presented up until 2000.

Buffett said the "eclectic group, which sells products ranging from Dilly Bars to B-737s" earned $1.3 billion on $32.1 billion of revenues in 2003. The resulting 20.1% return on average tangible net assets (tangible equity) was evidence of their above-average economic characteristics. While we don't have information from 2002 to compare, we know the Manufacturing, Service, and Retailing businesses earned higher returns in the past. In 1994 (the first year of the former presentation), after-tax return on equity was 32.4%. Returns dropped to the low 20%-range by the late 1990s as Berkshire acquired additional businesses. The new businesses were very good, just not quite as good as the earlier ones. Struggles in footwear and publishing hurt results, too.

Buffett judged businesses and their operating managers based on returns on capital employed. But Berkshire paid a premium to acquire many of its subsidiaries and he judged himself based on total purchase price, which included goodwill. Berkshire's after-tax return on carrying value for the MSR businesses was just 9.2% in 2003.* Berkshire separated purchase accounting and goodwill accounts to enable shareholders to distinguish the true quality and performance of the businesses and their accounting representation.

The building-materials businesses (Acme Brick, Benjamin Moore, and MiTek) earned 21% on tangible net worth. This was quite an impressive statistic for boring businesses. The businesses collectively earned $559 million pre-tax (up 8%) on revenues of $3.8 billion (up 4%), benefitting from strong housing demand.

---

* Goodwill and intangibles totaled $8.35 billion.

Shaw also benefitted from the strong housing market and earned $436 million pre-tax (up 3%) on revenues of $4.7 billion (up 8%) In November Shaw acquired a related carpet business from Dixie Group, which added $240 million to its revenues.

Fruit of the Loom, under the direction of John Holland, returned to profitability and now accounted for 42% of the men's and boys' underwear sold by large retailers. Its women's and girls' share increased to 14%.

Two of Berkshire's furniture retailers opened new stores during 2003. RC Willey opened a hugely successful store in Las Vegas (which was even more impressive given its closed-on-Sunday policy) and Nebraska Furniture Mart opened a large store in Kansas City, Missouri.

Revenues for the retail segment (which included the jewelry businesses) increased 10% to $2.3 billion, but pre-tax earnings remained flat at $165 million due to start-up costs for new stores.

Flight Services continued to experience some turbulence. Combined pre-tax earnings fell 68% to $72 million. FlightSafety earned $113 million after writing off $37 million in obsolete simulators. NetJets (Executive Jet now went by this name) lost $41 million as it continued to struggle despite being the dominant player in the fractional jet industry. The NetJets loss included a $32 million loss on aircraft inventory on top of continued operating losses building out its European business. Buffett remained upbeat on both businesses and noted that both FlightSafety and NetJets were leaders in their fields.

The apparel businesses continued to struggle. While the additions of Fruit of the Loom and Garan increased reported pre-tax earnings to $289 million on revenues of $2.1 billion, revenues declined 5% and earnings declined 11% on a comparative basis.

Investments

Berkshire's portfolio of equity securities moved just faster than glacial speed in 2003. Buffett reminded shareholders its major positions hadn't changed in a long time: Coca-Cola (1994), American Express (1998), Gillette (1989), Washington Post Company (1973), and Moody's (2000). The one exception was Wells Fargo, whose cost basis* increased by $157 million. This raised Berkshire's position by 3.2 million shares and brought its ownership interest to about 56.5 million shares and 3.3% of the company.

Two new companies made the $500 million threshold be included in the Chairman's letter: HCA, Inc., a company that ran hospitals, and PetroChina, an oil and gas company. Berkshire had 15.5 million shares in HCA, representing a 3.1%

---

* Cost basis is the original cost of an investment. The cost basis of an investment changes when shares are purchased or sold, or in other cases such as a return of capital from the company. Usually the basis for tax purposes and financial reporting purposes is the same, but they can differ.

interest in the company. At year-end 2003, it had 2.3 billion shares in PetroChina, representing a 1.3% interest in the Chinese company.

Buffett expressed neutral feelings on the portfolio, both in his letter to shareholders and at the next year's Annual Meeting. "We are neither enthusiastic nor negative about the portfolio we hold. We own pieces of excellent businesses—all of which had good gains in intrinsic value last year—but their current prices reflect their excellence." While the intrinsic values of these companies increased, so did their share prices. This did not create a price/value discrepancy wide enough to make major changes.

Buffett also discussed Berkshire's default position, which was to place any surplus cash in US Treasuries. He said Berkshire would "never 'reach' for a little more income by dropping our credit standards or by extending maturities. Charlie and I detest taking even small risks unless we feel we are being adequately compensated for doing so." Knowing that markets could turn quickly, and valuing certainty, Berkshire placed its excess cash in the safest, most liquid securities available.

Governance

Berkshire added four new board members to its roster in 2003. This brought its total to eleven. The four, all friends of Buffett, were David Gottesman, Charlotte Guyman, Don Keough, and Tom Murphy.

Don Keough, a former Coca-Cola executive who now served as chair of Allen and Company, and Tom Murphy, of Capital Cities/ABC, were already known to Berkshire shareholders through Buffett's writings and comments over the years. Buffett had known David "Sandy" Gottesman for almost as long as he had known Munger. Gottesman had partnered with Buffett and Munger in the Hochschild-Kohn department store acquisition in the mid-1960s, which was purchased via Diversified Retailing, the entity that was eventually merged into Berkshire Hathaway.

The last addition was Charlotte Guyman. Guyman retired from Microsoft in 1999,[76] and at the time of her appointment to the Berkshire board she was chair of the finance committee of the University of Washington Medical Center.

All of Berkshire's directors shared common traits essential to Buffett. To start, each director and his/her family owned at least $4 million of Berkshire stock that they had, importantly, acquired themselves and held over many years. Six had fortunes that included hundreds of millions of dollars worth of Berkshire stock. This meaningful level of ownership aligned their interests with those of "rank and file shareholders," wrote Buffett. He said the common trait among the group was "business savvy, a shareholder orientation, and a genuine interest in the company."

Buffett valued their independence, even though not all of them met the strict SEC test. Buffett's wife, Susan, and son, Howard, clearly failed the test as family members. Their role was to ensure the culture of Berkshire continued intact once he was no longer in control. Ron Olson also failed the test because his firm, Munger, Tolles, Olson, performed legal work for Berkshire. Buffett reasoned that the single-digit percentage of income Olson received from Berkshire would not be enough to cause him to lose his independence. Buffett pointed to the directorship of other corporations, including mutual funds, whose directors derived a significant percentage of their income from directors' fees but were nonetheless considered independent per SEC rules. Berkshire would comply with the SEC rules, though it would do it in such a way that ensured it was to Berkshire's shareholders' benefit, not just to meet a technical test. Buffett defined true independence not by family or financial ties but as "the willingness to challenge a forceful CEO when something is wrong or foolish."

Gifts Program

Berkshire's designated gifts program had directed $197 million to thousands of charities since its inception in 1981. In 2003, that program was terminated due to politics. Individuals and groups who were pro-life had begun to boycott Pampered Chef because of Berkshire's donations (at the direction of shareholders) to pro-choice charities. Buffett said it did not matter to these groups that other Berkshire shareholders had donated to pro-life organizations. Buffett and Munger terminated the program after judging the negative impact to the independent consultants as greater than the benefit.

Burlington Industries

In early 2003, Berkshire placed a bid for bankrupt former competitor, Burlington Industries. Burlington had labored on long after Berkshire got out of the textile business. Not surprisingly, it struggled mightily. The bid was a $500 million offer to the bankruptcy court to buy Burlington. Ultimately the court decided that Berkshire's $14 million breakup fee (less than 3% of the offer) was too rich.

2004

Berkshire just missed matching the S&P 500 in 2004. Its 10.5% increase in per share book value fell 0.4% behind the benchmark. The cause was the self-forged anchor Buffett long predicted. Berkshire's operating businesses, with their .400 sluggers, were hitting it out of the park. But that success and the resulting growing cash pile in Omaha had no immediate profitable outlet. As was typical of Buffett, he blamed himself for not finding operating businesses or marketable securities to put Berkshire's now $43 billion cash pile to work.

Insurance

Buffett devoted a few pages of his Chairman's letter to a history of how Berkshire had grown from a $20 *million* float business in 1967 to its 2004 collection of excellent insurance businesses with over $46 *billion* of float. He asked: how had Berkshire overcome the "dismal economics of the industry"? The answer: discipline, correct incentives, and capital strength.

The Chairman's letter presented a Portrait of a Disciplined Underwriter, a summary table of National Indemnity's key metrics from 1980 to 2004. Over that time, it had some loss years but overall wrote to a profit. It also survived a decade-long slump in premiums that tested its managers and employees. National Indemnity had grown to $366 million of written premiums in 1986 and then endured thirteen years of declines in volume, ending 1999 with just $54.5 million of premiums written before rocketing back to $606 million in 2004. Importantly, in each of those thirteen down years National Indemnity wrote to an underwriting profit (subsequently the only loss year was 2001).

Buffett contended that other insurance companies could not or would not endure the unrelenting decline in volume. Where its competitors were focused primarily on volume, National Indemnity focused solely on profitability. Even though huge volumes of business were available, National Indemnity only accepted risks it understood and could price to a profit.

Part and parcel to the disciplined underwriting were incentives that encouraged such behavior. Starting with National Indemnity, employees of Berkshire's insurance companies were rewarded based on profitability, not volume. The incentives at National Indemnity extended to a no layoff policy, which dissuaded writing business to justify an employee's existence. This did not mean indiscriminate spending on personnel. Costs would have to be controlled, but Berkshire tolerated higher levels of operating expenses than its competitors.[*]

National Indemnity and Berkshire's other insurance businesses also possessed above-average (and usually far above-average) capital strength. Capital strength was less important to National Indemnity in its primary operations. (After all, no one bought an auto policy based on name brand; price was usually the deciding factor.) But capital strength allowed Berkshire's insurance companies to market themselves to knowledgeable buyers, including other insurance companies via its reinsurance operations.

Once Berkshire entered the reinsurance field Buffett quickly realized that capital strength could be a huge advantage. Primary insurers looking to shed risks they might have to collect on years in the future understandably sought out a well-capitalized reinsurer to pay the bill. So too would buyers of super cat policies with large covers. Berkshire, bolstered by its conservatism and capital, was (and is) a standout.

---

[*] National Indemnity's expense ratio topped 41% in 1999, up from 25.9% in 1986.

Another way to prosper in a commodity-like business is to be the low-cost operator, and GEICO was among the best. Its direct-to-consumer distribution model provided a price advantage over rivals. Though the company had lost its underwriting discipline in the 1970s, it avoided bankruptcy. Under Berkshire's complete ownership it had flourished as a disciplined and much larger enterprise with an almost 6% market share.

Perhaps Buffett's most important job as overseer of the insurance managers was to monitor and reinforce the culture of discipline. His guidance was needed after General Re stumbled, but Berkshire was blessed to have managers like Tony Nicely at GEICO, Ajit Jain at Berkshire Hathaway Reinsurance Group, and many others within the Primary Group who operated with strong discipline.

Each of Berkshire's major segments within the Insurance Group reported a profit in 2004. On $21 billion of premium volume, the group earned $1.6 billion pre-tax, producing Buffett's highly valued negative cost of float. Float increased by 6% to $46.1 billion at year-end.

Table 6.35: Berkshire Hathaway—Insurance Underwriting

($ millions)	2004	2003
GEICO Corporation		
Premiums written	$9,212	$8,081
Premiums earned	8,915	7,784
Underwriting gain/(loss) - pre-tax	$970	$452
General Re		
Premiums written	$6,860	$8,021
Premiums earned	7,245	8,245
Underwriting gain/(loss) - pre-tax	$3	$145
Berkshire Hathaway Reinsurance Group		
Premiums earned	$3,714	$4,430
Underwriting gain/(loss) - pre-tax	$417	$1,047
Berkshire Hathaway Primary Group		
Premiums earned	$1,211	$1,034
Underwriting gain/(loss) - pre-tax	$161	$74
Total underwriting gain/(loss)	$1,551	$1,718
Year-end average float - total	45,157	42,722
Cost of float	(3.4%)	(4.0%)
Aggregate adverse (favorable) loss development	$419	$480

Note: Berkshire Hathaway Primary Group and BHRG written premiums were not detailed.
Sources: Berkshire Hathaway Annual Report 2003–2004 and author's calculations.

GEICO

GEICO continued to shower profits on Berkshire. In 2004, its 89.1% combined ratio produced a pre-tax profit of almost $1 billion. Premiums earned grew 14.5%, reflecting an 11.8% increase in policies-in-force* on top of a 2% rate increase. Part of the growth resulted from expanding into a new state during the third quarter of 2004. Prior to this, the state of New Jersey had a tough regulatory climate and GEICO chose not to do business there. GEICO now served 140,000 customers in New Jersey, or about 4% of the state—a clear vote of confidence in GEICO's ability to save its customers money.

While GEICO held its overhead in check,** it was the loss experience that really boosted the results for the year. GEICO experienced lower claims frequencies in physical and bodily damage, which more than offset the increased severity it saw in both categories.

General Re

Berkshire's former problem child demonstrated it was refocused on the one thing that mattered: profitability. It raised prices and rejected unsound risks. Consequently, it allowed written premiums to fall 14.5% to $6.9 billion. Earned premiums declined 12% to $7.2 billion. General Re earned a second year of underwriting profits with a $3 million gain. The profit meant its cost of float was technically negative but the pullback in writing new business caused float to shrink 2% to $23 billion.

North American property/casualty earned premiums fell 15% to $3 billion. Current year gains of $166 million included $120 million of catastrophe losses from four hurricanes that hit the US. Unfavorable loss development of $155 million brought the profit down to $11 million.

International property/casualty business earned premiums fell 22% to $2.2 billion. Hurricane-related catastrophe losses of $110 million and $102 million of unfavorable loss development contributed to a pre-tax underwriting loss of $93 million.

Global life/health earned premiums grew 9% and reported an $85 million underwriting profit. Over half of the premium growth was a result of a weaker dollar against foreign currencies.

---

* The larger preferred segment grew 8.8% and the non-preferred grew 21.6%, according to the footnotes to the financial statements.
** Underwriting expenses ticked up slightly from 17.7% to 17.8% of earned premiums.

Berkshire Hathaway Reinsurance Group (BHRG)

Berkshire's untarnished reinsurance gem was hitting on all cylinders. It reported an overall profit of $417 million on earned premiums of $3.7 billion (down 16%) and grew float 9.5% to end the year at $15.3 billion. BHRG's float represented one-third of Berkshire's total float.

Declines in volume in the retroactive reinsurance and multi-line segments echoed Gen Re's experience, which was a general pullback due to inadequate pricing. Earned premiums in multi-line business declined 20% to $2.1 billion but profits grew 36% to $444 million on gains from aviation coverage and commutations.

Retroactive reinsurance almost fell off the map in 2004. From a high of almost $4 billion in 2000, earned premiums had fallen each year to $188 million in the current year. That line booked a $412 million loss, which was largely attributable to amortization of deferred charges.

The catastrophe and individual risk segment would have declined during the year had it not been for several contracts reinstated after the hurricane losses.* Even after $790 million of hurricane-related catastrophe losses, the catastrophe and individual risk segment reported a $385 million profit.

Berkshire Hathaway Primary Group

The Primary Group had another good year in 2004. Earned premiums grew 17% to $1.2 billion and favorable claims experience led to a 118% increase in underwriting profit, to $161 million. Its float ballooned 30% to $1.7 billion.

Manufacturing, Service, and Retailing

Berkshire's "eclectic group" of Manufacturing, Service, and Retailing businesses continued to produce good results despite some acute cost pressures. A separate balance sheet and income statement reappeared in the Chairman's letter and provided additional detail. The MSR businesses earned $1.5 billion on revenues of $44 billion in 2004. The addition of McLane in 2003 made a comparison to prior years difficult. A better comparison, return on tangible equity, improved from 20.7% in 2003 to 21.7% in 2004. Strong growth in the US economy, led by housing, played a part in the improved results.

The strong construction market led the building products segment to increase revenues 13% to $4.3 billion. Pre-tax earnings increased 15% to $643 million (earnings

---

* Primary insurers, not wanting to go uncovered, often had what amounted to auto-renewing policies. If a loss event triggered a claim, the insurer would have to buy coverage for subsequent catastrophes to protect itself.

would have increased just 11% if not for a fire the year before at an insulation plant). Digging into some unit-specific results, MiTek, the building products business and a heavy user of steel, experienced a 100% increase in steel costs. Other businesses in this group also experienced increased input costs which negatively impacted margins.

At Shaw, input costs for carpet increased significantly due to rising oil prices (many synthetic fibers are made from oil). Shaw's input cost increases were followed by price increases to customers, though on somewhat of a lagging basis. Shaw nonetheless turned in an excellent year. Its revenues increased 11% to $5.2 billion on higher volume and higher pricing, and from the two acquisitions the year before. Its pre-tax earnings rose 7% to $466 million, which represented a 26% return on tangible equity.

Fruit of the Loom increased its unit sales by 10%, including a 31% increase in the women and girls' segment. That carried the apparel segment to a 6% increase in revenues, to $2.2 billion. Pre-tax earnings in apparel improved 12% to $325 million. Margin pressures at Fruit of the Loom kept its contribution to earnings at half, while H.H. Brown, Justin, and Garan contributed the rest. (Dexter by this time had been merged into H.H. Brown and its specific results weren't disclosed.)

Berkshire's jewelry and furniture retailers were buoyed by the strong US economy.[*] Ben Bridge and RC Willey particularly stood out. Ben Bridge had 11.4% growth in same-store sales, topping off a decade where annual same-store sales growth averaged 8.8%. RC Willey, against Buffett's better judgement, expanded its Las Vegas presence with a second store located within 20 miles from the first. The result was a huge success. While retailing revenues increased 13% to $2.6 billion, same-store sales in 2004 increased just 2.4%. Pre-tax earnings declined 1% to $163 million as start-up costs associated with the new stores weighed on profits.

FlightSafety earned a 15.1% return on tangible equity during 2004. This was up from 8.4% in 2003 as a result of a return to higher usage of the company's simulators by corporate and regional airlines. The 2004 result was after another write-down of simulators, but not to the same degree as the prior year. FlightSafety's founder, Al Ueltschi, while still involved in the business, turned over the CEO position to Bruce Whitman, a 43-year veteran employee.

Buffett disclosed that Berkshire subsidiary NetJets (formerly Executive Jet) was FlightSafety's largest customer. This was not surprising given the average of eighteen days NetJets pilots spent in training annually, and the fact that the business was growing rapidly. NetJets captured 70% of net new business in 2004. Part of that growth was a result of a new non-affiliated company that was essentially further fractionalizing NetJets ownership. The Marquis Card, offered by Marquis Jet Partners, gave customers the ability to purchase flight time in twenty-five-hour increments.

---

[*] U.S. real GDP growth was 3.8% in 2004 according to the St. Louis Federal Reserve (FRED).

Buffett and NetJets apparently were okay with this arrangement, perhaps because it fed volume into the system without additional overhead on their part.

NetJets' profitability continued to lag with some US profits offset by expenses in building out its European business. Buffett pointed to the volume of US customers taking intercontinental and intracontinental European flights as reason to stay the course to become the market leader in Europe.

McLane, the distribution business acquired in May 2003, increased its revenues by 6% to $23 billion and its earnings by 1% to $228 million compared to its full prior year results.

Finance and Financial Products

Given Buffett's activities within this segment, large fluctuations were not uncommon. In 2004 pre-tax operating earnings fell 6% to $584 million with some important changes in the details.

Perhaps the most important segment within Finance and Financial Products was Clayton Homes (this included manufacturing). The company was doing well under Berkshire's ownership. Buffett even ventured to use the word synergy to describe the benefits to both parties of Berkshire financing Clayton's financing activities. At year-end 2004, these interest-bearing liabilities had risen $1.5 billion to $3.6 billion (by January 2005 the total had risen to $7.35 billion.*)

Buffett used the word inadequate to describe the poor but improving earnings at CORT, the office furniture-leasing business held under Wesco. He also noted that XTRA, the trailer-leasing business, had taken a play from GEICO. XTRA refocused on its core trailer-leasing business and dropped the container and intermodal businesses it previously entered. The strategy appeared successful as pre-tax earnings rebounded from $34 million in 2003 to $92 million in 2004.

One accounting-related change to this segment was Value Capital. Accounting rules dictated that large owners such as Berkshire Hathaway fully consolidate the financials of investees.** Since Value Capital had found additional investors, Berkshire would be spared this requirement.

Lastly, Buffett commented on the ongoing wind down of General Re's derivatives business. He said that even in a benign market, the portfolio had been stubbornly hard to liquidate. This fact served to reinforce his and Munger's view that derivatives were "weapons of mass destruction."

---

* The footnotes to the 2004 financial statements disclose that Berkshire issued $1.6 billion in notes in 2004 and an additional $3.75 billion of notes in January 2005 to finance the Clayton portfolio.

** In response to the Enron fiasco, accounting rules were changed to require the consolidation of Variable Interest Entities, or VIEs. Enron had abused the prior accounting which allowed it to hide significant risks off balance sheet.

Regulated Utility Businesses

MidAmerican, in addition to its Iowa-based electric business, had grown to include a UK utility business and several pipelines. The company also owned a California geothermal operation that turned out to be a rare stumble for MidAmerican's management team.

MidAmerican's geothermal operation offered a tantalizing opportunity to recover and monetize zinc from the brine in its geothermal wells. Starting in 1998 and lasting four years, MidAmerican spent hundreds of millions of dollars trying unsuccessfully to make the project viable. It was ultimately shuttered when progress never materialized. The financial impact was a $579 million pre-tax loss in 2004 that included the project's write-off and followed a $46 million operating loss the year before.

The zinc project offered a broader lesson. Because of the many steps involved in the zinc recovery process, even small chances of failure at each step would compound into a very low overall success rate. Buffett reminded shareholders it was better to stay with simple propositions, bringing to mind his dictum to "avoid trying to clear 7-foot bars and focus on finding one-footers."*

Despite the zinc blunder, the core of MidAmerican's business was doing well and improved earnings in each segment. Berkshire's 80.5% share of MidAmerican's earnings fell 45% to $237 million largely due to the write-off of the zinc project. Berkshire also had slightly lower interest income as a result of MidAmerican using $100 million of excess cash to repay some debt owed to Berkshire.

Investments

Berkshire's common stock investments changed little in 2004, but the cutoff to make the Chairman's list grew to $600 million. There was one new name on that list and it carried some historical significance. White Mountains Insurance Company was the remnants of the Fireman's Fund, the insurer former GEICO CEO Jack Byrne ran after leaving his post.[77]

Four companies accounted for 65% of the $37.7 billion portfolio. They were American Express, Coca-Cola, Gillette, and Wells Fargo. One statistic reflected Berkshire's business-owner mindset, as contrasted to a short-term trader's mindset: Berkshire's equity investments had been held for an average of twelve-and-a-half years.** Holding these investments through ups and downs (like an owner of a private business would), the normalized earnings from just those four now amounted to $1.2 billion, almost a third of their $3.8 billion purchase price.

---

* About a decade later, your author committed an investing mistake related to a zinc-recovery investment, proving that the study of history is not a sure antidote to making foolish decisions.
** Buffett calculated the dollar-weighted purchase date as being July 1992.

Foreign Currency Investments

At year-end 2004, Berkshire owned $21.4 billion* of foreign exchange contracts across eight currencies. This was a decided change for Berkshire, which owned no foreign exchange contracts before March 2002. The investments were an example of Buffett putting his (and his shareholders') money where his mouth was. Over the past year or so, he became more vocal in public about America's worsening trade situation and even wrote an article in *Fortune Magazine*. The crux of the matter was that the United States was overconsuming.** Buffett thought the inevitable balancing effect would be depreciation of the dollar.

Buffett's focus was almost always on microeconomics, or the bottoms-up workings of the economy. But he was also well-versed in macroeconomics. Now the macro picture had changed significantly, providing Buffett with some certainty that something had to change, and he could profit from it. It was admittedly outside of his normal scope of investment activity. Judging there to be a probability of a decline of the dollar, he bet on currencies. Buffett said he would have made the same decision had he owned 100% of Berkshire, and was prepared to risk embarrassment if he was wrong.

Buffett pined for something intelligent to do with the now $43 billion of cash on Berkshire's balance sheet. The marginal changes in the investment portfolio and the foreign currency investments were just activity around the edges. Buffett would remain disciplined just like his insurance companies and wait for an opportunity to swing the investing bat. His comment at the 2005 Annual Meeting was prescient: "I think you will get a chance to do something that is more screamingly intelligent in not too many years—and maybe a lot shorter—than the alternatives that you're offered now."

The Oracle of Omaha would be proven remarkably right.

Decade in Review

The word transformational could aptly be used to describe any decade of Berkshire's history. The 1995–2004 decade was notable for the wave of acquisition activity—in particular, the growth in insurance through the acquisitions of General Re and the remainder of GEICO. It was also notable for how little had changed. While the business world and economy were changed by the internet boom, Berkshire remained on the sidelines. Textiles were firmly in the past, but the lessons of investing in industries with sound economics was Berkshire's guide. Internet companies failed that test.

---

* Notional value, or the underlying asset in a derivative trade.
** Buffett used the analogy of a large farm in which pieces were being sold off to fund consumption. The technical term for this is current account deficit, which should not be confused with a budget deficit.

Berkshire expanded in the two broad areas that now defined its business activities: insurance and non-insurance. The insurance businesses provided the double benefit of profits and showers of float to invest. Buffett shared his formula in his 1995 Chairman's letter: Berkshire had "benefitted greatly—to a degree that is not generally well-understood—because our liabilities have cost us very little." Buffett said a company's profitability is determined by three factors: "1. What its assets earn; 2. What its liabilities cost; and 3. Its utilization of 'leverage'." Berkshire did a good job earning high returns on assets, but its liabilities also contributed to its outsized success. Not only did float provide leverage to enhance Berkshire's return on equity, it came at a negative cost and was therefore profitable.

The hardships of the prior decades gave Berkshire a complete understanding of how to maximize the value of an insurance operation. The secret was as obvious and simple as it was difficult: discipline. Berkshire's insurers possessed a culture that prized profitability over volume, and this paid off handsomely.

Table 6.36: Reconciliation of shareholders' equity, 1965–2004

(*$ millions*)	1965–74	1975–84	1985–94	1995–04	1965–04
Beginning of period shareholders' equity	$22	$88	$1,272	$11,875	$22
Net income - operations	57	366	2,869	19,344	22,636
Net income - realized gains	7	199	1,354	14,096	15,657
Unrealized appreciation of investments	0	486	5,877	15,000	21,363
Mergers/divestitures	0	133	433	25,085	25,651
Dividends/treasury stock	(3)	0	69	0	66
Issuance of Class-B stock	0	0	0	565	565
Other/misc.	4	0	0	(65)	(60)
End of period shareholders' equity	$88	$1,272	$11,875	$85,900	$85,900
Change in equity during period	$66	$1,184	$10,602	$74,026	$85,877

Note: Figures may not add due to rounding.
Sources: Berkshire Hathaway Annual Reports and author's calculations.

Table 6.37: Contribution toward change in equity during period

	1965–74	1975–84	1985–94	1995–04	1965–04
Net income - operations	86%	31%	27%	26%	26%
Net income - realized gains	11%	17%	13%	19%	18%
Unrealized appreciation of investments	0%	41%	55%	20%	25%
Mergers/divestitures	0%	11%	4%	34%	30%
Dividends/treasury stock	(4%)	0%	1%	0%	0%
Issuance of Class-B stock	0%	0%	0%	1%	1%
Other/misc.	7%	0%	0%	(0%)	(0%)
Total	100%	100%	100%	100%	100%

Note: Figures may not add due to rounding.
Sources: Berkshire Hathaway Annual Reports and author's calculations.

Comparing the sources of Berkshire's shareholders' equity growth between decades we see that some sources changed little while others changed significantly. Net income from operations contributed about the same as it had in the prior two decades. Realized gains are also about the same proportion as in prior decades. Unrealized appreciation, however, had noticeably decreased.

The big standout is in mergers/divestitures. During the ten years ending in 2004, Berkshire made numerous acquisitions in both the non-insurance and insurance fields. By far the largest was General Reinsurance, with $22 billion of shares issued in connection with the merger. Numerous other acquisitions completed in whole or in part with shares, as well as the SQUARZ notes, comprised the $3 billion balance. In total about one-third of the increase in Berkshire's net worth could be chalked up to shares issued.

All sources of equity considered, Berkshire increased its overall net worth by $74 billion during the 1995–04 decade—a 623% increase. However, as Buffett frequently pointed out, the increase in overall net worth was not the real measure of success. The most important concern for shareholders was the change in per-share value. The increase in net worth translated into an annual rate of change of 21.9%. However, adjusting for the increase in shares outstanding the per-share rate of book value change was 18.7% per annum.

Berkshire's stock price increased at an even slower (but by no means unsatisfactory) rate. A shareholder holding on at the average price between the fourth quarter 1994 and 2004 would have earned 15.6%. This three percentage point per annum deficit is explained by Berkshire's price-to-book value decline over the ten years.* While we cannot know for sure the reason for the decline in price/book, it wasn't interest rates. (The 10-year Treasury declined yet again, from 7.8% in December 1994 to 4.2% in December 2004.) The more likely reason was reversion to a proper range of valuation guided by Berkshire's communications.

Berkshire's market capitalization rose from an average of $24 billion at year-end 1994 to over $130 billion in 2004. Berkshire found itself fourteenth on *Fortune Magazine*'s 500 largest company's list.

Figure 6.1: Berkshire Hathaway stock price, 1995–2004

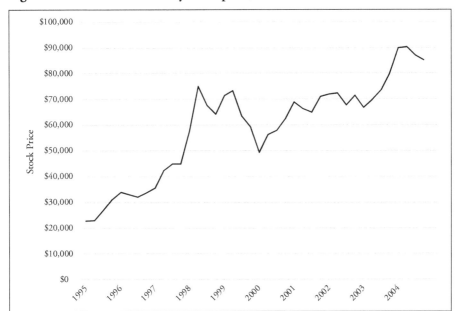

Sources: *Of Permanent Value* (Kilpatrick, 2015), Berkshire Hathaway Annual Reports 1995–2004, and author's calculations.

---

* One can see how much worse the result would have been for shareholders of the foiled Berkshire unit trust who would have bought in at a higher price and faced frictional costs along the way.

Figure 6.2: Berkshire Hathaway price-to-book ratio, 1995–2004

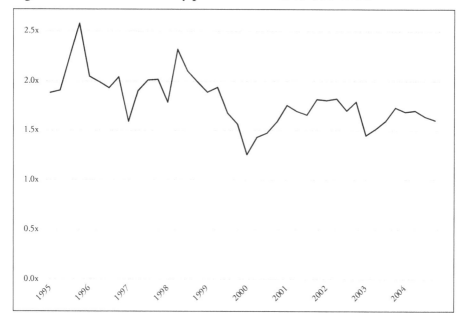

Sources: *Of Permanent Value* (Kilpatrick, 2015), Berkshire Hathaway Annual Reports 1995–2004, and author's calculations.

Berkshire went on a spending spree during the decade. The additional capital from float (which increased from an average of $3 billion at year-end 1994 to $45 billion at year-end 2004) and profits from existing operating businesses fueled the expansion.

Berkshire made two very important insurance investments and a host of non-insurance investments. In 1996, it paid $2.3 billion to acquire the half of GEICO it did not already own, and in 1998 it made the largest acquisition in its history with the $22 billion purchase of General Re. Both became catalysts for future growth in profits and float, though Gen Re went through some very difficult times to earn its worth.

Berkshire created mini powerhouses in jewelry and furniture retailing. It purchased jewelers Helzberg and Ben Bridge, and acquired furniture retailers RC Willey, Star Furniture, and Jordan's Furniture. In each case, Buffett allowed their managers complete autonomy to operate independently post-acquisition.

Berkshire also shunned the tech boom and doubled down on decidedly low-tech but proven cash-generating businesses important to everyday life. Some were household names; others were important to the workings of the economy but largely unknown to the average consumer. Berkshire welcomed Justin Industries, Benjamin Moore, Shaw Industries, MiTek, Albecca (Larson-Juhl), CTB, Garan, The Pampered Chef, Clayton Homes, and McLane. In addition, three new operating subsidiaries,

Johns Manville, Fruit of the Loom, and International Dairy Queen, came to Berkshire after stumbling on their own.

Berkshire's capital allocation strategy was subtly beginning to shift with the acquisition of a majority economic interest in MidAmerican. Finding it difficult to deploy capital into either wholly-owned business or part-ownership interests in common stocks, Berkshire found an outlet for some of its cash in highly stable though capital-intensive utility businesses. Returns from these investments would not come close to the potential of other, non-regulated businesses. But their relative certainty, coupled with the ability to put large incremental sums of capital to work, represented a logical outlet for Berkshire's excess cash.

Opportunities to put Berkshire's cash to work could not come fast enough to keep it from piling up at headquarters. Even with the large volume of acquisitions during this period Berkshire ended the decade with $40 billion of readily investible cash.* Compounding the problem was the relative scarcity of good opportunities in marketable securities, Berkshire's next go-to area of capital allocation.

Some opportunities had presented themselves. In 1994, Berkshire's balance sheet listed $15.2 billion of equity securities and another $2.4 billion in bonds.** Ten years later at the end of 2004, the balance sheet had $37.7 billion in equities, $22.8 billion in bonds, and $2.3 billion of other investments.

Viewing Berkshire's equity portfolio on a point-to-point basis (below), we see remarkably little change. Five of its investments at year-end 1994 remained over the ten-year period: American Express, Coca-Cola, Gillette, Washington Post and Wells Fargo. In addition, one investment at year-end 1994, GEICO, turned into a wholly-owned subsidiary.

The net $3.5 billion of additional investment in the equity portfolio during the decade is somewhat misleading since the portfolio did generate substantial capital gains. Berkshire sold or otherwise disposed of its investment in Salomon/Travelers, Capital Cities ABC/Walt Disney, and McDonalds, among others.

In the minds of Buffett and Munger, the equity portfolio was largely a category of less-than-100%-owned businesses to complement their wholly-owned subsidiaries. They would not have minded if the stock market did not give them quoted values for their holdings at all. All they wanted was to increase their holdings at favorable prices. At year-end 1994, Berkshire's investment in American Express, Coca-Cola, Gillette, and Wells Fargo represented 57% of the entire portfolio. Fast forward ten years and those same four represented 65% of the portfolio. Two, Coke and Gillette,

---

* I'm only including the Insurance and Other category. The cash held within Finance and Financial Products was debt-funded. I'm assuming cash held at other operating entities was needed for operations.

** Included in the bond category are $1.8 billion of fixed maturity securities and the Salomon, Inc. convertible preferred of $580.6 million.

went untouched during the period while Berkshire added to its holdings in American Express, and to a lesser extent Wells Fargo.

Table 6.38: Berkshire Hathaway—equity portfolio, select detail

($ millions)	2004 Cost	2004 Market	1994 Cost	1994 Market	Change Cost	Change Market
American Express	$1,470	$8,546	$724	$819	$746	$7,727
The Coca-Cola Company	1,299	8,328	1,299	5,150	0	3,178
The Gillette Company	600	4,299	600	1,797	0	2,502
Wells Fargo & Company	463	3,508	424	985	39	2,523
Washington Post	11	1,698	10	419	1	1,279
All other	5,213	11,338	2,526	6,066	2,687	5,272
Total equity securities	$9,056	$37,717	$5,583	$15,236	$3,473	$22,481

Sources: Berkshire Hathaway Annual Reports 1994, 2004; and author's calculations.

Berkshire's balance sheet remained fortress-like. Its $189 billion of 2004 year-end assets were financed by $86 billion of equity and just $3.5 billion of true debt. The balance sheet was funded with other real liabilities, but these were of a different nature. The largest were the insurance-related liabilities including losses and loss adjustment expenses, and unearned premiums. In all, these insurance liabilities amounted to $59 billion. Berkshire also had a $12 billion year-end deferred tax liability that provided capital to fund assets. While very much a real liability, deferred tax liabilities were payable only if/when Berkshire sold its appreciated investments or stopped investing in capital expenditures in excess of its depreciation costs.

The last category of liabilities, amounting to $20 billion, were the Finance and Financial Products liabilities. These liabilities included borrowings to finance Clayton Homes' mortgage portfolio, Scott Fetzer's finance arm, and other bank-like activities. Considering that the $20 billion of liabilities were backed by $30 billion of assets (including $3.4 billion in cash), this Berkshire mini bank was very conservatively financed. The $9.7 billion of equity attributable to Finance and Financial Products was akin to a 32% capital ratio—far in excess of anything seen in a typical bank.

As the decade progressed, Berkshire became less concentrated in insurance (see Table 6.39). Not only was Berkshire moving more into non-insurance operations but as we've seen the many businesses it acquired over the preceding decade were very diverse.

Table 6.39: Relative size of Berkshire's insurance subsidiaries

($ millions)	2004	1994
Insurance assets	$114,759	$18,494
Percentage of total BRK assets	61%	87%
Pre-tax underwriting profit	$1,551	$130
Pre-tax net investment income	$2,824	$419
Pre-tax income from non-insurance	$3,302	$333
Year-end float	$46,094	$3,057

Sources: Berkshire Hathaway Annual Reports 1994, 2004; and author's calculations.

The shift away from the concentration in insurance was a natural consequence of Berkshire's growth, and the non-insurance businesses reinforced the insurance businesses. Berkshire was well poised to take on huge insurance risks others could not or would not take on themselves because it had a growing and diverse stream of non-insurance earnings. The insurance companies were strong on their own, but to have assets and earnings streams not tied to insurance gave Berkshire confidence to expand into the reinsurance field when opportunities arose. Neither the economics of the business (the ability to take the lumpiness as it came), nor the accounting, were impediments.

The little debt that Berkshire incurred during this time was structured in Berkshire's favor and done cheaply. In 1996, it issued a $500 million convertible issue. Berkshire also issued the first negative interest rate security with its $400 million SQUARZ issue in 2002. Other debt was incurred in the Finance and Financial Products area to support the FINOVA/Berkadia transaction and Clayton Homes' lending activities, and to fund certain arbitrage situations managed by Buffett. Otherwise, very little debt was used at Berkshire by design. The one exception was MidAmerican. Being a utility, MidAmerican had the stability of earnings to borrow appropriately. Importantly, this debt was not guaranteed by Berkshire.

There were more than a few instances of share issuances during the decade. The largest was the $22 billion issued in connection with the General Reinsurance acquisition. Numerous other acquisitions during the decade, including Helzberg, RC Willey, Flight Safety, Executive Jet (NetJets) and Dairy Queen, had all or some Berkshire stock involved.

The issuance of the Class-B shares brought $565 million of net proceeds to Berkshire not tied to any acquisition. Increasing Berkshire's share count by about 1% it prevented investors from being duped by a stock promotor that sought to cash in on Berkshire's well-earned reputation. But it was otherwise, in Munger's words, a non-event. What would have been a real event was if any of the attempts to create unit trusts using Berkshire stock had been successful. That would have harmed the reputation of Berkshire and Buffett, as investment returns would necessarily have lagged Berkshire's underlying business results.

Berkshire was well-positioned to enter a fifth decade under Buffett's control. It had $40 billion of cash to work with, additional cash coming in from diverse streams, and reasonable expectations of additional capital via growth in float. It faced real challenges, to be sure, including its massive size, earning it the number fourteen spot on the Fortune 500. Its size would prevent it from earning the types of returns it had in the past. But Berkshire would have plenty of opportunities in future years to grow into a conglomerate in a class of its own.

Forty years in, Buffett and his longtime business partner, Charlie Munger, acted as if they were just getting started.

Lessons: 1995–2004

1. A well-structured liability like insurance float can be just as valuable as equity. Under the right conditions (such as within Berkshire's Insurance Group where profits were placed ahead of growth), float acted more like equity. Better yet, it did not dilute existing shareholders' equity and could grow without additional capital investment. Just as important is the acknowledgement that others recognized the value of float and competed vigorously (sometimes irrationally) for premium volume, which drove down pricing.

2. There are many ways to earn a satisfactory return on investment. Focusing on just one number can be misleading. A great extreme example is McLane. With its 1% pre-tax margin on revenues, McLane might not seem like a good business. Yet with extremely high capital turnover, that slim margin turns into a much larger (and satisfactory) return on capital. An opposite example is FlightSafety. With low capital turnover, its hefty near-30% pre-tax margin turns into a lower-but-still-good return on capital. (Better is See's, which had a 20%+ profit margin and low capital requirements but little opportunity for reinvestment. Nirvana was Coke with the ability to reinvest at very high rates of return.)

3. Economics is more important than accounting. Berkshire accepted different types of insurance business that greatly impacted its financial statements. Since Berkshire was focused on long-term profitability, it ignored (but communicated to shareholders) the accounting treatment which made the business look much worse than it was. Berkshire did not have stock options of its own, but Buffett wrote about the pernicious effects of their accounting. "If options aren't a form of compensation what are they? If compensation isn't an expense, what is it? And, if expenses shouldn't go into the calculation of earnings, where in the world should they go?"

4. Thinking through basic economics is important (and profitable). The internet craze that took the world by storm tricked many, but not Berkshire's managers. They correctly considered the implications of the internet and concluded the exact opposite of many participants: that competition would negate most advantages offered by technology, and that some costs simply could not be eliminated due to the internet (grocery sales, for example, still required delivery vehicles). The internet would change the world, but in the early 2000s profits were still elusive and many investors ultimately lost money. It would take another decade for the industry to mature and develop into an investment landscape capable of attracting the attention of serious value investors.

Table 6.40: Berkshire Hathaway—select parent-level financial information

($ millions, except per share data)	2004	2003	2002	2001	2000	1999	1998	1997	1996	1995
Revenues:										
Insurance premiums earned	$21,085	$21,493	$19,182	$17,905	$19,343	$14,306	$5,481	$4,761	$4,118	$957
Sales and service revenues	43,222	32,098	16,958	14,507	7,000	5,918	4,675	3,615	3,095	2,756
Interest, dividend, and other investment income	2,816	3,098	2,943	2,765	2,685	2,314	1,049	916	778	629
Interest and other revenues of finance and financial products businesses	3,763	3,041	2,234	1,928	1,322	125	212	32	25	27
Investment gains [1,4,5]	3,496	4,129	918	1,488	4,499	1,365	2,415	1,106	2,484	194
Total revenues	$74,382	$63,859	$42,235	$38,593	$34,849	$24,028	$13,832	$10,430	$10,500	$4,563
Earnings:										
Net earnings [1,2,3]	$7,308	$8,151	$4,286	$795	$3,328	$1,557	$2,830	$1,901	$2,489	$795
Net earnings per share [2,3]	$4,753	$5,309	$2,795	$521	$2,185	$1,025	$2,262	$1,542	$2,065	$670
Year-end data [6]:										
Total assets	$188,874	$180,559	$169,544	$162,752	$135,792	$131,416	$122,237	$56,111	$43,409	$28,711
Borrowings under investment agreements and other debt (excluding finance businesses)						$2,465	$2,385	$2,267	$1,944	$1,062
Notes payable and other borrowings of insurance and other non-finance businesses	3,450	4,182	4,775	3,455	2,611					
Notes payable and other borrowings of finance businesses	5,387	4,937	4,513	9,049	2,168					
Shareholders' equity	85,900	77,596	64,037	57,950	61,724	57,761	57,403	31,455	23,427	16,739
Common shares outstanding, in thousands [7]	1,539	1,537	1,535	1,528	1,526	1,521	1,519	1,234	1,232	1,194
Shareholders' equity per outstanding share	$55,824	$50,498	$41,727	$37,920	$40,442	$37,987	$37,801	$25,488	$19,011	$14,025

Footnotes:

1. After-tax investment gains were as follows:

	2004	2003	2002	2001	2000	1999	1998	1997	1996	1995
	$2,259	$2,729	$2,729	$923	$2,746	$886	$1,553	$704	$1,605	$125

2. Includes pre-tax underwriting loss of $2.4 billion ($1.5 billion after-tax; $982 after-tax per A-share) in connection with the September 11, 2001 terrorist attack.
3. Beginning in 2002 goodwill was no longer amortized. Amortization charges after-tax relating to goodwill were $636 million ($416 per share) and $548 million ($360 per share) in 2001 and 2000, respectively.
4. 1997 capital gain includes $678 million pre-tax ($427 million after-tax) from the acquisition of Salomon, Inc. by Travelers Group, Inc.
5. 1996 capital gain includes $2.2 billion pre-tax ($1.4 billion after-tax) from the acquisition of Capital Cities/ABC, Inc. by The Walt Disney Company.
6. Year-end data for 1998 includes General Re, acquired on December 21, 1998.
7. Class A-equivalent shares.

Note: Data was taken from the 2004 (2000–2004) and 1999 (1995–1999) Annual Reports to maintain consistency with the reporting for each five-year period. Slight differences exist for any particular year depending on the report year.

Sources: Berkshire Hathaway Annual Reports 1999, 2004.

Table 6.41: Reconciliation of shareholders' equity

($ millions)	2004	2003	2002	2001	2000	1999	1998	1997	1996	1995	1994
Prior year equity[1]	$77,596	$64,037	$57,950	$61,724	$57,761	$57,403	$31,455	$23,426	$16,739	$11,652	$10,140
Current year net income/(loss)	7,308	8,151	4,286	795	3,328	1,557	2,830	1,902	2,489	795	553
Change in common - issue 517,500 "B" shares									565		
Change in paid-in capital[2]	117	123	421	83	315	88	22,803	73	708	346	
Treasury stock[2]							3		3	3	
Other[3]											
Change in unrealized appreciation of securities, net of tax[4]	674	5,141	1,416	(4,579)	428	(1,382)	381	6,054	2,923	3,944	958
Change in comprehensive income[5]	205	144	(36)	(73)	(108)	95	(69)				
Ending equity	$85,900	$77,596	$64,037	$57,950	$61,724	$57,761	$57,403	$31,455	$23,426	$16,739	$11,652
Shares outstanding at end of period											
Class A	1,268,783	1,282,979	1,311,186	1,323,410	1,343,904	1,341,663	1,349,535	1,197,888	1,206,120	1,193,512	1,177,750
Class B	8,099,175	7,609,543	6,704,117	6,144,222	5,469,786	5,366,955	5,070,379	1,087,156	783,755		
Total Class A-equivalent shares	1,538,756	1,536,630	1,534,657	1,528,217	1,526,230	1,520,562	1,518,548	1,234,127	1,232,245	1,193,512	1,177,750

Footnotes:

1. The beginning 1994 (ending 1993) shareholders' equity is $288.3 million lower due to the restatement of the financials associated with the 1996 GEICO merger.

2.
1995: 15,762 shares issued in connection with acquisition of Helzberg Diamond Shops and RC Willey Home Furnishings.
1996: 17,728 "A" shares and 112,655 "B" shares issued in connection with acquisition of FlightSafety.
1997: 1,866 "A" shares and 165 "B" shares issued in connection with acquisition of Star Furniture.
1998: 272,200 "A" share-equivalents issued in connection with the General Re acquisition. Remaining 12,221 A-equivalent shares attributable to the stock portion of the International Dairy Queen and Executive Jet acquisitions. Also note that in 1998 Berkshire eliminated/retired its outstanding Treasury stock.
1999: $88 million attributable to the exercise of stock options in connection with acquisitions.
2000: $224 million or 3,572 A-shares issued in connection with the acquisitions of USIC and Ben Bridge. Remainder or $91 million related to the exercise of options in connection with acquisitions and SQUARZ warrant premiums.
2001: $83 million additional paid-in capital relating to the exercise of stock options in connection with acquisitions and SQUARZ warrant premiums.
2002: 4,505 A-shares and 7,063 B-shares issued in connection with unspecified acquisitions ($324 million); $97 million attributable to the exercise of options related to acquisitions and SQUARZ warrant premiums.
2003: $123 million attributable to the exercise of stock options in connection with acquisitions and SQUARZ warrant premiums.
2004: $117 million attributable to the exercise of stock options in connection with acquisitions and SQUARZ warrant premiums.

3. Other category included in the 1997 financial statements but not specified. Certain lines contain data that round to zero.

4. In 1998 and 1999, only the gross amounts for unrealized appreciation of investments and reclassification adjustment for appreciation included in net earnings are presented. The figures included for 1998 and 1999 use an estimated tax rate of 36%.

5. Includes foreign currency translation, transactions relating to pension plans, other, and amounts applicable to income taxes.

Sources: Berkshire Hathaway Annual Reports, 1996–2004, and author's calculations.

Table 6.42: Berkshire Hathaway Insurance Group balance sheets, 1994–2000

($ millions)	2000	1999	1998	1997	1996	1995	1994
Assets							
Investments							
Fixed maturities at market[1]	$32,381	$30,217	$21,216	$10,028	$5,462	$1,369	$2,482
Equity securities at market:							
American Express Company	8,147	8,218	5,067	4,315	2,732	2,001	794
Capital Cities/ABC, Inc.						2,406	1,662
The Coca-Cola Company	12,159	11,622	13,368	13,306	10,500	7,407	5,138
The Walt Disney Company	0	2,803	1,489	2,083	1,680		
Freddie Mac	146		3,885	2,683	1,773	1,044	644
GEICO[2]						2,393	1,678
McDonalds Corporation					1,356	505	
The Gillette Company	3,468	3,954	4,590	4,821	3,732	2,502	1,797
Wells Fargo & Company	2,964	2,316	2,466	2,208	1,917	1,427	958
Other	12,008	10,256	8,629	6,526	3,862	2,363	2,452
	71,273	69,386	60,710	45,969	33,014	23,416	17,605
Cash and cash equivalents	4,700	2,981	13,081	516	514	2,329	90
Deferred costs	3,508	2,309	1,226	608	438	411	468
Other	12,808	9,490	7,745	1,287	1,022	315	302
	$92,289	$84,166	$82,762	$48,380	$34,987	$26,470	$18,466
Liabilities							
Losses and loss adjustment expenses	$33,022	$26,802	$23,012	$6,851	$6,274	$3,699	$3,430
Unearned premiums	3,885	3,718	3,324	1,274	1,184	374	307
Funds held under reinsurance assumed				397	450	379	307
Accounts payable, accruals and other				1,256	802	239	255
Policyholder liabilities and other accruals	6,986	6,537	6,419				
Income taxes, principally deferred	9,729	9,430	11,432	10,372	6,612	5,483	3,209
	53,622	46,487	44,187	20,150	15,321	10,174	7,509
Equity							
Minority shareholders'	1,157	1,337	1,554	359	258	196	137
Berkshire shareholders'	37,510	36,342	37,021	27,871	19,408	16,100	10,820
	38,667	37,679	38,575	28,230	19,666	16,296	10,957
	$92,289	$84,166	$82,762	$48,380	$34,987	$26,470	$18,466

Footnotes:
1. Includes Salomon, Inc.
2. In 1996 GEICO became a wholly-owned subsidiary of Berkshire Hathaway.

Note: Berkshire discontinued this presentation after 2000.
Sources: Berkshire Hathaway Annual Reports 1994–2000.

Table 6.43: Berkshire Hathaway Insurance Group income statements, 1994–2000

($ millions)	2000	1999	1998	1997	1996	1995	1994
Premiums written	$19,662	$14,667	$5,476	$4,852	$4,105	$1,024	$916
Premiums earned	$19,343	$14,306	$5,300	$4,761	$4,118	$958	$923
Losses and loss expenses	17,326	12,518	3,904	3,420	3,090	612	564
Underwriting expenses	3,602	3,182	1,131	880	806	325	229
Total losses and expenses	20,928	15,700	5,035	4,300	3,896	937	793
Underwriting gain (loss) pre-tax	(1,585)	(1,394)	265	461	222	21	130
Net investment income	2,811	2,488	974	882	726	502	419
Realized investment gain	3,920	1,364	2,462	1,059	2,290	181	92
Other than temporary decline in value of investment in USAir Group, Inc. Preferred Stock							(261)
Earnings before income taxes	5,146	2,458	3,701	2,403	3,238	703	380
Income tax expense (benefit)	1,604	672	1,186	705	1,007	149	52
	3,542	1,786	2,515	1,698	2,232	554	329
Minority interest	230	35	17	15	8	8	4
Net earnings	$3,312	$1,751	$2,498	$1,683	$2,224	$547	$324
Net investment income detail:							
Dividends	*$493*	*$476*	*$363*	*$458*	*$418*	*$385*	*$362*
Interest	*2,340*	*2,030*	*621*	*431*	*322*	*100*	*92*
Equity in net income/(loss) of Salomon, Inc.						*18*	*(32)*
Investment expenses	*(22)*	*(18)*	*(10)*	*(6)*	*(14)*	*(1)*	*(4)*
Total net investment income	*$2,811*	*$2,488*	*$974*	*$882*	*$726*	*$502*	*$419*

Sources: Berkshire Hathaway Annual Reports 1994–2000.

Table 6.44: Berkshire Hathaway Insurance Group key ratios and figures, 1994–2000

	2000	1999	1998	1997	1996	1995	1994
Loss ratio	89.6%	87.5%	73.7%	71.8%	75.0%	63.9%	61.1%
Expense ratio (against written premiums)	18.3%	21.7%	20.7%	18.1%	19.6%	31.7%	25.0%
Combined ratio (statutory)	107.9%	109.2%	94.3%	90.0%	94.7%	95.6%	86.1%
GAAP combined ratio	108.2%	109.7%	95.0%	90.3%	94.6%	97.9%	85.9%
Change in premiums written	34.1%	167.8%	12.9%	18.2%	300.8%	11.9%	24.2%
Change in premiums earned	35.2%	169.9%	11.3%	15.6%	330.1%	3.7%	41.9%
Premiums written / average equity	51.5%	38.5%	16.4%	20.3%	22.8%	7.5%	8.4%

Sources: Berkshire Hathaway Annual Reports 1994–2000 and author's calculations.

Note: The following table was broken up into multiple sections and spans several pages

Table 6.45: Berkshire Hathaway—insurance underwriting detail

($ millions)	2004 Amount	%	2003 Amount	%	2002 Amount	%	2001 Amount	%	2000 Amount	%
GEICO Corporation										
Premiums written	$9,212		$8,081		$6,963		$6,176		$5,778	
Premiums earned	8,915	100.0%	7,784	100.0%	6,670	100.0%	6,060	100.0%	5,610	100.0%
Losses and loss expenses	6,360	71.3%	5,955	76.5%	5,137	77.0%	4,842	79.9%	4,809	85.7%
Underwriting expenses	1,585	17.8%	1,377	17.7%	1,117	16.7%	997	16.5%	1,025	18.3%
Total losses and expenses	7,945	89.1%	7,332	94.2%	6,254	93.8%	5,839	96.4%	5,834	104.0%
Underwriting gain (loss) - pre-tax	$970		$452		$416		$221		($224)	
Statutory combined ratio	88.5%		93.5%		93.1%		96.0%		103.5%	

General Re ($ millions)	2004 Amount	%	2003 Amount	%	2002 Amount	%	2001 Amount	%	2000 Amount	%
Premiums written:										
North American property/casualty	$2,747		$3,440		$3,975		$4,172		$3,517	
International property/casualty	2,091		2,742		2,647		2,553		3,036	
Life/health	2,022		1,839		1,899		2,005		2,263	
Total Gen Re premiums written	$6,860		$8,021		$8,521		$8,730		$8,816	
Premiums earned:										
North American property/casualty	$3,012		$3,551		$3,967		$3,968		$3,389	
International property/casualty	2,218		2,847		2,647		2,397		3,046	
Life/health	2,015		1,847		1,886		1,988		2,261	
Total Gen Re premiums earned	$7,245		$8,245		$8,500		$8,353		$8,696	
Underwriting gain (loss) pre-tax:										
North American property/casualty	$11	99.6%	$67	98.1%	($1,019)	125.7%	($2,843)	171.6%	($656)	119.4%
International property/casualty	(93)	104.2%	20	99.3%	(319)	112.1%	(746)	131.1%	(518)	117.0%
Life/health	85	95.8%	58	96.9%	(55)	102.9%	(82)	104.1%	(80)	103.5%
Total Gen Re underwriting gain (loss) - pre-tax	$3	100.0%	$145	98.2%	($1,393)	116.4%	($3,671)	143.9%	($1,254)	114.4%

Note: GAAP combined ratio shown in %.

Continued...

...Continued from prior page

Berkshire Hathaway Reinsurance Group

($ millions)	2004 Amount	2004 %	2003 Amount	2003 %	2002 Amount	2002 %	2001 Amount	2001 %	2000 Amount	2000 %
Premiums earned:										
Catastrophe and individual risk	$1,462		$1,330		$1,283		$553		$321	
Retroactive reinsurance	188		526		407		1,993		3,944	
Quota share					1,289		220		22	
Other	2,064		2,574		321		225		425	
Total BHRG premiums earned	$3,714		$4,430		$3,300		$2,991		$4,712	
Underwriting gain (loss) pre-tax:										
Catastrophe and individual risk	$385	73.7%	$1,108	16.7%	$1,006	21.6%	($150)	127.1%	$196	38.9%
Retroactive reinsurance	(412)	319.1%	(387)	173.6%	(446)	209.6%	(371)	118.6%	(191)	104.8%
Quota share					(86)	106.7%	(57)	125.9%	(3)	113.6%
Other	444	78.5%	326	87.3%	60	81.3%	(69)	130.7%	(164)	138.6%
Total BHRG underwriting gain (loss) - pre-tax	$417	88.8%	$1,047	76.4%	$534	83.8%	($647)	121.6%	($162)	103.4%

Note: GAAP combined ratio shown in %.

BHRG - Combined

	2004 Amount	2004 %	2003 Amount	2003 %	2002 Amount	2002 %	2001 Amount	2001 %	2000 Amount	2000 %
Premiums written	3,714		4,430		3,300		$3,254		$4,724	
Premiums earned	3,714	100.0%	4,430	100.0%	3,300	100.0%	2,991	100.0%	4,712	100.0%
Losses and loss expenses							3,443	115.1%	4,760	101.0%
Underwriting expenses							195	6.5%	114	2.4%
Total losses and expenses	3,297	88.8%	3,383	76.4%	2,766	83.8%	3,638	121.6%	4,874	103.4%
Underwriting gain (loss) - pre-tax	$417	88.8%	$1,047	76.4%	$534	83.8%	($647)	121.6%	($162)	103.4%

Berkshire Hathaway Primary Group

($ millions)	2004 Amount	2004 %	2003 Amount	2003 %	2002 Amount	2002 %	2001 Amount	2001 %	2000 Amount	2000 %
Premiums written	1,211		1,034		712		501		325	
Premiums earned[1]	1,211	100.0%	1,034	100.0%	712	100.0%	501	100.0%	325	100.0%
Losses and loss expenses										
Underwriting expenses										
Total losses and expenses	1,050	86.7%	960	92.8%	680	95.5%	471	94.0%	300	92.3%
Underwriting gain (loss) - pre-tax	$161	86.7%	$74	92.8%	$32	95.5%	$30	94.0%	$25	92.3%
Aggregate adverse (favorable) loss development[2]	$419	2.0%	$480	2.2%	$1,540	8.0%	$1,165	6.5%	$211	1.1%

...Continued from prior page

($ millions)	1999 Amount	%	1998 Amount	%	1997 Amount	%	1996 Amount	%	1995 Amount	%	1994 Amount	%
GEICO Corporation												
Premiums written	$4,953		$4,182		$3,588		$3,122		$2,856			
Premiums earned	4,757	100.0%	4,033	100.0%	3,482	100.0%	3,092	100.0%	2,787	100.0%		
Losses and loss expenses	3,815	80.2%	2,978	73.8%	2,630	75.5%	2,434	78.7%	2,254	80.9%		
Underwriting expenses	918	19.3%	786	19.5%	571	16.4%	487	15.8%	441	15.8%		
Total losses and expenses	4,733	99.5%	3,764	93.3%	3,201	91.9%	2,921	94.5%	2,695	96.7%		
Underwriting gain (loss) - pre-tax	$24		$269		$281		$171		$92			
Statutory combined ratio	98.7%		92.6%		91.5%		94.3%		96.3%			

($ millions)	1999 Amount	%	1998 Amount	%	1997 Amount	%	1996 Amount	%	1995 Amount	%	1994 Amount	%
General Re												
Premiums written:												
North American property/casualty	$2,801		$2,707									
International property/casualty	2,506		2,072									
Life/health	1,736		1,305									
Total Gen Re premiums written	$7,043		$6,084									
Premiums earned:												
North American property/casualty	$2,837		$2,708									
International property/casualty	2,343		2,095									
Life/health	1,725		1,292									
Total Gen Re premiums earned	$6,905		$6,095									
Underwriting gain (loss) pre-tax:												
North American property/casualty	($584)	120.6%	$21	99.2%								
International property/casualty	(473)	120.2%	(101)	104.8%								
Life/health	(127)	107.4%	(290)	122.4%								
Total Gen Re underwriting gain (loss) - pre-tax	($1,184)	117.1%	($370)	106.1%								

Note: GAAP combined ratio shown in %.

Continued...

...Continued from prior page

Berkshire Hathaway Reinsurance Group

($ millions)	1999 Amount	1999 %	1998 Amount	1998 %	1997 Amount	1997 %	1996 Amount	1996 %	1995 Amount	1995 %	1994 Amount	1994 %
Premiums earned:												
Catastrophe and individual risk	$880											
Retroactive reinsurance	1,507											
Quota share												
Other												
Total BHRG premiums earned	$2,387											
Underwriting gain (loss) pre-tax:												
Catastrophe and individual risk	($159)	118.1%										
Retroactive reinsurance	(97)	106.4%										
Quota share												
Other												
Total BHRG underwriting gain (loss) - pre-tax	($256)	110.7%										

Note: GAAP combined ratio shown in %.

BHRG - Combined

($ millions)	1999 Amount	1999 %	1998 Amount	1998 %	1997 Amount	1997 %	1996 Amount	1996 %	1995 Amount	1995 %	1994 Amount	1994 %
Premiums written	$2,410		$986		$955		$715		$777		$690	
Premiums earned	2,382	100.0%	939	100.0%	967	100.0%	758	100.0%	718	100.0%	688	100.0%
Losses and loss expenses	2,573	108.0%	765	81.5%	676	69.9%	573	75.6%	522	72.7%	477	69.3%
Underwriting expenses	65	2.7%	195	20.8%	163	16.9%	193	25.5%	217	30.2%	131	19.0%
Total losses and expenses	2,638	110.7%	960	102.2%	839	86.8%	766	101.1%	739	102.9%	608	88.3%
Underwriting gain (loss) - pre-tax	($256)		($21)		$128		($8)		($21)		$81	

Berkshire Hathaway Primary Group

($ millions)	1999 Amount	1999 %	1998 Amount	1998 %	1997 Amount	1997 %	1996 Amount	1996 %	1995 Amount	1995 %	1994 Amount	1994 %
Premiums written					$309		$268		$247		$226	
Premiums earned[1]	262	100.0%	328	100.0%	313	100.0%	268	100.0%	240	100.0%	235	100.0%
Losses and loss expenses					114	36.5%	92	34.2%	90	37.5%	88	37.6%
Underwriting expenses					146	46.6%	119	44.2%	109	45.6%	98	41.8%
Total losses and expenses	240	91.6%	311	94.8%	260	83.1%	210	78.4%	199	83.1%	187	79.4%
Underwriting gain (loss) - pre-tax	$22		$17		$53		$59		$41		$48	
Aggregate adverse (favorable) loss development[2]	($192)	(1.3%)	($195)	(1.7%)	($131)	(2.8%)	($90)	(2.2%)	$56	1.5%	$60	6.5%

Continued...

...Continued from prior page

Footnotes:

1. Beginning in August 2000, the Berkshire Hathaway Primary Group included the results of the United States Investment Corporation ("USIC").

2. Per the notes to the financial statements. Percentage is the ratio of loss development to earned premiums.

3. The results for 2000 at General Re include five quarters. In 2000 General Re International and Global Life/Health changed its reporting from a one-quarter lag.

Notes:

1. Unless otherwise stated, the ratios presented are on a GAAP basis. Statutory ratios were either unavailable or incalculable.

2. 1995: There is an inconsistency in the financial statements with respect to consolidated pre-tax underwriting income. The financial statements report the same $19.6 million consolidated pre-tax gain; however, Buffett's table reports a figure of $20.5 million. It is possible this is due to Buffett having removed Structured Settlement losses.

3. 1996: The consolidated underwriting gain amounts to $221.4 million in this table, and in the notes to the financial statements. However, Buffett's Sources of Reported Earnings table, and the non-GAAP financials at the end of the annual report, list a figure of $222.1 million.

4. In 1996 Berkshire stopped reporting loss development in each business line.

5. 2000: BHRG: The figure for earned premiums in the 2000 annual report is $4,705. In the 2002 presentation it is listed as $4,712. Likewise, the pre-tax underwriting loss, as originally presented, was $175. This changed to a loss of $162 in the 2002 presentation. I have used the 2002 figures and adjusted the losses and loss expenses, which were not detailed in the 2002 presentation, by the difference (reasoning it is more likely the loss estimate was off vs. the expenses, which should have been known).

2000: General Re: The results presented here for 2000 include 15 months. Berkshire subsequently corrected for this. The narrative contains results for the 12-month period.

Sources: Berkshire Hathaway Annual Reports 1995–2004 and author's calculations.

Table 6.46: Berkshire Hathaway—insurance underwriting overview

($ millions)	2004	2003	2002	2001	2000	1999	1998	1997	1996	1995	1994
GEICO Corporation											
Premiums written	$9,212	$8,081	$6,963	$6,176	$5,778	$4,953	$4,182	$3,588	$3,122	$2,856	
Premiums earned	8,915	7,784	6,670	6,060	5,610	4,757	4,033	3,482	3,092	2,787	
Underwriting gain/(loss) - pre-tax	$970	$452	$416	$221	($224)	$24	$269	$281	$171	$92	
General Re											
Premiums written	$6,860	$8,021	$8,521	$8,730	$8,696	$7,043	$6,084				
Premiums earned	7,245	8,245	8,500	8,353	8,696	6,905	6,095				
Underwriting gain/(loss) - pre-tax	$3	$145	($1,393)	($3,671)	($1,254)	($1,184)	($370)				
Berkshire Hathaway Reinsurance Group											
Premiums written	3,714	4,430	3,300	$3,254	$4,724	$2,410	$986	$955	$715	$777	$690
Premiums earned				2,991	4,712	2,382	939	967	758	718	688
Underwriting gain/(loss) - pre-tax	$417	$1,047	$534	($647)	($162)	($256)	($21)	$128	($8)	($21)	$81
Berkshire Hathaway Primary Group											
Premiums written	$1,211	$1,034	$712	$501	$325	$262	$328	$309	$268	$247	$226
Premiums earned[1]								313	268	240	235
Underwriting gain/(loss) - pre-tax	$161	$74	$32	$30	$25	$22	$17	$53	$59	$41	$48
Total underwriting gain/(loss)[2]	$1,551	$1,718	($411)	($4,067)	($1,615)	($1,394)	$265	$462	$222	$21	$130
Year-end average float - total	45,157	42,722	38,366	31,690	26,585	24,026	15,070	7,093	6,702	3,607	3,057
Cost of float	(3.4%)	(4.0%)	1.1%	12.8%	6.1%	5.8%	(1.8%)	(6.5%)	(3.3%)	(0.6%)	(4.3%)
Aggregate adverse (favorable) loss development[3]	$419	$480	$1,540	$1,165	$211	($192)	($195)	($131)	($90)	$56	$60

Footnotes:
1. Beginning in August 2000, the Berkshire Hathaway Primary Group included the results of the United States Investment Corporation ("USIC").
2. 1998: Total does not include General Re (only owned for 10 days).

Notes:
1. In 1996 Berkshire stopped reporting loss development in each business line.
2. The results for 2000 at General Re include five quarters. In 2000 General Re International and Global Life/Health changed its reporting from a one-quarter lag.

Sources: Berkshire Hathaway Annual Reports 1995–2004 and author's calculations.

Table 6.47: Berkshire Hathaway Insurance Group float, select data and information

			Year-end Float (in $ millions)				
Year	GEICO	General Reins.	Other Reins.	Other Primary	Total	Avg. Float	Float Cost
1994						3,057	(4.3%)
1995						3,607	(0.6%)
1996						6,702	(3.3%)
1997	2,917	n/a	4,014	455	7,386	7,093	(6.5%)
1998	3,125	14,909	4,305	415	22,754	15,070	(1.8%)
1999	3,444	15,166	6,285	403	25,298	24,026	5.8%
2000	3,943	15,525	7,805	598	27,871	26,585	6.1%
2001	4,251	19,310	11,262	685	35,508	31,690	12.8%
2002	4,678	22,207	13,396	943	41,224	38,366	1.1%
2003	5,287	23,654	13,948	1,331	44,220	42,722	(4.0%)
2004	5,960	23,120	15,278	1,736	46,094	45,157	(3.4%)

			Year-end Float Growth %			
Year	GEICO	General Reins.	Other Reins.	Other Primary	Total	Avg. Float
1994						16.5%
1995						18.0%
1996						85.8%
1997						5.8%
1998	7.1%	n/a	7.2%	(8.8%)	208.1%	112.5%
1999	10.2%	1.7%	46.0%	(2.9%)	11.2%	59.4%
2000	14.5%	2.4%	24.2%	48.4%	10.2%	10.6%
2001	7.8%	24.4%	44.3%	14.5%	27.4%	19.2%
2002	10.0%	15.0%	18.9%	37.7%	16.1%	21.1%
2003	13.0%	6.5%	4.1%	41.1%	7.3%	11.4%
2004	12.7%	(2.3%)	9.5%	30.4%	4.2%	5.7%

			Year-end Float % Total Float		
Year	GEICO	General Reins.	Other Reins.	Other Primary	Total
1994					
1995					
1996					
1997	39.5%	n/a	54.3%	6.2%	100.0%
1998	13.7%	65.5%	18.9%	1.8%	100.0%
1999	13.6%	59.9%	24.8%	1.6%	100.0%
2000	14.1%	55.7%	28.0%	2.1%	100.0%
2001	12.0%	54.4%	31.7%	1.9%	100.0%
2002	11.3%	53.9%	32.5%	2.3%	100.0%
2003	12.0%	53.5%	31.5%	3.0%	100.0%
2004	12.9%	50.2%	33.1%	3.8%	100.0%

Sources: Berkshire Hathaway Annual Reports, and author's calculations.

Table 6.48: Berkshire Hathaway property and casualty loss development

($ millions)	2004	2003	2002	2001	2000	1999	1998	1997	1996	1995	1994
Net unpaid losses net of discounts/deferred charges end of year[1]	$40,087	$39,709	$37,769	$34,373	$27,278	$22,751	$20,077	$5,883	$5,473	$5,045	$2,625
Liability re-estimated:											
1 year later		40,618	39,206	36,289	28,569	22,239	19,663	5,673	5,324	4,936	2,662
2 years later			40,663	38,069	30,667	22,829	18,132	5,540	5,220	4,901	2,707
3 years later				40,023	32,156	24,079	18,464	5,386	5,093	4,859	2,690
4 years later					33,532	25,158	19,750	5,293	4,973	4,795	2,696
5 years later						26,894	20,581	5,304	4,906	4,707	2,658
6 years later							21,172	5,246	4,920	4,647	2,622
7 years later								5,311	4,891	4,673	2,600
8 years later									4,958	4,660	2,617
9 years later										4,728	2,611
10 years later											2,662
Cumulative deficiency (redundancy)		909	2,894	5,650	6,254	4,143	1,095	(572)	(515)	(317)	37
Cumulative foreign exchange effect		(490)	(1,485)	(1,909)	(1,827)	(869)	(550)	0	0	0	0
Net deficiency (redundancy)		419	1,409	3,741	4,427	3,274	545	(572)	(515)	(317)	37
Cumulative payments:											
1 year later		8,828	8,092	6,653	5,352	5,825	4,509	1,811	1,385	1,166	210
2 years later			14,262	11,396	8,744	8,289	7,596	2,463	2,379	1,912	436
3 years later				16,378	11,625	9,889	9,384	3,330	2,891	2,732	775
4 years later					15,608	11,513	10,436	3,507	3,372	3,129	1,309
5 years later						13,840	11,421	3,598	3,465	3,310	1,460
6 years later							12,221	3,694	3,518	3,357	1,591
7 years later								3,752	3,586	3,388	1,624
8 years later									3,635	3,449	1,639
9 years later										3,491	1,686
10 years later											1,716
Net deficiency (redundancy) above		419	1,409	3,741	4,427	3,274	545	(572)	(515)	(317)	37
Deficiency from deferred charge amortization and discount accretion		332	333	334	335	336	337	338	339	340	341
(Redundancy) deficiency before deferred charge amortization and discount accretion		87	1,076	3,407	4,092	2,938	208	(910)	(854)	(657)	(304)

Footnote:

1. The full loss development table in the 10K report starts with gross unpaid losses and includes such items as reserve discounts, ceded reserves, and deferred charges. I've chosen to begin the table here due to space limitations.

Source: Berkshire Hathaway 10K filing, 2004.

Table 6.49: Manufacturing, Publishing, and Retailing businesses—balance sheets, 1994–2000

($ millions)	2000	1999	1998	1997	1996	1995	1994
Assets							
Cash and cash equivalents	$400	$370	$281	$103	$61	$125	$77
Accounts receivable	1,226	923	823	624	563	455	309
Inventories	1,215	806	727	599	579	556	398
Investments in MidAmerican Energy	1,719						
Properties and equipment	2,250	1,509	1,190	892	863	286	220
Other	921	388	331	156	98	34	30
Total assets	$7,731	$3,996	$3,352	$2,375	$2,164	$1,455	$1,033
Liabilities							
Accounts payable, accruals and other	$1,674	$908	$761	$532	$523	$398	$293
Income taxes	187	196	166	157	127	20	31
Term debt and other borrowings	1,213	740	442	217	193	151	22
Total liabilities	3,074	1,844	1,369	906	844	569	346
Equity							
Minority shareholders'	59	75	75	52	52	40	40
Berkshire shareholders'	4,598	2,077	1,908	1,417	1,269	847	648
Total equity	4,657	2,152	1,983	1,470	1,321	886	688
Total liabilities and equity	$7,731	$3,996	$3,352	$2,375	$2,164	$1,455	$1,033

Notes:

1. Berkshire discontinued this presentation after 2000.

2. Includes: Dexter as of Nov. 7, 1993; Helzberg's Diamond Shops as of Apr. 30, 1995; R.C. Willey Home Furnishings as of Jun. 29, 1995; FlightSafety as of Dec. 23, 1996; Star Furniture as of Jul. 1, 1997; International Dairy Queen as of Jan. 7, 1998; Executive Jet as of Aug. 7, 1998; Jordan's Furniture as of Nov. 13, 1999; CORT Business Services as of Feb. 18, 2000; MidAmerican Energy as of Mar. 14, 2000; Ben Bridge Jeweler as of Jul. 3, 2000; Acme Building Brands and Justin Brands as of Aug. 1, 2000; Benjamin Moore as of Dec. 18, 2000.

Sources: Berkshire Hathaway Annual Reports, 1994–2000.

Table 6.50: Manufacturing, Publishing, and Retailing businesses—income statements, 1994–2000

($ millions)	2000	1999	1998	1997	1996	1995	1994
Revenues:							
Sales and service revenues	$7,326	$5,918	$4,675	$3,578	$3,062	$2,756	$2,352
Income from MidAmerican Energy	197						
Interest income[1]	18	11	8	45	39	25	9
Sundry income	0	0	0	0	0	0	0
	$7,541	$5,929	$4,683	$3,622	$3,101	$2,781	$2,361
Costs and expenses:							
Costs of products and services sold	$4,893	$4,061	$3,010	$2,179	$1,876	$1,698	$1,443
Selling, general and administrative expenses	1,657	1,126	1,014	899	832	741	579
Interest on debt	85	31	19	20	15	9	4
	6,635	5,218	4,043	3,098	2,723	2,449	2,025
Earnings from operations before income taxes	906	711	640	524	378	332	336
Income tax expense	334	267	234	200	138	126	122
	572	444	406	325	239	206	214
Minority interest	21	5	5	6	5	5	5
Net earnings	$551	$439	$401	$319	$234	$201	$209

Footnote:
1. It appears some interest income was included in Sales and Service revenues prior to 1998 and Berkshire changed the presentation going forward.

Sources: Berkshire Hathaway Annual Reports, 1994–2000.

Table 6.51: Manufacturing, Publishing, and Retailing businesses—ratios and key figures, 1994–2000

	2000	1999	1998	1997	1996	1995	1994
Change in revenues	27.2%	26.6%	29.3%	16.8%	11.5%	17.8%	19.8%
Change in pre-tax profit (operating income)	27.4%	11.1%	22.0%	38.9%	13.7%	(1.1%)	23.3%
Gross margin	33.2%	31.4%	35.6%	39.1%	38.7%	38.4%	38.7%
Pre-tax margin	12.0%	12.0%	13.7%	14.5%	12.2%	11.9%	14.2%
Return on invested capital (avg.) - pre-tax	20.7%	26.7%	31.1%	32.8%	29.6%	38.0%	49.3%
Return on invested capital (avg.) - after-tax	13.1%	16.7%	19.8%	20.3%	18.8%	23.6%	31.3%
Return on average equity - pre-tax	26.6%	34.4%	37.1%	37.6%	34.2%	42.2%	51.0%
Return on average equity - after tax	16.8%	21.5%	23.5%	23.3%	21.7%	26.1%	32.4%
Debt/equity	26%	34%	22%	15%	15%	17%	3%

Sources: Berkshire Hathaway Annual Reports 1994–2000; and author's calculations.

Table 6.52: Manufacturing, Service, and Retailing Operations—balance sheets, 2003–2004

($ millions)	2004	2003
Assets		
Cash and equivalents	$899	$1,250
Accounts and notes receivable	3,074	2,796
Inventory	3,842	3,656
Other current assets	254	262
Total current assets	8,069	7,964
Goodwill and other intangibles	8,362	8,351
Fixed assets	6,161	5,898
Other assets	1,044	1,054
	$23,636	$23,267
Liabilities and Equity		
Notes payable	$1,143	$1,593
Other current liabilities	4,685	4,300
Total current liabilities	5,828	5,893
Deferred taxes	248	105
Term debt and other liabilities	1,965	1,890
Equity	15,595	15,379
	$23,636	$23,267

Sources: Berkshire Hathaway Annual Reports, 2003, 2004.

Table 6.53: Manufacturing, Service, and Retailing Operations— income statements, 2002–2004

($ millions)	2004	2003	2002
Revenues	$44,142	$32,106	$16,970
Operating expenses	41,604	29,885	14,921
(Including depreciation)	676	605	477
Interest expense (net)	57	64	108
Pre-tax income	2,481	2,157	1,941
Income taxes	941	813	743
Net income	$1,540	$1,344	$1,198
Pre-tax earnings breakdown:			
Building Products	$643	$559	$516
Shaw Industries	466	436	424
Apparel & Footwear	325	289	229
Retail Operations	215	224	219
Flight Services	191	72	225
McLane[1]	228	150	
Other businesses	413	427	328
	$2,481	$2,157	$1,941

Footnote:
1. Includes McLane starting May 23, 2003.

Sources: Berkshire Hathaway Annual Reports, 2003, 2004.

Table 6.54: Manufacturing, Service, and Retailing Operations—ratios and key figures, 2003–2004

	2004	2003
Return on avg. equity after-tax	9.9%	10.4%
Return on avg. tang. equity after-tax	21.6%	
Notes payable/equity	7.3%	
Total assets/total equity	1.52	1.51

Sources: Berkshire Hathaway Annual Reports 2003, 2004; and author's calculations.

Table 6.55: Finance Businesses—balance sheets, 1994–2000

($ millions)	2000	1999	1998	1997	1996	1995	1994
Assets							
Cash and cash equivalents	$341	$623	$907	$56	$11	$41	$16
Fixed maturity investments:							
Held to maturity, at cost	1,826	2,002	1,227	971	742	529	539
Trading, at fair value	5,327	11,277	5,219				
Available for sale, at fair value	880	999	743				
Trading account assets	5,429	5,881	6,234				
Securities purchased under agreements to resell	680	1,171	1,083				
Installment and other receivables				226	228	196	173
Deferred tax assets				18	23	14	6
Other	2,346	2,276	1,576			1	2
	$16,829	$24,229	$16,989	$1,271	$1,004	$781	$736
Liabilities							
Annuity reserves and policyholder liabilities	$868	$843	$816	$697	$435	$117	$41
Securities sold under agreements to repurchase	3,386	10,216	4,065				
Securities sold but not yet purchased	715	1,174	1,181				
Trading account liabilities	4,974	5,930	5,834				
Notes payable and other borrowings	2,116	1,998	1,503	326	381	524	602
Accounts payable, accruals, and other	3,004	2,304	2,428	126	124	77	32
	15,063	22,465	15,827	1,149	940	717	674
Equity							
Berkshire shareholders	1,766	1,764	1,162	122	64	64	62
	$16,829	$24,229	$16,989	$1,271	$1,004	$781	$736

Note:

1. Berkshire discontinued this presentation after 2000.

Sources: Berkshire Hathaway Annual Reports 1994–2000; and author's calculations.

Table 6.56: Finance Businesses—income statements, 1994–2000

($ millions)	2000	1999	1998	1997	1996	1995	1994
Revenues:							
Annuity premiums earned	$0	$0	$95	$248	$260	$75	$36
Interest and fees on loans and financed receivables				38	39	38	38
Interest and dividends on investment securities				75	55	44	35
Interest income	910	740					
Other revenues	595	247	293				
	$1,505	$987	$388	$360	$353	$157	$109
Expenses:							
Interest expense	$798	$596	$27	$24	$33	$39	$36
Annuity benefits and underwriting expenses	55	54	146	287	277	81	38
General and administrative	123	87	16	21	21	17	14
	976	737	189	332	330	136	87
Earnings from operations before income taxes	529	250	199	28	23	21	22
Income tax expense	187	32	70	10	8	8	8
Net earnings	$342	$218	$129	$18	$15	$13	$15

Sources: Berkshire Hathaway Annual Reports 1994–2000; and author's calculations.

Table 6.57: Finance Businesses—ratios, 1994–2000

	2000	1999	1998	1997	1996	1995	1994
Total assets/total equity	9.5	13.7	14.6	10.4	15.7	12.2	11.9
Capital ratio (inverse of above)	10.5%	7.3%	6.8%	9.6%	6.4%	8.2%	8.4%
Return on average assets (after tax)	1.67%	1.06%	1.41%	1.58%	1.67%	1.66%	1.80%
Return on average equity (after tax)	19.4%	14.9%	20.1%	19.4%	23.3%	20.1%	24.1%

Sources: Berkshire Hathaway Annual Reports 1994–2000; and author's calculations.

Table 6.58: Non-operating activities—balance sheets, 1994–2000

($ millions)	2000	1999	1998	1997	1996	1995	1994
Assets							
Cash and cash equivalents	$163	$484	$220	$383	$765	$250	$106
Investments:							
Fixed maturities:							
	184	2	30				
Bonds				206	943	8	287
Preferred stocks				64	42	47	76
Equity securities	365	339	267	307	199	187	113
Unamortized goodwill and property account adjustments	18,831	18,489	18,613	3,099	3,150	748	520
Deferred tax assets	62	80	130	136	31	2	8
Other	69	50	128	105	259	57	186
	$19,674	$19,444	$19,388	$4,298	$5,388	$1,299	$1,297
Liabilities							
Accounts payable, accruals, and other	$163	$76	$40	$39	$816	$51	$62
Income taxes	236	86	158	152	143	94	67
Borrowings under investment agreements and other debt	1,372	1,693	1,863	2,016	1,718	919	799
	1,771	1,855	2,061	2,208	2,677	1,064	929
Equity							
Minority shareholders'	53	11	15	45	25	29	23
Berkshire shareholders' equity	17,850	17,578	17,312	2,045	2,686	207	345
	17,903	17,589	17,327	2,090	2,711	235	368
	$19,674	$19,444	$19,388	$4,298	$5,388	$1,299	$1,297

Sources: Berkshire Hathaway Annual Reports 1994–2000; and author's calculations.

Table 6.59: Non-operating activities—income statements, 1994–2000

($ millions)	2000	1999	1998	1997	1996	1995	1994
Revenues:							
Interest and dividend income	$35	$39	$63	$41	$55	$38	$31
Realized investment gain (loss)	35	1	40	53	195	13	(1)
	70	40	103	94	249	51	30
Expenses:							
Corporate administration	6	6	6	7	5	5	5
Shareholder-designated contributions	17	17	17	15	13	12	10
Amortization of goodwill and property account adjustments	876	739	210	105	76	27	23
Interest on debt	98	106	96	101	91	55	59
Other (income) expense				(7)	(3)	(1)	2
Other than temporary decline in value of investment in USAir Group, Inc. Preferred Stock							8
	997	868	329	222	182	98	107
Loss before income taxes	(927)	(828)	(226)	(128)	67	(47)	(76)
Income tax expense (benefit)	(55)	(119)	(33)	(17)	44	(13)	(23)
	(872)	(709)	(193)	(111)	23	(34)	(53)
Minority interest	5	1	5	8	8	1	(1)
Net loss	($877)	($710)	($198)	($119)	$16	($35)	($53)

Sources: Berkshire Hathaway Annual Reports 1994–2000; and author's calculations.

Chapter 7
2005–2014

Table 7.1: Decade snapshot: 2004–2014

	2004	2014
Business:	Insurance, utilities, flight services, building products, furniture retailing, candy, jewelry, encyclopedias, home cleaning systems, shoes, newspapers, various finance businesses, miscellaneous manufacturing, significant stakes in several public companies.	Insurance, utilities, railroad, numerous industrial, building, and consumer products businesses, numerous service and retailing businesses, major interest in a branded food product business, significant stakes in several public companies.
Key managers:	Chairman & CEO: Warren E. Buffett; Vice Chair: Charles T. Munger	Chairman & CEO: Warren E. Buffett; Vice Chair: Charles T. Munger
Annual revenues:	$74 billion	$195 billion
Stockholders' equity:	$86 billion	$240 billion
Book value per A share:	$55,824	$146,186
Float (average):	$45 billion	$81 billion

Major capital allocation decisions:

1. Acquired Iscar for $6.05 billion ($4 billion for 80% in 2006 and $2.05 billion for 20% in 2013).
2. Acquired Marmon for $9 billion cash ($4.5 billion for 60% in 2008 and $4.5 billion for the remainder between 2011–13).
3. Invested $14.5 billion over two weeks in three private lending transactions: $5 billion in Goldman Sachs, $6.5 billion in Wrigley, and $3 billion in General Electric (2008).
4. Acquired BNSF railroad for $33.5 billion (aggregate cost). Cost included the issuance of 94,915 Class-A equivalent shares worth $10.6 billion. (2010).
5. Acquired Lubrizol for $8.7 billion cash (2011).
6. Acquired NV Energy for $5.6 billion (2013) and Alta Link for $2.7 billion cash (2014).
7. Invested $12.25 billion to take Heinz private with 3G Capital (2013).
8. Invested over $73 billion in capital expenditures ($36 billion more than depreciation expense) (2005–2014).
9. Increased stake in Wells Fargo by $11.4 billion (various years) and established a major investment in International Business Machines (IBM) at a cost of $13.2 billion (2011–14).

Noteworthy events:

1. In mid-2006, Warren Buffett pledged to give the bulk of his fortune (worth over $40 billion) to philanthropy. The major recipient was the Bill & Melinda Gates Foundation.
2. Between 2007 and 2009 the boom of the mid-2000s goes bust, freezing credit markets worldwide and causing the Great Recession. Markets bottom in early 2009.
3. Class-B shares split 50:1 in connection with the BNSF acquisition. Afterward they have the economic equivalent of 1/1500th of a Class-A share.
4. Berkshire adds new board members: Stephen Burke (2009) and Meryl Witmer (2013).
5. Berkshire Hathaway celebrates 50 years under present management (2014).

Table 7.2: Berkshire Hathaway pre-tax earnings

($ millions)	2014	2013	2012	2011	2010	2009	2008	2007	2006	2005	2004
Insurance Group:											
Underwriting:											
GEICO	$1,159	$1,127	$680	$576	$1,117	$649	$916	$1,113	$1,314	$1,221	$970
General Re	277	283	355	144	452	477	342	555	526	(334)	3
Berkshire Hathaway Reinsurance Group[1]	606	1,294	304	(714)	176	250	1,324	1,427	1,658	(1,069)	417
Berkshire Hathaway Primary Group	626	385	286	242	268	84	210	279	340	235	161
Investment income	4,357	4,713	4,454	4,725	5,145	5,459	4,722	4,758	4,316	3,480	2,824
Total Insurance Group	7,025	7,802	6,079	4,973	7,158	6,919	7,514	8,132	8,154	3,533	4,375
BNSF[2]	6,169	5,928	5,377	4,741	3,611						
Berkshire Hathaway Energy[3]	2,711	1,806	1,644	1,659	1,539	1,528	2,963	1,774	1,476	523	237
Manufacturing, service and retailing[4]	6,792	6,160	5,586	5,037	4,274	2,058	4,023	3,947	3,526	2,623	2,481
Finance and financial products	1,839	1,564	1,393	774	689	653	787	1,006	1,157	822	584
Unallocated interest expense	(313)	(303)	(271)	(221)	(208)	(101)	(35)	(52)	(76)	(72)	(92)
Eliminations and other	(199)	(834)	(997)	(819)	(358)	(292)	(217)	(155)	(94)	(132)	(138)
Subtotal - pre-tax operating earnings	**24,024**	**22,123**	**18,811**	**16,144**	**16,705**	**10,765**	**15,035**	**14,652**	**14,143**	**7,297**	**7,447**
Investment and derivatives gains/losses	4,081	6,673	3,425	(830)	2,346	787	(7,461)	5,509	2,635	5,494	3,489
Total pre-tax earnings	28,105	28,796	22,236	15,314	19,051	11,552	7,574	20,161	16,778	12,791	10,936
Income taxes and minority interests	8,233	9,320	7,412	5,060	6,084	3,497	2,580	6,948	5,763	4,263	3,628
Net income	$19,872	$19,476	$14,824	$10,254	$12,967	$8,055	$4,994	$13,213	$11,015	$8,528	$7,308

Footnotes:
1. 2009: The attentive reader will notice BHRG underwriting profit of $250 million in this table contrasts with that of the $349 million figure presented elsewhere. In 2010, Berkshire moved the life and annuity business from finance and financial products under BHRG.
2. BNSF beginning February 12, 2010.
3. In 2014 MidAmerican changed its name to Berkshire Hathaway Energy. Amounts in 2004–2006 were classified as equity in earnings of MidAmerican.
4. In 2014 Marmon's leasing operations began to be included in Finance and financial products. This table uses data from 2014 which adjusts 2012 and 2013 for the new presentation.

Sources: Berkshire Hathaway Annual Reports 2006, 2008, 2011, 2014.

Table 7.3: Berkshire Hathaway after-tax earnings

($ millions)	2014	2013	2012	2011	2010	2009	2008	2007	2006	2005	2004
Insurance - underwriting	$1,692	$1,995	$1,046	$154	$1,301	$949	$1,739	$2,184	$2,485	$27	$1,008
Insurance - investment income	3,542	3,708	3,397	3,555	3,860	4,271	3,610	3,510	3,120	2,412	2,045
Railroad[1]	3,869	3,793	3,372	2,972	2,235						
Utilities and energy[2]	1,882	1,470	1,323	1,204	1,131	1,071	1,704	1,114	885	523	237
Manufacturing, service and retailing[3]	4,468	3,877	3,357	3,039	2,462	1,113	2,283	2,353	2,131	1,646	1,540
Finance and financial products[4]	1,243	1,008	899	516	441	411	469	632	732	514	373
Other	(145)	(712)	(797)	(665)	(337)	(246)	(166)	(159)	(47)	(124)	(154)
Operating earnings	**16,551**	**15,139**	**12,597**	**10,775**	**11,093**	**7,569**	**9,639**	**9,634**	**9,306**	**4,998**	**5,049**
Investment and derivative gains/losses	3,321	4,337	2,227	(521)	1,874	486	(4,645)	3,579	1,709	3,530	2,259
Net earnings attributable BRK shareholders	$19,872	$19,476	$14,824	$10,254	$12,967	$8,055	$4,994	$13,213	$11,015	$8,528	$7,308
Common shares outstanding at year-end[5]	1,643	1,644	1,643	1,651	1,648	1,552	1,549	1,548	1,543	1,541	1,539

Footnotes:
1. 2010: Includes earnings of BNSF from February 12.
2. In 2014, MidAmerican changed its name to Berkshire Hathaway Energy. Amounts in 2004–2006 were classified as equity in earnings of MidAmerican.
3. 2011: Includes earnings of Lubrizol from September 16.
4. In 2014, Marmon's leasing operations began to be included in Finance and financial products. This table uses data from 2014 which adjusts 2012 and 2013 for the new presentation.
5. A-share equivalent, in thousands.

Sources: Berkshire Hathaway Annual Reports 2006–2014.

Introduction

T he fifth decade of Berkshire Hathaway under Warren Buffett's direction was one of enormous growth for the conglomerate. Cumulative operating earnings for the decade topped $100 billion and net worth grew to a level surpassed by very few corporations. But as the dollars increased, the *rate* of increase in shareholders' equity continued to decline. The decade proved what Buffett had been saying all along: size was an anchor to performance. Still, Berkshire's multiple levels of redundant capital and liquidity proved to be an enormous asset. Berkshire was ready when the Great Recession of the late 2000s struck, and it emerged from the decade stronger than ever.

This decade included the addition of many new operating subsidiaries. Among them were an entire railroad (Burlington Northern Santa Fe) and many other major acquisitions costing tens of billions of dollars in aggregate. Nearly $75 billion was spent on existing operations (including in the newly acquired businesses) for capital expenditures, about half of which represented capital to grow the businesses and strengthen their competitive positions. As a result, 70% of the change in net worth during this period came from operations—the largest proportion since the 1965–1974 decade.

Berkshire's insurance operations contributed more than their share. The Insurance Group reported an underwriting profit in *each* of the years of this decade. Better yet, they almost doubled float from $45 billion to $81 billion. Berkshire's superior financial strength and its reputation allowed it to write some of the largest reinsurance contracts in history, including one single premium worth $7 billion.

The financial crisis that came mid-decade provided Berkshire with ample opportunity. Berkshire became the go-to source for near-instantaneous capital during the height of the crisis and invested many billions over a very short period. It also invested tens of billions into its equity portfolio—and the market value of the portfolio nearly tripled in size during the decade. Yet with all this capital allocation, Berkshire still found itself with over $63 billion in idle cash at the end of 2014. A modicum of share repurchases in the latter part of the decade provided glimpses into Berkshire's future, when it would begin returning capital to shareholders.

Table 7.4: Select information 2005–2014

	2005	2006	2007	2008	2009	2010	2011	2012	2013	2014
BRK book value per share - % change	6.4%	18.4%	11.0%	(9.6%)	19.8%	13.0%	4.6%	14.4%	18.2%	8.3%
BRK market value per share - % change	0.8%	24.1%	28.7%	(31.8%)	2.7%	21.4%	(4.7%)	16.8%	32.7%	27.0%
S&P 500 total return	4.9%	15.8%	5.5%	(37.0%)	26.5%	15.1%	2.1%	16.0%	32.4%	13.7%
US GDP Growth (real %)	3.5%	2.9%	1.9%	(0.1%)	(2.5%)	2.6%	1.6%	2.2%	1.8%	2.5%
10-year Treasury Note (year-end %)	4.5%	4.6%	4.1%	2.4%	3.6%	3.3%	2.0%	1.7%	2.9%	2.2%
US inflation (%)	3.4%	3.2%	2.9%	3.8%	(0.3%)	1.6%	3.1%	2.1%	1.5%	1.6%
US unemployment (%)	5.1%	4.6%	4.6%	5.8%	9.3%	9.6%	8.9%	8.1%	7.4%	6.2%

Sources: Berkshire Hathaway Annual Reports 2018, 2019 and Federal Reserve Bank of St. Louis.

2005

From a quantitative standpoint, Berkshire's book value increased 6.4% in 2005. This was below the rate Buffett preferred to see on an absolute basis, but still 1.5 percentage points ahead of the S&P 500 for the year. The Insurance Group reported an overall profit, despite being hit by losses from major hurricanes. Ever on the quest to find new outlets for Berkshire's cash, capital allocators Warren Buffett and Charlie Munger closed three acquisitions and lined up two more to close the following year. Berkshire's businesses were thriving.

Buffett shared updated figures for his two-column method of tracking Berkshire's progress.* Breaking down the longer-term track record highlighted the shift toward growth in operating earnings relative to growth in investments. This shift was a direct result of Berkshire's many acquisitions during the preceding decade. The policy of retaining all its earnings (in addition to shares issued for acquisitions) funded this expansion. The result of that capital allocation is evident in the rate of growth in investments compared to pre-tax operating earnings during the 1995–2005 decade compared to the 1965–2005 period (see Figure 7.1). Importantly, the base and ending years did not artificially skew the analysis.

---

* Investments per share were $74,129 and pre-tax earnings per share were $2,441. Continuing the rough valuation exercise from the previous chapter, we can estimate Berkshire's intrinsic value in 2005 at approximately $98,500 per share. For reference, Berkshire's Class A shares traded in a range of $78,800 to $92,000 during the year. (It is important to note here that insurance underwriting did not skew the analysis up or down. Significantly above- or below-average underwriting experience is an important adjustment.)

Figure 7.1: Growth rates for per-share investments and per-share pre-tax earnings, select periods

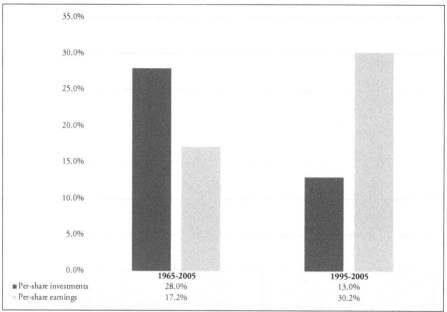

	1965-2005	1995-2005
■ Per-share investments	28.0%	13.0%
▪ Per-share earnings	17.2%	30.2%

Source: Berkshire Hathaway Annual Report 2005.

Table 7.5: Berkshire Hathaway—select data

($ per A-share)	Investments	Operating earnings
1965	$4	$4
1975	159	4
1985	2,407	52
1995	21,817	175
2005	74,129	2,441

Source: Berkshire Hathaway Annual Report 2005.

Buffett reiterated his and Munger's goal to provide shareholders with the key pieces of information they would want if roles were reversed. He thought the task of estimating Berkshire's intrinsic value could be accomplished more accurately than other companies. Why? Because Berkshire had the following characteristics:

1. A wide variety of relatively stable earnings streams
2. A lot of liquidity
3. Minimum debt

He was quick to note that simply looking at the consolidated parent-level financial statements was not enough. Shareholders did not need to examine the detail of *every* business—but a few broad delineations were important. "We have attempted to ease this problem by clustering our businesses into four logical groups," he said. Those groups were presented for the first time in 2003:

1. Insurance
2. Regulated Utilities (MidAmerican)
3. Manufacturing, Service, and Retailing
4. Finance and Financial Products

Insurance

Berkshire's insurance businesses suffered from three major hurricanes (Katrina, Rita, and Wilma) that hit the United States in the latter part of the year. This was the most Category 5 hurricanes recorded in a single season, breaking the old record of two Category 5 hurricanes set in 1960 and 1961, and cost Berkshire $3.4 billion.[78] Hurricane Katrina was the worst in insurance industry history, creating a need for the reinsurance operations to either firm up pricing to compensate for increased super cat risk or begin scaling back volume. Berkshire's losses from Katrina alone cost it $2.5 billion.

Considering its significant hurricane-related losses, a $53 million pre-tax underwriting profit for the Insurance Group in 2005 was a great result. It provided Berkshire with the all-important negative cost of float, which now totaled $49.3 billion at year-end and amounted to almost 10% of float for the entire American property/casualty industry.

Table 7.6: Berkshire Hathaway—Insurance Underwriting

($ millions)	2005	2004
GEICO		
Premiums written	$10,285	$9,212
Premiums earned	10,101	8,915
Underwriting gain/(loss) - pre-tax	$1,221	$970
General Re		
Premiums written	$6,155	$6,860
Premiums earned	6,435	7,245
Underwriting gain/(loss) - pre-tax	($334)	$3
Berkshire Hathaway Reinsurance Group		
Premiums earned	$3,963	$3,714
Underwriting gain/(loss) - pre-tax	($1,069)	$417
Berkshire Hathaway Primary Group		
Premiums earned	$1,498	$1,211
Underwriting gain/(loss) - pre-tax	$235	$161
Total premiums earned	$21,997	$21,085
Total underwriting gain/(loss) - pre-tax	53	1,551
Average float	47,691	45,157
Cost of float	(0.1%)	(3.4%)
Aggregate adverse (favorable) loss development	($357)	$419
Discount accretion and amortization charges included above	$386	$538

Note: Berkshire Hathaway Primary Group and BHRG written premiums were not detailed.
Sources: Berkshire Hathaway Annual Reports 2004–2005 and author's calculations.

GEICO

The shining gem of the Insurance Group was GEICO, and it again delivered spectacular results for both its customers and Berkshire. Buffett once more gushed about GEICO's brilliant CEO, Tony Nicely, who over the past two years had reduced headcount by 4% yet grew policy count by 26%. The result was increased market share to 6.1%, increased profits, and the ability to give more value back to its customers—all of which strengthened the brand.

Digging into GEICO's 2005 financial results, earned premiums grew 13% to $10.1 billion. Part of that growth came from GEICO's entrance into the New Jersey market. Overall, GEICO benefitted from a broad-based lower claim frequency offset by higher severity in injury and physical damage. Despite $200 million of losses attributable to Hurricanes Katrina, Rita, and Wilma, GEICO posted a $1.2 billion pre-tax underwriting gain—a combined ratio of 87.9%. Such strong profitability was above GEICO's 4% underwriting profit target (96% combined ratio), so GEICO reduced premiums and passed more savings to customers.

General Re

Hurricane-related losses at Gen Re were estimated at $685 million and led to its underwriting loss of $334 million.

The bulk of the hurricane-related losses at General Re were in its North American property/casualty line, which reported a pre-tax underwriting loss of $307 million on earned premiums of $2.2 billion. Results in that segment were better than at first glance since $480 million came from hurricane-related losses. Other North American property/casualty underwriting turned in profits of $220 million related to current-year accident gains less $47 million of adverse loss development for prior years.* In short, the (hopefully) irregular large super cat losses overshadowed better underwriting discipline in other North American property casualty lines.

Gen Re's international property/casualty segment reported pre-tax underwriting losses of $138 million on earned premiums of $1.9 billion. Included in losses were $205 million from US hurricanes and a windstorm in Europe. It booked $108 million of favorable loss development.

The life/health business reported another increase in underwriting profits, up 30% to $111 million on earned premiums that grew 14% to $2.3 billion. The business benefitted from favorable mortality trends, primarily in international operations. Results also included $66 million of losses from a US-based health business that was in runoff.

Berkshire Hathaway Reinsurance Group

BHRG gave up almost two years of underwriting profits to hurricane-related losses. In 2005, it reported a pre-tax underwriting loss of $1.1 billion on earned premiums of $4 billion. Irregularity was the hallmark of the Berkshire Hathaway Reinsurance Group. While hurricane losses surely stung, the catastrophe and individual risk segment was operating as designed. For one, profits from other underwriting activities within the segment partially offset $2.4 billion of hurricane losses and reduced the loss by half to $1.2 billion. Second, looking at the longer-term track record of catastrophe and individual risk, it earned cumulative underwriting profits of $1.2 billion between 1999 and 2005. This is to say nothing of the value from its float.

BHRG's retroactive reinsurance line stood out for its third year of decline in premiums earned. Retroactive premiums earned fell from $526 million in 2003 to $188 million in 2004—and then plummeted 95% to just $10 million in 2005. Berkshire

---

* This $47 million figure was the net result of many different factors, both positive and negative, and included: $228 million of increased reserves in workers' compensation, $136 million related to deferred charge amortization on retroactive reinsurance contracts and $102 million of increases to reserves for asbestos and environmental development. This was offset by a net $419 million of decreases, including $72 million related to Berkshire's liabilities stemming from the September 11th terrorist attacks.

gave no reason for the precipitous decline in retroactive policies, which indemnified others for past loss events. It was most likely due to a lack of appropriately priced business. Even though Berkshire recorded a $46 million gain from settling one retroactive reinsurance contract, and another $75 million in reduced loss reserves, the large amount of annual deferred charge amortization led the business line to record a $214 million loss in 2005.

Unamortized deferred charges related to BHRG's retroactive reinsurance business amounted to $2.13 billion at year-end 2005. This would all work its way into underwriting expense over time. Berkshire also slowed its deferred charge amortization in 2005 as a result of slower than expected loss payments. This meant float was sticking around longer.

Pre-tax underwriting earnings from BHRG other multi-line were $323 million on $2.3 billion of earned premiums. Its profits were after $100 million hurricane-related losses from Katrina, Rita, and Wilma.

In addition to the physical hurricanes inflicting pain on Berkshire during 2005, it also contended with the improper dealings of several of General Re's former executives (which was naturally picked up by the press). General Re's misbehavior boiled down to improperly using reinsurance contracts to hide underlying issues instead of actually transferring risk.* Berkshire quickly severed ties with the executives as their guilt came to light in mid-2005.[79]

Berkshire Hathaway Primary Group

Berkshire's not-so-hidden gem of primary insurers continued to have consistent underwriting profits. Earned premiums grew 24% to $1.5 billion and underwriting profits ballooned 46% to $235 million. But part of that growth was due to a new addition to the team.

Berkshire acquired Medical Protective Company (MedPro) from GE Insurance Solutions, a subsidiary of General Electric, on June 30, 2005. It came about after Buffett struck a deal with General Electric CEO Jeff Immelt. MedPro was based in Fort Wayne, Indiana, and had been in business for 106 years. It provided professional liability insurance for physicians, dentists, and other health care providers. For $825 million cash, Berkshire acquired the AAA-rated insurance company with over $700 million in premium volume and $2 billion of statutory assets.[80]

---

* Gen Re was paid a fee to allow accounting that hid improper loss reserving at other insurers. The contracts worked by inflating loss reserves so that it appeared to have appropriate levels. Little or no actual transfer of risk occurred. The two insurers purchasing the contracts were Reciprocal of America, and American International Group.

Regulated Utility Business

There were two big pieces of news in the Regulated Utility Business segment in 2005. The most important economic development was the agreement to acquire PacifiCorp. PacifiCorp was an electric utility serving 1.6 million customers in California, Idaho, Oregon, Utah, Washington, and Wyoming. MidAmerican purchased it from Scottish Power PLC. To fund the deal, which closed in 2006, Berkshire would purchase $3.4 billion of additional capital stock in MidAmerican, which would in turn issue $1.7 billion of long-term debt to meet the $5.1 billion cash purchase price.

After the PacifiCorp closing, Berkshire's economic interest in MidAmerican would increase to approximately 88.6%, or 86.5% on a fully diluted basis. It would also increase MidAmerican's revenues by $3.3 billion and its assets by $14.1 billion.

The second big piece of news was the repeal of the Public Utility Holding Company Act (PUHCA) on August 8, 2005. Since its original purchase of MidAmerican, Berkshire had operated under a somewhat unique arrangement giving it a majority economic interest but leaving the voting interest with the minority partners (Walter Scott, David Sokol, and Greg Abel). That arrangement had been necessary under law since Berkshire was a holding company. Repeal of the law allowed Berkshire to convert its preferred stock into voting common shares on February 6, 2006, and allowed its voting interest to mirror its economic interest. This ended what Buffett called the "convoluted corporate arrangement PUHCA had forced on us."

The repeal also caused an accounting change. Berkshire's increased voting interest required the full consolidation of MidAmerican into Berkshire's financial statements for accounting purposes. Like the exercise Buffett had performed with Scott Fetzer in 1986 (with old and new columns presenting the same company under different accounting), nothing would change from an economic perspective. But Berkshire's financial statements would look different. For this reason, Berkshire included a separate unaudited pro forma 2005 balance sheet in its financial reports to highlight the changes. The most noticeable changes were entries on both the asset and liability sides entitled Utilities and Energy, with the corresponding balance sheet items formerly detailed in the notes to the financial statements. Berkshire's consolidated 2005 assets would increase from $198 billion under the old (current-year GAAP) format to $214 billion under the new (future-years' GAAP) format. Berkshire's $91.5 billion of total shareholders' equity remained unchanged, which was to be expected.

Manufacturing, Service, and Retailing

The MSR businesses generated almost $47 billion of revenues and earned $2.6 billion pre-tax during the year. The $1.7 billion of after-tax earnings from these businesses represented a 22.2% return on average tangible equity. Because of the premium Berkshire paid above and beyond the tangible equity for these businesses,* Berkshire's return on carrying value was a lower-but-still-satisfactory 10.1%. Furthermore, the businesses operated with very little debt.** With two years of balance sheet data we can see the pre-tax return on tangible invested capital improved from 24.5% to 25.1%, which is additional evidence of the underlying quality of these businesses as a group.

The MSR Group gained a new business on August 31, 2005 with Berkshire's acquisition of Forest River. Forest River, a recreational vehicle manufacturer based in Elkhart, Indiana, was founded by Pete Liegl. After Liegl sold a predecessor company, Cobra Industries,[81] to a leveraged buyout operation, it promptly fired him and almost as quickly went bankrupt. Liegl then purchased Cobra's assets out of bankruptcy and rebuilt the business under the name of Forest River.

Although the terms of the sale were not disclosed by Berkshire directly, an article[82] included with the 2005 Berkshire Hathaway Annual Report put the figure at around $800 million. The company had annual revenues of $1.6 billion and operated out of sixty plants with 5,400 employees.

Several of Berkshire's MSR businesses were impacted by higher input costs in 2005, though most nonetheless reported higher profits. Strong prevailing economic conditions caused prices for raw materials, energy, and transportation (among others) to rise, sometimes sharply. Building products, which contained Acme Building Brands, Benjamin Moore, Johns Manville, and MiTek, the result of Berkshire's mini spending spree in the early 2000s, turned in pre-tax profit of $751 million (up 17%) on revenues of $4.8 billion (up 11%). Shaw earned $485 million pre-tax, up 4%, though its margins slipped due to increased raw material costs. Even though profits were up, and moats gave these businesses pricing power, it would take time to raise customer prices to counter rising input costs.

The apparel category (which included footwear) increased its pre-tax earnings 7% to $348 million on revenues up 4% to $2.3 billion. Result in apparel were largely driven by Fruit of the Loom, the largest business in that segment, which increased its market share in all categories. The footwear businesses were shadowed by Fruit of the Loom. H.H. Brown Shoe Group and Justin Boots turned in a respectable 5.3% increase in sales (profitability was not disclosed).

---

* Goodwill and intangibles amounted to $9.3 billion. Some intangibles existed, such as those related to MiTek's software, but the bulk of it was of the purchase-accounting goodwill type.
** Long-term debt represented just 8.7% of equity.

Buffett's Chairman's letter conveyed his delight at Ben Bridge and RC Willey, which increased same-store sales by 6.6% and 9.9%, respectively. Together, same-store sales for the jewelry and home furnishing businesses increased 2.5%. The increase at RC Willey was that much more impressive considering its closed-on-Sunday's policy. RC Willey's newest location in Reno, Nevada contributed to results and it planned to open another store in Sacramento, California. Jordan's Furniture also opened a new store in 2005, a 60,000 clearance center in Avon, Massachusetts.

The Chairman's letter also reported that Chuck Huggins, Sees Candy's long-time CEO, had passed the reins to Brad Kinstler. Kinstler previously headed Cypress Insurance and Fechheimer, and impressed Buffett greatly. He was the "obvious choice for the See's job," Buffett said.

All told, the jewelry, home furnishings, and candy segment increased pre-tax profit 20% to $257 million.

Within the flight services segment, results were mixed. Increased demand for simulator time at FlightSafety resulted in higher utilization. Profits were up 10% to $200 million. With the increased demand came expansion plans, including a $100 million project underway for fifteen new simulators at a major facility in Farnborough, England. This would bring its total facility count to forty-two.

Results at NetJets were a different story. The business reported a loss of $80 million. The cause: struggles maintaining the European operation thought necessary to dominate the worldwide fractional ownership industry. Even though European contracts increased 37%, its low efficiency resulted in red ink.*

With profits off 5% to $217 million, McLane was a fairly steady generator of revenues and profit. Part of that steadiness was due to Walmart, its former corporate parent, which remained a large customer.** Due to the low value-add nature of its business, McLane generated over half (51%) of the MSR Groups' total revenues—yet only 8% of its pre-tax profit.

The individual results of the MSR businesses highlighted the strength of the US economy in 2005 (when there was a 3.5% increase in real GDP[83]). The ability of the building products businesses to pass through input costs over time highlighted the strong housing market and the strength of the businesses. Results from Berkshire's retailers were proof of strong consumer demand.

In hindsight, we know this period was the beginning of a crescendo that would end in disaster. Buffett's comments at the 2006 Annual Meeting suggested caution. He pointed to the "ridiculous credit being extended" to homeowners, and the slowdown in home sales seen at MidAmerican's Home Services business as areas of concern.

---

* Buffett commented at the 2006 Annual Meeting that he thought NetJets would have more economies of scale.
** According to the footnotes to the 2005 Annual Report, Walmart represented 33% of McLane's 2005 revenues.

Finance and Financial Products

The Finance and Financial Products segment contained a wide variety of businesses. They were an eclectic mix of financial-type businesses and operations. From Clayton Homes, a manufactured housing company (included because of its large financing arm), to the remnants of General Re's securities operations, to Buffett's own proprietary trading, and more, the group was nonetheless very important to Berkshire.

Buffett said the star of the finance sector was Clayton Homes. It was not hard to see why. The company had grown to include thirty-six manufacturing plants since Berkshire's purchase in 2003. This included twelve acquired via the bankruptcy of competitor Oakwood in 2004. Another four plants came from the purchase of Karsten, a West Coast-based operation, in 2005. Clayton's manufacturing operations were dwarfed only by the size of its lending business, which provided financing for Clayton's customers and others.

Clayton as of 2005 serviced $17 billion of loans, of which $9.6 billion was owned by Clayton. To finance that $9.6 billion, Clayton had borrowed from Berkshire, which had in turn borrowed at an attractive interest rate. To compensate Berkshire for the use of its pristine credit rating, Berkshire charged Clayton a 1 percentage-point spread which, in 2005 cost Clayton $83 million.*

Over the years the Finance and Financial Products segment had grown sizable. At year-end 2005 the segment collectively held $24.5 billion of assets This included:

1. $4.1 billion cash
2. $3.4 billion fixed maturity securities
3. $11.1 billion of loans and finance receivables

That last category that contained the Clayton portfolio in addition to other loans and receivables, such as those from World Book and Kirby customers.

The liability side of the Finance and Financial Products segment balance sheet was equally large. The $20.3 billion of debt within this segment was less worrisome than at first glance since it operated more like a bank. Over half or $10.9 billion of liabilities were longer-term notes payable and borrowings used to finance the interest-bearing loans and receivables portfolio. Berkshire took pains to structure its debt to avoid the possibility of an immediate need for liquidity since, unlike a bank, it did not have reliable sources of deposits as funding. There were another $5.1

---

* The $416 million of earnings reported by Clayton was after this $83 million interest cost.

billion of derivative contract liabilities in addition to some residual liabilities related to Gen Re Securities.*

These trading activities and the irregular losses from unwinding General Re Securities meant the earnings of the Finance and Financial Products segment were irregular at best. From a profit of $584 million pre-tax and pre-capital gains in 2004, the segment reported an $822 million profit in 2005. Just over half of the 2005 profit ($416 million) was from Clayton Homes. Most of the remaining profit came from Buffett's trading ($200 million), and leasing operations of XTRA and CORT ($173 million).

Investments

Buffett thought general stock market levels already reflected a positive economic outlook: "Expect no miracles from our equity portfolio." Setting characteristically low expectations, Buffett thought Berkshire's portfolio of equity securities might double over the next decade—an annualized rate of return of about 7%. Still, he and Munger found a few intelligent things to do during 2005. Berkshire increased its Wells Fargo holdings substantially over the preceding year—almost doubling its shares to 95 million shares in 2005. Berkshire now owned 5.7% of the West Coast bank. In addition, Berkshire purchased stakes in two other companies, brewer Anheuser-Busch Company in St. Louis, Missouri, and Walmart Stores, Inc., the Bentonville, Arkansas-based retailer long admired by Buffett and Munger.

Two other names found their way onto the list of investments with a market value greater than $700 million (notice the minimum amount keeps going up). Both were accounting-related more than economics, and the result of corporate actions outside of Berkshire's control. The first was the spinoff of Ameriprise Financial from American Express. Berkshire now owned 12.1% of Ameriprise (roughly equal to its 12.2% stake in American Express), with a cost of $183 million and a market value of $1.2 billion. Second, during the fourth quarter of 2005, Gillette merged into Procter & Gamble. This created a lot of accounting noise and much less economic change, providing one of Buffett's famous accounting lessons.

Berkshire did not sell a single share of Gillette. It simply accepted the 0.975 shares of Procter & Gamble stock for each Gillette share it owned. However, GAAP rules required a $5 billion non-cash, pre-tax gain** be booked through the income account. Many people would rightfully ask why? This was a perfect example of economics vs. accounting. In economic terms, Berkshire's cost basis in Gillette at the time of the merger was $600 million. Berkshire's cost basis for tax purposes in Procter & Gamble

---

* The notes to the financial statements disclose that Berkshire had written equity index options and credit default swap contracts "during the last two years". Gen Re Securities was in run-off mode and would not have engaged in these types of transactions.
** $3.25 billion after-tax.

was $940 million.[84] This was because Berkshire purchased $340 million of Procter & Gamble to an even 100 million shares. In accounting terms, the cost basis increased to $5.96 billion, reflecting the non-cash gain booked through the income statement.[*]

With the wind largely at its back, Berkshire had a relatively good year in 2005. The Insurance Group, though not without struggles, turned in the all-important cost-free float and its non-insurance businesses largely did well despite signs of a peak in the booming economy. Berkshire used $2.4 billion of its excess cash to complete acquisitions of Medical Protective and Forest River, in addition to several other bolt-on acquisitions. The following year would see more acquisitions, including Berkshire's first major acquisition overseas.

2006

Berkshire's results in 2006 were probably at the high end of what could be expected for a conglomerate its size. With revenues approaching $100 billion and 217,000 employees, Berkshire Hathaway was the 12th largest US corporation according to *Fortune* magazine.[85] Berkshire's $16.9 billion increase in net worth year over year translated into an 18.4% increase in per share book value.

Buffett wanted shareholders to keep expectations in check going forward. While overall Berkshire's seventy-three business units did outstanding, the Insurance Group benefitted from a large dose of luck. This was not Buffett displaying his usual modesty; the year 2006 for insurers was all good news.

The wind was also at Berkshire's back on the capital allocation front. Berkshire spent $6 billion closing the PacifiCorp, Business Wire, and Applied Underwriters acquisitions that were pending at year-end 2005. It spent an additional $4 billion on Iscar (its first foreign acquisition), $1.2 billion on Russell Corp., plus several other tuck-in acquisitions at MiTek, CTB, Shaw, and Clayton.

Insurance

A combination of luck and continued underwriting discipline was behind the large jump in underwriting profit in 2006. Premiums earned grew 9% to $24 billion aided in part by the addition of Applied Underwriters on May 19, 2006. The real story, though, was Berkshire's loss experience—or rather, lack thereof. While each major segment did not contribute to premium growth, all contributed to a $3.8 billion underwriting profit, which was up from just $53 million in 2005. On top of that, float increased 5% to $50 billion, providing even more capital to put to work.

---

[*] Its financial accounting cost basis increased on par with the capital gain booked through the income account. This was offset by a corresponding decrease in unrealized investment gains (again, only for financial accounting purposes; for tax purposes it was still unrealized). See p. 62 of the 2005 Berkshire Hathaway Annual Report.

Table 7.7: Berkshire Hathaway—Insurance Underwriting

($ millions)	2006	2005
GEICO		
Premiums written	$11,303	$10,285
Premiums earned	11,055	10,101
Underwriting gain/(loss) - pre-tax	$1,314	$1,221
General Re		
Premiums written	$5,949	$6,155
Premiums earned	6,075	6,435
Underwriting gain/(loss) - pre-tax	$526	($334)
Berkshire Hathaway Reinsurance Group		
Premiums earned	$4,976	$3,963
Underwriting gain/(loss) - pre-tax	$1,658	($1,069)
Berkshire Hathaway Primary Group		
Premiums earned	$1,858	$1,498
Underwriting gain/(loss) - pre-tax	$340	$235
Total premiums earned	$23,964	$21,997
Total underwriting gain/(loss) - pre-tax	3,838	53
Average float	50,087	47,691
Cost of float	(7.7%)	(0.1%)
Aggregate adverse (favorable) loss development	($612)	($357)
Discount accretion and amortization charges included above	$459	$386

Note: Berkshire Hathaway Primary Group and BHRG written premiums were not detailed.
Sources: Berkshire Hathaway Annual Reports 2005–2006 and author's calculations.

General Re

The favorable insurance climate was most apparent in the two reinsurance units. Underwriting at Gen Re swung from a loss of $334 million in 2005 to a profit of $526 million in 2006, despite premiums earned falling 6% to $6.1 billion.

Gen Re's underwriting discipline was starting to show. Its North American property/casualty segment recorded a pre-tax underwriting gain of $127 million even as earned premiums fell 18% to $1.8 billion. Including gains from current year business and favorable loss development, property lines produced a gain of $348 million. Casualty/workers' compensation reported a loss of $221 million, which included discount accretion, deferred charge amortization, and additional loss reserves.

The International segment reported profits of $246 million on flat volume of $1.9 billion. More net gains from aviation lines and no catastrophe losses led to a strong gain of $360 million, while $114 million in casualty losses reduced profits for the segment. Casualty losses included an unspecified amount of costs related to the ongoing regulatory investigations surrounding misconducts by former executives.

An underwriting gain of $153 million on volume of $2.4 billion continued a long string of profits from Gen Re's life/health segment.

Berkshire Hathaway Reinsurance Group

The story was much the same (but even better) at Berkshire Hathaway Reinsurance Group in 2006. Premiums earned grew 26% to $5 billion and profits rebounded strongly from a loss of $1.1 billion in 2005 to a profit of $1.7 billion in 2006.

BHRG benefitted from both higher rates and higher volumes after other insurers pulled back following large hurricane losses in 2005. It was rewarded for staying the course: Premium volume in catastrophe and individual risk grew 32% to $2.2 billion, and profits rose sharply, from a loss of $1.2 billion in 2005 to a gain of $1.6 billion in 2006. Underwriting results in 2006 included $200 million unfavorable loss development, primarily tied to revised estimates of losses associated with Hurricane Wilma (which occurred during the fourth quarter of 2005).

The big news at BHRG was its huge $7.1 billion retroactive reinsurance deal with Equitas—the largest reinsurance contract in Berkshire's history and very likely the largest in insurance history at the time. Though finalized in 2006, the policy would not begin until 2007.

Equitas was an entity created by Lloyd's of London, the London-based association of insurers and reinsurers. Equitas was an entity created to hold all the risk incurred by thousands of names[*] or underwriters on contracts written by the Lloyd's syndicates prior to 1993. Those names were still on the hook for any losses—no matter how far into the future. The development of latent asbestos and environmental losses caused a pullback in their willingness to write new policies on *any* type of business. This uncertainty froze the market.

Ajit Jain and Buffett offered a policy to insure all 27,972 names backing Equitas. In exchange for $7.1 billion in cash and securities, Berkshire wrote a policy that covered all future claims (on policies in effect prior to 1993) up to a limit of $13.9 billion. Buffett and Jain reasoned that the payment of future claims would either be lower in amount or longer in duration, making the transaction a good bet for Berkshire. The transaction was like a loan, but with an unknown repayment schedule. The sooner and higher the ultimate payments, the higher the cost, and vice versa. The two certain variables were the upfront cash and the upper limit of the policy. Time would reveal the cost of this float.

---

[*] Names are participants in syndicates.

Before leaving the Equitas transaction, it's worth highlighting Buffett's accounting lesson on reinsurance from his 2006 Chairman's letter. Laying out the debits and credits, he explained exactly how the Equitas accounting worked:

> "The major debits will be to Cash and Investments, Reinsurance Recoverable, and Deferred Charges for Reinsurance Assumed (DCRA). The major credit will be to Reserve for Losses and Loss Adjustment Expense. No profit or loss will be recorded at the inception of the transaction, but underwriting losses will thereafter be incurred annually as the DCRA asset is amortized downward … . Eventually, when the last claim has been paid, the DCRA will be reduced to zero. That day is 50 years or more away."

It's important to reiterate the economics vs. accounting for a reinsurance transaction like Equitas. From an accounting standpoint, there was no impact to profitability on day one. Subsequent periods would show underwriting losses as the DCRA was amortized into expense. From an economic standpoint, any earnings from the $7.1 billion received upfront would be recorded in investment income. Retroactive insurance contracts always produce underwriting losses. The question is whether the float generated via the cash received upfront produced investment income exceeding those losses. Buffett made no guarantee on this bet but wanted shareholders to have the facts. He stressed this by jabbing Enron for its purposely unintelligible 10K filings.

BHRG's retroactive business in 2006 reported an underwriting loss of $173 million on $146 million of earned premiums, which was primarily a result of deferred charge amortization and gains from commuted/amended contracts.

Other multi-line had a gain of $243 million on premiums of $2.6 billion, which reflected strength in workers' compensation and aviation lines that offset a decline in quota-share volume.

GEICO

GEICO's results were simply splendid—no surprise there. The company grew policies-in-force 10.7% overall and ended 2006 with 8.1 million policies.* Its $1.3 billion pre-tax underwriting gain on $11.1 billion of earned premiums produced an 88.1% combined ratio and led GEICO to reduce rates in certain markets.

---

* The growth came from 11.3% growth in the preferred risk category and 8.6% in the standard category.

Berkshire Hathaway Primary Group

Berkshire's Primary Group earned $340 million pre-tax, an 18% underwriting profit on $1.9 billion of premiums earned. Each of its component businesses reported an underwriting gain, and results were bolstered by MedPro, which closed in mid-2005, and Applied Underwriters, which officially joined Berkshire on May 19, 2006.

Applied Underwriters

In December 2005, Berkshire agreed to acquire a majority stake in Applied Underwriters, a writer of workers' compensation insurance to small businesses as well as a provider of payroll services.[86] Even though most of its customers were based in California, the business was based in Omaha. Berkshire purchased an 85% ownership interest** and the remaining 15% of the business was retained by Sid Ferenc and Steve Menzies, whom Buffett praised for having built Applied Underwriters from nothing just over a decade before.

The favorable loss experience and strong underwriting profitability in insurance in 2006 suggested conditions were expected to deteriorate soon. Buffett pointed to the flood of capital entering the super cat field. He told shareholders that Berkshire would employ a lesson from investing to the insurance field: "Be fearful when others are greedy, and be greedy when others are fearful." For the time being, Berkshire would reduce exposure to wind-related events but stand by willing to assume risk at an appropriate price.

Manufacturing, Service, and Retailing

Like the Insurance Group, Berkshire's MSR segment had a good year in 2006. It could be traced to several factors, including a strong US economy and acquisitions of additional businesses. Net earnings grew 29% to $2.1 billion—a very respectable 25.1% return on tangible equity.*** Pre-tax return on tangible capital expanded four percentage points to 29.1%.

Iscar Metalworking Companies was the most significant newcomer to the MSR Group. The Israel-based company first came on Buffett's radar when Chairman Eitan Wertheimer sent him a short letter in October 2005. The company faced a familiar challenge transferring ownership to the next generation of a large family, and Wertheimer

---

* According to one source, the deal was valued at $288.8 million, which would have put the implied value of the business at about $340 million.
** The footnotes to the 2006 financial statements disclose that "Under certain conditions, existing shareholders of Applied may acquire up to an additional 4% interest in Applied from Berkshire."
*** Berkshire's carrying return (due to purchased goodwill) was a lower-but-still-good 10.8%.

thought Berkshire the perfect fit. Buffett agreed. On July 5, 2006, Berkshire paid $4 billion for an 80% stake in Iscar (valuing the whole business at $5 billion).

Iscar produced cutting tools used in conjunction with expensive machine tools.[*] Iscar's business was a very good one. Although not many details are known, the fact that almost $2.1 billion remained as goodwill on the Iscar balance sheet post-transaction was a major clue.

In thinking through Iscar, we can envision the superior economics at work. Its cutting tools were a crucial element of any metalworking project. While the price of each consumable cutting tool might be very high, its relative price to the overall project was likely relatively low.[**] Iscar can therefore deliver an excellent economic result for itself while continually reinvesting in R&D to further enhance the value delivered to its customers.

Other newcomers and bolt-on acquisitions in 2006 bolstered the MSR Group. Fruit of the Loom spent $1.2 billion (including assumed debt) to purchase Russell Corp., an athletic apparel business; and in December it agreed to purchase the underwear portion of Vanity Fair Corp.[***] Elsewhere, CTB, Shaw,[****] Clayton, and MiTek acquired other businesses during the year. Buffett highlighted MiTek's acquisition of fourteen businesses for $291 million since Berkshire acquired it in 2001. MiTek was now debt free, having repaid all the $200 million Berkshire lent it at the time of its acquisition. These types of expansionary capital allocation activities were prized by Buffett since they widened the scope of the businesses and managers he knew well.

Berkshire's newest service business was Business Wire, a global wire service that distributed corporate news, including regulatory filings. Acquired February 28, 2006, Business Wire came across Buffett's desk much like Iscar. In November 2005, CEO Cathy Baron Tamraz wrote Buffett a short two-page letter that piqued his interest. Lorry Lokey founded Business Wire in 1961 and grew it to serve over 25,000 clients in 150 countries. Buffett was particularly impressed with the company's relentless focus on value creation. Citing Tamraz in his Chairman's letter, he talked about the parts of the pitch he liked best: keeping unnecessary spending under wraps but investing where there were gains to be had. Buffett shared this approach. The price was not disclosed.

The existing manufacturing businesses, many of which were tied to the building industry, reported higher revenues and earnings during 2006, although weakness was

---

[*] The end of the 2006 Berkshire Hathaway Annual Report lists the company as having 6,518 employees. The footnotes to the report also disclose that it did business in 61 countries and had manufacturing facilities in Israel, Korea, the United States, Brazil, China, Germany, India, Italy, and Japan.

[**] IMC's products are often the last link in a chain of equipment needed to shape metal. Opting for a lower-quality product at the last step is akin to introducing a weak link in a chain.

[***] The transaction closed on April 1, 2007.

[****] Shaw benefitted from two vertical acquisitions late in 2005 that allowed it to lower and stabilize input costs.

seen going into 2007 as the construction industry began to slow. Shaw, one of the largest, increased revenues just 2% to $5.8 billion, but pre-tax earnings ballooned 22% to $594 million. Shaw was successfully passed along higher prices to customers (7% on average), which resulted in the surge in profits on lower unit volume.

The story was much the same at the other manufacturing businesses including Acme, Benjamin Moore, Johns Manville, and MiTek, which had similarly good years (no specifics disclosed) but looked forward with caution. While these businesses performed well themselves, the addition of Forest River to the segment beginning in mid-2005 was largely responsible for a 29% increase in revenues to $12 billion and a 32% increase in pre-tax earnings to $1.8 billion.

Within the service sector, NetJets' dominance of the fractional jet industry returned it to profitability. NetJets produced a profit of $143 million, finally realizing economies of scale from its large fleet of planes. That fleet was now larger than its three largest competitors combined.

If NetJets was the formerly difficult business getting better, *The Buffalo News* was the formerly great business getting worse. Because of its small size, the paper remained consolidated within dozens of other sister companies for reporting purposes. The Chairman's letter pointed to the deteriorating economics of the newspaper industry and highlighted a once shining star now dimmed. Earnings were down 40% from its peak.* As a newspaper business, *The Buffalo News* was one of the best and had one of the highest penetration ratios in the country. Yet a plethora of online information from low-cost competitors was destroying the once-great economics. Buffett highlighted one of Berkshire's Owner's Manual principles to calm any nerves: "Unless we face an irreversible cash drain, we will stick with *The News*, just as we've said that we would." He continued, "I think we will be successful. But the days of lush profits from our newspaper are over."

Berkshire's retailing businesses were the same story of good results in 2006. Revenues within the segment grew 7% to $3.3 billion and pre-tax profits rose 12% to $289 million. Strong consumer spending bolstered results. RC Willey opened two new stores that added $77 million in revenues. Same-store sales for the home furnishings businesses increased 6% over the prior year. See's was the major contributor in this segment, responsible for $27 million of the $32 million increase in retailing pre-tax profits.

McLane's pre-tax earnings rebounded to 2004 levels. Revenues increased 7% to $25.7 billion and earnings increased 6% to $229 million. These results came in the face

---

* At the 2007 Annual Meeting, Buffett said the paper's earnings were "certainly down over 40% from the peak." The highest earnings *The Buffalo News* reported before being consolidated into other businesses in 2000 was $56 million pre-tax in 1997. That would put its 2006 earnings at less than $28 million.

of losing a large customer and lower restaurant service revenues. Its grocery business expanded but faced lower margins from higher competition.

Regulated Utility Businesses

Berkshire's MidAmerican Energy Holdings was the parent of its utility operations. It acquired PacifiCorp on March 21, 2006. From no utilities six years earlier, Berkshire now controlled major utility operations spanning the globe. The utility operation lacked the potential for outsized investment returns because of its heavy regulation. But it contained the ability for outsized *additional* investment. It could take the large amounts of capital generated elsewhere within Berkshire and deploy it in relatively safe, long-term assets. Just the PacifiCorp deal alone required $3.4 billion from Berkshire that would likely produce steady returns into the future.

Berkshire's now 86.6% diluted stake in MidAmerican Energy Holdings generated $885 million in net earnings in 2006. This amount included the interest MidAmerican paid to Berkshire on a $1 billion loan, as well as earnings from PacifiCorp, which was acquired in March 2006. Excluding EBIT from PacifiCorp beginning on its acquisition date. Save for one operating segment, each of MidAmerican's businesses reported an increase in profits in 2006.

The one laggard in the segment was HomeServices. With lower residential real estate demand, earnings in that segment fell 50% to $74 million. Buffett did not let the current climate distract Berkshire from its long-term potential. "[W]e will be seeking to purchase additional brokerage operations. A decade from now, HomeServices will almost certainly be much larger."

Finance and Financial Products

Gen Re's derivative operation was now largely in the history books. From the time the wind down began in 2002 through the end of 2006, Gen Re Securities had recorded a $409 million loss across over 23,000 contracts. At one time, their value was blessed by accountants. Charlie Munger later quipped that the derivatives contracts were "good until reached for."

Clayton Homes was the largest contributor, making up almost half of the segment's $1.2 billion in pre-tax earnings. In addition to earnings, Berkshire received an $86 million fee from Clayton to use Berkshire's credit to finance its $10 billion+ portfolio of mortgages. The industry was unprofitable in 2006. Unit sales were just one-third of 1999 and Clayton itself had its lowest sales volume since 1962. But Clayton was an anomaly. Unlike other homebuilders, Clayton's earnings were largely tied to its portfolio of mortgage receivables (which is why it was included in the Finance and

Financial Products segment). Claytons earnings grew 23% to $513 million on 12% higher revenues ($3.6 billion).

Investments

Berkshire's investment portfolio grew to $61.5 billion at year-end 2006. Buffett was pleased with the operating performance of the businesses in the portfolio, singling out stellar results from the CEOs of American Express (per-share earnings up 18%), Coca-Cola (+9%), Procter & Gamble (+8%), and Wells Fargo (+11%). All exceeded the 6% to 8% range he thought earnings would increase over the next ten years, in aggregate.

Buffett then summarized the profits Berkshire made over the preceding six years in foreign currency and used that as a launching point to discuss the US trade deficit. His long-standing conviction that the US trade deficit would negatively impact the US currency led Berkshire to make sizable foreign currency bets across a portfolio of currencies. From 2002 to 2006, profits from those operations totaled $2.2 billion.

Buffett strongly believed the United States was like a large, rich farm that traded off pieces of the family estate to finance current consumption. In the year 2006, the US had a trade deficit of $760 billion worth of imports above and beyond its "honest-to-God" trade of $1.44 trillion where exports matched imports. This deficit, accounting for 6% of GDP, was what Buffett called "IOU's to the rest of the world".

The evidence against the strength of the dollar was so strong that Buffett couldn't help but find a way to profit from it. He did that using derivatives—even though he had spoken out forcefully against their existence.

"Why, you may wonder, are we fooling around with such potentially toxic material? The answer is that derivatives, just like stocks and bonds, are sometimes wildly mispriced. For many years, accordingly, we have selectively written derivative contracts—few in number but sometimes for large dollar amounts. We currently have 62 contracts outstanding. I manage them personally, and they are free of counterparty credit risk."

In other words, Buffett's derivative activities involved him taking advantage of a few mispricings in the market, not a large-scale operation with the potential to explode like mortgage-back securities would in the future.

Governance

Buffett concluded his 2006 Chairman's letter with an announcement that Malcolm "Kim" Chace was retiring from the board. Kim replaced his father on Berkshire's board in 1992. Buffett was now on the lookout for a director who was "owner-oriented, business-savvy, interested and truly-independent." He found such a candidate in Susan Decker, CFO of Yahoo!.

Buffett: Philanthropist

In July 2006, Buffett pledged 85% of his Berkshire stock (which was comprised of 474,998 A-shares[87]) to five charities. The largest was the Bill & Melinda Gates Foundation, which was to receive 10 million Class B shares over time, or about $31 billion at the time of the gift. The four other charities were the Susan Thompson Buffett Foundation, the Howard G. Buffett Foundation, the NoVo Foundation, and The Sherwood Foundation.[*]

The gifts were the ultimate display of rationality. Buffett could continue to do what he did best (run Berkshire) and let others do the hard work of giving. Since the shares would be distributed over time and conclude no earlier than ten years after his death, the net effect on Berkshire was effectively nil.[**]

Buffett was quick to point out he was in good health and had an actuarial expected lifespan of twelve years. The actuaries would be proven wrong.

2007

The year 2007 could best be described as the calm before the storm. Berkshire and most other businesses did well, but cracks were beginning to appear in the economy. And no one had better insight into the broader economy than Buffett and Munger, with front-row seats to Berkshire's diverse businesses.

Berkshire's 2007 operating performance delivered a $12.3 billion gain in net worth and an 11% gain in per share book value—exactly double the S&P 500's performance for the year.[***] Most of its businesses did well, except for the canary in the coal mine—housing, which showed signs of weakness foreshadowing what was coming in the next few years. Calm described the insurance market, which again provided a good underwriting year. But its profitability foretold a familiar storm: the entrance of new capital and inadequate pricing.

---

[*] The first three are charities run by Buffett's children Susan, Howard, and Peter, respectively. The last was formerly the Susan T. Buffett Foundation, a charity formed by Buffett's late wife, who died in 2004.

[**] The actual mechanics called for 5% of shares to be distributed annually with each subsequent year based on the residual value. In this way, the gifts could grow in value if Berkshire's share price increased greater than 5%. It would also spread the sales out over a number of years and thus have very little negative impact on Berkshire's share price. Buffett estimated it would take twenty-five years for all the shares to be distributed and sold.

[***] An update on the two-column valuation method figures: Per share investments in 2007 were $90,343. Per share pre-tax earnings were $4,093 but also included about $2,200 in insurance underwriting gains.

Insurance

Berkshire's collection of world-class insurance companies ended 2007 with $58.7 billion of float—up 15% in large part due to the Equitas deal described earlier. Better still, underwriting profits came in at $3.4 billion, though this was admittedly due to another year of calm weather with its resulting lack of super cat events.

Table 7.8: Berkshire Hathaway—Insurance Underwriting

($ millions)	2007	2006
GEICO		
Premiums written	$11,931	$11,303
Premiums earned	11,806	11,055
Underwriting gain/(loss) - pre-tax	$1,113	$1,314
General Re		
Premiums written	$5,957	$5,949
Premiums earned	6,076	6,075
Underwriting gain/(loss) - pre-tax	$555	$526
Berkshire Hathaway Reinsurance Group		
Premiums earned	$11,902	$4,976
Underwriting gain/(loss) - pre-tax	$1,427	$1,658
Berkshire Hathaway Primary Group		
Premiums earned	$1,999	$1,858
Underwriting gain/(loss) - pre-tax	$279	$340
Total premiums earned	$31,783	$23,964
Total underwriting gain/(loss) - pre-tax	3,374	3,838
Average float	54,793	50,087
Cost of float	(6.2%)	(7.7%)
Aggregate adverse (favorable) loss development	($1,478)	($612)
Discount accretion and amortization charges included above	$315	$459

Note: Berkshire Hathaway Primary Group and BHRG written premiums were not detailed.
Sources: Berkshire Hathaway Annual Reports 2006–2007 and author's calculations.

General Re

Gen Re continued to stay the course, rejecting inadequate risks and earning a $555 million pre-tax underwriting profit, up 6% from 2006. This won CEO Joe Brandon and President Tad Montross Buffett's praise for restoring its luster. Though premiums earned were flat in 2007, at $6.1 billion, two factors caused them to be higher than they otherwise would have. The first was the weakening US dollar, which meant Gen Re's non-US business translated into more dollars upon conversion. The other was $114 million from a reinsurance to close transaction with a Lloyd's of London syndicate.

A reinsurance to close transaction is usually associated with Lloyd's of London, an insurance and reinsurance market where syndicates join to insure and spread risks. In a reinsurance to close transaction, a reinsurer takes on the risks and rewards of a particular year. This allows the syndicates to close the books for that year and determine a profit or loss—thus the name reinsurance to close.

In this case, Gen Re was paid a $114 million premium to increase its share of the Lloyd's Syndicate 435 2001 account from 60% to 100%. This reinsurance to close transaction was similar to the Equitas contract. The key difference was the assumption of risk of one year of a particular syndicate, whereas the Equitas deal was for many years covering many syndicates.

In 2007, Gen Re began consolidating its North American and International property/casualty segments into one property/casualty reporting line. This new consolidated segment reported an underwriting gain of $475 million, up 27% on a comparative basis. Gen Re benefitted to the tune of $429 million of favorable loss experience on prior years' property business. On top of that, the current underwriting year produced a gain of $90 million even after $192 million in catastrophe losses.[*] These were offset by $44 million in net losses from the casualty/workers' compensation line, which was heavily impacted by amortization charges.

Life/health reported 48% lower earnings, but the $80 million underwriting profit continued a long streak of profitable operations.

Berkshire Hathaway Reinsurance Group

Berkshire Hathaway Reinsurance Group reported a 139% increase in earned premiums to $11.9 billion. Pre-tax underwriting profit fell 14% to $1.4 billion. The large increase in premium volume was due to the $7.1 billion Equitas reinsurance transaction. The Equitas deal masked a 28% drop in earned premiums from catastrophe and individual risk business as competition and inadequate pricing resurfaced. A lack of major super cat events in 2007 meant $1.5 billion of the $1.6 premiums earned in that segment fell to the bottom line.

Although the Equitas deal provided a large boost to earned premiums, its retroactive nature meant the earned premium was offset by associated incurred losses. Further, while the entire $7.1 billion was available to earn investment income, deferred charge amortization caused the retroactive segment loss to balloon 116% to $375 million.[**]

---

[*] While this dollar amount is large, the footnotes classified it as a low loss level.

[**] The footnotes disclose that deferred charge amortization was $156 million for contracts written in 2007, which was primarily related to the Equitas contract.

The third major segment within BHRG was other multi-line, which reported flat premium volume of \$2.6 billion.* The other multi-line segment turned in 34% higher profit, to \$325 million, largely due to favorable loss experience in both property and workers' compensation.

GEICO

The successful march forward continued at GEICO. With earned premiums up 6.8% to \$11.8 billion and 656,000 more voluntary auto policies-in-force, GEICO now boasted a 7.2% market share. Buffett disclosed it also had a 6% share of the motorcycle market, had started lines covering recreational vehicles and, working with National Indemnity, covered select commercial accounts. Based on prior comments about returning value to customers, GEICO's decline in profitability was intentional. Even after allowing average premiums per policy to decline, the year's profitability represented a 90.6% combined ratio—good for over \$1.1 billion in pre-tax profits.

Berkshire Hathaway Primary Group

The Primary Group reported a \$279 million pre-tax profit which produced a 14% underwriting gain on \$2 billion of premium volume. Premiums grew largely as a result of the impact of MedPro, Applied Underwriters, and the newest addition to the team, BoatU.S. Very little was disclosed about BoatU.S; this included its price. Headed by Bill Oakerson, BoatU.S. provided services to an association of about 650,000 boat owners, including a boat insurance offering. It must have been a very small tuck-in acquisition as it was not included in the footnotes at all.

Regulated Utility Business

With a full year of operations from Western utilities (PacifiCorp), in addition to more customers and higher usage due to warmer weather, pre-tax earnings from Mid-American grew 18% to \$2 billion. On an after-tax basis Berkshire's share, including the interest on a portion of the company's debt, grew 25% to \$1.1 billion. EBIT was flat if PacifiCorp's results were excluded.

Perhaps the biggest news at MidAmerican, though not the best, came from its smallest unit, HomeServices. Pre-tax earnings went from a high of \$148 million in 2005, halved to \$74 million in 2006 and just about halved again in 2007 to \$42 million.

---

* The footnotes to the financial statements disclosed that the workers' compensation casualty business in BHRG was transferred to the Primary Group. No reason for this change was given. It can be surmised that the Primary Group was better equipped to handle these transactions.

The cause was the dramatic slowdown in residential real estate sales. Still, Buffett saw the long-term potential of the business and said Berkshire would look to grow where it made sense. HomeServices was already the second largest real estate brokerage firm in the country, with twenty firms and 18,800 agents.

Manufacturing, Service, and Retailing

Including the recent additions, the MSR segment reported overall pre-tax earnings of $2.4 billion (up 10%) on revenues of $59.1 billion (up 12%). Even with the headwinds faced by the building products businesses and some of the retail businesses, the group earned 22.8% on tangible equity. This translated into a 9.8% return on Berkshire's investment, all while maintaining a strong balance sheet. Pre-tax return on tangible capital slipped 1.5 points to 27.6%.

Buffett laid out the wreckage in the building products market: pre-tax earnings fell significantly at Shaw (-27%), Acme Brick (-41%), Johns Manville (-38%), and MiTek (-9%). Combined pre-tax earnings from these businesses fell 27% to $941 in million compared to 2006. Despite these challenges, Shaw, MiTek, and Acme found tuck-in acquisitions.

Down markets provide an opportunity to examine the dynamics of economies of scale. Consider Shaw, the largest building-related business in the segment. With carpet volumes down 10%, revenues decreased 8% to $5.4 billion. The ratio between volumes and revenues determines the company's relative need to pass through price increases.[*] Working down the earnings statement, Shaw's gross profits decreased 17% due to the lower volume and higher input costs. Management at Shaw was only able to cut overhead costs (selling, general and administrative) by 6%, and as a result pre-tax earnings declined by the 27% seen above. Similar stories likely played out at the other building products businesses.

In addition to having a full year of Iscar included in its results, the manufacturing businesses had two other additions in 2007 with the acquisitions of Vanity Fair Corp. and Richline Group.

- Vanity Fair Corp.: Berkshire acquired the intimate apparel business of Vanity Fair Corp. on April 1, 2007, though it was announced in 2006. The business was tucked-in to Fruit of the Loom along with Russell Corporation, which was acquired in 2006.

---

[*] Higher volumes translate to lower per unit costs as fixed costs are spread over more units. Lower volumes can result in higher costs, as fixed costs are spread over a smaller number of units. Buffett confirmed the difficulty in passing through cost increases at the 2008 Annual Meeting.

• Richline Group: This was a newly formed jewelry supplier. Dennis Ulrich, a vendor of Ben Bridge, contacted Buffett with a plan to combine his company, Bel-Oro with that of Aurafin, another supplier, to form Richline. The deal came about after Buffett visited a Ben Bridge jewelry store in Seattle for a talk to vendors. Richline then made two smaller acquisitions. Buffett noted that the combined enterprise was far below the threshold normally considered for an acquisition by Berkshire, but he was confident the company would grow and maintain good returns on capital employed.

A new business, TTI, Inc., joined the service segment of the MSR Group on March 30, 2007.[*] TTI is a distributor of electronic components that was founded by Paul Andrews, Jr. in the early 1970s. The business was brought to Buffett's attention by John Roach of Fort Worth, Texas. Roach was Chairman of Justin Industries, which Berkshire bought in 2000. Beginning in the 1970s, Andrews built the business from $112,000 in revenues to over $1.3 billion by 2007. The company was based in Fort Worth and had distribution centers globally.

Berkshire's other service businesses performed well in 2007, with gains coming from the Business Wire acquisition in 2006 in addition to growth from FlightSafety and NetJets, which posted a second consecutive year of profits after struggling the prior year. Buffett noted that FlightSafety trained about 58% of US corporate pilots, and its growth seemed to reflect strong demand. Its revenues and pre-tax profits grew 14% and 20%, respectively. The other service businesses as a group earned $968 million on revenues of $7.8 billion, which were up from earnings of $658 million on $5.8 billion of revenues in 2006.

The retailing businesses fared less well than service, though they were not without pockets of good and bad. On the whole, pre-tax earnings from the retailing businesses declined 5% to $274 million, with the fall attributed to the jewelry operations. Among the furniture retailers Nebraska Furniture Mart stood out. "In a disastrous year for many furniture retailers, sales at Kansas City increased 8%, while in Omaha the gain was 6%." Buffett reported that each store had sales of over $400 million in 2007, which placed them at the top of home furnishing stores in the US by a big margin. See's also had a good year with pre-tax earnings of $82 million on revenues of $383 million.[**]

McLane continued its steady progress. Pre-tax earnings increased 1.3% to $232 million on revenues of $28.1 billion (up 9%).

---

[*] The original deal was struck in December of 2006 and discussed in the 2006 Chairman's letter.
[**] Buffett provided these numbers in his Chairman's letter without comparable figures.

Finance and Financial Products

Even though the primary driver of earnings in the Finance and Financial Products segment came from Clayton (the housing-related business), earnings were not impacted nearly as much as the building products manufacturers. In fact, earnings at Clayton rose 2.5% to $526 million, even as Finance and Financial Products pretax, pre-capital gains income fell 13% to $1 billion. That's because Clayton was both a manufacturer and financer of homes. A detailed breakdown was not provided, but Clayton's finance operations would have been the primary driver of results. Its year-end outstanding loan balances amounted to $11.1 billion, with good credit quality metrics.*

Berkshire's leasing businesses, XTRA and CORT, reported a 39% drop in earnings. XTRA was singled-out as the primary reason because its utilization of trailers declined considerably during the year (another example of economies of scale working in reverse).** Another reason for the overall decline in earnings in Finance and Financial Products was the life and annuity business, which swung from a profit of $29 million in 2006 to a $60 million loss in 2007 (based on a change to mortality assumptions on certain contracts).

Investments

Berkshire's investment portfolio saw more than its usual glacial pace of change during 2007. Net purchases of equity securities amounted to over $11 billion, funded in part by $3.5 billion of net reductions in fixed maturity investments. Here were the major changes:

- Elimination of its stake in PetroChina, which netted Berkshire $4 billion, about 5.7 times its original investment (after paying the US government taxes of $1.2 billion).
- Purchase of a 17.5% stake in Burlington Northern Santa Fe (BNSF) railroad at a cost of $4.7 billion.
- Purchase of an 8.1% stake in Kraft Foods at a cost of $4.2 billion.

Buffett had teased excitedly and anonymously about two investments, Kraft and BNSF, in his 2006 Chairman's letter but there was no discussion in 2007 and very little at the 2008 shareholders meeting.*** Both were destined to play much larger roles at Berkshire in future years. Kraft was the well-known, highly profitable, packaged food company Berkshire had owned two-and-a-half decades before through its investment

---

* The footnotes disclose that loan charge-offs fell to $197 million from $243 million. This represented a charge-off rate of about 1.65% on the average loans and finance receivables portfolio.
** Fixed costs included deprecation.
*** The news became public in April of 2007 when Berkshire filed its securities holdings as of year-end 2006.

in General Foods. Buffett did comment on the railroad industry in general at the 2008 shareholders' meeting, stating that the economics had improved significantly from twenty-five or thirty years before. With less regulation, little new capacity, and a fuel advantage over long hauls compared to trucks, the railroad business was a better business now but still very capital intensive.

Buffett gave away a hint at his expectations for Berkshire at the 2008 Annual Meeting. He noted that Berkshire would be happy with a 10% pre-tax return from its investment portfolio over time, including dividends and capital gains. The admission of the lower expectations was another reminder to shareholders of the difficulty of growing a very large conglomerate at anywhere near the rates of return achieved in the past.

Opportunities for Berkshire would still exist. In fact, some major future opportunities were foreshadowed by certain discontinuities Berkshire took advantage of during the year. One was high-grade municipal bonds (a big market) that for a short period traded at yields in the 3% to over 10% range. In hindsight, it is easy to see this event as a precursor to the major market disruptions that would happen over the coming months. A large market like municipal bonds is usually very orderly with yields moving tightly within any given band of credit quality. That yields temporarily spiked meant liquidity was hard to come by—a foreshock of the coming major financial earthquake.

Businesses – The Great, the Good and the Gruesome

Buffett's 2007 Chairman's letter included a lesson on what he saw as the three broad types of businesses. Overall, Buffett and Munger looked for businesses they understood and that had favorable long-term economics, able and trustworthy management, and a sensible price tag. Within these parameters they further sorted businesses into great and good, with gruesome businesses to be avoided.

- Great Businesses: Possess an enduring moat protecting excellent returns on invested capital.
  - » Example: See's, a "prototype of a dream business."

Berkshire paid $25 million for See's in 1972. Over the course of Berkshire's ownership, See's only got better. Its pre-tax return on capital, already very good at over 60%, grew to over 200%. This happened in conjunction with significant growth in revenues. See's was a great business because it earned more with very little investment. To achieve its dramatic growth required incremental investment of just

$32 million.* Meanwhile, some $1.35 billion in cumulative profit between 1972 and 2007 was sent to Omaha to pay tax and reinvest elsewhere. A dream indeed.**

Table 7.9: See's Candies—select data

($ millions)	2007	1972	Change
Revenues	$383	$30	12.8x
Pre-tax earnings	82	5	16.4x
Capital required	40	8	5.0x
Pre-tax return on capital	205%	63%	3.3x

Sources: Berkshire Hathaway Annual Report 2007 and author's calculations.

The only problem with a business like See's was that it had very little reinvestment opportunity. See's was limited to a few western states (in addition to the Berkshire faithful). Try as they might (and they did) Berkshire couldn't find ways to materially reinvest in the business at anywhere near the returns earned in the current business. Buffett said it wasn't surprising businesses like See's were rare. He elaborated:

> "Typically, companies that increase their earnings from $5 million to $82 million require, say, $400 million or so of capital investment to finance their growth. That's because growing businesses have both working capital needs that increase in proportion to sales growth and significant requirements for fixed asset investments.
>
> "A company that needs large increases in capital to engender its growth may well prove to be a satisfactory investment. There is, to follow through on our example, nothing shabby about earning $82 million pre-tax on $400 million of net tangible assets. But that equation for the owner is vastly different from the See's situation. It's far better to have an ever-increasing stream of earnings with virtually no major capital requirements. Ask Microsoft or Google."

- Good Businesses: Deliver good benefits to owners but require significant reinvestment of earnings to grow.
  » Example: FlightSafety

Over the course of Berkshire's ownership, FlightSafety increased earnings, but only did so by increasing its investment in fixed assets (see Table 7.10 on page 514).

---

* Buffett also noted that the business required seasonal debt (read: a line of credit) to handle the large seasonal volumes.
** Buffett elaborated on just how this result was achieved, from a financial standpoint: "First, the product was sold for cash, and that eliminated accounts receivable. Second, the production and distribution cycle was short, which minimized inventories."

FlightSafety's simulators, like most investments in fixed assets, were expensive and generated much lower revenues per dollar of incremental investment. The slightly outsized increase in earnings compared to fixed assets indicates the company increased its capital efficiency over that time, but it was nothing like the experience at See's. Buffett laid out the cold truth about good businesses:

"Consequently, if measured only by economic returns, FlightSafety is an excellent but not extraordinary business. Its put-up-more-to-earn-more experience is that faced by most corporations. For example, our large investment in regulated utilities falls squarely in this category. We will earn considerably more money in this business ten years from now, but we will invest many billions to make it."

Berkshire's growing size, and the rarity of finding See's-like businesses of the magnitude needed to move the needle, meant its future would be built mainly within the good category. A more capital-intensive business like MidAmerican Energy Holdings might fall on the low side of the return spectrum, but still in the good category.

Table 7.10: FlightSafety—select data

($ millions)	2007	1996	Change
Pre-tax earnings	$270	$111	2.4x
Net fixed assets	1,079	570	1.9x

Sources: Berkshire Hathaway Annual Report 2007 and author's calculations.

- Gruesome Businesses: "The worst sort of business is one that grows rapidly, requires significant capital to engender the growth, and then earns little or no money."[*]
  » Example: Berkshire's former textile business. Enough said.

Marmon

Berkshire shareholders woke up to a Christmas gift: the announcement of a major new operating subsidiary. Berkshire made many large acquisitions during its forty-two years with Buffett at the helm, but the deal inked on Christmas Day 2007 was one of the largest cash purchases for an acquisition in Berkshire's history: $4.5 billion

---

[*] Buffett went on to say "Think airlines." He then went on to offer a typical Buffett remark: "Indeed, if a farsighted capitalist had been present at Kitty Hawk, he would have done his successors a huge favor by shooting Orville down." The economics of airlines have changed since this time, now perhaps falling into the good category.

for a 60% initial interest in Marmon. "Charlie and I finally earned our paychecks," Buffett joked. The deal would not close until March 18, 2008. Marmon, which will be described more fully in the section on 2008, was a conglomerate of 125 separate businesses across nine sectors that employed 20,000 people.

Berkshire not only ended the year on a high note but had many reasons to celebrate throughout 2007. With tens of billions of dollars of surplus cash on hand and a fortress-like balance sheet, Berkshire was well positioned to weather any storm—and the one coming would be a doozy.

2008

Any account of 2008 necessarily includes the worldwide economic turmoil considered by many economists as the worst recession since the Great Depression. Since much has been written about the Great Recession of the late 2000s, this book will not attempt to provide a comprehensive explanation. Instead, the focus will remain on Berkshire Hathaway: How Berkshire's businesses managed through the recession, and the ways Berkshire's unique financial strength allowed it to proactively respond to once-in-a-generation-type opportunities.

For just the second time under Buffett's leadership, Berkshire's change in book value was negative, declining 9.6% (compared to a 37% falloff for the S&P 500). Berkshire's relative 27.4% outperformance highlighted its resiliency and focus on insurance and utilities. Neither were highly affected by the economic downturn. To a lesser degree, the strength of its business franchises (both from an operating and balance sheet perspective) protected them and allowed some to use the turmoil to go on the offensive. Still, Berkshire's many businesses tied to the residential construction and retailing sectors were acutely affected.

Insurance

Berkshire's Insurance Group earned $2.8 billion pre-tax, with each of its four major segments turning in an underwriting profit. Overall insurance earnings were down from 2007 due to increasing competition, but its continued profitability in the face of various economic challenges proved the group was what Buffett called an economic powerhouse. The Insurance Group ended the year with $58.5 billion of float[*] and, due to another year of underwriting profits, the sixth consecutive year of negative cost float.

---

[*] Year-end float decreased less than 0.5%, but this deficit was more than offset by underwriting profits.

Table 7.11: Berkshire Hathaway—Insurance Underwriting

($ millions)	2008	2007
GEICO		
Premiums written	$12,741	$11,931
Premiums earned	12,479	11,806
Underwriting gain/(loss) - pre-tax	$916	$1,113
General Re		
Premiums written	$5,971	$5,957
Premiums earned	6,014	6,076
Underwriting gain/(loss) - pre-tax	$342	$555
Berkshire Hathaway Reinsurance Group		
Premiums earned	$5,082	$11,902
Underwriting gain/(loss) - pre-tax	$1,324	$1,427
Berkshire Hathaway Primary Group		
Premiums earned	$1,950	$1,999
Underwriting gain/(loss) - pre-tax	$210	$279
Total premiums earned	$25,525	$31,783
Total underwriting gain/(loss) - pre-tax	2,792	3,374
Average float	58,593	54,793
Cost of float	(4.8%)	(6.2%)
Aggregate adverse (favorable) loss development[1]	($1,140)	($1,478)
Discount accretion and amortization charges included above	$550	$315

Note: Berkshire Hathaway Primary Group and BHRG written premiums were not detailed.
Sources: Berkshire Hathaway Annual Reports 2007–2008 and author's calculations.

General Re

General Re earned praise in Buffett's Chairman's letter for its outstanding year. Now led by CEO Tad Montross,[*] Gen Re reported favorable run-off in its property lines and profits from current year underwriting. This was a 180-degree reversal from when Gen Re first joined Berkshire and brought years of suffering from past underwriting mistakes. With earned premiums of $6 billion and pre-tax profits of $342 million (down 38% from the year before), its third consecutive year of profits resulted from Gen Re's new culture of underwriting discipline and rejecting unsound risks.

The property/casualty segment reported an underwriting profit of $163 million on earned premiums of $3.4 billion. Property business included $395 million in favorable loss development offset by $120 million of current year losses stemming largely from

---

[*] Joe Brandon stepped down in 2008 under good circumstances. The footnotes to the financial statements disclosed that in February 2008 certain former Gen Re executives had been convicted of various crimes committed in prior years.

Hurricanes Gustav and Ike, as well as storms in Europe. Casualty losses amounted to $112 million in large part due to loss reserve discount accretion and deferred charge amortization, and included unspecified amounts of costs associated with regulatory investigations. General Re also agreed to another reinsurance to close transaction with Lloyd's (like the one completed in 2007), for $205 million, which had a neutral effect on underwriting profit in 2008.*

Gen Re's life/health business reported profits of $179 million on earned premiums of $2.6 billion.

Berkshire Hathaway Reinsurance Group

BHRG reported its third year of billion dollar underwriting profits, earning $1.3 billion on premium volume of $5.1 billion. The comparative headline premium numbers were skewed due to the large one-time Equitas transaction in 2007 (premiums that year were $11.9 billion).

Retroactive reinsurance reported another year of red ink, a loss of $414 million. But losses were expected given the large amount of float it generated and the ongoing accounting charges bearing little connection to economic reality. After the large Equitas deal in 2007, premiums fell to just $204 million in 2008. The retroactive reinsurance business was chiefly responsible for the $24.2 billion of float at BHRG at year-end 2008.

The catastrophe and individual risk business let premiums fall 39% as increasing industry capacity softened pricing. Even after $270 million of losses from Hurricanes Gustave and Ike, the catastrophe and individual risk segment reported significant profits of $776 million in relation to its $955 million premium volume. Profits included $224 million from a contract that would have required Berkshire to purchase up to $4 billion of revenue bonds issued by the Florida Hurricane Catastrophe Fund Finance Corporation under certain conditions.** The entire premium went to the bottom line as the $25 billion threshold for losses wasn't met. The economics of the transaction were favorable to Berkshire since it represented a commitment to lend rather than coverage of losses. In effect Berkshire was paid a 5.6% fee on the $4 billion commitment for incurring credit risk related to the fund and its participating insurance companies.*** The fund was willing to enter the transaction because of uncertainty in credit markets.[88]

---

* Specifically, it was the Syndicate 435 2000 year of account, from 39% to 100%. It increased premiums earned but the net effect on 2008 underwriting results was neutral because increases losses and loss reserves offset premiums earned.

** Insurers pay premiums to the fund which in turn can borrow money to reimburse losses of participating insurers.

*** Berkshire was in effect betting that there was less than a 1 in 17 chance that a series of events would occur: a) hurricane losses exceed $25 billion *and* b) the fund borrows all $4 billion *and* c) the fund defaults causing a 100% loss. Such a series of events seemed unlikely enough that one of the three-person board in Florida approving the

The other multi-line segment benefitted from a five-year, 20% quota-share contract with Swiss Re, which increased premiums 50% to $3.9 billion. Underwriting profits swelled from $325 million in 2007 to $962 million in 2008 largely from a $930 million adjustment to its foreign-denominated liabilities. The worldwide turmoil in 2008 led to a significant strengthening of the dollar as it became a safe haven.

In the turmoil of 2008, Ajit Jain found more opportunity for BHRG. At the end of 2007 BHRG formed Berkshire Hathaway Assurance Corporation, which wrote insurance on municipal bonds.[*] This new entity, licensed in forty-nine states and seeded with $1 billion of capital, wrote $595 million in premium volume during 2008. Some of that was secondary insurance, where Berkshire was paid for taking on the risk of the primary insurer going broke.[**] In 2008, Ajit and Berkshire were paid handsomely for their willingness to make calculated bets based only on logic while panic gripped almost every financial market.[***] As Buffett put it, "The investment world has gone from underpricing risk to overpricing it."

GEICO

GEICO's operating results showed continued strength and growth. By allowing premiums per policy to fall, the company passed along more savings to its customers. This, combined with additional advertising expenditures, led to an 8.2% increase in voluntary auto policies-in-force, a 7.7% market share, and strong profits of $916 million on $12.5 billion of earned premiums.

Berkshire Hathaway Primary Group

The Primary Group continued to produce consistent profits and float for Berkshire, even though volume and underwriting profits declined. Pre-tax underwriting profit fell 25% to $210 million on $1.95 billion of earned premiums (down 2.5%). Buffett assured the managers of the many companies in this group that he and Munger recognized and appreciated their contributions to Berkshire even though Berkshire's other insurers dwarfed them in comparison.

---

transaction with Berkshire voted against it.

[*] At the Annual Meeting the next year, Buffett quipped that Berkshire was now insuring financial hurricanes in addition to natural ones.

[**] Berkshire would then be obligated to provide insurance on the underlying bonds.

[***] Buffett notes in his Chairman's letter that Berkshire received rates averaging 3.3%—a huge sum considering the primary insurer likely received just 1%. Berkshire wrote $15.6 billion of such coverage in 2008.

Regulated Utility Business

Berkshire's utilities (under the umbrella of MidAmerican Energy Holdings) thrived in 2008. EBIT from its operating units grew 3% to $2 billion and a large one-time gain swelled the bottom line. At Kern River, approved rate increases and stronger demand drove EBIT up 26%. Its PacifiCorp and UK utilities units maintained steady earnings. HomeServices was the glaring exception to the general rule of stability in MidAmerican's operations and swung to a $45 million pre-tax loss as home sales fell.

MidAmerican earned almost $1.1 billion pre-tax during 2008 (on top of regular operating earnings) from an investment in Constellation Energy Holdings, another energy holding company. Constellation was within hours of bankruptcy when MidAmerican acquired it, proving the value of being able to move very quickly. Buffett told shareholders at the Annual Meeting the next year that "we literally went from a phone call that Dave [Sokol] made to me at noon or 1 o'clock to handing them a firm bid that evening in Baltimore." Within months of agreeing to the deal, Constellation reneged in favor of another suitor. Berkshire was left without a new operating subsidiary—but with a $175 million breakup fee and a $917 million profit on a last-minute preferred stock investment that provided Constellation with liquidity to keep operating.

MidAmerican's ability to make deals quickly rested on its financial strength and its good reputation with regulators. As Buffett proudly told shareholders in his Chairman's letter, a 2009 report on customer satisfaction with pipelines ranked Kern River and Northern Natural first and third, respectively, a significant improvement from ninth and thirty-ninth when Berkshire acquired them in 2002. MidAmerican's Iowa electric operations had not increased electric prices since 1995 and did not plan to do so until after 2013. By focusing on efficiency and without the need to distribute earnings,* Berkshire's utility operations could maintain a strong balance sheet and invest any sums necessary to provide the best service. In return, said Buffett, "we have been allowed to earn a fair return on the huge sums we have invested."

Manufacturing, Service, and Retailing

The diversity of the MSR businesses led to diverse results amid the backdrop of the accelerating recession. Buffett said the full-year results were satisfactory, but "many businesses in this group hit the skids in [the] fourth quarter." Ominously he added, "Prospects for 2009 look worse." The businesses tied to construction and retail suffered the most, though some subsidiaries reported improved results. This group was also joined by a very large sister company during 2008, Marmon Holdings (discussed

---

* Buffett noted that MidAmerican had not paid a dividend since Berkshire's investment in 2000.

below). These businesses collectively earned a 21.8% pre-tax return on tangible capital (down from 27.6%) and 17.9% on average tangible equity (down from 22.8%).

Shaw, Berkshire's largest existing MSR business and one directly tied to building and real estate, saw a 6% decline in revenues to $5 billion. Its earnings fell 53% to $205 million as raw material costs eroded gross margins and lower demand prevented economies of scale. Shaw closed some manufacturing plants and laid off some employees, an unwelcome but necessary reality that also hurt earnings.

The other manufacturing segment included many economically sensitive businesses. Within this segment, pre-tax earnings for Berkshire's building products manufacturers fell 28%. Earnings in apparel fell 34%, and at Forest River, especially subject to consumer spending being in the outdoor recreation equipment business, earnings dropped 56%. Like Shaw, some of these businesses were forced to reduce headcount to right-size operations. The only business in this category identified as growing was Iscar.[*]

Berkshire's only standalone service business was its distributor, McLane. Because the SEC based segment reporting requirements on revenues and not profits, McLane could not be grouped with Berkshire's other service businesses.[**] In 2008, revenues increased 6% to $29.9 billion and earnings increased 19% to $276 million. The company benefitted from additional customers, higher prices, and slightly wider gross margins.

In the other service segment, which included NetJets, FlightSafety, TTI, Business Wire, The Pampered Chef, and International Dairy Queen, the impact of the recession was minimal until the last quarter of 2008 as the recession intensified. Overall, revenues of the other service businesses increased 8%, however, had TTI (the new electronics components distributor acquired in 2007) not been included, revenues would have increased just 2%. The segment's pre-tax earnings of $971 million were on par with the prior year, but augmented in 2008 with the full year of earnings from TTI. NetJets wrote down its fleet by $54 million.

With its direct line to consumer spending, the change in economic fortunes impacted retailing most. This group included Berkshire's four furniture retailers, three jewelry retailers, and See's Candies. Together, revenues in this segment declined 9% to $3.1 billion, with all but one (unidentified) business experiencing a decline. Every one of the businesses, however, had lower earnings and pre-tax earnings, which overall declined 41% to $163 million compared to 2007. If that wasn't bad enough, the fourth quarter was the worst (revenues and pre-tax earnings down 17% and 33%) and conditions were expected to worsen going into 2009.

---

[*] Note that the Annual Report only provides the aggregate revenues and earnings for the other manufacturing category. The percentages listed were the only detail provided.

[**] McLane's annual revenues were greater than 10% of Berkshire's consolidated revenues. If the test was based on profits, McLane would not have met the threshold.

Amid the weakening economic landscape of 2008, Berkshire's MSR businesses took steps to improve their long-term economic positions via acquisitions. This was the moat building Buffett praised so highly. To be sure, these businesses reduced overhead and personnel where necessary. But while others were myopically focused on today, many of the building products subsidiaries made tuck-in acquisitions that bolstered their long-term earning power. The most noteworthy acquisition of the year in the MSR segment was Iscar's acquisition of Japanese-based Tungaloy for $1 billion.[*][89]

Marmon Group, Inc.

Berkshire's newest operating subsidiary was itself a large conglomerate with a long history. It was also Berkshire's largest cash acquisition. Berkshire's $4.5 billion purchase of 60% of Marmon on March 18, 2008, implied a $7.5 billion valuation for the entire business. Marmon's results were included in the MSR segment.

The paths of one of Marmon's founders, Jay Pritzker, and Buffett, crossed in 1954 when Buffett worked in New York for Graham Newman. Over the ensuing decades Jay, and his brother, Bob, grew Marmon to an over 100-business conglomerate operating across many different sectors.

As of 2008, Marmon had 130 independently operated businesses within eleven sectors, and operated more than 250 manufacturing, distribution, and service facilities primarily in North America, Europe and China.

---

* In November 2008, Iscar purchased Tungaloy, "a leading Japanese producer of small tools," according to Buffett's letter.

Table 7.12: Marmon's operating sectors

Sector	Description
Engineered Wire & Cable	Energy-related markets, residential and non-residential construction, and other industries
Building Wire	Produces copper electrical wiring for residential, commercial and industrial buildings
Transportation Services & Engineered Products	Includes railroad tank cars and intermodal tank containers
Highway Technologies	Primarily serves the heavy-duty highway transportation industry
Distribution Services for specialty pipe and steel tubing	n/a
Flow Products	Producing a variety of metal products and materials for the plumbing, HVAC/R (R is for refrigeration), construction and industrial markets
Industrial Products	Metal fasteners, safety products, metal fabrication, and other products
Construction Services	Leases and operates mobile cranes, primarily to the energy, mining and petrochemical markets
Water Treatment equipment for residential, commercial, and industrial applications.	n/a
Retail Store Fixtures	Store fixtures and accessories for major retailers worldwide
Food Service Equipment	Food preparation equipment and shopping carts for restaurants and retailers worldwide

Source: Berkshire Hathaway Annual Report 2008.

Table 7.13: Marmon Group—select data

($ millions)	2008	2007	2006	2005
Revenues	$6,960	$6,904	$6,933	$5,605
Operating income[1]	977	951	884	556
Operating income %	14%	14%	13%	10%
Total assets	7,390	8,079	7,708	7,758
Shareholders' equity	4,311	5,037	4,486	4,495

Footnote:
1. Before interest income and interest expense

Source: Berkshire Hathaway Annual Report 2008, 2012 Marmon Brochure, and author's calculations.

We do not have access to the same detailed historical financial reports as Buffett. But the summary information for the three years ending 2007 (the data Buffett had when he made the deal) support the conclusion that he most likely saw a group of well-established businesses with consistent earning power.* All the sectors listed above were well established and critical to the economy over the long term. We can also assume they met Buffett's tests of having good management in place and a reasonable purchase price given the quality of the underlying business.

The purchase also included assumed debt and goodwill/intangibles.** If we assume Marmon's 2007 and 2008 financial performance was representative of the long-term earnings power of the business, Berkshire acquired a business earning solid double-digit pre-tax returns on tangible capital. Even after considering the premium Berkshire paid for the company, it would still earn more than the 10% pre-tax Buffett expected of Berkshire's stock market investments. It's possible the general economic weakness or weakness in the equity and/or credit markets played a role in keeping the price down.

Table 7.14: Marmon Holdings, Inc.—acquisition analysis

(*$ millions*)	2007
Revenues	$6,904
Revenues/tangible capital	$1.24
EBIT margin	14%
Return on capital - pretax	17%
BRK price/tangible capital	1.34x
BRK return - pre-tax	12.8%

Source: Berkshire Hathaway Annual Report 2008; 2012 Marmon Brochure and author's calculations.

Berkshire also agreed to purchase the remainder of the company over time based on a formula tied to earnings. By the end of 2008, Berkshire had acquired an additional interest, ending the year at 63.6% ownership.

Finance and Financial Products

Berkshire's Clayton Homes subsidiary was at the center of the recession and credit crisis. Its business of building homes and financing them contained many lessons, and Buffett chose to devote over two pages of his Chairman's letter to the subject.

---

* Marmon has periodically published a brochure that includes select financial information. Its 2012 report included return on equity figures beginning in 2005, which indicate Marmon had a consistent history of earning returns in the high-teens.

** Total debt assumed with the transaction was $1.07 billion and goodwill/intangibles were $1.9 billion.

A major lesson was the power of incentives. Brokers earning commissions upon the sale of a home or lenders earning them upon closing a loan transaction had every incentive to see the deals go through—up to and including forging information. Compounding the problem, and perhaps part of the cause of it, was that commissions and fees were earned at closing with no negative repercussions if problems later developed. Lending institutions often securitized loans into packages that were carved up and sold to unsuspecting investors.* No one, sometimes not even the homeowners, had much skin in the game.

Home prices reached their peak in 2006. By 2007, they began a two-year nosedive. During the rise, buyers and lenders pushed the envelope. Buyers bid up house prices fast and far. Lenders offered creative and cringeworthy loan terms to accommodate this, sometimes even resorting to forged incomes. Interest-only payments on loans meant the outstanding loan balances would never decline, and in some cases negative amortization loans (where the interest is higher than the loan payment) allowed principal to grow over time.

"Both parties counted on 'house price appreciation' to make this otherwise impossible situation work," Buffett told shareholders. This price appreciation incented builders to construct new housing. And build they did. Two million housing units were created despite demand of just 1.3 million units.[90] Once supply eclipsed this fundamental demand, housing prices had to fall. Housing starts then receded below demand, but it would take a while for the excess supply to be absorbed.**

Against this backdrop, Clayton was bruised but not broken. It avoided the major mistakes of its industry cousins by staying out of the fray. Where its peers securitized their loans, Clayton retained a portfolio of $12.6 billion of its own and others' loans. Its credit standards required a down payment of at least 10% and verified income. Losses from two hurricanes also inflicted pain during this period.

Clayton's business was negatively affected by the recession in two major ways:

1. Lower volumes of units sold resulted in a 9% decrease in manufactured home sales and presumably the loss of certain economies of scale in manufacturing.*** Clayton countered the lower unit volume by closing certain manufacturing facilities, costing it related write-downs and charges.

---

* Investors' senses were dulled by the fact that rating agencies allowed the packaged, repackaged (and in some cases packaged many more times) loans to be given investment-grade ratings. This kept demand for loans high.
** That housing starts would need to remain low had clear implications for Berkshire's building products businesses.
*** Buffett noted that the industry's volume had fallen 78% since its peak in 1998. Even though Clayton's 27,499 units sold in 2008 represented 34% of the industry, that figure was in relation to a sharply lower industry base.

2. A higher delinquency rate, while better than the industry average, resulted in higher loan loss provisions to cover future losses.* Even though Clayton's average borrower had a credit score below the national average, its prudent lending was rewarded with a delinquency rate of just 3.6% in 2008 (compared to a national average of 5%).

These factors combined resulted in Clayton's pre-tax earnings falling 61% to $206 million.

Paradoxically, Clayton's financial strength negatively affected its business. In order to help the country at large, the US government and the Federal Reserve provided funding to banks and other financial companies at rates far below what their creditworthiness would otherwise have allowed. This meant that the seven AAA-rated** companies in the United States, including Berkshire, were penalized for their strength and had a higher cost of borrowing than financially shakier competitors. "At the moment, it is much better to be a financial cripple with a government guarantee than a [Rock of] Gibraltar without one," Buffett wrote.

Pre-tax earnings from the Finance and Financial Products segment declined 22% to $787 million from the year before. Clayton's decline in earnings was a large reason for the deterioration, and the leasing operations also experienced a 22% decline in earnings, though each remained profitable.

Investments

Berkshire's investment portfolio usually changed at a glacial pace, and this was okay with Buffett. "Beware the investment activity that provides applause. The great moves are usually greeted by yawns," he wrote. Unfortunately, 2008 was memorable in the wrong way. A $15.1 billion after-tax decline in unrealized appreciation of the investment portfolio more than offset Berkshire's $5.0 billion of net earnings—and was in fact the primary reason Berkshire reported a decline in book value. The silver lining was that stocks were now on sale and Berkshire could invest additional sums at attractive valuations. It did just that, investing a net $3.3 billion in equity securities during the year, as well as additional sums in negotiated transactions.

Comparing the equity portfolio between 2007 and 2008, five names disappeared, and one new investment made the $500 million reporting threshold. Gone were Anheuser-Busch, which was sold to InBev, a Belgium-based beer conglomerate; USG Corp., which remained in the portfolio but fell below the cutoff; and White Mountains

---

* The footnotes disclosed a $125 million increase to the loan loss provision. Earnings were also impacted by $25 million from losses due to Hurricanes Gustav and Ike, and $38 million from asset write-downs and plant closures.
** A triple-A rating was the highest rating available.

Insurance Group, whose shares were sold. Additional purchases of BNSF stock made by Berkshire and share repurchases by Moody's caused them to fall off the list.

At the close of the year, Berkshire owned 70.1 million shares (or 20.7%) of BNSF, and its 48 million shares of Moody's, unchanged since 2000, now represented a 20.4% ownership interest. With that level of ownership, accounting rules required that Berkshire begin using the equity method. The change in methods required a $626 million increase in Berkshire's shareholders' equity to bridge the gap between the underlying shareholders' equity and the fair value of the investments.[*]

Two equity purchases are of note. The lone new name on the Chairman's table was Swiss Re, a Swiss-based reinsurer, of which Berkshire owned 3.2% at year-end. Another was an almost $6 billion increase (at cost) in ConocoPhillips stock which Buffett told shareholders was a mistake. "Without urging from Charlie or anyone else, I bought a large amount of ConocoPhillips stock when oil and gas prices were near their peak," he confessed. The mistake cost Berkshire $2.6 billion between year-end 2007 and 2008.

Investment opportunities were plentiful in the public stock and bond markets, and in private transactions that leveraged Buffett's and Berkshire's reputation. Over two weeks in October 2008, Berkshire invested $14.5 billion in three companies. The deals were reminiscent of the Convertible Preferred Stock investments of the late 1980s:

- October 1: A $5 billion issue of Cumulative Perpetual Preferred Stock of Goldman Sachs that carried a 10% coupon and came with warrants to purchase shares in the investment bank.[**]
- October 6: A $6.5 billion investment in Wrigley to assist Mars, Inc.'s acquisition of the chewing gum maker.[***]
- October 16: A $3 billion investment in 10% Cumulative Perpetual Preferred Stock issued by General Electric. That investment also came with warrants to purchase shares in GE.[****]

---

[*] Readers interested in the finer details of accounting may also be interested in the $1.8 billion other-than-temporary impairment charge booked in 2008 and relating to the declines in values of twelve securities. The charge only impacted the cost basis of the investments, with shareholders' equity remaining unchanged because they were already carried at fair value. See Berkshire's response to the Securities and Exchange Commission comment dated May 22, 2009 (available on SEC EDGAR).

[**] Berkshire acquired warrants allowing it to purchase 43,478,260 shares at $115 per share, expiring in 2013. The Preferred Stock could be redeemed by Goldman Sachs at 110% of par at any time.

[***] The Wrigley investment consisted of $4.4 billion of 11.45% subordinated notes due 2018 and $2.1 billion of preferred stock with a 5% coupon and a redemption tied to Wrigley's future earnings. Of historical note, Berkshire purchased 1,600 shares of Wrigley common stock in 1968.

[****] Berkshire acquired warrants allowing it to purchase 134,831,460 shares at $22.25 per share, expiring in 2013. The Preferred Stock could be redeemed by General Electric beginning in October 2011 at 110% of par.

Unlike the Gillette or Salomon investments of the early 1990s, these three new investments didn't carry any serious risk to Berkshire's well-being. Where Salomon represented an investment approaching 10% of Berkshire's equity capital at the time, these were comparatively modest against Berkshire's average equity of $115 billion.

To fund these commitments, and others, Berkshire sold investments it otherwise would have held onto. This included halving its stake in Johnson & Johnson and reducing stakes in other marketable securities. It was a matter of opportunity cost, said Buffett, as well as ensuring Berkshire always had enough cash on hand to meet its obligations.*

Buffett also took advantage of mispricing in the derivatives market during 2008. Such moves were seemingly un-Buffett-like given his outspoken criticism of derivatives. That Berkshire wrote four derivatives contracts during the year did not reflect a change in attitude. Buffett's logic instead rested on the fact that even under a worst-case scenario, the four put contracts would amount to a long-term loan with a very reasonable interest rate.** The four deals brought in $4.9 billion of premiums that would only pay out if the underlying major indexes declined between then and their expiration dates (which were far into the future).*** In the meantime, Berkshire could invest the premiums as it saw fit and had no requirements to post collateral.

Berkshire also wrote $4 billion of credit default swap contracts**** during 2008. In this case, however, it spread the risk over 42 companies because it faced counterparty risk in collecting the $93 million of annual premiums it received.

Berkshire's businesses were negatively impacted by the Great Recession, but not as much as other businesses. Led by Buffett, Berkshire's managers focused on building for the long term. Berkshire spent over $6 billion for acquisitions, which bolstered its earning power even if results would take time to materialize. Its major investments during the year (an additional $3.3 billion, net, in equities and another $14.5 billion in arranged deals) were made on very favorable terms but served as a counterforce in the sea of selling and negativity. Berkshire Hathaway's actions***** and Buffett's own words (he wrote an op-ed piece in *The New York Times* in October urging investors

---

* In addition to unfunded commitments, Berkshire had insurance obligations to others stretching decades into the future.
** The maximum payout was $37.1 billion if all the indexes went to zero at expiration, a highly improbable event. Buffett said a 25% decline across the indexes would cost Berkshire $9 billion (using the weighted average life of 13.5 years this equates to an implied interest rate of 4.6%; a total loss would imply a cost of capital of 16%).
*** The indexes were the S&P 500, FTSE 100, Euro Stoxx 50, and the Nikkei 225. The expiration dates ranged from September 2019 through January 2028 with a weighted average life of 13.5 years at year-end 2008. Unlike American-style options which allowed the purchaser to exercise the option anytime up to expiration these were European-style options which could only be exercised on the *day* of expiration.
**** A credit default swap is akin to insurance in that it protects the owner of a debt instrument if the underlying company goes bankrupt or defaults. A few of the CDS contracts required posting of collateral, which amounted to $550 million at year-end 2008.
***** Berkshire spent $6.1 billion on capital expenditures during 2008—a full $3.3 billion more than its depreciation of $2.8 billion.

to "Buy American, I am"[91]) backed his conviction that America had the right recipe and would do fine over time.

As Buffett indicated in his communications with shareholders, the pain of 2008 was just the start of what was to come. The economic recession would continue into 2009 and drag on longer than almost anyone imagined. The stock market itself would bottom in early 2009 before finally reaching positive territory at year-end. Berkshire soldiered on, ever on the lookout for opportunities.

2009

Like the year before, 2009 brought both challenges and opportunities for Berkshire Hathaway. The economy was still reeling from the deepest economic slowdown in generations. There were negative effects to be sure, but there were also unique opportunities. In the latter part of the year, Berkshire lined up one of its largest acquisitions yet, the railroad company Burlington Northern Santa Fe (BNSF). In 2009, Berkshire showed once again that a long-term approach to business and capital allocation was best.

Warren Buffett's high-level performance metric of change in book value gave up some ground during 2009, falling 6.7 percentage points behind its benchmark, the S&P 500. Still, Berkshire's absolute gain of 19.8% was just a half point behind its forty-five-year average, a highly satisfactory result for the 11th largest company on the Fortune 500.[92] With the BNSF acquisition completed when he penned his account of 2009,[*] Buffett reminded all shareholders new and old that "our defense has been better than our offence, and that's likely to continue." In other words, just as in 2008, Berkshire's relative outperformance came in the down years.

Insurance

Berkshire's Insurance Group reported another year of underwriting profits and topped it off with an increase in float. It's $1.6 billion pre-tax underwriting gain marked the seventh consecutive year of underwriting profitability, enough evidence for Buffett to tell shareholders he thought Berkshire's insurers would write to a profit in "most—though certainly not all—future years." Berkshire's significant reinsurance operations, particularly the catastrophe business, would all but guarantee some down years. Each of Berkshire's major insurance segments found ways to grow float except for General Re, where it remained flat. Their combined total float grew 6% to $62

---

* The BNSF acquisition was completed on February 12, 2010. Buffett's 2009 Chairman's letter was dated February 26, 2010.

billion at year-end. As usual, GEICO and Berkshire Hathaway Reinsurance Group were the standout performers.

During 2009, General Re acquired the remaining part of Cologne Re it did not already own. Berkshire owned a controlling interest in the German reinsurance operation since the 1998 Gen Re deal and gradually increased its ownership in the ensuing years. Buffett planned to celebrate with a visit to the operation later in 2010.

Table 7.15: Berkshire Hathaway—Insurance Underwriting

($ millions)	2009	2008
GEICO		
Premiums written	$13,758	$12,741
Premiums earned	13,576	12,479
Underwriting gain/(loss) - pre-tax	$649	$916
General Re		
Premiums written	$5,721	$5,971
Premiums earned	5,829	6,014
Underwriting gain/(loss) - pre-tax	$477	$342
Berkshire Hathaway Reinsurance Group		
Premiums earned	$6,706	$5,082
Underwriting gain/(loss) - pre-tax	$349	$1,324
Berkshire Hathaway Primary Group		
Premiums earned	$1,773	$1,950
Underwriting gain/(loss) - pre-tax	$84	$210
Total premiums earned	$27,884	$25,525
Total underwriting gain/(loss) - pre-tax	1,559	2,792
Average float	60,200	58,593
Cost of float	(2.6%)	(4.8%)
Aggregate adverse (favorable) loss development	($905)	($1,140)
Discount accretion and amortization charges included above	$602	$550

Sources: Berkshire Hathaway Annual Reports 2008–2009 and author's calculations.

General Re

For the fourth straight year, General Re posted underwriting profits, earning $477 million on premiums of $5.8 billion and Buffett's praise. Property risks appeared well managed and produced a $173 million underwriting gain from current year business along with $305 million of favorable loss development on prior year events. Current year gains were after $48 million of catastrophe losses from a winter storm in Europe, bushfires in Australia, and an earthquake in Italy. Casualty/workers' compensation again posted a loss. Higher loss trends on business written that year necessitated additional reserves and the usual accounting charges for loss reserve discount accretion and deferred charge amortization amounting to $118 million led to a $178 million loss from the casualty segment. The life/health business earned $177 million. Gen Re's float was $21 billion at year-end 2009 and represented a third of Berkshire's total float.

Berkshire Hathaway Reinsurance Group

Berkshire Hathaway Reinsurance Group (BHRG) benefitted from no meaningful catastrophe losses in 2009. It posted a smaller underwriting gain of $349 million compared to $1.3 billion the year before. Considering the accounting headwinds from the amortization of deferred charges on retroactive reinsurance contracts, and $280 million of losses in multi-line from a weaker dollar that revalued foreign-denominated liabilities, this result was highly satisfactory. Berkshire benefitted from both profits and float that grew 8.3% to $26.2 billion.

With a new audience of BNSF Railroad shareholders Buffett again recounted the story of Ajit Jain's arrival at Berkshire.[*] He praised Jain and his small team of thirty employees at Berkshire Hathaway Reinsurance Group for their contributions. The team found other ways to increase business even though softening markets restrained volumes generally.

One contribution was a fifty-year life reinsurance contract that would start in 2010 and which might amount to $50 billion of premiums over time. Another was a $1.7 billion[**] retroactive reinsurance contract with Swiss Re known as an adverse loss development policy. The complex policy basically covered Swiss Re in the event its estimates of incurred loss proved incorrect.[***] Swiss Re found itself in trouble after losing 6 billion Swiss francs and the retro policy with Berkshire was one way of shoring up its balance sheet.[93]

Berkshire came to the aide of Swiss Re in another way. Early in 2009, it invested $2.7 billion in a 12% convertible perpetual security that provided the insurer additional capital. Berkshire now had three relationships with Swiss Re: as a partner via the quota-share agreement from 2008, a part owner of the firm via its investment in common equity, and as a creditor.

While BHRG's overall earned premiums grew 32% to $6.7 billion in large part because of the two Swiss Re contracts, it slowed down its written premium volume. Written premiums in catastrophe and individual risk fell 34% to $725 million and other multi-line volume would have fallen 46% if not for the Swiss Re contract. This

---

[*] While it's impossible to know exactly how many new shareholders came with the BNSF acquisition because of shares held with brokers, the 2009 BNSF 10K report lists 29,000 shareholders of record.

[**] The contract was 2 billion Swiss francs and translated into dollars.

[***] The policy was for Swiss Re's non-life insurance losses and provided for 5 billion Swiss francs coverage over the 58.725 billion Swiss Francs loss reserves, less 2 billion Swiss francs.

was both self-imposed and due to softening markets. As its net worth declined due to the significant drop in equity prices during the first quarter, BHRG reduced volumes to maintain a more conservative premium-to-equity ratio.[*]

Another reason to pull back was the pending acquisition of BNSF, which would be held within National Indemnity[94] and soak up liquidity. Only at Berkshire Hathaway would an entire railroad be placed under the corporate umbrella of an insurance company. Why do this? BNSF's consistent earnings would be a natural offset to the volatility inherent in reinsurance.

A drastic reduction in premiums written at the newly formed Berkshire Hathaway Assurance Corporation highlighted the market's shifting willingness to bear risk. During 2008, it wrote $595 million as fear gripped the markets. Volume in all of 2009 was concentrated in the first half of the year and amounted to just $40 million. Berkshire's approach was not the norm. Buffett said other municipal bond insurers took on more risk when premiums became too thin. That risk had reared its ugly head during the credit crisis. Berkshire had the discipline to walk away from bad deals.

GEICO

GEICO's bottom line was in the black thirteen out of the fourteen years under Berkshire's ownership. But that was only part of the luster. While 2009 profits were *just* $649 million on $13.6 billion of earned premiums, the 95.2% combined ratio was right in the company's sweet spot of delivering profits to its owner and value to its customers. Profits in the prior two years were too high and GEICO allowed premiums per policy to fall over that time. Higher accident frequency and severity also played a part. During the recession, GEICO added policies at a record rate and increased its market share from 7.7% to 8.1%. This was counter to an expectation that some might look to reduce insurance costs during tough times by dropping policies. Instead, GEICO's ability to save money for its customers translated into more business as people became more cost conscious with their purchases.

A big part of GEICO's value was its float. At Berkshire, profitability was rule number one; after that growth in float drove value. On that front GEICO delivered: premium growth over the past three years had swelled float by over a third, to $9.6 billion.

Ever on the lookout to expand GEICOs reach, Buffett informed shareholders of a failed experiment to offer credit cards to policyholders. He reasoned its generally

---

[*] We do not know what Berkshire targets for a premium-to-equity ratio, if any. However, Buffett would likely want to maintain a healthy margin of safety, and probably chose to reduce the amount of business versus stretch the balance sheet.

above-average drivers were above-average credit risks. He was wrong. Instead, Buffett's idea—which GEICO managers disagreed with—cost the company over $50 million.

Berkshire Hathaway Primary Group

Premium volume and profits fell in the primary lines. Underwriting profit of $84 million was down 60% from the year before on earned premiums of $1.8 billion (down 9%). Competition hit each insurer under this group except for BoatUS.

Regulated Utility Businesses

Berkshire's collection of utility businesses demonstrated their resiliency as essential services, but also proved they weren't immune to the effects of recession. Earnings before interest and taxes (EBIT) declined 16% from the year before (adjusting for the one-time earnings from Constellation Energy in 2008).* While some of the decline was due to depreciation on additional assets, unfavorable exchange rates, and milder temperatures, a portion was attributable to reduced demand due to the recession.

Berkshire Hathaway HomeServices, tucked into the utilities segment, returned to profitability in 2009. Its EBIT increased to $43 million from a loss of $45 million the year before. The company added a Chicago firm to its roster of brokerages and continued to build out its business amid the ongoing recession.

Buffett compared the acquisition of BNSF (discussed in more detail in 2010) to Berkshire's utility operations. He noted both had certain "social compacts" with society due to the crucial role each played in the economy. Both also had similar economic characteristics of providing essential fundamental services, requiring large investments in excess of depreciation, and being subject to price regulation. He added they would both use "substantial amounts of debt that is *not* guaranteed by Berkshire." Like the utilities, the railroad would also retain most of its earnings once under the Berkshire umbrella. As economic cousins, the utilities and railroad would share the same reporting segment in Buffett's Chairman's letter going forward.

---

* The steepest decline in EBIT came from MidAmerican Energy Company, which dropped 33% to $285 million due to lower revenues and higher depreciation on new wind farms. This was partially offset by lower input costs.

Manufacturing, Service, and Retailing

Berkshire's MSR businesses were hit hard by the recession. Consequently, pre-tax earnings were cut in half (down 49%) to $2.1 billion. Pre-tax return on tangible capital fell from 21.8% to 9.7% and after-tax return tangible equity fell from 17.9% to 7.9%. But some of the businesses in this category managed to do better despite the challenges.

Buffett specifically identified and praised nine businesses and their CEOs for delivering higher profits despite lower revenues.* Special praise was reserved for Grady Rosier who led McLane to both higher revenues and profits.

Not surprisingly, the manufacturing businesses were hit hardest. Revenues at Marmon, Berkshire's newest large acquisition, declined 27%. Owing to improved margins (which earned CEO Frank Ptak Buffett's praise), earnings declined at a slower 26% rate.** That earnings fell just about in-line with sales is notable for Marmon since one would expect to see lower revenues negatively affect margins. With a large drop in carpet sales volume, Shaw's revenues declined 21% to $4 billion and its pre-tax earnings fell 30% to $144 million. Shaw's economic sensitivity was somewhat breathtaking: In just three years, pre-tax earnings fell by 67% on 25% lower revenues.

The smaller manufacturing businesses experienced similar pain. Revenues in apparel fell 11%, building products 20%, and other manufacturing businesses were off 16%. Earnings for this sub-segment were hit even harder, falling 51% compared to 2008, to $814 million.

McLane, the largest standalone service business, rightly earned Buffett's praise during 2009. Revenues increased 5% to $31.2 billion as increased grocery business more than offset a decline in food service business. Earnings swelled 25% to $344 million due in part to the increase in revenues and lower operating costs. Another reason, however, was a substantial inventory price change gain related to tobacco product inventory. Manufacturers of tobacco products raised their prices ahead of an increase in taxes, which allowed businesses already in possession of inventory to book a one-time windfall.

Taken as a group, the other service businesses generated the almost unthinkable: a pre-tax *loss* of $91 million. A closer look reveals the cause was one bad apple: NetJets. NetJets had a massive $711 million loss and was the overwhelming cause of the red ink. It had more planes than needed and the company incurred costs of $676 million to downsize operations. An operating loss made up the difference. Buffett pointed to the sad reality that NetJets' cumulative pre-tax losses since Berkshire acquired the company amounted to $157 million, and its debt had swelled from $102 million to $1.9 billion. He also put David Sokol, "the enormously talented builder and operator

---

* The businesses were: Benjamin Moore, Borsheims, CTB, Dairy Queen, H.H. Brown, Nebraska Furniture Mart, Pampered Chef, See's, and Star Furniture.
** The 13.5% pre-tax profit margin was a record according to Buffett.

of MidAmerican Energy" in charge of NetJets in August 2009. Sokol immediately began to right-size the company and generate a profit.

Excluding NetJets, the other service businesses were impacted by the recession but to a lesser degree. Pre-tax profits fell 18% to $620 million.

Results in the retail segment weren't as bad as manufacturing or service. Revenues dropped 8%, with home furnishings revenues sliding 7% and jewelry off 12%. Pre-tax earnings were flat at $161 million. And even though the year was difficult, See's, Star Furniture, and Nebraska Furniture Mart managed to increase earnings, which garnered Buffett's praise and recognition.

Finance and Financial Products

Clayton was now the largest modular home manufacturer in the US as the three previous industry leaders all went bankrupt (including Oakwood, which Berkshire purchased in 2004). The industry was in shambles. Clayton suffered from broader housing-related issues and manufactured home-specific challenges*—but it remained profitable. Its earnings were down 64% from their peak of $526 million in 2007 to $187 million in 2009.

Berkshire's leasing operations, which included CORT Furniture and XTRA, barely eked out a profit in 2009 as fixed costs swamped their income statements. A revenue decline of 14% to $661 million translated into an 84% decline in pre-tax earnings, far below the $182 million earned in 2006.

Because of a jump in life and annuity earnings** (the sole line item to see an increase during the year), the Finance and Financial Products segment overall earnings dropped less than 1% to $781 million.

Berkshire's old partners at Leucadia came knocking again at the end of 2009 with another opportunity. The two companies had joined forces in 2001 as Berkadia to buy troubled finance firm FINOVA. With FINOVA successfully liquidated and the name available, the new venture was also called Berkadia (which prompted Buffett to remark that it should be called Son of Berkadia and jokingly look forward to a Grandson of Berkadia someday).

The present Berkadia was Berkadia Commercial Mortgage.*** Like the 2001 Berkadia, this one was the result of a failed company. Capmark Financial Group, Inc. filed for bankruptcy after overextending itself. Berkshire and Leucadia came to the rescue with a deal to buy the assets out of bankruptcy. They then rehired many former employees.[95]

---

* The main challenge with the industry was a bias toward traditional homes over manufactured ones.
** No reason was given for the jump in life and annuity earnings from $23 million in 2008 to $116 million in 2009. In hindsight we know this was Ajit Jain beginning to ramp up Berkshire's operations in this area, a business that was transferred to the Berkshire Hathaway Reinsurance segment in 2010.
*** It serviced a $235 billion portfolio, according to Buffett, in addition to originating $10 billion annually.

Investments

With the stock market bottoming in March and companies in need of capital, Berkshire made some opportunistic changes to its equity portfolio and negotiated investments in additional non-traded securities. It also sold some investments to raise capital ahead of the BNSF acquisition.

Within the existing equity portfolio, Berkshire doubled its stake in Walmart, bringing its ownership to $1.9 billion at cost (from $942 million), or 1% of the company. It increased its investment in Wells Fargo too as bank stocks got punished. With almost one-fifth of the $59 billion equity portfolio in one company and over half in the top four, Berkshire continued its philosophy of concentration.

Figure 7.2: Berkshire Hathaway equity portfolio concentration

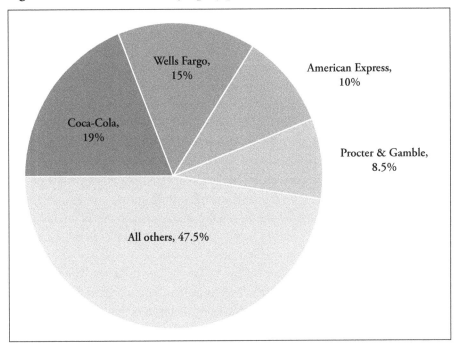

Source: Berkshire Hathaway Annual Report 2009.

One newcomer made the list in 2009, and it was unconventional in several ways. For starters, the idea came from Berkshire Vice Chairman Charlie Munger, a perennial skeptic who earned himself the nickname of the "abominable 'no' man" from Buffett. The investment was a $232 million stake (at cost) in China-based BYD Company, Ltd. that amounted to 9.9% of the company. This was the largest ownership stake allowed by the Chinese government.

BYD manufactured electric vehicles and lithium batteries. Munger compared company founder Wang Chuanfu, to Thomas Edison. While some outsiders saw the new holding as a venture capital-type investment, Munger saw otherwise: "This is not some unproven, highly speculative activity. What it is, is a damn miracle … ." Munger was impressed that Chuanfu had been born into poverty and founded BYD from nothing to successfully compete against well-established competitors. That the investment was worth nearly 8.5 times its cost (about $2 billion at year-end 2009) was enough to silence more vocal skeptics.

The year also brought additional opportunities to invest in non-traded securities like the Goldman Sachs, Wrigley, and General Electric deals completed in 2008. In addition to the $1.7 billion Swiss Re deal described earlier, Berkshire assisted Dow Chemical with its acquisition of Haas Company, investing $3 billion in a Cumulative Convertible Perpetual Preferred Stock. Another $1 billion went to Wrigley to assist Mars in the form of four- and five-year senior notes.

A $300 million investment in Senior Notes to Harley-Davidson provided insight into Buffett's decision-making process and how he thought about his circle of competence. In February 2009, Berkshire participated in a $600 million debt offering that carried a 15% coupon rate. The investment was too small to be identified in Berkshire's financial statements, but shareholders nonetheless picked up on it in Harley-Davidson's financials and so did the financial press. They all had the same question: Why did Buffett lend Harley-Davidson money rather than buy the equity, which had more than doubled within a year. Buffett's response was telling. He had no view on Harley-Davidson's equity value, since he couldn't gain clarity on the future of the motorcycle market or the company's margins or returns on capital. Lending to the company was relatively easy, however, since that decision was based on whether it was going to stay in business. He summed up the investment thesis in a way only Buffett could: "I like a business where your customers tattoo your name on their chest,"* he said.

The few equity sales that occurred in 2009 were made to fund new commitments. ConocoPhillips was reduced by about two-thirds and was admittedly a mistake.** Additional sales included Procter & Gamble and Johnson & Johnson, which were reduced modestly. Berkshire also sold some shares in Moody's, which reduced its holdings below the 20% threshold and therefore ceased reporting that investment on the equity basis.***

---

* In the credit offering Harley-Davidson's fixed charge coverage ratio (a measure of how many times the company earned its debt service) was *just* 10.7x as of the end of the third quarter 2008. This, and its history of coverage up to nearly sixty times indicated that Harley-Davidson's debt was a very safe credit risk.

** In his 2008 letter, Buffett recounted the "unforced error" he made buying ConocoPhillips when oil prices were high.

*** Buffett was asked about the Moody's position at the 2010 Annual Meeting. Keeping his cards close to his chest, he only said the ratings agencies remained wonderful businesses.

In a rare move, Buffett publicly criticized the management of an investee. Two inter-related capital allocation decisions made by Kraft Foods got his blood pressure boiling. One was its purchase of Cadbury, a candy company, which he thought overpriced. The other was the divestiture of its frozen pizza business to raise the capital needed to buy Cadbury. He thought the deal underpriced and tax inefficient. "I think the odds are that both deals were dumb. The pizza deal was particularly dumb," he told shareholders in response to a question at the Annual Meeting, adding Berkshire made its fair share of mistakes. Still, Berkshire didn't sell a share of Kraft stock.

The details of the pizza divestiture show the low multiple Kraft received on the net proceeds from the sale and illustrate Buffett's thinking process. It wasn't the headline sale price that mattered to him. The relevant facts were the net proceeds from the sale compared to the pre-tax earnings of the business (see Table 7.16).

Table 7.16: Analysis of the Kraft pizza business sale

($ millions)	
Sale price	$3,700
Less: income tax	(1,200)
Net proceeds	2,500
Pre-tax earnings	$340
Multiple	7.35x

Sources: Berkshire Hathaway Annual Meeting 2010 and Kraft 10K report 2009.

A major lesson from 2009: Big opportunities come in times of fear. Berkshire took advantage of the turmoil and made significant investments. In hindsight Buffett wished he did more:

> "When it's raining gold, reach for a bucket, not a thimble … It's been an ideal period for investors: A climate of fear is their best friend. Those who invest only when commentators are upbeat end up paying a heavy price for meaningless reassurance. In the end, what counts in investing is what you pay for a business—through the purchase of a small piece of it in the stock market—and what that business earns in the succeeding decade or two."

Berkshire's capital allocation activity in 2009 extended to acquiring additional interests from minority partners, a practice that was common. Within the footnotes of the 2009 Annual Report lay a particularly interesting accounting change related to these activities.* Effective that year, additional purchases of minority interests (that is,

---

* The accounting change was ASC 810 Consolidation, which also required non-controlling interests (aka minority interests) be separately identified on the balance sheet and income statement.

purchases of stock by Berkshire from non-controlling owners where Berkshire owned less than one hundred percent) would be recorded as changes to shareholders' equity. Prior to the change they were recorded as additional investments with any premium to book value placed on the balance sheet as goodwill. This was consistent with the accounting methodology at the time of the original investment. The purchases made this year, though, resulted in a $121 million *reduction* in equity because Berkshire paid a premium to acquire shares from minority partners. This accounting effectively required an immediate 100% write-off of goodwill created by subsequent investments when a brand-new investment would still place goodwill on the balance sheet. Under the prior accounting, no such reduction in shareholders' equity would have been required for additional investments of this kind.*

On December 22, 2009, Berkshire's board of directors announced it had elected Stephen Burke to its board. At the time Burke was COO of Comcast and served on the boards of JPMorgan Chase and the Children's Hospital of Philadelphia (as chairman). At 51 years old, Burke was the second youngest member of the Berkshire board (behind Susan Decker, then 47 years old).[96]

If the name sounded familiar, it's because Burke was the son of Daniel Burke, the former president of Capital Cities, who together with Tom Murphy built and ultimately sold the company to The Walt Disney Company. Stephen Burke cut his teeth at Disney before joining Comcast. Buffett clearly saw a pattern of successful businessmen in the Burkes, saying Stephen Burke was "business-savvy, owner-oriented, and keenly interested in Berkshire, the three ingredients we look for in directors."[97]

The value of the Berkshire operating model was on display during the stress of 2009. One characteristic was not requiring its managers to submit budgets or projections to Buffett in Omaha (some used budgets within their own operations, some didn't). Both Buffett and Munger knew the power of incentives. Buffett said if Berkshire required managers to submit budgets, they might become tempted to meet them by fudging numbers from time to time. Berkshire wanted to "create a structure that minimizes the weakness in human behavior." Its managers were instead expected to tell it how it was and act with integrity, even if it meant reporting bad news.**

---

* Taking things to the extreme to illustrate, if Berkshire acquired 51% of a company for $100 with underlying assets of $100 it would record $51 of shareholders' equity and $49 of minority interests. Consider the purchase of the remaining $49 the next year, however, at a premium of $10 (that is, for $59). Under this example the $10 would be deducted from Berkshire's shareholders' equity, leaving the $100 basis for $100 of assets. The $10 would simply disappear. Under the old system, a $10 entry for goodwill would have been recorded.

** At the Annual Meeting, Buffett referenced a study that had been conducted of corporate earnings, which showed it statistically impossible to find such low frequencies of the number four in the tenths spot in reported earnings. This meant managers were fudging numbers to get the five, which rounded up. (The paper was written by Nadya Malenko and Joseph Grundfest and entitled "Quadrophobia: Strategic Rounding of EPS Data," originally released in 2009.)

Berkshire allocated a great deal of capital during the prior two years of turmoil. With perfect hindsight more would have been possible, but the investments Berkshire made set it up for years of additional dividend and interest income. Its subsidiaries, while bruised, nevertheless remained secure within their castles, protected by the advantages of their economic positions.

2010

Berkshire's 13% growth in book value per share trailed the S&P 500 by 2.1 percentage points in 2010. It marked the second consecutive year of underperformance—a first in Berkshire's modern history. Many investors remained cautious about the state of the economy having just come through one of the worst economic recessions in US history. But Berkshire's capital allocators saw things differently. Some of its businesses, such as those tied directly or indirectly to construction, remained sluggish. Others, such as Marmon, Forest River, and Iscar, bounced back. Thanks to a focus on building businesses for the long term and good management, most of Berkshire's diverse operating businesses emerged from the recession stronger than before. They were also joined by a gargantuan newcomer. The Berkshire conglomerate swallowed an entire railroad—its largest acquisition to date by more than fivefold—providing no question that the United States remained a land of opportunity.

That opportunity, Buffett stressed, was only open to the fittest business: "Having loads of liquidity, though, lets us sleep well. Moreover, during the episodes of financial chaos that occasionally erupt in our economy, we will be equipped both financially and emotionally to play offense while others scramble to survive."

Despite Berkshire's good prospects, its share price in 2010 reflected pessimism. Whether it was a general caution or Berkshire specifically is unclear. The company's market capitalization ranged from a low of $160 billion to a high of $212 billion. This prompted Buffett to be more specific than usual about Berkshire's earning power to nudge shares closer to intrinsic value. Buffett estimated Berkshire's normal earning power at $17 billion pre-tax (or about $12 billion after tax) including the new BNSF acquisition and making allowances for insurance operation variability. His Chairman's letter also supplied the two numerical components he suggested using to estimate Berkshire's intrinsic value (per-share investments and per-share pre-tax operating earnings). These were not-so-subtle hints that Berkshire was meaningfully undervalued.*

---

* Investments per A-share were $94,730 and pre-tax earnings per share were $5,926. Using our 10x multiple from earlier, this equates to a value of $154,000 per A-share or a $250 billion market capitalization. The year-end stock price of $120,000 implied a value of $200 billion, 20% lower.

Burlington Northern Santa Fe (BNSF)

The largest acquisition in Berkshire's history-to-date occurred on February 12, 2010. The acquisition increased Berkshire's normal earning power by 40% pre-tax and over 30% after-tax.

BNSF was the culmination of 150 years of acquisitions and mergers that consolidated 400 railroad lines.[98] The industry had consolidated to the point of having just a handful of major Class I railroads serving large swaths of North America.* BNSF moved freight from many industries primarily across the Western part of the United States over 32,000 route miles.** Its revenues were classified in four broad categories (see Figure 7.3).

Figure 7.3: BNSF freight revenues by category, 2009

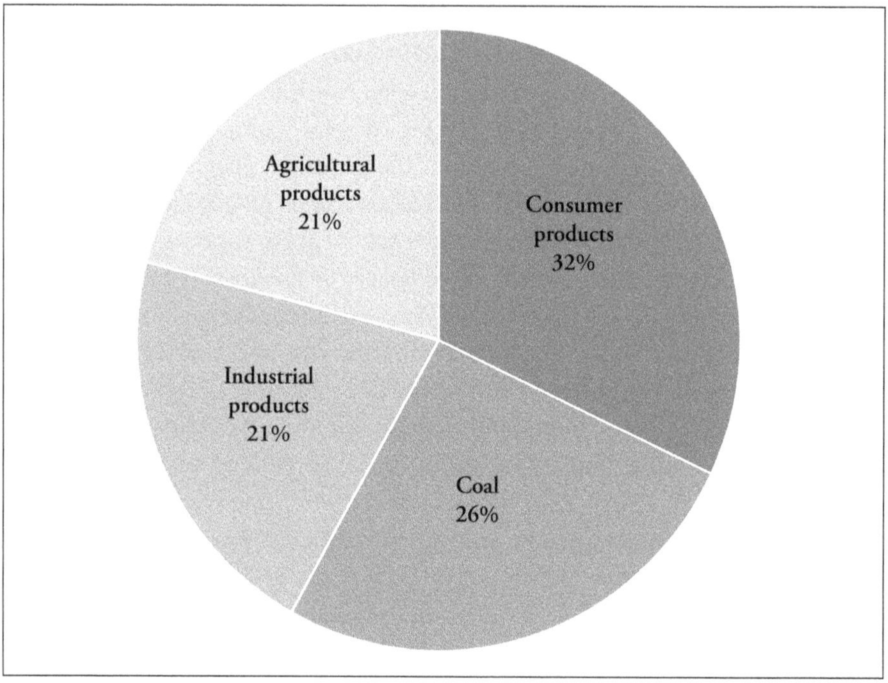

Note: Freight revenues in 2009 were $13.6 billion.
Source: BNSF Annual Report 2009.

---

* A Class I railroad is defined by the Surface Transportation Board as having annual revenues of $250 million or more in 1991 dollars.

** Of those, 23,000 miles were owned by BNSF.

What attracted Berkshire to BNSF, an industry historically full of woes? Charlie Munger summarized these past troubles as high capital intensity, heavy unionization, intense regulation, and a comparative disadvantage to long-haul trucks (the main alternative form of transport). That changed over time as the industry consolidated and deregulated. The railroads began successfully negotiating with unions to reduce labor costs and became more fuel efficient compared to trucking. By double-stacking freight cars (which required an investment in raising tunnels and strengthening bridges), the railroads became three times as efficient as trucks and could carry a ton of freight 500 miles on one gallon of fuel.

Buffett said agreeing to buy BNSF during the Great Recession was "an all-in wager on the economic future of the United States." Investing in the common stock of railroads (as Berkshire had done since 2006, including BNSF)[99] was one thing. It was something else to buy an entire railroad. Here are some factors that made BNSF attractive to purchase outright:

1. **Improved industry economics:** As noted above, railroads enjoyed improved operating margins and returns on capital compared to previous decades. Those returns were protected by a moat since the barriers to entry were sky-high. It would be virtually impossible to assemble the land and rights necessary to build a new long-haul railroad from scratch in the 21st century.

2. **Utility-like characteristics:** As "a major part of the American economy's circulatory system,"* the regulated railroad industry functioned like a utility, including known investment returns (just like MidAmerican) with the same social compact.

3. **Ability to invest huge sums:** Again, like MidAmerican, BNSF required huge amounts of capital investment to maintain its operations, and importantly, possessed the ability to invest more to expand. A known (but limited) return on additional capital investment would provide a place to invest cash generated from elsewhere within Berkshire.

4. **Western population expansion:** BNSF transported 11% of *all* inter-city ton-miles of freight in the United States. That was likely to increase as population growth in the Western United States outpaced that of the East. BNSF would benefit from having a near monopoly on Western rail traffic, including shipments of products originating in Asia to ports on the Western seaboard.

5. **Deferred taxes:** BNSF's need to grow (and its ability to take additional capital investment) came with tax benefits. The US allows companies to accelerate their depreciation for tax purposes compared to an asset's useful life. The result is an interest-free loan from the government (like deferred taxes on capital gains). BNSF's headline tax rate (total tax divided by taxable income) averaged between

---

* Buffett's words.

35% and 38% in the five years ended 2009. But it paid an average rate of just 27% on its pre-tax income during this period. In dollar terms, that amounted to $1.5 billion—no small sum.[*]

6. **Lower borrowing costs:** BNSF would benefit from Berkshire's credit rating even though Berkshire did not provide an explicit guaranty of BNSF's debt.

Taken together, the factors above shed light on what appeared to be a very low initial return for Berkshire (see Table 7.17). Berkshire could accept a slightly lower pre-tax return for the existing business since BNSF could defer a portion of its income tax each year. Additionally, any incremental investment BNSF made would be at pre-tax returns solidly in the double digits. And since the company functioned like a utility with stable revenues and earnings, some debt was appropriate and would serve to increase the return on equity capital. Importantly, Berkshire purchased the company during a time of economic weakness. Berkshire's return would thus be higher if BNSF earned the kind of return it had in the recent five-year period.

Table 7.17: Burlington Northern Santa Fe—acquisition analysis

($ millions)	2009	2008	2007	2006	2005
Total revenues	$14,016	$18,018	$15,802	$14,985	$12,987
Revenues/avg. capital	$0.64	$0.90	$0.85	$0.86	$0.79
EBIT margin	23%	22%	22%	23%	23%
Pre-tax return on capital	15%	20%	19%	20%	18%
Purchase price (equity)[1]	$34,194				
Assumed debt	10,335				
Effective purchase price	$44,529				
Purchase multiple	2.03x				
BRK going-in pre-tax return (2009)	7.3%				
Return using 5-year average ROC	9.0%				

Footnote:
1. This is the implied valuation for 100% of the equity based on the $26.5 billion paid for 77.5% of BNSF. The actual cost was $33.5 billion, which includes the $6.6 billion already owned plus $0.4 billion of equity awards. Upon acquiring the company, Berkshire recognized a $1 billion one-time holding gain on the shares it already owned.

Sources: Berkshire Hathaway Annual Report 2010; BNSF Annual Reports 2008–2009; and author's calculations.

---

[*] The Surface Transportation Board does factor in deferred taxes to its calculation of allowable return, but this is still a net plus since it comes at no cost from the government.

The price tag for BNSF was $44.5 billion, including debt assumed in the acquisition. The price accounted for the shares Berkshire already owned. The remainder of the purchase price of $26.5 billion was paid in cash (half borrowed) and Berkshire shares. (Berkshire issued 94,915 Class A share equivalents in connection with the acquisition.*) The implied valuation of Berkshire associated with the acquisition was about $184 billion. Berkshire's shares traded at what appeared to be a meaningful discount to its intrinsic value during 2010, but Buffett and Munger judged the acquisition worthwhile nonetheless.**

Simultaneous with the acquisition, Berkshire split its B-shares 50-to-1. This was done to allow more BNSF shareholders the opportunity to take Berkshire shares instead of cash. Before the split, each B-share represented 1/30th of each A-share. After the split, each B-share represented 1/1500th of each A-share. The voting rights were split accordingly, with each B-share having 1/10,000th the vote of each A-share. With BNSF gone from public markets, an opening was created in the S&P 500 index. Splitting the B-shares provided enough liquidity to meet the requirements, and Berkshire replaced BNSF in the index.

One last aspect of the BNSF acquisition highlights the benefits of the Berkshire conglomerate structure. Berkshire reported BNSF as a standalone entity, but the railroad was purchased and is legally owned first by National Indemnity Company. This bolstered the capital and earnings of its insurance companies. As noted in the discussion on 2009, BNSF had utility-like earnings that did not widely fluctuate, which was a natural offset to the variability in underwriting results associated with reinsurance operations.***

Regulated, Capital-Intensive Businesses

The pure utility businesses of MidAmerican Energy were joined by BNSF in this category beginning in 2010. Buffett considered the businesses very similar. "A key characteristic of both companies is the huge investment they have in very long-lived, regulated assets, with these funded by large amounts of long-term debt that is *not* guaranteed by Berkshire." Both operated with a social compact that required them to invest large amounts of capital into growth projects to support the growing needs of the country. In exchange, he expected regulators to be fair with their allowable returns.

---

* The shares accounted for $10.6 billion of the purchase price. It valued Berkshire at about $111,500 per A-share, or a market capitalization of $184 billion.

** Charlie Munger's comments at the 2011 Annual Meeting (which was held shortly after the BNSF acquisition closed) sheds some light on Berkshire's thinking: "When we did it, we knew it would be better for their shareholders than it was for ours, because, after all, they were getting into Berkshire. But we also thought it was good for our shareholders. And why should we care that it was better for theirs, if it was satisfactory for us?"

*** While this was true, insurance regulators discounted BNSF more for regulatory capital purposes as a 100%-owned entity than when National Indemnity owned its publicly traded shares.

Taken together, MidAmerican's operations reflected the inherent stability of a utility operation. Its various businesses, including electric generation and distribution, and its pipelines, delivered EBIT of $1.9 billion, up just 1% from the year before. Variability in results in some units couldn't be avoided altogether. EBIT from the pipelines declined 17% because of lower volume and pricing associated with specific economic conditions, and EBIT from the UK utilities swelled 34% from a gain on the sale of an asset in Australia. HomeServices, the real estate brokerage business, was as profitable in 2010 as the year before with EBIT of $42 million.

While BNSF's business was utility-like, it was more subject to business cycles than its MidAmerican cousin. BNSF's pre-tax earnings dipped 22% to $3.9 billion in 2009 along with the recession but rebounded 48% to $4 billion in 2010. Some questioned the wisdom of Berkshire buying BNSF. Its results in 2010 would convince most people it had been a good investment.

Insurance

Bolstered by the BNSF acquisition, Berkshire's Insurance Group ended 2010 with $94 billion of statutory capital, up 47%. Earned premiums grew 10% to $31 billion but still represented just a third of capital—indicating a rock-solid balance sheet. Berkshire's insurers also delivered another year of underwriting gains (up 38% to $2 billion) that produced the cherished negative cost of float. Float grew 6% to end the year at $65.8 billion. Berkshire's insurers were in very good shape.

Table 7.18: Berkshire Hathaway—Insurance Underwriting

($ millions)	2010	2009
GEICO		
Premiums written	$14,494	$13,758
Premiums earned	14,283	13,576
Underwriting gain/(loss) - pre-tax	$1,117	$649
General Re		
Premiums written	$5,632	$5,721
Premiums earned	5,693	5,829
Underwriting gain/(loss) - pre-tax	$452	$477
Berkshire Hathaway Reinsurance Group		
Premiums earned	$9,076	$6,706
Underwriting gain/(loss) - pre-tax[1]	$176	$250
Berkshire Hathaway Primary Group		
Premiums earned	$1,697	$1,773
Underwriting gain/(loss) - pre-tax	$268	$84
Total premiums earned	$30,749	$27,884
Total underwriting gain/(loss) - pre-tax	2,013	1,460
Average float	63,872	60,200
Cost of float	(3.2%)	(2.6%)
Aggregate adverse (favorable) loss development	($2,270)	($905)
Discount accretion and amortization charges included above	$356	$602

Footnote:
1. The attentive reader will notice BHRG underwriting profit of $250 million in this table contrasts with that of the $349 million figure presented in the discussion of 2009. In 2010, Berkshire moved the life and annuity business under BHRG.

Sources: Berkshire Hathaway Annual Reports 2009–2010 and author's calculations.

GEICO

Buffett used a section of his Chairman's letter to highlight the value GEICO had delivered to Berkshire and how that value was not always apparent. When Berkshire purchased the entirety of GEICO in 1996, it paid $2.7 billion over the company's net worth—equal to 97% of GEICO's annual premium volume. Since then the resulting goodwill was amortized from $2.7 billion to $1.4 billion. Yet GEICO's premiums rose from $2.8 billion in 1996 to $14.3 billion in 2010. Buffett was hinting that GEICO's value was not fully reflected on Berkshire's balance sheet. Clearly a company able to grow policies in force, and do so profitably, was worth a premium price. Buffett called GEICO the gift that keeps on giving. And it was: a combined ratio of 92.2% delivered another billion dollar underwriting profit in 2010 ($1.1 billion) and went along with a market share of 8.8%, up from 8.1% the previous year.

Berkshire Hathaway Reinsurance Group

Buffett credited Ajit Jain for creating the $30 billion float insurer that was Berkshire Hathaway Reinsurance Group. Jain still found ways to increase business volume amid an industry backdrop of weakening pricing. Earned premiums grew 35% to $9.1 billion and pre-tax underwriting profits declined from $250 million* to $176 million.

Earned premiums in catastrophe and individual risk contracted 24% to $623 million and pre-tax underwriting profits fell 67% to $260 million. Significant (but unspecified) losses of $322 million impacted results.

Retroactive premiums grew 32% to $2.6 billion largely from a $2.25 billion contract with CNA Financial Corporation to assume certain asbestos and environmental pollution liabilities. Ongoing deferred charge amortization was responsible for a $90 million loss reported by this line.

Other multi-line earned premiums fell 11% to $3.5 billion but underwriting profits expanded from $15 million to $203 million. More impressive, profits were after $308 million in catastrophe losses relating to earthquakes in Chile and New Zealand, floods in Australia, and the BP Deepwater Horizon oil rig explosion.

The Swiss Re life reinsurance deal negotiated the prior year incepted in 2010 and brought $2.1 billion of earned premiums that year. About $2 billion of annual premiums were expected to continue for decades. Accounting charges related to these contracts would mean significant reported losses, but the long-duration float made the economics of the business highly favorable. Berkshire moved the life and annuity business from Finance and Financial Products to BHRG as Jain expanded activities in this area. It reported a pre-tax underwriting loss of $197 million compared to a $99 million loss the prior year.

General Re

General Re reported another year of underwriting gains, proving it had taken Buffett's four-part test to heart.** That included the all-important last test of being willing to walk away if pricing wasn't adequate to cover risks, which happened in 2010. Earned premiums fell 2% to $5.7 billion and pre-tax underwriting profits declined 5% to $452 million.

---

* This figure is changed from the $349 million presented in the section in 2009 for comparative purposes. In 2010, Berkshire moved the life and annuity operation from Finance and Financial Products to BHRG.
** Buffett said a sound insurance operation had the following characteristics: (1) An understanding of *all* exposures that might cause a policy to incur losses; (2) A conservative evaluation of the likelihood of any exposure actually causing a loss and the probable cost if it does; (3) The setting of a premium that will deliver a profit, on average, after both prospective loss costs and operating expenses are covered; and (4) The willingness to walk away if the appropriate premium can't be obtained.

Its property/casualty line was hurt by several of the same natural disaster catastrophes that impacted BHRG. These cost $339 million and caused 2010 underwriting business to slip $96 million into the red. But favorable loss development of $332 million from business in prior years and $53 million in gains from the casualty segment brought it back into the black.

Favorable mortality trends led General Re's life/health business to a $163 million underwriting profit, down 8% from the year before but continuing a long string of gains in that area.

Berkshire Hathaway Primary Group

The Primary Group was constrained by weak pricing but still managed to report a combined ratio of 84.2%, a profit of $268 million on earned premiums of $1.7 billion.

Manufacturing, Service, and Retailing

The MSR businesses bounced back to report a profit of $2.5 billion and an after-tax return on tangible equity of 17.3%, up from 7.9% the prior year. Pre-tax return on tangible capital expanded from 9.7% in 2009 to 19.5% in 2010. But weakness remained in areas, particularly in those businesses tied to construction.

The largest single reporting unit was Marmon. The mini-conglomerate (remember Marmon was a group of 130 independently operated businesses across eleven sectors) increased pre-tax earnings 19% to $813 million. Except for Distribution Services, each of its eleven lines of business reported higher earnings in 2010, which reflected improvements in the general economy over 2009.

The big news with McLane was its entrance into the wine and spirits distribution business with its purchase of Empire Distributors and Horizon Wine and Spirits. This helped push revenues up 5% to $33 billion. Its pre-tax earnings remained tiny in proportion to revenues but grew 7% to $369 million.

With the addition of Marmon, Shaw lost its status as a single reporting unit and was included with Berkshire's various other manufacturing businesses. The fortunes of most businesses in this category improved, including those tied to building products. From the low of 2009, revenues of these businesses rebounded sharply: Forest River (up 57%), Iscar Metalworking Companies (up 41%), CTB (up 20%), and Johns Manville (up 12%). Overall, the other manufacturing businesses increased revenues 11% to $17.7 billion and pre-tax earnings nearly doubled to $1.9 billion. Looking closer things were better, but not good. Pre-tax earnings from Johns Manville, MiTek,

Shaw, and Acme Brick remained 72% below the $1.3 billion earned in 2006.* Each also made acquisitions during 2010.**

The other service businesses increased revenues 12% to $7.4 billion and pre-tax earnings rebounded from a loss of $91 million in 2009 to a profit of $984 million in 2010. Businesses in this category included Business Wire, Pampered Chef, Dairy Queen, *The Buffalo News*, and TTI. Strong worldwide demand for TTI's products and NetJets' return to profitability were responsible for restoring the group to profitability.

The largest business within other service businesses was NetJets. NetJets struggled during the previous year with too many planes. It was forced to downsize and write off almost $700 million of its jet fleet. Buffett placed NetJets under the direction of David Sokol, who built and operated MidAmerican Energy. Sokol received praise for turning a $711 million pre-tax loss the prior year into a $207 million profit in 2010.

Berkshire's subsidiaries enjoyed the advantage of operating autonomously. But that autonomy came with rules. Buffett said NetJets had unfairly used its ownership by Berkshire to obtain a lower cost of debt. To correct for this, Berkshire charged a $38 million guarantee fee like the spread it charged Clayton Homes for use of Berkshire's credit. (NetJet's profit was after paying this fee.)

Berkshire's retailing operations were comprised of its four home furnishing businesses, three jewelry businesses, and See's Candies. Though revenues increased just 2% to $2.9 billion, continued cost containment efforts helped collective pre-tax earnings jump 22% to $197 million compared to the prior year.

Finance and Financial Products

XTRA and CORT rightsized their businesses to account for revenues that remained unchanged from the prior year at $661 million. Earnings rebounded strongly compared to 2009 but remained below that of prior years. Pre-tax earnings of XTRA increased 105% to $35 million as its utilization ratios climbed. CORT swung from a pre-tax loss of $3 million to a profit of $18 million.

Clayton Homes remained small but mighty. It could boast producing 47% of the industry's total manufactured homes during 2010. But context matters. This was on an industry base of just 50,046 homes compared to a peak of 372,843 in 1998. Clayton's market share then was 8%. Buffett expressed continued frustration at government policies that favored site-built homes over those of manufactured

---

* Johns Manville, MiTek, Shaw, and Acme Brick had pre-tax earnings of $362 million in 2010.
** Acme purchased Jenkins Brick & Tile in Alabama which had been severely impacted by the recession, including one mothballed plant. It was an example of thinking beyond the current business climate. "Nobody else was bidding for a brick plant in Alabama with no customers to speak of," quipped Munger at the 2011 Annual Meeting. Sources: Berkshire Hathaway Annual Meeting transcript 2011, Birmingham Business Journal, January 24, 2011.

homebuilders like Clayton (it was harder and more expensive to get a mortgage on a manufactured home).

Buffett was proud of Clayton, which was prudent in its lending. Taking a stab at the recent housing crisis, Buffett told shareholders: "If we were stupid in our lending [at Clayton Homes], *we* were going to pay the price." Clayton retained most of its loans and was therefore incented to make good ones. Even though Clayton lent to people with questionable credit scores, its net loan losses remained remarkably stable and never rose above 2% in the prior five years. Its mortgage portfolio at year-end 2010 totaled $11.5 billion.

Investments

Perhaps the biggest news relating to Berkshire's investments wasn't an investment. It was a person. In 2010, Berkshire hired Todd Combs to manage a portion of Berkshire's $62 billion equity portfolio. Combs came to Berkshire after working as an analyst and then running his own hedge fund, Castle Point Capital. Hiring Combs was the first step toward a succession plan that would see Buffett's job split into three parts: Non-Executive Chairman, CEO, and one or more investment managers. Berkshire was on the lookout for one or two more individuals to join Combs. This was even more important after the retirement of Lou Simpson, the investment manager at GEICO whom Buffett kept on post-acquisition and praised as one of the investment greats.

Berkshire's equity portfolio changed little in 2010. The biggest change was an investment in Munich Re, a German reinsurer. Berkshire reported a cost basis of $2.9 billion at year-end.

In 2010, the country and the world were climbing out of the depths of the recession. An unfortunate consequence of this was the probable redemption of many of the large and highly profitable investments Berkshire had made during the prior two years. Its customized investments in Swiss Re, Goldman Sachs, General Electric, and Wrigley would soon be redeemed by those companies as redemption periods approached and credit markets provided more favorable terms. Goldman Sachs had already stated its intention to do so; the only thing holding it back was the Federal Reserve, which was expected to relax capital restrictions implemented during the recession. Even after accounting for large redemption premiums these companies would have to pay to break their financing arrangements with Berkshire, the conglomerate would be worse off.* Interest rates had declined into the low single digits. Finding replacements for securities earning upwards of 12% would not be easy and would cut into investment income.

---

* Buffett put the figure at $1.4 billion for the Goldman Sachs, General Electric, and Wrigley issues. Swiss Re redeemed its preferred in early 2011.

Financial Crisis Inquiry Commission Interview

In May 2010, members of the newly-formed Financial Crisis Inquiry Commission interviewed Warren Buffett in the hopes that the Oracle of Omaha might add some clarity to what caused the Great Recession and how to prevent something similar in the future. Within the transcript, which was twenty-three pages long (single-spaced), lay several pieces of timeless investing wisdom.

- Home prices as a function of replacement value: While it appeared that buying a home was a good investment because it grew in value over time, in reality the dollar was depreciating. Over time houses reflect replacement value. When home prices began rising, others jumped on board. This eventually caused investors and others to assume home prices could only go up, or at worst never decline on a national scale. When a correlated decline in home prices did happen nationally, many homeowners were left with houses they couldn't afford, and investors were left with loans that would never be repaid.*

- Farmland: Another real estate–related example. Buffett personally purchased a farm from the FDIC in 1986 because a bank had over-lent to many similar borrowers and subsequently went under because of poor underwriting standards. Buffett's analysis was as piercingly insightful as it was simple. The bank lent a farmer $2,000 per acre to buy a farm producing a normalized $60 per acre when interest rates were 10%. How could disaster not occur when the asset produced a loan yield of 3%?** Buffett purchased the farm from the Bank for $600 an acre, a 10% yield on cost (as of 2020 he still owns it almost thirty-five years later).

- Hedging at Burlington Northern Santa Fe: Buffett told the Commission that if he were running BNSF he would not hedge fuel costs, a major input cost at the railroad. Why? Because over time the plusses and minuses cancel out. And what's left? The frictional cost of the hedging program. Buffett knew why managements used hedging. It allowed for smooth earnings, which Wall Street rewarded.

- No substitute for US Treasuries: At Berkshire there were no substitutes for Treasuries. Even if a little more yield could be had investing surplus cash in commercial paper, Berkshire would not do it. Why? "Because I [Buffett] don't know what can happen tomorrow."

---

* Not content to take Buffett's word on it I checked the math. Between 1973 and 2018 (the latest data available), the median home price in the US rose 5.1% per annum. Over that same period the Consumer Price Index rose 3.8% per year. The median home size also rose by 1.0% per year during this time. This leaves 0.3% unaccounted for, which might be associated with general upgrades in standards of living. Sources: St. Louis Federal Reserve Bank FRED, United States Census Bureau Characteristics of New Housing.
** Take the $60 per acre yield divided by the $2,000 loan.

Tomorrow for Berkshire, like that of the United States and the world, held much promise.

2011

In 2011, Berkshire broke its two-year losing streak against the S&P 500, outpacing the benchmark by 2.5%. Its overall gain of 4.6% caused its compounded annual gain since 1965 to fall below 20% (to 19.8%). While this made it a middle-ground year, Buffett felt good about Berkshire's progress. Insurance delivered the all-important negative cost of float, and float grew yet again. The year saw improvements in Berkshire's various non-insurance operating businesses, though those tied to construction still lagged. Berkshire made three large investments in 2011: buying Bank of America Preferred Stock, investing in International Business Machines (IBM), and acquiring Lubrizol Corporation. The Lubrizol acquisition brought a rare scandal involving a long-time Berkshire lieutenant.

Berkshire's stock price continued to flounder and Buffett again included several not-so-subtle hints at Berkshire's value in his Chairman's letter. He also presented a novel solution—at least for Berkshire. Berkshire announced it would repurchase its shares up to 110% of book value. Just the year before Buffett had told shareholders "not a dime of cash has left Berkshire for dividends or share repurchases during the past forty years."* That changed in September 2011 when Berkshire repurchased $67 million of its own stock over a two-day period.** Why? Buffett said he favored share repurchases under two conditions: a company has ample funds (which for Berkshire at the time was cash equivalent holdings above $20 billion) and the stock is selling at a discount to the company's intrinsic business value, when calculated conservatively. Under these circumstances share repurchases increase per-share intrinsic value. The $67 million was the amount purchased before the price advanced beyond the 110% limit.

The purpose of Buffett's commentary and the share repurchase announcement was not to have Berkshire's shares trade at a high price. Over the years, Buffett had at times signaled to the market that Berkshire's stock was fully priced. Instead Buffett and Munger wished to have Berkshire's share price trade near its intrinsic value—not too high, not too low—so shareholders' financial results would roughly match that of Berkshire's underlying business results.***

---

* Buffett apparently forgot about the $433,055 spent in 1976 to repurchase 6,647 shares and the $229,162 spent in 1977 for 2,244 shares.

** Berkshire repurchased 98 Class A shares and 801,985 Class B shares, or 633 Class A-equivalent shares in total.

*** They went so far as to say they wished they could set a price once a year at which Berkshire's shares traded. This is similar to how private companies effect transfers of ownership.

Table 7.19: Berkshire Hathaway intrinsic value estimation

Per share (A-equivalent):	2011	2010
Investments	$98,366	$94,730
Pre-tax operating earnings (ex. investment income)	6,990	5,926
Estimated value (investments + 10x operating earnings)	168,266	153,990
Year-end share price	114,755	120,450
Year-end book value per share	99,860	95,453
Price/estimated value	0.68x	0.78x
Price/book	1.15x	1.26x
Value/book	1.69x	1.61x
Change in estimated value	9%	
Change in share price	(5%)	

Sources: Berkshire Hathaway Annual Reports 2010, 2011; and author's calculations.

Lubrizol Corporation

Berkshire acquired Lubrizol on September 16, 2011. The company was based in Cleveland, Ohio, and was founded in 1928. Lubrizol was a specialty chemical company that provided additives and advanced materials to industries including transportation, industrial and consumer markets.

Buffett may not have fully understood what the company did, but he loved its superior economics. Between 2004 and 2011 pre-tax profits increased almost tenfold to slightly over $1 billion. "It struck me as a business I didn't know anything about, initially. You're talking about petroleum additives. I never would understand the chemistry of it, but that's not necessarily vital."

Lubrizol had survived a long period of industry consolidation to become the leader in a relatively small market.* Lubrizol's financial results reflected this. Its returns on capital were consistently above 20% and shot up to over 45% in 2010, the year before Berkshire acquired it. Its financial statements show that major non-production costs remained in check while the topline continued to grow in the double digits (see Table 7.20) Additionally, the company's connection with customers, including that it often partnered with them to create additives when new engines were developed, gave it a sustainable competitive advantage—Buffett's beloved moat. Lubrizol also provided a product that was very cheap compared to the exponential impact it had on performance of an end product.

---

* Buffett said at the 2011 Annual Meeting he thought the market was $10 billion annually.

Table 7.20: Lubrizol Corporation—acquisition analysis

($ millions)	2010	2009	2008	2007	2006
Total revenues	$5,418	$4,586	$5,028	$4,499	$4,041
Revenues/avg. capital[1]	$2.19	$2.19	$2.78	$2.46	$2.30
EBIT margin[1]	21%	19%	10%	11%	10%
Pre-tax return on capital	45%	41%	27%	27%	23%
Purchase price (equity)	$8,700				
Assumed debt	1,352				
Effective purchase price	$10,052				
Purchase multiple	4.06x				
BRK going-in pre-tax return (2010)	11.1%				
Return using 5-year average ROC	8.1%				
Footnote: 1. Adjustments were made for goodwill and intangibles, in addition to a minor amount of write-offs and restructuring charges.					

Sources: Berkshire Hathaway Annual Report 2010; Lubrizol Annual Reports 2006–2009; Lubrizol 10K 2010; and author's calculations.

Lubrizol's price reflected its excellence. Berkshire paid $8.7 billion for the company. Considering the debt assumed in the acquisition, the purchase price reflected a multiple of 4x the underlying capital in the business. Such a price seemed to lend confidence to the company's level and sustainability of recent profits.* Buffett made it clear how the acquisition should be judged: "You have to judge us based on close to a $9 billion investment. You have to judge [CEO] James Hambrick in running the business based on the much lower capital that he has employed."**

The Lubrizol acquisition cost Berkshire more than billions of dollars. It also cost it a trusted lieutenant who many supposed was a leading candidate to someday succeed Buffett as Berkshire's CEO. The full story is long and nuanced but amounted to this: David Sokol (who first came to Berkshire with the MidAmerican acquisition and had recently been put in charge of NetJets) purchased stock in Lubrizol just before recommending Berkshire buy it. Sokol's actions suggested a significant lapse of judgement rather than an attempt to make a short-term profit. But the hit to Berkshire's reputation cost Sokol his job (he resigned). Buffett had a rule of thumb

---

* Even if the business reverted to earning returns in the mid-20% range Berkshire's return would be around 6.5%–7% and incremental growth would be at a very attractive rate.
** Buffett said the business employed about $2.5 billion of capital. That figure can be derived from the 2010 Lubrizol 10K as follows: $2,271 million shareholders' equity plus $1,352 million debt less $1,065 million goodwill and intangibles. Total capital employed in 2010 was $2,558 million; average capital employed was $2,479 million.

that employees should be willing to have their actions appear on the front page of the paper. This was not the kind of attention Sokol wanted.[*]

Just the year before, Buffett had included a copy of a biennial letter sent to Berkshire's managers at the end of the 2010 Annual Report.[**] The two-page letter emphasized the priority of each Berkshire employee: "The priority is that all of us continue to zealously guard reputation. We can't be perfect but we can try to be. As I've said in these memos for more than twenty-five years: 'We can afford to lose money—even a lot of money. But we can't afford to lose reputation—even a shred of reputation.'"

Insurance

Berkshire's Insurance Group delivered once again. Earned premiums grew 4% to $32 billion. Float grew 7% to $70.6 billion and came with underwriting profits. Profits declined from $2 billion in 2010 to just $248 million in 2011, but the result was even more impressive amid a backdrop of continued weak pricing industrywide and several large catastrophes. Remember, even breakeven insurance results produce significant economic benefits because of float. All of Berkshire's insurance units citied a constraint in volume due to pricing.

---

[*] Sokol bought Lubrizol shares two months before the Berkshire acquisition was announced. The deal increased the value of his shares by $3 million. The profits Sokol made in connection to Lubrizol paled in comparison to his earnings and net worth. Buffett defended Sokol, pointing to an incident years earlier in which Sokol voluntarily reduced his own compensation in favor of Greg Abel as an example of his good conduct. For more background, see the proxy report from the Lubrizol acquisition and the April 26, 2011 Berkshire Hathaway Audit Committee report.

[**] The letter was dated July 26, 2010. The 2010 Annual Report was released in February 2011, a month before Buffett learned of Sokol's improprieties.

Table 7.21: Berkshire Hathaway—Insurance Underwriting

($ millions)	2011	2010
GEICO		
Premiums written	$15,664	$14,494
Premiums earned	15,363	14,283
Underwriting gain/(loss) - pre-tax	$576	$1,117
General Re		
Premiums written	$5,819	$5,632
Premiums earned	5,816	5,693
Underwriting gain/(loss) - pre-tax	$144	$452
Berkshire Hathaway Reinsurance Group		
Premiums earned	$9,147	$9,076
Underwriting gain/(loss) - pre-tax	($714)	$176
Berkshire Hathaway Primary Group		
Premiums earned	$1,749	$1,697
Underwriting gain/(loss) - pre-tax	$242	$268
Total premiums earned	$32,075	$30,749
Total underwriting gain/(loss) - pre-tax	248	2,013
Average float	68,202	63,872
Cost of float	(0.4%)	(3.2%)
Aggregate adverse (favorable) loss development	($2,202)	($2,270)
Discount accretion and amortization charges included above	$342	$356

Note: Berkshire Hathaway Primary Group and BHRG written premiums were not detailed.

Sources: Berkshire Hathaway Annual Reports 2010, 2011; and author's calculations.

Berkshire Hathaway Reinsurance Group

Most of the newsworthy events took place at Berkshire Hathaway Reinsurance Group. Three of its four lines of business reported losses, all for different reasons, putting BHRG in the red for 2011 to the tune of $714 million on earned premiums which remained flat at $9.1 billion.

Catastrophe and individual risk pricing remained soft. A few new contracts and higher pricing on renewals led to earned premium growth of 21% to $751 million. Major earthquakes in Japan and New Zealand caused losses of $800 million, which led to a pre-tax underwriting loss of $321 million compared to a profit of $260 million the year before. Such a swing in profits was not atypical as a year with major catastrophes worldwide was expected from time to time.

Earned premiums in other multi-line grew 22% to $4.2 billion largely due to the 20% quota-share agreement with Swiss Re. The same two earthquakes that impacted catastrophe and individual risk, in addition to floods in Thailand, caused another

$933 million of catastrophe losses. After $455 million of profits on other contracts and foreign currency gains of $140 million, other multi-line reported an underwriting loss of $338 million compared to a profit of $203 million the year before.

The life and annuity line booked a $642 million charge relating to its contract with Swiss Re Life & Health to fix incorrect assumptions relating to mortality rates at the inception of the contract.* Pre-tax losses in the segment ballooned from $197 million the year before to $700 million in 2011. Earned premiums declined 9% to $2.2 billion, with most from the Swiss Re contract, as well as from the acquisition of Sun Life Assurance Company of Canada from its parent company.

Retroactive reinsurance was BHRG's only line in the black in 2011, reporting a $645 million underwriting profit compared to a loss of $90 million the year before. Premiums earned of $2 billion (down 23%) came mostly from a $1.7 billion retroactive contract with a subsidiary of American International Group (AIG). Since it was a retroactive contract, there was no immediate profit or loss associated with it. The primary reason for the large profit was an $865 million reduction in its estimated liability associated with the 2009 Swiss Re contract (this was a separate contract from the one above and covered Swiss Re's non-life insurance losses prior to 2009).

General Re

General Re managed to earn a profit in both its major reporting lines despite similar catastrophe losses as BHRG and the weak pricing environment. It reported a pre-tax underwriting gain of $144 million compared to $452 million the year before. Earned premiums grew 2% to $5.8 billion.

The property/casualty line eked out a $7 million profit even with $861 million of catastrophe losses. Profits of $741 million on other property/casualty contracts and $127 million from casualty/workers' compensation resulted in the small profit. Earned premiums were flat at $2.9 billion.

Gen Re's life/health unit increased earned premiums 6% to $2.9 billion on strength in international markets. It benefitted from favorable mortality in its life business and reported another profitable year with a gain of $137 million compared to a gain of $163 million the year before.

---

* Buffett was asked about the apparent contradiction between the higher mortality adjustment with the BHRG Swiss Re life insurance contract and a favorable adjustment relating to lower mortality with life policies at General Re. Buffett said mortality had developed worse than initially assumed, and that the adjustment made in 2011 was to bring reserves to a worst-case estimate.

GEICO

GEICO's profitability waned but remained impressive. Both policies-in-force and premiums grew as the company captured a 9.3% market share, up from 8.8% in 2010. GEICO's combined ratio crept up 4.1 percentage points but remained at a very satisfactory 96.3%. The main culprits were higher injury and physical damage severities. A $143 million increase in catastrophe losses (to $252 million) also caused the loss ratio to increase.

Berkshire Hathaway Primary Group

The Primary Group turned in a 14% underwriting gain, earning $242 million on premiums of $1.7 billion, compared to a profit of $268 million on similar premium volume the year before. MedPro and Applied Underwriters both reported favorable loss experience that bolstered results for the group. Berkshire's Home State insurers reported another year of losses, but no reasons were given. At the end of 2011, MedPro acquired Princeton Insurance, a New Jersey-based professional liability insurer. Princeton had annual written premiums of $140 million, surplus of $400 million, and brought $600 million of float. The price was not disclosed.

Manufacturing, Service, and Retailing

Results in the MSR Group reflected America's slow crawl out of the recession. The overall result (adjusting for Lubrizol) was a clear rebound in pre-tax earnings and an increase in return on tangible capital from 19.5% to 24.2%. The after-tax return on tangible equity improved from 17.3% to 22.9%. Even considering the full purchase price of these businesses (i.e. including goodwill), after-tax return on equity improved one percentage point to 8.9%. But those results also included the four housing-related companies, which remained in a distressed state (see Table 7.22).

Table 7.22: Manufacturing, Service, and Retailing—select data

($ millions)	2011	2010	2009
Housing-related businesses[1]	$359	$362	$227
Non housing-related businesses[2]	4,387	3,912	1,831
Lubrizol	291		
Total MSR pre-tax earnings	$5,037	$4,274	$2,058

Footnotes:
1. Acme, Johns Manville, MiTek, and Shaw (Clayton Homes was included in Finance and Financial Products).
2. Lubrizol separated for comparative purposes.

Source: Berkshire Hathaway Annual Report 2011.

Marmon continued to impress with revenues increasing 16% to $6.9 billion and pre-tax earnings rising 22% to $992 million. Marmon CEO Frank Ptak continued to expand the 140-business conglomerate with bolt-on acquisitions, including a recent partnership in an Indian crane company. Just one of Marmon's eleven sectors reported lower revenues and earnings. Reduced purchases by its largest customer led to weakness in the Retail Store Fixtures sector.

When Berkshire purchased 60% of Marmon in 2008, it also agreed to acquire the remainder of the company over time with the price tied to a multiple of earnings. This multiple was not made public, but Berkshire's subsequent transaction shed light on it. Berkshire spent $1.5 billion to buy 16.6% of Marmon in early 2011, implying a valuation of $9 billion for all of Marmon. That suggests a pre-tax multiple of 11x 2010 earnings, or an earnings yield of about 9%.[*]

Berkshire's growth gradually squeezed many large businesses into its "other" categories. Even Shaw, a business with annual revenues of $5 billion, had succumbed to that financial fate in 2010. Smaller businesses shared this fate in earlier years or immediately went below the surface unless Buffett chose to highlight them. One in particular was CTB, the agricultural equipment company managed by Vic Mancinelli. Since Berkshire's 2002 purchase for $139 million, the company had sent Berkshire $180 million, earned $124 million pre-tax in 2011 alone, and had $109 million cash on the books. It was quite a record.

As good at CTB's cumulative record was, it did not come close to that of See's. Berkshire purchased See's in 1972 for $25 million. See's had earned a total of

---

[*] An interesting accounting footnote is appropriate here. In connection with the additional purchase of Marmon, Berkshire was required to write off $614 million of the purchase price. This was the difference between the amount paid and the prior carrying amount of the non-controlling interests acquired. The adjustment was made retroactively to December 31, 2010 since that is the date that the valuation was fixed and determinable. It was as if the $614 million just disappeared. In acquisitions where there is no existing controlling interest, the difference is booked as goodwill. See the accounting discussion on page 159.

$1.65 billion pre-tax, including $83 million in 2011 alone. No wonder Buffett referred to the managers of Berkshire's various operating subsidiaries as members of the all-star team.

Jordan Hansell took over as head of NetJets after David Sokol resigned. The business had another good year with pre-tax earnings up 10% to $227 million.

Nebraska Furniture Mart had good news—and it wasn't just for record-setting earnings coming in at ten times the amount it earned when Berkshire purchased it in 1983.* The big news was its newly acquired 433-acre plot of land north of Dallas. The company planned to construct another mega store that was expected to rival that of its Omaha, Nebraska and Kansas City, Missouri stores. Each of those stores had revenues of over $400 million in 2011 and ranked among the largest (if not *the* largest) furniture retailers in the United States. Nebraska Furniture Mart's expansion coincided with its familial expansion, now with a fourth generation involved in the business.

Regulated, Capital-Intensive Businesses

Berkshire's share of net earnings from MidAmerican (which included interest on debt owed to Berkshire) grew 6% to $1.2 billion. MidAmerican's EBIT grew at the same rate to $2 billion. Utilities may be boring by design, but the earnings were not. Northern Powergrid, the United Kingdom-based distribution unit, grew earnings before interest and taxes by 41%. Part of the increase was a result of real improvements in the business, but a weaker dollar also made its earnings look comparatively bigger.

Berkshire's ownership of MidAmerican provided a tax advantage over other utilities. It could fully utilize tax credits because income tax was paid at the holding company level, and Berkshire had a large base of taxable income. Other utilities often had little or no taxable income because tax rules already allowed them to accelerate depreciation on investments. MidAmerican was therefore incentivized to invest in renewable energy projects. At the end of 2011, MidAmerican committed to two solar projects (one in California, another in Arizona), and had committed $6 billion to wind generation. That would make the utility the largest wind generator among regulated utilities nationwide.

Results for BNSF reflected the general improvement in the American economy. Unit volume increased 7% in both consumer and industrial products categories offset by a 4% decline in coal. Agricultural volumes were flat. The resulting 3% increase in volume and a 12% increase in revenues per unit combined to grow revenues 16% to $19.5 billion. Pre-tax earnings jumped 19% to $4.7 billion as operating expenses remained in check. This was even more impressive considering efficiencies lost due to severe weather, including over key coal routes that caused flooding.

---

* Buffett failed to mention the number, but it would have been around $70 million pre-tax.

BNSF's operating performance was better than at first glance. Usually once a subsidiary is acquired by another, much detail is lost. This was the case with many of Berkshire's acquisitions—but not the utilities. BNSF and MidAmerican had to report to the Securities and Exchange Commission because they are regulated entities with public debt. Remember the discussion of deferred taxes from 2010? BNSF's 10K filing for 2011 revealed that it incurred a $1.8 billion tax on $4.7 billion of pre-tax income. Of that amount, just $260 million was due currently, meaning a full $1.5 billion was deferred and remained in BNSF's checkbook. Huge outlays for capital expenditures (including $3.3 billion or over twice depreciation charges in 2011) would create favorable economic outcomes for years.

Finance and Financial Products

The performance in this segment was buoyed by a return to profitability of CORT and XTRA. Berkshire's two leasing companies grew earnings almost threefold to $155 million. This reflected the significant operating leverage (fixed costs as a percentage of total costs) the companies had as part of their business models. It took just 12% revenue growth to drive the large increase in profits.

Clayton struggled in 2011. The culprits were a combination of lagging home sales causing units sold to decline 14%, a consumer shift toward some of Clayton's lower-priced units, and the government subsidy of mortgages on traditional stick-built homes. On top of that, a federal tax credit program expired the previous year. Clayton's 12.5% decline in pre-tax earnings to $154 million did not look so bad considering these challenges.

Buffett said he expected Clayton's earnings to improve once the country's excess housing inventory was worked off. But he also said the intrinsic value of Clayton, XTRA, and CORT were not significantly different than their current book value, providing another hint at their intrinsic value. These were good businesses, but there was no hidden value in them like GEICO or See's.

Investments

Buffett characterized the changes to Berkshire's investments in equities as few but important. The first was a purchase of 63.9 million shares of International Business Machines (IBM) that cost $10.9 billion. This was the largest outlay for a single security Berkshire had ever made. It represented a 5.5% ownership interest in IBM and almost 7% of Berkshire's average equity capital.

Buffett said it took him only fifty years of reading IBM's annual reports to gain enough comfort to buy its stock. What did he see in IBM? Here are three things:

1. A long history: IBM had reinvented itself many times over the years. Its strong track record, including results through 2010 that seemed to back the assertion it had a strong competitive position, was reason to believe its recent good performance would continue.
2. Low capital requirements: IBM was not capital intensive and its capital efficiency was improving.
3. Shareholder-friendly management: The company returned over $56 billion to shareholders in dividends and net-share buybacks over the previous five years, including $14.8 billion in 2010 alone.*

Table 7.23: IBM investment analysis

($ millions)	2010	2009	2008	2007	2006
Total revenues	$56,868	$55,128	$58,892	$54,057	$48,328
Revenues/avg. capital	$2.31	$2.10	$1.60	$1.30	$1.20
EBIT margin	35%	34%	30%	28%	28%
Pre-tax return on capital	81%	71%	47%	36%	34%
Purchase valuation[1]	$197,382				
Total debt	28,624				
Total enterprise value	$226,006				
Purchase multiple	9.75x				
Implied going-in pre-tax return (2010)	8.4%				
Implied return assuming 5-year average ROC	5.5%				
Footnote: 1. Implied valuation based on Berkshire's purchase of 5.5% of IBM for $10,856 million.					

Sources: Berkshire Hathaway Annual Report 2010, IBM Annual Reports 2006–2010, and author's calculations.

Bank of America was the other major equity investment in 2011. A $5 billion preferred stock investment carried a 6% dividend rate and warrants to purchase 700 million shares of Bank of America stock at $7.14 per share. Buffett initiated the investment thinking Bank of America and Berkshire could benefit. Berkshire would lend the Buffett seal of approval to a bank Buffett saw as very good, but which Wall Street found unattractive due to prior troubles.

Buffett conveyed some insight into how he generated investment ideas. He said he dreamed up the Bank of America investment while in the bathtub. Better yet, when he went to communicate his idea to Bank of America CEO Brian Moynihan, he first

---

* In his 2011 Chairman's letter, Buffett used IBM as an example of how an investor benefitted when a company's share price remained low. This was especially true if the company repurchased its own shares in the market. His logic was that the remaining shareholders would be left with a higher ownership of the company (and therefore a higher share of future earnings) if the share price lagged.

tried reaching him through the call center. Buffett's assistant ultimately contacted the right parties at Bank of America to get Moynihan on the phone.

Berkshire also added $1 billion to its stake in Wells Fargo. This brought its investment to 7.6% of the West Coast bank.

Buffett was candid about some negative developments at Berkshire during the year. One was a $2 billion investment in Energy Future Holdings, an electric utility based in Texas. "That was a mistake—a *big* mistake." Why? Because the company's future was tied to natural gas prices, which tanked after Berkshire purchased it. The investment was written down to $878 million at year-end. Another negative was the return of capital from Swiss Re, Goldman Sachs, and General Electric, three of the unique negotiated investments Berkshire made during the tough years of the Great Recession. Each company paid Berkshire a premium for calling them away early, but the income they generated would be hard to replace in the prevailing low interest rate environment. (The 10-year Treasury Note dipped below 2% at the end of 2011.)

In 2011, Berkshire hired Ted Weschler to join Todd Combs in managing a portion of Berkshire's investment portfolio. Like Combs, Weschler ran his own hedge fund, Peninsula Capital Advisors, before joining Berkshire. To incentivize the managers and foster collaboration, Buffett compensated each manager with a base salary and a performance fee benchmarked to the S&P 500, with 80% tied to individual performance and 20% to the other man.[*]

Berkshire made another investment in 2011 that largely went under the radar. In June, Berkshire acquired the remaining 20% of Wesco Financial Corporation it did not already own. It paid $543 million, including $298 million cash and the remainder in Berkshire shares. Munger remarked that he felt Wesco had finally arrived at its port.

Three Investment Choices

A section of Buffett's 2011 Chairman's letter contained an investing lesson. In it, Buffett sought to convince readers that ownership of productive assets was the only sure way to prosper over the long run. He lumped the investing universe into three categories, and his main takeaways were as follows:

1. Currency-based investments: These included cash, money-market funds, bonds, and mortgages. The key takeaway here was the ravaging effect of inflation. Nations had a clear bias toward inflation, and this meant the purchasing power of any investment in this category would likely go down over time. Berkshire would

---

[*] It was later disclosed that Weschler and Combs each made a base salary of $1 million per year. Buffett noted that even with the performance arrangement, each man was giving up far more by joining Berkshire than could be gained at a hedge fund with the usual fee arrangement of 2% of assets and 20% of profits. Their incentive compensation would be paid on a rolling three-year basis, based on 10% of the amount they outperformed the S&P.

only make such investments if there were prospects for large gains. Berkshire's large holdings in US Treasuries would remain no matter how low the interest rate as a near-guarantee of liquidity for when cash was needed.

2. Commodities: This category included anything that did not produce, the most well-known example being gold. The logic was compelling. "If you own one ounce of gold for an eternity, you will still own one ounce at its end." Gold and other commodities were usually held by those fearful of runaway inflation, or because they thought others would buy it from them at a higher price. A visualization really drove home the point. All the gold in the world could be melted together into a 68-foot square cube worth $9.6 trillion that would never grow. Instead, at the current price of gold, one could buy all the farmland in the United States (400 million acres), sixteen Exxon Mobil-sized companies—*and* have $1 trillion left over.

3. Productive assets: This category included businesses, farms and real estate. Continuing the example from above, a century in the future the gold would still be sitting there while the Exxon Mobil-sized companies and farmland would continue producing. Such productivity would remain no matter what the currency or how much it depreciated. Buffett's logic led him to one conclusion: Over the long run, this category of assets was by far the safest. He called them "commercial cows" and said they would "live for centuries and give ever greater quantities of 'milk' to boot. Their value would be determined not by the medium of exchange but rather by their capacity to deliver milk."

Once again Buffett displayed his penchant for teaching and logic. He wanted shareholders to know he was comfortable with uncertainty, and that investments made based on sound economic reasoning may not be foolproof but were most likely to be profitable. Those who preferred a short game and more certain outcomes were likely to disagree, but Berkshire Hathaway was living proof that Buffett's logic was very profitable.

2012

"When the partnership I ran took control of Berkshire in 1965, I could never have dreamed that a year in which we had a gain of $24.1 billion would be subpar … . But subpar it was." This was Buffett's way of explaining why the enormous gain in book value—14.4%—was not as good as it seemed. Why? Because it fell behind the S&P 500 for the ninth time in forty-eight years (1.6 points in 2012). Berkshire's performance over longer periods held, however. It outperformed the S&P forty-three consecutive times when measured in five-year stretches. "We do better when the wind is in our face," he said. That statement reflected Berkshire's ability to invest large sums when the stock market is weak, and a willingness to write large volumes of insurance during times of acute stress. Buffett also lamented that he had come up short yet again in finding a major acquisition.

But it wasn't all bad news. Each of the major operating segments reported higher earnings despite some mixed results within each category. That included the Insurance Group, which produced underwriting gains in each insurance unit. While Buffett might have failed to land an elephant-sized acquisition, Berkshire did make numerous investments in 2012:

1. $2.3 billion: Twenty-six companies acquired via bolt-on acquisitions that were folded into existing operations.
2. $1.4 billion: An additional 10% of Marmon.
3. $4.6 billion: Capital expenditures in excess of depreciation, mostly concentrated within the capital-hungry railroad and utility operations.*
4. $1.3 billion: Repurchases of Berkshire shares.
5. $712 million: Net increase in equities (including $2.6 billion additional investment in IBM and Wells Fargo).

Berkshire's shares remained undervalued despite meaningful business progress. During 2012, shares traded between $113,855 to $136,345 compared to an estimated intrinsic value that approached $195,000. Berkshire took advantage of the opportunity to buy back 9,200 Class A shares, spending $1.3 billion or $131,000 per share.** Buffett provided no ambiguity on his conviction that Berkshire's shares were undervalued: "It's hard to go wrong when you're buying dollar bills for 80 cents or less."

---

* Total capital spending was $9.8 billion.
** The shares were bought from the estate of Al Ueltschi, the founder of FlightSafety International, who died in October 2012. The move required Berkshire's board to authorize an increase in the buyback threshold from 1.10x to 1.20x book value to accommodate the purchase of the Ueltschi shares at 1.16x book value.

Table 7.24: Berkshire Hathaway intrinsic value estimation

Per share (A-equivalent):	2012	2011
Investments	$113,786	$98,366
Pre-tax operating earnings (ex. investment income)	8,085	6,990
Estimated value (investments + 10x operating earnings)	194,636	168,266
Year-end share price	134,060	114,755
Year-end book value per share	114,214	99,860
Price/estimated value	0.69x	0.68x
Price/book	1.17x	1.15x
Value/book	1.70x	1.69x
Change in estimated value	16%	
Change in share price	17%	

Sources: Berkshire Hathaway Annual Reports 2011, 2012; and author's calculations.

Berkshire's share repurchases in 2011 and 2012 were also a subtle admission it had excess capital. The repurchases were only incidental to this fact, although its inability to put large amounts of capital to work could have weighed on the share price. Berkshire would not have repurchased shares if they weren't meaningfully undervalued. Dividends, at least for the moment, remained off the table as a means for returning capital to shareholders. Buffett took three pages of his Chairman's letter to explain why:

1. Berkshire's price-to-book value in the market allowed more than one dollar of value to be created for every dollar retained. Paying out retained earnings in dividends meant a loss of value.
2. Shareholders could choose their own dividend policy by selling shares. Not only would they receive more (because of the premium to book value above), but Berkshire would not impose one dividend policy on all shareholders. Some shareholders were in accumulation mode and didn't want a dividend, while others might wish to sell shares equal to the entirety of earnings each year (or more).
3. Dividends are taxed in their entirety, while the capital gains tax only applied to the gain over one's cost basis. Shareholders wishing to retain capital in Berkshire would have to pay tax on the dividend *and* invest it back in at a premium to the underlying book value.

Buffett used the example of his regular donations of Berkshire shares to illustrate how a sell-off approach made more sense. Since 2006, he had donated an average of 4.25% of his shares to philanthropy. His ownership in Berkshire since that time had fallen from 712 million shares (B-equivalent) to 529 million shares (down 26%). Yet his investment in Berkshire in dollar terms had risen from $28.2 billion to $40.2 billion (up 43%). That was because the retained earnings in Berkshire more than offset the annual selling of shares. Buffett was clear that Berkshire would always consider a dividend when it made sense, but for the time being shareholders were left with a viable yet nonintuitive way to receive capital from their investment in Berkshire.* Buffett also used the example of purchasing BNSF, what he called a whale, which would benefit shareholders for years to come and was only possible because Berkshire did not pay dividends and had cash on hand.

Insurance

"Our insurance operations shot the lights out last year," Buffett said, using a familiar phrase to describe 2012. The Insurance Group delivered its tenth consecutive year of underwriting profit. Over that time, Berkshire's insurers delivered a total of $18.6 billion of pre-tax underwriting profit, which came on top of billions of dollars of incremental float. Not all four major units had a positive underwriting result each year, but in 2012 they did, with pre-tax earnings totaling $1.6 billion. They also proved Buffett wrong. He had written in his previous Chairman's letter that float was not likely to grow very much from its base of $70.5 billion. Yet float grew 3.6% to $73 billion. These results were even more impressive considering significant losses from Hurricane Sandy (pre-tax cost of $1.1 billion) and other natural disasters, and continuing soft reinsurance pricing. The Insurance Group was built to withstand anything and ended the year with statutory surplus of $106 billion.

---

* The Chairman's letter also provided a hypothetical example of a private company whose owners chose between a dividend policy and a sell-off policy. It is worth reading in its entirety.

Table 7.25: Berkshire Hathaway—Insurance Underwriting

($ millions)	2012	2011
GEICO		
Premiums written	$17,129	$15,664
Premiums earned	16,740	15,363
Underwriting gain/(loss) - pre-tax	$680	$576
General Re		
Premiums written	$5,984	$5,819
Premiums earned	5,870	5,816
Underwriting gain/(loss) - pre-tax	$355	$144
Berkshire Hathaway Reinsurance Group		
Premiums earned	$9,672	$9,147
Underwriting gain/(loss) - pre-tax	$304	($714)
Berkshire Hathaway Primary Group		
Premiums earned	$2,263	$1,749
Underwriting gain/(loss) - pre-tax	$286	$242
Total premiums earned	$34,545	$32,075
Total underwriting gain/(loss) - pre-tax	1,625	248
Average float	71,848	68,202
Cost of float	(2.3%)	(0.4%)
Aggregate adverse (favorable) loss development	($2,126)	($2,202)
Discount accretion and amortization charges included above	$381	$342

Note: Berkshire Hathaway Primary Group and BHRG written premiums were not detailed.
Sources: Berkshire Hathaway Annual Reports 2011–2012 and author's calculations.

GEICO

GEICO led the pack. Its $680 million underwriting profit and combined ratio of 95.9% was even better than at first glance. GEICO faced $490 million of catastrophe losses from Hurricane Sandy alone, which inflicted three times the loss Hurricane Katrina had in 2005 because of its large market share in the New York area.* GEICOs results were also penalized by an accounting change. Effective 2012, US accounting rules eliminated the inclusion of most advertising costs in deferred premium acquisition costs. For 2012, that rule added $410 million of expenses compared to the prior method.

The two factors above weren't enough to counter earned premium growth of 9% and growth in policies-in-force of 6.5%. Had the accounting change not been made, GEICO's combined ratio would have been 93.5% (even with the losses from Sandy).

---

* Total catastrophe losses were $638 million in 2012 compared to $252 million in 2011. It wasn't unusual for GEICO to have catastrophe losses in any given year but the magnitude of the loss in 2012 was exceptionally high.

The losses from Sandy also offset lower claims frequencies, including a 10% drop in comprehensive coverage frequencies.*

General Re

General Re increased earned premiums 1% to $5.9 billion, which were negatively affected by currency effects. Its pre-tax underwriting gain grew from $144 million in 2011 to $355 million in 2012.

Property/casualty earned premiums were flat at $2.9 billion. Underwriting profits bounced back to a pre-tax gain $399 million from a near breakeven $7 million gain the prior year. Property business reported a profit of $352 million despite $266 million of catastrophe losses tied primarily to Hurricane Sandy, an earthquake in Italy, and tornadoes in the Midwest. Casualty/workers' compensation reported gains of $47 million.

General Re's life/health line reported its first loss since 2002 with a loss of $44 million from changes in reserves on a prior business line and worsening results in an Australian business line.** Premiums grew 3% to $3 billion.

Berkshire's culture of conservatism is illustrated by its reserve adequacy compared to other insurers. At year-end 2012, General Re's recorded liability for mass tort claims (those relating to mass claims for asbestos and hazardous waste claims) totaled $1.2 billion. Over the previous three years its payouts averaged $80 million. That meant General Re had reserved over fifteen years of estimated payouts. This ratio is called the survival ratio (how long the reserves will survive the current payout). The industry's survival ratio, by contrast, was just 8.8 years.***

Berkshire Hathaway Reinsurance Group

Results at Berkshire Hathaway Reinsurance Group reflected some of the same challenges as its reinsurance sister company. Ajit Jain's group found ways to increase business even with self-imposed constraints on volume due to weak pricing. It bounced back from an overall loss of $714 million in 2011 to a $304 million profit in 2012 on premiums that grew 6% to $9.7 billion.

---

* The notes to the financial statements disclose a $736 million favorable loss adjustment relating to lower frequency and/or severity assumptions. That figure amounted to 4.4% of premiums earned and 7.2% of prior year loss reserves.

** Two factors were to blame: a premium deficiency reserve established on a runoff book of business and adverse development in a book of business in Australia. Runoff is coverage of operations that have ceased producing new business. This can happen when a primary insurer goes out of business, merges, or if it simply stops writing certain policies.

*** BHRG's survival ratio was not disclosed. However, if we use the $12.4 billion liability figure from 2012 and divide it by the $862 million (a figure close to those of the prior two years) claims paid that year relating to those policies we come up with fourteen years, which is comparable to General Re's survival ratio.

Catastrophe and individual risk returned from an underwriting loss of $321 million to earn $400 million on earned premiums that grew 9% to $816 million. That was after $96 million of losses from Hurricane Sandy.

Premiums in the retroactive line fell sharply, from $2 billion in 2011 to $717 million in 2012, mostly due to the large contract with AIG the prior year. Volume in 2012 came from several smaller contracts. A $201 million loss in that segment was mainly due to deferred charge amortization stemming from previous contracts.

Other multi-line property/casualty improved from a $338 million loss to a $295 million gain, even after $268 million in catastrophe losses from Hurricane Sandy. Premiums grew 26% to $5.3 billion This year would mark the last of the four-year, 20% quota-share arrangement with Swiss Re, which was responsible for $3.4 billion of premium volume in 2012.

New contracts increased BHRG's life/health earned premiums 31% to $2.8 billion. Its underwriting loss improved from a loss of $700 million in 2011 to $190 million in 2012. Losses from life reinsurance amounted to $12 million, an improvement from the $582 million loss in 2011, which was from the large reserve adjustment that year. Annuity losses were $178 million and largely due to accounting charges.*

Berkshire Hathaway Primary Group

For once, the excitement in the Primary Group was due to more than financial results, though those were again very good. The segment now included a full year of business from Princeton Insurance, the professional liability insurer Berkshire acquired at the end of 2011. In the fourth quarter, the Primary Group also welcomed GUARD Insurance Group, a provider of commercial property and casualty insurance coverage to small and mid-sized businesses. GUARD was based in Wilkes-Barre, Pennsylvania, and had premium volume of $300 million. The purchase price was $221 million, about its book value at the time. With the two newcomers in place, premiums in this segment grew 29% to $2.3 billion and profits grew 18% to $286 million (87% combined ratio).

Manufacturing, Service, and Retailing

The MSR Group continued to make progress. Including a full year of results from Lubrizol, pre-tax earnings increased 22% to $6.1 billion and represented a return on average tangible capital of 25.3% (up from 24.2%). After-tax earnings increased at the same rate to $3.7 billion and represented a 21.4% return on average tangible equity

---

* Periodic discount accretion is an accounting charge that reflects the time value of money inherent in life insurance policies. As policies (and the underlying policyholders) age, the present value of the liability also grows. Interest rates also factor in. These factors are considered at the inception of the contract, and like other assumptions can change over time.

(down from 22.9%)*—an impressive result considering the businesses employed on average just 15% of debt compared to equity capital. There were pockets of difficulty, but overall the MSR businesses rebounded from the recession.

Marmon increased revenues 3.6% to $7.2 billion and pre-tax earnings 14.6% to $1.1 billion. A quarter of the increase in profits came from increased operating margins and the rest from bolt-on acquisitions. Marmon, like Berkshire's insurers, focused on profitability first and foremost, and had an eye on expanding into specialized niche markets that allowed a high operating margin and good returns on capital.

Marmon's growth caused the purchase price for the remainder of the company to go up. Berkshire acquired another 10% of Marmon from the Pritzker family during the fourth quarter of 2012. This brought its ownership to 90%. Berkshire paid $1.4 billion but Buffett said the purchase price implied a valuation of $12.6 billion. Buffett's figure is consistent with the 11x multiple Berkshire paid in 2011 for an additional 16.6% of the company.**

McLane, Berkshire's distribution business, made a large acquisition of its own in 2012 that increased revenues and earnings. On August 24, 2012, it acquired Meadowbrook Meat Company, Inc. of Rocky Mount, North Carolina. The purchase price was not disclosed. Meadowbrook Meat Company provided food distribution to national restaurant chains and had annual revenues of $6 billion. Including the results from the acquisition, McLane's revenues grew 12.5% to $37.4 billion and pre-tax earnings increased 9% to $403 million.

Berkshire's other manufacturing businesses rebounded moderately, but there were pockets of weakness. Revenues increased 26% to $26.8 billion and pre-tax earnings increased 38% to $3.3 billion. Excluding Lubrizol, revenues and earnings both increased 6%. Forest River, the recreational vehicle manufacturer, increased revenues 27% on higher volumes and pricing. That was an indication the US consumer was in better shape. Building products revenues increased just 4%, continuing their slow ascent from the depths of the recession. Shaw benefitted from higher sale prices and stable input prices. Weak commercial and industrial business hurt results at Scott Fetzer, Iscar, and CTB, with slowing economies overseas impacting the latter two particularly.

Buffett took the rare action of replacing a manager of Benjamin Moore, one of Berkshire's autonomously operated subsidiaries in the building products segment. The CEO of Benjamin Moore made strategic moves that threatened the company's independent network of dealers. This included a deal to have its paint sold in a

---

* The apparent discrepancy between ROIC and ROE comes from leverage declining from 21% to 15%.
** Using Marmon's pre-tax earnings of $1,137 million against the $12.6 billion valuation. The purchase also required a $700 million write-off like that taken in 2011. It's possible that the $140 million differential (the difference between the $1.4 billion paid for 10% of the company vs. the $1.26 billion Buffett's figure implied) represented undistributed earnings of minority interests.

major home improvement store. That was contrary to the promise Buffett made when Berkshire acquired the company in 2000 to soothe fears that Berkshire would shift away from its longtime distribution system of independent dealers. The incident proved there were limits to the autonomy Buffett would afford his managers and showed how closely he guarded Berkshire's (and his own) reputation.[100]

Revenues in the other services segment grew 10% to $8.2 billion mainly due to the inclusion of bolt on acquisitions at TTI, and the BH Media Group, which is discussed below. Pre-tax earnings fell 1% to $966 million despite the acquisitions, from weak demand and intense competition at TTI. NetJets and FlightSafety, the two aircraft-related businesses, performed on par with the prior year.

Retailing was up slightly in 2012, with revenues and pre-tax earnings growing 4% to $3.7 billion and 2% to $306 million, respectively. Results were bolstered by the acquisition of the Oriental Trading Company, on November 27, 2012, for $500 million.[101] The retailer sells party supplies, school supplies, and toys and novelty gifts.

Buffett's discussion of the MSR businesses in his Chairman's letter highlighted a flaw he saw in Generally Accepted Accounting Principles (GAAP). He thought amortization charges were an area that analysts should pay close attention to, since there were some important divergences from underlying economics. GAAP previously required the amortization of goodwill, which Buffett disagreed with. But amortization still applied to some items from business acquisitions. One such item was amortization expense related to customer relationships, which was not a real expense.

Other intangibles were very real. Buffett used the example of software that would become obsolete over time as a real amortization expense. He said he included just 20% of the year's GAAP amortization expense in the table presented in the Chairman's letter that laid out results for the MSR businesses. (The full amount was included with the GAAP-compliant results presented in the financial statements.) Buffett's goal was to provide shareholders with the clearest view of how their businesses were performing, and that meant thinking hard about how to translate the language of accounting into economic reality.

Regulated, Capital-Intensive Businesses

As large and important as they were (representing 24% of Berkshire's total assets and 37% of pre-tax operating income in 2012), MidAmerican and BNSF's results do not require much discussion from year to year. That's as it should be. Both were purchased to provide limited but stable earnings year in and year out. Still, some commentary is appropriate.

BNSF increased revenues 7% to $20.8 billion and pre-tax earnings 13% to $5.4 billion. Increased pricing (up 4%) and volume (up 2%) resulted in the topline growth, and operating leverage swelled the bottom line. The modest unit growth masked a 13% increase in industrial products volume from petroleum and construction products and a 6% decline in coal shipments. Consumer products unit volume increased 4% and agricultural products declined 3%. BNSF spent $3.5 billion on capital expenditures during the year. The sum was more than double its $1.6 billion depreciation expense and proof that BNSF and Berkshire saw much opportunity ahead.

Berkshire's share of MidAmerican's after-tax earnings grew 10% to $1.3 billion. The company continued to take advantage of tax incentives and invest in renewable projects, making an analysis of after-tax earnings more useful than a strict EBIT analysis (EBIT declined 1% to $1.6 billion). MidAmerican generated 6% of the wind power in the US and would have 14% of all solar production when several projects were completed. In all, MidAmerican's renewable portfolio cost $13 billion. The company spent $3.4 billion on capital expenditures during 2012 compared to depreciation of just $1.4 billion. That was another reminder of something Buffett often alluded to: "Money will always flow toward opportunity, and there is an abundance of that in America."

MidAmerican's HomeServices business increased pre-tax earnings 110% to $82 million. While small, it is noteworthy for a view into the housing industry. HomeServices participated in $42 billion of home sales in 2012, up 33%. The company also purchased two-thirds of a Prudential franchise operation that would further increase business. HomeServices planned to rebrand itself Berkshire Hathaway HomeServices, taking advantage of the Berkshire brand.

Finance and Financial Products

Pre-tax earnings in the Finance and Financial Products segment jumped 10% to $848 million. Earnings were buoyed by Clayton Homes, which increased its pre-tax earnings 66% to $255 million. That was despite the continued headwind from subsidies given to traditional home manufacturers. During 2012 Clayton sold 14% more units, but at a lower average selling price, which increased overall revenues 9%. Earnings ballooned for three reasons:

- Increased unit volume allowed for manufacturing efficiencies.
- Lower insurance claims and lower credit losses bolstered the bottom line.
- Lower interest rates on borrowings more than offset the lower earnings from its loan portfolio.

Combined pre-tax earnings at Berkshire's two leasing companies fell 5% to $148 million. This result followed an almost tripling of earnings the prior year. The decline in 2012 was from additional depreciation expense at XTRA and due to lower foreign exchange gains. The additional depreciation stemmed from investments XTRA was making in its business to take advantage of future opportunities. Like its larger sister companies MidAmerican and BNSF, XTRA spent twice its annual depreciation expense, or $256 million, on capital expenditures during the year. Some business leaders used the uncertain economic landscape to justify holding back on investing. Buffett said Berkshire didn't hold back. "While competitors fret about today's uncertainties, XTRA is preparing for tomorrow."

Pre-tax earnings in the other category were greater than Clayton's. This collection of assets generated solid profits every year. In 2012 these amounted to $445 million, down 4% from the year before. They included Berkadia, Berkshire's 50% commercial mortgage servicing partnership with Leucadia National Corporation, and a portfolio of bond and stock investments Buffett managed himself. Also included were charges to Clayton for use of Berkshire's credit, and the guarantee fee paid by NetJets.

Investments

There was modest activity in the investment portfolio during 2012. Berkshire pared down its stake in ConocoPhillips, an oil producer, by $800 million, while increasing its investment in IBM by $824 million, Well Fargo by $1.8 billion, and Walmart by $944 million. One new name on the list, DIRECTV, wasn't purchased by Buffett. Either Todd Combs or Ted Weschler made the $1.1 billion investment (Buffett wouldn't say). Each man managed around $5 billion for Berkshire by year-end.

Newspapers

Berkshire's purchase of twenty-eight daily newspapers for $344 million (around but not entirely in 2012) caused some to scratch their heads. But the purchases, which included Buffett's hometown newspaper, the *Omaha World Herald*, provided lessons on investing and a history of the media industry.

Buffett summed it up this way: "News, to put it simply, is what people don't know that they want to know." The longer historical version included how newspapers used to be powerhouses before the television and internet ages. What people then didn't know was a lot and newspapers were the only source for sports, stock prices, and local and national news. This primacy attracted advertisers and newspaper owners made *a lot* of money (including Berkshire with *The Buffalo News*).

Slowly but surely television and the internet came along and provided a faster (and cheaper) way to deliver news. With each passing year, more and more people dropped their subscription. The downward spiral of fewer readers led to fewer advertisers, leading to lower profits, and so on.

Buffett thought just a few newspapers would ultimately survive and would need to adapt to the online world. Big national newspapers such as *The Wall Street Journal*, *The New York Times*, and *The Washington Post* would all do well. So would the smaller local papers that provided information readers couldn't get anywhere else. They would also struggle, but newspapers in tightly-knit communities had the best chance.

Buffett readily admitted nostalgia played a part in the purchase. Afterall, he loved reading newspapers and had even delivered two as a boy. But as a businessman, the financials mattered too. Newspapers were shrinking. Buffett said their earnings were certain to decline. So why would he buy them? At a low enough price, the economics made sense.[*]

2013

By *almost* all accounts, 2013 was a very good year for Berkshire. The one glaring exception was a 14.2 point underperformance to its self-selected benchmark, the S&P 500, which rose 32.4%. Buffett had anticipated Berkshire's relative underperformance in periods of strong gains by the S&P 500 and had written the prior year that Berkshire's unbroken history of beating the S&P 500 over five-year periods could end if the market rose strongly in 2013.[**] His confidence lay with Berkshire Hathaway's underlying businesses, which made significant and meaningful progress during the year.

Continuing our methodology of estimating Berkshire's intrinsic value from earlier, Berkshire's progress was a meaningful 13% increase. Shares rose by over a third, which put the valuation beyond the 1.20x threshold Berkshire established for repurchases.

---

[*] Charlie Munger would later use an analogy that expressed the economics perfectly. He said newspapers were no different than an oil well that depletes over time. What was the difference between an oil well with a known limited quantity of value to extract and a newspaper with a limited quantity of cash to extract?

[**] Buffett said he expected a modest outperformance over market cycles with Berkshire doing better in down or flat years. Charlie Munger pointed out that Berkshire's past performance is even that much better considering that its after-tax book value performance was tracked against the S&P 500, which is pre-tax.

Table 7.26: Berkshire Hathaway intrinsic value estimation

Per share (A-equivalent):	2013	2012
Investments	$129,253	$113,786
Pre-tax operating earnings (ex. investment income)	9,116	8,085
Estimated value (investments + 10x operating earnings)	220,413	194,636
Year-end share price	177,900	134,060
Year-end book value per share	134,973	114,214
Price/estimated value	0.81x	0.69x
Price/book	1.32x	1.17x
Value/book	1.63x	1.70x
Change in estimated value	13%	
Change in share price	33%	

Sources: Berkshire Hathaway Annual Reports 2012, 2013; and author's calculations.

Berkshire fired on all cylinders during 2013. Its many operating businesses increased their earnings and competitive positions. Berkshire also put tens of billions of capital to work in new acquisitions:

- $12.25 billion for a major interest in ketchup maker H.J. Heinz
- $5.6 billion for NV Energy, a large West Coast utility company
- $3.5 billion for the remaining ownership interests in Marmon and Iscar
- $3.1 billion for twenty-five bolt-on acquisitions by existing subsidiaries

In addition, Berkshire spent $11.1 billion on capital expenditures, which was $5.7 billion more than its depreciation. It also spent $4.7 billion, net, on equity securities.

H.J. Heinz Company

On June 7, 2013, Heinz was acquired by a partnership formed between Berkshire Hathaway and 3G Capital. Buffett loved flagship brands with high, stable market shares and high returns on capital. Under this new template, 3G Capital from Brazil oversaw operations and Berkshire was the financing partner. Heinz was well-known for its signature brand of tomato ketchup and had a family of other brands including, sauces, soups, beans, pasta, infant foods, and Ore-Ida potato products. The company also produced licensed brands such as Weight Watchers and T.G.I. Friday's snacks. Its business was broken down by segment:

Figure 7.4: H.J. Heinz 2013 revenues by segment ($ billions)

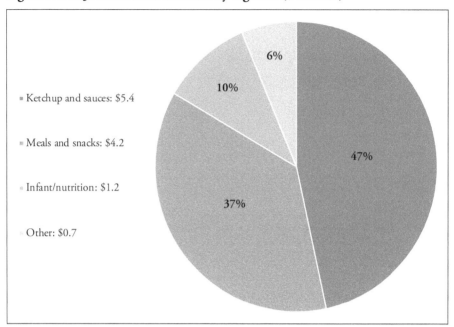

Note: Total revenues = $11.5 billion
Source: H.J. Heinz 2013 10K.

The company was headquartered in Pittsburgh, Pennsylvania, but had worldwide operations. Geographically, about a quarter of revenues were from North America, a quarter from Europe, 20% from Asia/Pacific, and the remainder split between a US Foodservice business and the rest of the world.

The strength of its brands was evidenced by its pre-tax return on tangible capital (see Table 7.27). Between 2009 and 2013 the company's average return on tangible capital was a mouthwatering 56%. Its flagship brand of Heinz ketchup commanded a 60% market share in the United States (and even higher overseas).[102] That the runner up (Hunts) accounted for just 20% was evidence of the company's dominance. Most people cannot even name a third ketchup brand.

3G Capital was a force in the investment world. The investment fund was led by Jorge Paulo Lemann, whom Buffett knew during their time serving on the Gillette board together. Prior to the Heinz deal, 3G Capital had taken Burger King private. It also created one of the world's largest beer brewers when a company it controlled, InBev, acquired the Anheuser Busch Company. The partners of 3G Capital, which included Lemann, Alex Behring, and Bernardo Hees, were known as excellent business operators. Their key operating philosophy was zero-based budgeting, a technique that requires all expenses be justified each period. Their past successes using that methodology, and the steep price that Berkshire and 3G paid for Heinz, suggested they would look to improve margins at Heinz.*

The total purchase price for Heinz, including debt assumed in the acquisition, was $29.1 billion. That represented a whopping 7.7 times the company's underlying tangible capital and what appeared to be a low initial return in the mid-single digits. The margin of safety in the deal stemmed from the company's strong historical returns on capital. Future growth could bring the initial return up, as would any improvement in margins the team at 3G Capital could squeeze out. But the price was steep. Buffett admitted they stretched a little because of the qualities of Heinz and what they saw in the 3G Capital management team.

Table 7.27: Heinz—acquisition analysis

($ millions)	2013	2012	2011	2010	2009
Total revenues	$11,529	$11,508	$10,559	$10,495	$10,011
Revenues/avg. capital[1]	$3.07	$3.80	$3.91	$4.25	$3.88
EBIT margin[1]	15%	13%	16%	15%	15%
Pre-tax return on capital	45%	51%	64%	65%	60%
Purchase price (equity)	$8,500				
Berkshire preferred stock	8,000				
Debt	12,600				
Effective purchase price	$29,100				
Purchase multiple	7.74x				
BRK going-in pre-tax return (2013)	5.9%				
Return using 5-year average ROC	7.4%				
Footnote: 1. Adjustments were made for goodwill and intangibles.					

Note: The company's fiscal year was 52 weeks ended in April.
Sources: Berkshire Hathaway Annual Report 2013; H.J. Heinz Annual Reports 2009–2013; H.J. Heinz 10Q 10/27/13; and author's calculations.

Berkshire and 3G Capital each invested $4.25 billion, with each receiving half of the company's common equity.** Berkshire also invested $8 billion in a 9% preferred stock issue. The remainder of the purchase price came from traditional bank debt. That one entity (Berkshire) would provide both equity and debt financing was somewhat unusual. It allowed Berkshire to put more money to work at a lower relative risk than

---

* Buffett was asked at the shareholder's meeting if 3G's techniques could be applied to Berkshire. Buffett and Munger thought Berkshire was already lean, but also dismissed 3G's involvement in operations at Berkshire. He said that while he admired 3G Capital, the two systems would not blend well. A very strong reason against such involvement was Berkshire's system of letting its managers run their businesses without any interference.

** Berkshire and 3G Capital each acquired 425 million shares in a new holding company that purchased the public company. Berkshire also had warrants to purchase an additional 46 million shares, and another 39.6 million shares were reserved for stock options.

if all the non-equity financing was borrowed. "We have a less-leveraged position in the capital structure than they have. They wanted more leverage, and we provided that leverage on what I regard as fair terms and what they regard as fair terms." The structure of the deal reflected the governing partnership, which allowed Berkshire to put capital to work with a team of managers already in place. "We [Berkshire] have more money than operating ability at the parent company level, and they have lots of operating ability and wanted to maximize their return on $4 billion."

Table 7.28: Heinz capital structure and leverage

($ millions)	Amount	Leverage[1]
Debt	$12,600	1.00x
Preferred stock	8,000	1.58x
Equity	8,500	2.42x
Total capital	$29,100	
Berkshire Hathaway total leverage:		
Preferred + equity	$12,250	1.87x
Footnote:		
1. Leverage as measured by the sum of capital more senior in priority divided by source.		

Sources: Berkshire Hathaway Annual Report 2013; H.J. Heinz Annual Reports 2009–2013; H.J. Heinz 10Q 10/27/13; and author's calculations.

Insurance

Berkshire's Insurance Group delivered big in 2013. Each operating unit produced an underwriting profit (the 11th year in a row), which resulted in a 4.1% negative cost of float. Better still, year-end float grew 6% to $77 billion. Buffett reminded shareholders that both gifts (negative cost of float and higher float) were not a given. He cautioned that future gains in float would be hard to come by and that Berkshire's float might shrink. Unlike debt, which could be called away requiring large cash resources, float could not place a large demand on liquidity. He said any future decline in float might only be around 3%. That comment sheds some light on why Buffett was reluctant to include underwriting gains in the calculation of Berkshire's earning power (and therefore intrinsic value calculations). If in future years Berkshire's float did shrink, underwriting gains would be offset by the outflow of capital from the decline in float. The resulting economics would still be very favorable because the cumulative underwriting profit would replace the float, leaving the same amount of capital available for Berkshire to use. Including underwriting profits in earnings would therefore be inappropriate.

Figure 7.5: Hypothetical 3% decline in float concurrent with a 3% underwriting gain

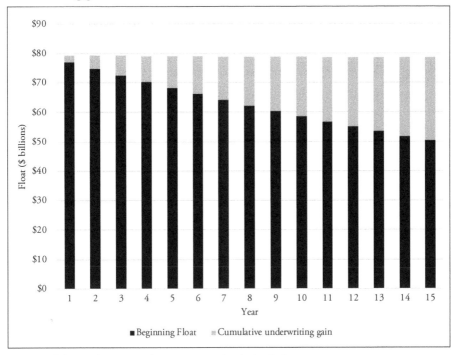

Source: Berkshire Hathaway Annual Report 2013 and author's calculations.

Table 7.29: Berkshire Hathaway—Insurance Underwriting

($ millions)	2013	2012
GEICO		
Premiums written	$19,083	$17,129
Premiums earned	18,572	16,740
Underwriting gain/(loss) - pre-tax	$1,127	$680
General Re		
Premiums written	$5,963	$5,984
Premiums earned	5,984	5,870
Underwriting gain/(loss) - pre-tax	$283	$355
Berkshire Hathaway Reinsurance Group		
Premiums earned	$8,786	$9,672
Underwriting gain/(loss) - pre-tax	$1,294	$304
Berkshire Hathaway Primary Group		
Premiums earned	$3,342	$2,263
Underwriting gain/(loss) - pre-tax	$385	$286
Total premiums earned	$36,684	$34,545
Total underwriting gain/(loss) - pre-tax	3,089	1,625
Average float	75,183	71,848
Cost of float	(4.1%)	(2.3%)
Aggregate adverse (favorable) loss development	($1,752)	($2,126)
Discount accretion and amortization charges included above	$186	$381

Note: Berkshire Hathaway Primary Group and BHRG written premiums were not detailed.
Sources: Berkshire Hathaway Annual Reports 2012, 2013; and author's calculations.

GEICO

Front and center in insurance was GEICO. When discussing float, Buffett was quick to point out that GEICO's float would almost certainly grow. Why such certainty? Because GEICO's business model as the low-cost provider created a moat. It could save customers real money, and that meant growth could be expected. In 2013, GEICO had a market share of 10.2% and passed Allstate to become the second largest auto insurer in the United States after State Farm's 18.5% share. Premiums earned swelled 11% to $18.6 billion, and it wrote to 93.9% combined ratio.[*]

---

[*] Buffett stated in the Chairman's letter that GEICO's true economic goodwill was approaching $20 billion, as compared to the carrying value of $1.4 billion for its accounting goodwill. Based on his previous comments, it would suggest confirmation that GEICO's goodwill was worth a little more than its annual premium volume.

Berkshire Hathaway Reinsurance Group

From a standing start in 1985, Ajit Jain created BHRG, which as of 2013 had float of $37 billion and cumulative underwriting profits. During the year, Jain went a step further by forming Berkshire Hathaway Specialty Insurance, a company that would provide direct commercial insurance. Jain placed Peter Eastwood in charge of the new company, one of several executives that sought out a place at Berkshire from competitors. The new entity would be a part of the Primary Group.*

The insurance landscape continued to be tough from a pricing perspective, which constrained volume. Still, the division overall outperformed itself over the previous year. Total premiums earned at BHRG fell 9% to $8.8 billion, but profits rebounded strongly, up 325% to $1.3 billion.

Results were expected to be volatile, and in 2013 a lack of major catastrophes led to the second year of profits within the catastrophe and individual risk segment, up 45% to $581 million on earned premiums that fell 2% to $801 million. Catastrophe losses totaled just $20 million from floods in Europe compared to losses of $96 million in 2012 and $800 million in 2011.

Retroactive premiums fell for the third year in a row, from $2 billion in 2011 to $717 million in 2012 to $328 million in 2013. A small number of contracts were responsible for current year volume and deferred charge amortization caused the line to report a loss of $321 million from a loss of $201 million the year before. Gross unpaid losses from retroactive reinsurance contracts totaling $17.7 billion demonstrate the huge amount of float from these activities. Offsetting unpaid losses were unamortized deferred charges amounting to $4.25 billion at year-end, an amount that was slowly working its way into loss expenses over time and impacting reported results.

Volume in other multi-line fell 18% to $4.3 billion largely from expiration of the Swiss Re 20% quota-share agreement at the end of 2012. Residual premiums of $1.5 billion were earned in 2013 from that contract, far below the $3.4 billion earned in 2012. As with the catastrophe and individual risk segment, other multi-line incurred low levels of catastrophe losses. Losses in 2013 amounted to just $16 million from floods and a hailstorm in Europe compared to $268 million the year before from Hurricane Sandy. As a result, pre-tax underwriting profits swelled 122% to $655 million.

BHRG's life and annuity business was impacted by three large contracts. Earned premiums jumped 17% to $3.3 billion due to two new pieces of business. The increase in life and annuity premiums would have been greater if not for a contract amendment with Swiss Re Life & Health America, Inc. that reversed earned premiums of $1.3

---

* Buffett was asked why Berkshire didn't just buy a commercial primary operation. His answer was that a good operation would likely be pricey. Berkshire could build its own from scratch at book value and would not have any of the baggage that came from buying another company.

billion but produced a one-time pre-tax gain of $255 million* Underwriting results rebounded from a loss of $190 million to a profit of $379 million in 2013.

General Re

"It can be remembered that soon after we purchased General Re, the company was beset by problems that caused commentators—and me as well, briefly—to believe I had made a huge mistake. That day is long gone. General Re is now a gem." Buffett's praise for General Re and Tad Montross reflected the company's eighth consecutive year of underwriting profits, which fell 20% to $283 million on earned premiums up 2% to $6 billion.

Property/casualty earned premiums increased 3.5% to $3 billion but would have been flat without positive currency effects. While pre-tax underwriting profits fell 63% to $148 million, the result was after $400 million of catastrophe losses from a hailstorm and floods in Europe. Property lines recorded $375 million of favorable loss adjustments on prior year business and $178 million in gains on current year business. Casualty/workers' compensation reported a loss of $5 million, almost overcoming $141 million of accounting charges.

Gen Re's life/health business bounced back from a $44 million loss in 2012 to report a $135 million profit in 2013. The improvement was a result of lower than expected mortality and the absence of a large charge taken the prior year.

Berkshire Hathaway Primary Group

Premiums earned at Berkshire Hathaway Primary Group jumped 48% to $3.3 billion. The increase was largely due to the inclusion of GUARD and Princeton for the full year, and from the new commercial specialty insurance business. Total underwriting profit grew 35% to $385 million, a strong 85% combined ratio. Favorable claims experience and the addition of the newcomers drove the increase in profit.

Manufacturing, Service, and Retailing

Pre-tax earnings from Berkshire's MSR businesses increased 10% to $6.7 billion. But the rate of return on tangible capital fell from 25.3% to 21.5% and after-tax return on tangible equity fell from 21.4% to just 16.7%.** At least part of the reason had to do with excess cash building up on the books. For the first time, the net debt position

---

* The gain was for accounting purposes. BHRG paid Swiss Re a $675 million. Losses under the contract had been booked in prior years that more than offset the gain in 2013.
** Return on carrying value (which includes goodwill) fell from 8.7% to 8.3%.

of the MSR Group was negative, meaning cash on the books exceeded total debt.* Over the previous five years, the MSR Group had gone from a net debt position of $5.1 billion to a net cash position of $605 million. Cash was piling up faster than it could profitability be used; this despite additional bolt-on acquisitions and spending on capital expenditures in excess of depreciation.

Table 7.30: Manufacturing, Service, and Retailing Businesses—net debt (cash)

($ millions)	2013	2012	2011	2010	2009
Total debt	$6,020	$7,280	$7,825	$8,426	$8,082
Cash	6,625	5,338	4,241	2,673	3,018
Net debt (cash)	($605)	$1,942	$3,584	$5,753	$5,064

Sources: Berkshire Hathaway Annual Reports 2009–2013 and author's calculations.

Marmon further organized its businesses. Previously it had classified its 160 businesses across eleven sectors. Those sectors remained but were grouped into three separate companies. The new layout was as follows:

Table 7.31: Marmon Group operating sectors and companies

Company	Sector
Marmon Engineered Industrial & Metal Components (Engineered Components)	Electrical & Plumbing Products Distribution, Distribution Services, Industrial Products
Marmon Natural Resources & Transportation Services (Natural Resources)	Transportation Services & Engineered Products, Engineered Wire & Cable, Crane Services
Marmon Retail & End User Technologies (Retail Technologies)	Highway Technologies, Water Treatment, Retail Store Fixtures, Food Service Equipment, Retail Home Improvement Products

Source: Berkshire Hathaway Annual Report 2013.

Results across Marmon's many businesses were mixed. Overall, the unit grew pre-tax earnings 3.4% to $1.2 billion even as revenues fell slightly to $7 billion. Its pre-tax margin grew again, from 15.9% in 2012 to 16.9% in 2013. Results from Marmon's businesses displayed the same bob around pattern Buffett described years earlier with various industry and business-specific changes impacting results from year to year. All the while it continued looking for ways to improve margins and deploy capital into new niches, including through bolt-on acquisitions. It was a successful strategy.

---

* The debt/equity ratio fell from 15% in 2012 to 11.2% in 2013. The MSR Group paid down $1.26 billion in total outstanding debt during the year.

During 2013, Berkshire acquired the remaining portion of Marmon it did not own. Berkshire paid $1.47 billion for 9.7% of the company. That implied a valuation of $15.2 billion for Marmon and represented a multiple of 12.9 times earnings.[*]

Berkshire increased its ownership in Iscar during 2013. The Wertheimer family exercised a put option it held and elected to sell the remaining 20% of the business the family had retained since the sale in 2006. Berkshire paid $2.05 billion, which valued the entire company at $10.25 billion. That meant the company was worth twice as much as when Berkshire first purchased it in mid-2006.[**] Its earnings were flat compared to 2012.

The other manufacturing segment, which included results from Iscar, reflected strength from consumers. Revenues increased 8.7% to $29.1 billion and earnings increased by the same rate to $3.6 billion. Forest River had another strong year and experienced 24% higher revenues and 32% higher profits, highlighting its manufacturing efficiencies on higher volumes. The building products businesses increased revenues 8% and pre-tax earnings 13%, and the apparel businesses increased revenues 3.5% and pre-tax earnings 25%. Lubrizol's earnings were unchanged from the prior year. Bolt-on acquisitions also contributed to results in this segment.

Earnings from other service businesses increased 10% to $9 billion and included strong showings from TTI (up 11%) and NetJets (up 7.5%). The newspapers, under the heading BH Media, saw 66% higher revenues but only because of acquisitions. Pre-tax earnings for the segment increased 13% to $1.1 billion and included TTI (up 10%), FlightSafety (up 11%), and NetJets (up 7%).

In the retailing segment, a full year of results from Oriental Trading Company led to a 15% increase in revenues to $4.3 billion and a 23% increase in pre-tax earnings to $376 million. The combined effect of an increase in earnings from the home furnishing and jewelry businesses and lower earnings from See's and Pampered Chef was neutral on the segment's earnings.

McLane's revenues increased 23% to $45.9 billion and pre-tax earnings increased 21% to $486 million. Revenues and earnings growth came from Meadowbrook Meat Company, which it acquired in 2012, double-digit organic growth in existing business, and a pre-tax gain of $24 million from the sale of a logistics business in Brazil.

---

[*] This multiple is higher than the 11x multiple paid in previous transactions. It's possible the improved margins drove the higher price. Another reason might have been the large acquisition it had pending at year-end. Or, it might have been due to excess cash on the books that belonged to the selling family (i.e. retained earnings accrued but not paid as dividends).

[**] Berkshire paid $4 billion for the initial 80% stake in Iscar, which valued the company at $5 billion. The Marmon and Iscar purchases required similar write-offs as in prior years. This year the total was $1.8 billion of the $3.5 billion spent; the amount greater than the carrying value of the non-controlling interests. Buffett expressed his amazement that such an accounting procedure was required. He said it was another reason Berkshire's intrinsic value far exceeded book value.

Regulated, Capital-Intensive Businesses

The big news in utilities was the acquisition of NV Energy. NV Energy was an energy holding company that served 1.2 million electric customers and 200,000 natural gas customers in Nevada through two main operating segments: Nevada Power Company and Sierra Pacific Power Company. MidAmerican paid $5.6 billion for the company.* The deal closed on December 19, 2013, and as a result had little effect on Berkshire's 2013 results.

The price tag Berkshire paid suggests it was a fair deal for both sides. MidAmerican would gain a platform to invest in the West, a growing area where Buffett got a foothold with the purchase of BNSF three years earlier. NV Energy would be able to invest in more renewable energy projects, such as solar generation, now that it was part of MidAmerican. And those projects would serve to lower the company's taxable income through accelerated depreciation and deferred taxes, as well as direct tax credits for the renewable projects.

Table 7.32: NV Energy—acquisition analysis

($ millions)	2013	2012	2011	2010	2009
Total revenues	$2,930	$2,979	$2,943	$3,280	$3,586
Revenues/avg. capital	$0.34	$0.35	$0.34	$0.38	$0.42
EBIT margin	25%	26%	21%	20%	16%
Pre-tax return on capital	8.5%	9.2%	7.1%	7.5%	6.6%
Purchase price (equity)	$5,596				
Assumed debt	4,921				
Effective purchase price	$10,517				
Purchase multiple	1.22x				
BRK going-in pre-tax return (2013)	7.0%				

Note: Data for 2013 are the trailing twelve months ending 9/30/13 and the balance sheet values as of that date.
Sources: Berkshire Hathaway Annual Report 2013; NV Energy 10K filings 2009–2012; NV Energy 10Q 9/30/12; NV Energy 10Q 9/30/13; and author's calculations.

MidAmerican's existing operations performed well during 2013. Its EBIT grew 7% to $2.1 billion and Berkshire's share of net income grew 11% to $1.5 billion. Broken down further, the news was mixed:

---

* The purchase price was financed as follows: $2.0 billion of new debt issued by MidAmerican and $3.6 billion additional equity from MidAmerican shareholders, which included $3.5 billion from Berkshire. The remaining $0.1 billion came from MidAmerican's minority shareholders.

- PacifiCorp drove a large part of the gain. It received regulatory approval in 2012 to raise rates, but a costly fire offset the higher revenues. With no adverse event in 2013, PacifiCorp's EBIT swelled 33% to $982 million.
- HomeServices increased its earnings by 70% to $169 million from a combination of the additional brokerages it had acquired and higher volumes of sales on higher sales prices.
- Northern Powergrid EBIT fell 16% to $362 million due to lower revenues and the strength of the US dollar against the UK pound.

BNSF railroad continued to do well for Berkshire. In 2013, it recorded yet another year of increases in revenues and earnings. Revenues grew 5.7% to $22 billion and pre-tax earnings grew 10% to $5.9 billion. BNSF moved 4.5% more units and received higher prices on those units. Three of its four major segments increased volumes in 2013. Industrial products volume grew 11% (driven by strength in petroleum products), consumer products grew 6% and coal was up 3%. The only exception was agricultural products, which declined 4% amid lower US exports.

Finance and Financial Products

The largest business in this segment, Clayton Homes, increased pre-tax earnings 63% to $416 million. Increased unit volumes led to higher manufacturing efficiencies and allowed an outsized increase in pre-tax earnings on just 6% higher revenues. During and after the recession, its manufacturing volumes dropped precipitously. That caused the high fixed costs associated with manufacturing to put a drag on earnings. Without the lending business, Clayton's earnings might well have been negative during those years. Clayton produced 29,547 homes in 2013, which represented 4.7% of all single-family homes in the United States and made it the country's largest builder, even including site-built homes.

Pre-tax earnings from CORT and XTRA increased 11% to $165 million. Together with $404 million of other income, the Finance and Financial Products segment increased pre-tax earnings 16% to $985 million.

Investments

Berkshire's major investment moves in 2013 amounted to hitting a repeat button. Berkshire added another $1 billion to its Wells Fargo stake, ending the year with 9.2% of the company worth $22 billion. It also added modestly to its IBM position, increasing it from 6% to 6.3% of the company worth $12.8 billion at year-end.

In a surprise purchase, Berkshire disclosed it had amassed close to a 1% stake in Exxon Mobil worth $4.2 billion at year-end. Commentators speculated the company's low price/earnings ratio and the company's history of returning capital to shareholders attracted Buffett.[103] A lack of commentary by Buffett, both in the Chairman's letter and at the Annual Meeting, suggested the purchase was not overly important. That lack of importance would soon be confirmed; it would be sold the next year.

Buffett provided two very interesting and timeless investing lessons in 2013. Both related to non-intuitive transfers of value that tripped up managers and investors alike. One was his logic for thinking through issuing options, which came as a result of a management compensation plan put forth by Coca-Cola. A second was his thinking on pensions, which included a memo he had written to Washington Post Co. CEO Katharine Graham in 1975.

The nineteen-page memo Buffett wrote to Graham in 1975 was included as an appendix to the 2013 Berkshire Hathaway Annual Report and is worth reading. In his 2013 Chairman's letter, Buffett called pensions and other related promises made today with tomorrow's checkbook a "gigantic financial tapeworm". His thoughts hadn't changed much since writing that letter. The problem was that many people in companies and governments across the country vastly underestimated the value transferred by making promises to pay sums in the future. As an example, Buffett said that a promise to pay him $500 a month for life was really a transfer in value of $65,000. And if an "earthquake risk" materialized, such as a combination of high salary inflation coupled with muted investment returns, the present value of such a promise could skyrocket.

Companies set aside assets to pay for these future promises, which were usually managed by an outside investment manager. As the liabilities mounted, so too did the requirement to contribute assets to a fund to cover them. These contributions directly impacted the profitability of companies since they were included as an expense. Over time, the value of pension assets sometimes eclipsed the net worth of the companies that sponsored them. Buffett used US Steel Company as an example in his 1975 memo. As of 1972, US Steel had a net worth of $3.6 billion and its pension fund assets amounted to $2.2 billion. The pension fund of US Steel was basically a separate operating division.

Despite these large promises, some managers neglected their pension assets even though the investment returns would drive future pension costs (and therefore a company's future profitability). To Buffett, a company had to be viewed in its entirety, and that included its sometimes-significant pension assets/liabilities. The risks around pensions and post-retirement benefits are so large that they are the only other item, besides large capital expenditures or acquisitions, that Buffett requires his company's managers check with him first before committing.

There is one last item related to pensions which is important to understand. Investments in a pension fund can reasonably be expected to earn a return. Consequently, future returns are projected alongside assumptions of future liabilities. It is a human bias for a management team to make optimistic assumptions about future returns since it lowers the amount a company must contribute in the present. Management's assumptions about future returns are disclosed in financial reports. Some companies, even in times of low interest rates (such as during the mid-2010s), assumed double-digit returns. Buffett has commented on how these assumptions are too high. Berkshire's own pension assumptions in 2013 included an expected long-term rate of return on plan assets of 6.7%. By contrast, the public pension fund median assumed rate of return was 7.75%.[104] The percent difference may seem small, but the difference represents billions of dollars. Berkshire's lower assumptions were another indicator of its conservatism.

In 2013, Coca-Cola's management team put forth a management compensation plan that by many accounts was excessive. The plan called for the issuance of 500 million shares over four years,[*] which on the surface amounted to possible dilution for existing shareholders of 16.8%. Coke's plan led one investor to publicly call out the management team for transferring billions in value from shareholders to management. The spat was covered by the business press.

Berkshire Hathaway owned 9.1% of Coke that was worth $16.5 billion. What did Buffett think? That was the very first question posed by Carol Loomis at the 2014 Annual Meeting. Buffett was not supportive of the plan but felt others' fears of outsized dilution were overblown. He explained his thinking. Even if all the shares were issued at the current price, dilution would be far less than suggested. Coca-Cola would receive proceeds from those exercising the options and a tax benefit from the transfer of value. Both would serve to reduce dilution if shares were repurchased. The figure Buffett calculated was 2.5%—a lot lower than 16.8%. "I don't like dilution and I don't like 2.5% dilution. But it's a far cry from the numbers that were getting tossed around." In the end, Berkshire voted to abstain on the management plan and had conversations with Muhtar Kent, Coke's CEO. Those were enough to cause Coke to scale back the plan and extend it over ten years instead of four.

---

[*] This figure included the 2014 plan and those leftover from previous plans.

Table 7.33: Buffett's calculation of Coca-Cola dilution

($ millions)	
Number of shares	500,000,000
Assumed strike price per share	$40
Assumed share price at exercise	$60
Transfer of value (exercise - strike)	$10,000
Exercise proceeds	20,000
Tax benefit (at 35% of value transfer)	3,500
Total proceeds	$23,500
Share repurchases (at exercise price)	391,666,667
Net share issuance	108,333,333
Dilution rate on 4.4 billion shares	2.46%

Source: Warren Buffett comments at the 2014 Berkshire Hathaway Annual Meeting.

Other news

Berkshire added a new director in 2013. Meryl Witmer was the first new addition to the Berkshire Hathaway board of directors since Stephen Burke in 2009. Witmer, 51 years old, was a managing partner and investment manager at Eagle Capital Partners, L.P. The addition of Witmer expanded the board from twelve to thirteen members.

On the proxy ballot that year (for vote in early 2014) was a suggestion that Berkshire pay a dividend. Shareholders overwhelmingly voted not to have Berkshire pay a dividend. The support was there even after removing Buffett's shares from the count. It was a vote of confidence for Berkshire's capital allocators and the strategy of retaining all earnings.

2014

The numbers for 2014 were reason enough to celebrate. Shares advanced 27% against the S&P 500's gain of 13.7%. Berkshire's book value per share increased 8.3%. The year also brought an important milestone for Berkshire Hathaway. It marked fifty years since Warren Buffett took control of the company and built it into one of the world's largest and most admired corporations. (See Chapter 8 beginning on p. 625 for an examination of Berkshire's fifty-year history under Buffett.)

Buffett marked the anniversary with a new measurement in the performance table presented at the beginning of the Annual Report each year. Shareholders were used to seeing the historical change in book value per share and the total return of the S&P 500, Berkshire's selected benchmark. Now presented alongside those figures was the historical record of changes in Berkshire's share price. Buffett's reasoning was that Berkshire's shift toward owning businesses in their entirety made book value an inferior gauge of performance as many companies were worth far more than carrying value. In early years, Berkshire's assets were mostly in securities, where book value and intrinsic value were closely aligned. Now assets were concentrated in operating companies and there was a wide gap.

One might have been suspicious of why the preferred metric was being changed in a year that showed Berkshire in a favorable light. Buffett noted the limitation of market prices over the short run, but said that over decades the market correctly tracked Berkshire's intrinsic value.

Revisiting our rough estimate of Berkshire's intrinsic value, we can observe that the market was roughly right during 2014. Berkshire's intrinsic value appears to have increased more than book value but less than the strong advance of its shares. The 13% increase in estimated value nearly matched the S&P 500 that year and is consistent with Buffett's observation that Berkshire would struggle to beat the market in up years.

Table 7.34: Berkshire Hathaway intrinsic value estimation

Per share (A-equivalent):	2014	2013
Investments	$140,123	$129,253
Pre-tax operating earnings (ex. investment income)	10,847	9,116
Estimated value (investments + 10x operating earnings)	248,593	220,413
Year-end share price	226,000	177,900
Year-end book value per share	146,186	134,973
Price/estimated value	0.91x	0.81x
Price/book	1.55x	1.32x
Value/book	1.70x	1.63x
Change in estimated value	13%	
Change in share price	27%	

Sources: Berkshire Hathaway Annual Reports 2013, 2014; and author's calculations.

How Berkshire achieved its gain in intrinsic value is the story of 2014. The year was mostly a good one for Berkshire. Its operating subsidiaries increased earnings and found ways to expand both organically and through bolt-on acquisitions. Buffett loved bolt-on acquisitions because they meant "no more work for us, yet more earnings." Insurance delivered yet another year of underwriting gains and more float. Berkshire also found other profitable outlets for its growing cash pile during the year. One was a multibillion-dollar acquisition in Canada that expanded Berkshire's utility operations. Another deal with 3G Capital presented itself during the year, as did opportunities to acquire both operating businesses and some of Berkshire's own stock via tax-savvy moves. The major blemish was an operating disruption at BNSF that Buffett appeared to bemoan more for its impact on customers and reputation than Berkshire's bottom line.

Insurance

The Insurance Group delivered its twelfth consecutive year of profits with a $2.7 billion pre-tax underwriting gain on earned premiums of $41.3 billion. That represented a negative cost of float of 3.3%. Float grew again in 2014, ending the year up 8.6% to $83.9 billion. All of Berkshire's insurance units benefitted from a year of no catastrophe losses.[*]

Table 7.35: Berkshire Hathaway—Insurance Underwriting

($ millions)	2014	2013
GEICO		
Premiums written	$20,962	$19,083
Premiums earned	20,496	18,572
Underwriting gain/(loss) - pre-tax	$1,159	$1,127
General Re		
Premiums written	$6,418	$5,963
Premiums earned	6,264	5,984
Underwriting gain/(loss) - pre-tax	$277	$283
Berkshire Hathaway Reinsurance Group		
Premiums earned	$10,116	$8,786
Underwriting gain/(loss) - pre-tax	$606	$1,294
Berkshire Hathaway Primary Group		
Premiums earned	$4,377	$3,342
Underwriting gain/(loss) - pre-tax	$626	$385
Total premiums earned	$41,253	$36,684
Total underwriting gain/(loss) - pre-tax	2,668	3,089
Average float	80,581	75,183
Cost of float	(3.3%)	(4.1%)
Aggregate adverse (favorable) loss development	($1,365)	($1,752)
Discount accretion and amortization charges included above	$128	$186

Note: Berkshire Hathaway Primary Group and BHRG written premiums were not detailed.
Sources: Berkshire Hathaway Annual Reports 2013, 2014; and author's calculations.

Berkshire Hathaway Reinsurance Group

Berkshire Hathaway Reinsurance Group, led by Ajit Jain, contributed the bulk of the increase in float during the year. Float at BHRG grew 14% to $42.5 billion and now represented over half of Berkshire's total float. Earned premiums grew 15% to $10.1 billion and pre-tax underwriting gains amounted to $606 million (a decline from $1.3 billion the prior year).

---

[*] Berkshire defined catastrophe losses as losses of $100 million or more from a single event.

In 2014, BHRG consolidated its other multi-line property/casualty reporting segment with the catastrophe and individual risk segment. On a comparative basis, earned premiums in property/casualty fell 21% to $4.1 billion but pre-tax underwriting gains swelled 36% to $1.7 billion. The Swiss Re 20% quota-share agreement expired at the end of 2012 but contained policies in runoff that contributed $1.5 billion to earned premiums in 2013 and $200 million in 2014.* The Swiss Re contract also contributed $283 million to underwriting gains in 2014 from reduced loss estimates. A lack of catastrophe events led to a $700 million gain in property business and foreign currency exchange gains added $315 million to the bottom line.

Retroactive reinsurance earned premiums grew from $328 million to $3.4 billion primarily from a $3 billion contract with Liberty Mutual Insurance Company.** The retroactive policy insured Liberty Mutual against adverse development of its asbestos and environmental book prior to 2005 and workers' compensation claims prior to 2014. Berkshire's exposure was capped at $6.5 billion after a $12.5 billion retention (the loss amount the primary or ceding insurer must incur first). Pre-tax underwriting losses from retroactive reinsurance swelled 182% to $905 million due to increases in deferred charge amortization and an $825 million unfavorable adjustment to prior year loss estimates. Total unamortized deferred charges grew 81% to $7.7 billion at year-end 2014. This amount would continue to be amortized into underwriting expense and be a drag on future earnings. Gross unpaid losses grew 37% to $24.3 billion.

The life/annuity business swung from a gain of $379 million in 2013 to a loss of $173 million in 2014. Earned premiums fell 19% to $2.7 billion.

General Re

General Re reported another year of profits, with its underwriting gain falling 2% to $277 million. Earned premiums grew 4.7% to $6.3 billion.

The property/casualty segment increased earned premiums 3% to $3.1 billion and its underwriting gain grew 15% to $170 million. Gains of $466 million from property business reflected no significant catastrophe losses. Casualty/workers compensation reported a loss of $296 million, which included $123 million favorable loss development and recurring accounting charges amounting to $138 million in 2014.

---

* Calculated based on the dollar declines stated in the 2013 and 2014 Annual Reports.
** Buffett said he knew of just eight property/casualty policies in history with a single premium over $1 billion. *All* were written by Berkshire Hathaway. The Liberty Mutual policy was behind only the $7.1 billion Lloyd's of London contract written in 2007.

General Re's life/health business continued its steady stream of profits with a $107 million gain. The gain in 2014 was down 21% from the prior year in large part because of increased reserves directly associated with lower interest rates.* Earned premiums grew 6% to $3.2 billion.

GEICO

GEICO turned in another strong year with a $1.2 billion underwriting profit and a combined ratio of 94.3%. Its premiums crossed the $20 billion mark (up 10%). That result solidified its standing as the second-largest auto insurer in the United States with a 10.8% market share, up from 10.2% in 2013.

Berkshire Hathaway Primary Group

Premiums from the Primary Group rose 33% to $4.4 billion from organic growth and the addition of the new commercial unit formed by Ajit Jain. Pre-tax earnings from these insurers grew 62% to $626 million. As small as they were individually or collectively in relation to Berkshire's other insurance operations, the Primary Group deserved its annual praise from Buffett. Their consistent profitability, and float at year-end amounting to $8.6 billion, contributed meaningfully to Berkshire's intrinsic value.

Manufacturing, Service, and Retailing

Marmon, one of the newest and biggest members of the MSR Group, was partly reorganized for reporting purposes in 2014. Buffett moved Marmon's leasing operations into Finance and Financial Products now that it was entirely owned by Berkshire.** Results for the prior two years were restated for a clean comparison. Table 7.36 contains the new presentation and the figures as originally presented.

Using the 2014 presentation, pre-tax earnings increased 10% to $6.8 billion for the MSR Group. Net earnings (after tax and non-controlling interests) grew 15% to $4.5 billion. While increases are always better than decreases, it's important to remember these business units were continually making bolt-on acquisitions and employing capital that in some cases came from headquarters. A better way to keep check on their progress was return on tangible equity, which in 2014 came in at 18.7%.***

---

* Lower interest rates increase the present value of liabilities associated with business such as long-term care and disability insurance.

** This was for reporting purposes only. The business continued to be managed on a decentralized basis like before.

*** This is the figure Buffett quoted on average tangible equity of $24 billion. I've calculated 17.3% based on average tangible equity of $25.9 billion, which uses the old 2013 balance sheet. The difference arises due to

Table 7.36: Original and restated results for MSR businesses

($ millions)	Without Marmon Leasing			With Marmon Leasing	
	2014	2013	2012	2013	2012
Revenues	$97,689	$93,472	$81,432	$95,291	$83,255
Operating expenses	90,788	87,208	75,734	88,414	76,978
Interest expense	109	104	112	135	146
Pre-tax earnings	6,792	6,160	5,586	6,742	6,131
Income taxes and minority interests	2,324	2,283	2,229	2,512	2,432
Net earnings	$4,468	$3,877	$3,357	$4,230	$3,699

Sources: Berkshire Hathaway Annual Reports 2013, 2014.

Marmon's manufacturing operations were now included together with Berkshire's other manufacturing businesses. As a result, some details of its operations were lost compared to when it was a standalone reporting segment. Berkshire divulged some details in the notes to its financial statements, reporting revenues increased 15% to $6 billion and pre-tax earnings 19% to $708 million. These increases were largely due to the inclusion of IMI PLC, a British beverage dispensing equipment manufacturer Marmon acquired for $1.1 billion on January 1, 2014. Marmon's existing businesses increased revenues and found cost savings in certain lines of business that contributed to higher earnings.

Berkshire began including a new table in the notes to the financial statements that made viewing the manufacturing businesses easier (see Table 7.37). The table further classified the manufacturing businesses along three lines: industrial and end-user products, building products, and apparel.

Table 7.37: Detail on Berkshire Hathaway manufacturing businesses

($ millions)	Revenues			Pre-tax earnings		
	2014	2013	2012	2014	2013	2012
Industrial and end-user	$22,314	$20,325	$19,003	$3,460	$3,044	$2,912
Building products	10,124	9,640	8,953	896	846	748
Apparel	4,335	4,293	4,149	455	315	251
	$36,773	$34,258	$32,105	$4,811	$4,205	$3,911

Source: Reproduced from the 2014 Berkshire Hathaway Annual Report.

Berkshire included Marmon's many manufacturing businesses (discussed above) in the industrial and end-user products category. As a whole they increased revenues 10% to $22.3 billion while pre-tax earnings increased 14% to $3.5 billion. Bolt-on

---

the balance sheet figures associated with Marmon's leasing business, which isn't calculable from the financial statements. A comparative balance sheet for the prior years was not provided in the 2014 Chairman's letter. As a rough reference, the 2013 figure was 16.7%.

acquisitions led to most of the 10% increase in pre-tax earnings of Lubrizol. Higher unit sales at Forest River led to its 21% increase in pre-tax earnings. Higher revenues, a higher gross margin, and lower costs increased Iscar's earnings 18%. CTB was also included in this category, but Berkshire made no mention of its results.

Pre-tax earnings in the building products category increased 6% to $896 million on revenues that grew 5% to $10.1 billion. Johns Manville, Acme, and MiTek improved their top lines. MiTek also benefitted from bolt-on acquisitions. Shaw closed its rug division in 2014. Improvements in its hard flooring unit kept revenues flat, but raw material costs depressed earnings. Every other business in this category increased earnings including Benjamin Moore.

Pre-tax earnings in apparel jumped 44% to $455 million on revenues up 1% to $4.3 billion. Details on earnings were scarce. All that Berkshire disclosed is that some of the six businesses were restructured. Lower manufacturing and pension costs also helped earnings growth. Included in this segment were Fruit of the Loom (including Russell and Vanity Fair Brands), and formerly large parts of Berkshire's operations such as H.H. Brown Shoe.

Revenues in the service businesses category increased 10% to $9.9 billion led by TTI, NetJets, and FlightSafety. TTI grew from higher unit sales as well as bolt-on acquisitions. NetJets and FlightSafety both benefitted from higher utilization rates, including higher sales of aircraft at NetJets. NetJets and TTI led the group to 10% higher pre-tax earnings totaling $1.2 billion. Other businesses in this category included Business Wire, Dairy Queen, *The Buffalo News*, and the BH Media Group that included the *Omaha World Herald*, twenty-eight other daily newspapers and publications, and new in 2014 a TV station (discussed below).

The retailing businesses included Berkshire's four furniture retailers (Nebraska Furniture Mart, RC Willey, Star, and Jordan's), its three jewelers (Borsheims, Helzberg, and Ben Bridge), See's, Pampered Chef, and Oriental Trading Company. Nebraska Furniture Mart's pending megastore outside of Dallas, Texas weighed on the results from this group. Overall, revenues declined 3% to $4.4 billion and pre-tax earnings declined 9% to $344 million.

McLane was the only business to receive its own reporting line. Its $46.6 billion revenues required that because of reporting rules. Its revenues increased 1.5% from the year before from higher foodservice and beverage revenues, but pre-tax earnings declined 10% to $435 million (the decline was 6% excluding the $24 million pre-tax gain on the sale its Brazil-based logistics business in 2013). A decline in earnings from the foodservice business overshadowed higher earnings from grocery and beverage.

Berkshire acquired two MSR businesses during 2014 in a relatively unusual way. The first was a division of Phillips 66 that was renamed Lubrizol Specialty Products, Inc. Its main product line allowed oil to flow faster in pipelines and was a perfect fit for Lubrizol. The second such acquisition was WPLG, a Miami, Florida television station affiliated with the ABC network. It was placed in the BH Media Group alongside the newspaper properties. These two acquisitions were unusual in that Berkshire bought them in exchange for stock it already owned in Phillips 66 and Graham Holding Company (owner of the TV station and the renamed entity that held *The Washington Post*). This allowed Berkshire a way to sell its investments in Phillips 66 and Graham Holding Company tax-free.[*]

These types of transactions are called cash-rich split-offs and entail using a provision in the tax code allowing no capital gains to be incurred for tax purposes. This was perhaps most important with Graham Holding Company. Berkshire's cost basis, which originated in the 1970s, was just $11 million. Those shares were now worth $1.1 billion, which meant Berkshire would incur a large tax bill if it sold the investment outright. Instead, Berkshire traded its shares for the Miami TV station, cash, and Berkshire Hathaway shares that Graham Holding Company owned. (Berkshire effectively repurchased 2,107 Class A and 1,278 Class B shares via this transaction.) The value of the Berkshire shares alone amounted to roughly what it would have paid on the gain assuming the typical all-in corporate tax rate of 38%.[105] Berkshire realized a total capital gain for GAAP purposes of $2.1 billion related to these two transactions.

Table 7.38: Analysis of Berkshire's 2014 cash-rich split-offs

($ millions)	Value given	Value received
Graham Holding Company		
Graham Holding Company shares	$1,092	
Cash		$328
Miami TV station		364
Berkshire Shares		400
Total	1,092	1,092
Tax savings (assuming 38% rate)	$411	
Phillips 66		
Phillips 66 shares	$1,350	
Cash		$450
Specialty chemicals business		900
	1,350	1,350
Tax savings (assuming 38% rate)	$387	

Sources: Berkshire Hathaway Annual Report 2014 and author's calculations.

In November 2014, Berkshire agreed to another cash-rich split-off. It would acquire Duracell, the battery maker, from Procter & Gamble in a similar transaction in 2015.

---

[*] Buffett noted that Todd Combs worked on the Phillips 66 deal. Combs also worked on the acquisition of Charter Brokerage, a deal that largely went below the radar.

Regulated, Capital-Intensive Businesses

On April 30, 2014, MidAmerican Energy Holdings Company, the holding company that owned all of Berkshire's utility operations, changed its name to Berkshire Hathaway Energy Company. The HomeServices business had changed its name to Berkshire Hathaway HomeServices in 2012. Its corporate parent now followed suit, leveraging the Berkshire Hathaway name which was becoming a brand synonymous with good business and personal values.

Aside from the new branding, the highlight of the year at the utility business was the acquisition of AltaLink from SNC Lavalin Group on December 1, 2014. The company was based in Alberta, Canada. AltaLink's business was very simple. Unlike its new sister companies at Berkshire Hathaway Energy, it only handled the distribution of electricity. It boasted 12,000 kilometers of transmission lines serving 85% of the population of the province of Alberta.[106] Berkshire Hathaway Energy acquired AltaLink for $2.7 billion. The transaction was funded with loans from Berkshire's insurance subsidiaries and debt of $1.5 billion.

Berkshire Hathaway Energy's consolidated EBIT increased from $2.1 billion to $3.1 billion. A large part of the increase was directly a result of the NV Energy acquisition in 2013, which added $549 million in EBIT in 2014. Another other large contributor was Northern Powergrid. The UK-based utility saw EBIT jump 46%, which was from a combination of rate increases and favorable foreign currency exchange. Additionally, EBIT increased from new solar and wind assets placed in service during the year. Berkshire's share of net earnings grew from $1.5 billion to $1.9 billion.

The major blemish of 2014 came from BNSF. Buffett called the railroad Berkshire's most important non-insurance subsidiary. It was clear from the tone in his Chairman's letter that he was not happy about the reputational hit the company took from service disruptions. "During the year, BNSF disappointed many of its customers. These shippers depend on us, and service failures can badly hurt their businesses." There were several causes for the disruption. They included strong demand from agricultural shippers and demand for oil shipment from the Bakken region in combination with adverse weather in the first part of the year. BNSF's extensive work to increase system capacity also played a part, though to a lesser degree.[107]

Buffett gave BNSF management marching orders to repair its reputation. "Though weather, which was particularly severe last year, will always cause railroads a variety of operating problems, our responsibility is to do *whatever it takes* to restore our service to industry-leading levels." Buffett was clearly also disappointed in BNSF's financial performance, which lagged its main rival. The Union Pacific railroad (BNSF's main competitor in the West), though far underspending BNSF in new capital projects, gained market share and earned more money than Berkshire's railroad. Pre-tax earnings from BNSF grew 4% to $6.2 billion because of a 1.8% increase in volumes and higher pricing.* Union Pacific reported in its fourth quarter earnings release that pre-tax earnings grew 18% to $8.3 billion on 7% greater volume.

These missteps in 2014 notwithstanding, Buffett remained optimistic. BNSF planned to spend $6 billion or 26% of revenues on capital expenditures in 2015, a figure far higher than Union Pacific's 17%. These huge investments were expected to lead to a system with greater capacity, much better service, and improved profits.**

Finance and Financial Products

Pre-tax earnings in the Finance and Financial Products segment swelled 18% to $1.8 billion. That increase included Marmon's earnings from its leasing operations, which were presented on a restated basis looking back to 2012.

Every business in this sector except CORT improved during 2014. No reason was given for its decline from the prior year. Clayton grew its pre-tax earnings 34% on just a 3% increase in revenues. Such outsized improvements in earnings compared to revenues reflected an increase in manufacturing efficiencies. Clayton produced 45% of the manufactured home volume in the United States during 2014, up from 14% in 2003 when Berkshire purchased the company. Clayton's mortgage portfolio ended 2014 on par with the prior year at $13 billion.

Table 7.39: Finance and Financial Products earnings

($ millions)	2014	2013	2012
Berkadia (50% share)	$122	$80	$35
Clayton	558	416	255
CORT	36	40	42
Marmon - containers and cranes	238	226	246
Marmon - railcars	442	353	299
XTRA	147	125	106
Net financial income[1]	296	324	410
Total pre-tax earnings	$1,839	$1,564	$1,393
Footnote:			
1. Excludes capital gains or losses			

Source: Reproduced from the 2014 Berkshire Hathaway Annual Report.

---

* The unit volume increase came from industrial products (up 9%) and agriculture (up 16%). Consumer products was flat and coal volume decreased 2%.
** Through 2014, BNSF paid Berkshire a total of $16 billion in dividends. This was nearly half its purchase price just five years earlier.

Marmon's leasing operations were extensive and spanned 105,000 rail cars. Its annual volume was 6,000 units. Berkshire's book value of $5 billion for Marmon's rail fleet was understated because it manufactured all its own cars and did not register a profit when transferring the units to the leasing operation. A consequence of this was lower annual depreciation expense over the thirty-year life of each unit.

The nature of the transportation leasing businesses, such as Marmon's and XTRA, was one of high fixed costs. The most significant was depreciation. Higher usage and higher rates had a disproportionate effect on the bottom line of these companies. This was the case with these two businesses during 2014. Their earnings also increased due to higher units in service.

Investments

When Berkshire listed its fifteen largest equity positions in 2014, one did not make the list. Berkshire had warrants to buy 700 million shares of Bank of America which could be exercised by Berkshire any time prior to expiration in September 2021. The warrants were worth $12.5 billion at year-end 2014. If the warrants were converted to shares, Bank of America would have been the fourth largest investment. Because they weren't, the company didn't even make the list. This was another prime example of economics vs. accounting, where accounting skewed the actual economics.

The top investments on the list were familiar and successful, so much so that Buffett called them the Big Four: American Express, Coca-Cola, Wells Fargo, and IBM. Buffett used simple math and an example to show the value of the Big Four and non-controlling ownership stakes: Each increase of 0.10% in Berkshire's ownership raised Berkshire's portion of annual earnings by $50 million. "It's better to have a partial interest in the Hope Diamond than to own all of a rhinestone."

Buffett also admitted a mistake he made in taking too long to sell Tesco shares. The UK-based grocer ran into problems that turned into a management change, shrinking profits, and accounting mishaps. The real problem wasn't Berkshire's $444 million after-tax loss on its $2.3 billion investment. Buffett said he lost faith in Tesco's management and that led him to sell some shares, but not all. His mistake was acting slowly.

Another position is worth noting. At year-end, Berkshire owned 8.6% of DaVita HealthCare Partners, Inc., a kidney dialysis company. Berkshire did not disclose who of the three investment managers (Buffett, Todd Combs, or Ted Weschler) made each investment. But DaVita was a company long owned by Weschler through his hedge fund.

Another opportunity presented itself to work with 3G Capital, the investment firm that partnered with Berkshire to buy Heinz in 2013. This time 3G Capital was looking for a financing partner to assist with its acquisition of Restaurant Brands International, Inc (RBI). RBI owned the Canadian-based fast food chain Tim Hortons and the well-known US-based fast food chain Burger King. Berkshire invested $3 billion in a 9% cumulative compounding perpetual preferred stock.* A unique provision required RBI to pay Berkshire an additional amount, if necessary, to produce an after-tax yield as if the dividends were paid by a US company. That provision provided protection against changes in tax rates and significant appreciation of the US dollar (making the Canadian dollar payments worth less upon conversion). Buffett remained bullish on America, but after a half-century building Berkshire Hathaway into one of the strongest and most respected companies in the world, protection against risk remained at the forefront.

Decade in Review

The fifth decade of Berkshire Hathaway under Warren Buffett's control might be considered its penultimate. It was the last decade in which earnings could profitably be retained in their entirety, and it proved that size was in fact an anchor to future performance. Its earnings and increase in net worth over the 2005 to 2014 period were enormous. Earnings from operations topped $107 billion and net worth rose to almost a quarter of a *trillion* dollars.

The *rate* of increase in shareholders' equity, however, dropped sharply—from 22% to just 11%. Net shares issued in acquisitions drove the rate of book value growth per share to 10.1%. Significantly, this was still two percentage points better than the S&P 500. What Berkshire Hathaway gave up in ability to generate outsized returns it gained in financial strength, which was tested during the worst economic downturn since the Great Depression. Berkshire was a financial fortress as it closed the books on a half-century.

The decade that ended in 2014 saw a marked shift toward ownership of operating subsidiaries. Earnings from operations jumped to 70% of the total increase in shareholders' equity for the period. That level of contribution hadn't happened since the very first decade of Buffett's control. The sum of all acquisitions, net of cash acquired, amounted to $59 billion. Berkshire acquired literally hundreds of businesses during this time including the smaller bolt-on acquisitions made by subsidiaries. But it was the big acquisitions that really moved the needle—and they were collectively known as The Powerhouse Five:

---

* The preferred investment, together with warrants to acquire a small number of shares, gave Berkshire a 14.4% voting interest in RBI.

- *$6.05 billion*: Iscar, the Israel-based manufacturer of cutting tools was Berkshire's first major international acquisition. Berkshire acquired it in two stages: 80% in 2006 and another $2.05 billion in 2013. This valued the whole company at over $10 billion (equity value; we don't know what debt, if any, was on the books).
- *$9 billion*: Marmon, a conglomerate with 130 businesses across eleven sectors. Like Iscar, Marmon was acquired in stages: The first 60% in 2008 for $4.5 billion and the remainder for another $4.5 billion between 2011 and 2013.
- *$33.5 billion*: Burlington Northern Santa Fe (BNSF) joined Berkshire in 2010. So too did some of BNSF's shareholders that elected to receive Berkshire shares in the process. Considering debt and the value of the shares Berkshire owned before it bought the rest of the railroad, the deal was worth $44.5 billion.
- *$8.7 billion*: Lubrizol joined Berkshire's ranks in 2011.
- *$13.4 billion*: MidAmerican, whose name was changed to Berkshire Hathaway Energy in 2014, acquired PacifiCorp in 2005 for $5.1 billion (with Berkshire contributing $3.4 billion of additional capital to fund the purchase). It also acquired NV Energy for $5.6 billion in 2013, and Alta Link for $2.7 billion in 2014.

Of the Powerhouse Five, only Berkshire Hathaway Energy in its smaller form as MidAmerican was around in 2005. That year it earned $393 million pre-tax. In 2014 the Powerhouse Five collectively earned $12.4 billion pre-tax. For perspective, Berkshire's many other non-insurance businesses in the aggregate earned $5.1 billion pre-tax.* Over the decade, the Powerhouse Five had a cumulative $12 billion gain in earnings that came with only minor dilution. "That satisfies our goal of not simply increasing earnings, but making sure we also increase *per-share* results."

The Powerhouse Five, though, were not the only big investments of the decade. The third largest investment of the decade was the $12.25 billion deal where Berkshire and 3G Capital acquired Heinz. In that deal, Berkshire contributed 50% of the equity for $4.25 billion and partially financed the deal with $8 billion of preferred stock. It was a unique structure where Berkshire provided financing and 3G oversaw operations.

Berkshire also invested a massive $73 billion in property, plant, and equipment. About half represented replacement of existing fixed assets and half represented growth capital. The big spenders were the railroad and utility operations, which could soak up huge amounts of capital but at a lower regulated rate of return.

Berkshire's insurance operations expanded mostly organically between 2005 and 2014. The Insurance Group earned an underwriting profit every year, bringing the total over the twelve years of consecutive underwriting profit to $24 billion pre-tax. Each year also included net favorable loss development, a trend that proved

---

* Buffett stratified these into groups: two companies earned between $400 million and $600 million, six earned between $250 million and $400 million, and seven earned between $100 million and $250 million.

Berkshire's conservatism in estimation and accounting. Insurance results were bolstered by several smaller acquisitions (MedPro, Princeton Insurance Co., Applied Underwriters and GUARD), and from new entities formed in-house (Berkshire Hathaway Assurance Corp. to take advantage of municipal bond insurance and Berkshire Hathaway Specialty Insurance to take advantage of an opportunity in the primary commercial market). Over the decade GEICO moved into the number two spot as the second largest auto insurer in the United States behind State Farm.

Average float grew 80% to $81 billion, providing even more capital for Buffett and Munger to deploy. Earned premiums grew 95% from 2004 to $41 billion in 2014. A big contributor to both premium and float growth was Berkshire Hathaway Reinsurance Group, Led by Ajit Jain. Jain's group contained over half of Berkshire's total float at year-end and contributed 72% of the increase in float generated by Berkshire over the decade (see Table 7.40). BHRG wrote some of the largest reinsurance contracts in history:

- $7.1 billion: A retroactive reinsurance contract with Equitas in 2007, which provided retroactive coverage to thousands of Lloyd's of London underwriters.
- $1.7 billion adverse loss development contract with Swiss Re in 2009.
- $2.25 billion with CNA Financial Corporation for reinsurance in 2010 to assume asbestos and environmental pollution liabilities.
- $1.7 billion with AIG in 2011 to reinsure asbestos liabilities.

Other contracts written by BHRG and General Re included quota-share arrangements and large catastrophe risks. Buffett frequently praised General Re during this decade for sticking to the four insurance commandments and focusing exclusively on underwriting profitability.

Table 7.40: Berkshire Hathaway insurance float, select data

($ millions)	2014	2004	$ Change	% Change
GEICO	$13,569	$5,960	$7,609	128%
Gen Re	19,280	23,120	(3,840)	(17%)
BHRG	42,454	15,278	27,176	178%
Primary	8,618	1,736	6,882	396%
	83,921	46,094	37,827	82%

Sources: Berkshire Hathaway Annual Reports 2004, 2014; and author's calculations.

The most severe economic recession since the Great Depression of the 1930s arrived in 2008. It caused financial markets to fall and credit markets to freeze. Berkshire's financial strength allowed it to go on the offensive and provide capital to the market during this period. Berkshire put to work tens of billions of dollars in a series of privately negotiated transactions. These included:

- $14.5 billion over two weeks in 2008 to Goldman Sachs ($5 billion), Wrigley ($6.5 billion), and General Electric ($3 billion)
- $5.7 billion in 2009 to Swiss Re ($2.7 billion) and Dow Chemical Company ($3 billion)
- $5 billion in 2011 to Bank of America

The recession proved Berkshire's model of operating with multiple layers of protection was not unduly conservative but instead allowed it to go on the offensive when others were scrambling for liquidity. This translated into double-digit interest rates and often warrants to acquire shares at a bargain price.

Berkshire's equity investment portfolio grew substantially during the decade. It was funded by the gusher of cash coming into Omaha from the operating subsidiaries, and the billions in additional float from the insurance companies. Buffett's Big Four earned their moniker. The most meaningful change during this time period was the addition of IBM, which was a new investment costing $12 billion. Over ten years, Berkshire put another $11 billion into its favorite bank, Wells Fargo. Its investment in American Express and Coca Cola remained virtually untouched, but appreciation contributed billions to Berkshire's increase in net worth over the period. Concentration remained a hallmark, though the top four positions edged down from 65% of the portfolio in 2004 to 59% in 2014. Three of the four remained in the top position at both points of measurement (the IBM investment was first made in 2011).

Table 7.41: Berkshire Hathaway—equity portfolio, select detail

($ millions)	2014 Cost	2014 Market	2004 Cost	2004 Market	Change Cost	Change Market
American Express	$1,287	$14,106	$1,470	$8,546	(183)	$5,560
The Coca-Cola Company	1,299	16,888	1,299	8,328	0	8,560
The Gillette Company			600	4,299	(600)	(4,299)
Procter & Gamble	336	4,683			336	4,683
Wells Fargo & Company	11,871	26,504	463	3,508	11,408	22,996
IBM	13,157	12,349			13,157	12,349
All other	27,106	42,940	5,224	13,036	21,882	29,904
Total equity securities	$55,056	$117,470	$9,056	$37,717	$46,000	$79,753

Note: Gillette merged into Procter & Gamble in 2005.
Sources: Berkshire Hathaway Annual Reports 2004, 2014; and author's calculations.

Too numerous to mention are the other investments purchased and sold over the course of the decade as opportunities arose. Buffett quickly admitted his mistakes such as Energy Future Holdings and Tesco, both of which caused Berkshire permanent capital losses.

In 2014, Berkshire changed its yardstick from measuring progress based on change in book value to change in market value. It was done because the discrepancy between Berkshire's book value and its intrinsic value became too great. Buffett stressed that it was market value over time that was the best judge, not any given year. Part of the reason for the change was the shift toward owning more operating businesses, whose values were not regularly updated like the market prices of securities. This change was critical as Berkshire's contribution toward change in equity due to net income from operations almost tripled from 26% in 1995–2004 to 70% in 2005–2014.

In some cases, such as with Marmon and Iscar, huge write-offs (totaling $3.3 billion) were required for accounting purposes when Berkshire purchased the remaining ownership interests from the selling families.

Buffett provided many clues to Berkshire's true value during this decade. He even provided two quantitative measures (per-share investments and per-share operating earnings) to nudge shareholders in the right direction. Communications were designed to help shareholders understand Berkshire's true intrinsic value. Both Buffett and Munger desired to see Berkshire's shares sell as close to intrinsic value as possible so that business results would translate very closely to shareholder returns. Berkshire implemented a share repurchase program in 2011 and modified it in 2012 to allow the company to purchase shares at up to 1.20x book value.

Table 7.42: Reconciliation of shareholders' equity, 1965–2014

($ millions)	1965–74	1975–84	1985–94	1995–04	2005–14	1965–14
Beginning of period shareholders' equity	$22	$88	$1,272	$11,875	$85,900	$22
Net income - operations	57	366	2,869	19,344	107,301	129,937
Net income - realized gains	7	199	1,354	14,096	15,897	31,554
Unrealized appreciation of investments	0	486	5,877	15,000	25,720	47,083
Mergers/divestitures	0	133	433	25,085	12,816	38,467
Dividends/treasury stock	(3)	0	69	0	(1,763)	(1,697)
Issuance of Class-B stock	0	0	0	565	0	565
Other/misc.	4	0	0	(65)	(5,701)	(5,761)
End of period shareholders' equity	$88	$1,272	$11,875	$85,900	$240,170	$240,170
Change in equity during period	$66	$1,184	$10,602	$74,026	$154,270	$240,148

Note: Figures may not add due to rounding.
Sources: Berkshire Hathaway Annual Reports and author's calculations.

Table 7.43: Contribution toward change in equity during period

	1965–74	1975–84	1985–94	1995–04	2005–14	1965–14
Net income - operations	86%	31%	27%	26%	70%	54%
Net income - realized gains	11%	17%	13%	19%	10%	13%
Unrealized appreciation of investments	0%	41%	55%	20%	17%	20%
Mergers/divestitures	0%	11%	4%	34%	8%	16%
Dividends/treasury stock	(4%)	0%	1%	0%	(1%)	(1%)
Issuance of Class-B stock	0%	0%	0%	1%	0%	0%
Other/misc.	7%	0%	0%	(0%)	(4%)	(2%)
Total	100%	100%	100%	100%	100%	100%

Note: Figures may not add due to rounding.
Sources: Berkshire Hathaway Annual Reports and author's calculations.

Berkshire's shareholders' equity grew at a rate of 10.8% per year over the course of the decade. A negative 0.7% net effect from share repurchases in 2011 and 2012, and the cash-rich split-offs in 2014,* combined with shares issued (primarily for the BNSF acquisition) to bring the rate of per share book value growth down to 10.1% per year. Berkshire's share price advanced at a still slower rate of 9.9% because of the small decline in average price/book ratio the market placed on the shares. Berkshire's share price still outperformed the 7.7% average annual advance of the S&P 500—a solid 2.2% edge but far below its historical average. (For context, the 10-year Treasury Note declined from 4.2% at the end of 2004 to 2.2% at the end of 2014.)

Berkshire's market capitalization rose from an average of $131 billion at year-end 2004 to over $350 billion in 2014. Berkshire found itself up ten spots to fourth on the Fortune 500.

---

* Share repurchases above book value decrease shareholders' equity and book value per share but increase intrinsic value per share (assuming they are undervalued). Conversely, shares issued above book value increase book value per share but don't necessarily change intrinsic value.

Figure 7.6: Berkshire Hathaway stock price, 2005–2014

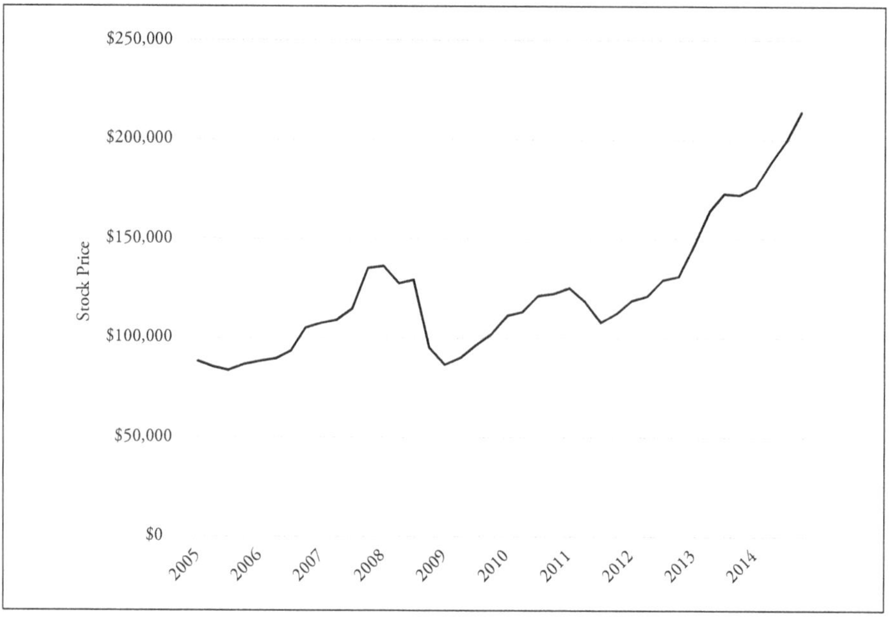

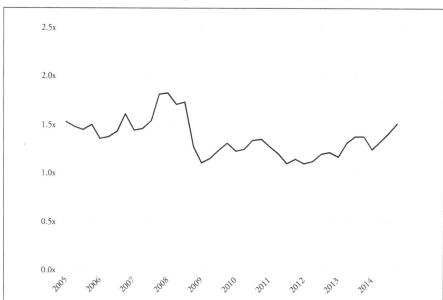

Sources: *Of Permanent Value* (Kilpatrick, 2015), Berkshire Hathaway Annual Reports 2005–2014, and author's calculations.

Figure 7.7: Berkshire Hathaway price to book ratio, 2005–2014

Sources: *Of Permanent Value* (Kilpatrick, 2015), Berkshire Hathaway Annual Reports 2005–2014, and author's calculations.

At year-end 2014, Warren Buffett and Charlie Munger oversaw the financial equivalent of the Rock of Gibraltar. Just as its size, diversity, and liquidity provided strength second only to sovereign nations, it also meant almost no chance of achieving returns like in prior decades. The fifth decade under Warren Buffett's control would be the last decade of full-steam-ahead growth. Berkshire ended 2014 with $63 billion in cash and equivalents even after the multibillion-dollar capital allocation decisions made during the decade. The share repurchases in 2011 and 2012 provided inklings of the shift toward returning capital to shareholders that was to accelerate during the next decade.

Berkshire Hathaway's place in the pantheon of business was secure after fifty years of careful building. The sixth decade would surely bring more opportunity for Berkshire, as well as its challenges. Warren Buffett and Charlie Munger would lead Berkshire Hathaway into a decade that would undoubtedly prove that the company they built was ready for them to step down. But much more lay ahead and the two men showed no signs of slowing down.

Lessons: 2004–2014

1. Large opportunities can present themselves very quickly. It pays to be ready. Berkshire Hathaway was able to put billions of dollars of capital to work during the Great Recession of 2008–09 because its balance sheet was very strong. During boom times it is tempting to push the envelope by borrowing too much or by reducing redundancies and introducing fragility into an organization. As Buffett says, you never know who's swimming naked until the tide goes out.

2. "[C]redit is like oxygen. When either is abundant, its presence goes unnoticed. When either is missing, that's *all* that is noticed." A company can substantially hurt itself or even go out of business under the right conditions if it faces a significant liquidity need at the wrong time. Berkshire's cash was placed in US Treasuries, which are the safest form of liquidity under almost any circumstance. It also kept its need for liquidity low by borrowing long term. Its float, while representing significant liabilities, was structured so it could never be a large drain on cash.

3. Businesses do not need to be sold during times of distress. Berkshire never thought of selling its wholly-owned businesses during the recession. That owner mentality also extended to many of its long-term equity investments. Business owners (whether in whole or part) don't panic and sell or seek to time the market. They instead look to the long-term cash-generating ability of the assets.

4. Share prices frequently diverge from intrinsic value. Berkshire's communications to shareholders often contained explicit hints to the company's value. Yet at times it sold for below what it was worth. Berkshire created value for continuing

shareholders by repurchasing its shares at a price below intrinsic value. Companies that buy back shares above intrinsic value (no matter the purpose) destroy value for continuing shareholders.

5. Capital intensive businesses can be satisfactory investments under the right conditions. Berkshire's growing size forced it to find outlets for mountains of cash. It found such an outlet in regulated businesses including traditional electric and gas operations and the railroad industry. The key attribute for both was the ability to earn a protected-but-limited return on equity capital.

6. High rates of return eventually forge their own anchor. Berkshire's growth in book value per share increased at its highest-ever dollar amount while increasing at the lowest-ever rate in its modern history. Larger and larger sums shrink the investable universe and make it harder to earn above-average returns over time. But as Berkshire demonstrated through its fifty-year modern history, a long run is possible.

Table 7.44: Reconciliation of shareholders' equity

($ millions)	2014	2013	2012	2011	2010	2009	2008	2007	2006	2005	2004
Prior year equity	$221,890	$187,647	$164,850	$157,318	$131,102	$109,267	$120,733	$108,419	$91,484	$85,900	$77,596
Current year net income/(loss)	19,872	19,476	14,824	10,254	12,967	8,055	4,994	13,213	11,015	8,528	7,308
Issuance of shares[1]	118	92	118	355	11,096	172	181	430	123	131	117
Treasury stock[2]	(400)		(1,296)	(67)							
Transactions with non-controlling interests[3]	(17)	(1,871)	(695)	(5)	(636)	(121)					
Adoption of equity method[4]							626				
Adoption of new accounting pronouncements								28	180		
Change in unrealized appreciation of securities, net of tax	1,585	14,829	9,647	(2,144)	2,838	13,143	(14,503)	(1,920)	4,962	(2,717)	674
Change in comprehensive income - other[5]	(2,878)	1,717	199	(861)	(49)	586	(2,764)	563	655	(358)	205
Ending equity	$240,170	$221,890	$187,647	$164,850	$157,318	$131,102	$109,267	$120,733	$108,419	$91,484	$85,900
Shares outstanding at end of period:											
Class A	826,339	859,043	894,955	938,244	947,460	1,055,281	1,059,001	1,081,024	1,117,568	1,260,920	1,268,783
Class B	1,224,855,488	1,177,366,608	1,121,985,472	1,068,843,376	1,050,990,468	744,701,300	14,706,996	14,000,080	12,752,431	8,394,083	8,099,175
Total Class A-equivalent shares	1,642,909	1,643,954	1,642,945	1,650,806	1,648,120	1,551,749	1,549,234	1,547,693	1,542,649	1,540,723	1,538,756

Footnotes:

1. With the exception of BNSF in 2010, the issuance of shares primarily relates to exercises under the SQUARZ notes and issuances related to prior acquisitions. Approximately $10.6 billion in 2010 is related to the BNSF acquisition.
2. The 2011 and 2012 treasury stock transactions were direct purchases. The 2014 transaction was connected to the Graham Holdings tax-free exchange, which included 2,107 Class A and 1,278 Class B shares.
3. Reductions in equity related to the acquisition of non-controlling interests; the excess of consideration paid over the previously recorded balance sheet carrying amount.
4. 2008: Berkshire adopted the equity method for its BNSF shares, which represented 20.7% of the company.
5. Includes foreign currency translation, transactions relating to pension plans, other, and amounts applicable to income taxes.

Sources: Berkshire Hathaway Annual Reports 2004–2014 and author's calculations.

Table 7.45: Berkshire Hathaway—select parent-level financial information

($ millions, except per share data)	2014	2013	2012	2011	2010	2009	2008	2007	2006	2005
Revenues:										
Insurance premiums earned[1]	$41,253	$36,684	$34,545	$32,075	$30,749	$27,884	$25,525	$31,783	$23,964	$21,997
Sales and service revenues	97,097	92,993	81,447	71,226	65,942	62,555	65,854	58,243	51,803	46,138
Railroad, utilities and energy revenues[2]	40,690	34,757	32,582	30,839	26,364	11,443	13,971	12,628	10,644	
Interest, dividend, and other investment income[3]	5,026	4,934	4,532	4,788	5,213	5,245	4,966	4,979	4,382	3,487
Finance and financial products sales and service revenues and dividend and interest income	6,526	6,109	5,932	5,590	5,571	4,579	4,931	5,103	5,111	4,633
Investment gains	4,081	6,673	3,425	(830)	2,346	787	(7,461)	5,509	2,635	5,408
Total revenues	$194,673	$182,150	$162,463	$143,688	$136,185	$112,493	$107,786	$118,245	$98,539	$81,663
Earnings:										
Net earnings attributable to Berkshire Hathaway[4]	$19,872	$19,476	$14,824	$10,254	$12,967	$8,055	$4,994	$13,213	$11,015	$8,528
Net earnings per A-share	$12,092	$11,850	$8,977	$6,215	$7,928	$5,193	$3,224	$8,548	$7,144	$5,538
Year-end data:										
Total assets	$526,186	$484,931	$427,452	$392,647	$372,229	$297,119	$267,399	$273,160	$248,437	$198,325
Notes payable and other borrowings:										
Insurance and other non-finance businesses[5]	11,894	12,440	12,988	13,179	11,803	3,719	4,349	2,680	3,698	3,583
Railroad, utilities and energy businesses[2]	55,579	46,655	36,156	32,580	31,626	19,579	19,145	19,002	16,946	
Finance and financial products businesses	12,736	13,129	13,592	14,625	15,145	14,611	13,388	12,144	11,961	10,868
Shareholders' equity	240,170	221,890	187,647	164,850	157,318	131,102	109,267	120,733	108,419	91,484
Common shares outstanding, in thousands (A sh.)	1,643	1,644	1,643	1,651	1,648	1,552	1,549	1,548	1,543	1,541
Shareholders' equity per outstanding share	$146,186	$134,973	$114,214	$99,860	$95,453	$84,487	$70,530	$78,008	$70,281	$59,377

Continued...

...Continued from prior page

Footnotes:

1. Insurance premiums earned in 2007 included $7.1 billion from a single reinsurance transaction with Equitas.

2. On February 9, 2006 Berkshire converted its non-voting preferred stock of MidAmerican to common stock, providing it with an 83.4% voting interest. MidAmerican began being consolidated in 2006 (it was previously carried using the equity method).

On February 12, 2010, BNSF became a wholly-owned subsidiary and began to be consolidated. Between December 31, 2008 and February 12, 2010 it was accounted for based on the equity method.

3. After-tax investment gains were as follows: $3,321 $4,337 $2,227   ($521) $1,874 $486   ($4,645) $3,579 $1,709 $3,530

4. 2005: Includes pre-tax underwriting loss of $3.4 billion ($2.2 billion after-tax) attributable to Hurricanes Katrina, Rita, and Wilma.

5. The 2005–09 presentation used "Insurance and other non-finance businesses" and the 2010–14 presentation used "Insurance and other businesses".

Note: Data taken from 2014 (2010–2014) and 2009 (2005–2009) annual reports to maintain consistency with the reporting for each five-year period. Slight differences exist for any particular year depending on the report year.

Sources: Berkshire Hathaway Annual Reports 2009, 2014.

Note: The following table was broken up into multiple sections and spans several pages

Table 7.46: Berkshire Hathaway—Insurance Underwriting

($ millions)	2014 Amount	%	2013 Amount	%	2012 Amount	%	2011 Amount	%	2010 Amount	%
GEICO										
Premiums written	$20,962		$19,083		$17,129		$15,664		$14,494	
Premiums earned	20,496	100.0%	18,572	100.0%	16,740	100.0%	15,363	100.0%	14,283	100.0%
Losses and loss expenses	15,924	77.7%	14,255	76.8%	12,700	75.9%	12,013	78.2%	10,631	74.4%
Underwriting expenses	3,413	16.7%	3,190	17.2%	3,360	20.1%	2,774	18.1%	2,535	17.7%
Total losses and expenses	19,337	94.3%	17,445	93.9%	16,060	95.9%	14,787	96.3%	13,166	92.2%
Underwriting gain (loss) - pre-tax	$1,159	5.7%	$1,127	6.1%	$680	4.1%	$576	3.7%	$1,117	7.8%
General Re										
Premiums written:										
North American property/casualty										
International property/casualty										
Property/casualty	3,257		2,972		2,982		2,910		2,923	
Life/health	3,161		2,991		3,002		2,909		2,709	
Total Gen Re premiums written	$6,418		$5,963		$5,984		$5,819		$5,632	
Premiums earned:										
North American property/casualty										
International property/casualty										
Property/casualty	3,103		3,007		2,904		2,941		2,979	
Life/health	3,161		2,977		2,966		2,875		2,714	
Total Gen Re premiums earned	$6,264		$5,984		$5,870		$5,816		$5,693	
Underwriting gain (loss) pre-tax:										
North American property/casualty										
International property/casualty										
Property/casualty	170	94.5%	148	95.1%	399	86.3%	7	99.8%	289	90.3%
Life/health	107	96.6%	135	95.5%	(44)	101.5%	137	95.2%	163	94.0%
Total Gen Re underwriting gain (loss) - pre-tax	$277	95.6%	$283	95.3%	$355	94.0%	$144	97.5%	$452	92.1%

Continued...

	2014 Amount	2014 %	2013 Amount	2013 %	2012 Amount	2012 %	2011 Amount	2011 %	2010 Amount	2010 %
Berkshire Hathaway Reinsurance Group										
Premiums earned:										
Catastrophe and individual risk	$4,064		$801		$816		$751		$623	
Property/casualty										
Retroactive reinsurance	3,371		328		717		2,011		2,621	
Other multi-line			4,348		5,306		4,224		3,459	
Life and annuity	2,681		3,309		2,833		2,161		2,373	
Total BHRG premiums earned	$10,116		$8,786		$9,672		$9,147		$9,076	
Underwriting gain (loss) pre-tax:										
Catastrophe and individual risk	$1,684	58.6%	$581	27.5%	$400	51.0%	($321)	142.7%	$260	58.3%
Property/casualty										
Retroactive reinsurance	(905)	126.8%	(321)	197.9%	(201)	128.0%	645	67.9%	(90)	103.4%
Other multi-line			655	84.9%	295	94.4%	(338)	108.0%	203	94.1%
Life and annuity[1]	(173)	106.5%	379	88.5%	(190)	106.7%	(700)	132.4%	(197)	108.3%
Total BHRG underwriting gain (loss) - pre-tax	$606	94.0%	$1,294	85.3%	$304	96.9%	($714)	107.8%	$176	98.1%
Berkshire Hathaway Primary Group										
Premiums earned[2]	$4,377	100.0%	$3,342	100.0%	$2,263	100.0%	$1,749	100.0%	$1,697	100.0%
Total losses and expenses	3,751	85.7%	2,957	88.5%	1,977	87.4%	1,507	86.2%	1,429	84.2%
Underwriting gain (loss) - pre-tax	$626	14.3%	$385	11.5%	$286	12.6%	$242	13.8%	$268	15.8%
Total premiums earned	**$41,253**	**100.0%**	**$36,684**	**100.0%**	**$34,545**	**100.0%**	**$32,075**	**100.0%**	**$30,749**	**100.0%**
Total underwriting gain/(loss) pre-tax	**2,668**		**3,089**		**1,625**		**248**		**2,013**	
Average float	**80,581**		**75,183**		**71,848**		**68,202**		**63,872**	
Cost of float	**(3.3%)**		**(4.1%)**		**(2.3%)**		**(0.4%)**		**(3.2%)**	
Aggregate adverse (favorable) loss development3	($1,365)		($1,752)		($2,126)		($2,202)		($2,270)	

Footnotes:
1. The $250 million pre-tax underwriting gain presented for BHRG in 2009 is the updated 2010 figure. The original amount was $349 million. In 2010, Berkshire moved the life and annuity business to BHRG from Finance and Financial Products.
2. 2010–2014: Earned premium figure for the Primary Group is calculated based on the total known earned premiums and the known other segment data. Footnotes disclose rounded figures.
3. Per the notes to the financial statements. Percentage is the ratio of loss development to earned premiums.

Note: Primary Group: Data on written premiums, losses and loss expenses, and underwriting expenses were not disclosed.

Sources: Berkshire Hathaway Annual Reports, 2004–2014, and author's calculations.

($ millions)	2009 Amount	%	2008 Amount	%	2007 Amount	%	2006 Amount	%	2005 Amount	%	2004 Amount	%
GEICO												
Premiums written	$13,758		$12,741		$11,931		$11,303		$10,285		$9,212	
Premiums earned	13,576	100.0%	12,479	100.0%	11,806	100.0%	11,055	100.0%	10,101	100.0%	8,915	100.0%
Losses and loss expenses	10,457	77.0%	9,332	74.8%	8,523	72.2%	7,749	70.1%	7,128	70.6%	6,360	71.3%
Underwriting expenses	2,470	18.2%	2,231	17.9%	2,170	18.4%	1,992	18.0%	1,752	17.3%	1,585	17.8%
Total losses and expenses	12,927	95.2%	11,563	92.7%	10,693	90.6%	9,741	88.1%	8,880	87.9%	7,945	89.1%
Underwriting gain (loss) - pre-tax	$649	4.8%	$916	7.3%	$1,113	9.4%	$1,314	11.9%	$1,221	12.1%	$970	10.9%
General Re												
Premiums written:												
North American property/casualty							$1,731		$1,988		$2,747	
International property/casualty							1,850		1,864		2,091	
Property/casualty	3,091		3,383		3,478							
Life/health	2,630		2,588		2,479		2,368		2,303		2,022	
Total Gen Re premiums written	$5,721		$5,971		$5,957		$5,949		$6,155		$6,860	
Premiums earned:												
North American property/casualty							$1,799		$2,201		$3,012	
International property/casualty							1,912		1,939		2,218	
Property/casualty	3,203		3,434		3,614							
Life/health	2,626		2,580		2,462		2,364		2,295		2,015	
Total Gen Re premiums earned	$5,829		$6,014		$6,076		$6,075		$6,435		$7,245	
Underwriting gain (loss) pre-tax:												
North American property/casualty							$127	92.9%	($307)	113.9%	$11	99.6%
International property/casualty							246	87.1%	(138)	107.1%	(93)	104.2%
Property/casualty	300	90.6%	163	95.3%	475	86.9%						
Life/health	177	93.3%	179	93.1%	80	96.8%	153	93.5%	111	95.2%	85	95.8%
Total Gen Re underwriting gain (loss) - pre-tax	$477	91.8%	$342	94.3%	$555	90.9%	$526	91.3%	($334)	105.2%	$3	100.0%

Continued...

...Continued from prior page

Berkshire Hathaway Reinsurance Group	2009 Amount	2009 %	2008 Amount	2008 %	2007 Amount	2007 %	2006 Amount	2006 %	2005 Amount	2005 %	2004 Amount	2004 %
Premiums earned:												
Catastrophe and individual risk	$823		$955		$1,577		$2,196		$1,663		$1,462	
Property/casualty												
Retroactive reinsurance	1,989		204		7,708		146		10		188	
Other multi-line	3,894		3,923		2,617		2,634		2,290		2,064	
Life and annuity												
Total BHRG premiums earned	$6,706		$5,082		$11,902		$4,976		$3,963		$3,714	
Underwriting gain (loss) pre-tax:												
Catastrophe and individual risk	$782	5.0%	$776	18.7%	$1,477	6.3%	$1,588	27.7%	$(1,178)	170.8%	$385	73.7%
Property/casualty												
Retroactive reinsurance	(448)	122.5%	(414)	302.9%	(375)	104.9%	(173)	218.5%	(214)	NM	(412)	319.1%
Other multi-line	15	99.6%	962	75.5%	325	87.6%	243	90.8%	323	85.9%	444	78.5%
Life and annuity[1]	(99)	n/a										
Total BHRG underwriting gain (loss) - pre-tax	$250	96.3%	$1,324	73.9%	$1,427	88.0%	$1,658	66.7%	$(1,069)	127.0%	$417	88.8%
Berkshire Hathaway Primary Group												
Premiums earned[2]	$1,773	100.0%	$1,950	100.0%	$1,999	100.0%	$1,858	100.0%	$1,498	100.0%	$1,211	100.0%
Total losses and expenses	1,689	95.3%	1,740	89.2%	1,720	86.0%	1,518	81.7%	1,263	84.3%	1,050	86.7%
Underwriting gain (loss) - pre-tax	$84	4.7%	$210	10.8%	$279	14.0%	$340	18.3%	$235	15.7%	$161	13.3%
Total premiums earned	**$27,884**		**$25,525**		**$31,783**		**$23,964**		**$21,997**		**$21,085**	
Total underwriting gain/(loss) pre-tax	**1,460**		**2,792**		**3,374**		**3,838**		**53**		**1,551**	
Average float	**60,200**		**58,593**		**54,793**		**50,087**		**47,691**		**45,157**	
Cost of float	**(2.6%)**		**(4.8%)**		**(6.2%)**		**(7.7%)**		**(0.1%)**		**(3.4%)**	
Aggregate adverse (favorable) loss development[3]	($905)		($1,140)		($1,478)		($612)		($357)		$419	

Footnotes:
1. The $250 million pre-tax underwriting gain presented for BHRG in 2009 is the updated 2010 figure. The original amount was $349 million. In 2010, Berkshire moved the life and annuity business to BHRG from Finance and Financial Products.
2. 2010–2014: Earned premium figure for the Primary Group is calculated based on the total known earned premiums and the known other segment data. Footnotes disclose rounded figures.
3. Per the notes to the financial statements. Percentage is the ratio of loss development to earned premiums.

Note: Primary Group: Data on written premiums, losses and loss expenses, and underwriting expenses were not disclosed.

Sources: Berkshire Hathaway Annual Reports, 2004–2014, and author's calculations.

Table 7.47: Berkshire Hathaway—Insurance Underwriting

($ millions)	2004	2005	2006	2007	2008	2009	2010	2011	2012	2013	2014
GEICO											
Premiums written	$9,212	$10,285	$11,303	$11,931	$12,741	$13,758	$14,494	$15,664	$17,129	$19,083	$20,962
Premiums earned	8,915	10,101	11,055	11,806	12,479	13,576	14,283	15,363	16,740	18,572	20,496
Underwriting gain/(loss) - pre-tax	$970	$1,221	$1,314	$1,113	$916	$649	$1,117	$576	$680	$1,127	$1,159
General Re											
Premiums written	$6,860	$6,155	$5,949	$5,957	$5,971	$5,721	$5,632	$5,819	$5,984	$5,963	$6,418
Premiums earned	7,245	6,435	6,075	6,076	6,014	5,829	5,693	5,816	5,870	5,984	6,264
Underwriting gain/(loss) - pre-tax	$3	($334)	$526	$555	$342	$477	$452	$144	$355	$283	$277
Berkshire Hathaway Reinsurance Group											
Premiums earned	$3,714	$3,963	$4,976	$11,902	$5,082	$6,706	$9,076	$9,147	$9,672	$8,786	$10,116
Underwriting gain/(loss) - pre-tax[1]	$417	($1,069)	$1,658	$1,427	$1,324	$250	$176	($714)	$304	$1,294	$606
Berkshire Hathaway Primary Group											
Premiums earned[2]	$1,211	$1,498	$1,858	$1,999	$1,950	$1,773	$1,697	$1,749	$2,263	$3,342	$4,377
Underwriting gain/(loss) - pre-tax	$161	$235	$340	$279	$210	$84	$268	$242	$286	$385	$626
Total premiums earned[2]	$21,085	$21,997	$23,964	$31,783	$25,525	$27,884	$30,749	$32,075	$34,545	$36,684	$41,253
Total underwriting gain/(loss) - pre-tax	1,551	53	3,838	3,374	2,792	1,460	2,013	248	1,625	3,089	2,668
Average float	45,157	47,691	50,087	54,793	58,593	60,200	63,872	68,202	71,848	75,183	80,581
Cost of float	(3.4%)	(0.1%)	(7.7%)	(6.2%)	(4.8%)	(2.6%)	(3.2%)	(0.4%)	(2.3%)	(4.1%)	(3.3%)
Aggregate adverse (favorable) loss development[2]	$419	($357)	($612)	($1,478)	($1,140)	($905)	($2,270)	($2,202)	($2,126)	($1,752)	($1,365)
Discount accretion and amortization charges included above	$538	$386	$459	$315	$550	$602	$356	$342	$381	$186	$128

Footnotes:
1. The $250 million pre-tax underwriting gain presented for BHRG in 2009 is the updated 2010 figure. The original amount was $349 million. In 2010, Berkshire moved the life and annuity business to BHRG from Finance and Financial Products.
2. Per the notes to the financial statements. Percentage is the ratio of loss development to earned premiums.

Note: Berkshire Hathaway Primary Group and BHRG written premiums were not detailed.

Sources: Berkshire Hathaway Annual Reports 2004–2014 and author's calculations.

Table 7.48: Berkshire Hathaway Insurance Group float, select data and information

				Year-end Float ($ millions)				
Year	GEICO	General Reins.	BH Reins.	Other Primary	Total	Avg. Float	Float Cost
2004	5,960	23,120	15,278	1,736	46,094	45,157	(3.4%)
2005	6,692	22,920	16,233	3,442	49,287	47,691	(0.1%)
2006	7,171	22,827	16,860	4,029	50,887	50,087	(7.7%)
2007	7,768	23,009	23,692	4,229	58,698	54,793	(6.2%)
2008	8,454	21,074	24,221	4,739	58,488	58,593	(4.8%)
2009	9,613	21,014	26,223	5,061	61,911	60,200	(2.6%)
2010	10,272	20,049	30,370	5,141	65,832	63,872	(3.2%)
2011	11,169	19,714	33,728	5,960	70,571	68,202	(0.4%)
2012	11,578	20,128	34,821	6,598	73,125	71,848	(2.3%)
2013	12,566	20,013	37,231	7,430	77,240	75,183	(4.1%)
2014	13,569	19,280	42,454	8,618	83,921	80,581	(3.3%)

			Year-end Float (% Growth)			
Year	GEICO	General Reins.	BH Reins.	Other Primary	Total	Avg. Float
2004	12.7%	(2.3%)	9.5%	30.4%	4.2%	5.7%
2005	12.3%	(0.9%)	6.3%	98.3%	6.9%	5.6%
2006	7.2%	(0.4%)	3.9%	17.1%	3.2%	5.0%
2007	8.3%	0.8%	40.5%	5.0%	15.3%	9.4%
2008	8.8%	(8.4%)	2.2%	12.1%	(0.4%)	6.9%
2009	13.7%	(0.3%)	8.3%	6.8%	5.9%	2.7%
2010	6.9%	(4.6%)	15.8%	1.6%	6.3%	6.1%
2011	8.7%	(1.7%)	11.1%	15.9%	7.2%	6.8%
2012	3.7%	2.1%	3.2%	10.7%	3.6%	5.3%
2013	8.5%	(0.6%)	6.9%	12.6%	5.6%	4.6%
2014	8.0%	(3.7%)	14.0%	16.0%	8.6%	7.2%

		Year-end Float (% Total)			
Year	GEICO	General Reins.	BH Reins.	Other Primary	Total
2004	12.9%	50.2%	33.1%	3.8%	100.0%
2005	13.6%	46.5%	32.9%	7.0%	100.0%
2006	14.1%	44.9%	33.1%	7.9%	100.0%
2007	13.2%	39.2%	40.4%	7.2%	100.0%
2008	14.5%	36.0%	41.4%	8.1%	100.0%
2009	15.5%	33.9%	42.4%	8.2%	100.0%
2010	15.6%	30.5%	46.1%	7.8%	100.0%
2011	15.8%	27.9%	47.8%	8.4%	100.0%
2012	15.8%	27.5%	47.6%	9.0%	100.0%
2013	16.3%	25.9%	48.2%	9.6%	100.0%
2014	16.2%	23.0%	50.6%	10.3%	100.0%

Sources: Berkshire Hathaway Annual Reports and author's calculations.

Table 7.49: Berkshire Hathaway property and casualty loss development

($ millions)	2014	2013	2012	2011	2010	2009	2008	2007	2006	2005	2004
Net unpaid losses net of discounts/deferred charges end of year[1]	60,589	57,452	57,216	56,727	53,530	52,537	49,487	48,876	42,779	42,834	40,087
Liability re-estimated:											
1 year later		55,421	55,557	54,787	51,228	49,955	48,836	47,288	41,811	42,723	39,002
2 years later			53,961	53,600	49,960	47,636	47,293	46,916	40,456	42,468	39,456
3 years later				52,526	49,143	46,793	45,675	45,902	40,350	41,645	39,608
4 years later					48,262	46,099	45,337	44,665	39,198	41,676	38,971
5 years later						45,630	44,914	44,618	38,003	40,884	39,317
6 years later							44,659	44,406	37,946	39,888	38,804
7 years later								44,355	37,631	40,088	38,060
8 years later									37,192	39,796	38,280
9 years later										39,472	38,189
10 years later											37,943
Cumulative deficiency (redundancy)		(2,031)	(3,255)	(4,201)	(5,268)	(6,907)	(4,828)	(4,521)	(5,587)	(3,362)	(2,144)
Cumulative foreign exchange effect		666	461	280	361	590	381	961	540	85	618
Net deficiency (redundancy)		(1,365)	(2,794)	(3,921)	(4,907)	(6,317)	(4,447)	(3,560)	(5,047)	(3,277)	(1,526)
Cumulative payments:											
1 year later		11,381	10,978	10,628	8,854	9,191	8,315	8,486	8,865	9,345	7,793
2 years later			17,827	17,260	14,593	14,265	13,999	13,394	13,581	15,228	12,666
3 years later				21,747	18,300	17,952	16,900	17,557	16,634	18,689	16,463
4 years later					22,008	20,907	19,478	19,608	19,724	20,890	18,921
5 years later						22,896	21,786	21,660	21,143	23,507	20,650
6 years later							23,339	23,595	22,678	24,935	22,865
7 years later								24,807	23,892	26,266	24,232
8 years later									24,831	26,928	25,430
9 years later										28,031	26,624
10 years later											26,917
Net deficiency (redundancy) above		(1,365)	(2,794)	(3,921)	(4,907)	(6,317)	(4,447)	(3,560)	(5,047)	(3,277)	(1,526)
Deficiency from deferred charge amortization and discount accretion		128	306	645	989	1,698	1,806	1,970	2,157	2,591	2,726
(Redundancy) deficiency before deferred charge amortization and discount accretion		(1,493)	(3,100)	(4,566)	(5,896)	(8,015)	(6,253)	(5,530)	(7,204)	(5,868)	(4,252)

Footnote:
1. The full loss development table in the 10K report starts with gross unpaid losses and includes such items as reserve discounts, ceded reserves, and deferred charges. I've chosen to begin the table here due to space limitations.

Source: Berkshire Hathaway 10K filing, 2014.

Table 7.50: Regulated, Capital-Intensive Businesses

($ millions)	2014	2013	2012	2011	2010	2009	2008	2007	2006	2005
Berkshire Hathaway Energy										
(formerly known as MidAmerican Energy)										
UK utilities	$527	$362	$429	$469	$333	$248	$339	$337	$338	$308
Iowa utility	298	230	236	279	279	285	425	412	348	288
Nevada utility	549									
PacifiCorp (primarily Oregon and Utah)	1,010	982	737	771	783	788	703	692	356	
Gas Pipelines (Northern Natural and Kern River)	379	385	383	388	378	457	595	473	376	309
HomeServices	139	139	82	39	42	43	(45)	42	74	148
Other (net)	236	4	91	36	47	25	186	130	226	115
Operating earnings before corporate interest and taxes	3,138	2,102	1,958	1,982	1,862	1,846	2,203	2,086	1,718	1,168
Constellation Energy[1]							1,092			
Interest	427	296	314	336	353	376	443	420	395	357
Income taxes	616	170	172	315	271	313	1,002	477	407	248
Net earnings	$2,095	$1,636	$1,472	$1,331	$1,238	$1,157	$1,850	$1,189	$916	$563
Net earnings applicable to Berkshire[2]	$1,882	$1,470	$1,323	$1,204	$1,131	$1,071	$1,704	$1,114	$885	$523
Burlington Northern Santa Fe (BNSF)	2014	2013	2012	2011	2010	2009	2008	2007	2006	2005
Revenues	$23,239	$22,014	$20,835	$19,548	$16,850	$14,016	$18,018	$15,802	$14,985	$12,987
Operating expenses (including depreciation)	16,237	15,357	14,835	14,247	12,355	10,762	14,106	12,316	11,508	10,102
Operating earnings before interest and taxes	7,002	6,657	6,000	5,301	4,495	3,254	3,912	3,486	3,477	2,885
Interest (net)	833	729	623	560	507	613	533	511	485	437
Income taxes	2,300	2,135	2,005	1,769	1,529	920	1,253	1,128	1,105	917
Net earnings	$3,869	$3,793	$3,372	$2,972	$2,459	$1,721	$2,126	$1,847	$1,887	$1,531

Footnotes:
1. Constellation Energy consists of a $175 million breakup fee and $917 million profit on investment.
2. Earnings applicable to Berkshire consist of its share of net earnings plus after tax interest income from debt owed to Berkshire from MidAmerican.

Notes:
1. BNSF owned from February 12, 2010. Historical data provided for reference.
2. PacifiCorp owned from March 21, 2006.

Sources: Berkshire Hathaway Annual Reports 2006, 2008, 2010, 2012, 2014; BNSF Annual Report 2006; BNSF 10K 2009.

Table 7.51: Manufacturing, Service, and Retailing businesses—balance sheets, 2004–2014

($ millions)	2014	2013	2012	2011	2010	2009	2008	2007	2006	2005	2004
Assets											
Cash and equivalents	$5,765	$6,625	$5,338	$4,241	$2,673	$3,018	$2,497	$2,080	$1,543	$1,004	$899
Accounts and notes receivable	8,264	7,749	7,382	6,584	5,396	5,066	5,047	4,488	3,793	3,287	3,074
Inventory	10,236	9,945	9,675	8,975	7,101	6,147	7,500	5,793	5,257	4,143	3,842
Other current assets	1,117	716	734	631	550	625	752	470	363	342	254
Total current assets	$25,382	$25,035	$23,129	$20,431	$15,720	$14,856	$15,796	$12,831	$10,956	$8,776	$8,069
Goodwill and other intangibles	28,107	25,617	26,017	24,755	16,976	16,499	16,515	14,201	13,314	9,260	8,362
Fixed assets	13,806	19,389	18,871	17,866	15,421	15,374	16,338	9,605	8,934	7,148	6,161
Other assets	3,793	4,274	3,416	3,661	3,029	2,070	1,248	1,685	1,168	1,021	1,044
	$71,088	$74,315	$71,433	$66,713	$51,146	$48,799	$49,897	$38,322	$34,372	$26,205	$23,636
Liabilities and Equity											
Notes payable	$965	$1,615	$1,454	$1,611	$1,805	$1,842	$2,212	$1,278	$1,468	$1,469	$1,143
Other current liabilities	9,734	8,965	8,527	15,124	8,169	7,414	8,087	7,652	6,635	5,371	4,685
Total current liabilities	10,699	10,580	9,981	16,735	9,974	9,256	10,299	8,930	8,103	6,840	5,828
Deferred taxes	3,801	5,184	4,907	4,661	3,001	2,834	2,786	828	540	338	248
Term debt and other liabilities	4,269	4,405	5,826	6,214	6,621	6,240	6,033	3,079	3,014	2,188	1,965
Non-controlling interests	492	456	2,062	2,410							
Equity	51,827	53,690	48,657	36,693	31,550	30,469	30,779	25,485	22,715	16,839	15,595
	$71,088	$74,315	$71,433	$66,713	$51,146	$48,799	$49,897	$38,322	$34,372	$26,205	$23,636

Note: In 2014 Marmon's leasing operations began to be included in the Finance and Financial Products sector. The 2014 Annual Report provided a restatement of 2012 and 2013 for comparative purposes. This presentation contains the original presentations.

Sources: Berkshire Hathaway Annual Reports 2004–2014.

Table 7.52: Manufacturing, Service, and Retailing businesses—income statements, 2004–2014

($ millions)	2014	2013	2012	2011	2010	2009	2008	2007	2006	2005	2004
Revenues	$97,689	$95,291	$83,255	$72,406	$66,610	$61,665	$66,099	$59,100	$52,660	$46,896	$44,142
Operating expenses	90,788	88,414	76,978	67,239	62,225	59,509	61,937	55,026	49,002	44,190	41,604
(Including depreciation)				*1,431*	*1,362*	*1,422*	*1,280*	*955*	*823*	*699*	*676*
Interest expense (net)	109	135	146	130	111	98	139	127	132	83	57
Pre-tax income[1]	6,792	6,742	6,131	5,037	4,274	2,058	4,023	3,947	3,526	2,623	2,481
Income taxes and non-controlling interests	2,324	2,512	2,432	1,998	1,812	945	1,740	1,594	1,395	977	941
Net income	$4,468	$4,230	$3,699	$3,039	$2,462	$1,113	$2,283	$2,353	$2,131	$1,646	$1,540

Footnote:
Excludes purchase-accounting adjustments.

Sources: Berkshire Hathaway Annual Reports 2004–2014.

Table 7.53: Manufacturing, Service, and Retailing businesses—ratios and key figures, 2004–2014

	2014	2013	2012	2011	2010	2009	2008	2007	2006	2005	2004
Tangible capital	$28,954	$34,093	$29,920	$19,763	$23,000	$22,052	$22,509	$15,641	$13,883	$11,236	$10,341
Revenues/average tangible capital	$3.10	$2.98	$3.35	$3.39	$2.96	$2.77	$3.47	$4.00	$4.19	$4.35	$4.27
EBIT margin	7.1%	7.2%	7.5%	7.1%	6.6%	3.5%	6.3%	6.9%	6.9%	5.8%	5.7%
Pre-tax return on tangible capital	21.9%	21.5%	25.3%	24.2%	19.5%	9.7%	21.8%	27.6%	29.1%	25.1%	24.5%
Return on average equity - after-tax	8.5%	8.3%	8.7%	8.9%	7.9%	3.6%	8.1%	9.8%	10.8%	10.1%	9.9%
Return on average tangible equity after-tax	17.3%	16.7%	21.4%	22.9%	17.3%	7.9%	17.9%	22.8%	25.1%	22.2%	21.6%
Net debt (cash)	($531)	($605)	$1,942	$3,584	$5,753	$5,064	$5,748	$2,277	$2,939	$2,653	$2,209
Notes payable/equity	10.1%	11.2%	15.0%	21.3%	26.7%	26.5%	26.8%	17.1%	19.7%	21.7%	19.9%
Total assets/total equity	1.37	1.38	1.47	1.82	1.62	1.60	1.62	1.50	1.51	1.56	1.52

Sources: Berkshire Hathaway Annual Reports 2004–2014 and author's calculations.

Table 7.54: Finance and Financial Products businesses—select earnings data

($ millions)	2014	2013	2012	2011	2010	2009	2008	2007	2006	2005	2004
Net investment income	$296	$324	$410	$440		$278	$330	$272	$274	$200	$264
Gen Re Securities[1]								(60)	(5)	(104)	(44)
Life and annuity operation[2]						116	23		29	11	(57)
Value Capital[3]									6	(33)	30
Berkadia	122	80	35	25							1
Leasing operations											
CORT[4]	36	40	42	29							
XTRA[4]	147	125	106	126							
Marmon – Containers and Cranes[4]	238										
Marmon – Railcars[4]	442										
Leasing operations – subtotal[4]	863	165	148	155	53	14	87	111	182	173	92
Manufactured housing finance (Clayton)	558	416	255	154	176	187	206	526	513	416	220
Other[5]					460	186	141	157	158	159	78
Pre-tax earnings	$1,839	$985	$848	$774	$689	$781	$787	$1,006	$1,157	$822	$584

Footnotes:
1. Gen Re Securities ceased in 2006. Cumulative pre-tax loss since 2002 was $409 million on 23,218 contracts.
2. Beginning in 2010 the life and annuity operation was moved to Berkshire Hathaway Reinsurance Group.
3. Investment in Value Capital ceased in 2006.
4. In 2014 results included Marmon's leasing operations. The report that year included a restatement of the prior two years for comparative purposes. Data here are the original presentation. The restated total pre-tax income for 2013 and 2012 was $1,564 million and $1,393 million, respectively.
5. Included in Other are fees paid to Berkshire from Clayton and Netjets for use of its credit.

Notes: Beginning in 2010 Berkshire stopped producing this table in the Chairman's letter. In 2012 data again began to be presented in the letter. Amounts for Leasing and Clayton in 2010 are from the footnotes and are included for continuity.

Sources: Berkshire Hathaway Annual Reports 2004–2014 and author's calculations.

Table 7.55: Berkshire Hathaway deferred tax analysis

($ millions)	2014	2013	2012	2011	2010	2009	2008	2007	2006	2005	Total
Earnings before income taxes	$28,105	$28,796	$22,236	$15,314	$19,051	$11,552	$7,574	$20,161	$16,778	$12,791	$182,358
Current taxes	3,302	5,168	4,711	2,897	3,668	1,619	3,811	5,708	5,030	2,057	37,971
Deferred taxes	4,633	3,783	2,213	1,671	1,939	1,919	(1,833)	886	475	2,102	17,788
Total taxes as reported	7,935	8,951	6,924	4,568	5,607	3,538	1,978	6,594	5,505	4,159	55,759
Cash paid for tax during period	4,014	5,401	4,695	2,885	3,547	2,032	3,530	5,895	4,959	2,695	39,653
Current rate	11.7%	17.9%	21.2%	18.9%	19.3%	14.0%	50.3%	28.3%	30.0%	16.1%	20.8%
Deferred rate	16.5%	13.1%	10.0%	10.9%	10.2%	16.6%	(24.2%)	4.4%	2.8%	16.4%	9.8%
Headline tax rate	28.2%	31.1%	31.1%	29.8%	29.4%	30.6%	26.1%	32.7%	32.8%	32.5%	30.6%
Current as % total	41.6%	57.7%	68.0%	63.4%	65.4%	45.8%	192.7%	86.6%	91.4%	49.5%	68.1%
Deferred as % total	58.4%	42.3%	32.0%	36.6%	34.6%	54.2%	(92.7%)	13.4%	8.6%	50.5%	31.9%
Total tax	100.0%	100.0%	100.0%	100.0%	100.0%	100.0%	100.0%	100.0%	100.0%	100.0%	100.0%
Cash tax as % EBIT	14.3%	18.8%	21.1%	18.8%	18.6%	17.6%	46.6%	29.2%	29.6%	21.1%	21.7%

Sources: Berkshire Hathaway Annual Reports 2005, 2008, 2011, 2014; and author's calculations.

Chapter 8
The First Fifty Years: 1965–2014

"It is not necessary to do extraordinary things
to get extraordinary results."
—Warren Buffett

E xtraordinary is the only word that singularly captures the arc of Berkshire
Hathaway's fifty-year transformation under Warren Buffett's control.
The company that existed at the end of 2014 looked *nothing* like it did
fifty years earlier despite bearing the same name. The struggling textile company
that once formed the foundation of Berkshire Hathaway had cracked, leading to
major structural issues that once rebuilt became a well-respected conglomerate. Its
extraordinary transformation took place using what in hindsight were fairy ordinary
and timeless basic principles of business. Applied step by step, year by year, and
decade by decade, the ordinary was molded into the extraordinary.

Berkshire's transformation can easily be attributed to the one man who was the
constant during this time. Yet Buffett is only part of the story—albeit a big part. The
other man is Charlie Munger, whom Buffett credited as the architect of Berkshire
Hathaway for his influence turning Berkshire's focus toward buying good businesses
to hold for the long term. "The blueprint he gave me was very simple. Forget what
you know about buying fair businesses at wonderful prices; instead buy wonderful
businesses at fair prices."

These businesses were deceptively simple. Yes, they were in understandable industries
such as insurance, retail, manufacturing, newspapers, and financing. But many shared a
trait that most businesses only wish for: an economic moat or a sustainable competitive

advantage. Berkshire's protective umbrella and autonomous operating philosophy were a system that maximized human potential and allowed businesses to flourish.[*]

Berkshire Hathaway's story also includes hundreds of owners and families that built up the many companies Berkshire came to own after shifting focus away from textiles. It includes the hundreds of thousands of employees that worked along with them. And it includes the hundreds of thousands of shareholders who made a long-term commitment to the company. Berkshire, then, is an amalgamation of these parts, all working together over a very long period.

In 1965, when Buffett took over, Berkshire Hathaway did not make the Fortune 500 list.[**] In 2014, it was number four behind Walmart, Exxon Mobil, and Chevron and ahead of Apple.[108] We can see the evolution of the company by examining its history in the broad decades-long periods outlined in this book.

1965–1974

Table 8.1: Select data

($ millions)	1974	1964	Change
Revenues	$101.5	$50.0	103%
Pre-tax operating earnings	6.5	0.5	1,128%
Average float	79.1	0	n/a
Shareholders' equity	88.2	22.1	298%
Book value per share	$90.02	$19.46	363%

Sources: Berkshire Hathaway Annual Reports 1965, 1974.

After taking control of Berkshire in May 1965, Buffett quickly learned how difficult it was to operate a commodity business in a declining industry. Buffett's raw material was a dying textile company with $22 million in net worth, no durable competitive advantage, and high capital costs. He quickly set to work redeploying as much of the available capital as possible into other businesses.

Two seminal acquisitions occurred during this decade that shaped the future trajectory of Berkshire Hathaway. One was the acquisition of National Indemnity, which became the platform for future expansion into insurance. Buffett quickly grasped the value of low-cost liabilities in the form of float to fuel expansion in other areas. The beginnings of Berkshire's insurance activities provided valuable lessons on the importance of focusing on underwriting profitability above all else. The second influential acquisition was See's Candies. See's provided lessons on the value in buying

---

[*] To the extent the businesses had the potential to flourish. No system could have stopped the few businesses that floundered, such as Dexter.
[**] Its last appearance was 1959 when it ranked 499th.

great businesses for keeps. It set the bar very high for future acquisitions and was a marked contrast to its sister textile companies.

Buffett made other important capital allocation decisions during this time. Berkshire purchased a newspaper, a bank, and made investments in marketable securities. One of those marketable securities was Blue Chip Stamps. Deploying the float in the shrinking trading stamps business, Buffett and Munger used Blue Chip Stamps as a platform to acquire See's, and eventually other good businesses before the core trading stamps business withered to almost nothing.

By the end of the decade, textiles had shrunk from the entirety of Berkshire Hathaway's business to about 30% of consolidated revenues and just 5% of total assets. The decline came from a combination of shrinking textile operations and expanding into new business lines. Textiles remained much longer than they probably would have had Buffett not chosen Berkshire as his investment vehicle.

1975–1984

Table 8.2: Select data

($ millions)	1984	1974	Change
Revenues	$729	$101.5	618%
Pre-tax operating earnings	82.0	6.5	1,165%
Average float	253	79	220%
Shareholders' equity	1,272	88.2	1,342%
Book value per share	$1,109	$90.02	1,132%

Sources: Berkshire Hathaway Annual Reports 1974, 1984.

The decade that ended in 1984 was marked by continued expansion of insurance operations and the acquisition of other non-insurance operating businesses. Written insurance premiums swelled 129% from $61 million in 1974 to $140 million in 1984 as Berkshire expanded operations organically and by forming numerous insurance companies. Its entry into reinsurance meant not only more float, but also longer-lived float. The big news of the decade was the acquisition of 36% of GEICO. Berkshire's share of GEICOs premium volume amounted to $336 million—which dwarfed its home-grown operations.

This decade also witnessed the mergers of Diversified Retailing and Blue Chip Stamps into Berkshire. With Blue Chip Stamps came Wesco, yet another platform for expansion, this time into banking and insurance. Through Blue Chip Stamps, Berkshire acquired other non-insurance operations including *The Buffalo News* and Precision Steel.

The non-insurance companies acquired during this decade illustrated Buffett's appreciation of locally dominant businesses. While *The Buffalo News* experienced some initial threats, Buffett and Munger saw that one-newspaper towns would create a protective moat allowing for superior returns on capital. Buffalo was a two-paper town at the time of the acquisition but became a one-paper town within five years with *The Buffalo News* the last one standing. Buffett also correctly identified Nebraska Furniture Mart as a dominant local business whose competitive advantage was created and reinforced by low margins coupled with huge volumes.

Berkshire's investment activities during this period showed the value of taking partial ownership interests in wonderful companies. Gains from the investment portfolio were responsible for 58% of the increase in Berkshire's net worth during this decade compared to just 11% the prior decade. The investment portfolio reflected lessons learned elsewhere. Berkshire's success owning *The Washington Post* stock and *The Buffalo News* led it to invest in other media company stocks including American Broadcasting Companies, Inc., Capital Cities, and Time, Inc. Other stocks acquired during this time were mostly in simple, understandable businesses whose share prices had declined out of line with their underlying intrinsic values.

Like a threadbare shirt, the last bit of Berkshire Hathaway's original business held on through this decade. By the end of 1984, though, the writing was on the wall for textiles. Almost immediately after acquiring Waumbec Mills, it was recognized as a mistake. The additional textile mill was eventually shuttered and faded along with the remainder of Berkshire's original textile operations. Textiles were no longer a profitable business.

1985–1994

Table 8.3: Select data

($ millions)	1994	1984	Change
Revenues	$3,847	$729	428%
Pre-tax operating earnings	839	88	857%
Average float	3,057	253	1,108%
Shareholders' equity	11,875	1,272	834%
Book value per share	$10,083	$1,109	809%

Note: The figure for 1984 operating earnings presented here uses the revised presentation for comparability with 1994.
Sources: Berkshire Hathaway Annual Reports 1984, 1994.

The decade that ended in 1994 marked when Berkshire hit its stride. During this decade, Berkshire perfected its understanding of insurance. It lost money in all but two of these years (1993–94) and used those lessons to engrain in the entire organization a philosophy of underwriting profitably first and foremost. Berkshire moved confidently into reinsurance and generated huge amounts of float to invest in marketable securities. Its strong balance sheet provided a double benefit. One was little restriction on where it could invest its float. Another was the ability to advertise its financial strength to attract additional reinsurance business.

The major capital allocation decisions made during this decade were not complicated. Some of the businesses, such as Scott Fetzer and Fechheimer, were easy to understand but had been shunned by others. Berkshire provided a permanent home for these and many other simple businesses, and importantly allowed managers to operate with autonomy almost unheard of in corporate America. Buffett could do this because of a basic tenet he followed "to go into business only with people whom I like, trust, and admire."

The marketable securities portfolio was responsible for 68% of the increase in Berkshire's net worth during this period. Here too the investments were not complicated and easy to fully understand in hindsight. Berkshire's experience with See's Candies led it to acquire a large stake in The Coca-Cola Company. Other investments during the decade included banks and consumer goods companies. Some of the investments, such as *The Washington Post*, ABC (which had merged with Capital Cities), and GEICO remained undisturbed and were viewed as near-permanent investments. Buffett's commentary to shareholders highlighted the large look-through earnings* the portfolio represented to Berkshire and by extension its shareholders.

The decade was not without its mistakes. Buffett later pointed to the acquisition of Dexter Shoe as the worst in Berkshire's history because of the shares issued to acquire a business whose value quickly evaporated. Two of Berkshire's investments in convertible preferred stocks also caused trouble. USAir almost caused a loss. And its Salomon preferred caused a major distraction for Berkshire when Buffett temporarily took the helm of the investment bank to save it, something he had never done before. This short stint proved the advantages of allowing subsidiaries much autonomy.

Berkshire Hathaway ended 1994 free of the financial and managerial drag of the dying textile business, having shuttered the last of the operations in 1986.

1995–2004

Table 8.4: Select data

($ millions)	2004	1994	Change
Revenues	$74,382	$3,847	1,834%
Pre-tax operating earnings	7,447	839	787%
Average float	45,157	3,057	1,377%
Shareholders' equity	85,900	11,875	623%
Book value per share	$55,824	$10,083	454%

Sources: Berkshire Hathaway Annual Reports 1994, 2004.

---

* Berkshire's share of retained earnings not paid out as dividends.

The 1995–2004 decade represented a rounding out and expansion of Berkshire's core operations. It also set the stage for the next phase of Berkshire's existence. During this decade Berkshire purchased the remaining half of GEICO it did not already own. It also acquired General Re by issuing shares. These insurance acquisitions were the final two pieces of Berkshire's insurance empire, which now included a major auto insurer, two reinsurance operations, and a host of smaller primary insurers that filled various niches of the insurance world. The acquisitions and organic growth swelled average float nearly fifteenfold to $45 billion.

Berkshire acquired dozens of simple and essential non-insurance businesses during this decade. Many were shunned over emerging tech companies during the dot-com boom of the early 2000s. The numerous larger acquisitions in the non-insurance category were bolstered by many more bolt-on acquisitions. These fell under the direction of existing management and caused little to no additional work at headquarters.

The acquisition of MidAmerican set the stage for Berkshire's future. In the utility Berkshire obtained an outlet for its growing streams of cash. Future returns would be lower in more capital-intensive businesses like utilities, but the certainty attached to those capital outlays and ability to invest large sums of incremental capital made it an attractive platform. Berkshire's large base of taxable income elsewhere within the conglomerate provided an added advantage to its utility operations not available to its standalone peers.

Berkshire ended the decade with $40 billion in cash and not enough attractive outlets to invest in despite the frenzy of acquisition activity. The idle cash was a symptom of Berkshire's growing size and the shrinking universe of investment opportunities available to move the needle.

2005–2014

Table 8.5: Select data

($ millions)	2014	2004	Change
Revenues	$194,673	$74,382	162%
Pre-tax operating earnings	24,024	7,447	223%
Average float	80,581	45,157	78%
Shareholders' equity	240,170	85,900	180%
Book value per share	$146,186	$55,824	162%

Sources: Berkshire Hathaway Annual Reports 2004, 2014.

The decade that ended in 2014 may well have been the last where Berkshire was able to retain most of its earnings. Its rate of growth in book value per share slowed dramatically as cash accumulated without enough investment opportunities.

Berkshire implemented a buyback policy and bought back its own shares on two occasions totaling $1.7 billion.

The acquisitions made during this decade were numerous. It ended the decade with the Powerhouse Five, consisting of Iscar, Marmon, BNSF, Lubrizol, and Berkshire Hathaway Energy (formerly MidAmerican). Only the last was around in 2005. These businesses were easy to understand and provided a product or service sure to be needed long into the future. Two of them (BNSF and Lubrizol) were large public companies before joining Berkshire. With BNSF, Berkshire gained another utility-like operation that could take massive amounts of capital investment. These and numerous other acquisitions (including many bolt-on acquisitions) resulted in 70% of the change in net worth coming from operations, up from 26% the previous decade.

Berkshire's size and cash reserves had its advantages. During the Great Recession of the mid-2000s, it made very attractive fixed maturity investments at a time of very low interest rates when other businesses were short on cash. Berkshire also secured significant equity stakes along with them. Berkshire's unparalleled balance sheet strength created reinsurance opportunities other companies couldn't offer, including a single premium totaling $7.1 billion.

Concentrated Investments

Examining the broad arch, we can see that this half-century of Berkshire Hathaway's history consisted of a series of large, concentrated capital allocation decisions mixed with many smaller ones (see Table 8.6). At the end of the decade, Berkshire's equity investments were highly concentrated, with the Big Four (American Express, Coca-Cola, IBM, and Wells Fargo) accounting for 59% of the portfolio. Berkshire's acquisitions were similarly concentrated. The largest acquisition in each decade represented no less than 15% of equity capital at the time of acquisition. Berkshire's capital allocation strategy was one of patient opportunism. It made or held large partial interests in companies via the stock market and acquired successively larger companies as each decade went on.

Table 8.6: Significant capital allocation decisions by decade

Decade ended:	1974	1984	1994	2004	2014
Common stock portfolio:					
Largest single common stock investment (% of portfolio[1])	23%	31%	34%	23%	23%
Top four common stock investments (% of portfolio)	47%	75%	57%	65%	59%
Top four (% of average equity at end of year)	20%	79%	78%	30%	30%
Acquisitions (% average equity capital at time of purchase):					
Illinois National Bank & Trust (1969)	44%				
National Indemnity (1967)	28%				
Buffalo News (1977)[2]		15%			
Nebraska Furniture Mart (1983)		6%			
Scott Fetzer (1986)			19%		
Dexter Shoe (1993)			4%		
General Re (1998)[3]				18%	
GEICO (1996)[4]				12%	
BNSF (2010)[5]					18%
Heinz (2013)[6]					6%

Footnotes:
1. Washington Post (1974); GEICO (1984); Coca-Cola (1994); American Express (2004); Wells Fargo (2014).
2. Buffalo News acquisition price compared to the combined average equity of Berkshire Hathaway, Blue Chip Stamps, and Diversified Retailing.
3. Size of General Re acquisition based on the 272,000 shares issued divided by the 1,518,548 shares outstanding at the end of the year.
4. Using the $2.33 billion purchase price for the remaining half of GEICO Berkshire did not already own.
5. Using the $26.5 billion purchase price for the 77.5% of BNSF Berkshire did not already own.
6. Using the $12.25 billion equity + preferred investment.

Sources: Berkshire Hathaway Annual Report 1974, 1984, 1994, 2004, 2014; and author's calculations.

Rocket Fuel: Insurance Float

Insurance float was perhaps the single most important factor driving Berkshire's growth over the first fifty years. Float produced both capital to deploy advantageously and substantial underwriting profits. Berkshire was in the insurance business forty-eight of the first fifty years of its modern existence. Discounting the partial first year in 1967, there was a negative cost of average float for twenty-seven years. In just eight of those years was Berkshire's cost of funds higher than that of the long-term US government bond. As time went on, Berkshire perfected its underwriting. This double benefit (increasing float *and* a loss experience that improved over time) resulted in substantial profits. Most of Berkshire's cumulative underwriting profits came in the last decade (see Table 8.7).

Table 8.7: Berkshire Hathaway pre-tax underwriting gain/(loss) by decade

($ millions)	
1968–1974	($5)
1975–1984	(93)
1985–1994	(285)
1995–2004	(3,248)
2005–2014	21,259

Sources: Berkshire Hathaway Annual Reports and author's calculations.

Figure 8.1: Berkshire Hathaway insurance cost of float 1968–2014

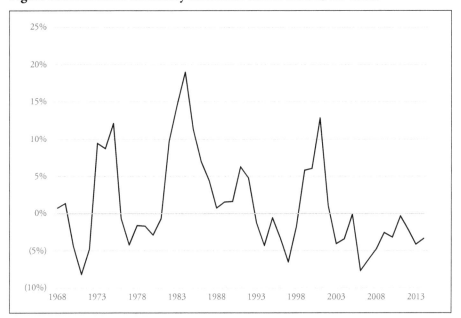

Source: Berkshire Hathaway Annual Reports.

A Self-Forged Anchor

Berkshire Hathaway was the victim of its own success. As the conglomerate grew larger and larger by retaining earnings, the universe of investment opportunities shrank dramatically. Compounding the problem was a market for businesses (either in part via the stock market or in whole) that became more efficient as the years went by. In Berkshire's early years, good companies were available for bargain prices. It bought the Illinois National Bank & Trust Company and *The Buffalo News* at book value, and the discarded Scott Fetzer and Fechheimer at premiums that still produced going-in pre-tax returns in the mid-20% range. During the decade ended in 2014, it purchased a variety of businesses, some with underlying returns on capital well into the double digits. But the prices paid for these acquisitions cut the going-in returns down to the low double-digit or even single-digit range.

By charting a sample of Berkshire's acquisitions by purchase multiples and going-in returns, we can see both the value of different companies and a hint of the market situation when they were purchased (see Figure 8.2). Generally, the better the business was, the higher its price (as represented by purchase multiple paid compared to the company's underlying value). The return on capital of the underlying businesses (the company-level return) ranges widely.

The three major outliers are See's, Scott Fetzer, and Fechheimer. See's was one of Berkshire's earliest purchases and was made when markets were not as efficient. The low Scott Fetzer and Fechheimer purchase multiples reflected that Berkshire could act as a safe port amid the leverage buyout storm of the mid-1980s. By contrast, Lubrizol and Heinz were excellent companies earning great returns on capital, but the price Berkshire paid reflected the market's correct appraisal of that fact.

Figure 8.2: Distribution of Going-In Returns, Select Acquisitions*

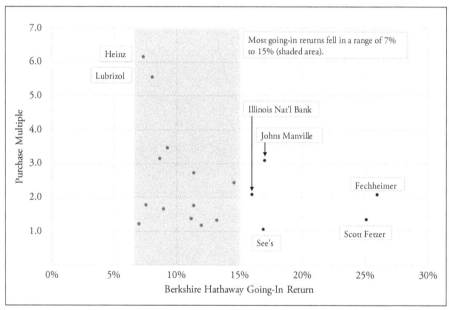

*Limited to acquisitions where the purchase multiple and going-in return were calculable.
Source: Berkshire Hathaway Annual Reports.

We can see the outperformance of Berkshire's book value and market values compared to the total return of the S&P 500 decline over its fifty-year history (see Figure 8.3). Its advantage in compounding book value per share peaked at 20% in the early 1980s and steadily declined to the single-digit percentage point range at the end of 2014.

Buffett was direct in his 2014 special letter discussing Berkshire's past, present, and future: "The bad news is that Berkshire's long-term gains—measured by percentages, not by dollars—cannot be dramatic and will not come close to those achieved in the past 50 years. The numbers have become too big. I think Berkshire will outperform the average American company, but our advantage, if any, won't be great."

Figure 8.3: Trailing ten-year difference between Berkshire Hathaway's per-share book value and market value to S&P 500 (with dividends)

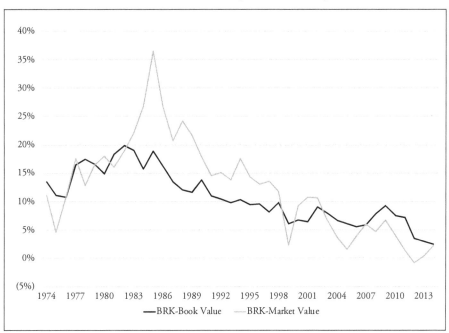

Source: Berkshire Hathaway Annual Report 2014 and author's calculations.

Figure 8.4: Berkshire Hathaway price-to-book ratio, 1965–2014

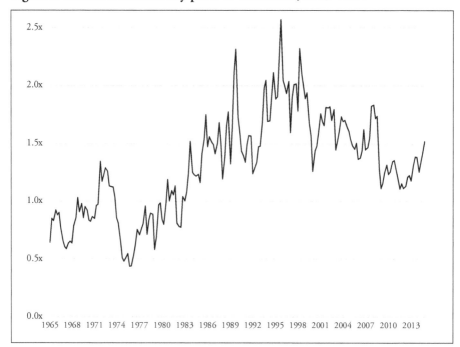

Sources: *Of Permanent Value* (Kilpatrick, 2015), Berkshire Hathaway Annual Reports 1965–2014, and author's calculations.

Broad Lessons

Examining Berkshire's fifty-year history through 2014 several major lessons stand out:

- **Circle of competence:** Buffett and Munger, for the most part, stayed within their circle of competence. Building Berkshire used common sense and a focused strategy of choosing long-term businesses and investments with good economics that they understood well.
- **Business focus:** A central guiding principal was to focus on the underlying business. It did not matter whether the actual investment was a whole company, part of a company via stocks, or lending to a business via fixed income investments. A focus on the long-term economic characteristics of businesses was paramount to Berkshire's success. This included seeking businesses with strong economic moats.
- **Financial and operational conservatism:** Berkshire benefitted to an enormous degree from the float in insurance, and to a lesser extent the trading stamp business at Blue Chip Stamps (before it faded). Some debt was used when it was available on attractive terms, and later the utility businesses used debt as

appropriate. Berkshire did not seek to increase returns by employing leverage. Its conservatism also extended to accounting. Countering the tendency toward optimism (and under-reserving) its loss reserving consistently overestimated insurance losses, which led to many years of favorable loss development. Berkshire took calculated risks with its capital and never suffered a large loss in relation to equity. It moved forward quicker by avoiding significant backward steps and common pitfalls.

- **Opportunism:** Building Berkshire was an exercise in patience combined with opportunism and a reminder that opportunity cost matters. There was no grand strategy. Rather, Berkshire stood ready to make decisions as they arose. Each new investment was measured against what was already available. This included if and when to issue or repurchase its own shares. Related, Buffett maintained an entrepreneurial spirit that encouraged those within Berkshire to continually push the boundaries. Some of these entrepreneurial ventures failed, such as some of the early Home State operations, GEICO's credit card, and multiple attempts to expand See's beyond the West Coast.

- **Concentrated investments:** As was discussed above, Berkshire combined its patience and its financial resources to make large investments when they became available. On more than one occasion, Buffett and Munger made investments that would not have been made if their objective was to avoid any risk.

- **Conglomerate structure:** The conglomerate structure conferred many advantages to Berkshire. The two biggest were the ability to move capital seamlessly between operating segments and take advantage of tax benefits not available to others. Berkshire's purchase of several public companies meant those companies no longer had to spend time attracting capital for worthwhile projects or otherwise appease a sometimes shortsighted investor base. Buying for keeps also meant Berkshire could offer a permanent home for businesses built by individuals or families whose primary motivation was not to maximize the sale price. (Berkshire's conglomerate structure will be discussed in more detail in Part 10.)

- **Autonomy:** Related to the conglomerate structure, the extreme autonomy given to operating managers meant the company could scale almost without limit and not become unwieldy. Autonomy had the added benefit of providing managers with a sense of ownership that motivated them outside of any monetary benefits. Berkshire maximized business potential by maximizing human potential.

The transformation Berkshire underwent during the 1965–2014 period was nothing short of breathtaking.

Chapter 9
2015–2019

Table 9.1: Half-decade snapshot: 2014–2019

	2014	2019
Business:	Insurance, utilities, railroad, numerous industrial, building, and consumer products businesses, numerous service and retailing businesses, major interest in a branded food product business, significant stakes in several public companies.	Insurance, utilities, railroad, numerous industrial, building, and consumer products businesses, numerous service and retailing businesses, major interests in branded food product businesses, significant stakes in several public companies.
Key managers:	Chairman & CEO: Warren E. Buffett; Vice Chair: Charles T. Munger	Chairman & CEO: Warren E. Buffett; Vice Chair: Charles T. Munger
Annual revenues:	$195 billion	$255 billion
Stockholders' equity:	$240 billion	$425 billion
Book value per A share:	$146,186	$261,417
Float (average):	$81 billion	$126 billion

Major capital allocation decisions:
1. Acquired Van Tuyl Automotive Group for $4.2 billion cash (2015).
2. Invested an additional $5 billion in Heinz to acquire Kraft Foods Group (2015).
3. Acquired Precision Castparts Corp. (PCC) for $32.6 billion cash (2016).
4. Acquired Duracell from Procter & Gamble in a cash-rich split-off transaction for $4.2 billion, gross of $1.8 billion acquired cash (2016).
5. Invested $8.9 billion in the four largest US airlines.
6. Acquired 38.6% initial stake in Pilot Flying J for $2.8 billion (2017).
7. Sold entire investment in IBM for approximately $13 billion (2017).
8. Acquired Medical Liability Mutual Insurance Company for $2.5 billion cash (2018).
9. Acquired a significant stake in Apple, Inc.: $6.7 billion (2016), $14 billion (2017) and $15 billion (2018) for a total investment of $36 billion or 5.4% of the company.
10. Sold 81% interest in Applied Underwriters for $920 million (2019).
11. Invested $10 billion in Occidental Petroleum preferred stock.
12. Invested over $71 billion in capital expenditures ($32 billion more than depreciation expense) (2015–2019).
13. Repurchased $6.4 billion of its own stock (2018–2019).

Noteworthy events:
1. The Insurance Group breaks its 14-year record of consecutive underwriting profits with a pre-tax loss of $3.2 billion. GEICO reports its first underwriting loss since 2000. (2017)
2. Completes the largest retroactive reinsurance deal in history with a $10.2 billion premium with AIG (2017).
3. Buffett wins a ten-year bet that an index fund will beat a group of hedge funds (2017).
4. Congress passed the Tax Cuts and Jobs Act of 2017 which reduces the US Corporate tax rate from 35% to 21%.

Table 9.2: Berkshire Hathaway pre-tax earnings

($ millions)	2019	2018	2017	2016	2015	2014
Insurance Group:						
Underwriting:						
GEICO	$1,506	$2,449	($310)	$462	$460	$1,159
General Re	*Consolidated with BHRG*			190	132	277
Berkshire Hathaway Reinsurance Group	(1,472)	(1,109)	(3,648)	822	421	606
Berkshire Hathaway Primary Group	383	670	719	657	824	626
Total underwriting	417	2,010	(3,239)	2,131	1,837	2,668
Investment income	6,600	5,503	4,902	4,482	4,550	4,357
Total Insurance Group	7,017	7,513	1,663	6,613	6,387	7,025
BNSF	7,250	6,863	6,328	5,693	6,775	6,169
Berkshire Hathaway Energy[1]	2,618	2,472	2,584	2,973	2,851	2,711
Manufacturing, service and retailing (MSR)[2]	12,365	12,308	9,243	8,462	7,115	6,792
Finance and financial products[3]	*Consolidated with MSR*		2,058	2,130	2,086	1,839
Unallocated interest expense	(416)	(458)	(1,494)	(230)	(374)	(313)
Equity method investments[4]	1,176	(2,167)	2,938	1,103	730	694
Corporate, eliminations and other	79	(75)	(1,610)	(1,381)	(971)	(893)
Subtotal - pre-tax operating earnings	30,089	26,456	21,710	25,363	24,599	24,024
Investment and derivatives gains/losses	72,607	(22,455)	2,128	8,304	10,347	4,081
Total pre-tax earnings	102,696	4,001	23,838	33,667	34,946	28,105
Income taxes and minority interests[5]	21,279	(20)	(21,102)	9,593	10,863	8,233
Net income	$81,417	$4,021	$44,940	$24,074	$24,083	$19,872

Footnotes:
1. In 2014, MidAmerican changed its name to Berkshire Hathaway Energy.
2. In 2014, Marmon's leasing operations were rolled into Finance and financial products.
3. In 2018, the Finance and financial products businesses were consolidated with the MSR businesses.
4. 2018: Includes intangible asset impairment from Kraft Heinz.
5. 2017: Includes $28.2 billion benefit from the Tax Cuts and Jobs Act of 2017.

Sources: Berkshire Hathaway Annual Reports 2014, 2016, 2017, 2019.

Table 9.3: Berkshire Hathaway after-tax earnings

($ millions)	2019	2018	2017	2016	2015	2014
Insurance - underwriting	$325	$1,566	($2,219)	$1,370	$1,162	$1,692
Insurance - investment income	5,530	4,554	3,917	3,636	3,725	3,542
Railroad	5,481	5,219	3,959	3,569	4,248	3,869
Utilities and energy	2,840	2,621	2,083	2,287	2,132	1,882
Manufacturing, service and retailing (MSR)	9,372	9,364	6,208	5,631	4,683	4,468
Finance and financial products[1]	*Consolidated with MSR*		1,335	1,427	1,378	1,243
Other[2]	424	(1,566)	(826)	(343)	30	(145)
Operating earnings	23,972	21,758	14,457	17,577	17,358	16,551
Investment and derivative gains/losses	57,445	(17,737)	1,377	6,497	6,725	3,321
Tax Cuts and Jobs Act of 2017			29,106			
Net earnings attributable BRK shareholders	$81,417	$4,021	$44,940	$24,074	$24,083	$19,872
Common shares outstanding at year-end[3]	1,625	1,641	1,645	1,644	1,643	1,643

Footnotes:
1. Beginning in 2018, the Finance and Financial Products businesses were consolidated with the Manufacturing, Service, and Retailing businesses.
2. Includes $2.7 billion after-tax intangible asset impairment charge from Kraft Heinz.
3. A-share equivalent, in thousands.

Sources: Berkshire Hathaway Annual Reports 2014–2019.

Introduction

B erkshire Hathaway entered its sixth decade of transformation in uncharted territory. It wasn't just that one man held the reins for so long, though that is noteworthy. A conglomerate of Berkshire's size simply hadn't existed before. How would the playbook change as capital began to accumulate faster than it could profitably be allocated? Since this book is being finalized in 2020, we must wait to see the longer story unfold. The first five years of the 2015–2024 decade looked much like the decade that preceded it. In short, Berkshire continued to make the most intelligent decisions at any time.

The conglomerate generated huge amounts of capital between 2015 and 2019 thanks to retained earnings and the effects of compounding. Berkshire continued to benefit from a playbook that included options to allocate capital into wholly-owned businesses or stocks. It found some smart uses of capital in the face of sky-high business valuations and an ever-advancing stock market fueled by continued low interest rates. One major acquisition materialized, as did a host of smaller bolt-on acquisitions that soaked up some capital. So too did Berkshire's partnership with 3G Capital, which allowed it to add another household name to the roster of businesses it owned or controlled.

Berkshire's future in a post-Buffett world became clearer during this time. It restructured management and promoted two long-time lieutenants to vice chairmen. However, the question of who would succeed Buffett as CEO remained. The gusher of cash found a partial relief valve in an expanded share repurchase program. Berkshire modified the criteria and returned a modicum of capital to shareholders in the form of buybacks. Would Berkshire have opportunity to return more cash through buybacks? Would it institute a dividend? These questions remained as cash built to a record $128 billion at year-end 2019 despite best efforts to use it.

One fact remained very clear. Warren Buffett and Charlie Munger weren't done shaping Berkshire Hathaway.

Table 9.4: Select information 2015–2019

	2015	2016	2017	2018	2019
BRK book value per share - % change	6.4%	10.7%	23.0%	0.4%	23.0%
BRK market value per share - % change	(12.5%)	23.4%	21.9%	2.8%	11.0%
S&P 500 total return	1.4%	12.0%	21.8%	(4.4%)	31.5%
US GDP Growth (real %)	3.1%	1.7%	2.3%	3.0%	2.2%
10-year Treasury Note (year-end %)	2.2%	2.5%	2.4%	2.8%	1.9%
US inflation (avg. annual %)	0.1%	1.3%	2.1%	2.4%	1.8%
US unemployment (avg. annual %)	5.3%	4.9%	4.3%	3.9%	3.7%

Sources: Berkshire Hathaway Annual Reports 2018, 2019 and Federal Reserve Bank of St. Louis.

2015

Berkshire's gain in net worth during 2015 amounted to $15.4 billion, an increase of 6.4%. This was significantly ahead of the 1.4% gain recorded for the S&P 500. But in 2014, Buffett had switched his preferred yardstick to Berkshire's change in market value per share, which fell 12.5%. These were two competing data points. Which to believe? Buffett was confident the market value metric would prevail over time. He knew Berkshire's share price, like that of the market in general, would rise and fall but eventually settle close to intrinsic value. A single year was not enough data to draw any definitive conclusion. Buffett preferred to look at Berkshire's progress building normalized earnings power (earnings excluding any gains or losses from marketable securities or derivatives) to evaluate a single year, and he thought Berkshire had a good year on that front.

The Powerhouse Five, the largest non-insurance businesses (comprised of Berkshire Hathaway Energy, BNSF, Iscar, Lubrizol, and Marmon), reported record earnings. That included a turnaround by BNSF, which earned Buffett's praise in 2015 after disappointing the prior year. The dozens of other non-insurance businesses increased their earnings too. Insurance turned in its thirteenth consecutive year of underwriting profits and again increased float. Large capital expenditures and many bolt-on acquisitions increased the earnings power of Berkshire's existing businesses. The partnership with 3G Capital expanded again when Heinz merged with Kraft to create a consumer brand giant. Additional capital was put to work in equity securities.

In Buffett's Chairman's letter he provided an update on the two quantitative factors he thought useful for estimating Berkshire's intrinsic value. For the first time he included underwriting profit in the per-share operating earnings figure.* His

---

* Underwriting earnings per share amounted to $1,118 in 2015 and increased the intrinsic value estimate by 4%.

reasoning was the underwriting business had changed substantially; earnings were more stable than a decade or two ago and were less heavily influenced by catastrophe coverage. Still, Buffett was quick to point out that an underwriting loss remained possible as the super cat business hadn't gone away; it just diminished in relation to other business.

Table 9.5: Berkshire Hathaway intrinsic value estimation

	With insurance underwriting		W/out insurance underwriting	
Per share (A-equivalent):	2015	2014	2015	2014
Investments (Kraft Heinz at market)	$159,794	$140,123	$159,794	$140,123
Pre-tax operating earnings (ex. investment income)	12,304	12,471	11,186	10,847
Estimated value (investments + 10x operating earnings)	282,834	264,832	271,654	248,593
Year-end share price	197,800	226,000	197,800	226,000
Year-end book value per share	155,501	146,186	155,501	146,186
Price/estimated value	0.70x	0.85x	0.73x	0.91x
Price/book	1.27x	1.55x	1.27x	1.55x
Value/book	1.82x	1.81x	1.75x	1.70x
Change in estimated value	6.8%		9.3%	
Change in share price	(12.5%)		(12.5%)	

Sources: Berkshire Hathaway Annual Reports 2014, 2015; and author's calculations.

Insurance

The Insurance Group delivered a $1.8 billion pre-tax underwriting gain in 2015 in addition to increasing year-end float by 4.5% to $87.7 billion. Each major insurance segment was profitable, though not without their unique challenges.

Doing so also reduced the change in estimated intrinsic value if the $1,624 underwriting earnings per share in 2014 are included that year.

Table 9.6: Berkshire Hathaway—Insurance Underwriting

($ millions)	2015	2014
GEICO		
Premiums earned	$22,718	$20,496
Underwriting gain/(loss) - pre-tax	460	1,159
General Re		
Premiums earned	$5,975	$6,264
Underwriting gain/(loss) - pre-tax	132	277
Berkshire Hathaway Reinsurance Group		
Premiums earned	$7,207	$10,116
Underwriting gain/(loss) - pre-tax	421	606
Berkshire Hathaway Primary Group		
Premiums earned	$5,394	$4,377
Underwriting gain/(loss) - pre-tax	824	626
Total premiums earned	$41,294	$41,253
Total underwriting gain/(loss) - pre-tax	1,837	2,668
Average float	85,822	80,581
Cost of float	(2.1%)	(3.3%)

Sources: Berkshire Hathaway Annual Report 2016 and author's calculations.

GEICO

GEICO reported mixed results. In the plus column, a combination of rate increases and policyholder growth expanded earned premiums 10.8% to $22.7 billion. Its market share grew from 10.8% to 11.4%. Underwriting expenses (at 15.9% of premiums) had a fourth consecutive year of improvement. That's where the good news ended. Losses ballooned by 4.4 percentage points to 82.1% of premiums. The cause was an increase in both frequency and severity of claims. Such an increase could only be attributed to more drivers using smartphones.[*][109] The higher loss experience caused GEICO's underwriting profit to decline 60% to $460 million, a 98% combined ratio. It would have to increase premium rates even more to counter the higher loss experience and return to historical rates of profitability.

---

[*] The Insurance Information Institute partially corroborated this theory in an October 2016 report. It referenced a National Safety Council Survey where 74% of drivers reported using Facebook while driving. The title of that report told it all: More Accidents, Larger Claims Drive Costs Higher.

General Re

General Re also faced headwinds in 2015. High industry capacity depressed pricing and reduced Gen Re's appetite for new business. But Gen Re remained profitable, a reflection of its culture of aiming for underwriting profits irrespective of volume. Its overall pre-tax underwriting gain fell 52% to $132 million on earned premiums that declined 5% to $6 billion. Gen Re was the only insurance unit to experience a decline in float during the year, which fell 3.7% to $18.6 billion.

Earned premiums in property/casualty were $2.8 billion, a decline of 10% (2% adjusted for currency). Pre-tax underwriting profits fell 26% to $150 million. An explosion in Tianjin, China costing $50 million was the only major catastrophe loss, but higher loss ratios elsewhere weighed on profitability. Property gains totaled $289 million and benefitted from favorable loss development. Casualty losses of $139 million included charges for discount accretion on workers' compensation liabilities and deferred charge amortization on retroactive reinsurance contracts, a drag that would continue largely independent of year-to-year changes in premium volume. Consistent current year losses on casualty business largely stemmed from Gen Re's conservative underwriting. In each year since 2009 the casualty lines reported favorable development of prior year business. Gen Re's troubled history was close enough in the past to remind it that continued discipline was required for good results in reinsurance.

The life/health lines reported losses of $18 million compared to a $73 million gain the year before. Earned premiums were flat at $3.2 billion but would have increased 8% if not for currency headwinds. New business came from markets in Canada and Asia. Weakness in its North American long-term care business and in individual life caused profitability to decline.

Berkshire Hathaway Reinsurance Group

BHRG also faced headwinds from depressed pricing. It too remained profitable, though its pre-tax underwriting gain fell 31% to $421 million on earned premiums that declined 29% to $7.2 billion. Ajit Jain earned his usual praise from Buffett in the Chairman's letter. It's easy to see why. Even in the face of industry headwinds, Jain's group increased float 4% to $44 billion.

Earned premiums in property/casualty increased 8% to $4.4 billion but profits fell by 33% to $994 million—a stellar result by any measure. A new ten-year, 20% quota-share contract with Insurance Australia Group that started on July 1 more than offset declines in earned premiums from property catastrophe, property quota-share, and London markets. The only notable catastrophe loss was an $86 million loss from the same explosion in China that hurt Gen Re's results.

The retroactive reinsurance segment all but disappeared. Premiums written and earned amounted to just $5 million in 2015, down 99.9% from the $3.4 billion the year before. Such a large decline reflected Berkshire's willingness to walk away when business was not available at appropriate prices. Shutting off the spigot revealed the impact of the deferred charges Buffett frequently pointed to as a drag on reported earnings. The retroactive segment reported a loss of $469 million with all but $60 million stemming from deferred charge amortization.*

Earned premiums from life/health increased 4% to $2.8 billion. A loss of $54 million was an improvement from a $173 million loss the year before. In 2015, Berkshire broke down the life/health segment into three additional categories. Each category was tied to time-value-of-money concepts and produced accounting charges that hid the valuable economics of its float. The categories were:

1. *Periodic payment annuity*: Berkshire received upfront premiums and made payments stretching over decades. This type of business records no gain or loss upfront. Instead, charges are recognized over time like the deferred charge amortization on retroactive reinsurance business. In this case, they arise because liabilities are discounted upfront to account for the time value of money, and the charges (called discount accretion) are taken into earnings.
2. *Life reinsurance*: Berkshire took the risk from the direct writers of life insurance.
3. *Variable annuity*: This business guaranteed closed blocks of variable annuity business written by direct writers.

Berkshire Hathaway Primary Group

The Primary Group grew earned premiums 23% to $5.4 billion and pre-tax underwriting profit by 32% to $824 million (an 84.7% combined ratio). Major contributors were the new Berkshire Hathaway Specialty Group, NICO Primary, the Home State companies, and GUARD. BH Specialty Group grew premium volume to $1 billion, an incredible achievement considering the unit was formed in 2013.

Regulated, Capital-Intensive Businesses

In 2015 BNSF regained its good graces with Buffett by improving its service levels. Just as Buffett predicted the previous year, the railroad's financial performance followed suit. Pre-tax profits grew 10% to a record $6.7 billion. Bolstering growth were massive

---

* The notes to the financial statements state that a $150 million gain was realized from foreign currency effects and a $90 million loss was booked relating to readjustment of ultimate liabilities (unfavorable loss development net of additional deferred charges). Any gain or loss from the $5 million premium earned in 2015, if any, would have been trivial.

capital expenditures of $5.7 billion—almost three times depreciation charges.* This was as it should be. Berkshire's railroad carried 17% of all intercity freight in the US during the year.

BNSF's 5.5% decline in revenues to $22 billion illustrates the importance of understanding the underlying business model of a company and paying attention to the right variables. One of the largest expenses of any railroad is fuel, and most pass these costs through to shippers. A 41% decline in fuel costs during the year was the major reason why BNSF's revenues declined during 2015. Its freight volume was flat at 10.3 million units, which shows the railroad regaining control of expenses.

Berkshire Hathaway Energy (BHE) increased EBIT 6.8% to $3.4 billion. Berkshire's share of net earnings grew $13% to $2.1 billion. A large part of that increase came from the addition of Alta Link, the Alberta, Canada-based electric distribution business acquired in late 2014. BHE's existing businesses continued to generate the stability inherent in their business models. Two items of note affected the financials. One was a strong increase in the value of the US dollar. This had the effect of reducing reported revenues and earnings from UK-based Northern Powergrid. The other item affecting the financials was a decline in energy costs. Like BNSF, BHE passed along these savings to customers. This was to be expected from a heavily regulated business.

Manufacturing, Service, and Retailing

Berkshire again revised its presentation of the MSR business (nothing changed operationally). The businesses were split into two broad categories: manufacturing businesses, and service and retailing businesses. Both were further delineated into three main segments (see Table 9.7). McLane was reported separately because its revenues were large compared to Berkshire's total. Earnings for the group totaled $36.1 billion, down 2%. Comparative results (undisclosed) were poorer considering Berkshire made acquisitions in this segment during the year.

---

* Buffett did take pains to point out that GAAP depreciation underrepresented the amount the railroad would have to spend to remain competitive. He went so far as to suggest shareholders make a downward adjustment to Berkshire's earnings to account for it.

Table 9.7: Manufacturing, Service, and Retailing businesses—pre-tax earnings

($ millions)	2015	2014	% Change
Industrial products	$2,994	$3,159	(5%)
Building products	1,167	896	30%
Consumer products	732	756	(3%)
Subtotal - manufacturing	4,893	4,811	2%
Service	1,156	1,202	(4%)
Retailing	564	344	64%
McLane	502	435	15%
Subtotal - service and retailing	2,222	1,981	12%
Total pre-tax earnings	7,115	6,792	5%
Income taxes and non-controlling interests	(2,432)	(2,324)	5%
Earnings after tax	$4,683	$4,468	5%

Sources: Berkshire Hathaway Annual Report 2015 and author's calculations.

With so many businesses to report, the categories were logical. But some analysts pined for additional data. Results from large companies like Shaw, Lubrizol, IMC (as the parent company of Iscar*), and Marmon were aggregated and discussion squeezed into just a few paragraphs along with many other businesses instead of being individually reported. Some had previously been public companies that produced annual reports hundreds of pages long. Much of that data was now gone as part of Berkshire's reporting. Many of the businesses were similar enough that the consolidated data was still valuable. The report did identify specific businesses where the impact was meaningful, but Berkshire's growth diminished the importance of individual businesses compared to the whole.

Industrial Products (revenues of $16.8bn, down 5%): A big part of the 5% decline in pre-tax to $3 billion earnings from industrial products came from a stronger US dollar. IMC was likely responsible for most of the impact, as it was the largest business in the segment and located overseas. A slowdown in demand began over the second half of the year and was expected to continue into 2016.

Building Products (revenues of $10.3bn, up 1.9%): This was the only manufacturing segment to increase earnings. The large 30% jump in earnings to $1.2 billion on just a 2% increase in revenues was a result of higher unit volume, lower raw materials costs, and energy savings, offset by the strong US dollar and restructuring costs. Bolt-on acquisitions increased earnings as well. The large increase in earnings illustrated the pricing power of those businesses. The segment included Shaw, Johns Manville, Acme Building Brands, Benjamin Moore, and MiTek. These businesses did

---

* The original business was now one of numerous operating units.

not face price regulation and were not required (like Berkshire Hathaway Energy and BNSF) to pass along savings to customers. Crucially, their competitive positions did not require it either. Some unregulated businesses nonetheless face competition so intense they must pass on savings to customers to retain business.

Consumer Products (revenues of $9.1 bn, flat): Earnings from consumer products fell 3% to $732 million because of a loss at Fruit of the Loom (related to selling an unprofitable unit) and declines in footwear. Earnings at Forest River increased on higher unit sales and increased prices.

Service (revenues of $10.2bn, up 3.5%): This was the only service and retailing segment to see a decline in earnings, which fell 4% to $1.2 billion. NetJets expanded operations but faced lower margins and higher costs (including a one-time lump-sum payment related to a collective bargaining agreement) that weighed on the results of the entire segment. Newspaper revenues (and presumably profits) declined. Offsetting this was the addition of WPLG, the Miami, Florida television station Berkshire acquired in 2014, and the addition of Charter Brokerage.

Retailing (revenues of $13.3bn, up 214%): This segment welcomed two new businesses in 2015 which increased pre-tax earnings by 64% to $564 million. The first was the Van Tuyl Group, a group of eighty-one automotive dealerships located in ten (mostly western US) states. The acquisition also included Van Tuyl's two related insurance businesses, two auto auctions, and a distributor of automotive fluid maintenance products. Buffett met Larry Van Tuyl years before and the Van Tuyls decided Berkshire would be a good permanent home for the business. Upon joining Berkshire Van Tuyl was renamed Berkshire Hathaway Automotive. The business was built by Larry Van Tuyl and his father, Cecil, over sixty-two years. A key insight the Van Tuyls had, and Buffett shared, was creating a sense of ownership with each local manager. "We will continue to operate with extreme—indeed, almost unheard of—decentralization at Berkshire," he explained to shareholders. This allowed them to successfully grow the business to the fifth-largest auto group in the US.*

A limited amount of data was available on the Van Tuyl acquisition. Buffett put the company's annual sales volume at $9 billion. Industry commentators thought pre-tax earnings might be between $350 and $471 million.[110] The purchase price of $4.1 billion included $1.3 billion in cash and investments. Adjusting for cash, it appears Berkshire paid between six- and eight-times pre-tax earnings. This apparent bargain

---

* Buffett noted at the 2014 Annual Meeting that the advantages Van Tuyl had were largely at the local dealership level. It was a reminder that scale only matters in certain contexts. Economies of scale only arise from leveraging fixed costs and sharing resources. Dealerships do not benefit much from scale because more dealerships equal more fixed costs and marketing is local. Van Tuyl's profitability came from running many dealerships efficiently in their local markets rather than any major advantages gained from having multiple dealerships (such as buying power with the manufacturers). The distinction is subtle but important.

price looks less rich considering that light vehicle sales (sales of cars, vans, SUVs and smaller pickup trucks) were at or near recent highs of about 17 million annually.[111]

The second acquisition of 2015 in this segment was Detlev Louis Motorrad. The company was one of the largest retailers of motorcycle accessories in Germany. The acquisition was too small to be detailed in the Berkshire Annual Report. Some sources put its annual revenues at around 270 million Euros (about $300 million) and the purchase price at about 400 million Euros (about $444 million).[112] The deal was notable in another way. Buffett tapped Ted Weschler to negotiate the deal and then made him chairman to oversee the investment.

Earnings from Berkshire Hathaway Automotive and Detlev Louis Motorrad were the primary reason for the 64% increase in retailing earnings in 2015. Furniture retailing revenues increased 24% from the new Nebraska Furniture Mart store in Texas and increases from RC Willey and Jordan's.

McLane (revenues of $48.2bn, up 3%): Berkshire's only standalone business other than BNSF, McLane, increased volumes in foodservice (up 6%), beverage (up 8%), and grocery (up 2%). This was another business able to directly benefit (at least in the short run) from the decline in fuel costs. Pre-tax earnings grew 15% to $502 million. A $19 million gain (or about 4 percentage points) came from a one-time gain from the sale of an undisclosed subsidiary.

Finance and Financial Products

Pre-tax earnings in Finance and Financial Products jumped 13% to $2.1 billion. The major driver of the increase was a 27% increase (to $706 million) in earnings from Clayton. Clayton increased unit sales and benefitted from lower interest costs and lower delinquencies/foreclosures. Marmon's tank leasing business (UTLX) and XTRA's trailer leasing business were lumped into transportation equipment leasing. Pre-tax earnings of those businesses increased 10% to $909 million. Part of that increase was a $1 billion purchase of 25,085 tank cars from General Electric (bringing its total to 133,280). UTLX also acquired several businesses during the year to continue building out its full-service maintenance operation. Berkshire couldn't come close to the financing advantage of banks to conduct pure leasing operations. Both the tank leasing business and XTRA's trailer leasing business had important service components that added value above and beyond a simple financing arrangement. Everything else from CORT to Berkadia and the fees charged to Clayton and NetJets for use of Berkshire's credit fell to the other category. Earnings in that category increased 4% to $471 million.

Investments

Berkshire's investment portfolio saw few changes in 2015. A net $1.5 billion was invested in equities funded by a few sales. The most notable sales were Berkshire's positions in Swiss Re and Munich Re, two European-based reinsurers. The position in Munich was valued at $4 billion at year-end 2014; Swiss Re was too small to be specifically identified. Buffett elaborated on his reasoning for selling the investments at the 2016 Annual Meeting. He said it came down to two factors, and neither was related to management, which he continued to admire:

1. An influx of capital that flooded the reinsurance industry and pressured premium rates. This was likely to continue for some time.
2. Low interest rates made insurance float much less valuable. That was more important for European-based insurers since interest rates there were low or even negative. Berkshire would be hurt by the competition and low rates, but it had more options to invest its float, including the acquisition of non-insurance subsidiaries.

The largest additions to the investment portfolio were not new companies, but bigger investments in existing companies, in this case two of the Big Four investees: Berkshire increased its investment in Wells Fargo by an additional $859 million and IBM by $634 million. Berkshire's interest in the other two Big Four investees also increased as American Express and Coca-Cola repurchased shares during the year. Buffett estimated that a 1 percentage point increase in any of those companies increased Berkshire's portion of their annual earnings by $500 million. He was enthusiastic about their management and long-term potential and reminded shareholders why he didn't mind owning non-controlling interests in other companies. Having stocks as an outlet for capital allocation provided two other advantages. One was the ability to put capital to work when it represented the best opportunity available. The other was the reverse as "having a huge portfolio of marketable securities gives us a stockpile of funds that can be tapped when an elephant-sized acquisition is offered to us."

Kraft Heinz

Berkshire again found opportunity with 3G Capital. This time it was the purchase of Kraft Foods Group, Inc. Like Heinz, Kraft was a well-known consumer packaged food and beverage company that owned many iconic food brands. In addition to its signature Kraft-branded lines, the company owned Oscar Mayer, Philadelphia cream cheese, Velveeta, JELL-O, Cool Whip, Kool-Aid, and Maxwell House coffee, among many others. Kraft's business was broken down by segment:

Figure 9.1: Kraft 2014 revenues by segment ($ millions)

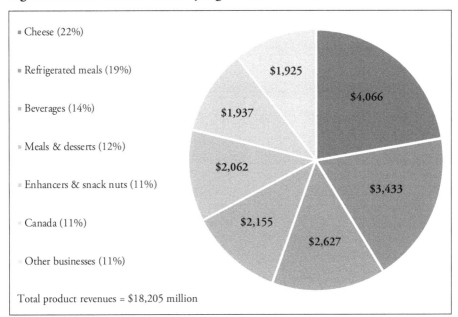

- Cheese (22%)
- Refrigerated meals (19%)
- Beverages (14%)
- Meals & desserts (12%)
- Enhancers & snack nuts (11%)
- Canada (11%)
- Other businesses (11%)

$1,925
$1,937
$4,066
$2,062
$3,433
$2,155
$2,627

Total product revenues = $18,205 million

Source: Kraft Foods 2014 10K.

The Kraft that merged with Heinz had a history with Berkshire Hathaway. Berkshire owned General Foods (Kraft's predecessor company) in the 1980s before it was taken over in a leveraged buyout. General Foods was later combined with Kraft, Inc., and in 2012 was split off from its renamed parent, Mondelez. Mondelez focused on international food and snack brands while Kraft contained the mostly US-based food and beverage brands.

The qualities that attracted Berkshire and 3G Capital to Heinz also attracted it to Kraft. Kraft's brands were iconic and had a long history of consumer purchasing habits. The quality of the brands resulted in significant amounts of goodwill and intangible assets on the balance sheet. Operating them required far less tangible capital, as evidenced by the strong historical pre-tax returns on capital (see Table 9.8).

The purchase price for Kraft reflected the quality of its underlying businesses and the expectation that the management team at 3G Capital could implement their cost-cutting playbook. To do that, the existing Heinz shareholders (3G Capital and Berkshire Hathaway) had to retain control of the post-merger company. The merger was structured such that 3G Capital and Berkshire would end up with 51% of Kraft Heinz, the new post-merger company. Existing Kraft shareholders would receive 49% of the company and a one-time $10 billion dividend funded by an additional equity contribution by 3G Capital and Berkshire. Because Berkshire owned slightly more of Heinz prior to the merger, it ended up with a 26.8% stake in Kraft Heinz.

Table 9.8: Kraft—acquisition analysis

($ millions)	2014	2013	2012	2011	2010
Total revenues	$18,205	$18,218	$18,271	$18,576	$17,797
Revenues/avg. capital[1]	$3.27	$3.35	$3.63	n/a	n/a
EBIT margin[2]	17%	16%	16%	17%	17%
Pre-tax return on capital	55%	55%	59%	n/a	n/a
49% of Heinz capitalization[3]	$14,334				
BRK & 3G equity contribution[4]	10,000				
Value given for 51% of Kraft equity	24,334				
Implied purchase price of 100% of Kraft equity	$47,714				
Debt	9,286				
Effective purchase price	$57,000				
Purchase multiple	10.8x				
BRK going-in pre-tax return (2014)	5.1%				

Footnotes:
1. Average capital calculated using specific working capital and fixed asset accounts for consistency. Data for 2011 did not contain comparable figures for accrued pension costs and accrued postretirement health care costs.
2. Adjustments were made to exclude changes to defined benefit plans.
3. Heinz capitalization at year-end 2014 consisted of equity ($7,336), total debt ($13,597) and preferred stock ($8,320).
4. Berkshire invested $5,260 and 3G invested $4,740.

Note: Balance sheet data for Kraft for 2010 was not available.

Sources: Berkshire Hathaway Annual Report 2015; Kraft Annual Reports 2012–2014; H.J. Heinz Holding Corporation S-4 registration statement filing; and author's calculations.

The Kraft Heinz merger was not without its accounting complications. The transaction included the issuance of shares, which reduced Berkshire's ownership from 52.5% to 26.8%. The equity method (the accounting applicable to Berkshire's ownership interest) accounts for that reduction in ownership as a sale. This holds true even though no cash changed hands. If Heinz had issued new shares in exchange for cash it would have had the same economic effect as Berkshire selling some of its shares. In this case, Berkshire was selling a part of its ownership in Heinz not for cash but in exchange for part of Kraft. As a result of the accounting requirement, Berkshire was required to book a $6.8 billion non-cash gain. Because it was only for accounting purposes, there were no tax implications.

Productivity and Prosperity

Productivity is the amount of output per hour of labor input. Buffett devoted a section of the 2015 Chairman's letter to productivity, connecting it to both Berkshire's and America's prosperity. The topic was timely (and probably prompted by) Heinz and Kraft, whose new management at 3G Capital were known for ruthlessly improving productivity, most often by reducing headcounts. Buffett thought the connection between productivity and prosperity was not entirely clear to some, so he provided examples.

- *Farming*: The most dramatic example was America's shift away from farming during the 20th century. In 1900, 40% of the country was employed growing America's food. As of 2015, just 2% of the population worked on farms. Productivity allowed this to happen, beginning with the invention and perfection of the tractor and extending to better farming techniques and seed quality.
- *Railroading*: After World War II there were 1.35 million workers employed in the railroad industry, and they moved 655 billion revenue ton-miles. Fast forward to 2014 and Class I railroads moved 1.85 *trillion* ton-miles with just 187,000 workers. The result was a 55% decline in the inflation-adjusted cost of moving a ton-mile of freight. Safety improved dramatically too. Using BNSF as an example, Buffett said injuries fell 50% from 1996.
- *Utilities*: Berkshire Hathaway Energy's (BHE) Iowa utility in 1999 employed 3,700 people and produced 19 million megawatt-hours of electricity. Fast forward to 2015 and it generated 29 million megawatt-hours while employing just 3,500 people. Such improvements in productivity allowed BHE to keep rates the same for sixteen years. Like BNSF, safety improved too.

The examples above proved that increased productivity resulted in real gains to civilization and allowed more to be employed in other industries. But they came with short-term costs, most notably the workers who lost their jobs. Buffett was aware of these costs and had experienced some up close. When Berkshire shuttered its mills in the mid-1980s (and at Dexter Shoe years later) it employed older workers with non-transferrable skills. Buffett thought the solution was social safety nets that cushioned the blow to the unfortunate workers while leaving productivity to continue working its magic for the benefit of society at large.* Both Buffett and Munger were clearly on the side of making operations at Kraft Heinz more efficient. They detested sloppy operations and were ever on the lookout for inefficiencies at Berkshire, noting

---

* There was also the political question of distribution of those gains, whether they accrued to the wealthy or the average citizen.

that once costs crept in, they tended to proliferate. A large and highly profitable conglomerate required continual diligence to protect itself from such tendencies.

2016

Berkshire's gain in net worth in 2016 was 10.7%. Its market value rose 23.4% against a gain in the S&P 500 of 12%. Business results in 2016 (and perhaps the strong rise in share price) reflected another good year. The acquisition of Precision Castparts Corp. sopped up some of Berkshire's excess cash. More importantly, it added to the conglomerate's normalized earnings power.* Buffett presented a history of Berkshire's progress adding to its earnings power in a table in the Chairman's letter (see Figure 9.2). The data show operating earnings grew irregularly but clearly upward over time as Berkshire retained earnings and added earning power.

Figure 9.2: Berkshire Hathaway After-Tax Operating Earnings and Capital Gains 1999–2016

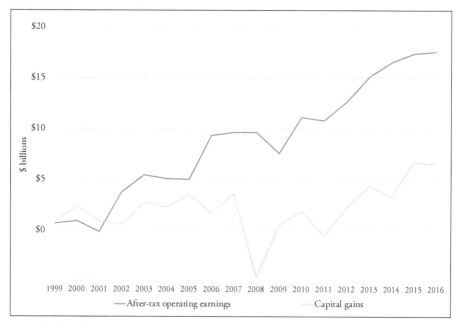

Source: Berkshire Hathaway Annual Report 2016.

---

* Normalized earning power is what a company could expect to earn in a normal year, free of any one-time factors pushing earnings up or down.

Buffett chose to start his analysis above in 1999 because it was the year after Berkshire acquired General Re by issuing shares. Issuance of additional shares since that time grew the share count by a modest 8.3%.* Over that time Berkshire's operating earnings grew steadily, with a few down years along the way. The only loss year during that time was 2001. After-tax operating earnings totaled $159 billion over the seventeen-year period. Capital gains were a different story; those were erratic. Berkshire made no effort to manage the timing or magnitude of capital gains and deemphasized their importance to any single year. Over time, net capital gains (totaling $39 billion since 1999) were an important source of funding to acquire additional operating businesses, he said.

Buffett's goal for Berkshire was to increase operating earnings over time without increasing shares, which would translate into satisfactory increases in per share value over time. After-tax operating earnings grew from $670 million in 1999 to $17.6 billion in 2016, a compounded annual rate of return of 20%. By this measure the goal has been met.

Precision Castparts Corp.

On January 29, 2016, Berkshire acquired Precision Castparts Corp. (PCC) for $32.6 billion in cash. PCC was based in Portland, Oregon, and made complex metal components and fasteners primarily for the aerospace and oil & gas industries. Buffett did not hesitate to credit Todd Combs with the idea. "The PCC acquisition would not have happened without the input and assistance of our own Todd Combs, who brought the company to my attention a few years ago and went on to educate me about both the business and Mark [Donegan, its CEO]."**

Many of its products were critical to the proper functioning of aircraft jet engines, airframes, and industrial turbines, among others. Aerospace represented a significant majority (70% in 2015) of PCC's business. PCC was one of just a few suppliers able to manufacture products of the size and quality needed for aircraft engine manufacturers and other customers. This technological know-how gave PCC a competitive advantage that was evident in the multi-year contracts it had with major customers. With lives and reputations at stake, PCC's customers thought twice before taking the low bid.

PCC's business results reflected its deserved success winning customers. Between 2011 and 2015, PCC increased revenues 61% to $10 billion (see Table 9.9). Its margins were remarkably stable and translated into a pre-tax return on tangible capital in

---

* The Gen Re acquisition increased Berkshire's shares by 21.8%. Buffett went so far as to say that issuing so many shares had been foolish and a terrible mistake. Most of the subsequent increase occurred with the purchase of BNSF in 2010.

** Berkshire owned a small number of shares prior to acquiring the whole company.

the mid-40% range. Buffett had high praise for Donegan. "Mark's accomplishments remind me of the magic regularly performed by Jacob Harpaz at IMC, our remarkable Israeli manufacturer of cutting tools. The two men transform very ordinary raw materials into extraordinary products that are used by major manufacturers worldwide. Each is the da Vinci of his craft."

Buffett's enthusiasm for PCC and Donegan was reflected in the acquisition price. Berkshire paid 6.7 times PCC's underlying capital, which gave it a pre-tax going-in return below 7%. He readily admitted that the low interest rate environment played a part in the price Berkshire paid for PCC.

Table 9.9: Precision Castparts Corp.—acquisition analysis

($ millions)	2015	2014	2013	2012	2011
Total revenues	$10,005	$9,533	$8,347	$7,202	$6,209
Revenues/avg. capital[1]	$1.79	$1.80	$1.77	$1.69	$1.67
EBIT margin[1]	26%	28%	26%	25%	24%
Pre-tax return on capital	46%	50%	46%	43%	41%
Purchase price (equity)	$32,658				
Debt	4,586				
Effective purchase price	$37,244				
Purchase multiple	6.66x				
BRK going-in pre-tax return	6.9%				
Footnote:					
1. Adjustments were made for goodwill and intangibles.					

Note: Fiscal years ended in March.
Sources: Berkshire Hathaway Annual Report 2016; Precision Castparts Corp. Annual Reports 2011–2015; and author's calculations.

Some wondered how Buffett could agree to spend such large sums of money so quickly. Andrew Ross Sorkin, a journalist invited to ask questions at the Annual Meeting, summed up the question as follows: "Other successful acquisitive companies use teams of internal people, outside bankers, consultants, and lawyers to due diligence, often over many months to assess deals … Speed may be a competitive advantage. You've done some amazing deals. But does your diligence process also put us at greater risk?" While the PCC deal was not as rapid as others in Berkshire's past (Buffett had a couple of years to study it), Berkshire's omission of the multitudes of personnel to assist in the transaction was much different than almost any other acquisition in the business world. Buffett's answer was instructive.

"It's interesting. We've made plenty of mistakes in acquisitions … the mistakes are always about making an improper assessment of the economic conditions in the future of the industry or the company. They're not a bad lease, they're not a specific labor contract, they're not a questionable patent. They're not the things that are on the checklist, you know, for every acquisition by every major corporation in America. Those are not the things that count. What counts is whether you're wrong about—whether you really got a fix on the basic economics, and how the industry is likely to develop or whether Amazon is likely to kill 'em, you know, in a few years, or that sort of thing. And we have not found a due diligence list that gets at what we think are the real risks when we buy a business."

Buffett was telling shareholders he has a different system for assessing acquisitions.* It might not have fit into the conventions of Wall Street, but the success of Berkshire was proof it worked well.

PCC contributed about $1.5 billion to Berkshire's normalized earning power. Yet the size of Berkshire Hathaway's existing operations meant it would be included alongside other manufacturing companies in Berkshire's results and not as a standalone business. The conglomerate had swallowed up another Fortune 500 company.

Duracell

Berkshire completed another cash-rich split-off** like the ones in 2014. This time it exchanged shares of Procter & Gamble for Duracell, the well-known maker of alkaline batteries. Buffett had been on the board of Gillette when it purchased Duracell in 1996.[113] The exchange was valued at $4.2 billion (including $1.8 billion in cash) and closed on February 29, 2016. The transaction resulted in a non-cash gain of $1.1 billion and likely saved Berkshire about $400 million in taxes.***

Although Duracell had a long history of operations and commanded a quarter of the market,[114] the company came to Berkshire needing improvement. In 2016, Duracell incurred $109 million in one-time restructuring and integration costs.****

---

* Munger's summation of the PCC deal and Berkshire's approach is too irresistible to pass over. After Buffett gave his lengthy explanation, Munger asked rhetorically, "How many people who, in this room, are happily married, carefully checked their spouse's birth certificate and so on? My guess is that our methods are not so uncommon as they appear." His remark had insight. Due diligence checklists had no way of assessing the qualitative factors of management that would have an outsize impact on future results.

** A cash-rich split-off is the exchange of (usually) appreciated shares of a company in exchange for an operating business and cash without incurring tax in the process.

*** Applying a 35% tax rate to the gain; other sources put the tax savings higher. It should also be noted that not just anyone could conduct a cash-rich split-off (otherwise everyone would do it to save taxes). Shares had to be held for at least five years, among other requirements.

**** Buffett explained more in his Chairman's letter, criticizing management teams that frequently put

Manufacturing, Service, and Retailing

Table 9.10: Manufacturing, Service, and Retailing businesses—pre-tax earnings

($ millions)	2016	2015	% Change
Industrial products	$4,209	$2,994	41%
Building products	1,178	1,167	1%
Consumer products	824	732	13%
Subtotal - manufacturing	6,211	4,893	27%
Service	1,161	1,156	0%
Retailing	659	564	17%
McLane	431	502	(14%)
Subtotal - service and retailing	2,251	2,222	1%
Total pre-tax earnings	8,462	7,115	19%
Income taxes and non-controlling interests	(2,831)	(2,432)	16%
Earnings after tax	$5,631	$4,683	20%

Sources: Berkshire Hathaway Annual Report 2016 and author's calculations.

Earnings from the MSR segment increased in 2016 due to the addition of PCC. The rest of Berkshire's businesses in both major categories (manufacturing, and service and retailing) were flat. Results varied widely depending on industry and sensitivity to both the US dollar and oil and gas prices. This group nonetheless earned an impressive 24% on average tangible equity of $24 billion.[*]

Industrial Products (revenues of $24.7bn, up 47%): With the addition of Precision Castparts, pre-tax earnings of industrial products grew 41% to $4.2 billion. Adjusting for PCC, revenues declined 5% as demand fell and competition pressured prices. Earnings of this segment would have fallen too without PCC but the magnitude wasn't disclosed. This segment was hit hardest by a decline in the price of oil. Lubrizol a specialty chemical company, was probably hit the hardest. It took a $365 million hit to its earnings to dispose of an unnamed underperforming business. IMC was one of the only businesses in this category to report a small earnings increase (unspecified).

Building Products (revenues of $10.8bn, up 4.4%): The decline in oil prices combined with increased demand for their products benefitted the building

---

forth adjusted earnings that added back restructuring costs. This was yet another chapter in the accounting versus economics story where managers seek to put the company's earnings in a more favorable light. Buffett considered these costs a part of doing business and noted that Berkshire incurred expenses every year that other management teams might add back when presenting results to shareholders. Instead of falling for what Buffett called baloney, the costs weighed on Berkshire's results.

[*] Buffett provided these figures in the Chairman's letter. The summary balance sheet and income statement disappeared from the Chairman's letter the next year.

products businesses modestly. Revenues and earnings increased, and both Shaw and MiTek completed bolt-on acquisitions during the year. Pre-tax earnings grew 1% to $1.2 billion.

Consumer products (revenues of $11.0bn, up 22%): These businesses shined in 2016. Pre-tax earnings grew 13% to $824 million despite a loss from Duracell (as a result of its restructuring costs). Revenues at Forest River, the recreational vehicle manufacturer, increased 12% and earnings grew even more, up 28%. Lower one-time costs compared to 2015 led to a 22% increase in apparel earnings. Footwear earnings declined by an unspecified amount.

Service businesses (revenues of $10.4bn, up 1.8%): Earnings were flat at $1.2 billion. TTI, the electronics components distributor, grew revenues 7% but changes in the sales mix and competitive pressures resulted in no change to earnings. This was a good reminder that what mattered was the bottom line profit. Earnings at NetJets increased 19%, but the comparison year had higher subcontracting expenses and asset impairments. Newspapers reported lower earnings, but no figures were provided. None of the other businesses in this category were discussed, including FlightSafety, Dairy Queen, and Business Wire.

Retailing (revenues of $15.1bn, up 14%): Pre-tax earnings increased 17% to $659 million and included a full year of results from Berkshire Hathaway Automotive and Louis, the German motorcycle accessory retailer. Earnings from those businesses and increased earnings at other unspecified retailers in this segment contributed to higher overall earnings. Both Nebraska Furniture Mart and Jordan's Furniture opened new stores during 2015 that contributed to results in 2016. Home furnishing revenues increased 8%.

McLane (revenues of $48.1bn, down 0.3%): McLane had the rare off year. Revenues were almost flat, but its earnings fell by 14% to $431 million. The cause was an increase in labor costs and a comparative year that included a $19 million gain from the sale of a subsidiary.

Insurance

The Insurance Group delivered its fourteenth consecutive year of underwriting profits. It was also the fifth straight year where each of the four major segments reported profits. Berkshire's insurers reported a consolidated pre-tax underwriting gain of $2.1 billion and grew year-end float by 4.4% to $91.6 billion (see Table 9.11). Buffett put forth Berkshire's not-so-secret reasons for its success, writing that "a sound insurance operation needs to adhere to four disciplines." It must:

1. Understand all exposures that might cause a policy to incur losses.
2. Conservatively assess the likelihood an exposure causes a loss, and the cost of it.
3. Set a premium that delivers a profit (on average) after prospective loss costs and operating expenses.
4. Be willing to walk away from business that is not profitable.

"Many insurers pass the first three tests and flunk the fourth," he said, but Berkshire was different. Berkshire often left the table with money in its pocket—in search of a better deal.* Its two reinsurers knew this playbook well and continued to swim well against a strong tide. New capital entering the industry continued to pressure rates. Buffett went so far as to say he thought the next ten years could be difficult, and almost certainly not as good as the previous decade. Notwithstanding the headwinds, both General Re and Berkshire Hathaway Reinsurance Group (BHRG) reported underwriting profits for the year.

Table 9.11: Berkshire Hathaway—Insurance Underwriting

($ millions)	2016	2015
GEICO		
Premiums earned	$25,483	$22,718
Underwriting gain/(loss) - pre-tax	462	460
General Re		
Premiums earned	$5,637	$5,975
Underwriting gain/(loss) - pre-tax	190	132
Berkshire Hathaway Reinsurance Group		
Premiums earned	$8,504	$7,207
Underwriting gain/(loss) - pre-tax	822	421
Berkshire Hathaway Primary Group		
Premiums earned	$6,257	$5,394
Underwriting gain/(loss) - pre-tax	657	824
Total premiums earned	$45,881	$41,294
Total underwriting gain/(loss) - pre-tax	2,131	1,837
Average float	89,650	85,822
Cost of float	(2.4%)	(2.1%)

Sources: Berkshire Hathaway Annual Report 2016 and author's calculations.

---

* It is interesting to note how Berkshire's patience in waiting out low prices effectively allows it to participate in the business at better rates later. It lets others rush in and make unprofitable deals and then turns around years later and takes the risk off their books in the form of retroactive or retrocessional reinsurance contracts.

GEICO

High expenses continued to weigh on GEICO's results, but its 98.2% combined ratio and $462 million profit were only poor in comparison to its past profitability. Losses from hail storms and flooding kept the loss ratio elevated even after the company instituted price increases. Those price increases and additional policies-in-force led to a 12% increase in earned premiums to $25.5 billion. Growth was good when GEICO was underwriting profitably. More appropriately priced policies-in-force would lead to more profits and more float—a simple recipe for success. Incentives were a key reason GEICO's market share continued to grow year after year, ending 2016 at 12%, up from 11.4%.

GEICO's incentive compensation system is beautifully simple. It consists of two primary variables. The first is growth in policies-in-force.* The second is the profitability of seasoned business. Everyone at GEICO from the frontlines up to the CEO depended on those two variables. (The more senior you are, the larger the incentive compensation is in relation to your base pay.) This accomplished Buffett's goal of having GEICO deliver both more business and profitable business. "It totally aligns the goals of the organization, in terms of compensation, with the goals of the owner," he told shareholders at the 2016 Annual Meeting.

Didn't other insurers use this simple (and almost obvious) two-pronged approach? Not necessarily. And why not reward employees for GEICO's bottom line? The answer lay in the way the incentive structure shaped behavior. Buffett knew focusing on GEICO's bottom line could have adverse effects. If employees were rewarded based on profits, an easy place to scale back would be its huge advertising budget. Such short-term thinking would hamper new business growth. On numerous occasions in the past, GEICO maintained large advertising expenditures when others were cutting back. This was again the case during the latter part of 2016.

The focus on the profitability of seasoned business (returning customers) accomplished two things. For one it properly incentivized underwriting for profitability, not just growth—a bedrock principle of *all* Berkshire's insurers. Second, those advertising expenditures cost a lot in relation to the premiums they generated. First-year customers are typically not profitable, but it really pays to have them stick around.**

GEICO first implemented this incentive structure in 1995. Two decades later, it was still proving its effectiveness.

---

* Specifically, GEICO rewards the number of policies-in-force, not premium growth. Premiums are a separate item and more related to profitability.

** At the 2017 Annual Meeting, Buffett said the loss ratio on first-year business ran 10 percentage points higher than renewal business.

General Re

General Re pulled back writing policies due to weak pricing and let earned premiums fall 6% to $5.6 billion. Pre-tax underwriting profits, however, grew 44% to $190 million as a rebound in life/health offset a decline in profits in property/casualty.

Property/casualty earned premiums fell 8% to $2.6 billion. Profits of $211 million on property business came after no significant catastrophe losses but declined from the prior year because of lower favorable loss development. Casualty/workers' compensation reported a $94 million loss, which came from the same pattern of current year losses from conservative reserving, favorable loss development on prior year business, and accounting charges related to discount accretion and deferred charge amortization. Gen Re's life/health line swung from an $18 million loss in 2015 to a $73 million profit in 2016 due to gains in international business, lower claims severity in North America, and reserving changes.

In 2016, Gen Re announced Tad Montross would be retiring at the end of the year after thirty-nine years at the company. Both Buffett and Ajit Jain (who would be elevated to oversee Gen Re in addition to BHRG), praised Montross for turning Gen Re around. Montross would be replaced by another longtime Gen Re insider, Kara Raiguel.

Berkshire Hathaway Reinsurance Group

BHRG earned premiums grew 18% to $8.5 billion and pre-tax underwriting profits nearly doubled (up 95%) to $822 million. Lower gains in property/casualty, lower losses in retroactive reinsurance, and a return to profitability in life and annuity were responsible for the increase in profits.

The property/casualty segment increased earned premiums 5% to $4.6 billion. The ten-year, 20% quota-share contract with Insurance Australia Group that began on July 1, 2015 represented 37% of earned premiums in this line. A catastrophe-free year led to another strong year of profits of $767 million but lower than the prior year because of lower reductions in prior year loss reserves (i.e. lower favorable loss development adjustments).

The retroactive reinsurance line sprang back to life after essentially taking a year off in 2015 (premiums were just $5 million). Almost all the $1.3 billion in premiums earned in 2016 in retroactive reinsurance came from three policies, including $670 million from a contract with Hartford Fire Insurance Company. That policy covered adverse development on asbestos and pollution claims losses (aggregate limit of $1.5 billion). The segment reported a $49 million loss, which would have been worse had the US dollar not appreciated and caused a $392 million currency gain from revaluation of liabilities in other currencies.

BHRG's life and annuity business reported an underwriting profit of $104 million on $2.6 billion of premium volume. That line was further delineated into three types of business based on implicit or explicit time value of money concepts, as described more fully earlier in the discussion on 2015.

Berkshire Hathaway Primary Group

Primary Group earned premiums grew 16% to $6.3 billion but underwriting profits fell 20% to $657 million. The combined ratio deteriorated from 84.7% to 89.5%. Causes of the lower profitability were declines in the level of favorable loss development and higher losses on current year business. The footnotes warned readers not to assume favorable loss development going forward. The primary insurers wrote a lot of business with long claim-tails, such as healthcare malpractice and workers' compensation business, that could develop unfavorable in future years.

Regulated, Capital-Intensive Businesses

BNSF fixed its internal service issues in 2015 only to be hit by external factors that negatively impacted results in 2016. A combination of carload volume declines and a reduction in shipping revenues largely driven by lower fuel costs resulted in a 10% decline in BNSF's overall revenues to $19.8 billion. Pre-tax earnings fell 16% to $5.7 billion.

Carload volume declined 5% as demand for industrial products fell and coal volume contracted sharply, down 21%. Agricultural volume increased 6% and consumer products increased 1%. Coal volumes decreased in part due to a long-term shift away from using it as a fuel for electrical generation. Low natural gas prices made coal relatively more expensive, leading utilities to stop using it or to just use existing stockpiles. The decline in industrial products reduced revenues from that segment by 14% and reflected weakness in oil and gas industries (its volume wasn't disclosed).

Berkshire Hathaway Energy EBIT grew 2.6% to $3.4 billion, while Berkshire's share of net earnings grew 7% to $2.3 billion. The flat result in EBIT masked a wide range of earnings at its many operating subsidiaries. Higher rates and volume combined with lower input costs to increase MidAmerican Energy Company's pre-tax earnings by 34% to $392 million. Part of the reason for the strong increase lay with an approved rate increase phased in over three years that MidAmerican received in 2014. The increase compensated the company for additional wind assets put in place that cut into returns on equity. The last time it increased rates was almost twenty years prior.[115]

On the negative side of the ledger, pre-tax earnings at Northern Powergrid fell 20% to $367 million. About half of the decline came from appreciation of the US dollar against the UK pound. The remainder of the decline came from lower distribution revenues and higher depreciation and impairment charges. Earnings fluctuated to a much smaller degree at BHE's other operating subsidiaries. Some benefitted from lower input costs, while others passed along most of the savings to customers. Fluctuations in temperatures also played a part in any year by impacting the demand for energy.

Finance and Financial Products

Pre-tax earnings in the Finance and Financial Products businesses grew 2.1% to $2.1 billion. Clayton's revenues grew 30% to $4.2 billion due to strong demand for homes and an expansion into site-built homes. Clayton purchased its first site-built homebuilder in 2015, added two more in 2016, and expected to acquire more in the future. Clayton's large mortgage portfolio overshadowed the manufacturing portion of its business, which resulted in its earnings growing just 5% to $744 million. The transportation equipment leasing businesses (Marmon's containers, cranes, and railcars; and XTRA) increased pre-tax earnings 5.5% to $959 million. Revenue growth of a similar magnitude and lower depreciation charges were responsible for the increase in earnings. A 9% decline in other earnings within Finance and Financial Products offset the increases at Clayton and transportation equipment leasing. Beginning in 2016 Berkshire began charging Marmon's rail and tank car unit for capital like it did for Clayton's mortgage portfolio. Curiously, NetJets wasn't included in that list, which appeared to indicate it paid off its debt or did not seek to benefit from Berkshire's strong credit rating.

Investments

Berkshire sold a net $12 billion of its equity portfolio in 2016. DaVita fell off the table presented in the Chairman's letter but remained unchanged. USG Corp., a drywall manufacturer, also went untouched but an increase in its market value caused it to make the cutoff. Some notable sales were AT&T, Deere & Company (the maker of John Deere equipment), and Walmart, which was mostly sold ($96 million, or 2.5% of the original investment, remained at year-end). Berkshire's Procter & Gamble shares were exchanged for Duracell.

The additions to the portfolio were notable and garnered much press. The biggest addition was Apple, the maker of iPhones, computers, and other technology. Over the year, Berkshire amassed a $6.7 billion stake valued at $7.1 billion. The purchase was made not by Buffett but by one or both of Todd Comb and/or Ted Weschler, Berkshire's two investment managers. Each managed over $10 billion at year-end

2016. Buffett gave them wide discretion over the money they managed and only learned about their moves in reviewing month end reports.[*]

The other big move was a series of investments in the airline industry. Berkshire initiated positions in American, Delta, Southwest, and United, together worth $8.9 billion at year-end.[**] Why was Berkshire interested in airlines, especially after almost losing its entire investment in USAir decades earlier and bemoaning the terrible industry economics many times afterward? "The worst sort of business is one that grows rapidly, requires significant capital to engender the growth, then earns little or no money. Think airlines." Over the ensuing decades, industry consolidation created stable market shares and less intense price competition. Spreading the investment over the four largest US carriers was a bet on the industry rather than one airline. Buffett also liked that the airlines were buying back a lot of their own shares.

Two of Berkshire's biggest investments weren't in the table at all as they were not simple common stock purchases. Its $5 billion investment in Bank of America preferred stock was worth $10.5 billion due to an option to purchase common shares. The other was Kraft Heinz, which was purchased with 3G Capital and had to be accounted for on an equity basis despite Berkshire owning publicly traded common stock. The accounting for Kraft Heinz proved that the value of private businesses could diverge quite drastically from their underlying value. The common stock cost $9.8 billion and was on the books for $15.3 billion. Yet its market value was over $28 billion. Extend the situation at Kraft Heinz to many of Berkshire's other businesses and one can see why Buffett considered book value an understated estimate of intrinsic value.

An ongoing scandal at Wells Fargo shed light on Berkshire's risk management practices. The Wells Fargo scandal involved the bank's incentive structure that rewarded cross-selling accounts. The system backfired when it led to improper account openings. Wells Fargo was Berkshire's largest marketable security holding at year-end and Carol Loomis used it as the subject of the first question for Buffett at the 2017 Annual Meeting.

> Loomis: "How do you satisfy yourself that Berkshire isn't subject to the same risk, with its highly decentralized structure and the very substantial autonomy given to senior leadership of the operating companies?"

Buffett's response boiled down to a couple factors. One was Berkshire's culture. "We count very heavily on principles of behavior rather than loads of rules." Buffett

---

[*] They were restricted from investing in certain existing investments that could cause regulatory headaches or might make it appear Berkshire had insider knowledge (such as with Microsoft and Berkshire board member Bill Gates) but otherwise were free to invest however they saw fit.

[**] It's not clear why the American shares, worth $2.2 billion at year-end, weren't included in the Chairman's table.

reinforced that behavior wherever he could. This included a biannual letter to Berkshire's managers instructing them never to go near the gray area and by airing a key part of Buffett's congressional testimony related to the 1980s' Solomon scandal every year at the Annual Meeting.

Buffett also said Berkshire was not completely hands-off. It had an internal auditing system that included ways to submit anonymous tips to headquarters in Omaha, a system that brought in over 4,000 tips annually. Some tips amounted to merely griping but others led to real change. Munger went so far as to say he believed Berkshire would be blindsided by something someday. Munger thought Berkshire would gain more by over-trusting, even if it meant they would miss something big now and again (which would garner an outsize share of press). The Wells Fargo scandal offered two lessons for managers.

1. Incentives work and must be crafted carefully to avoid unintended consequences. Even well-intentioned plans can backfire and cause misery.
2. It's important to act quickly when problems surface. The Salomon and Wells Fargo scandals proved that things only get worse, not better, by delaying.

Table 9.12: Berkshire Hathaway—equity portfolio, select detail

($ millions)	2016 Cost	2016 Market	2015 Cost	2015 Market	Change Cost	Change Market
American Express	$1,287	$11,231	$1,287	$10,545	$0	$686
Apple	6,747	7,093			6,747	7,093
AT&T			1,283	1,603	(1,283)	(1,603)
Charter Communications	1,210	1,955	1,202	1,367	8	588
The Coca-Cola Company	1,299	16,584	1,299	17,184	0	(600)
DaVita Healthcare Partners			843	1,291	(843)	(1,291)
Delta Airlines	2,299	2,702			2,299	2,702
Deere & Company			1,773	1,690	(1,773)	(1,690)
Goldman Sachs	654	2,727	654	2,053	0	674
International Business Machines	13,815	13,484	13,791	11,152	24	2,332
Moody's Corporation	248	2,326	248	2,475	0	(149)
Phillips 66	5,841	6,445	4,357	4,530	1,484	1,915
Sanofi	1,692	1,791	1,701	1,896	(9)	(105)
Southwest Airlines	1,757	2,153			1,757	2,153
Procter & Gamble			336	4,683	(336)	(4,683)
US Bancorp	3,239	5,233	3,239	4,346	0	887
United Continental Holdings	1,477	1,940			1,477	1,940
USG Corp.	836	1,253			836	1,253
Walmart			3,593	3,893	(3,593)	(3,893)
Wells Fargo & Company	12,730	27,555	12,730	27,180	0	375
All other	10,697	17,560	10,276	16,450	421	1,110
Total equity securities	$65,828	$122,032	$58,612	$112,338	$7,216	$9,694

Sources: Berkshire Hathaway Annual Reports 2015–2016 and author's calculations.

More of Berkshire's many investments made during the recession began winding down in 2016. In September, Wrigley redeemed its preferred stock for $4.6 billion, a hefty sum compared to the $2.1 billion investment and the preferred dividends received since 2008. In December, Dow elected to convert its $3 billion, 8.5% preferred stock investment into 72.6 million shares, which Berkshire immediately sold. In addition to these redemptions, Kraft Heinz repaid its $8 billion, 9% preferred stock for $8.3 billion. The pre-tax capital gains from these investments amounted to more than $4.2 billion. The total cash received was much higher and left Berkshire with more cash to add to its growing pile, now at $86 billion at year-end 2016.

2017

Berkshire's book value per share increased 23% during 2017. That result was 1.2 percentage points better than the S&P 500.* Berkshire's $65.3 billion gain in net worth was extraordinary for a conglomerate of its size. Had Berkshire's capital allocators finally found the secret to growing a company with a quarter-trillion-dollar net worth by almost a quarter in twelve months? Sadly, no. It came from a tax code change. In December 2017, Congress passed the Tax Cuts and Jobs Act of 2017. That legislation reduced the corporate tax rate from 35% to 21% (among other things) and diminished Berkshire's deferred tax liabilities by $29.1 billion. The lower tax rate meant Berkshire's shareholders were entitled to keep more of the conglomerate's profits, and those were growing.

Berkshire's operations contributed the other $36.2 billion or 12.8% of the prior year's net worth. On balance the year was a good one for Berkshire. Aided by the largest retroactive reinsurance deal in history, the Insurance Group increased float to record levels. On the negative side of the ledger, several catastrophe losses broke the fourteen-year streak of overall underwriting profitability. Most of Berkshire's many non-insurance subsidiaries did well during the year, although a few struggled with specific issues. A low interest rate environment made it difficult to compete for acquisitions and swelled Berkshire's cash hoard to $116 billion. Berkshire found modest success during the year on the acquisition front. It spent $2.7 billion on bolt-on acquisitions and made one notable partial acquisition.

---

* Berkshire's market value increased 21.9%.

Pilot Flying J

On October 3, 2017, Berkshire acquired a 38.6% interest in Pilot Travel Centers, LLC, based in Knoxville, Tennessee.* The company operated 750 travel centers across the US and Canada making it the largest in North America with $20 billion in annual revenues. Better known as Pilot Flying J (from the name of its travel centers), the company resulted from the 2010 merger of Pilot Travel Centers and Flying J, and was led by Jimmy Haslam III, whose father founded a predecessor company in 1958. Berkshire's initial purchase price went undisclosed, but sources later put the figure at $2.8 billion. That implied a valuation of about $7.25 billion for the company.[116]

Insurance

Berkshire's fourteen-year streak of overall underwriting profits ended in 2017. Six catastrophes, including three hurricanes in the United States and Puerto Rico, caused major losses.** The Insurance Group recorded a pre-tax underwriting loss of $3.2 billion on $60.6 billion of earned premiums (up 32%), which caused it to give back some of the $28 billion in pre-tax profit accumulated over the long winning streak. In that light, the loss wasn't so bad. Nor was the 3.1% cost of float on $103 billion of average float.***

Buffett repeatedly told shareholders to expect a loss year at some point. This was a fact of life for a big insurer. He estimated Berkshire's share of industry losses to be about 3% and placed a worst-case mega cat (mega-catastrophe) at $400 billion. Such an event would cost Berkshire $12 billion, a sum easily covered by Berkshire's non-insurance businesses—but one that would probably bankrupt other insurers.****

---

* Knoxville was also home to Clayton Homes. Buffett said Kevin Clayton, a friend of the selling family, played a part in helping the deal come through.
** Berkshire defined catastrophe losses as $100 million or greater pre-tax from a single event.
*** Year-end float increased from $91.6 billion in 2016 to $114.5 billion in 2017.
**** Buffett put the odds of such an event at 2% annually, a figure some thought too high.

Table 9.13: Berkshire Hathaway—Insurance Underwriting

($ millions)	2017	2016
GEICO		
Premiums earned	$29,441	$25,483
Underwriting gain/(loss) - pre-tax	(310)	462
Berkshire Hathaway Reinsurance Group		
Premiums earned:		
Property/casualty	$7,552	$7,218
Retroactive reinsurance	10,755	1,254
Life/health	4,808	4,587
Periodic payment annuity	898	1,082
Total premiums earned	24,013	14,141
Underwriting gain/(loss) - pre-tax:		
Property/casualty	(1,595)	895
Retroactive reinsurance	(1,330)	(60)
Life/health	(52)	305
Periodic payment annuity	(671)	(128)
Total underwriting gain/(loss) - pre-tax	(3,648)	1,012
Berkshire Hathaway Primary Group		
Premiums earned	$7,143	$6,257
Underwriting gain/(loss) - pre-tax	719	657
Total premiums earned	$60,597	$45,881
Total underwriting gain/(loss) - pre-tax	(3,239)	2,131
Average float	103,039	89,650
Cost of float	3.1%	(2.4%)

Note: In 2017, results for General Re were consolidated with BHRG. Results for 2016 were restated to conform to the new presentation.
Sources: Berkshire Hathaway Annual Reports 2017, 2019; and author's calculations.

Berkshire Hathaway Reinsurance Group

Beginning in 2017, General Re's results were consolidated with BHRG. The reporting was now delineated between four major lines of business: property/casualty, retroactive reinsurance, life/health, and periodic payment annuity, with some detail on activities from General Re separated for comparative purposes. A high-level analysis showed the NICO Group (BHRG's original operations) eclipsed General Re in property/casualty by about half. Gen Re's life/health business remained about double that of Berkshire Hathaway Life Insurance Company of Nebraska (BHLN Group, BHRG's original operations).

Led by Ajit Jain, Berkshire Hathaway Reinsurance Group underwrote the largest retroactive reinsurance deal in history. For a $10.2 billion premium, Berkshire agreed to pay up to $20 billion to cover losses AIG incurred prior to 2016.* The deal was attractive to both sides. It drastically lowered the risk that AIG would find itself with inadequate reserves and allowed Berkshire to put its superior financial strength to work. The AIG deal caused earned premiums for the retroactive reinsurance segment to grow from $1.3 billion in 2016 to $10.8 billion in 2017 and was responsible for BHRG overall earned premiums growing 70% to $24 billion. BHRG as a whole reported a pre-tax underwriting loss of $3.6 billion compared to a $1 billion gain the year before.

Remember that a retroactive reinsurance contract does not impact profitability on day one. Instead, future expected losses in excess of the premium received are booked as a deferred charge asset that is amortized into losses over the life of the contract. That amounted to $6.2 billion for the AIG contract alone. In theory this asset represented what Berkshire would earn on the premium it received upfront. The variables that would determine Berkshire's ultimate economic result were the timing and amount of future payments. More broadly, its ability to invest the float would also play a part. Even before year-end 2017, estimates were being revised. In the fourth quarter of 2017, Berkshire increased its estimate of ultimate claim liabilities on the AIG contract by $1.8 billion. It also increased the deferred charge asset by $1.7 billion because most of those losses would occur in the future. That left $100 million as the net hit to profits in 2017. The ultimate judge of its profitability would be seen over decades.**

Accounting charges dominated the retroactive reinsurance line. About $1 billion of the $1.3 billion underwriting loss in 2017 was due to deferred charge amortization.*** Charges of a similar magnitude would hit earnings in future years and create a strong headwind to an overall underwriting profit. Another $264 million foreign currency loss related to revaluation of foreign denominated liabilities also impacted results. The $100 million net adjustment from the AIG contract discussed above made up the difference.

Property/casualty earned premiums grew 5% to $7.6 billion. The 20% quota-share agreement with Insurance Australia Group from NICO Group represented 40% of its $4.5 billion earned premiums. Gen Re's property/casualty business increased earned premiums 21% to $3.1 billion despite continued headwinds from high industry capacity by adding new business and increasing participation for renewal business.

---

* The contract specified that Berkshire would indemnify AIG for 80% of losses up to $25 billion in excess of $25 billion retained by AIG.

** At the 2018 Annual Meeting, Buffett stated that about $15 billion had been paid by AIG to date. Berkshire's payments would kick in beginning at the $25 billion mark. He also noted that payments tended to slow down in future years, an effect that can be seen in historical claims duration statistics in financial filings.

*** Of the total $1.33 billion underwriting loss in retroactive reinsurance, $264 million related to changes in exchange rates and $100 million we know was from the AIG contract, so $966 million remained. The AIG deal was responsible for $10.2 of the $10.8 earned premiums in the retroactive segment, which left $700 million of other retroactive volume. The footnotes also disclosed that reserve development in retroactive "relatively insignificant in 2017 and 2016".

Losses from hurricanes Harvey, Irma, and Maria, an earthquake in Mexico, a cyclone in Australia, and wildfires in California caused $2.4 billion of losses for the combined property/casualty segment. Profit on other property/casualty contracts and $295 million favorable loss development mitigated the overall loss to *just* $1.6 billion.

A change to assumptions used in workers' compensation reinsurance illustrated the leeway management has over financial statements. Prior to the fourth quarter of 2017, Berkshire discounted its workers' compensation claim liabilities assumed under reinsurance contracts (reflecting the fact that payments in the future were worth less than in the present). The change eliminated the discount to make those contracts consistent with other contracts. This resulted in a $1.43 billion increase to losses and loss expenses and hit shareholders' equity to the tune of $931 million.* This move demonstrated Berkshire's conservatism and highlighted how managements could influence financial statements. Accounting for insurance was full of such assumptions and sometimes tempted unscrupulous management teams to hide losses—or even engage in outright fraud.** In every round of accounting versus economics, Buffett and Berkshire leaned toward realism, even if it made results looks worse.

A $52 million loss from the life/health line resulted from changes in underlying assumptions. Gen Re reported a loss largely from such charges related to its US long-term care business while gains were reported from Berkshire Hathaway Life Insurance Company of Nebraska related to its variable annuity business.

The periodic payment annuity business reported a $671 million loss. Part of that loss was due to depreciation of the US dollar against the UK pound and a reduced discount rate (which increased the liability).***

GEICO

GEICO reported its first underwriting loss since the year 2000, but growth in float more than offset the loss. Its 86.6% loss ratio was the highest on record under Berkshire's ownership and included $450 million (1.5% of earned premiums) of losses from hurricanes Harvey and Irma and $517 million (1.75% of earned premiums) from unfavorable loss development on prior year claims. The $310 million pre-tax underwriting loss represented a combined ratio of 101.1%. The topline was a different story. Earned premiums grew 15.5% to $29.4 billion driven by a combination of 8.6% growth in policies-in-force and 6.9% higher pricing. GEICO's float was not detailed but estimating float at 65% of premiums earned (its historical average) put

---

* The difference was a $502 million reduction in income tax liabilities.
** Retained earnings and shareholders' equity were restated for 2014–2016 to reflect the revised assumptions.
*** See the discussion of the economics of these time-value-of-money activities in the section on 2015.

it at approximately $19 billion, an increase of about $2.5 billion over the prior year. GEICO's market share increased from 12% to 12.8%.[117]

Berkshire Hathaway Primary Group

The Primary Group was in the black and delivered both 14% growth in premiums earned, to $7.1 billion, and 9% higher profit, to $719 million. Double-digit growth at GUARD (26%) and BH Specialty (23%) led the group, and growth from MedPro and the Home State companies also contributed to premium growth. Losses from the many catastrophe events in 2017 negatively impacted results. Favorable loss development amounted to ten percentage points compared to eight the prior year. In each of the last three years, favorable development occurred in healthcare malpractice and workers' compensation lines.

Regulated, Capital-Intensive Businesses

Revenues at BNSF grew 8% to $21.4 billion and pre-tax earnings 11% to $6.3 billion, with volumes and pricing contributing to results. Carload volumes increased in the mid-single digits in each of consumer products, industrial products, and coal; volume in agricultural products was flat. The full-year results masked somewhat slower growth in the second half of the year. The change in coal volume over the prior two years illustrated the basic economic principle of substitute goods (one that can be substituted for another). In the case of BNSF and coal, natural gas was the cheaper substitute good due to a decline in natural gas prices during 2016. This led consumers and electric utility generating plants to switch to natural gas. As natural gas prices rose during 2017, coal again became attractive and demand increased. Substitute goods are part of all business cycles, and which side a product or service falls on seals its financial fate.

EBIT at Berkshire Hathaway Energy was flat at $3.4 billion with little change in operational results at most units. The two natural gas pipelines increased EBIT 8% to $446 million. That resulted from a rate structure change at the beginning of the year which allowed Kern River to be more competitive with existing customers in order to retain more business.[118] AltaLink, the Alberta, Canada-based electric transmission utility, increased its revenues 39% due to a regulatory decision allowing it to recover construction-in-progress quicker.* Some units, such as Northern Powergrid (located in the UK) were hurt by foreign exchange rates, specifically a decline in the US dollar against the UK pound.

---

* AltaLink's pre-tax earnings were not disclosed. In the 2017 Berkshire Hathaway Energy 10K report filed with the SEC, AltaLink is consolidated with its US-based transmission assets. The increase in pre-tax earnings for that segment was 25%.

The accounting for interest expense illustrates the importance of understanding the nuances of accounting. During the year BHE completed a tender offer for some of its debt. This was favorable from an economic standpoint.* But the transaction caused a large one-time charge that accounting rules dictated be recorded on the interest expense line. On the books, it appeared interest expense increased from $465 million to $844 million, even though actual interest expense declined 7%. Including the accounting charge, Berkshire's share of net earnings fell 9% to $2.1 billion.

Impact of the 2017 Tax Cut

The 2017 tax law change that contributed to the outsized increase in net worth had an important subtlety. The key question was: Who would benefit from the lower tax rate? The answer depended on the industry:

- *Heavily regulated businesses: Customers*
  Utility businesses like BNSF and BHE were allowed a rate of return on equity calculated on an after-tax basis. Any benefit must be passed on to customers via lower prices. Berkshire put this figure at about $6 billion.
- *Unregulated businesses with strong moats: Companies*
  A business like See's would keep all or most of the benefit since it faced low pricing pressure from competition. (The reduced liabilities associated with deferred tax on unrealized investment gains accrued to Berkshire's benefit too.)
- *Unregulated businesses facing competition: Customers*
  These businesses would find they had to give most or all the benefit of lower taxes to customers in order to retain business. Businesses without a moat would have to lower prices to compete, thus losing most of the benefit of the lower taxes.

Manufacturing, Service, and Retailing

When Buffett told shareholders in 2016 that competitors read Berkshire's Annual Reports, he was setting the stage for a new format with less discussion of Berkshire's individual businesses. This new format was implemented in 2017, and the table summarizing the balance sheet and earnings for the MSR businesses was entirely gone. Only a rough calculation could be made using the business segment data provided in the notes to the financial statements.

---

* According to an offer memorandum published on December 28, 2017, the bonds redeemed had interest rates ranging from 5.95% to 8.48% and were replaced by borrowings with an average rate (according to the notes to the financial statements) of 2%.

Buffett suggested that more detail, while desirable to shareholders, wasn't as important as when Berkshire was smaller. "Be aware, though, that it's the growth of the Berkshire forest that counts. It would be foolish to focus over-intently on any single tree."

Buffett long counseled that profits must be analyzed in relation to the capital that produces them. Calculating return on tangible equity became all but impossible without the summary balance sheet historically provided to shareholders in the Chairman's letter. Information previously provided on the balance sheet was largely absent, aside from amounts for goodwill and identifiable assets at year-end.*

Table 9.14: Manufacturing, Service, and Retailing businesses—pre-tax earnings

($ millions)	2017	2016	% Change
Industrial products	$4,367	$4,209	4%
Building products	1,382	1,178	17%
Consumer products	1,112	824	35%
Subtotal - manufacturing	6,861	6,211	10%
Service	1,298	1,161	12%
Retailing	785	659	19%
McLane	299	431	(31%)
Subtotal - service and retailing	2,382	2,251	6%
Total pre-tax earnings	9,243	8,462	9%
Income taxes and non-controlling interests	(3,035)	(2,831)	7%
Earnings after tax	$6,208	$5,631	10%

Sources: Berkshire Hathaway Annual Report 2017 and author's calculations.

Industrial products (revenues of $26.4bn, up 6.8%): Earnings (up 4% to $4.4 billion) were hurt by one-time charges related to the Precision Castparts (PCC) acquisition, which led its pre-tax earnings to fall 12.5%.** Its earnings were not detailed. Nor were the earnings of IMC and Marmon. The footnotes disclosed strong revenue growth at those two companies (IMC up 13%, Marmon up 7%) but did not specify how much translated into earnings. Lubrizol's earnings were detailed. On just 3% revenue growth Lubrizol's pre-tax earnings grew 17% due to a combination of factors

---

* Many analysts and shareholders (the author included) bemoaned this change. The MSR businesses are a significant source of Berkshire's value and understanding the nuances of its businesses is important. A fun statistic: the 1987 Berkshire Hathaway Annual Report was 56 pages long. The 2017 report registered 148 pages. Said another way, Berkshire's Annual Report increased at a rate of just 3.3% per year over 30 years while its business expanded far beyond the budding conglomerate it was at the beginning of that period. Buffett: buster of footnote inflation.

** These one-time inventory and impairment charges were unrelated to the amortization charges Berkshire was required to take in connection with the acquisition. Buffett said there was a little over $400 million a year of amortization of goodwill related to PCC in 2017. Berkshire aggregated such purchase accounting-related charges into one line item as they were not considered useful in assessing the operating performance of the businesses.

including a lower comparable year in 2016 as a result of the $365 million write-off of an underperforming business.

Building Products (revenues of $11.9bn, up 10.8%): Pre-tax earnings grew 17% to $1.4 billion. Half of the increase in revenues was due to bolt-on acquisitions at Shaw and MiTek, which presumably also contributed to earnings. About half of the increase in earnings was a result of a lower base in 2016 from $107 million of asset impairments, pension settlements, and environmental claim charges from Shaw and Benjamin Moore.

Consumer Products (revenues of $12.1bn, up 10%): Earnings from the consumer products businesses swelled 35% to $1.1 billion. Forest River contributed to organic growth (growth from existing operations, not bolt-on acquisitions). Its revenues increased 14% and its earnings increased by 23% as strong demand for RVs bolstered results. Duracell bounced back strongly. Its results in 2016 were penalized by transition and restructuring costs. In 2017 its revenues increased 25% (compared to a ten-month period in 2016) and pre-tax earnings amounted to $82 million.[*] Apparel and footwear increased earnings 5%.

Service businesses (revenues of $11.2bn, up 8%): Segment pre-tax earnings grew 12% to $1.3 billion. Results at TTI and NetJets led the growth within the service segment. Higher demand for electronic components and increased flight hours translated into higher revenues and earnings for the two companies. Earnings for the service businesses increased strongly, even with lower earnings (unspecified) from FlightSafety, the media companies, and the logistics businesses.

Retailing (revenues of $15.1bn, flat): Berkshire's retailers had flat revenues but managed to increase earnings by 19% to $785 million. Earnings growth came from Berkshire Hathaway Automotive (which represented 63% of revenues within the segment), the home furnishings retailers, and the Pampered Chef. Results for the jewelers, See's, Oriental Trading Company, and Detlev Louis Motorrad were not discussed in detail.

McLane (revenues of $49.8bn, up 3.5%): McLane had a bad year. While revenues increased, earnings fell off a cliff, down 31% to $299 million. The large decline in earnings was attributed to a 57% decline in grocery business attributed to pricing pressures from competition and higher costs. Here too the analyst was left wanting reasons behind the large shift in business fortunes, especially one that had been relatively stable in prior years. Luckily, Buffett received a question from Jonathan Brandt, an analyst at Ruane, Cunniff & Goldfarb, one of three analysts invited to

---

[*] Duracell's earnings appear low compared to the $4.2 billion purchase price. Its earnings appear inadequate even when deducting the $1.8 billion cash from the purchase price. Duracell was a relatively small part of Berkshire. Buffett did note at the 2018 Annual Meeting that Duracell was expected to earn more after it finished working through ongoing transition problems. It appeared from Buffett's comments that management needed to right-size certain operations but was prevented from doing so, at least temporarily, because of employment laws, among other things.

ask questions at the 2018 Annual Meeting. The decline in grocery was worse than it appeared since McLane's liquor distribution business was relatively more profitable. McLane had large and strong suppliers on one side and equally formidable customers on the other side; what was left (less than 1% of revenues pre-tax) is what McLane had to live on. Buffett said McLane's woes would likely persist and were evidence of the competitive pressures of capitalism.

Finance and Financial Products

Pre-tax earnings in the Finance and Financial Products businesses declined 3% to $2.1 billion. Clayton's earnings increased 3% to $765 million on much stronger revenue growth of 18%. Clayton's $13.7 billion loan portfolio acted as a counterweight to manufacturing results (good or bad). Part of Clayton's revenue growth came from an increase in site-built homes. It acquired two additional site-built homebuilders in 2017.* Revenues from conventional construction were expected to top $1 billion in 2018, a large increase for Clayton but a tiny fraction of the overall industry. Clayton remained a powerhouse in manufactured homes—its 49% market share was three times its nearest competitor.

Earnings from transportation equipment leasing fell 9% to $869 million. Industry supply was part of the problem. Railcar capacity was thought to exceed demand, causing lower lease rates. Since depreciation and other fixed costs do not vary with revenues, a modest 2% decline in revenues translated into the larger drop in earnings.

Investments

Two investment moves in 2017 made big splashes—but neither were mentioned in the text of the 2017 Chairman's letter. If shareholders hadn't already heard about it in the business press, they would have noticed that IBM** disappeared from the list of top investments (where it was formerly third in market value) and Apple vaulted from fifth to second. Berkshire's initial stake in Apple was credited to one of the two investment managers, Todd Combs or Ted Weschler (Buffett again wouldn't specify). The enlarged Apple position, with a market value of $28 billion at year-end 2017, was Buffett's move. Buffett admitted to not understanding technology and being wary of such companies, so why divest of IBM and invest further in Apple?

The answer: Apple had a huge moat and IBM did not.

---

* The two were Oakwood Homes in Colorado and Harris Doyle in Alabama.
** At year-end 2017, two million shares worth $314 million remained, down from 81 million shares at year-end 2016.

Apple's moat was wide and deep. While its first successful business reinvention was the iMac personal computer in the late 1990s, the company hit true paydirt with the very portable iPod (which replaced bulkier CDs and CD players) and then again with the iPad (a tablet that can browse the internet) and iPhone (a smartphone that could be a telephone or used to browse the internet). These innovations made Apple more of a consumer products company than a technology company. They sold products people liked, and created an app technology ecosystem around those products that consumers invested in. Every time a new device or version of a device came out, people rushed to buy it. Having an iPhone was a status symbol, and Apple became a household name.

These consumer habits combined with significant switching costs created and maintained Apple's moat. Consumers would invest in apps and music that could only be used on Apple devices. Over time the market had consolidated to two large competitors: Apple and Google's Android system. Consumers had little incentive to adopt the competing system since it offered little added benefit compared to the large cost of repurchasing the apps and music already on their Apple system.

IBM, meanwhile, was a technology and service company. Its products are not as easily recognizable in day-to-day life, but that is not the reason for its narrow moat. IBM's products include supercomputers and various cloud computing services, including storage. That market proved to be more prone to competition from other large technology players such as Amazon, Microsoft, and Google than Buffett first realized. When Buffett first invested in IBM in 2011, he named it among four "exceptional companies" and praised its financial management. Years later, he admitted his investment had been a mistake. It was not that IBM did not make Berkshire money—it did, primarily through share repurchases and dividends—but another investment could have made Berkshire more. Berkshire's loss was one of opportunity cost. Its investment stagnated while the market advanced.

Apple's success as a business enterprise is captured in one remarkable statistic: The company required no tangible capital to operate.* Payables, accruals, and deposits exceeded everything needed to operate the business, from receivables, inventories, and fixed assets. In other words, Apple's suppliers and customers financed *all* its operations (and then some)—shareholders didn't need to supply any capital but were entitled to profits. What was such a company worth?

Berkshire paid $21 billion for its 3.3% stake in the company. This valued Apple at over $635 billion (see Table 9.15). Was Apple worth that much? The answer was yes, and more. Apple had $238 billion of cash and investments on the books at the end of its fiscal year in September 2016. Adjusting for excess cash and investments, and the debt the company had on its books, Berkshire's going-in pre-tax return was around

---

* This holds true even if we include goodwill and intangibles, and we capitalize R&D expenses.

12%. Berkshire's margin of safety was inherent in the quite-satisfactory going-in return and Apple's business moat (stemming from strong customer habits reinforced by high switching costs). That Apple could grow without needing additional capital was yet another benefit. "In effect we're betting on the ecosystem of Apple products led by the iPhone. And I see characteristics in that that make me think that it's extraordinary." Perhaps chastened by his experience with IBM, Buffett added, "But I may be wrong." He was not wrong, and nor was he alone in his bet. In July 2016, Apple hit the 1 billion mark in iPhone sales.

Apple also warmed Buffett's heart by buying back its own undervalued shares. "I'm delighted to see them repurchasing shares … with the passage of a little time we may own six or seven percent simply because they repurchase shares." A similar result played out with Berkshire's investment in American Express over its long holding period. Berkshire's initial position had grown from 13% of the company to almost 18% over the prior decade simply by virtue of share repurchases costing Berkshire nothing.

Table 9.15: Apple—investment analysis

($ millions)	2016	2015	2014	2013	2012
Total revenues	$215,639	$233,715	$182,795	$170,910	$156,508
Pre-tax operating income[1]	61,524	72,530	53,603	49,959	55,846
EBIT margin[1]	28%	30%	29%	29%	35%
Average tangible capital employed	(33,643)	(26,271)	(13,323)	(6,120)	(4,688)
Purchase price (equity)[2]	$635,182				
Debt	78,927				
Less: excess cash & investments[3]	(232,194)				
Effective purchase price	$481,915				
Average operating income (5 years)	58,692				
BRK going-in pre-tax return	12.2%				

Footnotes:
1. Adjustments were made for goodwill and intangibles.
2. Implied valuation based on Berkshire's cost of $20,961 million for 3.3% of the company.
3. Consists of cash & equivalents in excess of 2.5% of revenues plus long-term marketable securities.

Note: The company's fiscal year ended in September.
Sources: Berkshire Hathaway Annual Report 2017; Apple, Inc. Annual Reports 2011–2016; and author's calculations.

Berkshire exercised its Bank of America warrants in 2017 and exchanged its $5 billion preferred for 700 million shares of Bank of America. Those shares were worth $20.7 billion as of year-end, giving Berkshire a 6.8% stake in the bank.

Shares of Kraft Heinz had a market value of $25.3 billion at year-end. More exciting was the triple-play 3G Capital nearly pulled off in 2017. Berkshire and 3G Capital acquired Heinz in 2013 for $29 billion and then Kraft in 2015 for $57 billion. Two years later it was bidding for the consumer products giant Unilever. The price tag? $143 billion. The deal ultimately fell through after it was revealed the company wasn't interested in merging. The team at 3G Capital mistakenly thought Unilever was open to a friendly offer. Buffett told shareholders they were only interested in friendly transactions and the deal quickly died. Berkshire and 3G Capital were each prepared to inject an additional $15 billion of new equity to make the deal work.[119]

Restaurant Brands International redeemed Berkshire's preferred stock investment in December 2017. The $3 billion return of capital added to the growing cash pile at headquarters. The continued low interest rate environment meant Berkshire wouldn't be able to come close to matching the 9% yield it obtained on the investment made three years before.[*]

Protégé Bet

On December 19, 2007, Buffett made a ten-year bet through longbets.org that concluded on the same date in 2017. Long Bets was an organization set up to take long-term bets for periods of years stretching far into the future. Each side put up money, and the winner's charity received the proceeds after the bet concluded. Buffett bet that the S&P 500 index would outperform a portfolio of funds of hedge funds net of fees and expenses over the course of a decade. His bet put his own money (not Berkshire's) where his mouth had been for many years. He thought most investors would do better over time sticking to an unmanaged index, and that the fees hedge funds charged clients would negatively impact performance.

Buffett bet against Ted Seides, a co-manager of Protégé Partners who stepped up and contributed the $318,250 necessary to seed its $500,000 position. The money purchased zero-coupon bonds that would mature in ten years at the face value of the bond (no different than a savings bond). After an initial period of underperformance, the S&P 500 came out far ahead. At the end of the ten years, the S&P gained 125.8% (9.5% per year) compared to 36.3% (an average of 3% per year) for the group of five funds of funds. Buffett wrote that the managers of the 200-plus hedge funds and the fund of fund managers all had incentives to do well over that time. And all of them likely did well personally owing to the fees they charged. But in each case, the performance of the funds they managed fell short of an unmanaged index.

The bet offered an unforeseen lesson. The low-interest rate environment that accompanied the Great Recession drove the price of the zero-coupon bonds to almost

---

[*] The 10-year Treasury Note traded around 2.5% all year.

96% of par in just five years. Remember that the proceeds at maturity would be par or 100%. Buffett thought more money for charity could be had by switching from bonds to Berkshire stock. Protégé agreed to cash in the zero-coupon bonds and invest the proceeds in 11,200 shares of Berkshire Hathaway stock (B-shares). Buffett personally guaranteed their value would be at least $1 million at the end. At the conclusion of the bet, Girls Inc. of Omaha received much more. Over $2.2 million went to Buffett's charity and he also took home bragging rights. Buffett used the publicity to reinforce his message that fees matter and that an investor could do well by betting on America via a low-cost fund and sitting tight.

2018

Berkshire's 2018 business results were helped by the reduction in the corporate tax rate from 35% to 21%, which became law late in 2017. Operating results were strong in addition to (and perhaps partly because of) the reduction in the tax rate. Each of its major segments reported gains, including insurance, which returned to an overall underwriting profit. The dry spell for major acquisitions continued. But the stock market, including a downdraft late in the year, presented a chance to invest tens of billions into equities. Most of that money went into Apple, Berkshire's newest and largest holding.

A major change to accounting rules left Buffett opening his Chairman's letter with a lesson on accounting. Beginning in 2018, GAAP required unrealized gains and losses on equity securities to flow through the income statement instead of directly to book value as had been the practice for decades. Buffett primed shareholders on the change in his 2017 Chairman's letter and actual figures in 2018 proved the analytical limitations. Berkshire's record $24.8 billion of after-tax operating earnings resulted in $24.6 billion of net income under the old rules and a relatively dismal-seeming $4 billion net income under the new rules (see Table 9.16). Which should shareholders believe?

It came down to two questions: how best to present results to shareholders and what constituted earnings. The accounting authorities at the Financial Accounting Standards Board, the rulemaking body for GAAP, deemed the change beneficial to users of financial statements. Buffett and Munger disagreed. They suggested shareholders ignore *realized* gains and losses long before this rule change. Including *unrealized* gains and losses was going further in the wrong direction. Buffett warned in 2017 it would create "wild and capricious swings" in earnings that rendered the bottom line useless. That's exactly what happened in 2018. The accounting was at odds with the reality of common stock investment; owning stocks means owning businesses. Business values fluctuated but the magnitude of those changes was at odds with what the stock market would suggest through its frequent ups and downs.

Importantly, the accounting changes did not affect Berkshire's true economic performance. The unrealized gains or losses included in earnings were adjusted for taxes but did not create an actual tax bill. Like before, taxes would be due on realized gains only when a sale was made. From a financial statement presentation perspective, ASU 2016-01 (the name of the rule change) simply moved unrealized gains and losses from the statement of comprehensive income to the income statement. The statement of comprehensive income is an often-overlooked statement that contains items affecting net worth but not necessarily a component of income. This was another case of accounting versus economic reality. In both instances the unrealized gains and losses were presented net of taxes, so the impact to net worth was the same.

Table 9.16: Impact of ASU 2016-01 on Berkshire's reported earnings

($ billions, after tax)	Old rules	New rules
Income Statement:		
Operating earnings	$24.8	$24.8
Non-cash impairment[1]	(3.0)	(3.0)
Realized gains/losses	2.8	2.8
Unrealized losses		(20.6)
Net income	$24.6	$4.0
Statement of Comprehensive Income:		
Unrealized gain/losses	($20.6)	
Increase in shareholders' equity[2]	**$4.0**	**$4.0**

Footnotes:
1. Related to Kraft Heinz (discussed later).
2. Increase in shareholders' equity from earnings and securities gains. Does not account for share repurchases and certain other items.

Notes:
1. ASU 2016-01 is the accounting rule that changed the reporting of unrealized gains/losses.
2. Amounts are after non-controlling or minority interests.
Sources: Berkshire Hathaway Annual Report 2018 and author's calculations.

Buffett worried that too much emphasis would be placed on Berkshire's reported bottom line. Most reporters used the net income figure in their reporting and many, unfortunately, were not trained to dig much deeper. This was not as much of a problem at many companies. Berkshire was different in its huge holdings of marketable securities. The daily, quarterly, or yearly fluctuations of its $173 billion portfolio could overshadow the operating results at its many businesses. Buffett's advice to shareholders: "Focus on operating earnings, paying little attention to gains or losses of any variety." Capital gains, whether realized or unrealized, were important to Berkshire over time, but short-term movements were devoid of analytical information.

In years past, a solution to the accounting issue discussed above would be to focus on the change in book value per share. The fluctuations in marketable securities prices would find their way to book value under either accounting method. But that metric gradually lost its relevance as Berkshire allocated more capital to owning businesses in their entirety. Berkshire's change in book value per share made its last appearance in the 2018 Annual Report (it could still be easily calculated in the future). Preparing for this change, Buffett first presented market value data in 2014 as an imperfect but better guide over time.

Kraft Heinz is a perfect example of why book value was a bad metric. Berkshire's many companies were on the books at their purchase price and never revalued upward to their market value.* Although Berkshire didn't own 100% of Kraft Heinz, the accounting treatment was very close. Kraft Heinz was on Berkshire's books for $17.6 billion at year-end 2017, but its value based on publicly traded shares, was $25.3 billion. Nowhere on Berkshire's books did the excess value show up.** Berkshire's shift toward owning businesses in their entirety made book value an increasingly poor measure of performance as time went on. When marketable securities represented a larger portion of Berkshire's net worth their value was reflected in book value immediately.

Change in book value per share as a measurement tool would become even more problematic as Berkshire began returning capital to shareholders. In fact, Berkshire repurchased $1.3 billion in 2018 at an average price of $295,000 per A-share. We can be confident the price paid was below Berkshire's intrinsic value otherwise Buffett and Munger would not have done it. We know for a fact the price paid was above book value. Such repurchases would create a wider gap between intrinsic value and book value that would only intensify as time went on.

The Berkshire Forest

Buffett used the analogy of a forest and its trees to provide shareholders a way to estimate Berkshire's intrinsic value.*** Forget the mind-numbing exercise of trying to assess every tree, he said.

---

* Technically, retained earnings would be added to net worth. But to the extent that intrinsic value exceeded growth in book value it would not be reflected.
** I'm using 2017 here because of significant changes that occurred during 2018. These changes will be discussed later. The differential between the value carried on the financial statements and market value is instructive.
*** Buffett emphasized that it was an approximation.

"Fortunately, it's not necessary to evaluate each tree individually to make a rough estimate of Berkshire's intrinsic business value. That's because our forest contains five 'groves' of major importance, each of which can be appraised, with reasonable accuracy, in its entirety. Four of those groves are differentiated clusters of businesses and financial assets that are easy to understand. The fifth—our huge and diverse insurance operation—delivers great value to Berkshire in a less obvious manner … ."

The five groves are:

* *Grove #1: Non-insurance businesses with ownership between 80% and 100%*
  This most valuable grove includes Berkshire's many businesses "ranging from twigs to redwoods," from the smaller bolt-on acquisitions to giants BNSF and Berkshire Hathaway Energy. These businesses earned $16.8 billion after-tax in 2018. *All* expenses, including interest, depreciation, and corporate overhead, were deducted to arrive at that figure.
* *Grove #2: Equity securities*
  The market value of the second most valuable grove at year-end was $173 billion. But Berkshire would owe $14.7 billion in tax on the amount of unrealized gains. That left approximately $158 billion of net value.
* *Grove #3: Control group businesses*
  This grove contains businesses where Berkshire shares control with other parties. This included Berkshire's 26.7% ownership of Kraft Heinz, 50% of Berkadia and Electric Transmission Texas,* and 38.6% of Pilot Flying J. Together these companies earned $1.3 billion in 2018.
* *Grove #4: Cash, US Treasuries, Fixed Income (bonds)*
  At year-end, Berkshire had $112 billion of cash and $20 billion in fixed income investments. Buffett noted that $20 billion (a coincidence with the value of bonds) would always be reserved as a buffer.
* *Grove #5: Insurance*
  The insurance businesses were a source of value on the liability side of the balance sheet. Through the float they generated ($123 billion at year-end), Berkshire could hold far more assets than it otherwise would be able to. Buffett said float financed the first four groves but stopped short of saying it could be considered equity. Considering the long-term profitability of

---

* Electric Transmission Texas was a 50/50 joint venture formed a decade earlier between Berkshire Hathaway Energy and American Electric Power Company to own and operate electric transmission assets in Texas. Buffett mentioned it for the first time ever in his Chairman's letter in 2018. The company was relatively small. At year-end 2018, it was on BHE's books as an equity method investment for $527 million.

Berkshire's insurers, one could make the argument its float was at least as valuable as equity.*

"I believe Berkshire's intrinsic value can be *approximated* by summing the values of our four asset-laden groves and then subtracting an appropriate amount for taxes eventually payable on the sale of marketable securities." The analysis was an extension of the previous method of adding cash and investments per share to a capitalized amount of per share operating earnings. Buffett's equation left out one important variable in both cases. How should shareholders think about capitalizing the earnings from groves one and three? Berkshire's earnings might be worth more or they could be worth less depending on where interest rates went long term. That was a factor Buffett could not control, so he left it up to shareholders to decide.

We can approach the valuation problem in two ways. First by assuming an interest rate, and second by determining the going-in rate of return implied by Berkshire's market capitalization (see Table 9.17). To be consistent with our previous valuations of Berkshire, we'll use 15x after-tax earnings as our multiple to capitalize earnings. This is consistent with our use of 10x pre-tax earnings under the 35% tax rate. The decline in interest rates up to this time means our analysis is conservative, if anything.** For a business like Berkshire with modest levels of debt and subsidiary businesses earning good-to-great returns on capital, a meaningful margin of safety existed in the shares around 2018. The market appeared to completely discount any potential for growth or the optionality in its significant cash resources.*** Berkshire was undervalued by at least 14% under the first framework. Using the second method, the implied return of over 9% suggests the market discounted Berkshire's earnings too heavily.

---

* See the discussion of GEICO's float in the section on 1995 on page 342. If float declined someday (as Buffett expected) and the underwriting gain was equal to the rate of decline in float, its value would be akin to equity. That investments are counted in full without considering their funding source already incorporates this to a degree.

** Because we are using the same rate to discount earnings when interest rates have declined. Lower interest rates, all things being equal, would warrant a lower discount rate (higher multiple).

*** Buffett provided a major hint at the 2018 Annual Meeting. He said he thought Berkshire's normalized earnings power under the new tax environment was around $20 billion to $21 billion and pointed to the huge cash pile as the source of future earning power. At the 2019 Annual Meeting, he stated he and Charlie would have different answers to Berkshire's intrinsic value and that each would be a range within a band of 10%.

It should also be emphasized that Berkshire's debt was very modest. Debt at the parent company level amounted to $16.9 billion at year-end and total debt other than the railroad and utility businesses amounted to $35 billion. This amount could be repaid in less than two years of after-tax operating earnings. Additionally, it did not guarantee any debt of BNSF or BHE. Debt levels at those subsidiaries were also modest considering their business models. Finally, Berkshire's significant cash position dwarfed all debt, regulated businesses included.

Table 9.17: Berkshire Hathaway valuation, 2018

($ billions)	
Direct Calculation Method:	2018
Grove 1: Non-insurance[1]	$252
Grove 2: Equity securities[2]	158
Grove 3: Control group businesses[3]	20
Grove 4: Cash, Treasuries, bonds	132
Total	$562
Implied Yield Method:	
Implied market value[4]	485
Less: sum of Groves 2 & 4 above	(290)
Implied value of Groves 1 & 3	195
After-tax earnings of Groves 1 & 3	18
Going-in rate of return, after-tax	9.3%
Footnotes:	
1. 15x $16.8 billion after tax earnings.	
2. $173 billion less $15 billion tax on unrealized gain.	
3. 15x $1.3 billion after tax earnings.	
4. Based on Berkshire's 2018 share repurchases.	

Notes:

1. I've used Buffett's figures, which presumably represented something close to normalized earnings.

2. A 15x multiple is consistent with our use of 10x pre-tax earnings earlier in this book and assuming the new 21% tax rate.

Sources: Berkshire Hathaway Annual Report 2018; and author's calculations.

With book value no longer a worthwhile proxy, Berkshire's board authorized repurchases anytime Buffett and Munger thought the price went below intrinsic value, conservatively calculated. Previously, Berkshire could repurchase shares when they reached 120% of book value. Price-to-value would always be a key consideration for repurchases and Berkshire would always put its own businesses first. Growing existing operations and buying new businesses would come before share repurchases. All capital allocation decisions would be weighed against opportunity costs.

Insurance

The Insurance Group returned to profitability in 2018 with a $2 billion pre-tax underwriting gain on earned premiums down 5% to $57.4 billion. That brought the record of profits to $27 billion in fifteen of the prior sixteen years. Better still, float grew 7.2% to $122.7 billion at year-end.

A new acquisition bolstered results. On October 1, 2018, National Indemnity acquired Medical Liability Mutual Insurance Company (MLMIC) for $2.5 billion. The company changed its name to MLMIC Insurance Company upon joining Berkshire. MLMIC was a New York City-based writer of medical professional liability insurance that demutualized. The acquisition was a long time coming. National Indemnity first agreed to the acquisition in 2016 but the required demutualization process (which converted it from a mutual company owned by policyholders to a stock company) took some time. MLMIC wrote $400 million in premiums in 2018 and brought with it $5.4 billion of cash and investments.* Its results were reported with the Primary Group.

Table 9.18: Berkshire Hathaway—Insurance Underwriting

($ millions)	2018	2017
GEICO		
Premiums earned	$33,363	$29,441
Underwriting gain/(loss) - pre-tax	2,449	(310)
Berkshire Hathaway Reinsurance Group		
Premiums earned:		
Property/casualty	$8,928	$7,552
Retroactive reinsurance	517	10,755
Life/health	5,343	4,808
Periodic payment annuity	1,156	898
Total premiums earned	15,944	24,013
Underwriting gain/(loss) - pre-tax:		
Property/casualty	(207)	(1,595)
Retroactive reinsurance	(778)	(1,330)
Life/health	216	(52)
Periodic payment annuity	(340)	(671)
Total underwriting gain/(loss) - pre-tax	(1,109)	(3,648)
Berkshire Hathaway Primary Group		
Premiums earned	$8,111	$7,143
Underwriting gain/(loss) - pre-tax	670	719
Total premiums earned	$57,418	$60,597
Total underwriting gain/(loss) - pre-tax	2,010	(3,239)
Average float	118,616	103,039
Cost of float	(1.7%)	3.1%

Note: In 2017, results for General Re were consolidated with BHRG.
Sources: Berkshire Hathaway Annual Report 2019 and author's calculations.

---

* The footnotes to the 2016 Annual Report stated that the acquisition price would be equal to tangible book value (GAAP) plus $100 million. The company's policyholders received the proceeds of the sale. MLMIC's unpaid losses and loss adjustment expenses were $3.2 billion, which may be an estimate of the company's float.

Berkshire Hathaway Primary Group

The Berkshire Hathaway Primary Group (of which MLMIC was a part) grew earned premiums 13.6% to $8.1 billion. Written premiums increased 32% at BH Specialty, 19% at GUARD, 14% at NICO Primary, and the Home State companies increased volume 8%. Catastrophe losses of $190 million from Hurricanes Florence and Michael and wildfires in California, as well as lower favorable loss development, led profitability to slip slightly. The Primary Group's combined ratio of 91.8% in 2018 (compared to 89.9% in 2017) remained strong and reflected the strength of this collection of insurers.

GEICO

Buffett had nothing but praise for GEICO's Tony Nicely. Nicely retired as CEO in 2018 after almost sixty years with the company. Buffett credited him with leading GEICO to become the second largest US auto insurer with a market share of 13%. He estimated Nicely increased Berkshire's intrinsic value by $50 billion over his tenure leading GEICO from 1993 to 2018.* Nicely passed the reins to Bill Roberts, another longtime GEICO insider, and remained on as chairman.** He chose a fitting year to depart as CEO, as the company had one of its best years ever.

GEICO rebounded sharply in 2018. Earned premiums grew 13% to $33.4 billion from a combination of 3.3% policyholder growth and 6.4% higher premiums. GEICO successfully increased premium rates to compensate for the elevated levels of losses experienced over the prior two years. The loss ratio declined 7.8 percentage points compared to 2017 (to 78.8%), even after $105 million in catastrophe losses, leading GEICO's profit to swell to record levels at nearly $2.5 billion—a combined ratio of 92.7%. Favorable loss development of $222 million also played a part in the gain.

Berkshire Hathaway Reinsurance Group

Berkshire Hathaway Reinsurance Group was the only major insurance segment to report a loss, although that loss was significantly less than the prior year. A comparative year that included the world's largest retroactive reinsurance contract

---

* Buffett said pre-tax underwriting profits totaled $15.5 billion since Berkshire bought full control and float grew from $2.5 billion to $22.1 billion. Premiums earned increased about $30 billion from 1995 to 2018. If we use our prior conclusion that the company's goodwill was worth about its earned premiums and add the $15.5 billion in pre-tax profits we come close to the $50 billion figure Buffett cited. (An alternative method could assume a steady-state combined ratio of 4% produced $1.2 billion of annual profits; capitalize earnings at 10x then add the $15.5 billion in prior pre-tax profits plus incremental float of $19.6 billion.)

** That Berkshire's subsidiary companies retain boards of directors is an overlooked fact. Their function is more akin to an advisory board and is another way Berkshire keeps talent connected to the conglomerate.

(the $10.2 billion AIG deal) caused the unit's earned premiums to decline by a third to $15.9 billion. Earned premiums were up 13% over 2016. BHRG improved to a pre-tax underwriting loss of $1.1 billion from a loss of $3.6 billion in 2017. Considering the significant drag from accounting charges and a more normal year for catastrophe losses, such a result was not bad.

Property/casualty earned premiums grew 18% to $8.9 billion. The property/casualty line faced four catastrophe events in 2018 from Hurricanes Florence and Michael, Typhoon Jebi, and wildfires in California. Together these cost $1.3 billion and led to a $207 million loss.* Results were bolstered by $469 million of favorable loss development. Back-to-back years with catastrophe losses were expected occasionally. Berkshire remained committed to pricing appropriately regardless of the timing of catastrophe events. Annual repricing of policies is an important factor in catastrophe underwriting. Assumptions about the long-term impact of things like climate change could be worked into pricing over time. As a rule, Berkshire did not write catastrophe contracts for more than a year.**

After the record $10.2 billion AIG contract in 2017 that swelled earned premiums to $10.8 billion, retroactive reinsurance premiums fell to $517 million in 2018. The AIG contract alone was responsible for $611 million of the $778 million loss in this segment, most of which was related to deferred charge amortization. The retroactive line also benefitted from favorable loss development that contributed $185 million and exchange rate effects that added $169 million to segment results.*** Gross unpaid losses from retroactive reinsurance contracts were $41.8 billion at year-end and deferred charge assets amounted to $14.1 billion.

Life/health reinsurance was the only BHRG line to report a gain. It swung from a loss of $52 million in 2017 to a gain of $216 million in 2018 on earned premiums up 11% to $5.3 billion. The gain was due to lower losses from US long-term care business and gains (though lower than the prior year) from variable annuity guarantee contracts.

Earned premiums grew 29% to $1.2 billion in the periodic payment annuity business. Volumes in that business, like all of Berkshire's insurance lines, ebbed and flowed based on pricing. These produced a pre-tax underwriting loss of $340 million compared to a loss of $671 million in 2017. The losses included a $93 million gain in 2018 and a $190 million loss in 2017 from changes in foreign exchange rates.

---

* Of the $1.3 billion catastrophe losses, $1.1 billion occurred in the fourth quarter.

** Shareholder proposals have been put on the Berkshire proxy from time to time calling for action on climate change. Buffett discussed the effect on insurance companies in his 2015 Chairman's letter.

*** A finer detail for the interested reader: The actual decrease in reserves was $341 million. Part of the adjustment affected deferred charges and therefore did not impact the income statement.

Regulated, Capital-Intensive Businesses

BNSF benefitted from the strong US economy with a 4.1% increase in overall unit volume and 6.2% higher average pricing that increased revenues 11.5% to $23.9 billion. Car loadings totaled 10.3 million and increased in each freight category except for coal, which declined 0.8%. Volume increases came from industrial products (up 16% driven by strength in end markets) and agricultural products (up 9% driven by exports). The advantage of rail over trucks during a time of tight trucking capacity brought gains in consumer products freight, but an unspecified contract loss muted the overall volume increase in consumer products to just 2.9%. Pre-tax earnings grew 8.5% to $6.9 billion. Higher pre-tax earnings and the new lower Federal Tax Rate translated into a 32% increase in after-tax earnings to $5.2 billion.[*]

The new tax law immediately impacted Berkshire Hathaway Energy. Its regulated utilities began passing on savings to customers in various forms, including lower electric rates and regulatory modifications that indirectly affected consumer rates. The largest unit, PacifiCorp, experienced a 4% decline in revenues with most attributed to the impact of the tax cut. Pre-tax earnings, however, fell 34% to $745 million from a combination of reduced revenues and accelerated depreciation on a thermal generating facility. The increased depreciation expense was a non-cash charge in 2018 (after all, physical depreciation does not increase due to a change in tax rate), but it would lower the rate of assets on which future revenues could be based.

A similarly large decline in pre-tax earnings (26% to $417 million) occurred at NV Energy due to the tax cut. The natural gas pipelines benefitted from colder weather and higher volumes, leading to a 14% increase in pre-tax earnings. No major changes were reported from Northern Powergrid (the UK utility) or the other energy businesses. MidAmerican Energy Company (the Iowa and Illinois utility) was impacted by the tax bill but still reported 9% higher pre-tax earnings which reflected higher volumes and prices unrelated to the tax cut.

The net effect across all BHE utilities was a 14% decrease in EBIT to $2.9 billion and a 1% decline in pre-tax earnings to $2.5 billion. Berkshire's share of net earnings increased 29% to $2.6 billion in large part due to taxes. BHE's tax rate was negative in 2018, causing higher after-tax earnings than pre-tax earnings. Tax credits for wind-generating assets more than offset any tax liability. Berkshire Hathaway could take advantage of such credits immediately because it paid federal taxes on a consolidated basis. Such tax credits were less valuable to standalone utility companies. At year-end 2018, BHE's cumulative investment in renewables such as solar, geothermal, and biomass was $25 billion.

---

[*] BNSF's headline tax rate was 24% in 2018. Its ability to defer taxes led the rate to be just 18% compared to 23% the prior year.

Manufacturing, Service, and Retailing

Perhaps a result of the work classifying Berkshire's many businesses into groves, Berkshire consolidated the Finance and Financial Products businesses into the Manufacturing, Service, and Retailing businesses beginning in 2018.[*] As a result:

- Marmon's UTLX, the rail and mobile crane leasing business, went back with its parent company within industrial products.
- Clayton Homes became part of the building products segment.
- XTRA and CORT were reported with the service businesses.

These changes accounted for approximately $1.7 billion of 2017 pre-tax earnings reclassified to the MSR presentation. The remainder (about $375 million) went elsewhere. Table 9.19 contains the modified presentation with 2017 revised by Berkshire to reflect the new arrangement.

Table 9.19: Manufacturing, Service, and Retailing businesses—pre-tax earnings

($ millions)	2018	2017	% Change
Industrial products	$5,822	$5,065	15%
Building products	2,336	2,147	9%
Consumer products	1,208	1,112	9%
Subtotal - manufacturing	9,366	8,324	13%
Service	1,836	1,519	21%
Retailing	860	785	10%
McLane	246	299	(18%)
Subtotal - service and retailing	2,942	2,603	13%
Total pre-tax earnings	12,308	10,927	13%
Income taxes and non-controlling interests	(2,944)	(3,645)	(19%)
Earnings after tax	$9,364	$7,282	29%

Note: 2017 as revised to the presentation in 2018, which includes some businesses formerly reported in Finance and Financial Products.
Sources: Berkshire Hathaway Annual Report 2018 and author's calculations.

The MSR businesses performed impressively considering its 13% increase in pre-tax earnings was not affected by the tax rate explicitly.[**] After-tax earnings grew 29%

---

[*] For financial reporting purposes only. Management of the businesses remained as before.
[**] It's possible the lower tax rate improved economic conditions and led to the increases in operating performance indirectly.

to $9.4 billion through a combination of the gain in pre-tax earnings and lower taxes. Earnings were not boosted by acquisitions. Berkshire spent a total of $1 billion on bolt-on acquisitions in 2018 (not necessarily all within MSR). A strong US economy provided a tailwind to most MSR businesses, although specific factors impacted each differently. New tariffs imposed by the US hurt demand in certain businesses, while others reported higher earnings in part due to a weaker dollar.

Industrial Products (revenues of $30.7bn, up 7.4%): Pre-tax earnings grew 15% to $5.8 billion. Part of the strong gain in industrial products in 2018 resulted from one-time charges at Precision Castparts and Lubrizol the prior year.[120] Those charges notwithstanding, strong demand for aerospace parts and additives led to unit volume growth and higher pre-tax earnings at both companies. IMC grew revenues and earnings because of higher demand for its products and weakness in the dollar. CTB and Marmon were the only two businesses whose pre-tax earnings declined. Marmon achieved 6% higher revenues but weakness in the railcar leasing business, and its Foodservice Technologies and Retail Solutions sectors, weighed down results and caused a 6% decline in pre-tax earnings.

Building Products (revenues of $18.7bn, up 10.2%): Pre-tax earnings in this segment grew 9% to $2.3 billion, mostly due to strength at Clayton Homes and Shaw. Clayton Homes led the building products businesses with a 19% increase in pre-tax earnings to $911 million. Clayton now boasted eight site builders in addition to its manufactured home operations. Earnings at Berkshire's other building products companies increased just 3.1%. Shaw and Johns Manville both grew revenues in the high single-digits, but cost pressures left Johns Manville with lower earnings. The shortage of truck drivers that benefitted BNSF hurt the building products companies as their products required short-haul transport. They also faced higher input costs for raw materials, not all of which could be immediately passed on to customers. Some of the factors above might have played a part in Acme Brick closing several brick, concrete, and limestone plants in 2018.** Acme depended heavily on basic materials and short-haul trucking.

Consumer Products (revenues of $12.5bn, up 3.2%): Pre-tax earnings grew 9% to $1.2 billion but results from these businesses were mixed. Forest River's unit sales were flat year over year, but that belied significant changes throughout the year. Unit sales declined 7% during the second half of the year and the company was

---

* Precision Castparts's 2017 acquisition of a German pipe manufacturer fell apart almost immediately. The company fraudulently inflated its results prior to the acquisition. In April 2020 an American arbitration panel awarded Precision Castparts 643 million euros ($696 million). This was a partial refund of the 800 million euro purchase price ($912 million). Lubrizol in 2017 disposed of an underperforming unit that hurt earnings by $190 million. On a comparative basis Lubrizol's earnings would have increased 17%.

** After these closures, Acme operated 15 clay brick manufacturing facilities at 12 locations in seven states, and three concrete block plants in Texas.

negatively impacted by higher material costs. Fourth quarter earnings declined 28%. The company was lucky to escape the year with a pre-tax decline in earnings of 9%.[*] Larson Juhl's earnings also declined, though they were not detailed. The weakness in those businesses were more than made up by increased earnings at Duracell (also not detailed) and in the apparel and footwear businesses (up 6.4%).

Service businesses (revenues of $13.3bn, up 9.7%): TTI, the electronics components distributor, led the service businesses to a 21% increase in pre-tax earnings to $1.8 billion. Its results accounted for most (84%) of the increase in pre-tax earnings, a result of strong demand industrywide on top of acquisitions and favorable effects from a weaker dollar. Political advertising boosted revenues 21% at WPLG, the Miami, Florida television station. Charter Brokerage saw its topline grow by half; its earnings increased but were not disclosed. Earnings increased at XTRA and NetJets but FlightSafety again lagged. Lower margins on simulators and an impairment charge to fixed assets (likely on outdated simulators) reduced earnings.

Retailing (revenues of $15.6bn, up 3.6%): Pre-tax earnings grew 10% to $860 million. Berkshire Hathaway Automotive dominated the retailing segment, accounting for over 60% of its revenues. Berkshire did not disclose its earnings, only stated that BHA and Louis, the German motorcycle accessory retailer, were the primary reasons for the increase in pre-tax earnings. We can surmise that some of the other retailers, such as the jewelry businesses, See's, Dairy Queen, and Pampered Chef, also contributed at least something to earnings growth (as they were not identified). The home furnishings businesses were identified. Their revenues increased in part due to increased same-store sales from some markets and a new store. But their earnings fell 2.4% in part due to higher costs at Star Furniture.

McLane (revenues of $50.0bn, up 0.4%): Competitive pressures continued to weigh on McLane's results. Grocery revenues, which accounted for two-thirds of overall revenues, increased 1%. The loss of a large foodservice customer largely negated that gain. Higher operating costs ate into the company's already thin margins leading to another double-digit decline in earnings, which fell 18% to $246 million. Berkshire saw no let-up of the difficult operating conditions.

Investments

Apple took center stage in Berkshire's investment portfolio in 2018, with Berkshire investing an additional $15 billion in the iPhone creator. It ended the year with 255 million shares, or 5.4% of the company. At year-end, Berkshire's investment in Apple was worth over $40 billion—making it the largest holding and almost a quarter of

---

[*] The recreational vehicle business will always be subject to wide fluctuations in unit volume and earnings. Forest River's market share was estimated at 33% in 2018 behind industry giant Thor Industries at 48%.

the equity portfolio. The top five positions (in order: Apple, Bank of America, Wells Fargo, Coca-Cola, and American Express) represented 68% of the entire portfolio. Despite its size and the difficulties finding attractive investments in a continuing bull market, Berkshire hadn't lost its penchant for concentrating its investments.

Banks received the bulk of the remaining net investments made in 2018. Berkshire added to several of its holdings in banks and bought into a new one. Another $6.6 billion went into Bank of America, ending the year with 9.5% of the company. Berkshire also topped off its holdings in Bank of New York Mellon and US Bank but stopped short of breaching the 10% threshold. Crossing the 10% mark could bring unwanted regulatory headaches.* Berkshire sold shares in Wells Fargo to counter the effect of the bank repurchasing its own shares and remain below the threshold. Another $1.7 billion went into Goldman Sachs, and $5.6 billion into a new position in JPMorgan Chase.** Altogether, banks comprised 36% of the equity portfolio. And that wasn't counting the 8% of the portfolio in American Express, a financial services company.

Berkshire reported Kraft Heinz outside the investment portfolio because of its large ownership position. But it remained publicly traded. In 2018, the market value of Berkshire's Kraft Heinz shares fell 45% to $14 billion. Kraft Heinz took a massive $15.9 billion write-down of its goodwill and intangible assets that reflected weakness in its iconic brands. Remember, Berkshire and 3G Capital paid a huge premium over the net tangible assets of both Heinz and then Kraft. In 2018 Kraft Heinz management determined those intangible assets weren't worth as much and wrote them down.***

Berkshire's financial statements weren't affected by the precipitous drop in the share price of Kraft Heinz because it accounted for its investment using the equity method. (It hadn't been affected by the strong gains either.) It was as if the market for Kraft Heinz shares did not exist. If Berkshire's ownership in Kraft Heinz had been below the 20% threshold for equity method accounting, it would have necessitated flowing the market value decline through the income statement and reducing shareholders' equity by the after-tax amount of the decline. Instead, the asset impairment charges flowed proportionately to Berkshire and through its income statement. Berkshire's share was $2.7 billion after-tax. The equity method of accounting also meant its $814 million dividend received in 2018 was recorded as a reduction to Berkshire's investment in the company. But that cash was real, as were similar amounts received in the two prior years. Not a terrible result for an investment with a cost basis of $9.8 billion.

---

* The Bank Holding Company Act applies once ownership of a bank crosses 10%. A 10% ownership requires quicker filing if any purchases or sales are made. If an owner of 10% of a company sells any shares within six months, any profits must be remitted to the company (this is called the short-swing rule).
** Todd Combs was elected to the JP Morgan board in September 2016.
*** Kraft Heinz wrote down goodwill by $7 billion and intangible assets by $8.9 billion pre-tax.

The impairment charges taken by Kraft Heinz reflected real weakness in what Berkshire and 3G Capital originally thought it was worth. Buffett admitted they erred. "I was wrong in a couple ways on Kraft Heinz." The Heinz purchase was sensible but Berkshire and 3G Capital had overpaid for Kraft. While its brands were well known and continued to be purchased by consumers, it had lost some bargaining power with retailers due to the emergence of strong private label brands. For example, Costco's younger Kirkland Signature brand had revenues greater than all of Kraft Heinz. Costco customers choose Kirkland not just because it's at a lower cost, but because the products are high quality and easily recognizable. Kirkland brands accounted for about 27.5% of Costco's sales in fiscal 2018.[*][121] Store brands at many retailers have taken an increasing share while branded products lost ground.[122] Buffett was aware of these trends and competitive forces but concluded Kraft Heinz brands would be more resistant.

The issue wasn't so much the company; it was the purchase price. Kraft Heinz's underlying business was excellent. It earned approximately $6 billion pre-tax on $7 billion of net tangible assets. But the all-in purchase price was about $100 billion more. Berkshire thought it was paying a fair price for a great company. Instead, it found itself with a great company unable to produce the returns needed to justify the rich price its owners paid.[123]

Kraft Heinz was a reminder of three important investing concepts:

1. A great company could become a poor investment if the price paid is too high.
2. Competitive advantages aren't static. Competition and changing preferences can affect the strongest of companies.
3. A margin of safety protects the investor from unknowns, and it can come in the form of quality.

Kraft Heinz had many iconic brands that remained engrained in consumer purchasing habits. The underlying business reflected those advantages. The mistake of paying too much resulted in a lower rate of return than initially expected, but Berkshire hadn't lost money on Kraft Heinz. It intended to hold on to the investment and would continue to collect cash dividends.

Outside of the equity portfolio, Berkshire made a $2 billion secured loan to Seritage Growth Properties. Seritage was a real estate investment trust holding properties leased back to Sears, the struggling retailer. The loan was made by Berkshire Hathaway Life Insurance Company of Nebraska. Terms of the deal included an initial funding of $1.6 billion at an interest rate of 7%, with a 1% annual fee on the undrawn commitment of $400 million.

---

* Charlie Munger is on the Costco Board of Directors.

A Glimpse into Succession

Buffett received countless questions on Berkshire's succession planning over the decades. But as he neared the end of his eighties, and with Charlie Munger already into his nineties, the question came up more and more. Part of the question had been answered. His role would be split into a non-executive chairman (likely his son, Howard), a CEO, and two or more investment managers. Berkshire already had two highly capable investment managers in Todd Combs and Ted Weschler, and Howard's appointment was all but certain. That left the CEO post.

Berkshire's move in early 2018 removed some of the fog but left the question open. Berkshire's board voted Greg Abel (age 56) and Ajit Jain (age 67) as vice chairmen alongside Charlie Munger. Abel, the longtime Chairman and CEO of Berkshire Hathaway Energy, became vice chairman, non-insurance operations. Jain became vice chairman, insurance operations. Buffett said the move was long overdue. "You and I are lucky to have Ajit and Greg working for us. Each has been with Berkshire for decades, and Berkshire's blood flows through their veins. The character of each man matches his talents. And that says it all."

A layer of management between Buffett and the many managers of Berkshire's businesses left him and Munger with the primary job of investment and capital allocation. Not much would change for Buffett. Berkshire's policy of giving extreme autonomy to the managers of its many subsidiaries already made his job easier than almost any other CEO of a large conglomerate. The Salomon Brothers incident in the early 1990s already proved Berkshire could function without Buffett there day-to-day.

Uncle Sam: Business Partner

Discussion of taxes provided Buffett a unique way to explain the taxing power of governments. "Like it or not, the US government 'owns' an interest in Berkshire's earnings of a size determined by Congress. In effect, our country's Treasury Department holds a special class of our stock—call this holding the AA shares—that receives large 'dividends' (that is, tax payments) from Berkshire." The reduction in the US corporate tax rate from 35% to 21% equated to Congress appropriating 40% of its ownership back to Berkshire's other shareholders. Viewed this way it's easy to see that a reduced tax rate equated to a higher intrinsic value for all companies.

The key question was how much would remain after the effects of competition. Buffett touched on the subject in his prior Chairman's letter. BHE would give back all the benefit of lower taxes explicitly through regulation. Other Berkshire businesses would find competition erode the newfound profits. A few, such as See's, might be able to hang on to the entirety of the benefit. All things being equal, Berkshire was better off with a lower tax rate.

2019

Berkshire's results again required explaining thanks to another round of accounting versus economics. A strong stock market in 2019 following weakness in 2018 changed reported profitability significantly. But the nonsensical GAAP accounting rules caused Berkshire's bottom line to grow 1,900%. The GAAP requirement that unrealized gains and losses flow through the income statement made the bottom line useless for analytical purposes. Berkshire's results were good in 2019, just not *that* good. What really counted, operating earnings after-tax, amounted to $24 billion—a 3% decline from the prior year.*

Buffett reminded shareholders once again that it was the long game that counted and that reality trumped accounting, even when it showed results to be worse. "Charlie and I urge you to focus on operating earnings—which were little changed in 2019—and to ignore both quarterly and annual gains from investments, whether these are realized or unrealized."

The details of Berkshire's operating performance in 2019 revealed a year very much on par with the prior year. The Insurance Group delivered another year of underwriting profits. Growth in float brought more investable assets and higher investment income. The railroad and the utilities, along with the Manufacturing, Service, and Retailing businesses all reported higher profits. Berkshire found no major acquisitions. An opportunity to invest $10 billion in a negotiated preferred stock deal soaked up some of the continually growing cash pile. So too did repurchases that reduced Berkshire's share count by 1%. Nonetheless, cash and equivalents swelled to $128 billion at year-end. Amid the longest bull run in American history, Berkshire waited patiently for opportunity.

Valuation and Share Repurchases

Berkshire spent $5 billion repurchasing its shares in 2019. The sum was large but represented a small fraction of the company. We can estimate that Berkshire's intrinsic value increased by about 15% in 2019 using the same valuation methodology suggested by Buffett and presented in the section on 2018 (see page 684). Recall that Buffett divided Berkshire into five groves, four of which were used to calculate value (insurance was the fifth and supplied the float to fund the other groves). Those four groves were:

- Grove #1: Non-insurance businesses with ownership between 80% and 100%
- Grove #2: Equity securities

---

* Operating earnings appeared to increase 10%. However, adjusting for $3 billion of one-time non-cash intangible asset impairment charges (included in other) in 2018, the results in 2019 are seen to be lower.

- Grove #3: Control group businesses
- Grove #4: Cash, US Treasuries, Fixed Income (bonds)

It's unclear why Berkshire did not repurchase more of its own shares during the year. The discount between the calculated value (see Table 9.20) and the level at which Berkshire repurchased its shares appeared wide. The highest price paid during the fourth quarter implied a valuation of around $545 billion.* The price/value relationship appears favorable even if we use an average of the estimated year-end intrinsic values. Yet Buffett's comments suggested the repurchases were not a screaming bargain. "Calculations of intrinsic value are far from precise. Consequently, neither of us feels any urgency to buy an *estimated* $1 of value for a very real 95 cents."

Table 9.20: Berkshire Hathaway valuation, 2018 and 2019

(*$ billions*)		
Direct Calculation Method:	2019	2018
Grove 1: Non-insurance[1]	$266	$252
Grove 2: Equity securities[2]	216	158
Grove 3: Control group businesses[3]	15	20
Grove 4: Cash, Treasuries, bonds	147	132
Total	$644	$562
Implied Yield Method:		
Implied market value[4]	$508	$485
Less: sum of Groves 2 & 4 above	(363)	(290)
Implied value of Groves 1 & 3	145	195
After-tax earnings of Groves 1 & 3	19	18
Going-in rate of return, after-tax	12.9%	9.3%
Footnotes:		
1. 15x $17.7 billion (2019) and $16.8 billion (2018) after-tax earnings.		
2. Deducts $32 billion (2019) and $15 billion (2018) tax on unrealized gain.		
3. 15x $1 billion (2019) and $1.3 billion (2018) after-tax earnings.		
4. Based on Berkshire's share repurchases.		

Notes:

1. I've used Buffett's figures for 2018 (which presumably represented something close to normalized earnings) and followed the logic to 2019.

2. A 15x multiple is consistent with our use of 10x pre-tax earnings earlier in this book and assuming the new 21% tax rate.

Sources: Berkshire Hathaway Annual Reports 2018–2019; and author's calculations.

---

* Using the share count as of the end of the third quarter 2019.

Valuation and Share Repurchases – Berkshire Hathaway Energy

Berkshire wasn't the only entity that repurchased its shares in 2019. Little press has been given to Berkshire Hathaway Energy's (BHE) repurchases of its shares. This despite Buffett at times mentioning the modest increases in Berkshire Hathaway's majority ownership of the utility. When Berkshire first purchased BHE in 1999 its ownership amounted to 76%. Additional purchases of equity to assist BHE in making certain acquisitions and purchases of stock from BHE non-controlling shareholders raised its interest to almost 91% at year-end 2019. Its more recent purchases shed light on the value of the company (see Table 9.21) and backed up Buffett's assertion that BHE was worth far more than its carrying value.

Table 9.21: Berkshire Hathaway Energy—select data

Year	BRK ownership	Shares repurchased	Price per share	Implied value of BHE ($ millions)
2019	90.9%	447,712	$654.44	$50,097
2018	90.2%	177,381	603.22	46,553
2017[1]	90.0%	216,891	548.66	42,442
2016	89.9%	0	n/a	n/a
2015	89.9%	75,000	480.00	37,148
Footnote: 1. Series of two transactions: 35,000 shares for $19 million and 181,891 for $100 million (5% junior subordinated debenture).				

Note: Valuation is at the Berkshire Hathaway Energy level and includes investments such as BYD, Inc. (worth $1.1 billion at 12/31/19).

Source: Berkshire Hathaway Energy 10K filings 2015–2019 and author's calculations.

Regulated, Capital-Intensive Businesses

The higher implied valuation for BHE reflected its financial results. Pre-tax earnings grew 6% to $2.6 billion.[*] Another year of tax credits from wind power generation again caused after-tax income to exceed pre-tax income, which grew 7.5% to $3.1 billion. Beginning in 2019, Berkshire began presenting a table in the footnotes to the Annual Report detailing after-tax earnings of the utility businesses, "reflecting

---

[*] I'm using pre-tax earnings to highlight the effects of income taxes on net income. EBIT grew 5% to $4.5 billion in 2019.

how the energy businesses are managed and evaluated."* MidAmerican Energy, the Iowa and Illinois utility, had significant wind-generating capacity and experienced strong demand from industrial customers, even in the face of lower demand from residential customers because of weather. Its after-tax earnings grew 12% to $781 million and benefitted from higher tax credits. NV Energy experienced a similar increase in after-tax earnings, up 15% to $365 million; higher volumes and rates led to earnings of $422 million for the gas pipelines, up 9%; and Northern Powergrid increased earnings 7% to $256 million. PacifiCorp's earnings fell 3% to $773 million. The real estate brokerage division increased after-tax earnings by 10% to $160 million. This was largely driven by its mortgage business and acquisitions. No explanation was given for the lower volume and margin at existing brokerage offices, but a shortage of homes nationwide could have played a part.

Volumes declined 4.5% to 10.2 million units at BNSF. Revenues declined at a slower 1.4% to $23.5 billion because of an increase in average prices. Weather, including flooding, played a part. So too did competing forms of freight transport and international trade policies. Consumer products, agricultural products, and coal volumes fell by 5%. Industrial products volume fell 3%. Operating expenses benefitted from cost controls and the curtailment of a retirement plan (which more than offset higher weather-related costs). These were in addition to lower expenses due to lower volume. Pre-tax earnings grew 5.6% to $7.3 billion from a combination of lower operating expenses and higher average pricing.

Insurance

The Insurance Group underwrote to a second-consecutive year of profits. A $417 million pre-tax underwriting profit in 2019 brought the record to $27.5 billion in total profit in sixteen out of seventeen years. The lone loss year in 2017 was caused by numerous catastrophe losses. Float grew 5.5% to $129.4 billion at year-end.

---

* It makes sense that the managers of the individual units would be evaluated for finding ways to increase economic outcomes, tax advantages included.

Table 9.22: Berkshire Hathaway—Insurance Underwriting

($ millions)	2019	2018
GEICO		
Premiums earned	$35,572	$33,363
Underwriting gain/(loss) - pre-tax	1,506	2,449
Berkshire Hathaway Reinsurance Group		
Premiums earned:		
Property/casualty	$9,911	$8,928
Retroactive reinsurance	684	517
Life/health	4,883	5,343
Periodic payment annuity	863	1,156
Total premiums earned	16,341	15,944
Underwriting gain/(loss) - pre-tax:		
Property/casualty	16	(207)
Retroactive reinsurance	(1,265)	(778)
Life/health	326	216
Periodic payment annuity	(549)	(340)
Total underwriting gain/(loss) - pre-tax	(1,472)	(1,109)
Berkshire Hathaway Primary Group		
Premiums earned	$9,165	$8,111
Underwriting gain/(loss) - pre-tax	383	670
Total premiums earned	$61,078	$57,418
Total underwriting gain/(loss) - pre-tax	417	2,010
Average float	126,078	118,616
Cost of float	(0.3%)	(1.7%)

Sources: Berkshire Hathaway Annual Report 2019 and author's calculations.

GEICO

GEICO was the star of the show most years, and in 2019 it delivered again. Its value proposition led to over 1 million new auto policies-in-force, which represented unit growth of 6.4%. GEICO ended the year with a 13.6% market share, up from 13%. Lower average pricing offset some of the strong growth in policies-in-force as the company fine-tuned its pricing to balance profitability with passing savings on to customers. Higher loss severity drove losses up 2.5 percentage points (to 81.3% of premiums earned). Severities increased in the mid-single-digits for property and collision damage and in the high single-digits for bodily injury. The footnotes to the financial statements do not detail why bodily injury severity increased at such a high rate. Claims frequencies increased low single-digits. Earned premiums grew 6.6% to $35.6 billion and a 95.8% combined ratio delivered a pre-tax underwriting gain of $1.5 billion.

Berkshire Hathaway Primary Group

The Berkshire Hathaway Primary Group reported a strong 15% growth in premiums earned. But pre-tax underwriting profits fell 43% to $383 million (combined ratio of 95.8%) because of higher losses and lower (but still positive) favorable loss development. It is important to remember that insurance profitability comes from two components: underwriting and investing. Berkshire's insurance managers focused solely on underwriting, while the investing component was handled centrally in Omaha. A decline in underwriting profit is not as good as an increase, but it is still a satisfactory result because it means a negative cost of float. Additionally, the strong growth in premiums very likely led to an increase in float.* The value of Berkshire's insurers come from the low-cost capital they provide. That capital can come in the form of float and profits.**

A very rare event occurred in 2019 that affected the results of the Primary Group. In October, Berkshire sold its 81% interest in Applied Underwriters. The company increasingly came into conflict with other Berkshire insurance units selling the same workers' compensation product. Berkshire sold its ownership interest back to one of its founders, Steve Menzies, and an investment firm. The $920 million price tag valued the company at $1.1 billion, about equal to annual premium volume.[124] Berkshire purchased 85% of Applied Underwriters in 2006 for an estimated $290 million.***

Berkshire Hathaway Reinsurance Group

Premiums earned in the reinsurance unit increased 2.5% to $16.3 billion. Pre-tax underwriting losses widened from $1.1 billion in 2018 to $1.5 billion in 2019. Individual segment results reflected the basic design of the reinsurance units. Losses widened in retroactive reinsurance and periodic payment annuity (two lines tied to long-duration float with recurring accounting charges), and profits increased in property/casualty and life/health compared to the prior year.

Property casualty delivered underwriting profits of $16 million from a loss of $207 million on earned premiums up 11% to $9.9 billion. Volume included $1.7 billion from the 20% quota-share agreement with Insurance Australia Group. The barely breakeven profit was a good result considering it was after $1 billion in losses from

---

* Berkshire stopped providing specific detail on float at each major segment, but we can glean some information from the financial statements. The financials break out unpaid losses and allocated loss adjustment expenses (ALAE). Using this data, we can see that BH Primary Medical Professional Liability and BH Primary Workers' Compensation and Other Casualty unpaid losses and ALAE grew 9% net of reinsurance recoverable.

** From an economic standpoint, float and profits can be equal. If float is permanent/revolving, or at least stays for an exceptionally long time, it is indistinguishable from equity. Profits in one year become equity the next.

*** There was an option for existing shareholders to purchase 4% of the company from Berkshire.

catastrophe events (Typhoons Faxia and Hagibis, and wildfires in California and Australia). Favorable loss development added $295 million to the bottom line.

The life/health unit recorded underwriting profits of $326 million, up 51% from the year before. A contract amendment with an undisclosed major reinsurer was responsible for a one-time pre-tax gain of $163 million that swelled the bottom line in 2019 but reduced premium volumes. A single $228 million contract covering health insurance risks replaced some of that volume but still left earned premiums down 9% for the year to $4.9 billion.

Periodic payment annuity premiums declined 25% to $863 million and the loss widened from $340 million in 2018 to $549 million in 2019. Berkshire took pains to note that this business is almost entirely price dependent. Berkshire stood ready to write large amounts of business when other market participants stepped away for whatever reason and pricing firmed up. Like the retroactive reinsurance business, unpaid losses in periodic payment annuities were large. At year-end 2019, the discounted value of the liabilities (at a 4.1% rate) was $13.5 billion.

Premiums written and earned in retroactive reinsurance were the result of a few contracts booked during the year and amounted to $684 million, up from $517 million. Such low volume was typical of the business, which came in spurts. Results were penalized by $125 million of unfavorable loss development (net of changes to unamortized deferred charges) compared to favorable development of $185 million in 2018.[*] Deferred charge amortization related to contracts booked in prior years caused most of the reported loss of $1.3 billion.

Unamortized deferred charges (the asset placed on the books at inception of the contract comprising the difference between the premium received and estimated ultimate losses) related to retroactive reinsurance amounted to $13.7 billion at year-end. That sum would eventually work its way through the income statement along with any future loss development. The 2017 AIG contract alone was responsible for $646 million of deferred charge amortization in 2019 that directly flowed to the bottom line as a loss. Berkshire estimated that total deferred charge amortization would be $1.2 billion in 2020, an amount that would produce an underwriting loss absent any changes to reserves.

Cash flows often illustrate economics better than accounting (see Table 9.23). In 2019, Berkshire's income statement said it lost $1.3 billion on retroactive reinsurance. But it paid just $909 million to claimants under these policies. It also brought in $624 million of cash from premiums. That means just $225 million went out the door, net, costing less than 1% of average float. The result remains favorable even assuming no written/earned premium activity. Berkshire would eventually have to pay out the full amount of its incurred losses—a whopping $42.4 billion (assuming

---

[*] The gross values were a $378 million increase in reserves in 2019 and a $341 million decrease in 2018.

it reserved appropriately). In the meantime, it had a huge amount of float to invest for its benefit. The ultimate economic result hinged on the timing and amount of future payments.

Table 9.23: Economics of reinsurance float at BHRG, 2019

($ millions)			
Float:		2019	2018
Gross unpaid losses		$42,441	$41,834
Deferred charges		(13,747)	(14,104)
Net liabilities (float proxy)		$28,694	$27,730
Average float	(A)	$28,212	
		Data from 2019:	
		Economics	Accounting
Written premiums		$684	
Paid losses and adj. exp.		(909)	
Net cash flow	(B)	($225)	
Written premiums			$684
Foreign currency remeasurement			(76)
Increase estimated liabilities			(378)
Increase deferred charges			253
AIG deferred charge amortization			(646)
Other deferred charge amortization			(1,102)
Reported accounting loss	(B)		($1,265)
Cost of float (B / A)		(0.8%)	(4.5%)
Cost of float assuming no premiums		(3.2%)	(6.9%)

Sources: Berkshire Hathaway Annual Report 2019 and author's calculations.

Manufacturing, Service, and Retailing

The headline result of a 0.5% increase in pre-tax earnings from the MSR businesses masked a wide range of individual business results. Results from the six major sub-segments ranged from an increase of 17% to a decline of 8%.

Table 9.24: Manufacturing, Service, and Retailing businesses—pre-tax earnings

($ millions)	2019	2018	% Change
Industrial products	$5,635	$5,822	(3%)
Building products	2,636	2,336	13%
Consumer products	1,251	1,208	4%
Subtotal - manufacturing	9,522	9,366	2%
Service	1,681	1,836	(8%)
Retailing	874	860	2%
McLane	288	246	17%
Subtotal - service and retailing	2,843	2,942	(3%)
Total pre-tax earnings	12,365	12,308	0%
Income taxes and non-controlling interests	(2,993)	(2,944)	2%
Earnings after tax	$9,372	$9,364	0%

Sources: Berkshire Hathaway Annual Reports 2018–2019 and author's calculations.

Industrial Products (revenues of $30.6bn, flat): Pre-tax earnings fell 3% to $5.6 billion. Results lagged largely due to weakness at Lubrizol and IMC. A fire in one of Lubrizol's plants in France caused its pre-tax earnings to fall 15%, including a 50% drop in the fourth quarter, negatively impacting the segment. One of Lubrizol's major insurance companies was Berkshire Hathaway, an irony Buffett noted in his Chairman's letter. "In Matthew 6:3, the Bible instructs us to 'Let not the left hand know what the right hand doeth.' Your chairman has clearly behaved as ordered." That was perhaps a reflection of the breadth of Berkshire's operations and an illustration of how risks can combine within an entity.

IMC's pre-tax earnings fell 13% from a combination of foreign currency effects, sales of lower margin products, and impacts from an ongoing trade war between the US and China. Precision Castparts increased earnings 5%, although a part of the favorable comparison had to do with one-time gains in 2019 and one-time losses in 2018. The company did not expect the suspension of Boeing's 737 MAX aircraft, a new plane that was beset with major issues, to have a major impact on its business. Marmon's results were flat when considering the effects of a new acquisition. On October 31 it acquired 60% of Colson Medical companies and agreed to purchase the remainder over time. Colson was the second act for Marmon founder Robert Pritzker. Pritzker founded Colson to acquire companies in the orthopedic surgery field after he left Marmon.[125]

Building Products (revenues of $20.3bn, up 8.8%): Pre-tax earnings in building products increased 13% to $2.6 billion. Clayton Homes again led the strong results. Its pre-tax earnings swelled 20% to $1.1 billion from higher sales of manufactured and site-built homes. Strength in home sales also translated into strong 12% higher earnings in its financing unit. The other building products companies within the segment increased pre-tax earnings by 8% as a result of higher selling prices and lower costs. Earnings would have increased more if not for facility closure costs.

Consumer products businesses (revenues of $11.8bn, down 5.7%): Pre-tax earnings increased 4% to $1.3 billion. Duracell benefitted from a new product line. The apparel and footwear businesses experienced headwinds from private label products. Brooks, a running shoe company,[*] increased revenues 3.5% despite problems with a distribution center. Cost controls improved pre-tax margins for the consumer products businesses by a full percentage point to 10.6%. These factors more than offset continued weakness at Forest River, where revenues declined 13% on lower unit sales. Berkshire provided no information on its earnings.

Service businesses (revenues of $13.5bn, up 1.2%): Pre-tax earnings declined 8% to $1.7 billion. TTI and FlightSafety caused the decline in pre-tax earnings in this sector. TTI came off a strong year in 2018 and was hurt by softer demand for its products, lower margins, and higher expenses from acquired businesses. Currency-related losses and tariffs compounded the pain. The loss of a government contract hurt earnings at FlightSafety. Higher revenues and margins increased NetJets' earnings. Charter Brokerage divested a low margin business during the year but the impact on the bottom line wasn't disclosed.

Retailing (revenues of $16.0bn, up 2.5%): A small 2% increase in pre-tax earnings to $874 million hid wide differences in fortunes. Strong pre-owned car sales and financing activities led to a 23% increase in earnings from Berkshire Hathaway Automotive. That was the only good news in the segment. Pre-tax earnings at the home furnishings companies (representing 20% of overall segment revenues) fell 15% on a 1.3% decline in revenues and higher costs. The remainder of the segment, which included such companies as the jewelry retailers and See's Candies, fell 8%.

McLane (revenues of $50.5bn, up 0.9%): McLane's earnings rebounded strongly as its margin clawed back some ground lost in prior years. Pre-tax earnings grew 17% to $288 million. The business remained very competitive with no apparent end in sight. The comparison of McLane's earnings benefitted from an extra week of results since its business operated on a 52/53 week fiscal year.[**]

---

[*] Brooks was a subsidiary of Fruit of the Loom before being separated as a standalone unit in 2012.

[**] A 52/53 week reporting method is more common in retailing. The benefit is a more consistent measurement period since the fiscal year always ends on the same day of the week and 52 weeks isn't easily divisible without leaving off one day each year.

Investments

Berkshire's investment portfolio swelled along with strong double-digit advances in the overall stock market (the S&P 500 rose 31.5%). Berkshire sold $14 billion worth of equities and purchased $18.6 billion for a net purchase of $4.6 billion. But a privately negotiated $10 billion preferred stock investment was classified as an equity security. Adjusting the information presented on the statement of cash flows downward to reflect the preferred investment meant Berkshire *sold* a net $5.4 billion in other equities. Sales included 4.4 million shares of Apple, 3 million shares of Bank of New York Mellon, 104 million shares of Wells Fargo, and its entire stake in USG Corp. Berkshire added to its holdings of Bank of America, JP Morgan Chase, and US Bancorp.

Buffett used an obscure book from 1924 to illustrate the power of retained earnings. In *Common Stocks as Long Term Investments*, Edgar Lawrence Smith illustrated how companies grow by retaining earnings. In the case of Berkshire's ten largest holdings, their retained earnings were more than double dividends. Buffett reminded readers that only the dividends showed up in Berkshire's financials each year. He also pointed out that some of Berkshire's investees used their retained earnings to repurchase stock, "an act that enlarges Berkshire's share of the company's future earnings." Looking at the table Buffett provided, we can see that Berkshire's ownership in American Express increased from 17.9% in 2018 to 18.7% in 2019 without Berkshire buying a single share. Even more amazing was Apple. Berkshire's ownership increased from 5.4% in 2018 to 5.7% in 2019 despite the sale of some shares.

He also used a more recognizable historical reference to make his point. "It was no secret that mind-boggling wealth had earlier been amassed by such titans as Carnegie, Rockefeller, and Ford, all of whom had retained a huge portion of their earnings to fund growth and provide ever greater profits." These titans, like him, were among the most successful of their time.

The sale of shares in USG Corp. amounted to a relatively small dollar amount (under $2 billion). But it represented one of the rare occasions that Buffett both disagreed with and voted against proposed directors of a company. Berkshire owned 31% of USG Corp., a maker of gypsum wallboard (sheetrock), that it purchased in 2006.[126] The business struggled over the ensuing decade. In 2018, Knauf (a competitor) offered a buyout that Berkshire thought attractive, but USG's management team and certain board members opposed the deal. Buffett thought the deal was good value for shareholders and publicly criticized the directors saying they "did not represent our interests." After voting against the directors, the deal with Knauf was ultimately approved and the company was sold midway through 2019.

In August, Berkshire again acted as creditor in a privately negotiated preferred stock deal. Unlike prior deals it was not the result of a general pullback in available credit. Instead, the $10 billion deal assisted Occidental Petroleum with its acquisition of competitor Anadarko. The deal was almost immediately criticized—but not for Berkshire's involvement. The criticism fell on Occidental's management for providing an astute investor with a sweetheart deal to finance an overpriced acquisition. Leading the criticism was legendary investor Carl Icahn. Buffett received praise for his shrewd business deal that included an 8% dividend yield for Berkshire's preferred stock—a benefit worth $800 million a year. Berkshire also got warrants to purchase 80 million shares at $62.50 per share, and a 105% liquidation preference. The deal also included a provision that Occidental could pay its preferred stock dividend in shares.

Berkshire's cash continued to build amid the dearth of opportunities to allocate large amounts of capital amid sky-high valuations for public and private businesses. Yet it continued its practice of borrowing money when favorable terms were available. For the first time, Berkshire issued Japanese yen-denominated bonds, raising $4 billion to bolster its war chest.* Its $128 billion of cash at year-end 2019 was criticized by those wanting the Oracle of Omaha to return some of it to shareholders. But Warren Buffett's fifty-five year seat at the helm of Berkshire Hathaway gave him confidence that an intelligent use of capital would present itself sooner or later. Berkshire was prepared for anything.

Half-Decade in Review

In just five years, Berkshire Hathaway generated more capital than the entirety of the prior decade (see Table 9.25). Operations produced about half of it. High prices for businesses created headwinds that stemmed the flow of acquisitions. Those headwinds broke the trend of increasing contributions from wholly-owned operating subsidiaries. That holds true even if the one-time gain from the tax law change in 2017 is removed. Making that adjustment, operations produced 61% of the increase in net worth during the period. Strong gains in the stock market led to significant realized and unrealized gains for Berkshire's portfolio, but hurt Berkshire's relative stock performance. It also made it more difficult to find attractive places to put Berkshire's large and growing cash pile.

---

* The issue contained multiple tranches with maturities ranging from 2024 to 2049 and with a weighted average interest rate of 0.50%.

Table 9.25: Reconciliation of shareholders' equity, 1965–2019

($ millions)	1965–74	1975–84	1985–94	1995–04	2005–14	2015–19	1965–19
Beginning of period shareholders' equity	$22	$88	$1,272	$11,875	$85,900	$240,170	$22
Net income - operations	57	366	2,869	19,344	107,301	95,122	225,059
Net income - realized gains	7	199	1,354	14,096	15,897	20,299	51,853
Unrealized appreciation of investments	0	486	5,877	15,000	25,720	50,297	97,380
Mergers/divestitures	0	133	433	25,085	12,816	328	38,795
Dividends/treasury stock	(3)	0	69	0	(1,763)	(6,362)	(8,059)
Issuance of Class-B stock	0	0	0	565	0	0	565
Tax Cuts and Jobs Act of 2017	0	0	0	0	0	29,106	29,106
Other/misc.	4	0	0	(65)	(5,701)	(4,169)	(9,930)
End of period shareholders' equity	$88	$1,272	$11,875	$85,900	$240,170	$424,791	$424,791
Change in equity during period	$66	$1,184	$10,602	$74,026	$154,270	$184,621	$424,769

Note: Figures may not add due to rounding.
Sources: Berkshire Hathaway Annual Reports and author's calculations.

Table 9.26: Contribution toward change in equity during period

	1965–74	1975–84	1985–94	1995–04	2005–14	2015–19	1965–19
Net income - operations	86%	31%	27%	26%	70%	52%	53%
Net income - realized gains	11%	17%	13%	19%	10%	11%	12%
Unrealized appreciation of investments	0%	41%	55%	20%	17%	27%	23%
Mergers/divestitures	0%	11%	4%	34%	8%	0%	9%
Dividends/treasury stock	(4%)	0%	1%	0%	(1%)	(3%)	(2%)
Issuance of Class-B stock	0%	0%	0%	1%	0%	0%	0%
Tax Cuts and Jobs Act of 2017	0%	0%	0%	0%	0%	16%	7%
Other/misc.	7%	0%	0%	(0%)	(4%)	(2%)	(2%)
Total	100%	100%	100%	100%	100%	100%	100%

Note: Figures may not add due to rounding.
Sources: Berkshire Hathaway Annual Reports and author's calculations.

Figure 9.3: Sources of after-tax operating income 2015–2019 ($ millions)

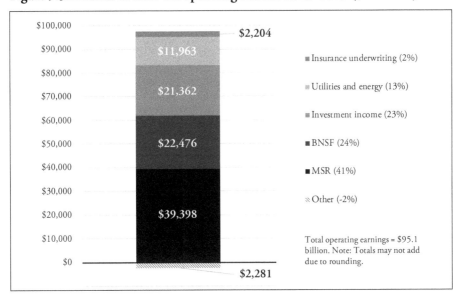

Sources: Berkshire Hathaway Annual Reports 2015–2019 and author's calculations.

Figure 9.3 breaks down the source of Berkshire's after-tax operating income for the half-decade. Taken together, BNSF and the utility businesses generated over a third of after-tax operating earnings in the period. Berkshire's fourteen-year record of underwriting profits came to an end in 2017 on the heels of six catastrophes. But it generated a profit in each of the other four years, which meant Berkshire's cost of float was negative. Better still, average float grew from $81 billion to $126 billion. A large part of the growth in float came from the retroactive reinsurance contract with AIG in 2017. The $10.2 billion premium Berkshire received was the largest in history and solidified Berkshire's reputation as one of (if not *the*) go-to reinsurer in the world.

Berkshire found reasonable opportunity to allocate capital during the five years under review. Acquisitions soaked up the most capital:

1. $4.2 billion: Van Tuyl Automotive Group joined the conglomerate in 2015 and changed its name to Berkshire Hathaway Automotive Group. Such renaming reflected the growing power and name recognition of the Berkshire Hathaway brand.
2. $33 billion: Precision Castparts was the only elephant or large acquisition that soaked up cash in 2016.
3. $2.8 billion: Pilot Flying J put one foot in the door with Berkshire's initial 38.6% stake in 2017. The deal called for Berkshire to increase its stake to 80% in 2023.
4. $2.5 billion: Medical Liability Mutual Insurance Company converted to a stock company to put itself up for sale to Berkshire in 2018.

5. $7.9 billion: Berkshire and its subsidiaries completed numerous bolt-on acquisitions.

Another cash-rich split-off transaction brought Duracell into the Berkshire fold. The partnership with 3G Capital found opportunity to invest another $5 billion in equity to acquire Kraft Foods Group.

Berkshire also invested an additional $32 billion in growth capital spending during the half-decade. The bulk of that capital went into BNSF and Berkshire Hathaway Energy. Berkshire also allocated additional capital to marketable securities. It continued its practice of concentrating its investments by buying $35 billion of Apple stock that was worth more than double the purchase price by year-end 2019. Berkshire also invested $10 billion in a privately negotiated preferred stock deal with Occidental Petroleum.

Table 9.27: Major capital allocation decisions 2015–2019

Acquisitions	$43,971
Capital expenditures, net	32,324
Net investment in equity securities	19,064
Share repurchases	6,362
	$101,721
Net increase in cash & fixed maturity investments	$115,022

Sources: Berkshire Hathaway Annual Reports 2014–2019 and author's calculations.

Two statistics from Berkshire's investment portfolio are too irresistible to pass over. Berkshire's share of 2019 earnings from American Express and Coca-Cola amounted to an exceptionally large proportion of their cost basis. Its share of American Express's 2019 earnings was $1.26 billion—almost equal to its $1.29 billion cost basis. Its share of Coke's earnings amounted to nearly two-thirds of the purchase price.[*] These statistics reflected the long holding periods and Berkshire's view of the investments as close to permanent. Both holdings were proof of the value of long holding periods. Deferred taxes on the significant unrealized gains allowed significantly more dividends than if the investments had been sold and reinvested elsewhere (or back into the same company).

---

[*] Another historical note: In 2010, Buffett wrote in his Chairman's letter that he expected Berkshire's share of Coke's earnings to equal its purchase price by 2021. Based on the $834 million figure for 2019 it appears it will take a few years longer to get to $1.299 billion.

Table 9.28: Berkshire Hathaway—equity portfolio, select detail

	2019		2014		Change	
($ millions)	*Cost*	*Market*	*Cost*	*Market*	*Cost*	*Market*
American Express	$1,287	$18,874	$1,287	$14,106	$0	$4,768
Apple, Inc.	35,287	73,667			35,287	73,667
Bank of America	12,560	33,380			12,560	33,380
The Coca-Cola Company	1,299	22,140	1,299	16,888	0	5,252
JP Morgan Chase	6,556	8,372			6,556	8,372
IBM			13,157	12,349	(13,157)	(12,349)
Moody's Corp.	248	5,857	248	2,364	0	3,493
US Bancorp	5,709	8,864	3,033	4,355	2,676	4,509
Wal-Mart Stores, Inc.			3,798	5,815	(3,798)	(5,815)
Wells Fargo & Company	7,040	18,598	11,871	26,504	(4,831)	(7,906)
All others	40,354	58,275	20,363	35,089	19,991	23,186
Total equity securities	$110,340	$248,027	$55,056	$117,470	$55,284	$130,557

Note: Investments with a market value of $5 billion or greater in either period.
Sources: Berkshire Hathaway Annual Reports 2014, 2019; and author's calculations.

Figure 9.4: Top Five Investment Portfolio Components, 2014 and 2019

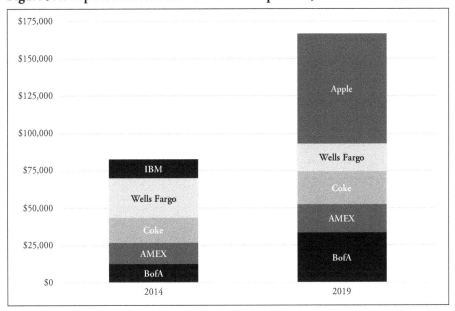

Sources: Berkshire Hathaway Annual Reports 2014, 2019 and author's calculations.

Berkshire's stock price continued to track the underlying progress being made in the business. Shares advanced past the $300,000 mark for the first time in late 2017 and Berkshire's market capitalization was in the $550 billion range by the end of 2019. While the price-to-book value during this time was steady, evidence pointed to the conglomerate being undervalued. Berkshire did its best to communicate this to shareholders and bring about a more rational valuation. When this failed, Berkshire repurchased undervalued shares to the benefit of continuing shareholders. Figures 9.5 and 9.6 present ten years of data for context.

Figure 9.5: Berkshire Hathaway stock price, 2010–2019

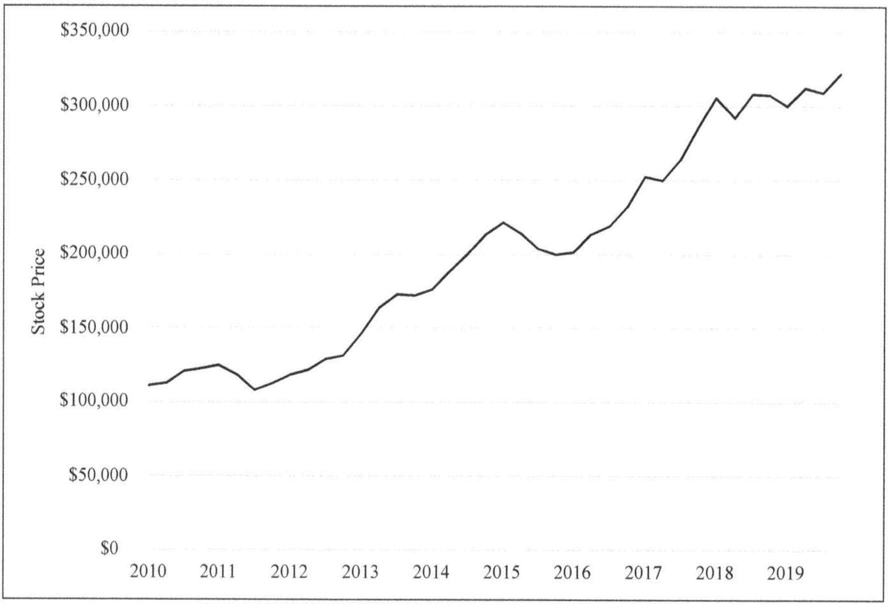

Sources: *Of Permanent Value* (Kilpatrick), Berkshire Hathaway Annual Reports 2010–2017, Yahoo! Finance, and author's calculations.

Figure 9.6: Berkshire Hathaway price to book ratio, 2010–2019

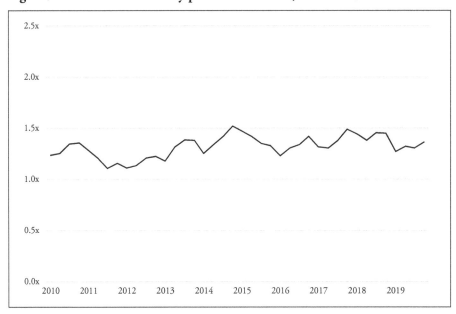

Sources: *Of Permanent Value* (Kilpatrick), Berkshire Hathaway Annual Reports 2010–2017, Yahoo! Finance, and author's calculations.

Lessons: 2015–2019

1. It is okay to admit you were wrong about an investment thesis. Acting to correct a wrong move is difficult but important. Buffett initially invested in IBM stock thinking the company had a stronger competitive advantage. A few years later, he realized he was wrong and sold Berkshire's investment in the company. Buffett also overcame the human tendency toward maintaining a commitment when you have publicly stated your opinion. Berkshire went on to purchase a large stake in Apple, which subsequently doubled in value.

2. Don't let cash burn a hole in your pocket. Berkshire's cash continued to build despite billions spent on growth capex and acquisitions. Buffett resisted pressure to invest cash in a market unsuitable for major investment and waited patiently for opportunity.

3. Compounding is a powerful force. In just five years, Berkshire generated more capital than the previous decade, and over 40% of the *entire* total since 1965. Assessing future capital allocation becomes that much more important for a company that retains a significant portion of its earnings.

4. Incentives are superpowers and can have unintended consequences. The scandal that enveloped Wells Fargo related to opening fraudulent new accounts was unintentional but unfortunately a result of the design of its incentive systems. Berkshire's businesses are managed in a very decentralized manner, but there are protections in place. For example, Berkshire maintains a hotline and a way to send direct and anonymous written communications to headquarters. When a problem arises the best thing to do is act quickly. Problems usually do not get better with time.

5. Focus on the right variables. Buffett said Berkshire's 2016 acquisition of Precision Castparts would undoubtedly come with some problems. He focused his thinking on the company's long-term economic position. Similarly, Buffett suggested an analyst would do better viewing Berkshire as a few collections of businesses rather than try to gain insight into each of Berkshire's many operating subsidiaries.

6. Accounting is a language and only the starting point. The 2018 accounting change that required unrealized gains to flow through the income statement caused Berkshire's bottom line to become analytically useless. Investors must understand the accounting rules as written and then use the financials to determine economic reality.

7. Productivity creates wealth for all citizens. The way a civilization advances its well-being is by producing more goods and services per individual. The process is disruptive in the short term as businesses figure out ways to do the same work with fewer workers. But in the long term productivity gains help all citizens. How to distribute those productivity gains and the best way to mitigate the impact on individuals affected are important political questions.

Table 9.29: Berkshire Hathaway—select parent-level financial information

($ millions, except per share data)	2019	2018	2017	2016	2015
Revenues:					
Insurance premiums earned	$61,078	$57,418	$60,597	$45,881	$41,294
Sales and service revenues	134,989	133,336	130,243	123,053	110,811
Leasing revenue	5,856	5,732	2,552	2,553	1,546
Railroad, utilities and energy revenues	43,453	43,673	40,005	37,447	39,923
Interest, dividend, and other investment income	9,240	7,678	6,536	6,180	6,867
Total revenues	$254,616	$247,837	$239,933	$215,114	$200,441
Investment and derivative gains/(losses)[1]	$72,607	($22,455)	$2,128	$8,304	$10,347
Earnings:					
Net earnings attributable to Berkshire Hathaway[2]	$81,417	$4,021	$44,940	$24,074	$24,083
Net earnings per share	$49,828	$2,446	$27,326	$14,645	$14,656
Year-end data:					
Total assets	$817,729	$707,794	$702,095	$620,854	$552,257
Notes payable and other borrowings:					
Insurance and other non-finance businesses	37,590	34,975	40,409	42,559	26,550
Railroad, utilities and energy businesses	65,778	62,515	62,178	59,085	57,739
Shareholders' equity	424,791	348,703	348,296	282,070	254,619
Common shares outstanding, in thousands (A-share equivalent)	1,625	1,641	1,645	1,644	1,643
Shareholders' equity per outstanding share (A-share equivalent)	$261,417	$212,503	$211,750	$171,542	$154,935

Footnotes:
1. After-tax investment gains were as follows: $57,445 ($17,737) $1,377 $6,497 $6,725
2. Beginning in 2018, investment gains/losses include the changes in fair values of equity securities during the period. Net earnings in 2017 includes a one-time net benefit of $29.1 billion attributable to the enactment of the Tax Cuts and Jobs Act of 2017.

Note: Data taken from the 2019 Annual Report to maintain consistency. Slight differences exist for any particular year depending on the report year.
Sources: Berkshire Hathaway Annual Report, 2019.

Table 9.30: Berkshire Hathaway—Insurance Underwriting

($ millions)	2019	2018	2017	2016	2016	2015	2014
GEICO							
Premiums earned	$35,572	$33,363	$29,441	$25,483	$25,483	$22,718	$20,496
Underwriting gain/(loss) - pre-tax	1,506	2,449	(310)	462	462	460	1,159
General Re							
Premiums earned	*Consolidated with Berkshire Hathaway Reinsurance Group*				$5,637	$5,975	$6,264
Underwriting gain/(loss) - pre-tax					190	132	277
Berkshire Hathaway Reinsurance Group							
Property/casualty	$9,911	$8,928	$7,552	$7,218			
Retroactive reinsurance	684	517	10,755	1,254			
Life/health	4,883	5,343	4,808	4,587			
Periodic payment annuity	863	1,156	898	1,082			
Premiums earned	16,341	15,944	24,013	14,141	$8,504	$7,207	$10,116
Property/casualty	16	(207)	(1,595)	895			
Retroactive reinsurance	(1,265)	(778)	(1,330)	(60)			
Life/health	326	216	(52)	305			
Periodic payment annuity	(549)	(340)	(671)	(128)			
Underwriting gain/(loss) - pre-tax	(1,472)	(1,109)	(3,648)	1,012	822	421	606
Berkshire Hathaway Primary Group							
Premiums earned	$9,165	$8,111	$7,143	$6,257	$6,257	$5,394	$4,377
Underwriting gain/(loss) - pre-tax	383	670	719	657	657	824	626
Total premiums earned	$61,078	$57,418	$60,597	$45,881	$45,881	$41,294	$41,253
Total underwriting gain/(loss) - pre-tax	417	2,010	(3,239)	2,131	2,131	1,837	2,668
Average float	126,078	118,616	103,039	89,650	89,650	85,822	80,581
Cost of float	(0.3%)	(1.7%)	3.1%	(2.4%)	(2.4%)	(2.1%)	(3.3%)

Note: The year 2016 is included twice to show the presentation before and after consolidating General Re into Berkshire Hathaway Reinsurance Group.

Sources: Berkshire Hathaway Annual Reports 2016, 2017, 2019; and author's calculations.

Table 9.31: Berkshire Hathaway Insurance Group float, select data and information

Year	Year-end Float ($ millions)							Year-end Float (% Growth)					
	GEICO	General Reins.	BH Reins.	Other Primary	Total	Avg. Float	Float Cost	GEICO	General Reins.	BH Reins.	Other Primary	Total	Avg. Float
1994						3,057	(4.2%)						16.5%
1995						3,607	(0.6%)						18.0%
1996						6,702	(3.3%)						85.8%
1997	2,917	4,014		455	7,386	7,093	(6.5%)						5.8%
1998	3,125	14,909	4,305	415	22,754	15,070	(1.8%)	7.1%	n/a	7.2%	(8.8%)	208.1%	112.5%
1999	3,444	15,166	6,285	403	25,298	24,026	5.8%	10.2%	1.7%	46.0%	(2.9%)	11.2%	59.4%
2000	3,943	15,525	7,805	598	27,871	26,585	6.1%	14.5%	2.4%	24.2%	48.4%	10.2%	10.6%
2001	4,251	19,310	11,262	685	35,508	31,690	12.8%	7.8%	24.4%	44.3%	14.5%	27.4%	19.2%
2002	4,678	22,207	13,396	943	41,224	38,366	1.1%	10.0%	15.0%	18.9%	37.7%	16.1%	21.1%
2003	5,287	23,654	13,948	1,331	44,220	42,722	(4.0%)	13.0%	6.5%	4.1%	41.1%	7.3%	11.4%
2004	5,960	23,120	15,278	1,736	46,094	45,157	(3.4%)	12.7%	(2.3%)	9.5%	30.4%	4.2%	5.7%
2005	6,692	22,920	16,233	3,442	49,287	47,691	(0.1%)	12.3%	(0.9%)	6.3%	98.3%	6.9%	5.6%
2006	7,171	22,827	16,860	4,029	50,887	50,087	(7.7%)	7.2%	(0.4%)	3.9%	17.1%	3.2%	5.0%
2007	7,768	23,009	23,692	4,229	58,698	54,793	(6.2%)	8.3%	0.8%	40.5%	5.0%	15.3%	9.4%
2008	8,454	21,074	24,221	4,739	58,488	58,593	(4.8%)	8.8%	(8.4%)	2.2%	12.1%	(0.4%)	6.9%
2009	9,613	21,014	26,223	5,061	61,911	60,200	(2.6%)	13.7%	(0.3%)	8.3%	6.8%	5.9%	2.7%
2010	10,272	20,049	30,370	5,141	65,832	63,872	(3.2%)	6.9%	(4.6%)	15.8%	1.6%	6.3%	6.1%
2011	11,169	19,714	33,728	5,960	70,571	68,202	(0.4%)	8.7%	(1.7%)	11.1%	15.9%	7.2%	6.8%
2012	11,578	20,128	34,821	6,598	73,125	71,848	(2.3%)	3.7%	2.1%	3.2%	10.7%	3.6%	5.3%
2013	12,566	20,013	37,231	7,430	77,240	75,183	(4.1%)	8.5%	(0.6%)	6.9%	12.6%	5.6%	4.6%
2014	13,569	19,280	42,454	8,618	83,921	80,581	(3.3%)	8.0%	(3.7%)	14.0%	16.0%	8.6%	7.2%
2015	15,148	18,560	44,108	9,906	87,722	85,822	(2.1%)	11.6%	(3.7%)	3.9%	14.9%	4.5%	6.5%
2016	17,148	17,699	45,081	11,649	91,577	89,650	(2.4%)	13.2%	(4.6%)	2.2%	17.6%	4.4%	4.5%
2017	*Detail no longer provided*				114,500	103,039	3.1%	*Detail no longer provided*				25.0%	14.9%
2018					122,732	118,616	(1.7%)					7.2%	15.1%
2019					129,423	126,078	(0.3%)					5.5%	6.3%

Sources: Berkshire Hathaway Annual Reports and author's calculations.

Table 9.32: Manufacturing, Service, and Retailing businesses—pre-tax earnings

($ millions)	2019	2018	2017 Restated	2017 Original	2016	2015	2014
Industrial products	$5,635	$5,822	$5,065	$4,367	$4,209	$2,994	$3,159
Building products	2,636	2,336	2,147	1,382	1,178	1,167	896
Consumer products	1,251	1,208	1,112	1,112	824	732	756
Subtotal - manufacturing	9,522	9,366	8,324	6,861	6,211	4,893	4,811
Service	1,681	1,836	1,519	1,298	1,161	1,156	1,202
Retailing	874	860	785	785	659	564	344
McLane	288	246	299	299	431	502	435
Subtotal - service and retailing	2,843	2,942	2,603	2,382	2,251	2,222	1,981
Total pre-tax earnings	12,365	12,308	10,927	9,243	8,462	7,115	6,792
Income taxes and non-controlling interests	(2,993)	(2,944)	(3,645)	(3,035)	(2,831)	(2,432)	(2,324)
Earnings after tax	$9,372	$9,364	$7,282	$6,208	$5,631	$4,683	$4,468

Note: In 2018, the Finance and Financial Products businesses were consolidated into the MSR businesses.
Sources: Berkshire Hathaway Annual Reports 2015–2019 and author's calculations.

Table 9.33: Manufacturing, Service, and Retailing businesses—balance sheets, 2004–2016

($ millions)	2016	2015	2014	2013	2012	2011	2010	2009	2008	2007	2006	2005	2004
Assets													
Cash and equivalents	$8,073	$6,807	$5,765	$6,625	$5,338	$4,241	$2,673	$3,018	$2,497	$2,080	$1,543	$1,004	$899
Accounts and notes receivable	11,183	8,886	8,264	7,749	7,382	6,584	5,396	5,066	5,047	4,488	3,793	3,287	3,074
Inventory	15,727	11,916	10,236	9,945	9,675	8,975	7,101	6,147	7,500	5,793	5,257	4,143	3,842
Other current assets	1,039	970	1,117	716	734	631	550	625	752	470	363	342	254
Total current assets	$36,022	$28,579	$25,382	$25,035	$23,129	$20,431	$15,720	$14,856	$15,796	$12,831	$10,956	$8,776	$8,069
Goodwill and other intangibles	71,473	30,289	28,107	25,617	26,017	24,755	16,976	16,499	16,515	14,201	13,314	9,260	8,362
Fixed assets	18,915	15,161	13,806	19,389	18,871	17,866	15,421	15,374	16,338	9,605	8,934	7,148	6,161
Other assets	3,183	4,445	3,793	4,274	3,416	3,661	3,029	2,070	1,248	1,685	1,168	1,021	1,044
	$129,593	$78,474	$71,088	$74,315	$71,433	$66,713	$51,146	$48,799	$49,897	$38,322	$34,372	$26,205	$23,636
Liabilities and Equity													
Notes payable	$2,054	$2,135	$965	$1,615	$1,454	$1,611	$1,805	$1,842	$2,212	$1,278	$1,468	$1,469	$1,143
Other current liabilities	12,464	10,565	9,734	8,965	8,527	15,124	8,169	7,414	8,087	7,652	6,635	5,371	4,685
Total current liabilities	14,518	12,700	10,699	10,580	9,981	16,735	9,974	9,256	10,299	8,930	8,103	6,840	5,828
Deferred taxes	12,044	3,649	3,801	5,184	4,907	4,661	3,001	2,834	2,786	828	540	338	248
Term debt and other liabilities	10,943	4,767	4,269	4,405	5,826	6,214	6,621	6,240	6,033	3,079	3,014	2,188	1,965
Non-controlling interests	579	521	492	456	2,062	2,410							
Equity	91,509	56,837	51,827	53,690	48,657	36,693	31,550	30,469	30,779	25,485	22,715	16,839	15,595
	$129,593	$78,474	$71,088	$74,315	$71,433	$66,713	$51,146	$48,799	$49,897	$38,322	$34,372	$26,205	$23,636

Notes:

Berkshire stopped reporting this data after 2016.

In 2014, Marmon's leasing operations began to be included in the Finance and Financial Products sector. The 2014 Annual Report provided a restatement of 2012 and 2013 for comparative purposes. This table contains the original presentations.

Sources: Berkshire Hathaway Annual Reports 2004–2016.

Table 9.34: Manufacturing, Service, and Retailing businesses—income statements, 2004–2016

($ millions)	2016	2015	2014	2013	2012	2011	2010	2009	2008	2007	2006	2005	2004
Revenues	$120,059	$107,825	$97,689	$95,291	$83,255	$72,406	$66,610	$61,665	$66,099	$59,100	$52,660	$46,896	$44,142
Operating expenses	111,383	100,607	90,788	88,414	76,978	67,239	62,225	59,509	61,937	55,026	49,002	44,190	41,604
(Including depreciation)						*1,431*	*1,362*	*1,422*	*1,280*	*955*	*823*	*699*	*676*
Interest expense (net)	214	103	109	135	146	130	111	98	139	127	132	83	57
Pre-tax income[1]	8,462	7,115	6,792	6,742	6,131	5,037	4,274	2,058	4,023	3,947	3,526	2,623	2,481
Income taxes and non-controlling interests	2,831	2,432	2,324	2,512	2,432	1,998	1,812	945	1,740	1,594	1,395	977	941
Net income	$5,631	$4,683	$4,468	$4,230	$3,699	$3,039	$2,462	$1,113	$2,283	$2,353	$2,131	$1,646	$1,540

Footnote: Excludes purchase-accounting adjustments.

Sources: Berkshire Hathaway Annual Reports 2004–2016 and author's calculations.

Table 9.35: Manufacturing, Service, and Retailing businesses—ratios and key figures, 2004–2016

	2016	2015	2014	2013	2012	2011	2010	2009	2008	2007	2006	2005	2004
Tangible capital	$33,033	$33,450	$28,954	$34,093	$29,920	$19,763	$23,000	$22,052	$22,509	$15,641	$13,883	$11,236	$10,341
Revenues/avg. tang. capital	$3.61	$3.46	$3.10	$2.98	$3.35	$3.39	$2.96	$2.77	$3.47	$4.00	$4.19	$4.35	$4.27
Pre-tax margin	7.0%	6.6%	7.0%	7.1%	7.4%	7.0%	6.4%	3.3%	6.1%	6.7%	6.7%	5.6%	5.6%
Pre-tax return on tangible capital	25.5%	22.8%	21.5%	21.1%	24.7%	23.6%	19.0%	9.2%	21.1%	26.7%	28.1%	24.3%	24.0%
Return on average equity - after-tax	7.6%	8.6%	8.5%	8.3%	8.7%	8.9%	7.9%	3.6%	8.1%	9.8%	10.8%	10.1%	9.9%
Return on average tangible equity after-tax	24.2%	18.6%	17.3%	16.7%	21.4%	22.9%	17.3%	7.9%	17.9%	22.8%	25.1%	22.2%	21.6%
Net debt (cash)	$4,924	$95	($531)	($605)	$1,942	$3,584	$5,753	$5,064	$5,748	$2,277	$2,939	$2,653	$2,209
Notes payable/equity	14.2%	12.1%	10.1%	11.2%	15.0%	21.3%	26.7%	26.5%	26.8%	17.1%	19.7%	21.7%	19.9%
Total assets/total equity	1.42	1.38	1.37	1.38	1.47	1.82	1.62	1.60	1.62	1.50	1.51	1.56	1.52

Sources: Berkshire Hathaway Annual Reports 2004–2016 and author's calculations.

Table 9.36: Regulated, Capital-Intensive Businesses

($ millions)	2019	2018	2017	2016	2015	2014
Berkshire Hathaway Energy (formerly known as MidAmerican Energy)						
UK utilities		$304	$311	$367	$460	$527
Iowa utility[1]		407	372	392	292	270
Nevada utility		417	567	559	586	549
PacifiCorp		745	1,131	1,105	1,026	1,010
Gas Pipelines (Northern Natural and Kern River)		507	446	413	401	379
Canadian transmission utility[2]				147	170	16
Renewable projects[2]				157	175	194
HomeServices		204	220	225	191	139
Other (net)[2]		296	296	73	49	54
Earnings before corporate interest and taxes		2,880	3,343	3,438	3,350	3,138
Interest		408	844	465	499	427
Pre-tax earnings	2,618	2,472	2,499	2,973	2,851	2,711
Income taxes	(526)	(452)	148	431	481	616
Net earnings	$3,144	$2,924	$2,351	$2,542	$2,370	$2,095
Net earnings applicable to Berkshire[3]	$2,840	$2,621	$2,033	$2,287	$2,132	$1,882
Burlington Northern Santa Fe (BNSF)	**2019**	**2018**	**2017**	**2016**	**2015**	**2014**
Revenues	$23,515	$23,855	$21,387	$19,829	$21,967	$23,239
Operating expenses (including depreciation)	15,195	15,951	14,043	13,144	14,264	16,237
Operating earnings before interest and taxes	8,320	7,904	7,344	6,685	7,703	7,002
Interest (net)	1,070	1,041	1,016	992	928	833
Income taxes	1,769	1,644	2,369	2,124	2,527	2,300
Net earnings	$5,481	$5,219	$3,959	$3,569	$4,248	$3,869

Footnotes:
1. For the 2016 presentation, Berkshire reclassified $22 million from Iowa utility to Other for results in 2015 and $28 million for results in 2014. The more recent presentation is included here.
2. Canadian transmission utility and renewable projects reported in other beginning in 2017.
3. Earnings applicable to Berkshire consist of its share of net earnings plus after tax interest income from debt owed to Berkshire.

Notes:
1. Berkshire stopped reporting this data in the Chairman's letter after 2016. Data for 2017–2019 taken from the Annual Reports.
2. In 2019, Berkshire changed the presentation of Berkshire Hathaway Energy to present consolidated income accounts and only detailed the after-tax results for each unit. Previous presentations included the pre-tax results.

Sources: Berkshire Hathaway Annual Reports 2016–2019.

Table 9.37: Reconciliation of shareholders' equity

($ millions)	2019	2018	2017	2016	2015	2014
Prior year equity	$348,703	$348,296	$283,001	$255,550	$240,170	$221,890
Current year net income/(loss)[1]	81,417	4,021	44,940	24,074	24,083	19,872
Issuance of shares[2]	21	59	76	119	53	118
Treasury stock[3]	(5,016)	(1,346)				(400)
Transactions with non-controlling interests[4]	(70)	(46)	(63)	(58)	(6)	(17)
Adoption of new accounting pronouncements[5]	111	(70)	(931)	0		
Change in unrealized appreciation of securities, net of tax		(354)	18,975	4,579	(7,022)	1,585
Change in comprehensive income – other[6]	(375)	(1,857)	2,298	(1,263)	(1,728)	(2,878)
Ending equity	$424,791	$348,703	$348,296	$283,001	$255,550	$240,170
Shares outstanding at end of period						
Class A	701,970	729,316	751,075	776,378	808,422	826,339
Class B	1,384,481,533	1,367,420,074	1,340,656,987	1,301,914,165	1,252,456,836	1,224,855,488
Total Class A-equivalent shares	1,624,958	1,640,929	1,644,846	1,644,321	1,643,393	1,642,909

Footnotes:
1. 2017: Includes a one-time gain from a reduction in the US Corporate income tax rate from 35% to 21%.
2. 2018: Beginning in 2018, unrealized gains and losses on equity securities are included in net income.
2. The issuance of shares primarily relates to prior acquisitions.
3. The 2014 transaction was connected to the Graham Holdings tax-free exchange, which included 2,107 Class A shares and 1,278 Class B shares.
4. Reductions in equity related to the acquisition of non-controlling interests; the excess of consideration paid over the previously recorded balance sheet carrying amount.
5. 2017: Related to Berkshire discontinuing the practice of discounting workers' compensation claim liabilities assumed under reinsurance contracts. Equity for the prior years was restated for 2014–2016 in the financial statements.
2018: Related to adoption of ASC 606 related to revenue recognition (affected fractional ownership interests).
6. Includes foreign currency translation, transactions relating to pension plans, OCI related to non-controlling interests, other, and amounts applicable to income taxes.

Sources: Berkshire Hathaway Annual Reports 2014–2019 and author's calculations.

Table 9.38: Berkshire Hathaway deferred tax analysis

($ millions)	2019	2018	2017	2016	2015	2014	2013	2012	2011	2010	Total
Earnings before income taxes	$102,696	$4,001	$23,838	$33,667	$34,946	$28,105	$28,796	$22,236	$15,314	$19,051	$312,650
Current taxes	5,818	5,176	3,299	6,565	5,426	3,302	5,168	4,711	2,897	3,668	$46,030
Deferred taxes[1]	15,086	(5,497)	3,386	2,675	5,106	4,633	3,783	2,213	1,671	1,939	$34,995
Total taxes as reported	20,904	(321)	6,685	9,240	10,532	7,935	8,951	6,924	4,568	5,607	81,025
Cash paid for tax during period	5,415	4,354	3,286	4,719	4,535	4,014	5,401	4,695	2,885	3,547	$42,851
Current rate	5.7%	129.4%	13.8%	19.5%	15.5%	11.7%	17.9%	21.2%	18.9%	19.3%	14.7%
Deferred rate	14.7%	(137.4%)	14.2%	7.9%	14.6%	16.5%	13.1%	10.0%	10.9%	10.2%	11.2%
Headline tax rate	20.4%	(8.0%)	28.0%	27.4%	30.1%	28.2%	31.1%	31.1%	29.8%	29.4%	25.9%
Current as % total	27.8%	(1612.5%)	49.3%	71.0%	51.5%	41.6%	57.7%	68.0%	63.4%	65.4%	56.8%
Deferred as % total	72.2%	1712.5%	50.7%	29.0%	48.5%	58.4%	42.3%	32.0%	36.6%	34.6%	43.2%
Total tax	100.0%	100.0%	100.0%	100.0%	100.0%	100.0%	100.0%	100.0%	100.0%	100.0%	100.0%
Cash tax as % EBIT	5.3%	108.8%	13.8%	14.0%	13.0%	14.3%	18.8%	21.1%	18.8%	18.6%	13.7%

Footnote:
1. 2017: Excludes (adds back) the $28,200 one-time gain associated with the Tax Cuts and Jobs Act of 2017.

Sources: Berkshire Hathaway Annual Reports 2011, 2014, 2016, 2019; and author's calculations.

Chapter 10
World's Greatest Conglomerate

The many pages written on Berkshire Hathaway thus far give away the ending. Berkshire Hathaway is the world's greatest conglomerate—and will remain the standard by which all future conglomerates are measured.

By any measure, Berkshire Hathaway has secured its spot in the pantheon of successful modern businesses. While Warren Buffett runs a conglomerate, he in some ways has more in common with the industrial greats than he does the historical conglomerate executives. Andrew Carnegie, John D. Rockefeller, Sr., Henry Ford and Cornelius Vanderbilt all built huge business empires and wealth within a particular industry that earned them lots of ink in history books and significant name recognition. These men had an outsized impact on the industrial revolution, directly impacting steel production, mass market car production, and the expansion of the railroads depending on the individual. Conversely, most people haven't heard of Charles Bluhdorn and Royal Little unless they are students of history or business. Yet those men were integral parts of the history of the conglomerate as a business structure.[127] Buffett too is a household name. Why? Because the success of Berkshire Hathaway earned him that reputation. Berkshire has stood the test of time as the standard-bearer for the best of business, investing, and value creation. This is Buffett's legacy: a formula for long-term sustainable success that maximizes human potential. Like the switch to mass-produced automobiles (Ford) and the revolution of steel production (Carnegie), Buffett's innovative business approach stands the test of time.

The conglomerate craze of the 1960s saw the rapid growth of conglomerates including Textron (founded by Royal Little), Litton Industries, Ling-Temco Vought and Gulf + Western (founded by Charles Bluhdorn). Their strategies included artificially inflating share prices and acquiring companies by issuing shares and borrowing heavily. Those companies made the usual lists and headlines for their successes and failures—but they weren't sustainable. The result of these strategies was often a whole that was eventually worth less than the sum of its parts (a conglomerate discount) and a company producing accounting fictions rather than real results. This often led to the companies being broken up, sold off, or both.

Berkshire achieved its position as the world's best conglomerate through a combination of business mastery and a bit of luck. The luck component is easy to observe. Warren Buffett and Charlie Munger were born at the right time to fill their sails, and that of their conglomerate, with incredible tailwinds. First, they were lucky to begin solidifying Berkshire's economic position when market inefficiencies were much more prevalent. Taking advantage of these inefficiencies paid handsomely. Second, the dawn of Berkshire Hathaway as the modern conglomerate powerhouse of today began at the end of the conglomerate craze of the 1960s. Buffett and Munger had the good fortune to observe what worked and what didn't. Critically, their minds wouldn't let go until they figured out why. These lessons were then applied to their canvas at Berkshire to create a masterpiece.

Business mastery is the only term sufficient to convey the decades of study and application necessary to forge one of the most respected companies in the world from a dying textile company. Yet that is what Warren Buffett and Charlie Munger did, along with much help—and a few mistakes. We can observe this business mastery in the way they maximized every element of business while allowing managers to independently run their businesses. Many of Buffett and Munger's techniques have since been copied by modern operators. And as they say, imitation is the sincerest form of flattery.

Capital Allocation

Berkshire's philosophy: Treat subsidiaries as investments, providing for operational independence. Use the cash flow from them, along with capital gains from investments, for organic expansion.

Early conglomerates: Acquire diverse businesses to achieve synergies or take a hands-on approach to managing them post-acquisition.

A successful business of any kind is the result of rational capital allocation over time. Berkshire Hathaway grew out of the philosophy Warren Buffett internalized from Benjamin Graham early in his career. A bedrock principle was that stocks represented ownership in a business. This framework gave Buffett an important vantage point to survey the economic landscape. No business or industry would be out of reach if Buffett could understand the business and its economics. Berkshire could allocate capital to wholly-owned businesses or buy pieces of businesses in the stock market, depending on which was more attractive at the time.

Crucially, the ownership philosophy set the stage for decentralization. Buffett and Munger's early years were spent buying stocks as part of a portfolio. Berkshire was constructed using what might be termed a portfolio approach. It became a collection of businesses and not one large business with operational oversight of multiple business activities. This is an important distinction. Berkshire's capital allocators were accustomed to acting as owners, not managers. If a hands-off approach worked for passive investments in stocks, why should the approach change much upon gaining control? Berkshire could view ownership of a subsidiary as equivalent to a stock in a portfolio and let it operate independently. The only difference between the two approaches was that Berkshire had a much higher threshold for divesting an operating subsidiary.

The advantages of buying good businesses arose organically. For example, Berkshire purchased The Illinois National Bank & Trust of Rockford because it was a good business. Once part of Berkshire, the Bank's tax bill was reduced by losses arising from its new sister companies. The acquisition was *not* made because of the tax savings, but a consolidated tax bill was one advantage. Another advantage was the ability to move capital between subsidiaries without tax consequences. Two stocks owned within a portfolio might have one common owner, but cannot share resources without tax implications. Once owned through a conglomerate, this barrier is removed.

The conglomerate structure also provided an important relief valve to subsidiaries. Berkshire's subsidiaries could grow to their optimal size and send surplus cash flow to headquarters. Buffett and Munger were in the best position to allocate capital to the highest use once it could not be used for expansion at the subsidiary level. This afforded Berkshire the opportunity to buy businesses with strong competitive positions but little growth potential. See's is perhaps the best example. The capital that remained within See's would earn a great return, and the cash it generated could earn a good return too, just not in See's.

Economics Over Accounting

Berkshire's philosophy: Act based on economics over accounting but present business results that are accurate, even if the economics are worse than the accounting.

Some early conglomerates: Use financial engineering to artificially increase earnings per share.

From Buffett's earliest communications with Berkshire shareholders, he stressed he cared more about economics than accounting. Berkshire's 1965 Chairman's letter highlighted that its reported earnings were significantly more than reality. That statement was made at a time when some other companies, but certainly other conglomerates, did everything in their power to make earnings look better. Buffett and Munger saw the spectacular rise and fall of the 1960s conglomerate leaders that were made possible by financial engineering designed to increase earnings per share. Their fatal flaw was reliance on accounting to paint a picture of robust health and growth that wasn't fully supported by the businesses they purchased with expensive shares. In short, their strategy wasn't sustainable.

Berkshire let others make business decisions based on accounting while it used opportunity cost as a guide. When more earnings could be purchased through the stock market, which was frequently the case, Berkshire purchased those. It didn't matter that only a part of the earnings accruing to its ownership interest was reflected in Berkshire's financials. That philosophy extended to its acquisition of entire businesses. "Accounting consequences do not influence our operating or capital-allocation decisions. When acquisition costs are similar, we much prefer to purchase $2 of earnings that is not reportable by us under standard accounting principles than to purchase $1 of earnings that is reportable." Berkshire's entry into the reinsurance field was aided by the fact that Berkshire cared more about the long-term economics of insurance than short-term accounting implications. It wrote huge retroactive reinsurance contracts and other time-value-of-money policies that penalized earnings immediately but were economically sound transactions long term.

Separate Management of Assets and Liabilities

Berkshire's philosophy: Opportunistic borrowing even when capital is not needed, and using low-cost insurance float to fund growth.
Other companies: Borrowed heavily and focusing on short-term returns over long-term gains.

Berkshire focused on maximizing the value of each side of its balance sheet largely independent of the other. Decisions on what assets to buy were not predicated on available financing, because ample resources were usually on hand. Conversely, availability of cheap financing did not by itself lead to asset purchases. The assets, whether whole companies or pieces of companies via stocks, had to stand on their own. Berkshire bought businesses with an all-equity mindset. It viewed acquisitions as entirely financed by equity even if some debt was used or assumed. Attention was on the economics of the underlying business and not what financial returns could be had by enhancing equity returns with debt. This properly focused attention on better businesses.

Insurance float is undoubtedly a major reason for Berkshire's rapid growth. It provided Berkshire with a low-cost way to finance the asset side of the balance sheet. Buffett recognized that float was only valuable if it could be obtained at a low cost, and he used the government's own borrowing rate as a benchmark. In most years,

Berkshire could finance at a lower cost than the US government. Beginning in the 1990s, it realized a consistent profit in underwriting.

Berkshire intentionally structured its insurance liabilities to ensure near permanence of capital. The primary insurers (including GEICO) were in short-tail lines that could consistently generate float so long as they maintained their cost and underwriting discipline. The reinsurance contracts stretched out over years and contained limits on maximum payouts. Underwriting discipline pervaded Berkshire's insurance underwriting culture—it only wrote business that made sense. Structured this way, Berkshire could never be called on to remit large amounts of capital at one time. If Berkshire's float did begin to decline, it would be very gradual and could be offset by underwriting profits. From an economic standpoint, Berkshire has structured its float to act very much like equity.

Some other insurance companies recognized the value in float but did not properly calculate its cost. These companies would push down premiums to be competitive. By exchanging long-term profits for short-term gains, their actions affected the entire industry. Berkshire maintained its discipline in the face of ebbs and flows of capital into the industry and only wrote business it thought had a reasonable expectation of profit. Its conservatism effectively allowed it to capture business from weaker pricing environments by writing more advantageously priced reinsurance deals later to shore up the balance sheets of competitors.

Modern day conglomerates have also used insurance as fuel for their growth too. Companies like Markel, Alleghany, and Canada-based Fairfax Financial—which are just a fraction of the size of Berkshire—have similar structures to Berkshire. All three employ largely the same strategy of discipline of underwriting insurance and reinsurance, and opportunistic acquisition of well-understood and profitable non-insurance operating businesses and marketable securities. The only disadvantage these modern conglomerates have is starting later when asset prices were more expensive than Berkshire's early purchases. Other even smaller mini-conglomerates have been formed to duplicate Berkshire's success in insurance in the modern era.

Discussion of Buffett's management of Berkshire's liabilities is often limited to insurance float. Float was a huge factor in Berkshire's success, but not the only one. On several occasions, Berkshire borrowed money with no clear immediate use for it. This was because the optimal time for financing did not necessarily coincide with the optimal time to buy assets. Even as late as 2019, Berkshire borrowed low-cost funds in Euros and yen at a time when it was flush with cash.

Berkshire's subsidiaries benefitted from lower borrowing costs by being a part of a conglomerate. In some cases, Berkshire borrowed the money directly then relent it to the subsidiary that needed the capital. An important aspect to financing arrangements like this was that the subsidiaries were charged a spread that amounted to a fee for using Berkshire's pristine credit and corporate guarantee. This reduced the distorting effects that a heavily subsidized interest rate might have on the subsidiary. Even BNSF and Berkshire Hathaway Energy, whose debt Berkshire does not explicitly guarantee, benefit to some degree by having a well-capitalized parent.

Deferred taxes are also a misunderstood liability that provided Berkshire with additional capital. While these arose from the primary objectives of holding investments for a long time (deferring capital gains taxes) and capital spending to buildout future earnings (deferring income taxes), they nevertheless provided Berkshire with real economic benefits.

Risk Management

Berkshire's philosophy: Take a long-term approach to business acquisition and investing that incorporates wide-ranging possibilities and probabilities.
Other companies: Place short-term profits ahead of considerations of long-term risks and fail to account for risk aggregation and correlation.

Berkshire benefitted from astute risk management. By using insurance float to fund assets, it could generate a higher return on equity while taking less risk. It consistently operated with far more capital than insurance regulators required. This conservatism allowed Berkshire to invest in better assets like businesses while its peers were restricted to lower-yielding bonds. What it gave up in additional underwriting premiums it gained in the certainty attached to equity ownership compared to cash-denominated investments over longer periods of time. Berkshire's stable of cash-generating, non-insurance businesses then backstopped the insurance businesses. This made them even stronger. The unsurpassed capital strength of the insurance company balance sheets brought reinsurance transactions in the billions that no other insurer could handle. It also allowed Berkshire to accept higher expected returns in exchange for bearing large but infrequent losses. Each individual risk mitigation factor looked unduly conservative on its own; taken together they provided Berkshire with valuable advantages.

Berkshire gained from judicious risk management in other ways. It was willing to accept huge risks for the right premiums in its insurance operations and make concentrated investments in marketable securities. When it came to Berkshire's cash, however, nothing but US Treasuries would do. Buffett only wished to make investments with certain payouts over long periods of time. In the short run, *anything* could happen. The September 11th terrorist attacks, and the Great Recession when markets froze, proved him right. Buffett's awareness of risk also saved Berkshire money by avoiding unnecessary costs. Taking the very long-term view, Buffett knew the cost of hedging over time resulted in unnecessary costs. When he was asked whether BNSF had insurance to cover large accidents, Buffett explained that Berkshire was basically self-insured. Why would Berkshire pay another insurer to cover the same type of risk its insurers would be willing to write itself?

Another nuanced risk Berkshire successfully managed was trust. Berkshire understood there were risks related to its policy of extreme autonomy. A delicate balance existed between maximizing human potential (and by extension business potential) by being hands off, all the while maintaining adequate oversight. Berkshire took the position that it was better to over trust and incur infrequent but public embarrassments than impose strict controls that were a net negative. It continually reinforced the message that it cared for Berkshire's reputation first and foremost.

Berkshire successfully managed risks in the businesses it purchased—but it did make mistakes. Berkshire lost money on those investments, but its winning bets *by far* exceeded losers. The largest loss Berkshire suffered was Dexter Shoe. Yet the shares issued for Dexter represented just 2% of Berkshire's outstanding shares—an extremely good result for a loss considering the degrees of concentration Berkshire employed elsewhere in businesses and investments. With insurance Berkshire had not only more assets working in its favor but safer assets too. The key was recognizing risk as a factor that could interrupt or destroy years of profitable compounding.* These examples of Berkshire's risk management prove it gained by thinking carefully and long term.

Governance

Berkshire's philosophy: Let managers run businesses independently.
Some early conglomerates: Meddled in subsidiary management and/or attempted to find synergies between subsidiaries.

Another element of Berkshire's success was its governance practices. Its policy of "delegation just shy of abdication" rested on first acquiring businesses that could be managed autonomously. Buffett's skill at recognizing managers who cared more about their businesses than money they would receive is often overlooked. By carefully selecting and then placing an enormous amount of trust in its managers, coupled with proper incentives, Berkshire created what amounted to ownership of individual subsidiaries. Managers were rewarded for the contributions they made to their specific businesses without any regard to Berkshire as a whole. Tying incentive compensation to factors like return on capital focused attention on the variables that would drive long-term business success for its owner, Berkshire.

---

* Berkshire's worst mistakes were errors of omission, investments that should have been made but weren't. These included not buying Walmart sooner and recognizing Google as a powerful and entrenched business.

Berkshire's acquisitions came intact and without any illusion that managerial skill would further enhance their operations. The wholly-owned businesses were managed much like Berkshire's investments in marketable securities. No attempt was made to find or create synergies between operating units. Buffett kept his distance even when opportunities for cross sales seemed obvious, because he knew meddling in the affairs of subsidiaries would ultimately cost Berkshire far more. No attempt was made to have Clayton Homes buy from Shaw, Johns Manville, or Benjamin Moore, for example. When Van Tuyl joined Berkshire with an insurance arm of its own, its new owner did not require it to offer GEICO insurance to buyers of its automobiles. The key was allowing operating managers to act independently and locally. Communication between operating units was inevitable and not discouraged, but it was organic and spontaneous, not forced.

Berkshire left its managers alone to focus on what they did best. The hallmark of a Berkshire manager is a long tenure with no required retirement age. Think Mrs. B.

Per Share Thinking

Berkshire's philosophy: Rarely issue shares to keep business and per-share results in line.

Some early conglomerates: Grew by issuing shares, often coupled with copious amounts of debt.

Berkshire Hathaway differentiated itself from the early conglomerates by a marked respect for the individual shareholder. This is not surprising given Buffett and Munger's pre-Berkshire days operating investment partnerships for close family and friends. They treated Berkshire Hathaway shareholders with the same respect as business partners.

Berkshire's share count increased by just 44% during the first fifty years of Buffett's control. The largest increase came with the 1998 acquisition of General Re and increased Berkshire's shares outstanding by 22%. Berkshire's reluctance to issue shares meant the results from its underlying businesses translated into nearly equivalent results for its shareholders. Berkshire understood that issuing shares was the economic equivalent of selling pieces of its existing businesses, which it was hesitant to do since those businesses were of such high quality.

The conglomerates of the 1960s that issued shares to grow (in some cases many multiples of their beginning share counts[*]) were forced to turn inward after the go-go years ended. Many of the conglomerates were turned over to managers that could attempt to maximize the value of assets accumulated during the prior decade. In

---

[*] Two of the worst offenders were Ling-Temco-Vought and Gulf + Western, which increased share counts by well over 1000%.

the worst cases, executives were fired and bankruptcies occurred. In the better cases, divestures shrunk the business and raised needed cash. In some cases, companies grew, but the executives were not as mindful or respectful of shareholders as Berkshire was.*

Reputation/Brand

Berkshire's philosophy: Acquire and invest in strong brands with good reputations that protected strong returns on capital and build a trustworthy brand in the insurance industry. Protect Berkshire's reputation first and foremost.
Some early conglomerates: Chose companies with well-known names but whose economics were often average.

Berkshire Hathaway recognized and maximized the power of reputation and brands. Buffett's appreciation for brands started before he took control of Berkshire. In the mid-1960s he purchased a stake in American Express for his investment partnership, Buffett Partnership Limited. The credit card company became embroiled in a then-famous salad oil scandal that almost took down the company. Buffett recognized the power of the American Express brand and put almost one-third of the partnership's assets into its stock. When the brand prevailed, Buffett and his partners realized a significant profit.

Charlie Munger also appreciated brands and pushed Buffett in the direction of buying better businesses at a fair price over fair businesses at a great price. The first was See's Candies, which had a powerful brand on the West Coast. Berkshire went on to acquire other companies that had a strong brand awareness that translated into valuable economic benefits. Berkshire's investments in publicly traded companies, such as Coca-Cola, reflected this strategy. Many of these businesses, due to their reputation and operations, also had business moats protecting them.

Berkshire grew the Insurance Group by leveraging its reputation. Insurance, Buffett said, is nothing more than a promise. The insured pays the premium and the insurance company promises to provide coverage as agreed. Nowhere is that promise more important than reinsurance. As Berkshire built its reinsurance operations, its reputation became more and more valuable. Berkshire was capitalized far greater than industry minimums (or even norms). Over time this became a powerful advantage that attracted reinsurance business that very few competitors could even have a shot at bidding on. Berkshire became the gold standard of the insurance industry, a reputational and brand advantage that will only grow as Berkshire grows.

---

* Teledyne, run by Henry Singleton (and cited favorably by Buffett and Munger), was one of the only conglomerates to reverse course and repurchase undervalued shares after they became cheap.

Over time, Berkshire cultivated a reputation for fast and fair business dealings with sellers of businesses. Families that built businesses over generations turned to Berkshire as a permanent home for their businesses. They could realize all the advantages of selling, such as liquidity, diversification, and estate planning, while maintaining what amounted to full operational control of the business if they so chose. In exchange for this operational control, the sellers accepted a slightly lower selling price than if they marketed the business more widely. Berkshire received a fair price and a turnkey operation that wouldn't require much from headquarters. Under the conglomerate's wing, the family businesses would be spared meetings with bankers, analysts, and investors, and they would have access to almost unlimited capital for worthwhile projects—a classic win-win scenario. Berkshire's promise never to sell unless under exceedingly rare circumstances and the way it treated its existing businesses created a powerful reputational and brand for the conglomerate.

Tax advantages

Berkshire's philosophy: Use the conglomerate structure to move capital without tax consequences.
Some early conglomerates: Let taxes drive business decisions or disregard the impact of taxes on long-term results.

The conglomerate structure provided meaningful tax advantages. Berkshire could move capital between subsidiaries without tax consequences. Capital could be taken from a business like See's that had strong returns on capital but little reinvestment opportunity and moved to opportunities elsewhere at sister companies. Businesses not united by a corporate parent, or smaller ownership stakes owned in a portfolio, would not have this advantage. The conglomerate structure also allowed Berkshire Hathaway Energy to maximize the tax incentives available to utilities. These tax savings represented real value creation.

While Berkshire took full advantage of the tax code, it did not let taxes drive the business. Some operators past and present have let taxes dictate business decisions, choosing companies to acquire based on the tax advantages they would bring. Short-term this could work, but businesses that are losing money are doing so for a reason, and there are often long-term consequences.

Other factors

The factors discussed so far could be considered a blueprint to create a successful conglomerate. As was discussed at the beginning, Berkshire also benefitted from a degree of luck, and this cannot be controlled. Other factors helped too. Buffett and Munger did not have to worry about outside shareholders or a board of directors that would second guess them. Buffett controlled enough of Berkshire's voting power for so long he could make the best long-term capital allocation decisions. Berkshire also treated shareholders as partners and cultivated like-minded manager-partners that shared their vision and reinforced this strategy.

Berkshire had one corporate office and one board of directors. The savings surely added up from the elimination of multiple boards of directors, proxy statements and annual reports, and other regulatory and compliance costs. Tenure at the company is another important factor. With a tenure closing in on sixty years, Berkshire benefitted from the compounding of business knowledge over time as Buffett, Munger, and many other managers remain committed to the business well beyond a typical corporate retirement age.

Berkshire even went so far as to minimize the costs of its own public company status. No corporate-level human resources, legal, or investor relations existed. Communication to shareholders consisted of the annual Chairman's letter and Annual Meeting, in addition to three quarterly reports and the Annual Report/10K. Berkshire shunned analysts and maximized the time its capital allocators could spend working on things that benefitted the business directly. As a testament to the efficiency at Berkshire, it prepares its quarterly reports in-house and doesn't consolidate the financial statements of its many businesses monthly.

Why Berkshire Hathaway is the World's Greatest Conglomerate

The factors above created a lollapalooza, to borrow a phrase from Charlie Munger. Its success stemmed from maximizing every aspect of business. Over a long period, Berkshire found the optimal financial structure, use of a permanent and low-cost source of capital, motivated and properly incentivized management teams, judicious risk management techniques, care for the individual shareholder, and a base of owners that supported the company's strategy.

It would be foolish to state categorically that the record of Berkshire Hathaway will never be overtaken. However, considering the alignment of all the factors discussed, the probabilities are against it. Berkshire added an element to the conglomerate structure, long-term sustainability, that was missing from the early conglomerates.

And it had the benefit of doing it first. Warren Buffett and Charlie Munger were driven by a desire to paint their own canvas and achieve business mastery. It's no surprise they did not succumb to the short-term strategies employed by the early conglomerators who sought short-term gains or a quick rise to fame.

Berkshire Hathaway's record transcends business history to enter the full pantheon of human achievement. Berkshire today represents an ideal of business and human accomplishment, not just in financial terms but in setting an example for taking the high road in all walks of life. Warren Buffett and Charlie Munger, and their many associates, have shown us how to conduct business in the very best way possible. Berkshire mastered its domain and left a complete record for anyone to see. Today there are a host of smaller contemporary conglomerates and a legion of followers emulating and building on their work. That is proof enough that Berkshire, Buffett, and Munger mastered not only business but the art conveying wisdom to future generations. Berkshire Hathaway is the world's greatest conglomerate because it was a good teacher—and that is perhaps the highest praise to bestow.

Chapter 11
Afterward—Berkshire After Buffett

T he question of Berkshire Hathaway after Warren Buffett has been asked since the beginning of his tenure running the company. It had more validity during the early years when a large part of the conglomerate was comprised of stocks, which Buffett managed. Back then, the question wasn't age but the proverbial bus. What would happen if Berkshire's shareholders woke up one morning to find Buffett no longer able to run the company? No one can argue that Berkshire would have been quite different if Warren Buffett left the scene prior to, perhaps, the mid-2000s. As Warren Buffett instead entered his tenth decade of life as this book was being finalized, different questions face Berkshire Hathaway and its shareholders. Buffett turned 90 years old in 2020. Biology guarantees Berkshire will one day be without the man synonymous with creating one of the world's most admired businesses. Buffett guaranteed the conglomerate had a bright future by hiring skilled investment managers, continually seeking companies with sound economics, and widely sharing his business principles. After all, as Buffett himself said, "If a business *requires* a superstar to produce great results, the business itself cannot be deemed great."

Management Succession

Not much will change in the immediate period surrounding Buffett's departure from Berkshire. Management of the individual business units will continue unchanged. The question of who will take over Buffett's role has already been partially decided. Buffett's role as chairman, CEO, and chief investment officer will be split into three parts:

1. *Non-executive chairman*: Buffett has strongly suggested his son, Howard Buffett, be chosen for this role. His sole purpose will be to ensure that the culture of Berkshire remains intact. That includes serving as a safety valve of sorts in the remote chance that the next CEO is unfit for the job.

2. *One or more investment managers*: The addition of Todd Combs in 2010 and Ted Weschler in 2011 largely completed this step.

3. *Chief executive officer*: The addition of Greg Abel and Ajit Jain in 2018 as vice chairmen supervising non-insurance and insurance operations, respectively, solidified the suspicions of outside observers that one of those two men would succeed Buffett. The background and skill set of Greg Abel suggests the board will choose him as CEO. The primary reason is his extensive experience with capital allocation. During his time running Berkshire Hathaway Energy, and later as vice chairman overseeing non-insurance operations, Abel oversaw many acquisitions. He is also much more comfortable in the spotlight, and about ten years younger than Jain, which would give him a longer run at the helm. Jain, by contrast, is a brilliant handicapper more comfortable evaluating insurance risks (though he is also one of the best executives in the world, having overseen acquisitions of his own).

Capital Allocation

Perhaps the single most important question regarding Berkshire is its future capital allocation. After all, Buffett acquired companies whose management he trusted to independently run operations and hired skilled managers, most importantly in the insurance business, who increased float. The excess money made by these businesses and their leaders was then sent back to Berkshire for redeployment. The conglomerate is already one of the world's largest companies and consistently in the top five on the Fortune 500. Most observers agree with Buffett and Munger that Berkshire's size makes matching the results of the past impossible. How then should Berkshire proceed?

Berkshire's earning power all but guarantees it will have enough cash to invest in worthwhile projects at the subsidiary level, and ample cash to make opportunistic acquisitions. That means cash will need to be returned to shareholders. Here Berkshire has two main options and a blended third.

1. *Pay a dividend*: This option is the most logical on its face as it immediately provides a relief valve. It is also something Berkshire avoided doing for years, and with good reason, as dividends have drawbacks. Perhaps the biggest is imposing a uniform standard on all shareholders of the company. Some shareholders might prefer receiving their share of earnings in cash to pay for retirement, say. Others might be younger and in savings mode and therefore prefer the company reinvest their

earnings without incurring unneeded taxes. But Berkshire's net profits continue to grow and have reached a level that will require returning capital to shareholders. Dividends may be the only option if repurchasing shares is unavailable.

2. *Share repurchases*: Returning capital to shareholders via repurchases makes the most sense from an economic standpoint. It allows the company to increase intrinsic value per share while reducing excess cash. Shareholders wishing to maintain or increase their ownership can hold their shares. Those wanting income can simply sell a portion of their shares to raise a desired amount of cash. Having the company in the market as a buyer means the price will be better (theoretically) than if it wasn't. The only drawback to share repurchases as the primary means of returning capital is that it is price dependent. The Berkshire board of directors would be limited to repurchases only during times of undervaluation. What happens when shares are fully valued?

3. *Combination of regular and special dividends, and share repurchases*: The middle ground option would see Berkshire implement a small regular dividend that provided an automatic relief valve to drain excess cash off the books. This might be set equal to 25% of normalized annual operating earnings. Then, irregular special dividends could be declared to reduce excess cash when earnings cannot be fully utilized internally or for share repurchases. If a large acquisition materializes, Berkshire's management would have an easy lever to pull to rebuild its cash position.

Should Berkshire Be Dismantled?

Some commentators have argued that Berkshire should be partially or wholly dismantled in the post-Buffett era. The idea is that the sum of Berkshire's parts would be worth more as separate businesses than as one. The logic of this argument rests largely on market multiples. The analyst takes Berkshire's many businesses and compares the multiple of revenues, earnings, or book value the market is valuing other similar companies. The analyst then arrives at the conclusion that Berkshire's conglomerate structure is causing a conglomerate discount (where the whole is worth less than the sum of its parts). Ergo, dismantling the company would unlock value for shareholders.

There are several flaws to the argument for dismantling Berkshire Hathaway. To summarize some of the points that have been discussed elsewhere in this book, Berkshire gains more from having its businesses under one roof. Here is why:

1. *Tax efficiency*: Capital can flow between operating units without taxation. And the utility subsidiaries can take full advantage of tax incentives because of Berkshire's consolidated tax bill.

2. *Diversification*: Berkshire can operate each business unit to its full potential because of the many businesses under its corporate umbrella. This also reduces the risk of the entire enterprise. The diverse collection of cash-generating businesses, combined with a conservatively financed balance sheet, additionally allows for lower borrowing costs.

3. *Capital allocation*: Diversification extends to Berkshire's opportunity set. There is value in having the ability to buy whole companies or invest in the stock market, buy bonds, or act as a merchant banker to facilitate an acquisition, all depending on relative availability and valuation. Separate companies would be restricted to reinvesting internally or be forced to pay the cash to shareholders (incurring taxes on dividends, if the shareholder is taxable, in the process).

Many of Berkshire's businesses and investments have been a part of it for decades. Breaking up Berkshire would face a major hurdle in the form of taxes on top of the lost advantages just enumerated. It is possible Berkshire might be required to spin off or sell a subsidiary for anti-competitive reasons or choose to for other reasons. This could be done in a tax efficient way. But a wholesale dismantling of its many businesses would face a large tax bill.

A policy of spinning off subsidiaries could harm Berkshire's future in another way. One of its major advantages is as a permanent home for family businesses. If Berkshire began selling off units to "maximize their value" it could lose out on future value creation if sellers thought this trust would be broken.

Perhaps the strongest argument for keeping Berkshire Hathaway whole is the problem of reinvestment. If broken up by selling off business units, Berkshire's shareholders would be trading productive assets (businesses) for an unproductive one (cash). Cash in hand, Berkshire's shareholders would face the problem of what to do with their newfound liquid wealth. They could leave it in cash, spend it on current consumption, or reinvest it (likely at high prices) into other businesses. Buffett put it succinctly in his Chairman's letter: "Truly good businesses are exceptionally hard to find. Selling any you are lucky enough to own makes no sense at all." A spin-off strategy where shareholders owned the exact same businesses with value "unlocked" (i.e. higher valuation) would lose the connecting conglomerate structure and create the same reinvestment problem at the company or shareholder level too. It seems likely that present value would be diminished, even considering a hypothetical higher breakup value of the parts compared to the consolidated whole.

The crux of the argument comes down to what constitutes value. Berkshire was built on the notion that value is independent of the market's appraisal of that value. The value of a company is the present value of all future cash flows. In short, the underlying cash flows of Berkshire's many subsidiaries would not change upon being separated into pieces. In fact, as separate businesses they would incur additional costs for boards of directors, financial filing requirements, and financing costs, among other factors. This is to say nothing of the very real but often invisible costs of lost time to attend to various internal and investor-related meetings. Even setting these added costs aside, cash flows and therefore value would not increase post breakup. The subsidiaries already take advantage of opportunities for organic investment and bolt-on acquisitions that come their way, and Berkshire has taken care of the reinvestment problem by allowing excess cash to be sent to headquarters. *No additional value could come from the underlying businesses themselves, which means the argument for breaking up Berkshire is a chimera.*

Without question, Berkshire Hathaway's potential for incremental value creation compared to a broadly diversified list of companies will be minimal going forward. That is okay so long as some value can be achieved—after all, compounding even a small edge adds up over time. Berkshire's future value creation will likely come in the form of minimizing the downside to allow infrequent but meaningful advantages to accrue and accumulate to the benefit of ongoing shareholders. Value can be created by:

1. *Time arbitrage*: Taking advantage of the short-term thinking that guides markets to properly evaluate and capture the long-term value of businesses, whether public or private.**
2. *Private market discount*: Berkshire's reputation as a permanent home for businesses will continue if nurtured and protected. The small amount of value given up by sellers for this permanence will accrue to Berkshire's shareholders.
3. *Alternative source of financing*: Berkshire will be able to act as a lender of last resort to businesses that need lightning-fast access to capital. The so-called Buffett blessing of the past will be replaced by the Berkshire blessing. Berkshire's prudence in lending in one-off situations will make it sought after for companies wishing to telegraph to the market their staying power during crises.
4. *Opportunistic share repurchases*: During times of market turmoil, or when Berkshire becomes out of favor, it can repurchase undervalued shares to the benefit of continuing shareholders.

---

* We can also use a thought experiment and consider we own all businesses, everywhere. With no one to buy or sell we're left with the business itself. It is a closed system, a zero-sum game. Any value created in breaking up Berkshire Hathaway would actually be a diminution of another investor's pocketbook to benefit Berkshire's shareholders.

** The stock market provides the most opportunity, but private business does too. Acme Brick buying a mothballed plant in a downturn is a good example. Berkshire knew it was a good long-term business and thought in terms of the complete business cycle.

Berkshire's operating structure and governance will not change much at all in the first decade following Buffett's death. This is because Buffett's estate will own a significant block of voting stock. These shares are all slated to go to charities, a process that will take time, perhaps upwards of a decade or more. During that time, Berkshire's board and management will have time to prove the system put in place by its modern founders can continue unabated. It will also allow Berkshire to double in size (assuming even a 7% compounding rate, Berkshire's equity will double in about ten years). This will make it extremely hard for corporate raiders on Wall Street to attempt to break up the conglomerate.

The ultimate fate of Berkshire Hathaway rests with its shareholders. As the owners of Berkshire's assets, shareholders hold the key to Berkshire's future governance and capital allocation. Shareholders have a duty and obligation to ensure the conglomerate holds true to its culture and values. This has always been true, but will become more important as Buffett, Munger, and the first generation of Berkshire's builders step down. This will happen during a period of transformation in ownership that sees some of Buffett's early partners and longtime Berkshire shareholders pass their ownership interests to the next generation. If this new generation of shareholders steward and safeguard the culture so carefully built and maintained by the first it will allow Berkshire to thrive for the next one hundred years. Berkshire will undoubtedly not look the same in twenty-five, fifty, or one hundred years, but it's not inconceivable that it maintains a reputation for upholding proven and timeless ideals of business and investing.

Berkshire's future after Warren Buffett has been studied extensively. In his book, *Berkshire Beyond Buffett, The Enduring Value of Values*, Lawrence A. Cunningham, a well-recognized Berkshire scholar, discusses the momentum the conglomerate already enjoys. That momentum is a result of the long history and cultivation of an enduring culture now separable from the man who put it all in motion. Buffett was once asked how Berkshire would continue to find the types of deals conducted under his tenure after he is gone. "I like to think I'll be missed a little bit, but you won't notice it."

The short answer to the question of Berkshire after Buffett is that the conglomerate will thrive without Warren Buffett. That is perhaps the highest praise one can give a man who took a blank canvas and turned it into one of the finest and most highly valued pieces of artwork the business world has ever seen.

Sources

1. Berkshire Hathaway Annual Reports/10K, 1955–2019
2. Warren Buffett's Chairman's letters, 1965–2019

Endnotes

Chapter 1: Through 1954

1 Joshua B. Freeman,. *Behemoth: A History of the Factory and the Making of the Modern World* (New York: W. W. Norton & Company, 2018), Kindle Edition, 45.

2 Ibid, 45.

3 Ibid, 46.

4 "Lowell Mill Girls and the factory system, 1840," Gilder Lehrman Institute of American History, accessed on August 19, 2018, https://www.gilderlehrman.org/content/lowell-mill-girls-and-factory-system-1840.

5 Ibid.

6 "Francis Cabot Lowell and the Boston Manufacturing Company," Charles River Museum of Industry & Innovation, accessed on August 12, 2018 https://www.charlesrivermuseum.org/francis-cabot-lowell-and-the-boston-manufacturing-company/.

7 Seymour Lewis Wolfbein, *The Decline of a Cotton Textile City: A Study of New Bedford* (New York: Columbia University Press, 1944), 9.

8 Freeman, Behemoth: A History of the Factory and the Making of the Modern World, 45.

9 Wolfbein, *The Decline of a Cotton Textile City: A Study of New Bedford*, 64.

10 Ibid, 67.

11 Ibid, 60.

12 Ibid, 60.

13 Ibid,73.

14 Ibid, 74–80.

15 Alice Schroeder, *The Snowball: Warrant Buffett and the Business of Life* (New York: Bantam Dell, 2008), 268.

16 Wolfbein, *The Decline of a Cotton Textile City: A Study of New Bedford*, 19.

17 "Valley Falls Mill Village," Woonsocket, My home town on the web, accessed on August 12, 2018, http://www.woonsocket.org/valleyfalls.html.

18 American Textile Reporter 1922, Google Books digitized production, 1177.

19 American Textile Reporter 1921, Google Books digitized production, 43.

20 Schroeder, *The Snowball*, 267.

21 Wolfbein, *The Decline of a Cotton Textile City: A Study of New Bedford*, 102.

22 Ibid.

23 David Whiteman, Impact of The Uprising of '34: a coalition model of production and distribution, *Jump Cut*, accessed on September 17, 2018, http://www.ejumpcut.org/archive/jc45.2002/whiteman/.

24 Wolfbein, *The Decline of a Cotton Textile City: A Study of New Bedford*, 130–1.

25 Ibid, 141.

26 Seabury Stanton, *Berkshire Hathaway, Inc.: A Saga of Courage* (New York: Newcomen Society of North America, 1962). Stanton made this address to the Newcomen Society in Boston on November 29, 1961.

27 Fortune 500 list for 1956, *Fortune magazine*, 1956, http://archive.fortune.com/magazines/fortune/fortune500_archive/companies/1956/B.html.

28 L.D. Howell, Marketing and Manufacturing Margins for Textiles, pdf version accessed (Washington, D.C.: U.S. Government Printing Office, 1952), 73.

29 Wolfbein, *The Decline of a Cotton Textile City: A Study of New Bedford*, 98.

30 Burlington Industries, 2002 Annual Report.

Chapter 3: 1965–1974

31 Schroeder, *The Snowball*, 273.

32 Schroeder, *The Snowball*, 299.

33 Berkshire Hathaway, 2017 Annual Report.

34 Berkshire Hathaway, 1971 10K report.

35 Management's Discussion and Analysis, Association of International Certified Professional Accountants, accessed on January 22, 2019, https://www.aicpa.org/Research/Standards/AuditAttest/DownloadableDocuments/AT-00701.pdf.

36 Alice Schroeder, *The Snowball: Warrant Buffett and the Business of Life* (New York: Bantam Dell, 2008), 407.

Chapter 4: 1975–1984

37 Moody's Manual, June 1966.

38 Blue Chip Stamps, 1971 Annual Report.

39 Letter from Warren E. Buffett to Charles N. Huggins, December 13, 1972.

40 Wesco, 1973 Annual Report.

41 Wesco, 1978 Annual Report.

42 Blue Chip Stamps, 1977 Annual Report, p.7.

Chapter 5: 1985–1994

43 Robert B. Reich, "Leveraged Buyouts: America Pays The Price," *The New York Times*, January 29, 1989, https://www.nytimes.com/1989/01/29/magazine/leveraged-buyouts-american-pays-the-price.html.

44 Robert P. Miles, *The Warren Buffett, CEO, Secrets from the Berkshire Hathaway Managers* (New Jersey: John Wiley and Sons, 2001), 274.

45 Wolfgang Saxon, Obituary of Richard Rosenthal, *The New York Times*, April 19, 1987, https://www.nytimes.com/1987/04/19/obituaries/richard-rosenthal-arbitrager.html.

46 Alice Schroeder, *The Snowball: Warren Buffett and the Business of Life* (New York: Bantam Dell, 2008).

47 Ellen Wulfhorst, "*Forbes* lists 400 richest Americans," UPI, October 10, 1989, https://www.upi.com/Archives/1989/10/10/Forbes-lists-400-richest-Americans/5214623995200/.

48 Schroeder, *The Snowball*; Carol Loomis, "Warren Buffett's Wild Ride at Salomon," October 27, 1997, *Fortune* magazine, http://fortune.com/1997/10/27/warren-buffett-salomon/.

49 Alina Selyukh, "Why The American Shoe Disappeared And Why It's So Hard To Bring It Back," NHPR, June 19, 2019, https://www.npr.org/2019/06/19/731268823/why-the-american-shoe-disappeared-and-why-its-so-hard-to-bring-it-back; David Purcell, "Maine's shoe industry struggles to survive. Determined to stay in business, firms look to Washington for some help in competing against imports," *The Christian Science Monitor*, April 4, 1985, https://www.csmonitor.com/1985/0404/nshoes-q.html; Pamela G. Hollie, Shoe Industry's Struggle, *The New York Times*, May 28, 1985, https://www.nytimes.com/1985/05/28/business/shoe-industry-s-struggle.html.

50 Schroeder, *The Snowball*, 503.

51 Financial Accounting Series, Financial Accounting Standards Board publication, December 2004, https://www.fasb.org/jsp/FASB/Document_C/DocumentPage?cid=1218220124271&acceptedDisclaimer=true.

52 The definitive collection: Buffett in his own words, CNBC archive, accessed on July 5, 2018, https://buffett.cnbc.com/.

Chapter 6: 1995–2004

53 Wesco, 1997 Chairman's letter, p. 4–5.

54 General Re, 1997 Annual Report.

55 Warren Buffett comment at 1999 Berkshire Hathaway Annual Meeting.

56 Alice Schroeder and Gregory Lapin, "The Ultimate Conglomerate Discount," research study by PaineWebber, January 1999.

57 "Remarks by Chairman Arthur Levitt," The Securities and Exchange Commission, September 28, 1998, https://www.sec.gov/news/speech/speecharchive/1998/spch220.txt.

58 Tad Montross, "The Battlefield," July 16, 2014, http://www.genre.com/knowledge/blog/the-battlefield.html.

59 Warren Buffett and Carol Loomis, "Mr. Buffett on the Stock Market," *Fortune* magazine archives, November 22, 1999, http://archive.fortune.com/magazines/fortune/fortune_archive/1999/11/22/269071/index.htm.

60 Berkshire Hathaway press release, "Berkshire Hathaway, Walter Scott and David Sokol to Acquire MidAmerican Energy Holdings," October 25, 1999, http://www.berkshirehathaway.com/news/oct2599.html.

61 MidAmerican, 1999 Securities and Exchange Commission 10-K filing, March 30, 2000, https://www.sec.gov/Archives/edgar/data/1081316/000108131600000009/0001081316-00-000009.txt.

62 Ibid.

63 "Rival Bidders Face Off Over Cort Furniture," *Washington Business Journal*, June 21, 1999. https://www.bizjournals.com/washington/stories/1999/06/21/story6.html, accessed 10/28/20.

64 "Berkshire to Acquire U.S. Investment Corp.," *Insurance Journal*, April 20, 2000, https://usli.com/about-us and https://www.insurancejournal.com/news/national/2000/04/28/10967.htm.

65 Justin Industries, 1999 Annual Report.

66 Carrick Mollenkamp and Devon Spurgeon, "Shaw Industries Got Berkshire As Investor Simply by Asking," *The Wall Street Journal*, November 20, 2000, https://www.wsj.com/articles/SB974678647739635225.

67 James R. Hagerty, "Shaw Industries Plans to Acquire Queen Carpet for $470 Million," *The Wall Street Journal*, August 14, 1998, https://www.wsj.com/articles/SB903043434761383500.

68 Ibid.

69 Johns Manville press release, "Johns Manville Chairman & CEO Jerry Henry Retires; Steve Hochhauser to Become Chairman, President & CEO," May 11, 2004, https://news.jm.com/press-release/historical-archive/johns-manville-chairman-ceo-jerry-henry-retires-steve-hochhauser-be.

70 Bethany McLean, "The Fall of Fannie Mae," *Fortune* magazine archive, January 24, 2005, http://archive.fortune.com/magazines/fortune/fortune_archive/2005/01/24/8234040/index.htm.

71 Corporate history book by MiTek, "MiTek: A Global Success Story," MiTek publication, 88.

72 Berkshire Hathaway, Securities and Exchange Commission 13f filing, February 14, 2001, https://www.sec.gov/Archives/edgar/data/1067983/000109581101001369/a69281e13f-hr.txt.

73 Ibid.

74 "Buffett Praises Amazon, Then Buys Its Debt," *Chicago Tribune*, Greg Wiles, Bloomberg News, April 12, 2003. https://www.chicagotribune.com/news/ct-xpm-2003-04-12-0304120174-story.html accessed 10/29/20.

75 "Enron Fast Facts," CNN, updated April 24, 2020, https://www.cnn.com/2013/07/02/us/enron-fast-facts/index.html.

76 Monte Enbysk, "Alumna revives her Microsoft passion at Save the Children," Microsoft Alumni Network, March 22, 2012, https://www.microsoftalumni.com/s/1769/19/interior.aspx?sid=1769&gid=2&pgid=252&cid=1773&ecid=1773&crid=0&calpgid=466&calcid=1401.

77 Susanne Sclafane, "Former White Mountains' Chair, GEICO Rescuer Byrne Passes Away," *Insurance Journal*, March 11, 2013, https://www.insurancejournal.com/news/national/2013/03/11/284185.htm.

Chapter 7: 2005–2014

78 NOAA press release, "Hurricanes and Tropical Storms-Annual 2005," June 2006, https://www.ncdc.noaa.gov/sotc/tropical-cyclones/200513.

79 Berkshire Hathaway press releases: May 20, 2005, http://berkshirehathaway.com/news/may2005.pdf; June 10, 2005, http://berkshirehathaway.com/news/jun1005.pdf; June 6, 2005, http://berkshirehathaway.com/news/jun0605.pdf.

80 Berkshire Hathaway press release, July 1, 2005, http://berkshirehathaway.com/news/jul0105.pdf.

81 *RV Business* magazine, December 2005 http://www.berkshirehathaway.com/letters/rvbiz.pdf.

82 Ibid.

83 Federal Reserve Bank of St. Louis accessed 10/25/20.

84 "Buffett profit no close shave," *CNN Money*, January 28, 2005, https://money.cnn.com/2005/01/28/news/newsmakers/buffett/index.htm.

85 "Fortune 500 2005," *Fortune* magazine, http://fortune.com/fortune500/2005/.

86 S&P reports, Berkshire Hathaway acquisition of AU Holding Company, Inc, parent company of Applied Underwriters, Inc, accessed on January 23, 2020, http://www1.snl.com/irweblinkx/mnahistory.aspx?iid=100501&KeyDeal=125872&print=1.

87 Carol J. Loomis, "Warren Buffett Gives it Away," *Fortune* magazine, July 10, 2006, http://berkshirehathaway.com/donate/fortune071006.pdf.

88 "Florida, Berkshire Hathaway Strike $224 Million Deal on Insurance Fund," *Insurance Journal*, Bill Kaczor, July 31, 2008. https://www.insurancejournal.com/news/southeast/2008/07/31/92371.htm accessed 11/6/20.

89 "Iscar Ltd of Israel acquired Japanese tungsten carbide tool maker Tungaloy for US$ 1 billion," Japan strategy, September 22, 2008, https://www.japanstrategy.com/2008/09/22/iscar-ltd-of-israel-acquired-japanese-tungsten-carbide-tool-maker-tungaloy-for-us-1-billion accessed 11/6/20.

90 According to data from the Federal Reserve Bank of St. Louis.

91 Warren E. Buffett, "Buy America. I am," *The New York Times*, October 16, 2008, https://www.nytimes.com/2008/10/17/opinion/17buffett.html.

92 2008 Fortune 500 list, *Fortune magazine*, May 5, 2008, https://money.cnn.com/magazines/fortune/fortune500/2008/snapshots/980.html.

93 David Jolly, "Swiss Re Gets $2.6 Billion From Berkshire Hathaway," February 5, 2009, https://www.nytimes.com/2009/02/06/business/worldbusiness/06swiss.html.

94 The first SEC filings for BNSF post-acquisition noted that it is owned by National Indemnity, an indirect wholly-owned subsidiary of Berkshire Hathaway: Burlington North Santa Fe, Securities and Exchange Commission, 10-k/A form, February 11, 2010,
https://www.sec.gov/Archives/edgar/data/934612/000095012310042892/c00146e1ovkza.htm.

95 "Berkadia Commercial Mortgage LLC Completes Acquisition of Capmark's North American Loan Origination and Servicing Business," *Business Wire*, December 11, 2009, https://www.businesswire.com/news/home/20091211005586/en/Berkadia-Commercial-Mortgage-LLC-Completes-Acquisition-Capmark%E2%80%99s.

96 Berkshire Hathaway, Securities and Exchange Commissions Schedule 14A filing, March 12, 2010, https://www.sec.gov/Archives/edgar/data/1067983/000119312510053975/ddef14a.htm.

97 Berkshire Hathaway press release, December 22, 2009, http://berkshirehathaway.com/news/dec2209.pdf.

98 *Of Permanent Value*. Kilpatrick. 2015 edition. p. 579.

99 *Of Permanent Value*. Kilpatrick. 2015 edition. p. 580.

100 Erik Holm, "Buffett Gets Hands-On at Benjamin Moore," *The Wall Street Journal*, June 27, 2012, https://www.wsj.com/articles/SB10001424052702304830704577493153732326984;

James Covert, "Warren Buffett fired Benjamin Moore CEO after Bermuda cruise," *The New York Post*, June 15, 2012, https://nypost.com/2012/06/15/warren-buffett-fired-benjamin-moore-ceo-after-bermuda-cruise/;

Sheeraz Raza, "The Wrath of Warren Buffett: How Benjamin Moore Almost Broke his Promise," *Value Walk*, September 27, 2014, https://www.valuewalk.com/2014/09/warren-buffett-benjamin-moore/.

101 Matt Wirz, "Berkshire Buys Oriental Trading," *The Wall Street Journal*, updated November 5, 2012, https://www.wsj.com/articles/SB100014240529702037076045780 95082919727020.

102 Javier E. David, "The Ketchup War that Never Was: Burger Giants' Link to Heinz," *CNBC.com*, updated February 17, 2013, https://www.cnbc.com/id/100464841.

103 Alex Crippen and Reuters, "Berkshire Hathaway takes $3.7 billion stake in Exxon Mobil," *CNBC.com*, updated December 3, 2013, https://www.cnbc.com/2013/11/14/ warren-buffetts-berkshire-hathaway-takes-40-million-share-stake-in-exxon-mobil-sec-filing.html.

104 Issue brief, "State Pension Funds Reduce Assumed Rates of Return," Pew Trusts, December 19, 2019, https://www.pewtrusts.org/en/research-and-analysis/ issue-briefs/2019/12/state-pension-funds-reduce-assumed-rates-of-return.

105 Antoine Gara, "Berkshire May Avoid $400 Million Tax Bill In Graham Holdings Swap," *The Street*, March 14, 2014, https://www.thestreet.com/markets/ mergers-and-acquisitions/berkshire-may-avoid-400-million-tax-bill-in-graham-holdings-swap-12529683.

106 Berkshire Hathaway Energy news release, "Berkshire Hathaway Energy Announces Acquisition of AltaLink L.P. and Joint Transmission Development Agreement with SNC-Lavalin," May 1, 2014, https://www.brkenergy.com/news/ berkshire-hathaway-energy-announces-acquisition-of-altalink-l-p-and-joint-transmi ssion-development-agreement-with-snc-lavalin.

107 Russell Hubbard, "Service problems in 2014 give BNSF 'a lot of work to do,' Buffett says," *The Omaha World-Herald*, March 1, 2015, https://www.omaha.com/ money/buffett/service-problems-in-give-bnsf-a-lot-of-workto/article_36d807e8-8644-5c92-a8d0-3e999299571d.html.

Chapter 8: The First Fifty Years

108 *Fortune magazine* archives: 2014 Fortune 500, https://fortune.com/for-tune500/2014/; 1965 Fortune 500, https://archive.fortune.com/magazines/fortune/ fortune500_archive/full/1965/401.html.

Chapter 9: 2015–2019

109 Robert P. Hartwig, James Lynch and Steven Weisbart, "More Accidents, Larger Claims Drive Costs Higher," Insurance Information Institute whitepaper, October 2016, https://www.iii.org/sites/default/files/docs/pdf/auto_rates_wp_092716-62.pdf.

110 Jamie Lareau, "$4 billion deal? A win all around, experts say," *Automotive News*, October 6, 2014, https://www.autonews.com/article/20141006/RETAIL/141009861/4-billion-deal-a-win-all-around-experts-say.

111 According to the Federal Reserve Bank of St. Louis.

112 Jonathan Stempel and Ludwig Berger, "Berkshire to buy German motorcycle equipment retailer," *Reuters*, February 20, 2015,

https://www.reuters.com/article/us-detlevlouis-m-a-berkshire/berkshire-to-buy-german-motorcycle-equipment-retailer-idUSKBN-0L01X120150220; *Bloomberg News* wire story, "Warren Buffett buys German motorcycle apparel firm," *The Kansas City Star*, February 20, 2015, https://www.kansascity.com/news/business/article10739990.html.

113 Jonathan Stempel and Devika Krishna Kumar, "Buffett's Berkshire Hathaway buys P&G's Duracell," *Reuters*, November 13, 2014, https://www.reuters.com/article/us-duracell-m-a-berkshire-hatha/buffetts-berkshire-hathaway-buys-pgs-duracell-id USKCN0IX1F020141113.

114 According to the Procter & Gamble annual report.

115 Staff story, "Iowa Utilities Board signs off on MidAmerican rate increase, but final order still pending," February 28, 2014, https://www.desmoinesregister.com/story/money/business/2014/02/28/iowa-utilities-board-signs-off-on-midamerican-rate-increase-but-final-order-still-pending/5899817/.

116 Nicole Friedman, "How America's Largest Truck Stop Owner Stays on the Right Path," *The Wall Street Journal*, October 19, 2019, https://www.wsj.com/articles/how-americas-largest-truck-stop-owner-stays-on-the-right-path-11571457602.

117 "Just 3 of the Top 10 Largest Auto Insurers Grew Market Share During 2018 in the U.S." *CollisionWeek*, March 27, 2019. https://collisionweek.com/2019/03/27/just-3-top-10-largest-auto-insurers-grew-market-share-2018-u-s/ accessed 10/26/20.

118 Federal Energy Regulatory Commission, Docket RP17-248-000 on Kern River, www.ferc.gov.

119 Martinne Geller and Pamela Barbaglia, "Kraft Heinz bids $143 billion for Unilever in global brand grab," *Reuters*, February 17, 2017, https://www.reuters.com/article/us-unilever-m-a-kraft/kraft-heinz-bids-143-billion-for-unilever-in-global-brand-grab-idUSKBN15W18Y; Antoine Gara, "Kraft Heinz Withdraws Its $143 Billion Bid For Unilever," *Forbes*, accessed on April 20, 2020, https://www.forbes.com/sites/antoinegara/2017/02/19/kraft-heinz-withdraws-its-143-billion-bid-for-unilever/#fdf47f440639.

120 Jonathan Stempel, "Berkshire Hathaway unit wins 643 million euro award over 'fraudulent' German pipemaker purchase," *Reuters*, April 15, 2020, https://www.reuters.com/article/us-berkshire-buffett-arbitration-award/berkshire-hathaway-

unit-wins-643-million-euro-award-over-fraudulent-german-pipemaker-purchase-idUSKCN21X29I.

121 Amit Singh, "How Costco Manages Its Inventory and Supply Chain," *Market Realist*, December 31, 2019, https://marketrealist.com/2019/12/analyzing-costcos-inventory-supply-chain-management-strategies/.

122 Allison Reck, "What is Driving the Growth of Private-Label/Store Brands?," Martec white paper, accessed on June 3, 2020, https://www.martecgroup.com/growing-private-label-store-brand-purchasing/.

123 Fred Imbert, "Buffett, after last week's stock plunge, says Berkshire Hathaway 'overpaid' for Kraft," *CNBC*, February 25, 2019, https://www.cnbc.com/2019/02/25/buffett-says-berkshire-hathaway-overpaid-for-kraft-following-last-weeks-stock-plunge.html.

124 Nicole Friedman, "Buyout of Berkshire Hathaway Insurance Unit Under Scrutiny," *The Wall Street Journal*, October 21, 2019, https://www.wsj.com/articles/buyout-of-berkshire-hathaway-insurance-unit-under-scrutiny-11571706822; Nicole Friedman, "Warren Buffett Is Doing Something Rare: Selling a Business," *The Wall Street Journal*, updated February 26, 2019, https://www.wsj.com/articles/warren-buffett-is-doing-something-rare-selling-a-business-11551221992?mod=article_inline.

125 Marmon press release, "Marmon Acquires Majority Interest in Colson Medical Companies," *Business Wire*, November 1, 2019, https://www.businesswire.com/news/home/20191101005396/en/Marmon-Acquires-Majority-Interest-Colson-Medical-Companies; Jonathan Stempel, "Berkshire's Marmon unit buys medical device provider from Pritzker company," Reuters, November 1, 2019, https://www.reuters.com/article/colson-ma-berkshire-marmon/berkshires-marmon-unit-buys-medical-device-provider-from-pritzker-company-idUSL2N27H0YG.

126 Naureen S. Malik, "Buffett Sees Value in Beaten-Down USG," *The Wall Street Journal*, October 9, 2006, https://www.wsj.com/articles/SB116040937003386976.

Chapter 10: World's Greatest Conglomerate

127 Eric Pace, "Royal Little, Pioneer in Forming Of Conglomerates, Is Dead at 92," *The New York Times*, January 14, 1989, https://www.nytimes.com/1989/01/14/obituaries/royal-little-pioneer-in-forming-of-conglomerates-is-dead-at-92.html; William G. Blair, "Charles G. Bludhorn, The Head of Gulf and Western, Dies at 56," *The New York Times*, February, 20, 1983, https://www.nytimes.com/1983/02/20/obituaries/charles-g-bluhdorn-the-head-of-gulf-and-western-dies-at-56.html.

Index

The numbers in *italic* refer to figures and those in **bold** refer to tables.